The

YOM KIPPUR WAR

Also by
ABRAHAM RABINOVICH

The Boats of Cherbourg

The Battle for Jerusalem

Jerusalem on Earth: People, Passions, and Politics in the Holy City

Israel

Jerusalem: The Measure of the Year

The

YOM KIPPUR WAR

THE EPIC ENCOUNTER THAT
TRANSFORMED THE MIDDLE EAST

Abraham Rabinovich

Schocken Books, New York

Library of Congress Cataloging-in-Publication Data

Rabinovich, Abraham.
The Yom Kippur War: the epic encounter that transformed the Middle East /
Abraham Rabinovich.
p. cm.
Includes bibliographical references and index.
ISBN 0-8052-4176-0
1. Israel-Arab War, 1973.   I. Title.

DS128.1.R33   2004   956.04'8—dc21   2003054353

www.schocken.com

Book design by Johanna S. Roebas

Printed in the United States of America
First Edition

2   4   6   8   9   7   5   3   1

TO MICHAL AND GUY,
DANA AND ELAN,
YARDEN, DAVID, AND BENNO

On Rosh Hashana it is written and on the day of the fast of Kippur it is sealed . . . who shall live and who shall die, . . . who by water and who by fire, who by the sword. . . .

—FROM THE YOM KIPPUR PRAYER BOOK

CONTENTS

CONTENTS xi

MAPS

Israel and Its Neighbors

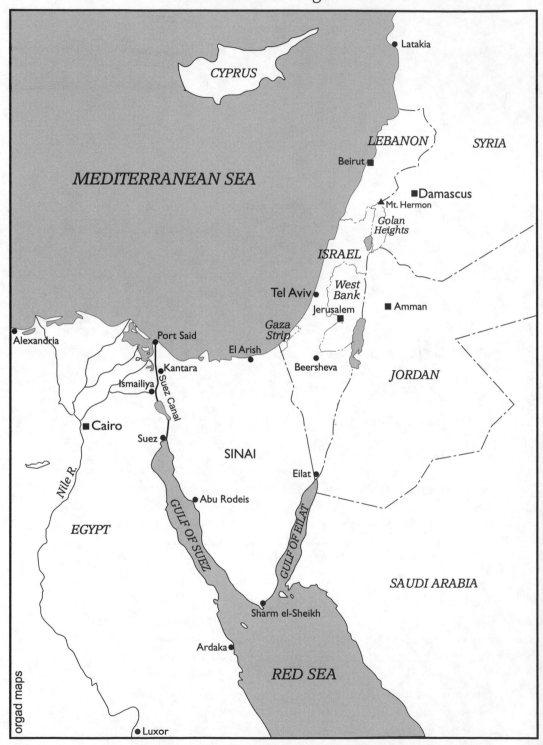

CYPRUS

Latakia

MEDITERRANEAN SEA

LEBANON

SYRIA

Beirut

Damascus

Mt. Hermon

Golan
Heights

ISRAEL

Tel Aviv

West
Bank

Amman

Jerusalem

Gaza
Strip

Alexandria

Port Said

El Arish

Beersheva

JORDAN

Kantara

Ismailiya

Suez Canal

Cairo

Suez

SINAI

Eilat

GULF OF SUEZ

GULF OF EILAT

Abu Rodeis

Nile R.

EGYPT

SAUDI ARABIA

Sharm el-Sheikh

Ardaka

RED SEA

Luxor

orgad maps

PREFACE

O N YOM KIPPUR AFTERNOON, 1973, Israel was caught by a surprise
attack on two fronts with the bulk of its army still unmobilized. When
the fighting ended less than three weeks later, its army was on the roads to the
Egyptian and Syrian capitals in one of the most remarkable turnabouts in
military history. Israel emerged from the war, however, more chastened than
triumphant.

Much has been published about the Yom Kippur War, but there has
been lacking a narrative that tells the extraordinary story with the inclusive
sweep it deserves. The passage of time has eased censorship restrictions—
most notably in the release of the findings of an Israeli inquiry commission
into the war—and permitted publication of valuable memoirs and analyses.
I have availed myself of this material and the human dimension provided by
130 interviews.

I covered the war as a reporter for the *Jerusalem Post*. On its fifth day, I
reached the northern part of the Golan Heights together with a colleague,
Joe Treen of *Newsday*. The battlefield was eerily quiet and the fatigued soldiers we encountered could tell us little of what had happened.

Unknown to us, the biggest tank battle since the Second World War had
just ended. A vastly outnumbered Israeli force had stopped the Syrian army,
which attacked with more than one thousand tanks. The last of the Syrians
had been driven back only hours before after desperate fighting, and Israeli

forces would the next morning launch a counterattack towards Damascus. The counterattack was to have been carried out this day, but entire battalions were falling asleep whenever their tanks stopped moving. The quiet we had stumbled into was that of two exhausted armies gathering strength for the next round.

I would learn much of this only twenty years later when I researched an article on the battle. Deeper familiarity with the subject made it clear that although I thought myself well informed about the war, what I knew were only disconnected episodes in a fuzzy matrix. Missing was the epic quality that could only be grasped by understanding both the decision-making processes of the high commands and the flow of events on the battlefield itself. I have spent the last five years trying to understand the war as a coherent narrative.

I am indebted to Professor Howard Sachar for his generous initiative in introducing me to my publisher. My thanks to the Israeli Armored Corps Center at Latrun for making available unit histories, to the Israeli Defense Forces Archive in Ramat Gan, and to the General Staff Library in Tel Aviv. Gratitude as well to Gen. Donn A. Starry, U.S. Army (ret.), who was sent to Israel by the American army to study the Yom Kippur War, for the insights he kindly offered me in Washington. My appreciation to all interviewees who shared their memories, including those who chose to remain anonymous. Most of what was remembered was remembered vividly, even after three decades. Particular thanks to Gen. Amnon Reshef (ret.), whose brigade was involved in the fiercest battles in Sinai, for making available his unit's war diary and for granting five long interviews. Thanks also to Avi Yaffe for letting me hear the tapes he recorded in a Suez Canal fort in the first days of the war. My former editor at the *Jerusalem Post*, Ari Rath, kindly agreed to read the manuscript, as did Benny Michaelson, former chief historian of the Israeli army, and journalist Malka Rabinowitz. My thanks to them for their comments. Errors that remain, of course, are mine alone.

Use of direct quotes is generally based on excerpts from official protocols or from memoirs based on transcripts of radio traffic.

For all those who lived through it, on whatever side, the Yom Kippur War—or, as it is known in the Arab world, the October War or Ramadan War—remains one of the defining moments of their lives. It is a defining moment too in the history of the region. Its reverberations are with us yet.

Abraham Rabinovich
Jerusalem
September 2003

The

YOM KIPPUR WAR

The Suez Front

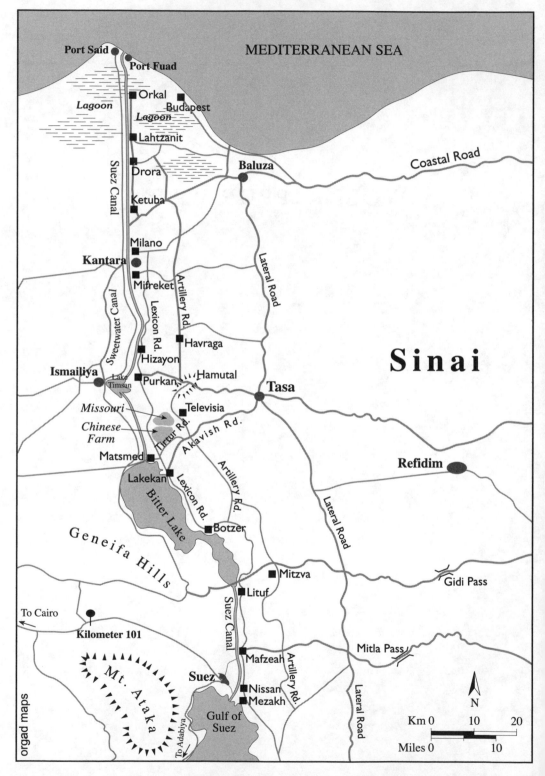

MEDITERRANEAN SEA

Port Said
Port Fuad

Orkal
Budapest
Lagoon
Lagoon
Lahtzanit

Suez Canal

Drora
Baluza
Coastal Road

Ketuba

Milano

Kantara

Mifreket

Sweetwater Canal

Lexicon Rd.

Artillery Rd.

Lateral Road

Havraga

Hizayon

Ismailiya
Lake Timsan
Purkan
Hamutal

Missouri
Televisia
Tasa

Chinese Farm
Tirtur Rd.
Akavish Rd.

Matsmed

Lakekan

Lexicon Rd.
Artillery Rd.

Refidim

S i n a i

Bitter Lake

G e n e i f a   H i l l s

Botzer

Mitzva

Lituf

Gidi Pass

Lateral Road

Suez Canal

To Cairo

Kilometer 101

Mitla Pass

Mt. Ataka

Mafzeah

Artillery Rd.

Suez

Nissan
Mezakh

Gulf of Suez

To Adabiya

Lateral Road

N

Km 0   10   20
Miles 0   10

orgad maps

PROLOGUE

A MILITARY SATELLITE beaming images of the Middle East to Earth late on the afternoon of October 5, 1973, would have confronted analysts with a perplexing picture.

On the west bank of the Suez Canal, five Egyptian divisions—100,000 soldiers, 1,350 tanks, and 2,000 artillery pieces and heavy mortars—were drawn up in full battle array. Bridging equipment and rubber boats positioned near the water's edge offered clear evidence of intent.

On the Israeli side, some 450 men could be counted in the strongpoints lining the canal. The Israelis were clearly able to see the preparations for a crossing on the Egyptian bank, but there was no sign that it troubled them even though they had only 44 artillery pieces along the hundred-mile front and 290 tanks in all of Sinai.

The pictures from the Golan Heights would have been even more puzzling. Here, too, five Arab divisions on maximum war footing confronted a thin Israeli defense line from which it was impossible to miss the Syrian deployment. But here there was no canal to serve as a barrier. The disparity in tanks was almost 8 to 1 in Syria's favor; in infantry and artillery, far greater. On the Syrian side, secondary defense lines were carved into the landscape between the front and Damascus, forty miles to the east. On the Israeli side, there was no secondary defense line at all, as if the enormous disparity in forces were in Israel's favor, not the other way around.

In Israel itself this Friday afternoon, the satellite would have detected no signs of alarm. There was hardly a person or moving vehicle to be seen on the country's streets. The setting sun would mark the onset of Yom Kippur and the country's three million Jews were at home preparing for this holiest of days. The only sign of unusual activity was at the headquarters of the Israel Defense Forces in the center of Tel Aviv. Long after the lights had gone out in the rest of the building, they were still on in the office of the chief of staff and in the army intelligence offices on the floor above.

In Jewish tradition, Yom Kippur is the climax of the Ten Days of Awe, during which man makes accounts with his Maker. On this Yom Kippur, Israel's days of awe were only beginning.

One
FOOTPRINTS IN THE SAND

CAPT. MOTTI ASHKENAZI WAS NOT A MAN to accept a perceived wrong without protest. The outpost in Sinai his unit of reservists took over two weeks before Yom Kippur was in an advanced state of neglect. Barbed-wire fencing had sunken almost entirely into the sand, trenches were collapsing, gun positions had insufficient sandbags, and the ammunition supply was short. When the officer he was relieving asked him to sign the standard form acknowledging receipt of the outpost in good condition, Ashkenazi declined. Without this formality, the unit being relieved could not depart. When Ashkenazi refused an order from his battalion commander to sign, the exasperated commander signed the form himself.

Ashkenazi's unit was part of the Jerusalem Brigade, which had never before been assigned to a tour of duty on the Bar-Lev Line. Unlike the units which normally undertook this task, the Jerusalem Brigade was a second-line formation which included men well into their thirties. Some were immigrants who had received only a truncated form of basic training before being relegated to the reserves. A sprinkling of younger reservists with combat experience stiffened the ranks, and officers too were generally veterans of combat units.

The assignment of such a unit to the Bar-Lev Line, once considered hazardous duty, reflected the relaxed situation on the Egyptian front. It was six years since Israel had reached the canal in the Six Day War, and three years since the intense skirmishing across the waterway—the so-called War of Attrition—had ended.

The reservists had grumbled as usual upon receiving their annual call-up notices for a month's duty, particularly since their tour began on the eve of Rosh Hashana, the Jewish New Year, and would last through Yom Kippur and the subsequent Succot holiday. However, by the time they boarded the buses that would take them to Sinai, some were looking forward to a month of camaraderie, far from the routine of work and home. The men brought books and board games, *finjans* (pots) for brewing coffee, even fishing rods. Ashkenazi, a thirty-two-year-old doctoral student in philosophy at Hebrew University in Jerusalem, took along his four-month-old German shepherd, Peng, because he had nowhere to leave him.

Unlike the other Bar-Lev forts, which were built along the canal bank, Ashkenazi's outpost, code-named Budapest, was ten miles east of the canal on a narrow sandspit between the Mediterranean Sea and a shallow lagoon. The outpost's purpose was to guard against an Egyptian thrust along the sandspit towards the coastal road to Israel. Budapest was the largest of the Bar-Lev Line fortifications, incorporating an artillery battery and a naval signals unit which maintained contact with vessels patrolling off the coast.

Towards evening on the day of his arrival, Ashkenazi, a deputy company commander, climbed the fort's observation tower and looked west along the sandspit towards Port Fuad at the entrance to the Suez Canal. This northwest corner of Sinai was the only part of the peninsula not captured by Israel in the 1967 war. Ashkenazi could make out a string of Egyptian outposts stretching along the sandspit. The one closest to him was only a mile away. Since the canal did not separate them, the only thing that could inhibit an Egyptian raid was a minefield that Budapest's previous commander had pointed out to him during their tour that morning.

As Ashkenazi watched, a pack of wild dogs emerged from the Egyptian lines and trotted down the sand towards the Israeli outpost. They appeared to be heading towards Budapest's garbage dump at the western edge of the position. As they approached the minefield, Ashkenazi braced for explosions. But the dogs passed through unharmed. Tides washing over the sands had dislodged or neutralized the mines. Ashkenazi decided to contact battalion headquarters in the morning to request additional fencing and sandbags.

Maj. Meir Weisel, an affable kibbutznik, was the most senior company commander in the battalion which moved into the Bar-Lev Line. In previous tours of reserve duty, his unit had clashed with Palestinian guerrillas along the Jordan River and taken casualties. "This time," a brigade officer had told him, "I'm sending you to the canal and you can rest." His company took over four forts in the canal's central sector and he positioned himself in Fort Purkan, opposite the city of Isamailiya on the Egyptian-held bank. The officer whom he replaced pointed out a villa across the canal which he said had belonged to the parents of foreign minister Abba Eban's wife, Suzie, who was from a prominent Egyptian Jewish family. It was not clear who lived there now but a gardener watered the plants every day. "As long as you see the gardener working there," said the officer, "everything is OK."

The limited forces Israel deployed on both the Syrian and Egyptian fronts opposite vastly larger enemy armies reflected a self-assurance induced by the country's stunning victory in the Six Day War. Israel believed it had attained a military superiority that no Arab nation or combination of nations could challenge. The euphoria that followed the lightning victory in 1967 over the Egyptian, Syrian, and Jordanian armies gave Israel a sense of manifest destiny similar to that which impelled the United States westward in the nineteenth century.

Its thin front lines belied a vast increase in military strength. Israel had twice as many tanks and warplanes in 1973 as it had in the Six Day War. Its largest armor formations were no longer brigades with one hundred tanks but divisions with three hundred. Veteran armor officers permitted themselves to fantasize about commanding a full armored division deploying into battle—two brigades forward, one to the rear, as they swept into the attack.

The armies of Egypt and Syria had grown more than Israel's in absolute numbers but the overall ratio in the Arab favor remained 3 to 1. Given the fighting ability of the Israel Defense Forces (IDF), this ratio was considered acceptable in Israel. The General Staff, in fact, was preparing to reduce the thirty-six months of service required of its conscript soldiers by three months. Convinced that it could stand up to an Arab world thirty times its size, Israel was waiting for the Arabs to formally recognize the Jewish state and agree to new borders.

The Arabs, however, refused to accept the humiliation of 1967. During the War of Attrition launched by Egypt in March 1969, hundreds of Israeli soldiers died in massive artillery bombardments. Deep penetration raids by Israeli warplanes and commandos forced Cairo to accept a cease-fire in August 1970. Since then, the Suez front had remained quiet. On the Syrian front, there were periodic exchanges of fire—"battle days," Israel termed them—but no serious challenge to Israel's dominance.

The seeming docility of the Arabs encouraged a sense of invulnerability in Israel. In August 1973, defense minister Moshe Dayan, in a speech to army officers, said that Israel's strength was a reflection not only of its military potential but of inherent Arab weakness. "It is a weakness that derives from factors that I don't believe will change quickly: the low level of their soldiers in education, technology, and integrity; and inter-Arab divisiveness which is papered over from time to time but superficially and for short spans."

A Mossad official posted abroad immediately after the Six Day War returned home five years later to find the country transformed. Israel was not just self-assured, he found, but self-satisfied, awash in a good life that seemed as if it would go on forever. Government and military officials traveled now in large cars and wrote off business lunches to expenses, a new practice in Israel. Arabs from the West Bank and Gaza Strip provided the working hands the fast-growing nation needed but were politically invisible. The sense of physical expanse was startling to someone accustomed to the claustrophobia of pre–Six Day War Israel. The border was no longer fifteen minutes from Tel Aviv or on the edge of Jerusalem but out of sight and almost out of mind—on the Jordan River, on the Suez Canal, on the Golan. People went down to Sinai now not to wage war but to holiday on its superb beaches.

The army had grown tremendously and so had its prominence in national life. There was a layer of brigadier generals, a newly created rank required by the expanding army. The Mossad official sensed arrogance in high places. Some generals had their offices redone to reflect their new status; some gave parties with army entertainment troupes singing in the background. All of this was foreign to the spartan ways the official had known as distinguishing features of Israeli public life only five years before. An attitude of disdain for Arab military capability had etched itself insidiously into the national psyche. The official was as yet unaware of the extent to which this disdain had led to distortions in the mind-set of the armed forces.

Sitting in a downtown Jerusalem café a few months before the war, Motti Ashkenazi had told a friend that war was inevitable unless Israel accepted Egypt's demand that it pull back from the canal in order to permit the waterway to be reopened. Now, in command of Budapest, he took his own warning seriously. After two days of badgering battalion headquarters, he was informed that his request for sandbags and barbed-wire concertinas was being met. The supply vehicle that arrived carried only a fraction of the material he had asked for. Nevertheless, he was able to fortify the area around the fort's gate and the vulnerable approach from the beach.

A week before Yom Kippur, Ashkenazi was in a half-track making a routine morning patrol along the sandspit towards his rear base when he saw fresh footprints in the sand on both sides of the road. Whoever made them seemed to have circled the area, as if examining the lay of the land. The road was shut at night because it was vulnerable to commando landings from the sea. If anyone came down the road by day, Budapest was supposed to be informed beforehand, but there had been no such notification. The footprints, thought Ashkenazi, could have been left by Egyptian scouts landing from the sea, on one side of the road, or coming on foot through the lagoon, on the other side. He radioed headquarters and a vehicle with two Bedouin trackers arrived. They examined the footprints and concluded that they had been made by standard Israeli army boots.

"If I were an Egyptian scout, I would use that kind of boot," said Ashkenazi.

The trackers laughed. "Do you think they're that clever?"

"Why not?" asked Ashkenazi.

Twice more in the coming days he would find footprints along the route.

Two

THE MAN IN THE PEASANT ROBE

Civilian clothing did little to mask the military bearing of the six men who descended from the Soviet liner docking in Alexandria on its regular run from the Syrian port of Latakia on August 21. It took a moment before Lt. Gen. Saad el Shazly, chief of staff of the Egyptian army, recognized his Syrian colleagues as they came through customs with their false passports, trying to look like tourists. Shazly, also in civilian clothing, escorted them to the officers' club and left them to settle in. Towards evening, the Syrians were driven to a former palace serving as Egyptian naval headquarters. Eight Egyptian generals joined them, including defense minister Ahmed Ismail. The Syrians included defense minister Mustafa Tlass and chief of staff Gen. Yusuf Shakoor. In intensive meetings over the next two days, the fourteen men coordinated their plans for a surprise two-front attack on Israel. When they rose, all was settled except the timing of D-Day. This would be left to the leaders of the two countries.

The humiliation of the Six Day War had cast its debilitating shadow over Egyptian president Anwar Sadat ever since he assumed office in October 1970. The War of Attrition undertaken by his predecessor, Gamal Abdel Nasser, had not budged Israel from the Suez Canal. Nor had diplomatic efforts by the international community. Israel insisted on achieving border changes in direct negotiations with the Arab countries. The Arabs refused to recognize Israel as a legitimate state, let alone cede territory to it.

Prime Minister Golda Meir, confident that Israel's geopolitical situation had never been better, was content to wait for the Arabs to bow to reality. She rejected defense minister Moshe Dayan's suggestion in December 1970 that Israel pull back twenty miles from the canal in order to enable its reopening and thereby reduce Egyptian motivation for going to war. Two months later, Sadat reshaped Dayan's proposal and adopted it as his own in an address to the Egyptian National Assembly. Unlike Dayan, the Egyptian leader saw a partial Israeli pullback as catalyzing, not indefinitely delaying, a final withdrawal.

Sadat astonished his audience by declaring his readiness to achieve a peace agreement with Israel, the first time an Arab leader had publicly suggested that possibility. But Israel, said Sadat, would have to commit itself to subsequent withdrawal, not only from all of Sinai but from all the other territories captured in the Six Day War—the West Bank, the Golan Heights, and East Jerusalem. The Palestinian refugee question must be resolved as well. As dire as were Egypt's straits economically and strategically, Sadat was not bidding for a separate settlement with Israel.

As an interim measure, U.S. secretary of state William Rogers attempted to persuade Israel to agree to a limited pullback but found it unyielding. After a fruitless trip to Jerusalem, his assistant, Joseph Sisco, paid a courtesy call on the prime minister and handed her a bouquet of flowers he had stopped to buy on the way. "Joe, you're saying it with flowers," Mrs. Meir said lightheartedly. "It won't do you any good."

A week after the Six Day War, the Israeli government had asked the United States to inform Egypt and Syria of its readiness to evacuate Sinai and the Golan, except for minor border modifications, in return for peace treaties. There was no response, but an Arab summit in Khartoum two months later rejected peace with Israel. The following month, the Israeli government rescinded its offer.

The international community made valiant attempts at a solution. In reply to a questionnaire submitted by UN envoy Gunnar Jarring in February 1971, Egypt declared its readiness to live in peace with Israel if it returned to the prewar border. In a parallel questionnaire submitted to Jerusalem, the reverse question was put—in return for peace, would Israel evacuate all Sinai? The reply was negative. Israel was prepared to withdraw to "mutually determined boundaries," not the prewar boundaries. Any peace achieved by pulling back to the vulnerable prewar borders, said Dayan, would be short-lived, because it would make another war too tempting for the Arabs. "If we really want to honor all the sovereign rights of the past and all the desires of every Arab, we won't be able to have a Jewish state here." The possibility of an interim settlement in Sinai had sunk into the desert sands.

As Israel saw it, it had twice in one generation—in 1948 and 1967—been forced into wars of survival by Arab states which wished to destroy it. Israel believed it had the moral right, the strategic need, and the military strength to demand border changes. The Arabs, for their part, regarded Israel as a usurper of Arab land. Sadat was willing to pay for Israel's withdrawal by offering it a sort of peace—one, he would later make clear, that did not include an exchange of ambassadors or normalized relations; in effect, a nonbelligerency pact. But he would not pay with territory.

Whether patient diplomacy could have won a peace agreement must remain a matter of conjecture, although the possibility seems in retrospect unlikely. The person who knew Sadat best, his wife Jehan, would tell an Israeli newspaper in 1987 that peace could not have been achieved without the two countries first passing through the cauldron of war. "Sadat needed one more war in order to win and enter into negotiations from a position of equality," she said. Henry Kissinger would testify that Sadat himself told him years later that if the United States had been able in 1973 to broker an Israeli pullback to the prewar border without Egypt being required to sign a peace treaty, he, Sadat, would have accepted it, but only reluctantly, because it would not have restored Egyptian pride.

Sadat had been regarded when he took office as a gray interim figure filling Nasser's shoes until some more charismatic personality took power. He would metamorphose into one of the most imaginative and daring national leaders of the twentieth century. He reveled in his peasant origins and was imbued with a mystic view of himself as the embodiment of Egypt's destiny. Sadat would often return to the poor Nile Delta village where he was born, Mit Abul-kum, to meditate. In what seemed to some to be ostentatious asceticism, he would accord interviews to visiting journalists as he sat on the ground under a tree in Mit Abul-kum dressed in a simple galabiya. However, the sustenance he received from this link to his roots and from his Islamic faith was clearly genuine. His mother was the daughter of a freed Sudanese slave, an origin reflected in his dark skin. Before pursuing a military career, he had attempted to become an actor. He failed to make it, but the political stage would afford him far greater scope for his sense of drama than any theater. His wardrobe attested to the variety of roles he pursued with flair: well-tailored Italian suits, medal-bedecked uniforms—of an admiral as well as a general—and peasant robes.

Sadat's desire as a young man to see an end to British hegemony in Egypt was accompanied by admiration for national leaders who fought for the liberation of their people. In this category he placed not only the likes of Mahatma Gandhi and Kemal Atatürk but also Adolf Hitler. He held him in esteem as a charismatic leader who rebuilt a shattered nation. Sadat abandoned this assessment, at least publicly, only after he became president. From that point on, he used the term "Nazi" as a pejorative, usually directing it at Israel.

Although a visionary, Sadat well understood the hard rules of autocracy. Within seven months of assuming the presidency he had arrested his main political opponents, who were plotting his ouster, and stabilized his regime. His declared readiness to make peace with the Jewish state, albeit on terms Israel was unwilling to accept, was a courageous departure from Arab political rhetoric.

With the failure of his call for a partial Israeli withdrawal, Sadat began preparing for war. His militancy bore elements of desperation that rendered him a quasi-comic figure to many. Halfway through 1971 he declared it to be "a year of decision." But the year ended without decision. So did the following year. "We had already lost credibility in the eyes of the whole world and we had begun to lose faith in ourselves," Sadat would acknowledge in a television interview in 1974.

The three years since Sadat had taken office—a period of no war, no peace—were the most demoralized in modern Egyptian history. The War of Attrition had at least offered a sense of fighting back, but now it was over and the nation stood naked before the impact of the Six Day War. A deep sense of humiliation and helplessness was reflected in literature and song and in the sardonic jokes about the army and the national leadership, particularly Sadat. A dessicated economy added to the nation's despondency.

War was a desperate option. If Egypt was defeated again, the impact on its self-image was too awful to contemplate. But Sadat saw no other way out. When he discovered that the army under Nasser had plans only for defense, Sadat would write, he ordered the generals to draw up plans for crossing the canal and coming to grips with the Israeli army. His assertion that he was prepared to sacrifice a million soldiers in the battle to recover Sinai made little impression on the Israelis. His army, as they saw it, was not ready for war. The Soviet Union, however, was altering that situation with a vast armaments and training program.

Egypt and Syria were major Cold War assets for the Soviet Union. They provided port facilities, landing rights for reconnaissance planes, and bases for electronic monitoring stations to keep track of the American Sixth Fleet in the Mediterranean, whose nuclear missiles were capable of striking the Soviet Union. Moscow had lost its previous foothold in the Mediterranean when Communist Albania shifted its allegiance to Red China. The Soviets were happy to cement relations with Egypt and Syria by selling them weapons for hard currency. Some fifteen thousand Soviet military experts were shaping the Egyptian armed forces into a modern army. A similar corps of advisers was attached to the Syrian army.

But the Soviets attempted to discourage the Arabs from a military confrontation with Israel that would endanger Moscow's warming relations with Washington. Moscow refused to provide certain offensive weapons systems the Egyptians demanded, such as long-range fighter-bombers. Transparent Soviet disdain for the fighting ability of the Egyptians further strained relations. On one occasion, Marshal Andrei Grechko, the Soviet defense minister, lectured Sadat on the three prerequisites for a successful war—arms, training, and the will to fight. "The first two you have," said Grechko.

The closer that détente brought the superpowers together, the more despondent Sadat grew. The communiqué that followed the first summit meeting between President Richard Nixon and Chairman Leonid Brezhnev in Moscow in May 1972 was termed by the Egyptian leader "a violent shock." Its advocacy of military relaxation in the Middle East meant to him one thing—perpetuation of Israeli occupation of Arab land. The Soviets had even agreed to the possibility of border changes.

It took fully seven weeks before Soviet ambassador to Cairo Vladimir Vinogradov presented the Egyptian leader with a report from the Kremlin on the Nixon-Brezhnev summit and its implications for Egypt. Sadat sat on a couch, he would later recount, leaning his head against his walking stick as the ambassador spoke. The message Vinogradov read out made no mention of pending Egyptian arms requests and ended by noting that Egypt was not yet ready for war. Sadat's reply was terse. He was herewith expelling all Soviet advisers from Egypt, he said. Looking at his watch, he turned to an aide. "What is the date? I can't see without my glasses." Upon being told it was July 8, he turned to Vinogradov and said, "All right then, I'm giving you ten days. The old way of doing business between Egypt and the Soviet Union is at an end."

Sadat's action was no spur-of-the-moment whim. The outcome of the summit had made it clear to him that he could not rely on the Soviets for support in regaining Sinai. His stunning move—the kind of grand political theater that would become his hallmark—was received with dismay in Moscow and delight in Israel, where it was taken as a guarantee that Egypt would not be going to war in the foreseeable future. In Washington too, Sadat was seen as having left himself with no military option.

To one astute observer in Jerusalem, however, the expulsion did not mean the shelving of Sadat's war option but its possible activation. Gideon Rafael, director general of the Foreign Ministry, after mulling over the expulsion for a couple of days, wrote a memo to his colleagues. It suggested that Sadat's move was intended to invite the Americans into the game in the hope that they would pressure Israel back to the international border. If this failed, wrote Rafael, Sadat intended to go to war, and in that case the massive presence of Soviet advisers was an impediment, given Moscow's known opposition to Egyptian military adventures. Sadat, argued Rafael, was preparing both political and military options. Although not taken seriously in Jerusalem, Rafael's analysis was a precise reading of Sadat's intentions.

It was more than half a year before there was a significant response to Sadat's move from Washington, with which Cairo had severed relations after the Six Day War. In February 1973, Sadat's national security adviser, Hafez Ismail, was invited to the United States to confer with his American counterpart, Henry Kissinger. Meeting secretly for two days on a businessman's estate in Connecticut borrowed for the occasion, Ismail spelled out Egypt's position. His country was willing to make peace with Israel, he said, but the process must begin with a declaration by Israel that it would return to its prewar borders on all fronts.

It was Kissinger's impression that the Egyptians were leaving an opening for border adjustments on the West Bank and even for an Israeli presence along the Jordan River, aimed at preventing any Arab army from linking up with the West Bank. Once Israel declared its readiness for a pullback, said Ismail, demilitarized zones would be created on both sides of the Israeli-Egyptian border. Israeli vessels would be permitted to use the Suez Canal and Egypt would end its boycott of companies trading with Israel. There would, however, not be diplomatic relations or open borders. This would have to await an Israeli settlement with Syria (including full withdrawal from the Golan Heights), Jordan, and the Palestinians. Arab control of East Jerusalem and the Temple Mount was nonnegotiable.

Kissinger was skeptical about Israel agreeing to these terms, even though they were far better than anything any Arab state had yet offered. Golda Meir was by now willing to discuss a partial Israeli pullback in Sinai, but it was clear that Israel would insist on border changes in any final settlement. In the view of the Israeli government—at least Mrs. Meir's "kitchen cabinet," where policy was shaped—the Arabs had no military option and would eventually have to accept the implications of that situation.

The message Ismail carried back to Sadat was that the United States could do nothing to change the situation. "My advice to Sadat is to be realistic," said Kissinger, according to the report submitted by Ismail. "The fact is that you have been defeated so don't ask for a victor's spoils. Either you can change the facts, and consequently our perceptions will naturally change with regard to a solution, or you can't change the facts, in which case solutions other than the ones you are offering will have to be found. I hope that what I am saying is clear. I'm certainly not asking Sadat to change the military situation. If he tries that, Israel will win once again and more so than in 1967. In such a situation, it would be very difficult for us to do anything."

Sadat did not dispute this view; in fact, he shared it, except for the inevitability of another Arab defeat. "It was impossible," he would write in his memoirs, "for the United States or, indeed, any other power to make a move if we ourselves didn't take military action to break the deadlock."

This is what he now prepared to do.

Three

DOVECOTE

Golda meir was not in a position to judge Gen. David Elazar's military acumen, but she was enough a judge of character to want him as her next chief of staff. He was, she felt, a resolute man who didn't compromise easily. He was also modest and easy to talk to. In addition, she would say, "he's a pleasure to look at."

Since the Six Day War, the annual intelligence assessment of the IDF had deemed war unlikely. At Elazar's first meeting with the General Staff after taking up his post on January 1, 1971, he changed that. "The likelihood of war is strong," he said. Sadat had virtually no other option, Elazar believed, if he wished to get a political process started.

Israel had nothing to gain from another war, Elazar told the generals. Should it break out, the object would be to win swiftly, in order to reduce the impact on the economy, and decisively, to discourage the Arabs from trying it again.

The relevance of the Bar-Lev Line was one of the first subjects Elazar reviewed with the General Staff. It had been built during the tenure of his predecessor, Gen. Haim Bar-Lev. Its name conjured up an image of massive interlocking fortifications like the Maginot or Siegfried Line. In fact, it was a string of small, isolated forts, each with garrisons of only twenty to thirty men. There were miles-wide gaps between the forts. They had been built to protect the troops from artillery fire during the War of Attrition. But they had come to be seen as having a role even in the event of an all-out Egyptian attack, slowing down the assault until the reserves deployed. Others, however, saw the Bar-Lev Line as a death trap—too thin to be a meaningful barrier, yet too thick to be an expendable tripwire. Gen. Ariel Sharon, who assumed command of the southern front in 1970, proposed sealing the forts and maintaining Israel's presence in the canal zone with armored patrols and observation posts set well back from the waterline. A similar position was taken by Gen. Israel Tal, Elazar's deputy. The forts, he argued, constituted static targets and should be evacuated the moment war began.

Elazar told the General Staff that he did not rest the defense of the canal area on the forts but on tank forces. However, since the strongholds already existed and could interfere with an Egyptian crossing in their immediate locales, there was no point in dismantling them. They also provided ongoing observation of the Egyptian lines. In addition, he said, flying the Israeli flag on the canal was an important political statement. "Even if I thought that the strongholds were worthless from the military point of view, I would be in a quandary over whether to abandon them from the political standpoint. When I factor in that they do help to secure the line and provide a little intelligence, I'm no longer faced with a dilemma." He had no objection, he said, to thinning out the line, but he would not abandon it. Sharon interpreted "thinning out" in his own fashion. By the time he left Southern Command in the summer of 1973, fourteen of the thirty forts had been shut down. But the Israeli defense of the canal zone was still tied to this string of outposts left over from another war.

The debate over the Bar-Lev Line reflected the paradox of Israeli military planning. Because of Israel's narrow boundaries, it was basic IDF doctrine before the Six Day War that in the event of an Arab attack the war must be carried swiftly onto enemy territory. That war had pushed the cease-fire line in Sinai 150 miles from Israel's border, but doctrine had not been changed to reflect this fact. Israel's objective in the event of an Arab attack was to prevent the enemy from achieving any gain and thereby discourage future attempts. This was interpreted to mean that the Egyptians must be prevented from gaining a foothold on the Israeli-held Sinai bank east of the Suez Canal.

But by thus drawing a political line in the sand at the very edge of the Suez Canal, Israel was waiving the major military asset it had won in the Six Day War—strategic depth. Despite having a broad desert to fall back into, the "no enemy gain" formula meant that the Israeli forces on the canal would have to fight with the same back-to-the-wall stubbornness as if defending Israel's heartland. Given the depth afforded by Sinai, it made eminent sense to fall back and draw the Egyptians into the desert in a war of maneuver, at which the Israeli armored corps excelled and the Egyptian army didn't.

Elazar was not indifferent to the merits of such a move. At a meeting of the General Staff in the spring of 1972, he permitted himself to fantasize. "If I know that they're going to attack in the morning, we could say—as an intellectual exercise—that under certain circumstances thirty kilometers in Sinai could be completely evacuated. We let them move five divisions into Sinai, and then we slam the door on them. Such a battle implies a number of political risks but it's a beauty and I'm sure it would make it into the military history books. We have no interest in war, but if one breaks out, it's an historic opportunity to deal a crushing military and political blow that would last for a very long time to come." It was, however, merely a passing reverie. Both in Sinai and on the Golan, Elazar stressed, there would be no tactical withdrawals. "We've got to kill them on the canal."

Intelligence believed that if war came it would likely be a renewed war of attrition consisting of artillery barrages and small-scale raids. Another possible scenario was an Egyptian attempt to seize a limited foothold on the Sinai bank and hold it until a cease-fire was imposed.

To deal with these possibilities, the IDF drew up a defense plan code-named Dovecote. It rested on the three hundred tanks of the Sinai Division—the only armored division of the standing army—and on the air force. So confident was the Israeli command of coping with an Egyptian foray that the plan dealt only sketchily with the defensive battle itself and focused instead on a swift counterattack across the canal.

In the event that the Egyptians attempted a full-scale crossing, a broader plan had been drawn up. Code-named Sela (Rock), it called for the deployment behind the lines of two reserve armored divisions which would be mobilized before the war on the basis of intelligence warnings. Like Dovecote, Sela dealt only in passing with the actual defensive phase, as if the swift destruction of Egyptian forces crossing the canal was too straightforward to require elaborate planning. It left the task of dealing with the Egyptian incursion, in fact, to the Sinai Division and the air force, as in Dovecote. The reserve divisions would be able to help out if needed, but their focus would be on a massive counterattack across the canal.

In the unlikely event that intelligence did not provide sufficient warning for the reserve divisions to deploy before the war started, the Sinai Division was expected to hold the Egyptian army off, with the assistance of the air force, until the reserves arrived. It was like expecting a napkin to serve as a tablecloth in a pinch. The planners did not provide a flexible alternative that would permit one division to hold off five divisions in the event of a surprise attack by falling back in a delaying action. The Sinai Division would in all circumstances stop the Egyptians on the canal.

In a war game staged by Southern Command in August 1972, four Egyptian divisions were depicted crossing the canal, with only a forty-eight-hour warning given by intelligence. In the exercise, dubbed Battering Ram, the Sinai Division wiped out the Egyptian bridgehead in half a day. On the third day, the first Israeli reserve division reached the front and crossed the canal near its northern end. The forty-eight-hour warning was regarded by participants as absurdly short notice given the quality of Israeli military intelligence—a warning of five or six days was considered closer to reality. The notion that the Egyptians might stage a full-scale crossing without even a forty-eight-hour warning was too far-fetched to waste time on in war games. Sharon said that the exercise proved that the Sinai Division could meet any Egyptian threat on its own. In view of the way the Arab armies had fallen apart in the Six Day War, it was hard to imagine otherwise.

There was one Israeli officer who thought it possible to thwart an Egyptian crossing before it even reached the Israeli side of the canal. Col. David Lascov headed a secret unit which developed special weapons and other devices. At sixty-six, Lascov was the oldest Israeli officer on active duty. Born in Siberia and trained in architecture, he became a target for the Soviet secret police because of his Zionist activities. He fled via China to Haifa in the 1930s, served in the British army in the Second World War, and was an early recruit to Israel's army. Over the years, he had come up with numerous ingenious solutions to operational problems. It occurred to him that if the Egyptians attempted to cross the canal, Israel might inflict a blow comparable to that inflicted on Pharaoh's army when it tried to follow the Israelites through the parted waters of the nearby Red Sea more than three thousand years before. Lascov intended to go the Almighty one better by setting the waters afire. It was a solution of biblical resonance but achievable with simple engineering.

Large fuel tanks were installed belowground for this purpose at two of the canal-side fortifications. Pipes led to the canal edge. From within the fort, the commander could release the fuel and ignite it with an electric spark. The system, dubbed Dusky Light, was tested in February 1971 at one of the forts. The flames and dense cloud of black smoke that covered the placid canal waters alarmed the Egyptians. The Israeli command was less impressed. The fire did not cover a large area and burned itself out too quickly. In addition, considerable maintenance problems developed with the system. Sharon, as front commander, preferred to invest the funds allocated to Dusky Light in roads. Sixteen dummy installations were built instead—outlet pipes meant to be seen and to serve as a deterrent. Gradually, the two real installations fell into neglect and their exact locations were unknown to most personnel serving on the front. But the Egyptians kept the threat firmly in mind.

On a line of sand hills five to six miles east of the canal—the first high ground inside Sinai—a second, thinner line of outposts was built. These served as tank and artillery staging areas. In the event of an Egyptian attack, tanks would race from here to the canal-side forts. The outposts were linked by a north–south road called the Artillery Road. Fifteen miles further east, another north–south road—the Lateral Road—served the rear area. A series of east–west roads linked the Lateral and Artillery Roads with each other and with the canal road, code-named Lexicon, a mile from the waterway itself. These three roads—roughly one, five, and twenty miles east of the canal and parallel to it—would be pivots around which future battles would unfold.

The post–Six Day War deployment of the IDF on the canal and on the Golan Heights had placed a special burden on military intelligence. The Egyptian and Syrian armies had in the past kept the bulk of their armies well back from their borders. When Egypt moved its divisions into Sinai before the Six Day War, signaling hostile intent, Israel had more than two weeks to fully mobilize and deploy. Israel lost this early warning buffer after the Six Day War since the Egyptian and Syrian armies were drawn up in strength only a few hundred yards from the new Israeli lines inside their territory.

In October 1972, after returning from posting as military attaché in Washington, Gen. Eli Zeira was appointed head of military intelligence, known by its Hebrew acronym, AMAN. Zeira had once served as Dayan's aide-de-camp and was said to be the general whom Dayan most respected. The brilliant, self-assured officer was already being mooted as a coming chief of staff. In some circles, however, his appointment created unease. After Zeira addressed a forum of senior officers in his new capacity, a colonel commanding a paratroop brigade remarked to a fellow officer as they left the hall that he was troubled by Zeira's overweening self-confidence. The colonel would have preferred an intelligence chief more open to uncertainty.

AMAN was the leader of Israel's intelligence community. It was responsible for formulating the "national intelligence estimate," which served not
only the General Staff but the government in decision making. The Mossad
was responsible for intelligence collection abroad, but for all its reputation, it
deferred to AMAN on assessments of Arab capabilities and intentions.

To ensure early warning in the new circumstances, AMAN under Zeira
no longer relied only on analysis of what the enemy was capable of doing—
he was now capable of attacking on very short notice—but principally on
analysis of what he *intended* to do.

This could normally be equated with a reading of entrails, particularly
when dealing with autocratic regimes where decisions lie mainly with a single man. But Zeira's belief that he understood Anwar Sadat's thinking rested
on more than his own analytical abilities. The intelligence chief had discovered when he assumed his post that Israel had access to a supersource who
would be described as "an economically well-established man in Egypt." It
was the kind of source that intelligence officers dream about, supplying high-
quality military-political information and insights from the heart of the
Arab world. He had walked into the Israeli embassy in London in 1969 to
offer his services. Despite initial skepticism, his claim to have access to
Egypt's political-military pinnacle had proven itself in the quality intelligence he provided. The Mossad ran extensive checks and concluded that he
was not a double agent. It was to him that Dayan referred years later when
he said that Israel's prewar intelligence on Egyptian thinking was based on
solid information. "I can say with total certainty that any intelligence service,
chief of staff, and defense minister in the world, having received this information and knowing its origins, would have come to the same conclusion."

It was from this agent—who would be referred to as "the Source" by a
postwar commission of inquiry—that Israel learned the key to Sadat's strategic thinking. The Egyptian leader was determined to regain all of Sinai and
would go to war if he had to. But he would not do so before two conditions
were met. He wanted first to receive from the Soviet Union fighter-bombers
capable of neutralizing the Israeli air force by attacking bases inside Israel.
And he wanted Scud missiles capable of hitting Tel Aviv. This was intended
to deter Israel from striking the Egyptian heartland. Israeli intelligence knew
from other sources that the Egyptians were indeed negotiating with the Soviets for long-range planes and Scuds. The Soviets had not yet supplied them
and therefore Egypt was not yet ready to go to war.

Zeira had inherited "the concept," as this assessment came to be called,
but he embraced it without reservation. It was Sadat's concept, not his, and

from an Egyptian point of view it made sense. Zeira assured the General Staff that whatever angry noises Egypt might make, it would not go to war until those two conditions were met. And Syria, which was far weaker, would certainly not go to war without Egypt.

Half a year after Zeira took over the intelligence branch, his analytical abilities and nerves were put to the ultimate test. In the spring of 1973, unprecedented movement was detected of Egyptian troops, artillery, and bridging equipment to the canal front. Intelligence assets, including "the Source," reported Sadat's intention to go to war. Cairo placed its army on high alert and expeditionary forces from Iraq, Algeria, and other Arab countries took up positions in the Egyptian line. Two squadrons of warplanes arrived in Egypt from Iraq and Libya. The latter squadron consisted of Mirages capable of reaching Israel. Intelligence sources cited a date in mid-May for the war to commence, and the IDF was placed on alert status— code-named "Blue-White."

On May 8, Prime Minister Meir visited army headquarters for a briefing. If the Egyptians intended to go to war, she was told, Israel would know about it. "How will we know?" she asked. "By the preparations?" If the entire Egyptian army was planning to cross the canal, Zeira assured her, the IDF would know. Syria was unlikely to join in, he said, unless it felt, after the battle with Egypt was already under way, that Israel was in difficulty. The Syrians had no barrier like the Suez Canal separating their capital from the IDF, and their air force had no chance against Israel's. Therefore they would be very cautious. In any event, the chances of an all-out war with Egypt, which alone might bring in the Syrians, were "very low," said Zeira. Mrs. Meir's simplistic-sounding question was more to the point than she realized, because Zamir's analysis was *not* in fact determined by Egypt's preparations but by his understanding of Sadat's thinking.

Elazar did not accept Zeira's "low probability" assessment. War was not a certainty but he ordered the General Staff to act as if it were. Blue-White preparations included the shifting of tank depots closer to the fronts, speeding up the creation of new units, and readying equipment to bridge the Suez Canal.

The head of the Mossad, Zvi Zamir, did not share Zeira's assessment either. He believed that Sadat was ready for war, regardless of "the concept." He did not go so far as to forecast war but he supported the preparations being undertaken by the IDF. Dayan also believed war a reasonable option for Egypt since it would end political stalemate and bring international intervention. If war came, he said, it would be all-out.

Zeira emerged from the Blue-White episode with his reputation, and his self-confidence, greatly enhanced. With alarm bells going off all around him and the nation's fate at stake, he had coolly maintained throughout the crisis that the probability of war was not only low but "very low." Even senior analysts on his own staff had challenged his assessment, but he stuck to it, unperturbed. It was AMAN's task, he would say, to keep the national blood pressure down and not sound alarms unnecessarily. Otherwise, the reserves would be mobilized every couple of months with devastating effect on the economy and on morale.

Appearing before the Knesset Foreign Affairs and Defense Committee in May, Zeira said, "If the Egyptian army is planning to cross the canal, warning indicators will reach us." Even in their current deployment, poised to spring, there were a number of specific steps the Egyptians and Syrians would have to take before opening fire. In fact, however, Zeira gave higher priority to his own analysis of Sadat's intentions than to these "warning indicators" on AMAN's checklist.

Zeira's triumph was an indirect rebuke for Elazar. Criticism was voiced in the government of the heavy expenditures the Blue-White logistical initiatives had involved and there was a clear risk that the chief of staff would be viewed as an alarmist if he again cried wolf. In future, he would think twice before challenging Zeira's evaluations.

In the general relief at the end of the crisis, little notice was given to a report coming across the Egyptian desk at intelligence headquarters. Only some of the bridging equipment and artillery that the Egyptians brought to the canal had been returned to bases in the rear. The remainder was still in storage areas in the canal zone.

Four

BADR

GENERAL ZEIRA'S READING OF EGYPT'S STRATEGY, which he would cling to confidently over the course of a year, was obsolete even before he adopted it. The very month Zeira took over AMAN, Anwar Sadat revealed to his senior commanders that he had abandoned the concept on which the Israeli assessment was based.

The Egyptian president told the Supreme Council of the Armed Forces on October 24, 1972, that he intended to undertake military action without waiting any longer for long-range aircraft and Scud missiles. His objectives in Sinai could be achieved with lesser means. "We have to manage our affairs with whatever we have at hand," he said.

He had made his decision about the time he expelled the Soviet advisers in July, ordering the minister of war, Gen. Mohammed Ahmed Sadek, to have the army ready for war by mid-November. When Sadat at the October meeting asked Sadek for a report on the army's readiness, the general leaned over in embarrassment to whisper that he had not passed the order on to most of the generals for fear that it would be leaked. Two days later, Sadat dismissed Sadek. "He didn't want to fight," Sadat would write in his memoirs. Also dismissed were two generals and an admiral who had expressed reservations at the meeting about embarking on war.

General Sadek had maintained that only a war that forced Israel out of Sinai and the Gaza Strip would achieve Egypt's objectives. That, however, was a formula for doing nothing, since it was clearly beyond Egypt's capacity. Simply gaining a foothold on the Sinai bank of the canal, Sadat believed, would be sufficient to trigger superpower intervention and set off a political dynamic that would eventually force Israel to withdraw to the international border. To achieve this goal, it was not necessary to neutralize the Israeli air force by attacking its bases, a dubious prospect in any case. Soviet-made SAM surface-to-air missiles would serve instead to keep it at bay.

This approach had been urged by General Shazly, whom Sadat had appointed chief of staff a year earlier. A charismatic paratroop officer, Shazly was selected for his post over thirty more senior generals. His appointment reflected Sadat's determination to go to war. Shazly's personal flair and his readiness to "eat sand" by prolonged stays with his men in the field made him an appropriate choice for restoring the self-confidence lost by the army in the disaster of 1967. Cairo newspaper editor Mohammed Hassenein Heikal, a shrewd judge of men, would conclude that Shazly was no military genius but that his energy and attention to detail would lead the army to success. "He knew what he was doing in using his glamour to achieve his military ends, above all raising the army's morale for the task it faced."

General Sadek had initially rejected Shazly's proposal for a limited Egyptian foothold in Sinai on the grounds that an Israeli counterattack could pin the Egyptian forces against the canal, the very image Elazar had conjured up. Eventually, he authorized Shazly to draw up a plan, with the assistance of Soviet advisers, for an attack up to the Gidi and Mitla Passes, thirty-five to forty miles east of the canal—a plan known as Granite 2.

Even this was regarded by Shazly as unrealistic since it would take the Egyptian forces beyond the SAM umbrella. He was finally authorized to draw up a still more limited plan. Named High Minarets, it envisioned an advance of only five or six miles eastward from the canal, a range just covered by the SAM batteries. In Shazly's view, this was Egypt's only realistic offensive option.

In the Six Day War, as a division commander, Shazly had barely escaped the Israeli onslaught, reportedly swimming back across the canal after his forces were destroyed. He had seen the devastation inflicted on the retreating army by Israeli warplanes operating with impunity over the battlefield. He did not want to put the army at risk again to an unfettered Israeli air force.

At the same time, Shazly did not accept the notion that Egypt could not go to war until its air force had neutralized Israel's air superiority. He expressed this view at a meeting of the Armed Forces Supreme Council attended by Sadat in June 1972. "If we are going to base our planning upon an adequate air force, we will have to postpone the battle for years and years," he said. "In fact, I believe the gap between our air force and the enemy's will tend to widen rather than narrow. We therefore have no choice but to prepare for a battle under conditions of enemy air superiority. We can do it by challenging that superiority with SAMs." It was a rational assessment which would be reflected in Sadat's revised strategy presented to the council four months later.

The person named by Sadat to replace Sadek as war minister, Gen. Ahmed Ismail, was the last man in the Egyptian army Shazly would have chosen to serve with, let alone under. The two men were longtime foes because of a squabble originating in the Congo in 1960. Ismail, heading an Egyptian military mission to the Congolese army, tried to interfere with Shazly's command of an Egyptian contingent that was part of a UN peace-keeping force. Shazly had thrown a punch at Ismail, who outranked him, and the two men thereafter maintained an icy relationship whenever their common career brought them into contact. Shazly regarded Ismail as both indecisive and a bully. He submitted his resignation in 1969 when Nasser appointed Ismail chief of staff. It was only Nasser's personal intervention that persuaded Shazly, then head of special forces, to remain. Six months later Ismail was dismissed following an Israeli armored raid on the Red Sea coast that met no resistance. Sadat had now recalled him as war minister, to general surprise.

Thrown together once again in a working relationship, Shazly and Ismail managed to suspend their mutual distaste. Shazly showed Ismail both the Granite 2 plan for reaching the passes and the limited High Minarets plan. The minister accepted Shazly's opinion that only the latter was feasible and told him to proceed with detailed planning. Thus, an entirely new Egyptian strategic concept began to take shape even as Israeli intelligence clung confidently to the old. In time, the name of the limited plan would be changed to Badr, the site of the Prophet Mohammed's first military victory in A.D. 624.

Shazly's plan was completed by January 1973 but would continue to be refined over the coming months. Its outline was simple, but in the myriad, interlocking details lay its grandeur.

Five Egyptian infantry divisions had been deployed along the canal since the 1967 war. Three divisions, occupying the northern part of the line, constituted the Second Army. The southern two divisions constituted the Third Army. It was a basic premise of any Egyptian plan that a canal crossing would be made simultaneously at points all along the hundred-mile canal line. This would play Egypt's best hand—its abundant manpower—against Israel's worst—its limited manpower.

The Egyptian army had been extensively revamped since the debacle of 1967. The heavily politicized General Staff had been purged and new commanders chosen on the basis of competence rather than connections. In the armored corps, illiterates, who had made up a significant percentage of tank crews, were replaced. University graduates, previously exempt from serving in the army, were now drafted, significantly upgrading the quality of the officer corps. Intensive training with the new Soviet military equipment honed the army's skills.

Before coming to grips with the Israelis, the Egyptians would have to overcome the obstacle of the canal itself. Some 180 yards wide, it was subject to tides which rose and fell up to two yards. From the canal edge on the Israeli side rose a steep sand barrier 60 feet high, forming the outer edge of the Bar-Lev Line.

The assault crossing would be carried out in rubber boats. The commandos in the first wave would be supplied with rope ladders which they would secure to the top of the Israeli barrier to make it easier for the subsequent waves to climb. After the assault waves secured the Sinai bank, the bulk of the army would cross by bridges and ferries after openings had been cut through the rampart. Experiments in blasting openings through sand ramparts with explosives proved disappointing. A young engineering officer finally provided the solution. Heavy water cannon, he noted, had been used during construction of the Aswan Dam to cut openings through sand dunes. Light pumps floated across the canal might do the same to the Israeli earthwork. Tests behind the Egyptian lines proved that the idea worked, and hundreds of pumps were purchased in Britain and Germany. Israeli intelligence was aware of the Egyptian plan to use water cannon to open breaches in the sand barrier but dismissed it as unfeasible.

High priority was given to neutralizing Lascov's "fire-on-the-water" system. An initial idea was to form firefighting units which would beat the flames out with palm fronds. Another proposal was to use chemical extinguishers. Shazly didn't think either approach efficient. He decided to try to block the fuel outlets on the Israeli bank just before the crossing or to rupture the buried fuel tanks with artillery fire. If these efforts failed, the crossings would be made upstream of the outlets, leaving the canal's current to carry the burning fuel away. In a worst-case situation, the crossing would simply have to be delayed until the fuel burned itself out.

In the back of every Egyptian's mind was the trauma of the 1967 rout and the fear that it might be repeated. Whether or not this would happen depended largely on Shazly and his planning staff, headed by Gen. Mohamed Abdel Ghani el-Gamasy, chief of operations. By not foraying beyond the SAM umbrella, the Egyptians believed they would be spared air attack, provided the Israelis had not figured out how to foil the SAM missiles. But what of the Israeli tanks? Egyptian intelligence knew the outlines of the Dovecote plan from documents they had captured in cross-canal raids and from observing the frequent training exercises along the canal. Within less than half an hour of the opening barrage, the first of the Israeli tanks would reach the canal from the Artillery Road. Egyptian tanks could not cross to challenge them until openings had been sliced through the sand barriers and bridges erected, which would take hours. Until then, the Israeli armor would have to be held off by foot soldiers with antitank weaponry.

There were two weapons the Soviets had supplied for this purpose. One was the shoulder-held RPG-7 (rocket-propelled grenade), a successor to the World War II bazooka-type weapons, which was highly effective at close range. It had been developed by the Soviets in 1961 to penetrate the armor of NATO tanks and would still be in use after the turn of the century. It could hit a target at 300 yards but was generally used at closer ranges. The other weapon, carried in what resembled a suitcase, was called the Malotka by the Soviets; in the West it was known by its NATO designation as the Sagger. The case opened to reveal a small missile connected to a length of thin wire and to a joystick. The operator would guide the Sagger to target with the joystick, which sent signals down the wire unreeling behind the missile. Its range was 3,000 yards, about the maximum effective range of a tank gun, and its impact was no less deadly than a tank shell.

The Egyptian infantrymen would be fighting alone during the critical early hours, but they would get covering fire from ramps the Egyptians had built on the west side of the canal. Instead of one continuous ramp the length of the canal, as on the Israeli side, the Egyptians raised scores of separate ramps at strategic locations. The Israeli ramp had initially been higher, and every time the Egyptians raised theirs, the Israelis raised theirs as well. But in 1972, the Egyptians undertook a massive construction project at the order of Ismail in which the Egyptian ramps grew to twice the height of the Israeli barrier.

The Israelis chose not to raise their ramp again. Instead, they built tank emplacements, which they called "fins," up to a mile behind their canal-side strongpoints. From here, protected by long, low earthworks shaped like inverted V's, whence the name "fins," they could duel with the tanks atop the

Egyptian ramp, relying on superior gunnery to overcome the Egyptian advantage in height.

The Egyptians had grasped Israel's operational mode and had formulated an effective strategy to counter it. The Israelis would respond aggressively to an Egyptian attack, attempting to destroy the SAMs with air attacks and rushing tank forces forward to destroy the bridgeheads. The Egyptian response would be judo-like, letting the enemy's forward thrust be his undoing.

The SAM air defense system supplied by the Soviet Union was one of the strongest in the world. It was backed by hundreds of antiaircraft guns defending against low-flying aircraft which the SAMs could not lock on to.

In the ground battle, the intention was to let the Israeli armor break against a defensive wall that included thousands of Saggers and RPGs. This was an antitank array no army had yet encountered. Shazly ordered all units not crossing in the early waves to transfer their Sagger contingents to those that were. Until the Egyptian tanks could cross, the infantry units in Sinai would form shallow, dense bridgeheads in order to concentrate their antitank fire. They would be supported by tanks and antitank guns firing across the canal from the Egyptian ramparts.

The Egyptian attack plan was impeccable. But there were major unknowns. How soon would Israeli intelligence become aware of the pending attack, and what steps would the IDF then take to thwart it? Also unknown was the ability of the Egyptian troops to bear up to whatever Israel was going to throw at them.

Five

ILLUSIONS

I T WAS OPERA, THOUGHT BENNY PELED, and bad opera at that.
Reviewing contingency plans upon his appointment as Israel Air
Force (IAF) commander in May 1973, General Peled found the proposals for
suppression of the SAM missile batteries complex to the point of absurdity.

Israel had encountered SAM-2s in the Six Day War and lost three planes
to them. But the missile batteries had been few and were easily destroyed by
low-level attack. In the War of Attrition, the nuisance became a nemesis.
Deployed in large numbers, the batteries, each with six missile launchers,
were now mutually supporting. The defenses had also been reinforced by
SAM-3s, which were more difficult to evade.

In July 1970, the air force tested a system devised by the Americans for
countering SAM-2s over North Vietnam. It was based on electronic pods
which sent signals distorting the missile's radar. Warplanes equipped with
these pods were required to maintain formation at precise altitudes even if
missiles were fired at them. The Americans themselves did not know if the
method was effective against SAM-3s. But the need for finding a solution to
the SAM threat was so critical that the commander of one of the IAF's two
Phantom squadrons, Col. Shmuel Hetz, pressed for the American system
to be put to the test.

Hetz led the first flight of twenty Phantoms into the missile zone. Activating the pods slung beneath their wings, the Phantoms held steady course

as the sky around them blossomed with exploding missiles. The planes got through to destroy four of the ten batteries targeted and damage three others. But one plane was downed on the way back. It was Hetz's, hit by a SAM-3. His navigator bailed out and was captured. Hetz did not manage to parachute. A Phantom flown by the other squadron commander, Col. Avihu Bin-Nun, was also hit, and he barely succeeded in landing at a base in Sinai, his plane running off the runway and plowing into the sand for one hundred yards. Five Phantoms, the pride of the Israeli air force, would be downed by missiles before the cease-fire went into effect three weeks later.

In the ensuing lull, the air force was left with the queasy realization that it no longer held unchallenged mastery of the skies. The technological edge it enjoyed over the Arabs had been reversed almost overnight. The problem became even more acute when the Egyptians, flouting the cease-fire, moved missiles into the canal zone, from which their reach extended over Israeli-held western Sinai.

The best minds in the air force were devoted in the coming years to the missile challenge. What Benny Peled found on his desk was a plan devised by a team headed by Bin-Nun that sought to make up with tactics what was lacking in technology. Code-named Tagar, it envisaged a complex aerial ballet executed by hundreds of planes performing exacting maneuvers at top speed and with stopwatch precision. A similar plan, code-named Dougman 5, was drawn up for the Golan Heights.

The Israelis eventually succeeded in creating a jamming system against the SAM-3s, but the appearance in 1972 of the SAM-6 posed a more menacing threat. The electronic parameters of the new missile were unknown even to the Americans. They would therefore have to be attacked without precise electronic foreplay, which greatly increased the risks. From war games, the air force had concluded that it could lose as much as one plane per SAM battery attacked. Given that there were eighty-seven batteries on the Egyptian and Syrian fronts—not to mention another ninety-five defending rear areas such as air bases—there was an immense price to be paid if this projection held, even if only the frontline batteries were attacked. Some air force officers maintained that Tagar and Dougman were too complex and too rigid to work. But no one offered a better solution.

Ironically, Peled was the only senior airman in the IAF who had not experienced missiles close-up. He had joined the air force as a mechanic and only later became a pilot, rising to squadron commander. But the technical side of flying always intrigued him. He was an unexpected choice for the top command. In a clubby organization filled with superb pilots and fighter aces,

Peled had never downed an enemy plane. He himself had been shot down in the 1956 Sinai Campaign. His extended absences on special development projects made him something of an outsider. But his intellect, organizational brilliance, and ample self-confidence left no question once he took over about who was running the shop. He had an acerbic tongue and did not suffer fools.

The missiles, he discovered, had traumatized the air force. For long virtually invulnerable in dogfights, the fliers had seen Hetz and other top pilots suddenly brushed away by a new weapon system that threatened to drive them all from the sky. Most of the air force's energies and much of its budget were dedicated to the missile question, diverting attention from critical subjects like strategic warfare and close support of ground forces. Meeting with the Tagar planners, Peled said he believed their scheme could work, but only in a perfect world. Success required that the operation be launched when the sun would be in the enemy's eyes and in good weather. It would need fresh intelligence, from the morning of the planned attack or the previous evening, fixing the exact location of the missiles. It would also need thirty-six hours' notice to prepare necessary electronic accoutrements to foil the enemy radar. Above all, it required a government decision to launch a preemptive attack which alone could ensure these ideal conditions. This meant relying on politicians. Peled determined to find another solution, but meanwhile Tagar and Dougman 5 remained on the books.

Shortly after taking command, Peled was paid a formal visit by Dayan, Elazar, and other members of the General Staff. They had come to hear the new air force commander's war plans. With Peled were Bin-Nun and the other Tagar and Dougman 5 planners who spelled out their "star wars" proposals, as Peled would sardonically label them. The visitors were impressed at the sophistication of the plans and were relieved to be told there was a solution to the missile problem. Before they left, Peled brought them back to earth. "You should know that these plans aren't worth the paper they're written on unless we get permission to strike first." As Peled would recall it, Dayan replied, "Do you think that if we have even a hint of an Arab attack we will not attack first?"

The visit by the heads of the defense establishment and the comfort they drew from the airmen's presentation betrayed one of the basic flaws of Israel's defense posture—overdependence on the air force. The IAF received fully half the military budget and had come to be seen as an almost mystical problem solver. The flimsiness of the frontline forces deployed opposite the Egyptian and Syrian armies rested on the presumption that the air force would slow the enemy down if necessary until the reserves were mobilized. But this now depended on prior suppression of the missiles. Tagar and Dougman 5 were untested, and the arrival of the SAM-6s rendered these already complex operations even more chancy.

Just as a sense of dolce vita had come to permeate the civilian sector, flabbiness of thought had overcome the senior military command. Israel had fallen victim to its own victory in 1967. A success of such dimensions, against such odds, evoked a sense of Israeli power and of Arab dysfunction that was too powerful to ignore. There were some who saw in this disparity a divine hand, but most presumed a civilizational difference—a divide between East and West that would not be bridgeable for generations to come. "The Arab soldier lacks the characteristics necessary for modern war," then chief of staff Haim Bar-Lev declared in 1970. These characteristics, he said, included rapid reaction, technical competence, a high level of intelligence, adaptability, and, "above all, the ability to see events realistically and speak truth, even when it is difficult and bitter."

However, the Egyptians had proven, as far back as the first Israel-Arab war in 1948, that in defensive battles they were stubborn opponents. The 1967 rout had been touched off by a premature fallback order by Egypt's high command on the second day of the war, before 80 percent of its army had been in contact with the enemy. A fleeing army may be dismissed as rabble. But that same army, infused by better leadership with motivation, could prove formidable. In the War of Attrition, which saw daring commando raids behind Israeli lines, the Egyptian army showed that it had another face.

Israel's tank corps was a particular victim of the victory syndrome. Its success in the 1956 Sinai Campaign and the Six Day War in breaking through heavily defended Egyptian positions reinforced the notion that the tank was king.

Israel's tank doctrine rested in good part on a concept developed by General Tal during his seven years as head of the armored corps, a concept which came to be called "the totality of the tank." Conventional doctrine, deriving from vast experience in World War II, called for a combined arms approach in which tanks advanced in tandem with infantry and artillery. The infantrymen served to protect the tanks from enemy ground troops wielding antitank weapons while artillery provided both with support. Engineers moved with the spearhead to clear minefields and other obstacles.

Tal, however, believed that on the desert battlefields of the Middle East the tank could for the most part manage alone. Visibility was far clearer than in hazy Europe and there was precious little brush for infantrymen with bazookas to hide behind. As for enemy antitank guns, these are easily spotted in the naked desert and could be hit at a distance with accurate gunfire. Tanks would advance swiftly to reduce exposure to enemy fire, not stopping till they had broken the enemy line. Such a charge would create an effect of "armor shock." Infantry would follow to mop up. Since the charging tanks would quickly outrun artillery, they would rely primarily on their own guns and on the air force. Fewer artillery pieces and fewer armored personnel carriers (APCs) or half-tracks for carrying infantry meant more funds that could be allocated to tanks. Tal stressed tank gunnery training, and Israeli tank crews opened fire at longer range than in any other army. A senior American armor general who closely studied the Israeli armored corps would term its gunnery the best in the world.

This "totality of the tank" approach had its opponents even within the armored corps, but the results of the Six Day War appeared to confirm its validity. Several times, Israeli tank columns broke through fortified Egyptian positions by brazen, head-on attacks with virtually no assistance from artillery or infantry. Critics would note, however, that the fact that it worked in the context of that war, in which the surprise Israeli assault had stunned the Egyptians, did not necessarily prove its applicability in every war. There were other battles in the 1967 war which were won by effective use of combined arms, including battles by Tal's division, but it was the dashing tank charge that seized the army's imagination.

In 1972 when the infantry corps requested better weapons, including rifles and antitank weapons, Tal—now deputy chief of staff—said the Belgian FN rifles it had were adequate. As for antitank weapons, he said, the IDF already had the best antitank system in the world, namely the armored corps.

The acquisition by the Egyptians and Syrians of the Sagger antitank missile made little impression on the Israelis. They had encountered a number of missiles in exchanges of fire across the lines during the War of Attrition and regarded them as just another antitank weapon along with conventional antitank guns, recoilless rifles, and tanks themselves, not a threat that required a basic revision of doctrine. AMAN printed booklets about the Sagger's characteristics based on information received from the United States, which had encountered the missile in Vietnam in 1972. The armored corps command had even developed tactics for dealing with the missile. But neither the booklets nor the suggested tactics had yet filtered down and few tank men were even aware of the Sagger's existence.

Its introduction, however, transformed the battlefield. Unlike conventional antitank guns, the Sagger was wielded by a single soldier. He did not need bushes to hide behind; lying behind a small pile of sand or in a shallow foxhole would be enough to render him invisible from a distance to tank crews. The Sagger operator would find it much easier to hit a tank than the other way around—and at ranges that matched the tank's.

Israel was also aware that masses of RPGs had been acquired by the Egyptians and Syrians but did not find convincing the thought of Arab infantrymen meeting a tank charge head-on.

Another technical advance in the Arab armies—the acquisition of infrared equipment for night fighting—was likewise noted and dismissed. Night fighting had been Israel's preferred mode in its War of Independence in 1948. Its lightly armed troops used the darkness to close on the enemy, something that would have been costly in daylight. But as the army over the years acquired heavier weapons, daylight came to be seen as the best time to exploit this strength. The IDF continued to train in night fighting and to engage in it periodically, and there remained a myth that the IDF preferred night fighting while the Arabs were afraid of it. However, in the 1970s few Israeli tanks had night sights. By contrast, Soviet tanks in Egyptian and Syrian hands came equipped with infrared projectors as well as infrared headlights and infrared sights for the crew. Night sights were also widely distributed among infantry units.

Israel had not turned its back on night fighting but it preferred not using infrared devices which could be detected by an enemy with infrared binoculars. The armored corps was planning to acquire night sights that magnified starlight. Meanwhile, however, the Arab armies were equipped with night-viewing equipment and the IDF was not.

The Israeli navy had been spared the self-satisfaction which overtook the rest of the IDF after the Six Day War. Its antiquated collection of ships dating from the Second World War had taken virtually no part in the fighting. The defense establishment regarded the navy as little more than a coast guard and would not expend funds to build a modern fleet. It was clear that Israel's fate depended on its army and air force; whatever happened at sea would not matter much one way or the other.

In 1960, the service's senior officers assembled to discuss the navy's future. From this two-day conclave, a revolutionary concept emerged. Israel's fledgling defense industry was developing a missile that it was trying to peddle, in different versions, to the air force and the artillery corps. Neither was interested. The missile could be fired from long distances but had to be guided onto target by a forward observer manipulating a joystick. If the missile could be adapted for use at sea, the naval officers fantasized, its large warhead would give a small, cheap patrol boat the punch of a heavy cruiser.

In the coming years, the navy invested prodigious efforts in creating a sea-to-sea missile and the missile boat that would launch it, a weapon system no country had. It would take thirteen years of rigorous work by the navy and the military industries for the pieces to come together. During development, the idea of guiding the missile with a joystick was improved upon. The missile, dubbed the Gabriel, was provided with an electronic brain that permitted it to home in on a target and pursue it on its own.

Halfway through the project, it was learned that the Soviets had developed their own missile boats and had supplied them to the Egyptian and Syrian navies. Four months after the Six Day War, Egyptian missile boats emerging from Port Said harbor demonstrated for the first time the lethality of seaborne missiles when they sank Israel's flagship, the destroyer *Eilat*. An Israeli naval electronics expert, calculating the sort of homing device his Soviet counterpart had probably devised, developed electronic countermeasures to foil it.

An embargo declared by France impounded the last five of twelve missile boat platforms Israel had ordered from a shipbuilder in Cherbourg. On Christmas Eve, 1969, in the midst of a force-9 gale that kept even large freighters in port, Israeli sailors who had slipped into Cherbourg raised anchor and took the five vessels out. When the authorities realized the boats were gone, the infuriated French defense minister threatened to send planes to bomb the boats, but cooler heads prevailed. The boats sailed into the Haifa harbor on New Year's Eve and a virtually round-the-clock effort was launched to turn them into operational missile boats, the first in the West.

Like the Israeli navy, the Arabs had been spared the smugness induced by victory. Answers were painstakingly hammered out to Israel's superiority in air and armored warfare, thousands of officers were sent to advanced military courses in the Soviet Union, and intelligence officers were trained intensively in Hebrew in order to permit them to monitor Israeli communications. If Israel's thinking had been lulled by hubris, Arab thinking was sharpened by desperation. The "on to Tel Aviv" bravado of earlier wars that led to disaster had given way to sober war preparations.

The bizarre disproportion of forces along the front line rested on Israel's confidence that it would have enough warning to mobilize the reserves—

two-thirds of its fighting strength—before the war started. In the highly unlikely event of an intelligence failure, the fallback would be the air force, which would block any Arab incursion.

The possibility that the air force might be neutralized by the SAMs was not considered despite the fact that the War of Attrition had ended without an answer to the missiles having been found. It was presumed that the solutions the air force had since come up with—Tagger and Dougman 5—would work, even though they had not been tested. To envision a failure of the air force on top of a failure of the intelligence services would be pushing imagination to the point of perversity. The General Staff made no contingency study of what would happen if the Sinai Division had to hold off a surprise attack by five Egyptian divisions without the reserves—and without the air force.

There was still another worst-case scenario the high command did not consider—that innovative Egyptian tactics would cripple Israel's armor.

If any one of these three scenarios became reality, it would confront the IDF with a major challenge. If all three became reality—meaning neutralization of the IDF's intelligence, air force, and armor—Israel faced catastrophe.

Six

SUMMER LULL

THE PHONE IN HENRY KISSINGER'S ROOM at President Nixon's retreat in San Clemente, California, rang shortly after he returned from a farewell dinner for Leonid Brezhnev. The Soviet leader had asked to retire early in order to set out the next morning, June 24, 1973, for Moscow. The caller was a Secret Service agent who notified Kissinger that Brezhnev, in an unusual deviation from protocol, was asking for an immediate meeting with the president, who had already gone to bed.

Kissinger telephoned to waken the president and was with him when Brezhnev arrived forty-five minutes later. The Soviet leader said he wanted to discuss the Middle East, a subject he had failed to bring up during a week of talks in Washington and San Clemente. The proposal he spelled out was identical with Egypt's position—total Israeli withdrawal to its 1967 border in return for a nonbelligerency pact. If this was not accepted, warned Brezhnev, "we will have difficulty keeping the military situation from flaring up."

Though delivered almost as an afterthought, it was a clear threat that the Soviets could not, or would not, restrain their Arab clients from going to war if Israel did not meet their terms. Kissinger believed that Brezhnev's late night maneuver was an attempt to catch Nixon off guard and elicit a verbal agreement in the absence of the president's advisers, principally himself. The Soviets, he would later deduce, had been told by their Arab clients that they intended to go to war and Brezhnev was hoping that Nixon, by agreeing to pressure Israel into concessions, would spare Moscow the embarrassment of seeing its clients suffer an ignominious defeat. If war did break out, the Soviets could at least say they had given warning. The president smoothly deflected the proposal with a version of "we'll look into it" and bid Brezhnev good night.

The Arabs and Israelis were not alone in the Middle East. Even while pursuing their own regional power games, they were doubling as proxies for superpowers engaged in a global confrontation. The relationship between patron and proxy, however, was not one of commander-subordinate. To safeguard their foothold in Egypt, the Soviets had agreed to renew arms shipments to Cairo despite the jarring expulsion of their advisers the previous year. Several hundred Soviet experts and their families had in fact returned to Egypt together with the arms.

In Israel, the amicable Brezhnev-Nixon summit was taken to mean that war had receded from the horizon. The Arabs appeared paralyzed while Israel was redrawing the map of the Middle East by establishing settlements in the occupied territories, including Sinai.

A major source of confidence was the charismatic Moshe Dayan, whose standing as a security icon went far beyond his function as defense minister. Chief of staff during the successful Sinai Campaign of 1956 against Egypt, he had, on the eve of the Six Day War, been forced upon a reluctant government as defense minister by popular demand when the massing of Arab armies on Israel's borders appeared to pose an existential threat. He became the symbol of Israel's astonishing victory, receiving much of the credit due chief of staff Yitzhak Rabin.

Dayan's freebooter style and popular appeal were not appreciated by his cabinet colleagues. But they bowed to his judgment on defense matters. A rakish private life only enhanced Dayan's public aura, as did the general's black eye patch; he lost an eye when a bullet hit a telescope he was looking through in South Lebanon in 1941 while scouting for a British incursion into Vichy-held territory. Dayan did little to hide his extramarital adventures. He found solace too in the illicit embrace of the ancients, digging for archaeological artifacts in violation of Israel's antiquities law. He transferred them to his own home, where he relaxed from affairs of state by gluing broken pottery together and mounting the artifacts in his garden. Pragmatic and nononsense in his daily life, he permitted himself a mystic attachment to the ancient people who had shaped the clay vessels he unearthed. It was Dayan who formulated policy towards the occupied territories. He was willing to envision the return of territory in exchange for peace treaties. But not all territory. In a reference to the southern tip of the Sinai Peninsula which controlled maritime passage to Eilat, he famously said, "Better Sharm el-Sheikh without peace than peace without Sharm el-Sheikh."

Dayan would unashamedly change his mind when circumstance warranted—only donkeys don't change their minds, he would say. On May 21, during the Blue-White alert, he told the General Staff to prepare for war in the second half of summer. "We the government tell you, the General Staff, 'Gentlemen, please prepare for war in which those who threaten to start the war are Egypt and Syria.' "

By the following month, however, the perceived threat had receded and Dayan's tone changed dramatically. In a speech atop the historic mount of Masada, he said that Israel's geopolitical circumstances were of a nature that "our people has probably never witnessed." In an interview with *Time* magazine, he predicted that there would be no war for ten years. To the General Staff, he now said, "We are on the threshold of the crowning period of the Return to Zion."

In Washington, a relatively junior analyst in the State Department's Bureau of Intelligence and Research, Roger Merrick, submitted a memo in May noting that Sadat's political alternatives were exhausted. Unless there was a credible U.S. peace initiative, he wrote, the chances of an Israeli-Egyptian war within six months were better than fifty-fifty.

Many in the Israeli hierarchy held similar views, but there was general agreement that war, while regrettable, would bring the Arabs, after their defeat, closer to accepting Israel's terms. "We're not interested in war," said General Elazar at a meeting at Golda Meir's home on April 18. But if war did break out, he continued, "I favor striking such a blow over a week or ten days that they'll need five years to lift their heads up again."

Mrs. Meir herself did not regard war as a strategic opportunity but as something to be avoided. If it appeared likely to break out, she said at the meeting, the Americans should be notified and asked to head it off. At this point, her closest political adviser, minister without portfolio Israel Galili, raised a delicate point. The danger of war, he noted, stemmed from Israel's unwillingness to withdraw to the 1967 borders. Referring to the meeting between Hafez Ismail and Kissinger in February, on which the Israelis had been briefed, he said, "If you take what Hafez said as a starting point—that [the Egyptians] are ready for peace . . . this is based on our complete pullback to the previous lines."

He later returned to this theme, as if fearing his previous remark may have been too oblique. "There is also a possibility that we can avoid all this mess [the danger of war] if we are prepared to enter into talks on the basis of returning to the previous border." From the protocol, Galili's remark sounds more like an observation than a proposal, but the fact that he voiced it twice suggests that the veteran political adviser, of hawkish bent, thought it perhaps worthy of exploration.

Mrs. Meir, however, declined to pursue it, either at this meeting with her kitchen cabinet and senior military officials or with the full cabinet. She was against war but she was also against total withdrawal from the territories. As she put it in a speech: "Neither war nor the threat of war" would move Israel from its insistence on defensible borders. "We will make every effort that these borders be accepted by our neighbors. We want defensible borders not only so that if we are ever attacked we will be able to defend them but so that the borders by their very existence will dissuade our neighbors from touching us."

Mrs. Meir had not informed the government either about the proposals Ismail had floated or about the indications of Egyptian war preparations that led to the Blue-White alert. Galili suggested that she do so in order to forestall complaints from ministers later in case war did break out.

In later years, a battle-tested Israeli paratroop general would lament the fact that Mrs. Meir had excluded the full cabinet from ongoing discussions on the crisis in the months before the war. "What we needed were ministers like [minister for religious affairs] Zerah Warhaftig [a Holocaust survivor], who was frightened by the prospect of war, saying 'Let's think this through again.' "

In July, Gen. Ariel Sharon stepped down as head of Southern Command, the most important of the IDF's regional commands, and retired from the army. He was replaced by Gen. Shmuel Gonen. The appointment by Elazar of this relatively inexperienced general drew criticism, particularly from some of Gonen's peers. Apart from the question of experience, they believed him clearly unsuited for the post. He had earned his reputation in the Six Day War when he commanded the tank brigade that broke through the Egyptian lines in northern Sinai and was the first to reach the Suez Canal.

His men would remember seeing him through the shell smoke in his open command half-track at the forefront of the battle, and they remembered the moving talk he had given at war's end. "We looked death in the eyes," he had said, "and it averted its gaze."

While admired as a brave and competent field commander, he terrorized subordinates and jailed soldiers wholesale for minor infractions. On an

inspection visit to one battalion, he reportedly ordered eighty-two men pun-
ished for various infractions, including buttons left unbuttoned. His theory
was that discipline was indivisible and that sloppiness in minor matters could
lead to indiscipline in battle at a critical moment. While the principle was
sound, his enforcement of it was tyrannical. He would regularly shout at
subordinates and would often throw things at them. On one occasion, when
a senior staff officer arrived late for a meeting, Gonen flung a microphone he
was holding, hitting the officer in the face. The officer, a reservist lieutenant
colonel, was a distinguished professor of economics in civilian life. Gonen
favored dark glasses and on speaking tours to American Jewish communities
enjoyed being billed as "the Israeli Patton."

Raised in Jerusalem's ultraorthodox community, Gonen had left that
insular world as a teenager during Israel's War of Independence to take part
in the fighting. Wounded several times, he remained in the army after the war
and was among the first to join the armored corps. As a young officer, he was
assigned to train Israel Tal and David Elazar, already senior officers, when
they transferred from the infantry to armor. The connection with these
important figures, who admired his expertise, was believed to have played a
role in his subsequent rise.

Gen. Avraham Adan, commander of the armored corps, had long been
disturbed by Gonen's behavior. Observing him during a large desert exercise,
Adan saw that Gonen's subordinates were afraid to report to him and did not
give straight answers for fear of his reaction. When the exercise was over,
Adan told Elazar, "Gorodish has no place in the IDF," using Gonen's original name, by which he was generally known. Elazar said only, "I'll speak to
him." But Gonen's advancement was not halted and he was now commanding Israel's major front.

As weeks passed uneventfully after the spring alert, tensions eased. Intelligence reported large arms shipments to Egypt and Syria in July, but there
was no sense of near-term conflagration, not even with the report on August
24 that the deterrence weapon long sought by Sadat, a brigade of Scud
ground-to-ground missiles, had arrived in Egypt. With a range of two hundred miles, the missiles could hit Tel Aviv from the Nile Delta. It would take
at least four months of training before they were to be handed over by the
Soviets to Egyptian crews. Along the canal front itself, there was no change
in the relaxed Egyptian deployment and their soldiers were daily seen fishing
in the canal.

Sadat, who had been hinting at imminent war since assuming office, had
switched to talk of "an extended struggle." Intelligence noted four speeches

during July in which he spoke of a "twenty-five-year strategy" to rectify the domestic situation and resolve the Israel-Arab question, a clear hint that the war option had been shelved for the foreseeable future.

Sadat's lowering of the rhetorical flames was part of an elaborate strategy embarked upon in May with the creation of an interministerial committee for deception. Rumors planted about the poor maintenance of Egypt's weapon systems were picked up by the foreign press, as were reports that Egyptian crews could not properly operate the SAMs. Rumors were also loosed about a falling-out between Egypt and Syria. War minister Ismail, on a visit to Romania, let drop that Egypt's military strength was insufficient for a confrontation with Israel. Central to the Egyptian deception was Sadat's ability to restrict knowledge about the coming war to a tiny number of civilian and military officials. Israeli intelligence would subsequently conclude that until late August only four persons in the Egyptian army were in on the secret.

Meanwhile, Cairo was executing a deception of another sort against Syria itself. A two-front war against Israel was basic to any Arab strategy; ragged Arab coordination had been a factor in Israel's victory in 1967 over Egypt, Syria, and Jordan. But Sadat and Syrian leader Hafez Assad had differing war aims. Sadat wanted a short, sharp blow aimed not at recapturing all Sinai, but at dislodging the political process from the status quo in which it was mired. Assad saw war as a vehicle for regaining by force the territory lost in 1967. Sadat did not believe the Syrian leader would risk war unless assured that Egypt was embarking on an all-out campaign that would tie down most of Israel's military strength.

Assad, a former air force commander, had seized power in Damascus in 1970, a month after Sadat assumed the reins in Egypt. His attitude towards Israel was far more implacable than that of Sadat. While the Egyptian leader was willing to contemplate peace with Israel—at least, a nonbelligerency agreement—Assad refused to acknowledge Israel's right to exist.

Coordination between Egypt and Syria for the coming round began in February 1973 when war minister Ismail flew to Damascus to inform Assad of Sadat's intentions. The minister cited three periods which Egyptian military planners found suitable for attack—time spans in May, August, and September–October. On April 23, Assad flew secretly to Egypt for two days of talks with Sadat. The pair agreed on the establishment of a coordinating council made up of senior military officers from both countries. It was this body that met in Alexandria in August to plan the opening blow. However, the two sides did not set up machinery for joint command during the rest of the war.

As Assad understood it, both countries would launch sustained attacks that would oblige Israel to split its forces between two fronts. At their April meeting, Sadat assured him that Egypt's army would drive for the Sinai passes in the first stage of the war. Assad hoped during this phase to regain the Golan Heights. It was the Syrian leader's understanding from Sadat that the Egyptian army, after regrouping, would move on from the passes to capture the rest of Sinai. This pressure would inhibit Israel from attempting a swift counterattack on the Golan before Syria had consolidated its position.

Sadat and his generals, however, had already decided that the Egyptian attack would halt well short of the passes so that the army remained under the SAM umbrella. Unlike Shazly, General Gamasy believed that Egypt should drive for the passes after an "operational pause." But Egyptian planners did not believe they could drive Israel by force from all Sinai and did not intend to try.

General Shazly was ordered by war minister Ismail just before Assad's April visit to revive Granite 2, the plan for reaching the passes. Shazly was appalled but Ismail said the order to dust off the plan had come from President Sadat himself. It would be shown to the Syrians, Ismail said, but would not actually be implemented unless unforeseen circumstances developed, like a sudden Israeli withdrawal. Syria, he explained, would not take part in an all-out war unless it understood that Egypt intended to drive into the heart of Sinai.

In his autobiography, Shazly would write, "I was sickened by the duplicity." Granite 2 was duly updated but Shazly told his generals that there was no intention of actually implementing it. In instructing their subordinates, they were to remain vague about the second phase of the battle. "After an operational pause, we will develop our attack to the passes," was the way they would put it.

Jordan's King Hussein was on uneasy terms with both Egypt and Syria and could not be relied on by them to take part even though his country shared the longest border with Israel. Hussein had been reluctantly dragged into the Six Day War by Egypt. He had placed his army under the command of an Egyptian general and lost half his kingdom—the West Bank—as a result. It was now his supreme strategic goal to avoid involvement in another war that would endanger what he still had left. The participation of other Arab countries in the war was counted on, even though none could be made privy to the date of D-Day beforehand.

Under the command of General Gamasy, the Egyptian army's operations staff studied tide schedules and even the Jewish calendar in order to select the precise date for the attack. The planners wanted a long night for the canal crossing, half in moonlight and half in darkness. The bridges would be assembled in moonlight and the tanks would cross in darkness, hidden to Israeli planes. One of the days within the optimal crossing period in October was Yom Kippur. It struck the Egyptian planners as fortuitous. Israeli reservists, they knew, were mobilized during emergencies by having unit code names broadcast on radio. On Yom Kippur, however, radio and television in Israel were shut down. The selection of D-Day would be left to Sadat and Assad, but the planners put a circle around October 6, Yom Kippur, noting its special advantage.

Yom Kippur, however, was the worst possible Arab choice. In the absence of radio, Israel had other ways of mobilizing its reserves—couriers, for instance. Unlike on any other day in the year, it is certain on Yom Kippur where virtually every reservist in the country can be found—at his home or at a nearby synagogue. The absence of traffic on this day would enable couriers to speedily reach the reservists and the reservists themselves to quickly reach their bases.

The October date also fell within the monthlong Moslem holiday of Ramadan. The planners saw this too as an advantage. The Israelis were less likely to suspect an attack during the holy month, when the Moslem faithful do not eat or drink during daylight hours.

War, then, would come at the most sacred time of the year for both sides, with sanctity itself accorded a tactical role.

Seven

A ROYAL VISIT

Fᴿᴼᴹ ᴀᴛᴏᴘ ᴏɴᴇ ᴏꜰ ᴛʜᴇ ᴠᴏʟᴄᴀɴɪᴄ ᴄᴏɴᴇꜱ on the Israeli side of the cease-fire line on the Golan Heights, Maj. Gen. Yitzhak Hofi could see the Syrian encampments straddling the road leading to Damascus to the northeast. The Syrians normally maintained three divisions opposite the Golan. They had pulled them out in April for annual training and units began to trickle back by midsummer. There were now, in mid-September, far more tanks and artillery out there than ever before.

Most worrying to Hofi, who headed Israel's Northern Command, was the presence since August of SAM-6 batteries. The SAM-6s covered the skies not only over the Syrian lines but over the entire Golan Heights and even over parts of the Galilee inside Israel proper. This meant that the air force would not be able to operate against Syrian ground forces until the missiles had been eliminated. The air force had already stopped flying over the Golan; only low-flying light planes, such as crop dusters, were now permitted.

On September 13, two pairs of Phantoms returning from a photo reconnaissance mission over Syria were jumped by Syrian MiG-21s off the Lebanese coast and an escort of Israeli Mirages intervened. In the ensuing dogfight, eight Syrian planes and one Israeli Mirage were shot down. The downed Israeli pilot managed to climb into a life raft. As his comrades circled overhead, waiting for a rescue helicopter, a second wave of Syrian planes attacked. Four more were shot down. The helicopter picked up the Israeli pilot as well as one of the Syrian pilots swimming nearby.

Four days later, at a meeting of the General Staff, General Zeira tried to calm Hofi's concerns. Despite the Syrian buildup, the intelligence chief said, the Arabs understood they had no chance of winning a war against Israel. It would be another two years before Egypt had sufficient long-range planes and Scuds to even contemplate war. As for Syria, it was axiomatic that it would not go to war without Egypt.

Hofi was not reassured. The Syrian deployment was growing more disturbing by the day. Artillery, normally deployed well to the rear, had been moved to forward positions. This made sense only if the Syrians intended to use it to support forces advancing into the Golan. The September 13 air battle was not the kind of blow Syria would take passively. Hofi did not believe the Syrians were thinking about full-scale war but they might attempt to capture one of the Israeli settlements on the Golan. There were now eight hundred Syrian tanks opposite the Israeli lines. All Hofi had was an understrength armored brigade with seventy-seven tanks. There were also two hundred infantrymen scattered in ten small outposts along the front line. And the two armies were only 200 to 400 yards apart.

The Blue-White alert in the spring had improved Hofi's defensive posture somewhat. A network of roads had been bulldozed through the rocky terrain for swifter deployment of tanks. The antitank ditch which had guarded only half the Israeli line was now almost completed and minefields had been thickened. The Syrians could bridge the ditch and get through the minefields, but the barriers would slow them down for a few precious hours. Firing ramps were prepared for tanks on high ground overlooking likely Syrian attack points. The two spans linking the Golan with the Galilee across the narrow Jordan—the Bnot Yaacov (Daughters of Jacob) Bridge and Arik Bridge—had their capacities doubled by the addition of parallel lanes. In an important move, some camps where reserve tank brigades would mobilize were moved to the foot of the heights from the other end of the Galilee to permit the units to reach the battlefront faster.

None of this, however, made up for the loss of air support. Hofi had until now been able to reassure himself that despite the disparity in ground forces, the air force would, in the event of a surprise attack, keep the enemy at bay until the reserves arrived. With the forward deployment of the SAM-6s, the air force would now be out of the picture for the critical opening hours— perhaps forty-eight hours—while it attended to Tagar and Dougman. The general decided to share his concern with his colleagues at the weekly meeting of the General Staff on September 24, which happened to be attended by Dayan. The main item on the agenda was the proposed acquisition of American F-15 warplanes. Hofi was the first of the participants scheduled to comment. "Before I express my opinion about whether to acquire the planes or not I'd like to talk about something else," he said. The situation on the Golan was "very serious." The Syrians were in position to strike without warning and there was no depth that would permit his forces to roll with the blow. The introduction of the SAM-6s meant that he was now deprived of air support. "To my mind the Syrians are more dangerous to Israel than the Egyptians." Having painted this dire picture, he went on to give his opinion about the F-15s.

The discussion about the planes and other strategic issues proceeded around the table, without any reference to Hofi's remarks. It was Dayan who brought the generals back to it. "The General Staff can't let Khaka's [Hofi's nickname] remarks pass without comment," he said. "I ask that you explore this to the full. Either his scenario doesn't hold water or it does. If it does, we need a plan for dealing with it." Rosh Hashana was only two days away; Dayan said he could not permit himself to go on holiday without getting an answer.

Although the Syrian army was not nearly as strong as Egypt's, Hofi was right about it representing the greater danger. The Egyptian army would have to cross 150 miles of desert before it reached sparsely populated Israeli territory in the far south, but the Syrians were less than 20 miles from villages and towns in the Galilee and far closer to settlements on the Golan itself. There was no canal to slow them down, and if the IDF were caught napping by a massive attack, the Syrians could be inside Israeli territory in hours.

Elazar sought to downplay Hofi's concerns. "I don't accept that the Syrians can conquer the Golan." Intelligence might not provide warning of a limited attack, the chief of staff said, but the forces deployed on the heights were sufficient to deal with such an eventuality. If the Syrians were planning full-scale war, intelligence was certain to pick up signals in time for reinforcements to reach the front. As for the SAMs, said the chief of staff, the air force was prudently keeping clear of their reach in a nonwar situation. In war, however, they would provide close support and pay the price necessary. "If it's a question of war, the missiles to my mind do not affect the ability of the air force to deal with the problem in half a day."

Dayan was not assuaged but did not wish to further interrupt the meeting. He asked Elazar to set up a special meeting to decide on appropriate measures for the Golan. It was fixed for the morning of the twenty-sixth, Rosh Hashana eve, two days hence.

On the night of the twenty-fifth, a helicopter landed at a security installation outside Tel Aviv and its occupants were led into a modest building serving the Mossad. While the others in the party were taken to a side room, two of the visitors were conducted into a conference room. Golda Meir awaited them. "Your majesty," she said to the short figure who strode forward to shake her hand.

Jordan's King Hussein took a seat at the table opposite the Israeli prime minister. Alongside him sat Jordanian prime minister Zeid Rifai. Alongside Mrs. Meir sat Mordecai Gazit, director of the prime minister's office.

The Arab monarch had maintained secret contacts with Israel's leaders for years in an effort to avoid misunderstandings that could lead to armed conflict. He had requested this meeting without indicating what he wanted to discuss. In an adjacent room, Lt. Col. Zussia Keniezer, head of the Jordanian desk in AMAN, monitored the conversation through earphones.

The king began by raising a minor border problem north of Eilat. Both he and Mrs. Meir then offered each other a leisurely *tour d'horizon* of the political situation in the region. Mrs. Meir had grown up in Milwaukee but she had lived in the Middle East long enough to wait patiently for the king to come to what really brought him. From time to time, her longtime personal assistant, Ms. Lou Kedar, brought in hot drinks. It was close to an hour before Hussein came to the point. The Syrians, he said, were in a "pre-jump-off position" for war. Lieutenant Colonel Keniezer straightened up. Are they going to war without the Egyptians, asked Mrs. Meir. The king said he didn't think so. "I think they would cooperate."

Lou Kedar had the clear impression that he was saying that war was coming and she felt that the prospect disturbed him greatly. Mordecai Gazit would afterwards assert that Hussein did not warn about an imminent coordinated attack. That was AMAN's conclusion as well. AMAN was fully aware of the Syrian deployment. As for Hussein's linkage to Egypt, it had only been conjectural.

As soon as the king left, Mrs. Meir asked Kedar to get Dayan on the phone. It was already midnight. The prime minister gave Dayan a brief résumé of the meeting and Dayan said he would call back. Mrs. Meir chain-smoked as she waited. When Dayan called ten minutes later, they spoke briefly and she left with Kedar for the prime minister's official residence in Jerusalem. Mrs. Meir was to depart the next day for Strasbourg to address the Council of Europe. When Kedar asked if they would still be going, Mrs. Meir said, "Why not?"

"I suppose we won't be going to Europe now," said Kedar as they drove.

"Why not?" asked Mrs. Meir.

It struck the incredulous Kedar that Mrs. Meir did not take Hussein's warning seriously. The prime minister's relaxed attitude stemmed from her conversation with Dayan, who had been briefed by someone in AMAN on the content and implications of the king's message. There had been other intelligence officers in the monitoring room besides Keniezer, and Dayan's source had evidently reported that there was nothing new in the king's remarks.

Lieutenant Colonel Keniezer's evaluation was precisely the opposite. The Jordanian king had met with Sadat and Assad in Alexandria two weeks before. Given the mutual suspicions prevailing among the Arab leaders, it was unlikely that he had been told of any specific war plans. But it was probable that Sadat and Assad had raised the prospect of war against Israel in more general terms to feel out the likelihood of Jordan joining in or at least preventing Israel from counterattacking Syria through Jordanian territory.

What electrified the intelligence officer was that for the first time a well-placed source was suggesting that Egypt and Syria would be going to war together. Until now, it had been assumed that, despite its warlike preparations, Syria would not undertake war without Egypt. And Egypt would not go to war because it still did not have long-range planes and Scuds. The import of Hussein's remarks was that "the concept" was no longer relevant.

Accompanying Keniezer as they emerged from the back room was a longtime friend, the senior officer in charge of field security in the IDF. "Stick with me," Keniezer said to him, "because I'm about to break field security and I'm going to do it twice."

He telephoned his direct superior, Gen. Arye Shalev, head of the Research section at AMAN and second in the hierarchy to Zeira. "The bottom line of what Hussein had to say was that there's going to be war with Egypt and Syria. I'll give you details in the morning." Keniezer then called the head of the Syrian desk, Lt. Col. Avi Ya'ari. Without revealing the source of his information, he notified Ya'ari of the prospect of a two-front war and suggested that he inform Northern Command.

The next morning at 8:15 Elazar met with the General Staff to discuss implementation of Dayan's demand two days before to beef up the Golan defenses—"if only to rest easy on Rosh Hashana," as Elazar put it. At Dayan's request, Elazar first sounded out the generals on Hussein's warning the previous night. "There's a report from a serious source that the Syrian army is prepared to launch war at any moment. It's not known if this is coordinated with Egypt."

Even Hofi dismissed the possibility of the Syrians embarking on full-scale war. Elazar summed up the consensus view by saying that the warning added nothing to what they already knew. It was unreasonable to think the Syrians would attack without Egypt. "I could almost say, I hope they try it. In any case, there's not going to be a war."

If the Syrians decided to react at all to the downing of their planes, the most likely way was with an artillery barrage, said Elazar. However, an attempt at a limited land grab could not be ruled out. It was decided to dispatch to the Golan two companies from the Seventh Armored Brigade stationed in the south. This would bring the number of tanks on the Golan to one hundred. "We'll have one hundred tanks against their eight hundred," said Elazar. "That ought to be enough." In that sentence, Elazar summed up official Israel's attitude towards the Arab military threat.

An artillery battery was also sent to the Golan, and the air force was put on alert, as were a number of ground units.

At 9 A.M., Dayan joined them and Elazar spelled out the steps that had been decided on. "I think there could be nothing more idiotic on Syria's part than to attack alone," he said. "There won't be war on both the Egyptian and Syrian fronts. I believe all indications point to that. Therefore I would not go onto a war footing in order to prevent war on the Golan Heights."

Dayan agreed that all-out war was unlikely but noted that the Syrians did not have to cross a major barrier to reach the Israeli lines. "And we have to consider that there will be some clever Russian advising them."

The defense minister informed Elazar that he intended after the meeting to fly up to the Golan and transmit a message to the Syrians through the journalists who would cover the visit. He also wished to prepare the Israeli public for the possibility, however remote, of a flare-up in the north. He asked Elazar to accompany him. The chief of staff tried to dissuade Dayan from making the trip on the grounds that it would disturb the tranquillity of the Golan settlers during the holiday period. Dayan, however, insisted. "They have to be prepared for something, but we will do it in a positive way."

Dayan and his party, which included General Zeira, were briefed on the Syrian deployment from a hill overlooking the Syrian lines by Maj. Shmuel Askarov, a tank officer. Pointing to the array of Syrian tanks and artillery positions to the east, Askarov said, "War is certain." Dayan gestured to Zeira, giving him the right of response. "There will not be another war for ten years," Askarov would remember Zeira saying.

In his meeting with Israeli and foreign journalists on the Golan just three hours before the onset of Rosh Hashana, Dayan said that if the Syrians chose to strike at Israel in retaliation for the September 13 air battle, "any blow they land will hurt them more than it will us." His remark was duly picked up by the Syrian media.

The two-day holiday passed peacefully and Elazar was able to get in a brief beach holiday with his family at Sharm el-Sheikh in Sinai. Duty officers in the intelligence community, however, were kept busy monitoring new developments on the hitherto quiet Egyptian front. Already on September 25, troops had been reported moving towards the Suez Canal. On September 28, the level of alert in the Egyptian air force, navy, and some ground units was raised. AMAN at first attributed these moves to fear of an Israeli attack somehow connected to the air clash with Syria. However, a more cogent explanation soon emerged. The Egyptians, it was learned, were planning a large-scale exercise, called Tahrir-41, in the canal zone from October 1 to 7.

On September 28, the anniversary of the death of Nasser, Sadat addressed the nation. The anniversary was normally an occasion for reaffirming the legacy of Nasser's struggle for restoration of the lost lands and Arab honor. Sadat made do with expressing hope for the nation's emergence from its present straitened circumstances to "a broad and glittering future." AMAN, in its analysis of the speech, interpreted it to mean that Sadat wished to indicate to the Egyptian public that there was at present no point in considering an armed struggle against Israel. But the fact that Sadat chose to keep silent about the struggle could have meant that it was not his own people he was seeking to lull.

Eight

SWORD FROM
THE SCABBARD

G ENERAL SHAZLY HAD ASKED FOR FIFTEEN DAYS' NOTICE before D-Day
to make final preparations. He got fourteen days. More importantly,
fourteen nights. It was at night that the convoys would move across the desert
from Cairo and other points to the staging areas along the canal.

Assad and Sadat, meeting secretly in Damascus on September 22,
agreed to launch the war on October 6. They had differed over zero hour.
Assad wanted it at 7 A.M. so that the Israeli forces facing east on the Golan
would have their vision obscured by the rising sun. Sadat wanted the joint
attack launched just before evening so that his engineers could span the canal
with bridges under cover of darkness. In an act of generosity about which he
would shortly have second thoughts, Assad bowed to the Egyptian leader's
preference. On his way to Damascus, Sadat had stopped off in Saudi Arabia
to discuss with King Faisal the unleashing of an oil embargo against the West
as part of a coordinated effort by the Arab world to bring pressure on Israel
and its supporters.

Shazly had 650,000 combat troops under his command. The Syrian
army numbered 150,000. Contingents from Iraq, Jordan, and other Arab
countries would add another 100,000 soldiers to the Arab frontline ranks.
The Israeli army numbered 375,000 soldiers, of whom 240,000 were
reservists. The rest were conscripts doing their three-year service and a small
regular army nucleus. A higher percentage of Israel's population served in
the reserves, well into middle age, than in any other nation.

Israel's 2,100 tanks were about half the combined number of Egyptian (2,200) and Syrian (1,650) tanks. Iraq and Jordan would send 650 more tanks after war was joined. Israel had 359 first-line warplanes, compared to a combined total of 680 for Egypt (400) and Syria (280).

If Israel had not mobilized its reserves, the odds at the beginning of war would be in the Arabs' favor by several orders of magnitude. The 100,000 Egyptian soldiers and 1,350 tanks west of the canal faced 450 Israeli soldiers in the Bar-Lev forts and 91 Israeli tanks in the canal zone. Another 200 tanks were posted deeper in Sinai. In artillery and heavy mortars, the Egyptians outgunned the Israelis along the canal by a 40 to 1 margin. On the northern front, the Syrians enjoyed 8 to 1 superiority in tanks and far greater in infantry and artillery. These odds would be drastically reduced once the Israeli reserves came into play, but until then the young conscripts on the front line and their regular army commanders would have to bear the brunt.

The five Egyptian divisions on the canal would attack out of positions they had been occupying for years, eliminating the need for an elaborate approach march that would tip their hand. The divisions would be reinforced by reservists, but the buildup would be gradual since two-thirds of the attack force was already in place.

Mobilization of the Egyptian reserves was correctly presumed in Cairo to be monitored by Israeli intelligence. Frequent mobilization exercises were held, both to perfect the system and to accustom Israeli intelligence to them. In the last week in September, some 120,000 reservists would be called up. On October 4, 20,000 would be released to lull the Israelis. (On the eve of the Six Day War, Dayan had carried out the same ruse with Israeli reserves.) To deceive the Soviet experts in their midst, the Egyptians told them they were taking precautions against a possible Israeli raid that intelligence had learned about.

The first large-scale movement of Egyptian troops was picked up by Israeli intelligence on the night of September 24–25. It involved an entire division proceeding from Cairo under heavy escort of military police. Every night following, there were further reports of convoys.

AMAN kept the military and political leadership abreast of ongoing developments through bulletins, issued several times a day. On September 30, it noted that a large-scale Egyptian military exercise would begin the following day and end on October 7. The exercise would involve mobilization of reserves, work on fortifications, troop movements, and mobilization of civilian fishing boats as troop transports. Henceforth, all unusual moves in the Egyptian army would be viewed by AMAN and the high command in this context, including cancellation of leaves and the manning of forward command posts. By this discounting a priori of any unusual movements by the Egyptian army as part of a military exercise, Israel's early warning system was effectively shut down.

The Syrians were also raising their alert status and mobilizing reserves. These moves were attributed by AMAN to Syrian fears that the IDF might follow up the September 13 air battle with another blow. At a lower level of probability, Syria might be preparing to retaliate with a limited strike of its own. Fed by this double illusion—an Egyptian exercise in the south and Syrian nervousness in the north—Israel looked on unperturbed as its two enemies prepared their armies for war in full view.

Eleven warnings of war were received by Israel during September from well-placed sources. But Zeira continued to insist that war was not an Arab option. Not even Hussein's desperate warning succeeded in stirring doubts.

Zeira would subsequently explain the close-ended nature of his official assessments by noting that he had spent most of his career as a commander who made clear-cut decisions, not as a staff officer. "My nature does not lead me to pass responsibility to my superiors, if that is at all avoidable," he would tell an official inquiry commission. "The best support that the head of AMAN can give the chief of staff is to provide a clear and unambiguous assessment, provided it is done in an objective manner." To have pointed out to Elazar that there was conflicting intelligence regarding Arab intentions and to have left the chief of staff to sort it out would have been to shirk his own responsibility, Zeira said. His attitude was indeed admirable in a commander but devastating in an intelligence officer.

Zeira was supported by his deputy, Brig. Gen. Arye Shalev, and by the head of the Egyptian desk, Lt. Col. Yona Bandman. The latter had won Zeira's high regard in the Six Day War as a young intelligence major. Asked his assessment of the Egyptian army on the eve of that war after it had deployed in Sinai, he predicted that it would disintegrate in combat. He proved right, and his assessment of the fighting quality of the Egyptian army had not changed much since.

The intelligence chiefs believed they knew a deeper truth—"the concept"—that rendered irrelevant all the cries of alarm going up around them. Zeira and his chief aides were to demonstrate the ability of even brilliant men to adhere to an idée fixe in the face of mountains of contrary evidence. Explaining away every piece of information that conflicted with their thesis, they embraced any wisp that seemed to confirm it. This included disinformation leaked by the Egyptians that should have been suspect since it came through channels the Egyptians clearly knew AMAN to be monitoring, such as the Arab press. They clung to their view even though the Egyptian deceptions were contradicted by the evidence of war preparations that AMAN's own departments were daily gathering. Virtually every move in the Arab armed forces was being monitored. But the deception succeeded beyond even Egypt's expectations because it triggered within Israel's intelligence arm and senior command a monumental capacity for self-deception. "We simply didn't feel them capable [of war]," Mossad chief Zvi Zamir would say later.

The tempo of war drums became more insistent on the evening of September 28. American intelligence passed on a report from a source it considered highly reliable—in fact, King Hussein—that a massive Syrian attempt to reconquer the Golan Heights could be expected imminently. Hussein, of course, had delivered the same warning to Mrs. Meir directly three days earlier. Now the Americans were finding it worthy enough to pass on. The next morning, Elazar held a meeting of senior staff to discuss the report. Most were unimpressed. The consensus remained that Syria would not go to war without Egypt, and AMAN held firm that Egypt was not going to war. The most that could be expected from Syria was a limited strike in retaliation for the downing of the planes on September 13.

There was one dissenting voice, that of General Tal. All signs, said the deputy chief of staff, pointed to war on the Golan. These included the forward deployment of bridging tanks which could throw spans across Israel's antitank ditch. The Syrian divisions on the line were in emergency deployment, which would enable them to launch an attack without further warning, and SAMs now covered the skies over the Golan. "The balance of forces has changed on the ground," he said at a General Staff meeting. "The only thing that can block a Syrian attack is the air force." Like Elazar, he believed the air force could cope with the SAMs. The weather, however, was another matter, particularly now that the rainy season had begun. "If the air force is neutralized, the Syrian army can sweep across the Golan. We can't take chances." He called for reinforcing the heights with the rest of the Seventh Brigade and a battalion of artillery. Elazar disagreed with his deputy's assessment but agreed to send up several more tank companies and artillery as well.

Still troubled after the staff meeting, Tal telephoned upstairs to Zeira and said he wanted to continue the discussion with him and Shalev in the intelligence chief's office. When they met, Tal said the only thing preventing Elazar from ordering mobilization was AMAN's assessment of the "low probability" of war. Zeira rejected Tal's request to reconsider that assessment. As far as understanding enemy intentions, said the intelligence chief, he and not Tal was the expert. Tal replied that he was the expert on tank warfare, and if the Syrians launched a surprise attack the Israeli force on the Golan stood no chance.

At 2 A.M. on October 1, AMAN received an alarming report from a normally reliable source that war would break out this very day on both the Egyptian and Syrian fronts. According to the report, the Egyptian exercise which was to begin at dawn would unfold into an actual crossing of the canal. Zeira did not waken Elazar or Dayan to pass on the report. "I saved you a night's sleep," he told the chief of staff in the morning at a meeting of the General Staff. Elazar took it in stride but Dayan sent Zeira a note during the meeting taking him to task for not reporting the warning to him immediately. Zeira sent a note back saying he and his staff had spent the night checking the report and concluded towards morning that it was groundless.

Zeira noted at the meeting that Egyptian mechanized divisions had been moved to the canal. So had bridging units and airborne troops. "There are several sources saying the exercise is not an exercise but is leading towards war," said Zeira. "This definitely does not seem likely to us, even though these are good sources."

Zeira's fixation on "the concept" was a not unfamiliar phenomenon in the world of intelligence. Roberta Wohlstetter, writing about the American intelligence failure at Pearl Harbor, noted that on several critical occasions prior to the Japanese attack, intelligence analysts failed to properly distinguish between irrelevant "noise" and "signals" hinting clearly at enemy intentions. "Pearl Harbor, looked at closely, shows how hard it is to hear a signal against the prevailing noise, in particular when you are listening for the wrong signal."

Elazar and Dayan were unaware that the confident assessments given them by Zeira and Shalev were not shared by all in the AMAN command structure. A number of dissidents insisted that the signs spoke clearly of war. Ever since monitoring King Hussein's meeting with Mrs. Meir on September 25, Lieutenant Colonel Keniezer was convinced that a two-front war was in the offing. He had gotten into a shouting match over the seriousness of the war threat with General Shalev, ignoring the rank that separated them.

The head of the Syrian desk, Lieutenant Colonel Ya'ari, had accepted AMAN's contention that Egypt was not going to war and that therefore Syria wasn't. This assumption was jarred by Keniezer's unauthorized report to him at midnight on September 25 of the warning about imminent war. Ya'ari would have been more upset had he known the source was none other than King Hussein. The warning had not been passed on to Ya'ari by his AMAN superiors, even though it directly concerned the Syrian front, his area of responsibility.

A warning of a two-front war passed on by the Mossad in the early hours of October 1 finally convinced Ya'ari that "the concept" no longer held.

Hussein's warning was being dismissed in AMAN as overwrought. But now another source, considered reliable, was also making a connection between the Syrian and Egyptian fronts. For Ya'ari the linkage was electrifying. If the Egyptians were preparing for war, then there was finally a clear explanation for the puzzling Syrian preparations of the past month. The intelligence colleague who passed on the war warning to Ya'ari noted that AMAN discounted it. For Ya'ari, however, the penny had dropped. Ignoring official channels and the late night hour, he telephoned the chief intelligence officer of Northern Command and suggested that he alert General Hofi immediately to the possibility of a two-front war breaking out this day.

When Ya'ari arrived at intelligence headquarters in the morning for the daily staff meeting, he was roundly chewed out by General Shalev for having thrown Northern Command into an uproar by his unauthorized warning— a warning, moreover, that contradicted AMAN's analysis. Shalev did not have to point out that war had not broken out; AMAN had been proven right again. Two days later, Ya'ari and the Northern Command intelligence officer were summoned to Shalev's office to have a formal rebuke entered into their records.

Col. Yoel Ben-Porat, the head of AMAN's Sigint (signal intelligence) section, which monitored radio communications in the Arab world and beyond, was among those lulled by Sadat's September 28 speech, which he listened to on a transistor as he relaxed on the Tel Aviv beach. "I heard Sadat's speech," he told a colleague the next day. "He talked about trees and stones, everything but war."

Ben-Porat was not a man normally lulled by events across the border. The essence of his professional being was edginess. His department was AMAN's prime bulwark against surprise attack. It was unlikely that an enemy could prepare for war without its radio signals leaving tracks. Ben-Porat had an obsessive interest in the possibility of surprise attack. As a boy of eleven living in Poland near the Russian border, he had personally witnessed the results of Operation Barbarossa, in which the German army overwhelmed the Russian army after an elaborate deception. Ben-Porat lost his family in the Holocaust and spent part of the war years with partisan bands roaming the forests. He had been sent by AMAN to Europe in 1969 to study the Soviet suppression of the Czech uprising the year before. In his report, he described the way Russian tank forces, carrying out what seemed routine maneuvers in neighboring Warsaw Pact countries, had suddenly descended on Prague.

"The only thing differentiating war from maneuvers is the last stage on the last day," he wrote. "The concentration of forces and the logistics is the same for both." He subsequently wrote a directive for the units under his command pointing up this lesson. "Whenever there is a military exercise in the region of unusual scale, relate to the possibility that it cloaks intentions of war." Twice in the past two years he had put his men on an emergency footing in response to Egyptian exercises.

The phone call that woke him at 3 A.M. on October 1 thus bore special resonance. It was from an AMAN officer passing on the report that the Egyptian exercise beginning this day would conclude with an attack across the canal and that the Syrians would join in a two-front war.

"What does Research say?" asked Ben-Porat.

"They say it's just an exercise."

Ben-Porat called the duty officer at Sigint headquarters and asked him to have key officers assembled there by 4:30 A.M., less than an hour away. Data accumulated in the coming hours increased Ben-Porat's suspicion that the Egyptians had hostile intent even if the exercise did not seem to be developing into a cross-canal attack this day. Failing to get Zeira on the phone, he spoke to Shalev later in the morning and voiced his belief that the warning was well founded. Shalev reminded him that he had said the same thing during the Blue-White alert in the spring. "You're wrong this time too," he said.

Ben-Porat asked whether "special means" had been activated. These were particularly sensitive listening devices which were to be called on only in emergencies since activation risked their exposure. Shalev said he had asked Zeira to activate them but that the reply thus far was negative.

When he finally got through to Zeira, Ben-Porat asked permission to mobilize two hundred intelligence reservists. Zeira's reply was firm. "Yoel, listen well. It is intelligence's job to safeguard the nation's nerves, not to drive the public crazy, not to undermine the economy. I don't permit you to think about mobilizing even a fraction of a reservist."

This definition of intelligence's role was one Ben-Porat did not accept. Despite the edge of annoyance in the voice on the line, he recommended activation of the "special means." Zeira refused. "What do these sources exist for," asked an exasperated Ben-Porat, "if not for situations like the one we're facing?"

"The situations you see," replied Zeira, "are not the ones I see."

Like others puzzled at the refusal of the AMAN hierarchy to bend to the overwhelming evidence accumulating of imminent war, Ben-Porat resigned himself to the notion that Zeira had access to other sources which apparently painted a very different picture.

Sigint operations officer Shabtai Brill was not assuaged by Zeira's reassurances. A red light had flashed for him on September 28 with a report that Syria had moved two squadrons of Sukhoi bombers to a forward airfield. Since the Six Day War, when much of its air force had been destroyed on the ground, Syria had been careful to keep its warplanes well out of the IDF's reach. To Brill, the move of the Sukhois to a base where they could easily be hit made no sense unless they were to support advancing troops. On the Egyptian front, a convoy of three hundred ammunition trucks had been detected making its way from Cairo to the canal zone. An exercise would not require that amount of ammunition, Brill argued. There were numerous other alarming moves, including the shifting of SAM batteries from the Damascus area to the Golan approaches. If the Syrians were fearful of an Israeli attack, as AMAN's leadership maintained, why were they weakening the defenses of their capital? From these and other signs, it was clear to him that war was in the offing. But his warnings made no more impact than did those of other dissidents within AMAN.

The northern half of the line on the Golan Heights was held by a tank battalion commanded by Lt. Col. Yair Nafshi. The day he assumed command the year before, he announced to the men his intention to focus on gunnery. The only way to overcome the numerical superiority of the Syrian tanks opposite them, he said, was to shoot faster and straighter. Turning to a gunner, he asked, "How long would it take to hit three tanks coming straight at you at 1,200 meters?" Four minutes, the gunner replied. Others thought they could do it in half that time. Not even a minute, said Nafshi. He let the laughter die down before saying he would demonstrate.

As the men walked with him to a nearby gunnery range, he briefed a crewman on a borrowed tank on how he wanted him to load the shells. The men sat on the ground to watch the demonstration, some of them holding stopwatches. The tank commander gave Nafshi, in the gunner's position, the order to fire. Nafshi hit three tank targets, spaced 50 yards apart, with three rapid shots and jumped down from the tank. The stopwatches showed less than 10 seconds.

Gunnery proficiency became the unit's hallmark. Nafshi cultivated "snipers" who could hit targets at long range. He had them wear gray uniforms instead of standard green to give them special status. Tanks which scored hits on Syrian tanks during skirmishes had tank silhouettes pasted to the side of their turrets to indicate their "kills." Nafshi instituted a series of written tests on subjects ranging from ballistics to the detailed history of

Israel's battles. Nafshi's efforts were rewarded when his battalion was cited for proficiency and chosen, from all the units in the armored corps, to host the corps' Passover seder in April, attended by the defense minister and chief of staff. By successfully "stealing" the *afikoman* matzo from Dayan—a ritual theft that is the prerogative of the youngest participant in a seder—the battalion won a basketball court.

During the turmoil over the Golan front in September, the Suez front had remained calm. Apart from the Bar-Lev forts, defense of the line was entrusted to an armored brigade commanded by Col. Amnon Reshef. The brigade had been on the line for three months after an intensive training period and was at the peak of efficiency. Strong emphasis was placed on gunnery drills and tactics. The young crewmen learned that modern tanks, properly handled, could cope far better with the treacherous sands than did the tank armies which fought in North Africa in the Second World War. Even high dunes, previously thought impassable, could be climbed if approached straight on; attempts to take them at an angle risked throwing a tread. Before passing over a dune crest, crewmen had to remember to turn the tank gun sideways to avoid smashing it into the ground on the steep decline. The units exercised "Dovecote" by day and night, the tanks rushing forward from rear deployment to take positions supporting the forts on the canal.

Reshef's tank brigade was one of three that made up the Sinai Division, commanded by Gen. Albert Mendler. A second brigade, commanded by Col. Dan Shomron, was stationed sixty miles to the rear in central Sinai. The third brigade, commanded by Col. Avigdor Ben-Gal, had already dispatched some of its units to the Golan in response to Hofi's alarm and the rest would follow.

Mendler was scheduled to transfer out of the division on October 7 to assume command of the armored corps from General Adan, who was to retire. Preparations were already under way for a series of farewell parties within the division, and staff officers were searching Tel Aviv shops for appropriate gifts. However, a report passed on to Mendler informally by a friend in AMAN early on October 1 created a new agenda. "Fantastic," he wrote in his diary. "0515 hours. Intelligence. War tomorrow. Farewell, transfer."

The division commander ordered Reshef to have his brigade ready to move out on five minutes' notice. Crews were to sleep with their clothes and boots on, and tanks were to be ready for immediate movement, fully armed and fueled. In the fortifications on the canal, the men were to be roused half an hour before dawn.

It was only on this day that the two senior Egyptian commanders on the Suez front, Gen. Saad Mamoun of the Second Army and Gen. Abdel Muneim Wasel of the Third Army, were summoned to Cairo and informed that D-Day had been set for October 6. Division commanders were not to be informed until October 3. Brigade commanders would be told the day after that, and battalion and company commanders only the day before hostilities commenced. With some exceptions, platoon commanders and the soldiers themselves would not be told until six hours before the battle.

Under cover of conducting the exercise, the Egyptian high command moved on October 1 to Center Ten, an underground complex in Cairo from which the war would be run. That evening, Sadat assembled the Supreme Council of the Armed Forces. Each commander in turn stepped up to an operations map, outlined his mission, and formally declared himself ready to carry it out. Sadat expressed his confidence in them and all joined in a brief prayer.

Sgt. Mahmud Nadeh introduced himself in his new notebook on the shore of the Bitter Lake. "We'll begin from the beginning. I serve as a sergeant in the armed forces. We'll be going to war in the next few days. I'm two and a half kilometers from the enemy. We've been told we will be the first to cross the canal to free our lands and expel the enemy." He promised, in the name of "historical truth," to keep an accurate account of events that awaited him and of the heroism and patriotism of the Egyptian soldier.

The notebook, which would fall into the hands of Israeli intelligence, revealed that some units in the Egyptian army were aware at least three days before October 6 that they were going to war. More tellingly, it offered an insight into the mind of a university-educated soldier whose kind was now to be found in large numbers in the Egyptian army alongside peasants and urban slum dwellers.

A third-year humanities student from Alexandria, Nadeh had trained as a commando but was now attached to an amphibious armored unit that was to cross the Bitter Lake. "We are to proceed with all possible speed to the Mitla Pass after an artillery barrage of fifty minutes," he wrote on Thursday. "I hope to emerge alive from the battle because I believe in God. There is a smile on everyone's face, even my officer's."

After addressing the Council of Europe in Strasbourg, Mrs. Meir flew on to Vienna in an attempt to persuade Austrian chancellor Bruno Kreisky to rescind his decision to close down a transit center for Jews arriving from the Soviet Union, most of whom were on their way to Israel. He had made his decision after two Palestinian gunmen seized a train and took five Jewish migrants and an Austrian border guard hostage. The meeting between the two leaders was tense and ended in disagreement.

Mrs. Meir's absence in Europe reassured the Arab command since the Israeli government was unlikely to decide on mobilization as long as she was out of the country. Egyptian intelligence, closely monitoring developments in Israel and in Sinai, reported no indication that Israel was taking cautionary steps. To the Egyptians' astonishment, the Israeli command seemed entirely unaware that large armies on its borders were preparing for war. The preparations did not, however, go unnoticed by the soldiers on the front line in Sinai and the Golan.

Four days before Yom Kippur, Sgt. Yoram Krivine's platoon took over Strongpoint 111, on the Golan cease-fire line. It was a routine changing of the guard but it struck the twenty-one-year-old paratroop sergeant that the soldiers they were relieving seemed unusually happy about leaving. The dark basalt blocks of the igloo-like fort were stout enough to withstand even direct artillery hits.

The hillock on which 111 was situated offered a view across the rocky Syrian plain. Krivine could see countless artillery pieces, tanks, and other vehicles nestling under camouflage netting. He had never before served on the Purple Line—a name given to the cease-fire line because of its color on the Israeli map—and did not know whether this massive deployment was routine. On a wall inside the fortification the men found a sign reading "111 Will Not Fall Again." Krivine learned that the post had indeed been broken into by the Syrians during a "battle day."

Opposite them was Tel Kudne, a Syrian military position on a volcanic cone that rose abruptly from the landscape. One hundred yards from the Israeli fortification was one of several UN observation posts situated along the line.

The day they arrived, Krivine's platoon was briefed by an intelligence officer belonging to the unit they had just relieved. The officer identified for them the Syrian units they were facing. "The whole Syrian army is out there," he said in conclusion. "I'm happy I won't be here when the war starts."

Nine

COUNTDOWN

Her contentious meeting with Chancellor Kreisky was still on Golda Meir's mind when she met with her senior security advisers on Wednesday, October 3, the morning after her return from Europe. "He didn't even offer me a glass of water," she complained. The newspapers carried extensive accounts of her European trip and the closing of the transit camp in Vienna. In one or two papers there was passing reference to tension on the northern border.

The meeting in the prime minister's office was described as a consultation by Moshe Dayan, who had requested it. He could not shake his concern over what was happening in the north and wanted to share it with the prime minister. Military symbol though he might be, he related to the seventy-five-year-old grandmother even on purely military matters with the deference due her position. There were reports, he said, that Egypt was bent on war, but the situation on the Syrian front was more troubling because of the immediate threat it posed to the settlements on the Golan. The Syrians had deployed their most advanced SAMs not around Damascus but opposite the Golan. "This is not a normal defensive deployment," he noted. If the Egyptians crossed the canal, Dayan said, they would find themselves in open desert with Israeli forces attacking them from every side. But the Syrians, with one quick thrust, could hope to push Israel off the Golan and then be protected against counterattacks by the steep heights, girdled by the Jordan River below.

General Shalev, filling in for Zeira, who was ill at home, gave AMAN's appraisal of the situation. "There are troubling reports on Syria and also Egypt," he confirmed. The Syrians were in emergency deployment and could launch an attack without warning. They had moved two squadrons of Sukhoi-7s to forward air bases and had deployed an unprecedented amount of artillery opposite the Golan. On the Suez front, the Egyptians were engaged in a large-scale military exercise. A worst-case situation, said Shalev, would be for Syria and Egypt to launch a two-front war. "Is this reasonable?" he asked rhetorically. "In my opinion, on the basis of much material received in recent days, Egypt believes it is not yet ready to go to war." And if Egypt was not going to war, then neither was Syria. Might Egypt not stage a diversion, asked Mrs. Meir, in order to let the Syrians attack? Assad and the Syrians know their limitations, replied Shalev. "They're aware of Israel's great advantage in the air." In short, the probability of war remained low.

General Elazar agreed with Shalev's analysis. Egypt and Syria indeed had plans for a coordinated attack, he said. "But I don't see a concrete danger in the near future." Should Syria attempt a full-scale attack on its own, he said, Israel would know beforehand. "We have good information. It's reasonable that if a big machine begins moving there will be leaks." He intended to keep the Israeli deployment on the Golan as it was, except for a slight beefing up. When Mrs. Meir asked about the possibility of more substantial reinforcement, he said, "That would either mean weakening the south or mobilizing reserves for an extended period." Despite her palpable unease, Mrs. Meir did not take it upon herself to challenge a roomful of generals counseling calm.

Shalev's upbeat bottom line had succeeded in reassuring her, at least for the moment. As the meeting broke up, she shook his hand and said, "Thanks for calming me." His words were so soothing that the security situation was no longer considered serious enough to be placed on the agenda of the cabinet meeting scheduled for the next day to hear Mrs. Meir's report on her European trip. The government thus had no idea that the possibility of war was even being mooted. Nor would the Arab buildup be referred to at Thursday's General Staff meeting. The sole subject on the agenda this day—two days before Yom Kippur—was discipline, with emphasis on the need for soldiers to adhere to the military dress code.

This relaxed posture was not warranted by what the men at the fronts were seeing or by what AMAN itself was picking up from its myriad sources. Lookouts along the canal had been reporting a massive buildup since the beginning of the week. Much of the information was not being passed upwards by the chief Southern Front intelligence officer, Col. David Gedalia. Adopting AMAN's no-war thesis, he regarded such reports as irrelevant "noise" attributable to the Egyptian exercise. Some of the information which he did pass on to the Egyptian desk in AMAN in turn was not passed on to Zeira and Shalev. But Zeira and Shalev were not passing on all the information reaching them either. The reports about Arab preparations that did reach Elazar and Dayan were packaged with reassuring explanations— Egyptian exercise, Syrian fears of an Israeli attack—that sapped them of their menace.

Even as Mrs. Meir was consulting Wednesday with Dayan and the others, the Egyptian war minister, General Ismail, was flying into Damascus for final coordination with his Syrian colleagues. To his dismay, the Syrians requested a forty-eight-hour postponement of D-Day in order to complete the draining of fuel tanks at Homs which they feared Israel might bomb. Ismail refused on the grounds that any delay risked the secrecy of the operation. The Syrians dropped their request but asked that zero hour be changed back from 6 P.M. The two sides compromised on 2:00 P.M.

The Syrian deployment had reached saturation point. The arrival of one armored brigade in particular, the Forty-seventh, raised eyebrows among Israeli intelligence officers. The brigade had been brought to their attention the previous year by one of several Syrian officers captured in a cross-border raid into Lebanon. The Syrians, reconnoitering the border area with a Lebanese escort, were seized in order to exchange them for Israeli pilots in Syrian hands. An officer who served on the Syrian General Staff mentioned that a new brigade, the Forty-seventh, was being formed to serve at Homs. The city was a hotbed of Islamic fundamentalist opposition to the regime in Damascus and President Assad wanted an armored brigade posted there to suppress any uprising.

"If you ever hear that the Forty-seventh is being sent to the front, you can be sure it's war," said the officer. On September 27, word was received that the Forty-seventh was heading towards the Golan. (In 1982, Assad would unleash his army against Islamic dissidents in Homs, killing an estimated 10,000 to 25,000 of his own citizens.)

On the Bar-Lev Line, lookouts reported feverish activity across the canal. Convoys were arriving every night. Descents to the water for rubber boats were being prepared at dozens of locations, and the Egyptians were working late every night to raise the height of their ramps overlooking the Israeli canal-side positions.

General Mendler began holding staff meetings twice a day to update situation assessments. It was becoming ever more apparent to him that the Egyptians were engaged not in a training exercise but in preparation for war. When the division commander passed his concern upwards to Southern Command, he was told that all of these activities, according to AMAN, were connected to the Egyptian exercise.

One junior intelligence officer in Southern Command begged to differ. Lt. Binyamin Siman-Tov was charged with monitoring the deployment of Egyptian forces. At a staff meeting on October 1, he submitted to Colonel Gedalia a memo suggesting that the Egyptian exercise was only a mask for "a real operation."

Why was there need for the Egyptian army to suddenly cancel courses and postpone officers' examinations if this was a scheduled exercise? Siman-Tov asked.

Why was Egyptian radio whipping up war fever if this was just an exercise and why were Egyptian officers being obliged to listen?

Why have the Egyptians prepared some forty descents for boats on the banks of the canal?

Why have tanks made an appearance along the canal in the (hitherto quiet) northern sector?

Why were the Egyptians making such extensive preparations for an exercise only one week long?

Why wasn't the Egyptian air force taking part in the exercise?

Why were they so assiduously stocking emergency ammunition and engineering supplies?

The last point struck some of the others present as particularly telling. If this was just an exercise, why were the Egyptians topping off their emergency ammunition supplies? As for the Egyptian air force, its absence could mean that there was no real exercise going on at all.

Gedalia was not impressed. He was, in fact, annoyed, since the lieutenant's appraisal ran directly counter to that of the intelligence chiefs in Tel Aviv. He first watered down the wording of the memo, then shelved it.

General Elazar, who was focused on the Syrian front and shielded by the cotton-wrapped AMAN assessments from the troublesome details, remained unaware that anything out of the ordinary was occurring in the south except for an extensive Egyptian military exercise similar to ones held in previous years.

So sanguine was the Israeli high command that no air photos of the

Egyptian lines were taken between September 25 and October 1, a week when large forces were streaming towards the canal every night. Reconnaissance flights were risky because of the SAMs and were not carried out frequently, but if there was a sense of urgency they would have been given top priority. A scheduled photo mission on October 2 was canceled because of bad visibility. It was rescheduled for the next day, but when the plane returned it was found that the camera shutter had failed to open. It would not be until the afternoon of the following day, Thursday, October 4, that the mission would finally be executed.

It was precisely during this critical period that the CIA, which had been monitoring Egyptian and Syrian movements, was itself blacked out in Egypt. The agency had reported bridging equipment and rubber boats being trucked to the canal on September 27 and noted that the air defense systems in Egypt and Syria were put on full alert shortly afterwards. An Agena reconnaissance satellite which covered the Middle East was launched on a routine mission from Vandenberg Air Force Base in California on September 27, but Agenas could not transmit from orbit: its pictures would not be developed until it landed in two weeks. A more sophisticated Big Bird satellite, which could send pictures from orbit, landed on September 28. Because of costs, these satellites were used sparingly and none was scheduled to go back up for a few weeks.

The blackout was extended to Cairo itself when Egyptian military headquarters suddenly switched from radio transmissions, monitored by the CIA, to landlines, which were not. The agency noted a number of oddities in Egyptian dispositions. Elite commando units were being deployed to new bases, larger than normal stockpiles of ammunition were being prepared, and more divisions were getting ready for maneuvers than was normal. In addition, a communications network was being prepared that was far larger than ordinary maneuvers would require.

The agency transmitted its concerns to Israel on September 30 through the office of Henry Kissinger, who had just been appointed secretary of state. The reply, transmitted by the prime minister's office in consultation with the Mossad, was that Israel was aware of the Arab moves and was studying their implications. Two days later, a fuller reply was sent to Washington. It expressed Israel's belief that Syria, for all its hostile intentions, did not believe itself capable of capturing the Golan Heights without Egypt's participation in a two-front war, although there was a small chance that it might try a limited attack. As for Egypt, Israel believed that the exercise being carried out along the canal was just that and not a camouflage for war.

The Americans, respectful of the Israeli intelligence services, deferred to AMAN's assessment.

On Thursday, October 4, as the Israeli General Staff was discussing dress codes, the heads of U.S. intelligence agencies met in Washington for the weekly meeting of the U.S. Intelligence Board's "Watch Committee." In reply to Kissinger's query, the CIA and the State Department's Bureau of Intelligence and Research (INR), basing themselves largely on the Israeli assessment, said that war in the Middle East was unlikely. The Defense Intelligence Agency went further, saying the Arab buildup was not even of a threatening nature, an evaluation that would cost three of the agency officials their jobs.

Direct superpower involvement in the looming crisis began on October 3 when Sadat summoned the Soviet ambassador in Cairo, Vinogradov, to inform him that Egypt and Syria had decided to go to war against Israel in order to break the Middle East deadlock. "What will the Soviet attitude be?" he asked. Sadat and Assad had agreed that the Soviets, upon whom they would be dependent for resupply and political support once the war started, would have to be told beforehand. But they would do it in such a way as to discourage any attempt by Moscow to restrain them. When the ambassador asked when the war would start, Sadat said the date had not yet been decided upon. He and Assad had agreed that more information would be given the Soviets the next day by the Syrian leader, whose relations with Moscow were better than Sadat's.

On Thursday, Assad duly summoned the Soviet ambassador in Damascus, Nuritdin Mukhitdinov, and told him the war would begin in the next few days. Syria's object, he said, was Israeli eviction from the Golan Heights and restoration of Palestinian rights. Assad said that he had in mind a war lasting only one or two days, not a protracted campaign. The Syrian army, he said, would position itself to block an Israeli counterattack once the Golan was taken. In his report to Moscow, Mukhitdinov said that Assad was interested in having the Soviet Union initiate a cease-fire resolution in the UN Security Council immediately after the initial stage of the battle in order to forestall an Israeli counterattack.

This was not the strategy that Sadat had agreed upon with Assad, who had asked him to press for the capture of all of Sinai. Assad hoped an ongoing Egyptian offensive would keep Israel from focusing its attentions on Syria. His request to the Soviets for an early cease-fire, made without Sadat's knowledge, was an extra insurance policy. Sadat had taken out his own insurance policy by ordering his army to stop well short of the Sinai passes, contrary to the plans shown Assad.

In Cairo, Ambassador Vinogradov passed on to Sadat a response to the Egyptian leader's query the day before about Moscow's attitude. It was a cautious message from Brezhnev that reiterated Moscow's preference for a political solution in the Middle East. A decision on war was a matter for the Egyptian leadership alone, said Brezhnev, but it had best be thought through carefully. He added that Moscow had decided to evacuate Soviet families from Egypt and Syria immediately. He asked permission for the Soviets to land four large passenger aircraft at an Egyptian military base the next day, rather than at Cairo's international airport, so as to keep the evacuation secret. Sadat was upset at the Soviet move, which he took to be a crude expression of nonconfidence in Egypt's military capability. However, he raised no objection.

The Soviet role in the developing conflict would remain ambiguous. In order to retain its standing with Egypt and Syria, it had supplied them with the modern armaments that would enable them to make war. However, Moscow did not want them to actually go to war since this would endanger the Soviet Union's relations with the West. Furthermore, virtually no Soviet military or political leader believed the Arabs capable of winning. Defeat would be another embarrassment for Soviet arms. In the unlikely event of an Arab victory, Arab dependence on the Soviet Union would be reduced. War was therefore a terrible option, but Egypt and Syria were Moscow's clients and, for better or worse, they would receive its backing.

In Moscow this Thursday evening, at almost the same time that Kissinger was being told by his intelligence advisers in Washington that there was no immediate prospect of a Middle East war, foreign minister Andrei Gromyko summoned aides to his study on the seventh floor of the ministry on Smolenskaya Square to tell them the opposite. What they were about to hear, he said, must be kept absolutely confidential. Egypt and Syria were to open war against Israel on Saturday at 2 P.M. Neither Sadat nor Assad had informed the Soviet ambassadors of zero hour, but the Soviets had other sources. The prospect of war disturbed Gromyko. It would have a negative impact on détente and undermine the chances of a durable Middle East peace. He was skeptical about the Arabs' chances but acknowledged that a surprise attack might improve their odds. When an aide said that the evacuation of Soviet citizens might reveal the Arabs' intentions to the Israelis and Americans, Gromyko said, "The lives of Soviet people are dearer to us." As the meeting broke up, the foreign minister told the others to get a good night's sleep. "You'll need your strength very soon."

Through the night, teams of Israeli photo interpreters worked on the films brought back by the reconnaissance plane which had returned late

Thursday afternoon. They counted every tank and artillery piece in a twenty-mile-wide swath west of the canal and made note of every change since the previous photographs nine days earlier. The results were anxiously awaited by General Elazar and the rest of the high command. General Mendler sent one of his intelligence officers up from Sinai with orders to phone him with the first results.

Even before the reconnaissance plane had returned to base, AMAN's Sigint branch picked up a report that finally ended the high command's complacency. Colonel Ben-Porat was notified at 4 P.M. Thursday that a radio transmission had been intercepted from the KGB in Moscow to its station chief in Damascus indicating that an emergency evacuation of the families of Soviet advisers was under way. The transmission had not been encoded, raising speculation that Moscow might have intended that it be intercepted, perhaps to disassociate itself from whatever was about to happen. A few hours later, it was learned that the evacuation also involved families of the Soviet experts who had returned to Egypt the previous year. This time, the relevant message had been sent to the Soviet embassy in Cairo more discreetly by telephone. Eleven Soviet planes were on their way to the Middle East, including six giant Antonov 22s, each with a capacity of four hundred passengers. The Soviet families were ordered to be at assembly points by midnight.

The hasty evacuation smacked of panic. What to make of it? AMAN's Research section suggested that there had been a falling-out between the Soviets and the Arabs similar to the one that had led to Sadat's expulsion of advisers the previous year. Zeira himself offered this explanation when Ben-Porat called him at home. The Sigint chief pointed out that the evacuation was not of the advisers but of their families. "This can't mean anything except war," he said. This conclusion seemed to be supported by a report from Israeli naval intelligence that Soviet warships were hastily departing Egyptian ports.

In London, it was after midnight when the phone rang in the home of a Mossad case officer. On the line was the Source. He wanted to meet the boss, he said. Urgently. It was 2:30 A.M. Friday in Israel when Mossad chief Zvi Zamir was wakened by a call from the case officer. Apologizing for the hour, the latter passed on the Source's request as well as a seemingly innocuous word he had let drop. It was the code word for war.

The Source was not infallible. He had twice—in December and in

April—given warnings of war that had not come to pass. It was still not clear whether his information on those occasions had been wrong to start with or whether Sadat had changed his mind after setting war preparations in motion. But such was the Source's proven value that Zamir decided to leave for Europe in the morning. The Source would be flying there to meet him. The Mossad chief was thinking about the call when the phone rang again. This time it was Eli Zeira, calling to report the evacuation of the Soviet advisers' families. Zamir told him of the call from the Source and of his planned departure in a few hours to meet him. For both men the confluence of these two events—the airlift of the Soviet families and the urgent call from the agent—created an uneasy resonance. Zamir, who worked directly for the prime minister, did not wish to waken Mrs. Meir and asked Zeira to advise her of his departure in the morning.

Early Friday, Dayan met in his office in Tel Aviv with Elazar, Tal, and other senior officers, including Zeira, who was back after several days in bed. The meeting was fraught with tension. Yom Kippur would begin at sundown but the transcendent nature of the holy day had been overshadowed by developments across the borders which had cosmic implications of their own for Israel. The air photos showed a stunning Egyptian buildup all along the canal. "You can get a stroke just from the numbers," said Dayan to the generals. "There are 1,100 artillery pieces compared to 802 on September 25. You people don't take the Arabs seriously enough."

The air photos liberated Elazar somewhat from ambiguity. For days now, lulled by the "low probability" mantra of AMAN, he had been forcing the evidence of Arab war preparations into molds—Egyptian exercise, Syrian nervousness—which were too shallow to contain them. He was still not certain of war and did not seek mobilization, but he was now concerned enough to order the armed forces onto a C alert, the highest state of alert short of war. It was the first time since the Six Day War that a C alert was declared. The emergency mobilization network was put on standby and all leaves in the armed forces canceled—an important step since a significant percentage of frontline soldiers were scheduled to be released in the coming hours for Yom Kippur. Elazar ordered the remainder of the Seventh Armored Brigade dispatched to the Golan. There would be 177 tanks there by the following morning and these, he felt, would be sufficient to cope, even against odds of 8 to 1. A brigade from the standing army commanded by Col. Gabi Amir was ordered to fly down from Israel to Sinai this night to replace the Seventh Brigade there.

The implications of the Soviet evacuation were not immediately clear.

Elazar thought it might indicate a political rupture between the Soviets and the Arabs. Dayan disagreed. "A political rupture isn't [evacuation only of] women and children," he said. "It could be they fear an attack by us."

AMAN was able to find a nonthreatening interpretation of the massive buildup across the canal—the Egyptians feared that Israel might use Egypt's military exercise as an excuse for attacking. However, if the buildup did not shake Zeira's certitude about no war, the evacuation of the Soviet families finally did. He admitted for the first time to a measure of puzzlement about Arab intentions and gave his blessing to the C alert. "The evacuation has introduced a new dimension," he said. It was not reasonable to assume the Soviets were evacuating civilians because they feared an Israeli attack, he acknowledged. If they had that fear, they would have turned to the United States to ask it to stay Israel's hand. The evacuation could, however, mean that the Soviets were aware of an Egyptian-Syrian plan to attack Israel and that Moscow feared the Israeli reaction. It could also be a way of showing the United States that the Soviets disapproved of something the Arabs were about to do. Although Zeira's analysis pointed to an Arab attack on Israel as the most likely scenario, he did not explicitly say so.

Another puzzlement was the nature of the Egyptian exercise. No radio traffic was being picked up except from outposts in the Aswan area far to the south. The Egyptians were confining their communication to landlines or messages sent by runners. This could mean that there was in fact no exercise, only a mustering of a huge army on the canal banks for some other purpose. (Egyptian units had been ordered not to use wireless communications until the war began in order to prevent the Israelis from getting a fix on their numbers and location.) Despite these admittedly troubling uncertainties, Zeira saw no reason to alter AMAN's basic assessment that Arab self-interest negated war as an option. "I don't see either the Egyptians or the Syrians attacking."

Zeira mentioned that Mossad chief Zamir had flown to Europe to meet an important source. "It may be that by tonight we'll be a lot wiser," he said.

Despite Dayan's long-held faith in Zeira's judgment, he had become uneasy about the intelligence chief's unbending position in face of the mounting evidence. He asked him now if he had activated the "special means." Elazar had put the same question to him earlier in the week. Zeira's answer to both was affirmative. Knowing the quality of these sources, Dayan and Elazar assumed that Zeira's "low probability" assessment, which seemed to defy logic, had substantive roots. However, Zeira had in fact not activated the devices until this day in order not to risk exposing them before an ultimate moment of truth when he would really need them. He had not believed, until now, that that moment had yet arrived.

Zeira's self-confidence no longer appeared to be shared by his closest associates. Sigint chief Ben-Porat, speaking to General Shalev by telephone midday Friday, thought Zeira's deputy sounded like a man struggling with reality. Ben-Porat's assistant told him that Yona Bandman on the Egyptian desk likewise sounded no longer certain about Egypt's intentions.

Leading a nation into a major war was not a role Golda Meir would ever have wished for. But she was coping so far with the steadiness that had marked her long public career. Born in Kiev, she had arrived in Milwaukee at the age of eight with her family, the memory of pogroms still vivid—a memory that would underlie her determination that the Jews must be strong. She trained as a teacher but in 1921 sailed with her husband for Palestine, where they settled in a spartan kibbutz. Strong-minded and articulate, she moved from social activity into politics, becoming in time part of the senior Zionist leadership of the state-in-the-making. In May 1948, four days before the state of Israel was to be proclaimed, she was dispatched across the Jordan River to meet with Jordan's King Abdullah. Dressed as an Arab woman and accompanied by a single colleague, she passed through an area where an Arab army was preparing to invade the Jewish state. Her attempt to persuade the king not to join in the attack failed. With the founding of Israel, she became its first ambassador to the Soviet Union and later was chosen foreign minister. Her pluckiness, wry sense of humor, and simple lifestyle earned her widespread popularity. But her uncompromising mind-set left little room for exploring the chances of peace, however slim, with the Arabs. Empathy was not something she extended to enemies, even as a tactical exercise. "Put yourself in Nassar's shoes," a relative said to her once. "Not a chance," replied Mrs. Meir.

Following the meeting of the military chiefs in Dayan's office Friday morning, most of the participants proceeded to Mrs. Meir's office nearby to brief her on the latest developments. "I still think that they're not going to attack," said Elazar, "but we have no hard information." Zeira, digging in, said that a joint Egyptian-Syrian attack was "absolutely unreasonable," and offered a new theory to account for the evacuation of the Soviet families. "Maybe the Russians think the Arabs are going to attack because they don't understand them well." In other words, the Russians who had been working alongside the Egyptians and Syrians for years, serving as their advisers and arms suppliers, did not understand the Arab mentality, while AMAN did.

Conceding that that was only speculation, Zeira said that in fact he could not explain the Russian move.

It was decided to pass a message to Egypt and Syria through the Americans saying that Israel had no intention of carrying out hostile action against them, in case this fear was what had prompted the massing of troops on the two borders. The Arabs were also to be told that if they themselves were planning a surprise attack, Israel was prepared. A message sent to the Americans giving Israel's evaluation of the situation said the likelihood of the Egyptians and Syrians launching a war against Israel was minimal. "Our assessment is that the alerts by Egypt and Syria are in part connected with maneuvers [as regards Egypt] and in part due to fears of offensive action by Israel."

At 11:30 A.M., the generals briefed those cabinet members who were in Tel Aviv. It was decided not to summon ministers living in Jerusalem because of the proximity of Yom Kippur, which would begin at sunset. Dayan and Zeira reviewed the fast-moving developments for the ministers. Zeira reiterated his conviction that the high state of alert in the Syrian and Egyptian armies stemmed from fear of an Israeli attack and that there was a "low probability" of war. The military options open to the Arabs were artillery bombardment, limited incursions, or a massive Egyptian crossing of the canal with the objective of reaching the passes in central Sinai. "All are low probability and the lowest of all is a crossing of the canal," Zeira said. "As long as they don't have the feeling they can achieve a reasonable situation in the air, they won't go to war, certainly not all-out war." The one thing for which he admittedly had no explanation was the evacuation of the Soviet civilians.

It was Mrs. Meir who challenged Zeira's reading of the situation, albeit obliquely. She expressed doubt that the Syrians, if they did intend to engage in hostilities, would make do with only an artillery barrage, given the massiveness of their deployment. She found further cause for concern in the translations of the Arab press that she had perused earlier. On the eve of the Six Day War, she recalled, the Arab media had been filled with false reports that Israeli troops were massing on the borders. Today they were writing the very same thing. "Maybe this should tell us something." Hers were the healthy instincts of a woman who knew nothing of military strategy but could recognize a bald fact staring her in the face.

Elazar said that if the Arabs decided to attack, there would be "additional indications" of this beforehand so that at least twelve to twenty-four hours' warning could be relied on. In response to a question by Israel Galili,

Mrs. Meir's closest adviser, Elazar said the IDF would not mobilize reserves unless there were further indications of war. Mobilization was not something to be lightly undertaken since a mass call-up would itself escalate tensions in the region and could lead to events spinning out of control. Dayan firmly opposed mobilization unless the Arabs made the first hostile move.

Elazar was confident that the "special means," which he believed had already been activated, would provide reasonable warning if war was indeed in the offing. With the Blue-White controversy of the previous spring still vivid, he also apparently wished to avoid being perceived as an alarmist by pressing for mobilization, particularly on the eve of Yom Kippur, when intelligence was saying "low probability." He might well have felt otherwise had he been aware of what frontline observers were seeing or of the fact that Zeira's views were disputed by senior members of his own staff who believed that war was at hand.

Ending the meeting, Mrs. Meir said the discussion would be resumed by the full cabinet on Sunday. At Galili's suggestion, the ministers authorized Mrs. Meir, who was remaining in Tel Aviv for the holiday, and Dayan to order mobilization on Yom Kippur if they deemed it necessary, without convening the cabinet. Mrs. Meir asked the ministers to leave telephone numbers with the cabinet secretary where they could be reached during the holy day.

Mrs. Meir's secretary, Lou Kedar, had been growing increasingly distressed by the snatches of conversation she was picking up during the morning. On the staircase outside the prime minister's office she encountered a group of officers, including Zeira. Seeing her expression of concern, he patted her on the shoulder and said, "Don't make a face like that. There won't be a war."

At that hour, Zeira's own staff was preparing an updated intelligence bulletin which, in forty-two paragraphs, spelled out unusual activities in Egypt and Syria that pointed to imminent war. But a forty-third paragraph negated the conclusion to be drawn from all the rest.

The items reveal something of the depth to which Israeli intelligence was monitoring the Arab armies:

Egyptian naval headquarters had the night before last ordered windows and car headlights at naval bases painted as a blackout precaution; soldiers had been ordered to break their Ramadan fast; military courses were being canceled; in the past two weeks seventy-three of the eighty-five boat descents to the waterline along the length of the canal had been improved; in the Gulf of Suez a force of naval commandos had been identified along with two dozen rubber boats; in Syria, ammunition had been transferred from Homs to a central depot opposite the southern Golan front; several sources reported a feeling among Syrian soldiers and officers that a large-scale war was in the offing.

These alarming details, coming on top of what was already known about the Arab buildup, should have been enough to remove any lingering doubts about Arab intent. The item about the Ramadan fast alone should have set off every alarm bell in the country. Why would a Moslem country with a strong religious ethos order its soldiers to violate a central religious obligation just for an exercise? Israel would certainly never ask its soldiers to eat on Yom Kippur just to carry out an exercise.

Such conclusions were offset by one paragraph inserted by Colonel Bandman of the Egyptian desk: "Although the emergency deployment along the canal appears to show clear evidence of aggressive intent, our best assessment is that there has been no change in Egypt's evaluation of its relative strength vis-à-vis the IDF. Thus, the chances that Egypt is planning to renew hostilities are low." Bandman would subsequently testify that he had added the forty-third paragraph because he felt obliged not just to provide information but to evaluate it as well. "From the point of view of real intent, in my view, they did not think themselves prepared for an offensive." Like the September 30 bulletin attributing, a priori, all unusual activity along the canal to the Egyptian exercise that was to begin the next day, this one, too, effectively shut off Israel's alarm system.

In the General Staff command bunker in Cairo, Center Ten, Gen. Ahmed Fuad Havidi, the head of the Israeli desk in Egyptian intelligence, studied the reports that had gathered since midmorning. Israel's Southern Command seemed to be showing signs of waking from the torpor which had gripped it for months. It had been evident to Havidi since General Sharon's replacement in the summer that the Israelis were not expecting war. If they had been, they would not have let such an experienced general leave that key position. There had been no reinforcement in recent days of Israeli units in Sinai, no large-scale training exercises. Even the beginning of the Egyptian exercise had failed to stir the Israelis. But Friday morning, bustle was reported by Egyptian signal intelligence and by Bedouin in Sinai serving as Egyptian spies. (Other Bedouin served as Israeli spies.) Senior Israeli officers were arriving at the large Refidim base in western Sinai, tank formations could be seen on the move, mechanics were checking generators. At noon

Havidi prepared a bulletin for distribution to the senior command. Its conclusion: Israel has discovered our intentions to attack and it also knows the scale of the attack.

General Gamasy, head of operations, was furious with Havidi when he read it. The bulletin could raise fears of an Israeli trap precisely at a time when high morale was critical. Havidi told Gamasy that there was no reason for concern. The Israelis had only just begun to move and there was no chance of any substantial reinforcements reaching Sinai before the war began.

Despite the alert, the Israelis had, in fact, not yet begun to move. In Tel Aviv shortly after noon, Elazar and Zeira hurried off to their fourth meeting of the day, this with the General Staff. The meeting had been called to pass on holiday greetings. "But as long as you're here," said Elazar, "we have some new information." Again, it was Zeira who gave the main briefing, including news of the Soviet evacuation and the results of the photo reconnaissance mission. "To sum up," he concluded, "I don't think we're going to war but there's a bigger question mark about it today, I would say, than twenty-four hours ago."

Elazar said that if the Arabs should attack without warning over the holiday, the troops holding the line, together with the air force, would block them until the reserves were mobilized. In conclusion, the chief of staff offered his generals the traditional holiday greeting for the coming Jewish year: May you be well inscribed in the Book of Life. In Jewish tradition, the heavenly book is opened on Rosh Hashana for the recording of one's fate in the coming year and sealed, after Ten Days of Repentance, on Yom Kippur.

Despite his attempts to be reassuring, Elazar was increasingly uneasy. In a departure from standing procedures, he authorized air force commander Benny Peled to call up his own reservists without clearing the move with Dayan. If it came to a worst-case situation, Elazar wanted to have at least the air force at full strength.

A hush had descended over the land by late afternoon as the Jewish population prepared for the onset of Yom Kippur at sundown. Although only a minority of the population described itself as religious, the bulk of Israelis fasted on Yom Kippur and spent at least some time during the day in synagogue. Traffic halted and the streets emptied of pedestrians. Elazar, however, remained in his office, going through reports and thinking about whether he had done everything possible to prepare for whatever lay ahead. Sometime in the next few hours, Zamir was to report from Europe on his meeting with the Source, who might be able to clarify whether the Arabs were going to war. Unknown to Elazar, an answer to that question had already arrived and lay on a desk one floor above him.

Sigint had that afternoon intercepted a message from an unimpeachable source who said that the reason the Soviets were evacuating their civilian personnel was that Egypt and Syria were about to open a two-front war against Israel. It was precisely what Elazar was waiting for, a reliable signal of Arab intentions that, together with all the other signs of war, would justify the beginning of mobilization. The message was passed on at 5 P.M. to the duty officer in Zeira's office at army headquarters. Instead of sending the message on to Elazar and others on the intelligence distribution list, the intelligence major first called his superiors. He was bounced from one to another until he ended up talking to Zeira himself, whom he reached at home. Knowing that the Sigint report would trigger mobilization, the intelligence chief told the duty officer to hold off on distributing it. He wanted to first hear from Zamir in Europe.

It was, even for Zeira, a breathtaking display of intellectual arrogance. Once again, he was preventing vital information contradicting his no-war thesis from reaching the decision makers, this at a time when even he acknowledged an alert to be justified. Elazar would later say that if he had received the report in time he would have immediately set the mobilization process in motion. This was the kind of "additional indications" he had told the cabinet ministers he needed before deciding on a call-up of reserves. Instead, as he finally drove home through the deserted streets at 9 P.M., he wondered whether he had not overreacted by putting the armed forces on C alert.

Footprints of intruders had been detected by an Israeli patrol Friday morning in the central Suez sector. The patrol tracked them to a barely perceptible opening in a sand dune deep behind Israeli lines. From it emerged an Egyptian intelligence-gathering team. The prisoners were transported to the rear for questioning.

For the past week, the men in the canal forts had been reporting nightly convoys, sometimes numbering hundreds of trucks, entering the Egyptian lines. What were suspected of being ground-to-ground missiles were deployed in darkness and covered with tarpaulins before daybreak. Groups of Egyptian officers were seen every day surveying the Israeli strongpoints with maps in their hands. Throughout the week, SAM batteries were moved to forward positions so as to extend their reach over Sinai.

The Egyptian rear, up to three miles from the canal, was overflowing with vehicles, pontoons, and fuel dumps. The sound of tanks moving behind the Egyptian ramps near the water's edge had become commonplace. So too the sound of mines being detonated in the water across the canal. The mines had been placed against the danger of an Israeli crossing. Their detonation meant either that the Egyptians intended to replace them with fresh ones, as had happened once before, or that they were clearing the way for their own crossing. Bulldozers worked late every night cutting openings through the Egyptian ramps to permit vehicular access to the canal bank. The Israelis had grown accustomed to seeing Egyptian soldiers on the far bank over the years walking about at leisure without arms or helmets. For several days now, a new type of soldier could be seen—armed, helmeted, and with the purposeful bearing of a combat soldier. The soldiers who had previously been manning positions along the canal itself remained in place, looking as indolent as ever and continuing to fish in the canal.

Pvt. Menahem Ritterband participated in a motorized patrol each morning from Orkal, the northernmost fort on the canal, to the neighboring fort of Lahtzanit. The task of the men in the half-track was to check the dirt track alongside the road for footprints. The track was raked each evening so that anyone infiltrating from across the canal during the night would leave fresh prints. From the beginning of the week there had been footprints every morning. Almost all were heading inland, few returning. Unless the infiltrators were crossing back elsewhere during the night, this meant that the Egyptians were putting men into Sinai in some numbers on long-range intelligence missions or as artillery observers. The footprints added to the tension already caused by the sound of tanks and other vehicles arriving each night behind the Egyptian ramparts. On Friday morning, there were so many footprints they couldn't be counted.

Arriving at Lahtzanit every morning, Ritterband would chat with the commander there, Lt. Muli Malhov, who had briefly served at Orkal at the beginning of the reserve tour. Malhov was one of the few men in the battalion to have served on the canal before. He had been expressing mounting unease at what he was seeing. Friday morning, Ritterband heard him telling their battalion commander, who was visiting the line, that the Egyptians were going to attack and that the forts didn't have a chance.

General Elazar remained oblivious to all of this. "For me, the week between October 1 and 6 in Southern Command is the most normal week," he would later say, reconstructing this period. "I distinguish nothing out of the ordinary."

From the Purkan outpost opposite Ismailiya on Friday, men in the lookout tower saw soldiers arguing with the gardener watering plants at the villa. A few moments later, the gardener was gone. So were other civilians normally seen in the area. Major Weisel, the fort commander, saw a large group of Egyptian officers surveying his position. Through binoculars, he could see that their shoulder boards carried lots of rank, including that of brigadier. Some of the officers had turned their epaulets upside down so that the rank could not be seen. Weisel reported his sighting to battalion headquarters and an intelligence team was sent forward, but by the time it arrived the Egyptians were gone.

The group across the canal had included General Shazly. The Egyptian chief of staff had abandoned the claustrophobic atmosphere of Center Ten for a last look at the front line before the battle. He knew Weisel's fortification by its Hebrew name of Purkan, one of the strongest forts on the Bar-Lev Line. An Israeli map giving the code names of every position and road in western Sinai had fallen into Egyptian hands and copies had been distributed to all units, particularly artillery batteries. Israeli units giving their location by radio could be precisely tracked. Studying Purkan through binoculars, Shazly was relieved to detect no sign of special alert. When he saw it next, he hoped, the fort would be a ruin.

Officers from Reshef's and Shomron's brigades drove to General Mendler's headquarters in Refidim on Friday for a farewell party for the division commander, who was to hand over his command on Sunday. They found that Mendler had other plans. His departure was being put off, he said, until the present tension had resolved itself. From the air photos he had seen that morning, it was clear to him that war was on the doorstep. Instead of a party, there was a war briefing. The general took the opportunity of his officers' presence to review the division's operational plans, particularly Dovecote. He was interrupted by a call from a colleague in Tel Aviv reporting on the cabinet meeting. The caller said something that caused Mendler to stare into the middle distance and hang up wordlessly. Turning to his officers, he said, "They're not mobilizing."

Colonel Reshef had hoped to be back at his headquarters in Tasa by sunset in time for Kol Nidre, the opening prayer of the Yom Kippur service, at the base synagogue. But when he emerged from the meeting with Mendler it was nearly dusk and his head was aswim with what he had just heard. Two Egyptian armies, with some fifteen tank brigades, were preparing to cross the canal. His brigade would be the only force in their way for hours.

Walking to his jeep, Reshef encountered the armored corps chaplain, who suggested he put off his return to Tasa, an hour's drive. Stay and pray with us, he said. Snapped out of his reverie, Reshef looked at the rabbi, an old acquaintance, and for the first time addressed him not by his title but by his first name. "Ephraim," he said, "there's going to be war tomorrow."

In Center Ten, the absence of visible Israeli preparations was as much a source of concern as of satisfaction. General Gamasy found it incomprehensible that the Israelis had been so completely deceived. The report earlier in the day that Israel was aware of the pending attack did not appear to be substantiated. There was still no report of Israeli mobilization and the front line had not been reinforced. There was a gnawing suspicion that the Israelis may have been secretly moving forces into Sinai and were preparing a major surprise.

Late that night, Egyptian scouting parties were sent across the canal at several points. They landed well away from the canal forts and stealthily made their way to their vicinity to observe. The reports from the scouts when they returned before dawn all carried the same message: The Jews are sleeping.

One Jew wide awake was Zvi Zamir. He was not fasting and had not heard Kol Nidre, but no Jew this Yom Kippur night was gripped by a greater sense of portent than he. Accompanied by the case officer, the Mossad chief met with the Source for an hour in a London apartment. The Source's message was blunt. Egypt would attack tomorrow before dark. The attack would be carried out according to the war plan already in Israel's hands, which meant a crossing of the canal by five divisions that would begin just before nightfall. Asked whether this might not prove a false alarm as in December and May, the Source said he could not rule out the possibility that Sadat might change his mind again at the last moment. Egypt feared that if its preparations were to become known there was a chance that "outside pressures," evidently Soviet, might dissuade Syria from going to war. He nevertheless estimated the chances of Egypt going to war at "99.9 percent."

Zamir knew that the Source's message would trigger immediate mobilization if he passed it on without softening the warning by pointing out the previous instances of "crying wolf." An emergency mobilization on Yom Kippur, even if a false alarm, would have far-reaching repercussions, domestically and regionally. But there had been too many other warning signals for this to be downplayed, and Zamir decided to pass it on without dilution. To save time needed to encrypt and transmit his message by secure means this Yom Kippur night, he decided to telephone its essence to Tel Aviv. The communication he sat down to formulate was necessarily elliptical in case it should be intercepted, but the message itself was stunning—before the blast of the shofar marked the end of Yom Kippur this coming night, before the last invocation calling on God to open the gates of heaven to receive his people's prayers, Israel would be at war on two fronts.

Ten

YOM KIPPUR MORNING

ISRAEL'S WAKE-UP CALL CAME in the early hours of Yom Kippur morning, an insistent ringing at the bedsides of the nation's political and military leaders. The message from Zamir was passed on to a small number of men, and one woman, who were wakened into the same bad dream.

Zamir had had difficulty getting through to his chief of bureau, Freddy Eini, by telephone after his meeting with the Source. The telephone operator, after checking with an operator in Tel Aviv, informed Zamir that it was a holiday in Israel. Zamir said he was aware of that and asked her to keep trying. Finally, the phone at the other end was lifted and Zamir heard Eini's sleepy voice. Speaking slowly to permit him to write down his words, Zamir read out the seemingly innocuous message he had carefully composed. It spoke of a business deal that was to be consummated this day "before dark" with the signing of a contract. The terms, he said, were those already known. Another part of the message indicated that the Soviets would not be involved.

According to an account published by Ofer Bar-Yosef and acknowledged by Zamir as accurate, the meeting with the Source ended about midnight Israel time. Zamir's message was received by Eini at 2:40 A.M. It was about 3:40 that Mrs. Meir's military aide, Gen. Yisrael Lior, was wakened by Eini. The next call was to Dayan's aide-de-camp. It was only at 4:30 that General Elazar, on whom time would press most of all, was wakened by his own aide-de-camp, Lt. Col. Avner Shalev (not to be confused with AMAN's Gen. Arye Shalev). Once Elazar was wakened, the pace picked up smartly. He asked that his deputy, General Tal, and other members of the General Staff be at headquarters by 5:15. The commanders of the northern and southern fronts were to be there by 6 A.M.

Within ten minutes of being wakened, Elazar placed his first call from home. It was to Benny Peled. "We have information that there will be war with Egypt and Syria by tonight. Are you ready?"

"I'm ready," said the air force commander.

"What do you want to do?"

Peled gave first priority to attacking the Syrian SAMs. Elazar agreed. "Roll it," he said. "I'll get permission." Authorization for a preemptive strike would have to come from Dayan and Golda Meir, but Elazar had no doubt it would be forthcoming. Peled said the air force would be ready by 11 A.M. to noon.

As Elazar dressed, his wife, Talma, sleepily asked what was happening. "This is it," he said. "War." The look on his face—"almost ceremonial"— was one she had seen before. Driving through the empty streets at high speed, Elazar had time for a quick overview of the situation. It had been a basic assumption that intelligence would provide five or six days' warning of war. This would have permitted full mobilization and allowed time for equipment to be put into proper working order and for the reservists to adjust to military mode. Two days' warning was the least expected, enough for mobilization. The present situation, just half a day's warning, was something he had never seriously thought possible.

Zeira, who arrived at headquarters shortly after Elazar, was still maintaining that Sadat would not go to war. The chief of staff chose to humor him. "Let's act as if there will be a war," he said.

For Elazar, the trap Israel found itself in was potentially calamitous. But psychologically the certainty of war had at last cleared the air. He had been clinging with increasing uneasiness to AMAN's assessment of "low probability" despite the Arab buildup and the inevitability, as he saw it, of the Arabs lashing out at some point in the absence of political movement. The fog had now dispersed and Elazar was totally focused on what lay ahead—"like a bulldog," as his aide-de-camp would put it. There was as yet no authorization for mobilization, but the chief of staff told General Tal to activate the network that would carry it out. Without waiting for authorization, he ordered the call-up of several thousand key personnel, including those filling staff positions at various command levels, as well as some commando units.

At 5:50, Elazar met with Dayan in the defense minister's office. An officer who took the official notes of the meeting was surprised at Elazar's seeming jauntiness. When he told Dayan he wanted to quickly smash the Syrians, Dayan asked what his hurry was. Elazar replied with a Jewish joke. An early riser in an eastern European shtetl is surprised to see a friend coming out of a brothel at 6 A.M. Why this early? he asks. I have a busy day ahead of me, says the friend. I just wanted to get this out of the way. To Elazar's astonishment, Dayan adamantly opposed a preemptive strike. Despite the warning passed on by Zamir, the minister doubted that war would break out. "We don't order full mobilization just on the basis of a report by Zvika [Zamir]," he said. There had been similar warnings in the past that had proved false, he noted. The Source was quoted as saying that Sadat still might desist if Israel let it be known that it was aware of Arab intentions. Zeira reinforced Dayan's thesis by noting that American intelligence services with whom he was in contact were reporting no sign of imminent war.

"We're in a political situation in which we can't do what we did in 1967," said Dayan, referring to the preemptive strike which opened that war. To attack, particularly when the Americans were saying the Arabs were not going to war, would in the world's eyes be to initiate hostilities. The only circumstance in which he was prepared to approve a preemptive strike, said Dayan, was if information was received that the Arabs were planning to attack Tel Aviv. The assurance he had given Peled a few months before that the government would authorize a first strike if the Arabs were seen preparing for war had not stood the test of reality.

The minister also opposed Elazar's proposal for an "almost full" mobilization of 200,000 to 250,000 men. In the absence of active hostilities, said Dayan, mobilization on this scale would itself be perceived as an act of war. At this stage, he said, only forces needed to buttress the defense, some 20,000 to 30,000 men, should be mobilized. The remainder of the reserves would be called up only if war actually broke out. Elazar said that defense alone would require 50,000 to 60,000 men. Certain that war was coming, he insisted that the entire reserve combat potential be mobilized—four armored divisions plus ancillary units—so as to be ready to counterattack as soon as the initial Arab drive had been stopped. Dayan agreed to accept the 50,000 to 60,000 figure for defense, but Elazar still insisted on 200,000. Instead of ordering mobilization of the 50,000 to 60,000 men about whom there was now agreement, the two men left the overall decision to Mrs. Meir, who was waiting for them.

Meanwhile, the argument over a preemptive strike had lost much of its relevance. Peled was at his desk at 7 A.M. when there was a knock on the door of his office and his chief meteorologist entered.

"What are you doing here?" asked Peled. "I don't need you now."

"I'm sorry, sir, but the Golan Heights are covered with clouds—base 800 feet, ceiling 3,000 feet."

Peled called Elazar to inform him that the strike against the missile batteries could not be carried out. However, visibility over the rest of Syria was unlimited and Peled suggested hitting Syrian air bases instead. Elazar consented. The mechanics who had been arming the planes for the strike against the missile batteries were ordered to remove those armaments and replace them with the types of bombs needed to damage runways and penetrate the concrete shelters in which the Syrian warplanes were kept.

The day before, General Peled had summoned his base commanders to Tel Aviv to confer on Dougman. He discovered that important elements were not yet in place. Some of the failings could be remedied within a day and Peled gave the order to do so. He warned his commanders, however, that if the situation developed into a full-blown war and the ground forces were in difficulty, the air force might have to go to their assistance even if the missiles had not been taken out. "Be prepared to go into the fire," he said. That was what they would now have to do.

Elazar put off the meeting with Mrs. Meir for an hour in order to confer with the generals who would lead the coming battles. He met first with the commanders of the northern and southern fronts, Generals Hofi and Gonen. Once the war started, he would have limited opportunity to communicate with them and he wanted to be sure that they were all thinking within the same parameters. The warning of war, he told them, was shorter than they had ever imagined. The standing army, however, was already on full alert. "We'll mobilize whatever they permit. The rest we'll call up under fire."

After brief talks with each officer separately, Elazar asked them to return to their headquarters and set their commands in motion. They were to come back to him at noon to tie up loose ends. Elazar then met with the commanders of the air force, navy, and armored corps. He told them that war would break out at 6 P.M. The Source had not mentioned a time, only that the attack would be launched according to the Egyptian war plan already in Israeli hands. The plan called for the crossing of the first wave to begin just before last light, which would be about 6 P.M., some forty minutes after sunset.

Elazar told his generals that the reserve divisions would organize for a counterattack while the standing army held off the enemy with the assistance of the air force. The Syrian front was of primary concern but Elazar was anxious about Sinai as well. Dovecote had not been designed to hold off an attack by five divisions; it was only a fallback in such a worst-case situation. "We're in for a difficult war," he said.

The meeting with the prime minister got under way at 8:05 A.M. Dayan began by saying that war was not a certainty. Children in the Golan settlements would be evacuated in late afternoon, he said, on the pretext that they were going on an outing. A reduction in tension during the day might obviate the need for this evacuation and thus avoid the ensuing public outcry at a government-organized excursion on Yom Kippur. Mrs. Meir, operating under her mandate as a grandmother rather than as prime minister, ordered that the children be brought down immediately. Dayan and Elazar then presented their respective cases on a preemptive strike and mobilization.

It was admittedly bizarre to have two generals, veteran warhorses at the pinnacle of Israel's military establishment, bringing their differences over vital military matters to a seventy-five-year-old grandmother. Mrs. Meir lit one cigarette after another as they spoke, filling the room with acrid smoke that caused those present to squint. Elazar expressed readiness to compromise on the mobilization at this stage of 100,000 to 120,000 men. Gathering that Mrs. Meir was leaning towards his view, he dispatched his aide shortly after 9 A.M. to make a phone call that would get mobilization started for two divisions.

Elazar argued for a preemptive strike against the Syrian airfields at noon and against the missiles at 3 P.M., by which time the sky should have cleared over the Golan. "Then, at five, the air force can hit the Syrian ground forces and put them out of action." Aware of Mrs. Meir's extreme sensitivity to casualties, he said that a preemptive strike would save many lives.

When the presentations were done, the prime minister hemmed uncertainly for a few moments but then came to a clear decision. There would be no preemptive strike. Israel might be needing American assistance soon and it was imperative that it not be blamed for starting the war. "If we strike first we won't get help from anybody," she said. As for mobilization, she agreed to Elazar's compromise proposal. "If war does break out, better to be in proper shape to deal with it, even if the world gets angry with us." Summing up the meeting, Dayan said, "The chief of staff will mobilize the entire force he has proposed." It was now 9:25 A.M. A sense of relief descended on those present despite the somberness of the moment. Indecision was over. The wheels had begun to turn.

Almost three precious hours had been lost by the disagreement between

Dayan and Elazar over mobilization. And there was even less time left than they thought.

Mrs. Meir made no pretense of understanding military matters. She would confess to her military aide, Gen. Yisrael Lior, that she had no idea what a division was. When he had telephoned her this morning with the report of imminent war received from the Mossad, she asked him, "Yisrael, what do we do now?" When she arrived at her office, her face had been gray and her step heavy. But she functioned well. Her decisions at the meeting with Dayan and Elazar had been sound, based on common sense and political instincts, and they would determine Israel's operational profile in the critical opening phase of the war. There would be no preemptive air strike, but the weight of Israel's reserve army would be brought to bear as quickly as possible. Her decision about the early evacuation of the Golan children would also prove critical. She would leave the running of the war to Dayan and Elazar, but her instincts would continue to serve her well whenever her input was required.

Elazar called the air force commander to inform him that a preemptive strike had been ruled out. Even if the attack on the airfields had been executed, it would not have altered the outcome of the war. Unlike in the Six Day War, the Arab planes were well protected in concrete shelters and difficult to destroy. More importantly, it was not the Syrian air force but the SAMs which would menace Israeli planes over the battlefield.

At 9:30, American ambassador Kenneth Keating and his deputy, Nicholas Veliotes, arrived at Mrs. Meir's office in response to her urgent summons. The diplomats were stunned when she described the situation. They had been assured by CIA reports and the Israelis themselves only the day before that there was no danger of war. Mrs. Meir told them that Israel would not carry out a preemptive strike. She asked that Washington, in the coming hours, try to stave off war by turning to the Soviets or directly to Cairo and Damascus. If the Arab moves were dictated by a misreading of Israeli intentions, the Americans were to assure them that Israel had no plans to attack. If the Arabs did initiate war, said Mrs. Meir, Israel would respond forcefully. As Veliotes rapidly made notes, the silver-haired Keating asked whether he could be sure that Israel would take no preemptive action. "You can be sure," Mrs. Meir said decisively. Keating said he would send his report to Washington with the highest security designation, which would mean that Kissinger would be wakened to read it.

Israel's ambassador to Washington, Simha Dinitz, was in the corridor outside Mrs. Meir's office when Keating emerged, looking pale. Dinitz had arrived in Israel a few days before to attend the funeral of his father and was now in the weeklong mourning period. A former director of the prime minister's office, he enjoyed Mrs. Meir's confidence and was one of the first persons she summoned. "You've got to return to Washington immediately," she said. He was first to consult with the defense ministry about armaments to be requested from the American administration. The prime minister saw Washington as a critical anchor for Israel in the coming storm. She asked her military aide to find a way to get Dinitz out of the country, no easy feat because there were no commercial flights into or out of Israel on Yom Kippur. Lior arranged for the government-owned Israel Aircraft Industries to roll out an executive jet. It flew Dinitz in the afternoon to Rome, where he boarded a commercial flight for the United States.

The brewing Middle East crisis jarred Henry Kissinger out of deep sleep in New York's Waldorf-Astoria Hotel. Without standing on ceremony, Joe Sisco, assistant secretary of state for Near Eastern affairs, had burst into his suite at 6:15 A.M. local time (12:15 P.M. Israel time) to announce that Israel and the Arabs were about to go to war. Sisco had just read the message from Keating. The ambassador quoted Mrs. Meir as saying, "We might be in trouble." Half an hour later, it was Kissinger's turn to rouse Soviet ambassador to Washington Anatoly Dobrynin from sleep. He passed on Mrs. Meir's message that Israel was not planning offensive action and asked Moscow to urgently get this message to the leaders of Egypt and Syria. Kissinger then called the Israeli chargé d'affaires in Washington to inform him of his conversation with Dobrynin and to ask Jerusalem to avoid any "rash moves."

General Zeira's senior staff members, summoned to an urgent meeting in his office, took their places at the conference table. Zeira began by turning to his deputy, General Shalev, to his immediate left. "Tell me, Arye, will there be war today or not?" General Shalev did not look his usual confident self. "I have no reason to change my view that the chances of war are low," he replied. Zeira pointed at the next person in line, Yona Bandman, and asked the same question. The head of the Egyptian desk said he stood behind Shalev. Zussia Keniezer, who had come in late and taken a place on one of the couches along the opposite wall, rose angrily. "Say what you think, not that you stand behind someone." The two men had been rivals for the Egyptian desk and Bandman had won. Keniezer, the head of the Jordanian desk, had been convinced war was coming since monitoring King Hussein's conversation with Mrs. Meir and had been riled at Bandman's insistence on no war. AMAN's official line regarding low probability remained unchanged but the voices of dissent were growing stronger. Meanwhile, Zeira had finally given the order to activate "special sources."

At 10 A.M., Elazar descended to the vast underground war room—"the Pit," in popular parlance—to meet with senior staff. Zeira offered a review of the Egyptian and Syrian war plans in Israeli hands. The Egyptians, he said, would begin with artillery and air attacks, to be followed by crossings in small boats along the entire canal front. They might also send helicopters bearing commandos into Sinai to cut roads and attack command posts. There would be five bridgeheads, but only three of them—opposite the main roads leading into the heart of Sinai—would constitute major points of attack. Under cover of the SAMs, the Egyptians intended to penetrate six miles into Sinai and then consolidate. What happened afterwards would depend on how the first stage played out. His description of Badr was accurate; so was his outline of Syria's attack plan. The three Syrian divisions on the line would send their infantry brigades forward to cross the Israeli tank ditch on foot, followed by bridging tanks which would lay spans across it. The tank brigades attached to each of these divisions would follow.

Dayan, who had joined them, asked for details of Israel's deployment in Sinai. Elazar said that one of the Sinai Division's armored brigades was presently positioned in the canal area and the two others were being held to the rear for use at Southern Command's discretion.

When will the reserves arrive? asked Dayan.

"At a very rough estimate," said Elazar, "three hundred tanks by tomorrow night, three hundred on Monday, and another three hundred on Tuesday." The total number of men already in uniform—conscripts, regular army personnel, and reservists who happened to be doing their annual service—was 100,000. Mobilization orders had already been issued for 70,000 men and the remainder would follow shortly.

When Dayan asked what offensive action he planned, Elazar said the unexpected circumstances required revision of existing plans. Earlier in the morning, Elazar had raised the possibility of reaching Damascus in a counterattack. The defense minister was not enthusiastic about the idea. He now made it clear to his generals that if war came, Israel had no new territorial ambitions. "I want to remind everyone," said Dayan, "that our main objective is destruction of enemy forces. Any move in the direction of Damascus would be in order to destroy forces, not to capture positions that I believe we will be obliged to pull back from. This is the line that will guide this forum."

Dayan still questioned, however, whether there would be war at all.

What will you do with all these reservists if war doesn't break out? he asked Elazar. If the threat is canceled and not just postponed, said Elazar, the men will be sent home. "A hundred thousand men will hang around a full day before they're sent home?" asked Dayan. He sounded as if he was still annoyed that Elazar had won Mrs. Meir's vote for a large mobilization.

"They won't hang around," answered Elazar. "They'll go down to the front. If it turns out that there's no war, we'll release them in forty-eight hours." Tal thought it would be more like four days. In any case, the task at the moment was getting the men into uniform, not out of it.

For health minister Victor Shemtov, riding in a car through the empty streets of Jerusalem on Yom Kippur was an unsettling experience even though he was not religiously observant. For his government driver, a religious man, it was excruciating. On Yom Kippur no vehicle normally moved unless it was carrying a pregnant woman or stricken person to the hospital. Shemtov had been telephoned at home the previous evening by the cabinet secretary, who informed him that an emergency cabinet meeting was to be held at noon in the prime minister's Tel Aviv office. He was to tell no one. Shemtov already had an indication of something unusual afoot Friday afternoon when his son was ordered to report immediately to his elite reconnaissance unit. Why on Yom Kippur eve? his son asked. Is anything happening? Nothing I know about, said the minister. Shemtov drove his son to his base in the Negev and got back to Jerusalem just before the onset of the holiday, puzzled over the call-up. The summons to the cabinet meeting came shortly afterwards.

Military vehicles with high antennas were parked outside the prime minister's office when Shemtov arrived. He bounded up the stairs and entered the room used by the cabinet when meetings were held in Tel Aviv rather than Jerusalem. Most of his colleagues were already seated around the large table. Only the religious ministers from Jerusalem had not come. Faces were taut and no one was speaking, itself ominous, given this voluble collection of politicians. As Shemtov eased himself into his chair, the minister next to him leaned over and whispered, "There's going to be war." It was an incredible statement. Shemtov had not attended the previous day's abbreviated cabinet meeting and had received no hint over the past months of possible war, not even in intelligence briefings. Mrs. Meir had not yet emerged from her office by the scheduled starting time, which was unusual. Shemtov went out to the corridor briefly and an army officer said to him, "They caught us with our pants down." Mrs. Meir entered the cabinet room at 12:30, together with

Dayan. She was pale and her eyes were downcast as she walked slowly to her chair. Her hair, normally neatly combed and pulled back, was disheveled and she looked as if she had not shut her eyes all night. For the first time, her ministers saw an old woman sitting in the prime minister's chair, slightly bent. She lit a cigarette, leafed briefly through a pile of papers in front of her, and declared the meeting open.

Mrs. Meir began with a detailed report of events over the past three days—the Arab deployment on the borders that had suddenly taken on ominous color, the evacuation of the Soviet families, the air photos, the insistence by AMAN that there would be no war despite mounting evidence to the contrary. The military men were divided, she said, over whether there would be a war, over whether there should be mobilization and a preemptive strike. She spoke in a monotone that sounded like a judge reading out a sentence. Then she reached the bottom line. In the early hours of this morning, word had been received from an unimpeachable source that war would break out at 6 P.M. this day on both the Egyptian and Syrian fronts.

The ministers were stunned. They had not been made privy to the Arab buildup on the borders. Furthermore, they had been told for years that even in a worst-case situation the IDF would have at least forty-eight hours to call up the reserves before war broke out. Now they were being told that a two-front war was less than six hours away, with the army still unmobilized.

Mrs. Meir asked Dayan to describe the situation along the two fronts. Despite her depressed look, her voice had been firm. But there appeared to be a tremor in Dayan's voice. He looked like a man whose certainties had suddenly crumbled.

At 12:30, Elazar met in the Pit with General Gonen, with whom he had talked briefly five hours before. Although Gonen had assumed command of the southern front three months before, he had not yet familiarized himself with relevant intelligence data. He was unaware, for instance, that the Egyptian war plans in AMAN's hands called for a crossing along the canal's entire length. He was also unaware that the Egyptian plan specified that the preliminary artillery barrage would last thirty to forty-five minutes. He believed that it would last several hours.

His counterpart on the northern front, General Hofi, had won significant reinforcement in the past few days by voicing concern over the Syrian buildup. But Gonen had accepted AMAN's assessment of "low probability" and made no effort to beef up his front even after the Egyptian buildup reached unprecedented levels. He had not attempted to form an independent judgment about whether AMAN's soothing estimates of "low probability" were justified by what the troops along the canal were reporting. Nor had he replaced the second-line Jerusalem Brigade reservists in the forts with a larger force of elite troops as called for in Dovecote.

On Thursday evening, when the air photos from the canal area were being anxiously awaited at General Staff headquarters and by Gonen's subordinate, General Mendler, Gonen himself chose to visit with a friend in Haifa.

Instead of moving Mendler's division in the early afternoon to forward positions, as called for in Dovecote, Gonen decided to wait until 5 P.M., an hour before the anticipated Egyptian attack. He had heard Zeira say in the morning that the attack was far from certain. Gonen thought that an early deployment might be taken by the Egyptians as provocation. He also feared that premature movement of the tanks to the front would give the Egyptians time to adjust their preset artillery and bombing plans to hit the tanks. Moving up only an hour before H-Hour would not leave them time enough for that.

A precautionary step that Gonen had taken the day before was to order Dusky Light to be implemented Saturday as a deterrent measure. An engineering team reached the canal Saturday morning and found the two fuel installations, at Forts Matsmed and Hizayon, inoperable. With the Source's warning now in hand, Gonen ordered repairs to be made to the installation at Matsmed and fixed ignition for 6 P.M., the presumed time of the Egyptian crossing.

If Dusky Light had largely slipped from the minds of the Israeli command over the years, it had remained prominent in the concerns of the Egyptians. They knew from commando incursions that some of the Israeli installations were dummy. They were, however, not sure about all. Late Friday night, Egyptian frogmen swam underwater across the canal to block all the outlet pipes.

Many of the Israeli soldiers in the Bar-Lev forts did not sleep all night as they listened to the activity across the canal. Egyptian soldiers could be seen dragging objects down to the water's edge and work was going on intensively in the storage areas behind the lines. In the morning, stacks of orange life preservers could be seen alongside bridging equipment.

For Dr. Avi Ohri, this was the day his month of reserve duty at the canal was supposed to end. It had been a pleasant enough tour for the young doctor, rotating among the canal forts to relieve colleagues on leave. He had done a good bit of reading, and when things got too boring he volunteered to fill in as a radioman or lookout. In some of the forts, men had fished in the canal and he had gotten to eat fish and chips. The heat and flies weren't pleasant, but he usually wore short pants and a T-shirt rather than a uniform unless the lookouts reported a vehicle approaching.

Reaching Tasa in midmorning on his way back to Israel, he was informed that a C alert had been declared. In view of the sudden emergency, his commander asked whether he would mind staying an extra day. Fort Hizayon was without a doctor and none would arrive until tomorrow. Ohri agreed. He was the only passenger on the army bus that took him to Hizayon and was surprised at the haste with which the driver turned around and sped back after dropping him off. The guard at the gate directed him to a bunker. A few soldiers inside were lying on cots. They got up when he entered. He introduced himself—"I'm Avi, I'm a doctor"—and began to spread his equipment. It was 1:30 P.M.

Col. Avigdor Ben-Gal, commander of the Seventh Brigade, which had arrived on the Golan piecemeal over the past ten days, was a commanding presence with a craggy, Lincolnesque face, large shock of unkempt hair, and tall frame. Born in Lodz, Poland, in 1938, he had lost his family in the Holocaust. He arrived in Palestine in 1944 with a group of orphaned children via the Soviet Union and Iran. In the absence of a family of his own, he adopted the army. To his officers and men he radiated authority and professionalism. "Yanush," as Ben-Gal was known, had a cutting tongue but some saw his toughness as a mask. Since assuming command of the prestigious brigade the previous year, he had insisted that training exercises emulate war conditions as closely as possible. He drilled his men intensely in gunnery and held exercises lasting a week or more in which the brigade operated only at night. Frequently, in the midst of an exercise, he would announce a change in mission, requiring rapid decisions by commanders and movement through unfamiliar terrain.

At 10 A.M. Yom Kippur morning, Ben-Gal was informed by Gen. Rafael (Raful) Eitan, the Golan divisional commander, of the war tidings passed on by General Hofi. Ben-Gal ordered his battalion and company commanders by radio to meet him immediately in an army camp in the northern Golan.

All present rose to their feet when he entered the meeting room and he waved them back to their seats. "We don't have much time," he said. "Who's here and what's the state of your tanks?"

"My deputy and five company commanders are in the room," said the senior battalion commander, Avigdor Kahalani. "The tanks are under camouflage netting."

The other two battalion commanders, whose units had arrived during the night, reported that most of their tanks were in place but that some were still moving up from the supply depots at the foot of the Golan.

"All right," said Ben-Gal. "Let's get down to business. Gentlemen, war will break out today." The looks around the table reflected disbelief. "Yes, just what you heard," he continued. "A coordinated attack by Egypt and Syria." After issuing instructions, Ben-Gal told the battalion commanders to return to their units and prepare them for action. The men were to be ordered to break their fast. The officers were asked to assemble again at 2 P.M. for a final briefing.

Frontline units reported no unusual Syrian activity. An exception was a tank platoon commanded by Lt. Yoav Yakir at the southernmost end of the line. All night long the men had heard the movement of Syrian tanks opposite, as if new forces were arriving. In the morning, Yakir tried to persuade those crewmen observing Yom Kippur to break their fast. To encourage them to eat, Yakir and his first sergeant, Nir Atir, made breakfast for the platoon, a treat to which most of the men succumbed.

At Strongpoint 107 in the northern sector, 2d Lt. Avraham Elimelekh spent an hour, twice as long as usual, reviewing with his men what each would do in the event of a Syrian attack. The garrison, normally numbering twelve, had been increased to nineteen in the past day. Of the ten strongpoints along the line, 107 was the only one not located on a rise that dominated its immediate surroundings. It sat flat on a plain that extended deep into Syria. The reason for the strongpoint's inferior siting was that it had been placed to cover the Damascus–Kuneitra road, two hundred yards away.

In the event of a serious attack, the strongpoint's survival would depend on the tank platoon posted to its rear. In the few weeks he had been at 107, Elimelekh had had intensive sessions with the platoon commander, Lt. Shmuel Yakhin, to work out cooperation in the event of an attack. The two officers identified elements of the topography together so that each would quickly understand what the other was referring to. They agreed that the tanks would deal with Syrian armor and the strongpoint with infantry. The battalion intelligence officer visited Yom Kippur morning and told Elimelekh that the Syrians might attempt to snatch a strongpoint in the coming battle day and take its garrison prisoner. A likely target, said the officer, making a snatching movement with his hand, was Strongpoint 107.

Colonel Ben-Gal drove to the front about noon and scanned the Syrian lines through binoculars. There was a large army out there but he could see nothing stirring. At the sound of chirping he lifted his head to see birds on a nearby tree. There was nothing unusual about the birds singing. What was odd was that he could hear them. The unnatural stillness seemed final confirmation that war was imminent.

In Sinai, General Mendler was meeting with his commanders when Gonen telephoned at 10 A.M. Passing on Gonen's message to his officers, the division commander said that something was expected to happen at dusk but it was not clear whether it would be war or only the end of the Egyptian exercise.

Mendler and his officers assumed that if the shooting started, it would be a resumption of the War of Attrition, with massive artillery strikes and possible raids. Mendler, indeed, focused the discussion not on defensive steps but on the offensive options embedded in Dovecote—an attack by one or two brigades across the canal while Reshef's brigade attended to any Egyptian forces which might cross.

At 12:20 P.M., a listening post picked up a message from a UN observation post on the Egyptian side of the canal—"special time check." It was, the Israelis knew, code for an imminent Egyptian artillery barrage. The canal-side forts were ordered to recall men from outlying posts and to prepare for incoming artillery. As a sergeant at an outpost started towards the half-track sent to fetch his squad, he saw an Egyptian soldier across the canal trying to catch his eye. The Egyptian tapped his watch and spread his hands in a gesture of "Why?" The Egyptians had ordered their "loungers" on the canal bank to continue signaling indolence by fishing and chewing sugarcane.

At 12:30, AMAN issued an updated bulletin noting extensive military preparations in Egypt and Syria. It acknowledged receipt of reports that war was imminent. However, noted the bulletin, "we assume that the strategic level in Egypt and Syria is aware of the absence of any chances of success." Even at this hour, AMAN was not to be stampeded by events into abandoning the clear logic of Sadat's strategic concept, as it understood it.

In the cabinet room, Dayan told his colleagues that if the Egyptians crossed the canal, they were heading for destruction. The situation on the Golan was more complex, he said. There was no significant barrier there to slow down the Syrians, and the defenders were much fewer than those deployed in Sinai. But the IDF believed it could hold the line. Justice minister Yaacov Shimshon Shapira asked what would happen if the Egyptians detected the Israeli preparations and advanced their zero hour. Dayan said that the air force was already sending patrols aloft to guard against such a contingency.

For Jerusalemites, it was the sound of a plane that offered the first intimation of unusual developments. Early worshipers at the Western Wall were startled by the sudden roar of a single Phantom low overhead as if some pilot had decided to get in a quick prayer. As the morning progressed, the awesome silence of the holy day was increasingly broken by the burr of tires as solitary military vehicles turned into residential neighborhoods. Couriers carrying mobilization orders stepped out to scan house numbers. Generally they were directed by neighbors to one of the local synagogues. Services were halted to permit the courier or a synagogue official to read out names. It was apparent to all that if mobilization was being carried out on Yom Kippur, it was not an exercise and that it must be because of a surprise Arab move.

At a synagogue in Jerusalem's Ramat Eshkol quarter, a young man wearing a prayer shawl rose from his seat when his name was called. His father, seated next to him, embraced him and refused to let go. The rabbi approached and said gently to the weeping father, "His place is not here today." The man released his son and the rabbi placed his hand on the young man's head to bless him. In the Bait Hakerem quarter, a sexton called on the congregation for silence and then read out the names handed him by a courier, pausing almost imperceptibly as he reached the name of his own son. Rabbis mounted the podium to tell their congregations that it was permissible for all those mobilized to break their fast and drive a car.

Throughout the country, men wearing skullcaps and prayer shawls could be seen incongruously driving or trying to hitchhike to assembly points. Many family men drove their wives and children to relatives before heading to their units. Resonant in the minds of all—those being called up and those left behind—was the "Unetaneh Tokef" prayer with its poignant melody that they had chanted this morning about the prospects for the year ahead. "On Rosh Hashana it is written and on the day of the fast of Kippur it is sealed . . . who shall live and who shall die, who in his allotted time and who not, who by water and who by fire, who by the sword. . . ."

In Cairo, President Sadat had donned his military uniform and was waiting at home when war minister Ismail arrived in a jeep at 1:30 to drive him to Center Ten. The officers of the Supreme Command sat on a low dais overlooking the operations room where the commanders of each branch of the armed forces and their senior staff sat by communication consoles. The room was dominated by situation maps projected onto a large screen. Orders had been given to break the Ramadan fast and clerics ruled that it was permissible also to smoke. Sadat could see no one in the room doing either. He ordered tea and lit up his pipe and soon others were doing the same. All eyes now were on the clock.

At 1:30 on the Israeli side of the canal, the soldiers in the forts were ordered to don flak jackets and helmets and to enter bunkers. Only fort commanders remained as lookouts, mostly in tiny "rabbit holes" built into an outer wall, safe from anything but a direct hit, where they could observe the enemy lines through a periscope. At Fort Matsmed, the commander chose to mount the observation tower. The only things he could see moving on the other side of the canal were farmers in a distant field working the land. At Budapest, Motti Ashkenazi also climbed the lookout tower. The enemy lines opposite were devoid of movement. For the first time, Ashkenazi noted, the Egyptian lookout towers were empty.

On the Golan Heights at 1:30, an artillery observer on Mount Hermon reported to Nafshi that the Syrians were removing the camouflage netting from their artillery and tanks. The battalion commander recalled that the Syrians were wont to start their battle days at 2 P.M. He ordered the tanks on his half of the front line to pull out of their regular positions and move some distance away. If the Syrians opened fire they would hit every fixed Israeli position marked on their maps.

In the cabinet room, Dayan was nearing the end of his briefing at 2 P.M. when an aide entered and handed him a note. The defense minister announced that Egyptian airplanes had begun to attack in Sinai. Even as Mrs. Meir declared the meeting closed, a siren wail rose in the street outside.

At Tasa in Sinai, Colonel Reshef heard the undulating signal for enemy air penetration on the radio net. Emerging from his headquarters, he saw planes diving on a nearby battalion encampment from which black smoke had begun to rise. The desert floor beneath his feet began to tremble. Twenty miles to the west, two thousand Egyptian guns and heavy mortars had opened up on the Bar-Lev Line.

Eleven

THE CROSSING

THE PLANES WENT IN FIRST, skimming low over the canal and then rising briefly for orientation before diving at their targets—Israeli command centers, Hawk antiaircraft missile batteries, artillery, air bases, radar stations, the main intelligence base in Sinai. One of the first Egyptian fatalities was the half brother of President Sadat, a pilot shot down in the attack on Refidim Air Base, where the main runway was knocked out for several hours and the control tower damaged.

When the planes had passed, the artillery opened up. In the first minute, more than ten thousand shells fell on the Israeli lines, mostly on and around the canal-side forts. With the Israeli defenders driven into their bunkers, flat-trajectory weapons and tanks were moved into position atop the Egyptian ramps and began firing directly at the forts opposite. The lookout towers in the Israeli forts were all shot away in the first minutes. Heavy mortars lobbed 240 mm shells into the fortifications with thunderous explosions, causing bunkers to shudder and trenches to collapse.

Fifteen minutes after the start of the bombardment, 4,000 commandos and infantrymen in the first wave slithered down from the Egyptian ramps to the water's edge along the length of the canal, where 720 rubber and wooden boats awaited them. Screened by smoke shells, they started across the water-way—some paddling, some propelled by outboard motors—to the chanting of "Allahu akbar" (God is great). General Shazly had arranged for loudspeakers to be set up at crossing points, repeatedly broadcasting the ancient battle cry, which was picked up by the soldiers.

In the forefront of the first wave were engineering teams which checked the "fire-on-the-water" outlets to ensure that they had been properly blocked by frogmen during the night.

Landing on the Sinai shore, generally out of sight of the Israeli forts, agile soldiers made their way up the steep sand embankment and affixed rope ladders to the top. Tank-hunting teams climbed after them and raced inland. Some carried the suitcase-like Sagger containers. Many more wielded RPGs. Ammunition and equipment too heavy to be carried were dragged in wheeled carts. Thousands of carts had been produced at the order of Shazly after he had seen one left behind by an Israeli raiding party in 1970. They would serve until supply vehicles could cross.

In many places, the soldiers reached the "fins"—the earthen barricades a mile inland—behind which the Israeli tanks intended to take up firing positions. Dust clouds to the east indicated that the tanks were fast approaching.

On the Bitter Lake, an amphibious brigade consisting of twenty floating tanks and eighty armored personnel carriers (APCs) began churning its way eastward. Lake Timsah to the north was crossed by an infantry company in amphibious vehicles. The Sinai shores of these lakes were largely undefended. On the northern end of the Suez line, a diversionary force of Egyptian tanks and APCs prepared to make its way along the sandspit that led to Fort Budapest.

South of the Suez Canal, in coves along the western shore of the Gulf of Suez, scores of fishing boats had been assembled to transport commando forces to southern Sinai after darkness. Other commandos were waiting to be helicoptered behind Israeli lines at dusk.

With the crossing of the first wave, seventy engineering teams, equipped with pumps and water hoses, began scouring holes in the Israeli embankment. The engineers had been allotted five to seven hours for the task.

The crossing would be carried out by 100,000 men with exemplary order. Large signs bearing luminous numbers were planted on the Israeli-held shore by the first wave. These matched the numbers on the color-coded signs along the routes taken by units moving up to the canal. Military police ensured that units did not go astray or become entangled with each other. Within two hours, 23,000 men had crossed and five tenuous divisional bridgeheads had been established on the Israeli bank, each one mile deep and five miles wide. Artillery now shifted to targets deeper in Sinai.

Large transporters bearing bridge sections backed up to the water's edge and slid them into the canal, where engineers began to assemble them. Other units began assembling thirty-one prefabricated ferries capable of carrying tanks. Monitoring the reports in Center Ten, Shazly sensed that the vast machine constructed for this day was working superbly. The Israelis appeared to have been taken by total surprise.

At 5:30 P.M., the twelfth and final wave of the initial assault force crossed the canal, bringing the total on the Sinai bank to 32,000 men. The bridgeheads were now two miles deep. The Israelis were reeling, and this before even a single Egyptian tank had crossed the canal. With the onset of dusk, dozens of helicopters crossed into Sinai. Many would be downed by Israeli planes and ground fire, but hundreds of commandos were landed behind Israeli lines.

At 6:30 P.M., water hoses opened the first breach in the Israeli sand barrier. Within another two hours, sixty passageways had been opened. In the southern canal sector, the claylike embankment yielded in the form of thick and slippery mud which made passage impossible. Ten planned openings in this sector were written off. But the remainder were now at the service of tanks and supply vehicles crossing by ferry even before the bridges were up.

The first bridge was completed at 8:30 P.M., six and a half hours after zero hour. Two hours later, all bridges were open—eight heavy bridges which could take tanks and four light bridges for light vehicles and men on foot. The bridges would be periodically floated opposite different breaches in the Israeli barrier so as not to provide a fixed target for artillery or air attack. The way into Sinai was open and the Egyptian armor was pouring through. Not since the construction of the Pyramids—at least not since construction of the canal itself—had Egypt seen such a massive and well-executed enterprise.

Capt. Motti Ashkenazi, atop Budapest's observation tower, had seen the planes before he heard them, four Sukhois flashing low over the lagoon to his left as they headed for the Israeli rear. He heard the outgoing Egyptian artillery, however, before the shells began crashing on his compound. The fort commander slid down the tower's ladder and dove into a "rabbit hole" where he could survey the surroundings through a periscope. The ground shook beneath him. This, he imagined, was what it would have been like at Normandy or Stalingrad. It was impossible to see anything because of the shell smoke. Fearing that enemy forces might already be advancing along the sandspit under cover of the shelling, Ashkenazi extricated himself and ran towards the western edge of the position where the smoke was thinner. He saw that the barbed wire had been blown apart.

Ashkenazi returned to the main bunker and told the men to remain under cover until he summoned them by radio. He did not want to lose anyone to shelling before the enemy was close enough to engage. Returning to the western perimeter, he saw personnel carriers emerging from Egyptian positions three miles to the west. Soon he could make out tanks as well and jeeps mounted with antitank weapons. The vehicles formed up and began moving along the sandspit.

The bazooka shells he had asked for had not arrived and Budapest was without antitank weapons of any kind. Ashkenazi believed, however, that he still had a fighting chance. The Egyptian tanks, which carried exterior fuel tanks, would have to pass below the elevated fighting positions of the fort and there was a possibility of igniting the fuel tanks from above with grenades. He was about to summon his men when the guard at the main gate reported two Israeli tanks approaching along the shore from the rear. Ashkenazi ran across the compound and climbed aboard the closest tank. Its hatch was closed and when he banged on it he was not heard above the shelling. Ripping off a shovel strapped to the side of the turret, he rapped again. A sergeant poked his head out. "Who's in command?" shouted Ashkenazi. The sergeant pointed at the other tank. By the time Ashkenazi reached it, its turret hatch had opened and Lt. Shaul Moses was looking in his direction.

Ashkenazi guided Moses westward along the shore to a point where the smoke began to thin. Moses made out the approaching Egyptian column. Five tanks, old T-34s, were in the lead, the closest 1,200 yards away. Infantrymen had already descended from the personnel carriers and were forming a skirmish line. There was sufficient smoke around the Israeli tanks to cloak them from the Egyptians' view. The two tanks opened fire. Within minutes all of the Egyptian tanks were burning. When the sergeant reported a turret malfunction in his tank, Moses continued firing alone, methodically working down the Egyptian column as the vehicles frantically tried to turn on the narrow sandspit, some of them colliding. He hit five APCs and three trucks. Soldiers abandoned the vehicles and ran back towards the Egyptian lines. Moses let them go.

In Fort Purkan, midway on the canal, Major Weisel, looking through his periscope, saw rubber boats crossing to the north. His call for artillery drew no response. The noise of the incoming Egyptian artillery was deafening. A tank on the ramp across the canal swiveled its gun in Weisel's direction and fired. The ground around the company commander shook. A moment later, two shells exploded nearby, emitting red smoke. Weisel thought at first it was gas, but the Egyptian artillery lifted and he understood that the smoke was a signal to the infantry to close on the fort. Weisel summoned his men into the trenches. Racing from the bunkers, they repulsed the Egyptian attack. Scattered shelling resumed. As the awesome thump from a 240 mm mortar shell died away, Weisel said to the men around him, "Fellows, that's as bad as it gets. The next heaviest thing is an atom bomb." Despite the massiveness of the shelling, the bunkers had held and only two men were wounded.

At Hizayon, north of Purkan, the commander, Lt. Rami Bareli, sank several boats with machine-gun fire. Other boats, however, made it across. From his post at the other end of the fortification, Sgt. Pinhas Strolovitz could see flames arching over the top of the positions facing the canal where the Egyptians were wielding flamethrowers. Strolovitz's own position was being heavily assaulted. The barrel of his machine gun had grown hot and had to be changed because of the danger of blockage, but the sergeant was afraid that if he stopped firing even briefly he would be overwhelmed.

Bareli, a former paratrooper, ran from position to position to encourage his men, most of whom were not combat soldiers. An hour after the battle started, a shell exploded alongside him, killing his radioman and virtually severing Bareli's left arm. He was carried to the medical bunker and had enough presence of mind to notice the unfamiliar face of the man leaning over him. "Who are you?" Bareli asked. Dr. Ohri introduced himself. "I've just arrived." The arm was beyond saving. Ohri cut it off and stilled the pain with morphine. The agony of Hizayon had begun.

At Fort Milano alongside the abandoned Egyptian town of East Kantara, the commander, Capt. Yaacov Trostler, a twenty-nine-year-old geology teacher, was cut in the head by the opening salvo. He resumed command after his wounds were dressed, but much of the responsibility now fell on his young deputy, Lt. Micha Kostiga, twenty-one, who had recently finished his regular army service. Less than an hour after the start of the shelling, a soldier reported hearing voices in Arabic outside the western perimeter fence where the ground fell sharply away towards the canal. Kostiga heard it too, someone shouting "Enter, enter." He climbed out of the trench. Just downslope were ten Egyptian soldiers moving towards the lip of the position, an officer urging them on. Kostiga fired before they did, emptying his Uzi in their direction. He jumped back into the trench, took his radioman's Uzi, and climbed back onto the sandbags to fire at the retreating Egyptians. Returning to the trench, he threw a dozen grenades downslope. As he did, he saw additional boats crossing the canal straight for the fort. The garrison sank them or drove them off. But attacks were coming all around the perimeter. Trostler had the noncombatants load magazines and bring up crates of grenades for the dozen men in the fighting positions.

An Egyptian flag went up on one of Milano's outposts five hundred yards to the south, which had been evacuated that morning. Kostiga called down artillery fire on it. With darkness, the men heard the hammering of a bridge being erected to their south. The sound gave way a few hours later to the rumble of tanks crossing. The men would later hear a bridge being constructed to their north. Israeli artillery groped for the spans, but neither could be seen from Milano so the fire could not be adjusted.

At Lituf, just south of the Bitter Lake, the fort commander was wounded in the first Egyptian assault; his deputy and the first sergeant were wounded in the second. The attackers reached within five yards of the outer fence before being driven back.

It was apparent from the radio net that the Egyptians had crossed in strength all along the line. The men of the Jerusalem Brigade, regarded dismissively as second-line troops, were fighting well, as were paratroopers from the standing army manning the three southernmost forts. But their impact on the Egyptian crossing was negligible. Not even the best fighting units could have made a difference, given the wide gaps through which the Egyptians passed unimpeded. The role of the Bar-Lev forts as a barrier against an all-out attack had proven a failure. But the besieged forts were now taking on a new and far more effective role—Egyptian bait that would lure General Mendler's tank division to its near destruction.

Twelve

THE HUMBLING
OF THE TANK

IN THE TANK STAGING AREAS along the Artillery Road, company commanders were giving final briefings when a wailing on the radio net signaled
enemy air penetration. Bombs struck the compounds before the tanks could
get away, but none were hit.

Speeding towards the canal, they covered the distance in twenty to thirty
minutes, but in most cases they lost the race. The sand barriers behind which
they were to take up firing positions were already covered by figures in light-
colored uniforms. From observing Dovecote exercises, the Egyptians knew
precisely where the tanks would be heading.

"Infantry to the front," called tank platoon commanders. "Attack." It
was a drill they had rehearsed repeatedly—racing forward to shoot, stampede, and literally crush the enemy. The Egyptians, however, had prepared a
different scenario. Commandos rising from shallow foxholes with RPGs on
their shoulders hit the leading tanks. Some of the commandos were cut
down but others continued to fire. Surprised at the resistance, tank commanders pulled back beyond effective RPG range, about 300 yards. It was not far
enough.

A platoon commander saw a red light waft lazily past him and explode
against a nearby tank. The commander of the impacted tank was propelled
from the turret by the pressure, like a cork from a bottle. Other lights floated
in from the Egyptian rampart across the canal which dominated the battle-

field. The platoon commander had no idea what they might be. The answer came over the radio net. "Missiles," said the company commander, the first to recognize the Saggers. Their 3,000-yard range was ten times that of the RPG and their impact more deadly.

For the first time since tanks lumbered onto the battlefields of the First World War, the greatest danger they faced was not from enemy tanks or crew-served antitank guns but from individual infantrymen. Bazookas had been used by infantrymen in previous wars but never in such quantity as the RPGs or with the range and lethality of the Saggers. The Egyptian troops had been provided the antitank weapons in prodigious numbers. At Shazly's orders, Saggers had been stripped from rear units and added to the spearhead forces. Each of the five attacking divisions had infantrymen armed with 72 Saggers and 535 RPGs. In addition, 57 antitank guns and 90 recoilless weapons added a more conventional but no less deadly tank-killing capability. This added up to close to 800 antitank weapons per division apart from the 200 tanks attached to each division. Never had such intensive antitank fire been brought to bear on a battlefield. Furthermore, Israeli tank commanders, who rode with their heads out of the turrets for better visibility, were vulnerable to the massive Egyptian artillery fire and to rifle and machine-gun fire from infantrymen all around them. The profusion of fire was stunning. So was the grit with which the Egyptian infantrymen defied the charging tanks.

The decision by Israel not to raise the embankment on its side of the canal to mask the Sinai bank from the Egyptian ramps severely aggravated the situation. Tanks, Saggers, and antitank guns on the ramps dominated not only the Israeli forts but an area up to two miles inland from the canal. Israel's idea of neutralizing the ramps with long-range fire from the shelter of the fins—the sand barriers a mile from the canal—had no validity now that RPG teams were dug in all around them.

The air force, on which Elazar had rested his hopes, was unable to stem the Egyptian tide. Because of the SAMs, the planes could not circle over the battlefield. The IAF executed 120 sorties over the Egyptian front this day and lost four planes, but the snap attacks made little impact. The Egyptian infantrymen were vulnerable to artillery but the IDF had fewer than 50 artillery pieces along the hundred-mile-wide front and these were under heavy counterbattery fire. Nor were the forts themselves a meaningful barrier. For the most part, the boats simply crossed between them.

Defense of the Suez front fell on Yom Kippur afternoon to Colonel Reshef's 91 tanks constituting the forward brigade of General Mendler's

Sinai Division and to the 450 men in the sixteen Bar-Lev forts. The four northern forts on the canal were strung along a causeway between the canal itself and a lagoon which covered most of the sector. The northernmost of the forts, Orkal, was, because of its remoteness, the only one to have tanks permanently posted there—a platoon of three. With the onset of war, pairs of tanks were dispatched to the three other causeway forts via a road through the lagoon. All were ambushed and destroyed.

One crew managed to escape on the road through the lagoon. The tankers came across a downed Israeli pilot with a broken leg who refused to be carried so as not to slow them down. He was taken prisoner before a rescue vehicle they sent reached him.

The tank battalion commander in this sector, Lt. Col. Yom Tov Tamir, led the rest of his battalion towards two forts south of the causeway. Egyptian soldiers had broken into the southernmost, Mifreket, and were using flamethrowers. Several tanks bogged down in marshes, difficult to discern because they were covered by sand. Others were disabled by surface mines laid by the Egyptians or were hit by RPGs or Saggers.

Responding to calls from the adjacent fort, Milano, Tamir dispatched three tanks via East Kantara to its assistance. Egyptian soldiers, who had already penetrated the ghost town, knocked out two of them.

As dusk approached, Tamir was ordered to send tanks to Fort Lahtzanit on the causeway, whose radio had gone dead. The fort's commander, Lt. Muli Malhow, who had warned of the coming attack, was dead. Tamir sent almost all his remaining tanks together with infantrymen on half-tracks. This force too was ambushed. The war was only four hours old and Tamir's battalion was almost entirely wiped out.

The fortunes of the two other battalions on the line were better, but not by much. In the central sector, where most of Egypt's Second Army was crossing, a report of four tanks destroyed on the Egyptian ramps sent a surge of optimism along the radio net. Another unit shot up an infantry company it surprised. But at 4 P.M. Egyptian infantrymen were spotted already three miles east of the canal, heading for the Artillery Road. A small force of Israeli infantry in APCs drove them back just before darkness.

In the southern sector, where the Third Army was crossing, Lt. Chanoch Sandrov halted his tank company six hundred yards from Fort Mafzeah and surveyed the terrain. There was no enemy in sight and no sign of activity on the Egyptian ramp opposite. As the company started forward again, RPG squads rose from the sand and set the lead tank afire. Simultaneously, Sagger missiles erupted from the Egyptian ramp and an artillery barrage descended.

A rescue tank approaching the burning tank was hit by a Sagger. The driver turned back with his three dead or dying comrades.

Sandrov was blinded in one eye by shrapnel and pulled back briefly to have a crewman apply a bandage. Resuming command, he ordered his deputy, Lt. Avraham Gur, to comb the area south of the fort with half the tanks while he swept north with the other half. When Gur passed close to the Israeli embankment, an Egyptian with an RPG rose on the slope above. Gur, standing in the open turret, ordered his driver to turn right. As the tank swung, throwing up a cloud of dust, the RPG shell exploded alongside. "When the dust settles," Gur shouted, "fire." A moment later the gunner said, "I see his face," and squeezed the trigger. Gur saw the soldier be lifted into the air and disintegrate.

He rejoined Sandrov's force just as a missile coming off the Egyptian ramp struck the company commander's tank. Gur ran to it and found Sandrov and his loader dead. The lieutenant took the other two crewmen, both wounded, into his own tank. Another tank fifty yards away was struck by a missile and Gur climbed onto that too. The tank commander was slumped inside the turret. Gur took his wrist but there was no pulse.

In late afternoon, the canal-side embankment began to fill again with Egyptian infantry clambering up from boats. Lt. Col. Emanuel Sakel, commanding the battalion defending the southern sector, formed armored personnel carriers carrying reconnaissance troops into line with Gur's remaining tanks and led a charge. The Egyptians broke and ran, many of them throwing away their weapons. The waterline had been regained in this sector, but the only tanks still in action were Sakel's and Gur's. Sakel told Gur to begin towing damaged tanks to the rear. He ordered the APCs to pull back as well. Artillery could not penetrate a tank but could easily destroy a thin-skinned personnel carrier. Sakel remained alone with his tank near Mafzeah to cover the fort against infantry attack.

Five miles south of Sakel, another of his companies, commanded by Capt. David Kotler, broke up an infantry attack on Fort Nissan. But no matter how many Egyptians were hit, more sprouted in their place. Kotler's deputy, Lt. Yisrael Karniel, saw a Sagger heading towards his tank just as he was shot in the shoulder. Falling back into the turret, he shouted "Hard right" and passed out. The tank swerved sharply and the missile exploded harmlessly beyond it. A platoon leader went to Karniel's aid but his own tank was struck a blow that brought it to a shuddering halt. A Sagger had hit just above the gun, where the metal was thickest. It did not penetrate and the driver was able to restart. Reaching Karniel, the officer tied a stretcher to the hull of his own tank and strapped him on it. As they started towards nearby

Fort Mezakh, the southernmost on the Bar-Lev Line, the tank was hit again, this time by an artillery shell. The stretcher was lifted into the air and slammed back down. The platoon leader was certain that Karniel was dead until he heard him groan. They reached the fort without further incident.

Towards evening, the doctor at Mezakh asked for urgent evacuation of a wounded man. Kotler headed there together with Lt. David Cohen. As they approached, Cohen's tank hit a surface mine. The commandos who had placed it rose from foxholes and fired at the stricken tank. Kotler drove them to ground with machine-gun fire and closed up behind Cohen's tank to take the crew aboard. At a rear staging area, Cohen took over a tank whose commander had been wounded. By now, only two tanks remained of the eleven Kotler had started out with three hours before.

The IDF was attempting to stem the massive Egyptian tide with unconnected, small-unit attacks along a 100-mile front. Instead of falling back or concentrating forces, it was futilely thrusting tiny fingers into a rapidly disintegrating dike.

A report half an hour before sunset of bridge sections being assembled in the water near Purkan was the first clear indication to Colonel Reshef that the Egyptians were not just raiding in strength, but intending to put an army into Sinai. He sent a company of reinforcements commanded by Lt. Moshe Bardash to attack the bridge. The setting sun was in Bardash's eyes when his eight tanks approached the area. An indistinct vision of infantrymen lining the road ahead was followed by a barrage of RPGs. The tankers fired back blindly into the haze. Several tanks were hit by RPGs and Saggers. Bardash, wounded, ordered his tanks to pull back.

Reshef's operations officer, Lt. Pinhas Bar, who had accompanied Bardash's force, assembled the tank commanders and explained the techniques developed in the past few hours for coping with the Sagger. Such impromptu lessons would be going on all along the front as new units took the field alongside tankers who had survived the day. The Saggers, the "veterans" explained, were a formidable danger but not an ultimate weapon. They could be seen in flight and were slow enough to dodge. It took at least ten seconds for a missile to complete its flight—at extreme range it could be twice that—during which time the Sagger operator had to keep the target in his sights as he guided the missile by the bright red light on its tail. From the side it was easy for the tankers to see the light. As soon as anyone shouted "Missile," the tanks were to begin moving back and forth in order not to present a stationary target. Movement would also throw up dust that would cloud the Sagger operator's view. Simultaneously, the tank should fire in his presumed direction, which itself could be sufficient to throw him off his aim.

As long as the Israelis were fighting near the water's edge, the Saggers were mainly deployed on the Egyptian ramp, from which they sniped at the Israeli tanks across the canal by day. But RPG teams lying in shallow foxholes were a close-up threat by day and night. The profusion of RPGs took the Israelis aback. Tank commanders learned during the day to carefully examine the terrain for possible ambushers before moving forward. There could be no such precaution at night.

It was clear to the tank crews that something revolutionary was happening—as revolutionary, it seemed, as the introduction of the machine gun or the demise of the horse cavalry. Tanks, which had stalked the world's battlefields for half a century like antedeluvian beasts, were now being felled with ease by ordinary foot soldiers. It would take time, in some cases days, before the implications of this extraordinary development would be grasped by higher command. Meanwhile, the tankers would have to figure out for themselves how to survive.

Emerging from the rabbit hole of his outpost near Fort Lituf when the shelling lifted, Sgt. Shlomo Shechori saw soldiers trying to get through the barbed wire. He thought they were reinforcements from the fort until he noticed the sand-colored uniforms and heard shouts in Arabic. When the Egyptians were ten yards away in the winding trench, he emptied his magazine at them and slipped through a hole in the fence. Halfway to the fort, he dropped to the ground. Lituf was surrounded by an Egyptian company pouring fire into it.

Shechori made his way to the nearby road and saw three tanks racing towards the fort, firing as they went. His dark uniform identified him as Israeli. The lead tank stopped alongside and Capt. Boaz Amir beckoned Shechori aboard. The officer, who commanded the northernmost of Sakel's three companies, posted the sergeant in the turret alongside him. Shechori tried to give him a grateful hug but the officer stopped him. "Save the kisses till this is over," he said, handing the sergeant a grenade. Other grenades were stashed within reach. "Anyone you see is Egyptian," said the officer. "Throw grenades and use your Uzi."

The tanks swept around the compound, spewing fire and running over enemy soldiers who tried to hit them with RPGs. Within minutes, the surviving Egyptians had pulled back. The tank officer decided that he too would have to withdraw because of antitank fire from the Egyptian ramp.

As he left the northern end of the compound, he saw three Soviet-make APCs. Soldiers aboard them waved in greeting. The IDF had incorporated

Soviet vehicles captured in the Six Day War, but the personnel carriers in front of him were painted the sand color employed by the Egyptian army. On the other hand, the Egyptians could not have bridged the canal this quickly. Captain Amir radioed headquarters and reported what he saw. Is there any Israeli unit with Soviet personnel carriers in the vicinity? he asked. "No," came the reply. "Hit them." A moment later the three vehicles were smoking hulks.

Lifting his gaze, the company commander saw a mass of sand-colored APCs and tanks approaching. They constituted the southern wing of the amphibious brigade which had crossed the Bitter Lake. The force's objective was the Gidi Pass.

It is not clear why an attempt was made to reach the pass, well beyond SAM coverage, when everywhere else along the line the Egyptians did not attempt to foray out from beneath the missile umbrella. The attack was to have been coordinated with a landing of commandos by helicopters at the pass itself. But with zero hour moved up from dusk to 2 P.M., the Egyptians were not willing to risk the dispatch of helicopters over the Israeli lines in daylight. Twenty-six amphibious vehicles, mostly APCs, were set aflame, with the loss of one Israeli tank. Egyptian infantrymen who escaped the APCs deployed with Saggers and RPGs. His ammunition depleted, Captain Amir ordered his three remaining tanks to fire short machine-gun bursts to keep them at bay until reinforcements arrived.

The sounds of the battle near Lituf reached 1st Sgt. Haim Yudelevitz on the roof of a building in the Mitzvah staging compound, four miles to the rear, from which the tanks had set out three hours before. A dozen soldiers, mostly technicians and medics, sheltered in a bunker from the intermittent shelling. A tank had returned from Lituf with its wounded commander. Another tank arrived now from a rear maintenance workshop. It had no machine guns and no crew except for the driver, Sgt. Moshe Rosman, who joined Yudelevitz on the roof. Towards evening, the pair saw a cloud of dust heading in their direction. As it drew closer, the sergeants identified ten Egyptian amphibious vehicles, including at least one tank.

Sergeant Rosman took command of the wounded officer's tank. He stripped it of its two machine guns—the commander's gun on the turret and one parallel to the tank gun—for use by the men in the compound and headed out. Yudelevitz had meanwhile gathered two nonfunctioning machine guns from a storeroom and, scavenging parts from one, made the other operable. He hauled it up to the roof with ammunition belts. The APCs halted a mile away. Officers formed the soldiers into line and they advanced, first slowly and then at a trot. Yudelevitz opened fire at 200 yards.

Many Egyptians went down, either hit or taking cover. Others began to edge around to the north. Yudelevitz descended again and deployed the men along the perimeter fence, ordering them to fire short machine-gun bursts at random in the gathering dusk.

Rosman meanwhile spotted a line of APCs at 1,500 yards. His gunner hit two. The others dispersed among the dunes. Rosman took up pursuit and hit two more. Yudelevitz returned to the roof and ranged him in on a tank a mile away which Rosman's gunner set aflame.

Darkness now descended. It seemed that the Egyptian force, what was left of it, had pulled back. But Rosman remained in his tank 700 yards from the compound. After half an hour, Yudelevitz said he could hear vehicles. Rosman turned and saw two armored personnel carriers at the entrance to the compound. His gunner dispatched them with two shells.

Rosman positioned the tank at the compound entrance and remained there with the engine off, the better to hear. After half an hour, he sensed movement to his front. Thirty Egyptian soldiers appeared out of the darkness, the closest only three yards away. They seemed to regard the silent tank as incapacitated. In a whisper, Rosman told the driver to start the engine. As it sprang to life, he tossed grenades into the darkness and shouted, "Run them down."

Two sergeants, acting on their own initiative with a pickup team of soldiers, had broken the armored drive towards the Gidi Pass in this sector.

With a preemptive strike canceled, Israeli air force activity this first afternoon of war was muted, in striking contrast to the frenzied opening hours of the Six Day War. General Peled had ordered patrols into the air at 12:30 P.M. as a precaution against an early Egyptian air attack. With the onset of war ninety minutes later, the rest of the air force was sent aloft. It was too late in the day to organize and execute Tagar or Dougman. Instead, the air force concentrated on protecting the country's airspace. Mechanics who had spent hours in the morning arming planes for the aborted attack on the Syrian missiles and then hours refitting them for the aborted attack on the Syrian airfields now had to feverishly strip them of their bomb loads once again and prepare them for aerial combat. Some pilots were ordered to take off and drop their bombs into the sea so that they could move immediately into their patrol sector.

The heightened alert quickly paid off. A reservist Mirage pilot patrolling over the Mediterranean shortly after 2 P.M. saw what seemed to be a MiG heading towards the coast. It moved sluggishly, and when he fired at it and sent it spinning into the water, it blew up with a ferocious bang. He had hit a Kelt air-to-ground missile fired from well offshore by an Egyptian Tupolev bomber which had already fled back towards Egypt. Another Kelt had been fired by a second Tupolev but had fallen into the sea. The Egyptian command was using the missiles, homing on a radar in the center of the country, as a warning that it could retaliate in kind if Israel struck its hinterland.

The most intensive air battle this day took place at Sharm el-Sheikh, the remote southern tip of the Sinai Peninsula, where Israel maintained small military bases. The IAF had allocated only two Phantoms to its defense. The pilots and navigators, all fresh out of flight school, were in their cockpits on the runway at 2 P.M. when the flight controller reported numerous aircraft approaching. The Phantoms took off and plunged into a formation of twenty-six MiGs from opposite ends. Within half an hour, the rookies had together downed seven planes, far better than any of the numerous aces in the Israeli air force would do this day. Although the runway had been holed by bombs, the pair managed to land safely.

Col. Oded Marom, a former Phantom squadron commander recently transferred to a desk job at air force headquarters in Tel Aviv, found himself superfluous Yom Kippur afternoon and drove to an air base in search of gainful employment. Two Mirages on standby were waiting at the end of a runway when his car passed. The pilots recognized him and one, who had to attend to a call of nature, beckoned to him to take his place. Marom did not recognize either of the pilots because of their helmet visors, but he hurried to a dressing room to don flying gear and returned to relieve the pilot. The latter had just disappeared from view when the control tower ordered the Mirages to take off. The air controller started the pair towards Sinai but then ordered them to turn north on full power. Over the Golan, the Mirages jumped four MiGs attacking Israeli ground forces, shooting down one apiece. Marom only now recognized his wingman from his voice as Mirage squadron commander Avi Lanir. Twenty minutes after taking off, they were back at base, where Marom handed over the plane to the original pilot, who was furious at having missed his first chance at a combat sortie. (Marom would continue flying for a few days with his old Phantom squadron, scoring more kills, before being recalled to duty at air force headquarters. Lanir would be shot down within a few days over the Syrian lines. He would die under interrogation.)

The main contribution of the air force to the ground forces in Sinai this day was the downing of helicopters trying to land commandos. Of the forty-eight helicopters dispatched by the Egyptians, twenty were downed by the IAF and by ground fire, some loaded with troops and some returning empty.

An opportunity to inflict a major blow from the air was missed, air force commander Peled would later state, because vital air photos were lost in a bureaucratic shuffle. Flying at 30,000 feet well inside Sinai, reconnaissance planes took detailed photographs of the Egyptian side of the canal on Yom Kippur. Although the air force took the photographs, it was AMAN which analyzed and distributed them. It was not until two weeks later that Peled would come across enlargements of the photographs showing Egyptian armored brigades lined up for miles, virtually bumper to bumper, waiting to move towards the bridges. It would have cost two to four planes, Peled would estimate, but the air force, had it known of this stationary target, would have caused greater destruction than it had wrought on the fleeing Egyptian army in Sinai in 1967. It would not be the air force's only missed opportunity.

Reshef's brigade had been holding the line alone for more than three hours when Mendler's two other brigades approached the battlefield shortly before dusk. Col. Dan Shomron was to take over the southern sector from the remains of Sakel's battalion. Col. Gabi Amir's brigade moved towards Reshef's northern flank, exposed by the destruction of Yom Tov Tamir's battalion. Each of the newly arrived brigades detached units to reinforce Reshef's tattered force in the center.

Shomron had been unable to make radio contact with division head-quarters while traversing the Gidi Pass. As soon as he emerged, he telephoned Mendler from a small base.

"What's the situation?" he asked.

"Grave," replied Mendler. "The Egyptians are crossing along the entire front. Do the best you can."

The brigade commander pressed for details. What was the status of Sakel's battalion, which was now to come under Shomron's command? How deep had the Egyptians penetrated?

Mendler said he didn't know. "Do the best you can," he repeated.

Shomron ordered a battalion under Maj. David Shuval to continue down the Gidi–Suez Canal road to Fort Lituf, near where Boaz Amir was holding out. Passing between high dunes, Shuval's battalion came on a score of Egyptian APCs and tanks, the northern wing of the amphibious brigade. The Israeli tank commanders were surprised to encounter Egyptian armor already more than six miles inside Sinai and made quick work of them. Boaz Amir's three tanks were down to their last machine-gun bullets when he saw Shuval's battalion topping a rise two miles to the rear with lights on. Shuval pushed past them and came on more than a score of intact Egyptian APCs closer to the shore of the Bitter Lake. By 9 P.M. all were burning and Shuval's tanks stood at the water's edge, without having suffered a loss. The sense of easy victory would not last long.

What concerned Reshef most were the unmonitored gaps between the forts. Some were wide enough to put an army through, which was precisely what was happening. At dusk, he ordered a newly arrived company under Maj. Avraham Shamir to reconnoiter the twelve-mile gap between Matsmed and Purkan in the center of the line. Reshef sent along an officer who knew the area as a guide. It was almost dark when the guide, in the lead, called out, "Infantry to the front. Break to the right." The day's experience had already amended the standing order of "Infantry to the front, charge." Infantry now merited a respectful distance.

Shamir, in the second tank, saw figures rise from foxholes and move aside. Shamir's tank was hit glancing blows by RPGs three times but none penetrated and he kept pressing westward. The fourth time, he was wounded. Reshef called to ask what was happening. The company commander was too dazed to immediately respond coherently. The officer guiding them was dead, the tanks were scattered, and radio contact had been lost with most. Reshef told him to pull back. Shamir retired a short distance and lit his projector. The remaining tanks, all with wounded aboard, converged on the light. Scorched by this baptism of fire, the company moved off to the rear. With the failure of the patrol, Reshef ordered a tank platoon guarding Fort Matsmed to reconnoiter northward. It too was driven back, its commander wounded.

A few miles to the north, a newly arrived battalion under Shlomo Nitzani moved cautiously towards the site of the Egyptian bridge being built between Purkan and Hizayon. Nitzani ordered the tanks to turn on their projectors to spot tank hunters, but the beams of light were broken by dust and drifting smoke laid down by the Egyptians to hide the bridge from Israeli aircraft. As the tanks neared Lexicon Road, they were attacked by RPGs. Within minutes, most were hit.

Nitzani called on the battalion to fall back but communications had broken down. So had discipline. A platoon commander reported that another platoon commander was wounded at the furthest point of advance and that he was going forward to get him out. The battalion commander, understanding now what they were up against, ordered him to pull back. The junior officer disregarded the order. He advanced two hundred yards with two other tanks and was ambushed. Only one tank returned but all the crewmen made it back, some of them wounded. Nitzani called for an air strike on the bridge. He heard planes go in but could not observe the results.

Adherence to Dovecote kept propelling small tank forces forward to the same grim fate. A company commanded by Lt. Zeev Perl resumed the attack towards Hizayon and was also ambushed. Once again, tanks under fire charged towards the source. Once again, most were hit. Perl was temporarily blinded and the gunner took his place in the turret. The company comman- der ordered his tanks to pull back, but his own crew lost its direction and the tank was still traveling towards the canal when it was hit again. Perl called to the loader and the gunner but got no response. Reaching out, he touched their bodies. Egyptian soldiers leaped on the tank in an attempt to drop grenades through the open turret. The driver swerved, throwing them off, and then ran over them. The tank stopped only when it went into a bog. The driver extricated Perl, who told him to take maps and canteens. They pro- ceeded east on foot, the driver leading the officer by the hand, for eight hours. Close to dawn they reached a staging area, where Perl was evacuated to an aid station. (He would regain his sight.)

As the night wore on, units were ordered to disengage and tow disabled tanks to the rear. Repairs were imperative if there was to be anything left of the division in the morning. Three tanks remained opposite Hizayon under Maj. Eliezer Caspi, who had already led two failed attempts to reach the fort. He tried once more, by a different route, but again ran into an ambush, this time involving at least ten RPGs. He too pulled back.

At 7:30 P.M., Mendler had ordered Reshef to send tanks to the canal, with hatches closed for protection, to scout the location of Egyptian bridges. Most of the tanks made it to the canal and back. They reported bridge build- ing along the length of the canal. Air force attempts to knock out the bridges were called off at midnight. It was more dangerous flying at night than by day because the pilots could not gauge the distance of SAMs fired at them in the dark and thus could not outmaneuver them. In any case, the air force was planning a major attack in the morning.

Although beginning to grasp the magnitude of the Egyptian attack, the Israeli command had still not absorbed the disastrous nature of its pre- planned response—Dovecote. The Egyptian plan had brilliantly converted an offensive initiative—the crossing of the canal—into a defensive battle. The Israeli tank crews and commanders were fighting with exceptional brav- ery, but their erosion was inevitable as they hurled themselves again and again at the masses of Egyptian infantry waiting for them to do precisely that. The concept of armor shock had been turned on its head by the Egyptians' new weapons and tactics—it was armor that was being shocked by infantry.

At 6:30 P.M. Elazar authorized Gonen to evacuate all canal-side forts except those that stood in the path of Egyptian main thrusts and could serve as observation posts. However, Southern Command did not issue any evacuation orders. Instead of pulling back to reorganize and rethink, Mendler and Gonen continued to try to stop the Egyptians on the waterline in adherence to a directive whose wisdom was dubious when conceived and made no sense at all now. Unlike the tank crews who were adjusting to the Saggers, neither the divisional nor the front commanders were coming to grips with the new reality. Instead, they clung mechanically to Dovecote even after it should have been clear that a single division could not hold the waterline against a five-division crossing and that the air force was unable to take up the slack.

The surprise attack had a paralyzing effect on much of the Israeli command. "You break into a cold sweat and your mind freezes up," a deputy division commander, one of Israel's most daring tank officers, would say later. "You have difficulty getting into gear and you react by executing the plans you've already prepared, even if they're no longer appropriate." Apart from the psychological shock, mental circuits were thrown out of kilter as commanders tried to simultaneously grasp what was happening, how it could have happened, and what had to be done.

The men in the field were spared these excruciating deliberations. They only had to figure out how to stay alive and beat back the enemy waves. This was true up to the position of battalion commander—the lieutenant colonels who were generally the senior officers in direct contact with the enemy. Their performance from the opening shots was superb, as was that of the officers beneath them. A brigade commander would later say that for officers in his category it generally took two days before the shock wore off and they returned to themselves, although from the start some seemed unaffected by the shock.

Operating out of his rear headquarters in Beersheva, 150 miles from the front, General Gonen tried to discern from the reports pouring in where the main Egyptian crossing points were, still unaware that the Egyptian plan in Israel's hands called for a crossing all along the canal. Around midnight, he asked Elazar for permission to attack an Egyptian position half a mile north of Orkal. He was oblivious to the fact that the causeway leading to Orkal was a death trap that had consumed every tank that reached it. Permission was not granted.

At 1:30 A.M., with most of Mendler's tanks already knocked out and the

Egyptian forces virtually unscathed, Gonen pronounced the Egyptian crossing a failure since they had not moved their armor across the canal. In fact,
several hundred Egyptian tanks had already crossed, although they would
not go into action until the morning. "Gonen arrived at conclusions without
taking counsel," General Adan would write. "Instead of having his staff officers take part in the process of assessing situations, he relied on his intuition,
based on his previous experience with the Egyptians, whom he held in deep
contempt." Not until 2 A.M., twelve hours after the war's start, did Gonen fly
by helicopter to his forward headquarters at Umm Hashiba, thirty miles
from the canal.

Division commander Mendler did not share Gonen's illusions, but he
did not draw the necessary conclusions from the picture unfolding before
him. At his headquarters, he sat quietly to the side, his eyes fixed on the large
wall map which his staff was constantly updating. Having issued his brigade
commanders their marching orders—basically, to defend the canal line—he
gave hardly any further instructions and rarely spoke on the radio net. His
injunction to Shomron—"Do the best you can"—was virtually the last directive the brigade commander received this day. To an officer at divisional
headquarters, Mendler seemed to wear a thin, bitter smile as he stared
fixedly at the map. "I said to myself," the officer would later recall, "Why
doesn't the man talk? A whole world that he built and trained for is collapsing in front of him and he keeps silent." The red circles and arrows his aides
drew on the map were a parody of Dovecote, indicating Egyptian bridgeheads expanding and Israeli units melting away. Periodically, Mendler would
disappear into his office until the next staff meeting. He did not have the
authority to order the evacuation of the forts but he did not request it.

The garrisons on the Bar-Lev Line could not understand why they were
being asked to remain in the beleaguered forts when the circumstances were
clearly hopeless. It was evident to them that the forts were traps to be
escaped, not assets to hang on to. But Gonen was intent on regaining the
waterline and crossing the canal and was unwilling to abandon existing
footholds. The decision not to evacuate the forts would prove calamitous for
both the garrisons and the tank forces trying to protect them. In some forts,
most of the men were already casualties. Those who weren't were mostly service personnel, not combat troops. They pleaded with the tankers who
reached them to take them out. The request was passed up the command
chain but the response was negative.

Darkness provided cover for the Egyptian tank hunters who were now
covering all the approaches to the forts. Capt. Yaron Ram, commanding the

force that had relieved Boaz Amir outside Lituf, dispatched two tanks to locate a disabled tank with wounded aboard. Both were ambushed. Shortly before dawn, one of their gunners came on the radio. Keeping his voice low, he said that only he and another crewman were still alive. They had been keeping off Egyptian soldiers for more than an hour, but ammunition was almost gone and they were now using grenades whenever enemy soldiers drew close. Captain Ram asked him to indicate his whereabouts by firing a shell. A moment later, a flash could be seen two miles away.

Three tanks were sent to the rescue. As they drew close, one was disabled by an RPG and the others driven back. Ram asked Major Shuval for permission to go himself with the three tanks remaining to him. Shuval refused. Ram's tanks constituted the only force blocking the road to the Gidi Pass. Ram told the gunner that his only chance was to play dead when the Egyptian soldiers climbed aboard. Two minutes later, the tank's radio went silent. When the tank was recovered the next day, the gunner and his comrade were found dead inside.

While the battle continued into the night along the canal, navy captain Ze'ev Almog at Sharm el-Sheikh, two hundred miles south, kept patrol boats at sea in anticipation of an Egyptian attempt to land supplies and reinforcements for the commandos helicoptered across the Gulf of Suez. At 10 P.M., two of his patrol vessels picked up radar images of dozens of small craft approaching across the Gulf of Suez. In the light of flares dropped by a patrolling plane, they saw rubber boats filled with commandos. The Egyptian boats fled into an area of reefs where the Israeli vessels could not follow and succeeded in making it back to the far shore.

The MiG attack during the day had knocked out radio communications between Almog and two patrol boats at the northern end of the gulf. At 10 P.M., the patrol commander, Ensign Zvi Shahack, was startled to be called directly by the commander of the navy, Adm. Binyamin Telem, speaking from the navy's war room in Tel Aviv. Intelligence was reporting Egyptian preparations to transport commandos to the Israeli-held shore that night in fishing boats. The admiral ordered the ensign to cross the gulf and attack any craft he found. Feeling his way down the dark Egyptian coast, Shahack entered a small anchorage at Marse Telemat while the other patrol boat remained outside. Switching on his projector, he saw fishing boats anchored around the rim of the bay. In the center was a large patrol boat attached to a buoy. Two rubber boats alongside were filled with commandos in wet suits.

Shahack and his crew opened fire as they moved counterclockwise around the anchorage. Points of light showed that Egyptians were shooting back. Midway the boat shuddered to a stop as it ran onto a reef. Shahack switched off the projector and summoned the other boat to sweep the harbor. Shahack's chief mechanic, shoving a sock into a hole in a water pipe, managed to get the engine started and Shahack worked the boat off the reef. The other boat also hung up briefly on a reef but freed itself. The two vessels left the anchorage with half their crews wounded and one man dead, but the sky behind them had turned red from burning boats.

Reshef received the last of the division's reserves at 1 A.M., a battalion under Lt. Col. Amram Mitzna. On its way towards Hizayon, it was fired on. The tanks wheeled and threw on projectors, revealing several dozen soldiers lying in shallow foxholes. As the tanks closed range, the Egyptian infantrymen rose with RPGs. Some managed to get off shots but most were cut down before they could. The commandos were tall blacks, apparently Sudanese. In a few moments, all were dead.

Resuming their westward progress, the battalion found itself passing between two rows of parked tanks, some of whose crews were sitting on the ground drinking coffee. It was an encampment of Egyptian T-55 tanks that had just crossed. The surprise was mutual. After a brief exchange of fire, Mitzna broke contact.

Twice during the night, Shazly would write in his war diary, Israeli tanks broke through to the canal and inflicted damage on bridges and ferries. "Through the night, commanders of [Israeli] subunits, even individual tanks, fight on. They are evidently made of better stuff than their senior commanders."

One of these units was a battalion commanded by Lt. Col. Amir Yoffe which had been ordered to link up with Mifreket and Milano in the northern sector. The thirty-three-year-old Yoffe, nephew of a distinguished general, had a reputation in the IDF as a hard-bitten, punctilious professional—the kind of officer, General Adan would say, whom you would not want to serve under in peacetime but to whom you would readily entrust your life in war. During the hasty organization of combat formations at his base the day before, he had not noticed that his younger brother, Eyal, a cadet in an officers' course, had been assigned to him as a tank commander.

Guided through the boggy terrain by Yom Tov Tamir, whose battalion had been destroyed in the area in the morning, Yoffe took half his tanks to

Mifreket, where they engaged RPG teams swarming over the approaches. Entering the fort, Tamir found a radioman in command. Tamir's request that the garrison be evacuated was denied.

Firing at a bridge north of the fort, a tank stalled on the canal embankment but continued shooting even though it was now a sitting target. The gunner, Sgt. Yadin Tannenbaum, nineteen, had been a musical prodigy. A flutist, he had been singled out for praise by conductor Leonard Bernstein. After hitting the bridge, Tannenbaum knocked out a bulldozer widening a passage through the Israeli ramp and then hit an Egyptian tank coming through the opening. A shell hit his tank, killing him and his tank commander.

Sgt. Eyal Yoffe followed his platoon commander, Lt. Michael Vardi, through the narrow S-shaped entrance into the Mifreket compound. He could hear shouts in Arabic in the trenches. He and his men fired into the darkness around them with the tank's machine guns and with Uzis. As they approached the main bunker, the surviving members of the garrison ran out and climbed atop Vardi's tank, expecting to be evacuated. The officer descended and led them back to the bunker. He had orders, he said, to evacuate only the wounded. He tried to assure the remainder that rescue would shortly come. Eyal Yoffe, in his tank outside, heard his brother on the radio ordering Vardi to join him north of the fort. Without identifying himself, Eyal said he would pass on the message.

It was difficult for the sergeant to grasp that this was reality, not another exercise. Darkness added to the disorientation. As they drove out of the fort, he saw an Egyptian tank thirty yards to his right. In his excitement, he forgot the proper way to issue a fire command. "Ehud," he shouted to his gunner. "Quick. A tank to the right. Fire." The first shot hit. In the light of the burning tank, its four crewmen descended and ran towards his tank. Eyal cut them down with his machine gun. He hit an Egyptian bulldozer and fired at the bridge. Reality had begun to disentangle itself.

From time to time, Eyal Yoffe and Vardi reentered Mifreket to strike at Egyptians who had returned and to encourage the men in the bunker with their fire. The garrison's wounded, together with wounded tankers, were placed aboard Eyal's tank for evacuation. One man had lost both legs and an arm. Eyal saw his brother issuing orders nearby. The battalion commander did not recognize him in the darkness until he heard his voice. He was startled to discover that his kid brother was serving under him.

"How you doing, Ili?" he asked.

"Doing fine," responded Eyal, taking off his tanker's helmet for this moment of intimacy.

He transported the wounded to the rear and returned to Mifreket as it began to dawn. Lieutenant Vardi, he discovered, was dead, killed in another attempt to enter the fort. Most of the remaining tanks were either mired in marshes or trying to extricate others which were mired.

Colonel Yoffe, together with his brother and another tank commander, fired on enemy vehicles moving inland from the bridge. Eyal was wounded by a Sagger and his brother had him placed inside his own tank. Eyal suffered burns on his face and could not speak but nodded to indicate to his brother that he was all right, or at least would be.

As Tamir had done, Yoffe requested evacuation of the Mifreket garrison. Colonel Shomron likewise asked permission to evacuate the forts in the southern sector. "If we don't do it now, we won't be able to do it in the morning," he said. Mendler said he had not been authorized to evacuate the forts.

Meanwhile, Tamir had gone back during the night to guide the rest of Yoffe's battalion to Milano, accompanied by brigade commander Gabi Amir. The tank column moved into Kantara, firing to either side in response to heavy fire. Some tanks got lost in side streets where they were destroyed by RPGs.

The situation in Milano contrasted sharply with that in Mifreket. The fort commander, Captain Trostler, told Amir that they had beaten off several attacks during the day and sunk a number of boats. He had lost four men but the defenses were intact and he was not in need of help. Since the fort was not to be evacuated and since it was too dangerous for the tanks to remain opposite the Egyptian ramp when daylight came, there was nothing to do but pull back.

Of the fourteen tanks which had started out for Milano, only five returned. Of the eighteen tanks Yoffe brought to Mifreket, another five returned. Had they been authorized to evacuate the forts, there would have been purpose to their sacrifice.

In the southern sector, the commander of a lone tank at Lituf with radio problems got through at dawn to report that he had stalled. He was told to put his gear into reverse and fire a shell. The recoil succeeded in starting the engine, and the tank commander was ordered to rejoin the remnants of Shomron's brigade which had fallen back to the Artillery Road, six miles to the east.

Mendler received permission in late morning from Gonen to evacuate the forts. But it was too late. They were all surrounded now by masses of Egyptian infantry. Mendler asked Shomron if he could evacuate the forts in his sector. "Maybe I can reach them," replied Shomron, "but every attempt will cost a battalion. It's your decision." Mendler decided to wait until the reserves counterattacked. For now at least, the Egyptians had won the battle for the waterline.

The fatal flaw of the Bar-Lev Line—its irrelevance in the face of a major attack—had been brutally exposed. If Dovecote had been fully deployed, with two armored brigades forward instead of one, with the forts manned at full strength and by elite troops as they were supposed to be, and if there had been serious artillery support, Egyptian losses would clearly have been much heavier. But senior Israeli officers would concede that the crossing would not have been stopped even then.

By the early hours of Sunday, the import of the past day's events were beginning to be absorbed by the IDF command. But by this time, two-thirds of the Sinai Division had been knocked out. Of the division's 290 tanks, only 110 were still operational. Reshef's brigade had only one-quarter of its tanks left.

Virtually every assumption by the Israeli command about the nature of the coming war had proven wrong—that AMAN would provide ample warning, that the air force could save the day, that the IDF could get by with limited artillery and infantry, that "armor shock" would stampede the enemy, that the Arab soldier was a pushover and the Arab military command inept.

The Israeli command had permitted itself to believe that given the nature of the enemy—"We're facing Arabs, not Germans," as one officer put it—Dovecote could be stretched to cope with a full-scale attack if necessary. The General Staff had failed to think through the implications of the massive amounts of antitank weaponry the Egyptian infantry was known to possess. Duels at fifty paces between tanks and individual soldiers wielding RPGs were not what armored warfare was supposed to be about.

Of all the fuzzy thinking that marked the preparations for war, reliance on air support was the fuzziest. Air force commander Peled had made clear that he would need the first forty-eight hours of war to deal with the SAMs. Yet Elazar and his generals permitted themselves to believe that the air force, still wreathed with the magical aura of the Six Day War, would somehow be able to deal with enemy ground forces if it became necessary. Relying on the air force, the IDF made do with a few dozen artillery pieces in Sinai. Without meaningful artillery and air support, the IDF lacked firepower even more than manpower. The Egyptians had provided themselves amply with both.

As for AMAN, its failure went deeper than the failure to warn of war. It did not prepare the IDF for the kind of war that was coming. It failed to indicate the innovative tactics the Egyptian army would employ or point to the motivation and training that would make the Egyptian soldier of 1973 different from the soldier of the Six Day War. A common factor behind all these failings was the contempt for Arab arms born of that earlier war, a contempt that spawned indolent thinking.

The surprise Arab assault would be a staggering psychological blow for Israel that would impact on the rest of the war by imposing a measure of caution on the Israeli command. But it was operational unpreparedness, not the surprise, that was responsible for the debacle on Yom Kippur. Even if there had been no surprise, the IDF was not prepared to cope with the Egyptians' new antitank tactics, the air force—held at bay by the SAMs—would have been unable to assist the ground forces, at least for the first day or two, and Dovecote would still have been a suicidal response.

For Israel, there was one bright spot—the professionalism, courage, and initiative displayed by the young soldiers and their commanders despite the disastrous tactics imposed on them.

The Sinai Division had been mauled, but not destroyed. Most of its damaged tanks would be returned to action, some within a day, and its command structure was still intact. Many of the wounded would return to duty as well and replacements would fill the gaps. Appropriate lessons for coping with the Saggers were already being drawn and implemented. But the reserve divisions now approaching the battlefield would have to learn these lessons for themselves.

Exhausted by the day's battle, the surviving Israeli tank crews pulled back before dawn to refuel and rearm. The men had hardly eaten since the onset of Yom Kippur, which seemed a lifetime ago. Thinking about what they had been through and what the morrow might bring, many fell into a brief and troubled sleep.

In the Egyptian lines this night, soldiers who could doze off did so on the wings of euphoria. There had not been a feat of Arab arms like this since Saladin defeated the Crusader army near the Sea of Galilee in the twelfth century. No matter what was yet to come, Egypt's soldiers had restored Arab honor.

Thirteen

MOBILIZATION

A GROUP OF WOMEN SAT IN FRONT of their apartment building late Saturday afternoon in the port city of Ashdod watching with mounting unease the extraordinary sight of vehicles moving through the streets on Yom Kippur. The husbands of all had received emergency call-up orders in the past few hours, except for one. It was she who stepped forward ruefully when a car pulled up and a courier emerged with a brown envelope in his hand. Her husband had returned from a month's reserve duty just two weeks before—on the Suez Canal, as it happened—and she had permitted herself to hope that he might be spared. When she entered the apartment she found him already packing his kit bag. As a member of an armored infantry battalion, he had no doubt that he would be called.

Downing a cup of coffee, he kissed his wife and set off for a nearby assembly point. Other men from his unit were already there. He could read in their eyes the same sense of surprise and apprehension that he felt himself. The consensus among them was that whatever was happening would be over in a couple of days. If the Arabs had forgotten the lessons of the Six Day War after only six years, they would be reminded soon enough. Nevertheless, the prospect of war was sobering. Two buses arrived at 6:30 P.M. As they moved off, the men began singing. Passersby looked up, then waved and applauded.

Army bases seethed with activity as reservists arriving from around the country reported to their units. First, the men were formally mobilized, handing over their reservists' identity cards to company clerks, who asked for the names of relatives to be informed "in case something happens." After receiving uniforms and personal weapons—not having to sign for them as they did during reserve stints—the men dispersed to the sheds of their respective battalions to equip and arm the tanks and personnel carriers.

More than 200,000 civilians were being transformed overnight into an army. The process had been set in motion shortly before 10:00 that morning with the transmission of code words to brigade mobilization centers. Couriers from each brigade were summoned to the centers by telephone and were provided with civilian vehicles that had been mobilized. The civilian owners were permitted to drive the vehicles themselves if they preferred not handing over the keys to army drivers. Most of the civilian bus fleet was mobilized as well to carry reservists to their bases. Some reservists reached their bases by early afternoon. Others, living in remote parts of the country where the buses had to stop at many rural settlements, did not arrive until after midnight. Some men, impatient at not having received their call-up notice, came on their own, sometimes even by taxi. Veteran warhorses long since mustered out of service showed up at their old units and asked to be taken on, a request usually granted.

While the mobilization process went smoothly, the scenes at the tank bases were of barely controlled pandemonium. The tanks had been stripped when put into storage and they now had to be equipped and armed from scratch. Tanks assigned to reserve brigades were used in training by various units and, like borrowed books, they were not always returned in their original condition. The army assumed that it would have at least forty-eight hours' warning of impending war to replace missing and damaged equipment. The depots were not ready to handle a call-up of the entire reserve army in one day without notice. Sometimes the tanks themselves were missing and officers had to scurry among army bases to track them down or find replacements. One brigade had to fetch its tanks from six different bases. Officers from one battalion almost came to blows with quartermasters who refused to release tanks they believed designated for another unit. Small but vital pieces of equipment like binoculars and flashlights were missing almost everywhere, while the availability of other items ranging from crew helmets to projectors was spotty. Far more grave, entire brigades had to set off for the front without machine guns, which would be more important than tank guns in the encounters with infantry that lay ahead.

Some problems were solved by local initiative. At the request of army officers, police in Beersheva, near where many army bases lay, summoned store owners at night to open their shops for the sale of binoculars and flash-lights. At a base in the south where no forklifts could be found to transfer crates of shells from ammunition bunkers, soldiers "borrowed" forklifts from an adjacent industrial area after breaking through a fence. In the north, a battalion commander took forklifts from his home kibbutz, which was near his unit's assembly area. Sharon telephoned a millionaire friend in the United States for binoculars. A shipment would arrive by air within a few days and be rushed directly to the front.

The men worked feverishly into the night to turn the metal behemoths into fighting machines. Technical teams swarmed over the tanks. Optical sights, drivers' periscopes, radio sets, and other equipment were fitted into their places. Water and battle rations were put aboard, and shells, passed from hand to hand, were stored in the turrets and bellies of the tanks. Offi-cers constantly pressed the men to move faster. "We'll lose the war because of you," was a standard spur. "Hurry. Hurry."

Despite the surprise and inadequacies, 85 percent of units would reach the front within the time planned. Many would reach it in half the time.

News from the front was scant but the men were aware that the small forces holding the line were fighting a desperate battle.

Gen. Yeshayahu Gavish (res.), who had commanded Israel's southern front in the Six Day War, drove down to his old headquarters in Beersheva on Yom Kippur afternoon to see whether the current commander, General Gonen, could use his services. He found him in his office going through papers. "How's it going, Shmulik?" he asked.

"We're going to screw them," said Gonen.

Gavish went into the war room to monitor the radio net for a sense of what was happening at the front. What he heard shocked him. Cries of des-peration were coming from the forts. "Where's the air force?" "We need help." Tank crews were plainly engaged in fierce battles. Gavish returned to Gonen and urged him to come out and listen for himself.

"Things aren't going well," said Gavish.

Gonen waved dismissively. "We're on top of it," he said. "Don't worry about it." Gavish gathered that Gonen had no task to offer him.

Someone else concerned by the voices on the radio net was Col. Uri Ben-Ari, who had arrived at the Beersheva headquarters to take up his reserve assignment as assistant to the front commander. He too suggested that Gonen come out of his office and listen. "It'll be over soon," Gonen had replied, remaining behind his desk.

In giving Ben-Ari his assignment, Elazar was balancing Gonen's limited experience with the steady hand of one of the most illustrious veterans of Israel's armored corps. The strapping German-born Ben-Ari looked like a Prussian officer. His grandfather had in fact been an *ulan,* a member of the kaiser's bodyguard. Ben-Ari himself was born Heinz Banner in Berlin. His father, a prosperous textile merchant, had sent him to Palestine at age fourteen, half a year before the onset of the Second World War, in order to get him out of Germany. All of Ben-Ari's relatives, some ninety persons, perished in the Holocaust. He himself served with distinction in the elite Palmach strike force in Israel's War of Independence—he was Elazar's commander at San Simon—and was one of the first to join the armored corps. In the 1956 Sinai Campaign, he commanded the Seventh Armored Brigade, which spearheaded the Israeli breakthrough. Gonen had served under him in that campaign. Ben-Ari left the army shortly afterwards, but as a reservist in 1967 he led a mechanized brigade in the battle for Jerusalem. Recalled to duty on Yom Kippur, he was surprised to learn that Gonen had not yet moved his headquarters to the forward command post at Umm Hashiba.

When they did reach Umm Hashiba twelve hours later, Ben-Ari found the underground facility barely functioning. He would devote his first day to putting it in working order. The most important task he assigned himself, however, was keeping an eye on Gonen. He had concluded on the basis of what he saw in the first hours that Gonen was totally unsuited for his post. Elazar, in countering critics of Gonen's appointment, had said that he would gain experience over the course of time. The war, however, had come at the beginning of Gonen's tenure. Beyond that, Ben-Ari believed that waging a multidivisional war on a broad front was simply beyond Gonen's intellectual powers.

Ben-Ari was also repelled by Gonen's coarse behavior—cursing, shouting, throwing telephones at personnel when he couldn't get a line. In Beersheva, Gonen had been relatively relaxed, but upon arriving at Umm Hashiba, with reality close to hand, he went out of control. He created an atmosphere of terror in which staff officers hesitated to call unpleasant facts to his attention. Orderly staff work practically ceased, so that it became difficult for Gonen himself to make decisions based on sound information. Ben-Ari decided that as long as the war lasted he would not go to sleep before Gonen and not waken after him. He asked his driver to be sure to waken him if he saw Gonen waking first. The front commander, he felt, must not be left alone.

The two reserve divisions assigned to Southern Command were commanded by generals whose rich military careers had seemed behind them—Avraham Adan and Ariel Sharon.

Adan, known to all as "Bren," was scheduled to retire in a month. The public knew him best from the photograph of him climbing a pole to raise the first Israeli flag in Eilat during the War of Independence twenty-five years before. He had now been commander of the armored corps for five years. In that time, he had overseen the doubling of the armored forces. There was a reserve about him that made him seem somewhat distant or shy. But he was regarded by his peers as a gentleman and a consummate professional.

Sharon was cut from different cloth. He had won fame as a commander of special forces, but his assertive character brought him into conflict with superiors and peers at virtually every stage of his military career. He was accused of being overaggressive, disobedient, and divisive. When Sharon transferred to the armored corps, Adan and other veteran tank commanders saw him as burdened by an infantryman's mentality. "He did not seem cut out to be an Armored Corps soldier," Adan would write in his memoirs. In addition, Adan found Sharon's views on strategic-political issues simplistic, if not extreme in their hawkishness.

However, Israeli military analysts would credit Sharon with having conceived and executed the one classic set-piece battle in Israeli military history—the night battle for Abu Agheila in Sinai in the Six Day War. It was a complex operation involving paratroopers landed by helicopters in the enemy rear to silence his artillery, flanking movements by infantry that avoided the enemy's main defenses, effective use of artillery, engineers clearing enemy minefields, and well-timed assaults by tanks. Each unit's combat potential was exploited to the maximum. The operation was executed almost exactly as planned, a model of a combined arms operation that was nevertheless overshadowed in Israeli military thought by the notion of the totality of the tank.

A general who knew Sharon since serving as his company commander in the War of Independence would say of him, "Arik can never execute someone else's plan, only his own." It was a trait not bound to endear him to his superiors. In the waiting period before the Six Day War, General Gavish had prepared a tentative plan calling for two divisions to attack while the third, commanded by Sharon, remained in defensive positions. When Sharon objected to his role, Gavish made a point of coming to the briefing Sharon gave the next day to his division staff. A look at the maps on the wall showed that Sharon was planning to attack, not defend. Gavish asked him to come outside. If Sharon did not intend to carry out orders, "Get on your jeep and go home," Gavish would recall saying. Instead of being put down by the rebuke, Sharon said, "Let's speak to Yitzhak," a reference to chief of staff Yitzhak Rabin. Calling Rabin in Gavish's presence, he said that Gavish was proposing a plan that made no sense. He then proceeded to outline his own plan. Rabin did not even ask to speak to Gavish. He told Sharon to either obey Gavish's order or hand over his command. From that moment, Gavish had no problem with him. In the end, plans were changed and Sharon got to execute his own at Abu Agheila.

Even Sharon's bitterest opponents acknowledged that he was a superb field commander—the best Israel had, in the view of many—a daring and imaginative officer who could read a battle as it unfolded and inspire his troops. He remained a field soldier even in high command, capable of studying a photostat of unfamiliar territory for a quarter hour, as a staff officer would testify, and then leading his unit through the terrain for an entire night without further reference.

He had reluctantly retired from the army after it was made clear to him that he had no chance to be appointed chief of staff and that his term as commander of the southern front was ending after three and a half years. On the morning of his retirement, he telephoned Dayan to plead for another year as front commander. War with Egypt was a real possibility, he said, and his battle experience and familiarity with the front were assets not to be cast aside lightly. Sharon heard a pause before Dayan replied, "There won't be war in the coming year."

Despite opposition by Elazar, Sharon had, with Dayan's support, been granted a commission as commander of a reserve division. Dayan appreciated Sharon's qualities as a fighting general even though he was well aware of his excesses. In the Sinai Campaign of 1956, Dayan, then chief of staff, had come close to court-martialing him for launching an attack at the Mitla Pass in defiance of orders that cost the lives of thirty-eight paratroopers. Nevertheless, Dayan believed it better to have a general who was too aggressive than one who was not aggressive enough.

In the three months Sharon had been a civilian, he had proved himself no less vigorous in the political arena. He was the driving force behind the formation of the new right-wing Likud Party headed by Menahem Begin and was himself a candidate for the Knesset in elections scheduled for the end of October.

Telephoning Gonen on Yom Kippur afternoon, Sharon urged him to move to his forward command post to get a better feel for the battle. Gonen did not appreciate the advice. Until three months before, he had been subordinate to Sharon. The delicate command situation made for a charged atmosphere and Sharon realized he would have to be cautious in dealing with Gonen. Both Sharon and Adan had far more combat experience than Gonen, whom they were now serving under, and both had more seniority. Both were also extremely skeptical about his command abilities. Neither, however, wanted his job. They were grateful to be leading divisions in the field rather than sitting behind a desk in rear headquarters.

As armored corps commander, Adan had attended the meeting at 7 A.M. with Elazar and Zeira in the Pit, where he learned of the Source's warning. He proceeded from there to his own headquarters, where, in his other capacity as commander of a reserve division, he met with his three brigade commanders. Adan's division was assigned the northern canal front and would proceed there along the Mediterranean coastal road. Sharon was assigned the central sector and would proceed through the heart of Sinai to Tasa. Mendler's division, what was left of it, would confine itself to the canal's southern sector as soon as the other divisions arrived.

Meeting with General Elazar later in the morning, Adan found the chief of staff calm and coping. They agreed that Mendler, who was to have been replaced the next day by General Kalman Magen, would remain at his post for the duration of the war.

The first tank transporters, bearing a reserve tank company commanded by Maj. Yitzhak Brik and a small force of infantry in half-tracks, set off for the front Saturday night at 10:30, just half a day after mobilization had been set in motion.

Sitting in the radioless cabin of the transporter as it moved through the desert darkness, Brik was cut off from the outside world. In the borderland between sleep and wakefulness, he reviewed the frantic events of the day, which had begun with the sound of warplanes overflying his kibbutz in southern Israel. He and a fellow kibbutz member belonging to his battalion had driven to their assembly point, assuring each other that whatever was happening would be over in a day or two. The storerooms in his mobilization depot had been in good shape, which accounted for the swift readiness of his unit. But the haste and the unclear orders with which he had been dispatched to the front did not bode well. He was to proceed along the road to Baluza, on the approaches to the canal, until he was flagged down. He was then to await further orders. His battalion commander, Assaf Yaguri, said that the situation along the canal was bad, with the Egyptians crossing en masse.

By dawn, Brik's transporters reached the environs of Baluza. The road was empty and no one flagged them down. The canal zone was not far ahead and Brik was wary. Should they encounter Egyptians while still aboard the transporters, they would be helpless. "We're unloading here," he said to the driver.

The tanks and APCs descended from the transporters and formed up behind the company commander. They had only proceeded a mile when Brik heard an explosion behind him. At the rear of the column, an APC was burning. Fire suddenly opened along the entire length of the column. Some 150 Egyptian commandos, landed by helicopter at dusk the day before, were dug in on either side of the road. Most of the fire was coming from the right. Brik ordered his driver to turn in that direction. As his tank closed on the heaviest source of fire, commandos rose from the sands all around him, firing and throwing grenades. Brik and the other tank commanders fired their machine guns and the drivers tried to run the commandos down. The tanks moved with difficulty through the dunes, and commandos tried to clamber aboard from the rear in order to drop grenades through the open turret hatches. Brik and the commander of a tank forty yards away fired their machine guns at each other's tanks to knock commandos off.

The other tank commander was hit and his crew pulled back, leaving Brik's tank alone. He fired his machine gun without pause until a rocket-propelled grenade literally brushed him, its heat igniting his shirt. Shouting to his gunner to take command, he leaped from the tank and rolled in the sand to extinguish the fire. The gunner rose into the turret and turned the machine gun on Egyptians closing in on Brik. One commando fell dead near the company commander. Brik found himself intact except for a badly singed face. Crawling back to the tank, which had meanwhile halted, he scrambled aboard. Several other tanks and an APC now joined him, and they pursued the Egyptians, who had begun pulling back. Brik finally called off the chase, leaving the commandos to be dealt with by infantrymen who would be following. The pursuit, however, would be abandoned by officers who presumed that the commandos had been effectively eliminated.

Cautiously resuming movement westward, Brik saw a solitary Israeli tank ahead and stopped alongside. The crewmen standing by it appeared stunned. They were young conscripts who had survived the battle at Mifreket the night before. From their account, and from what he himself had just experienced, Brik began to comprehend that they were not up against the Egyptian army they knew from the Six Day War.

The other reserve forces streaming towards Sinai still had no idea of what awaited them. Many, anticipating an upgraded replay of the Six Day War, were afraid they would miss the action. Others were afraid they wouldn't. A company commander assembled his men and said that reports from the front indicated that a tough battle awaited them. All were veterans of the War of Attrition, a gritty conflict that evoked no nostalgia. "Be careful," he said. "Use your heads. Good luck." To brigade commander Haim Erez of Sharon's division, luck was a flimsy crutch in the face of a surprise so total. "We're in a mess," said Colonel Erez prophetically to one of his battalion commanders. "This is going to end with 2,500 to 3,000 dead."

As units from Sharon's division passed through Beersheva on the way to the front, people on the streets applauded. At an intersection, a tank clipped a civilian car waiting at a red light. The car driver, a soldier, got out to examine the damage and waved reassuringly to the tank commander. "It's all right," he said. "It's a mobilized car, not mine." Passing out of the city, the vehicles were swallowed up by the desert, which stretched all the way to the canal.

The convoys grew longer and slower as the night progressed and more units joined the flow from camps dotting the Negev. Men drew reassurance from the long line of tanks, their commanders upright in the turrets. "The Egyptians have made the mistake of their lives," said one soldier, contemplating the sight. Others, however, sensed that this war was different. It was the Arabs who had seized the initiative, and the outcome could not be predicted.

The men fell silent as they traveled west, lost in their own thoughts. A doctor with Sharon's division was struck by the surreal nature of what had overtaken him and the others. "Only yesterday," he would write, "it was high-rise buildings, grassy lawns, synagogue, and children. Now it's armored vehicles, desert, khaki, and an endless road leading to war."

At times, the convoys had to pull over to make way for vehicles heading back to Israel. These were mostly empty tank transporters or buses carrying young women soldiers ordered out of the war zone. The girls made the V sign to the soldiers moving up to the front.

For Egyptian Sergeant Mahmud Nadeh, the first day's encounter with war had been enough to dispel all illusion about a stirring adventure. His amphibious battalion, which had crossed the Bitter Lake, had been savaged by Boaz Amir's tanks. "The amphibious tanks proved worthless beyond the crossing of the lake itself," Nadeh wrote in his diary the next morning. "Most of the tanks with me were set on fire, the rest scattered. It was the cruelest night we've ever experienced—death, hunger, thirst, fear, and cold. All of us fellows from Alexandria have gotten into one foxhole at the edge of the lake, so that we can die together. Some of the news they're broadcasting on the radio caused us to laugh out loud."

However, the broadcasts on Cairo Radio about Egyptian successes were truer than Nadeh and his comrades were in a position to appreciate in their isolated corner of the battlefield. Surveying the field reports Sunday morning in Center Ten, General Shazly could declare the battle of the crossing won, and by an astonishing margin. By 8 A.M. Sunday, 90,000 men had been put across the canal. By 2 P.M.—twenty-four hours after the war's start—the number would grow to 100,000 men. Also across were 1,020 tanks and almost 14,000 other vehicles, in what Shazly would describe as the largest first-day crossing of a water barrier in military history. The Egyptian high command had been prepared for 20,000 casualties in the crossing operation, but the number killed, according to the final Egyptian count, was 280.

Bridges had been hit during the night by Israeli planes, but the damaged modular sections were replaced within an hour. Shazly permitted himself a touch of ironic regret at the failure of the Israelis to have mobilized on time. Had their reserves been fully deployed, he thought, they would have rapidly followed up the Sinai Division's attack, repeating the same mistakes and suffering the same fate. It was an opinion that not a few Israeli officers would come to share.

General Adan had reached Baluza at 6:30 A.M., shortly before the Egyptians sprang their ambush on Brik. Fortunately for him, the Egyptians were waiting for heavier prey and did not reveal themselves by hitting the light vehicles carrying the divisional command. After reporting his arrival to Gonen, Adan set off to meet Gabi Amir. He found the brigade commander, an old comrade, and Yom Tov Tamir in a half-track alongside a handful of tanks. The faces of the two officers conveyed the harrowing nature of what they had been through. Colonel Amir gave a chilling description of the night's battles. Tamir was offended that Adan offered no words of solace about his battalion's destruction, but the general was too busy absorbing the dimensions of the setback to empathize. Instead of scattering the remains of Amir's shattered brigade among other units, Adan decided to keep it intact, in order not to destroy the morale of its men, and to attach fresh forces to it.

Gonen raised Adan on the telephone. "Good that you've arrived," said the front commander, sounding weary. "The situation along the canal is rough. Move your forces to prevent a breakthrough." Elazar had urged

Gonen to move back from Umm Hashiba for fear that commandos might be preparing to attack it. "I don't want a general taken prisoner," said Elazar. Gonen assured him he would never permit himself to be taken prisoner.

As Adan was deploying his units astride the east–west roads in his sector, he was informed that the commando force dispersed earlier by Brik had returned to block the coastal road. The commandos had fired on a convoy of half-tracks traveling from Baluza towards the rear for refueling. The vehicles got through except for the last half-track, which had engine trouble, and a jeep at the rear of the convoy. The thirteen men in the two vehicles dismounted. Nine were Israeli commando officers, the other three privates.

At the direction of Lt. Rafi Sa'id, who took command, they began moving towards the ambushers. On the way, Sa'id saw an Israeli tank sheltering in a fold in the ground. He signaled it to take the lead. As they closed on the Egyptians, Sa'id split his force into two groups, which proceeded under the covering fire of the tank towards the enemy flanks. This time it was the ambushers who were taken by surprise. The tank driver ran down enemy soldiers while Sa'id's men hit the disoriented Egyptians with precise fire. When the battle was over, the tank commander was dead and several Israelis were wounded but the bodies of ninety-two Egyptians covered the ground. The Egyptian commander was taken prisoner. All told, twenty-one Israelis were killed in the two phases of the battle on the coastal road. Five tanks and five other vehicles were knocked out. Lying on the roadside, they would constitute a warning to the arriving forces that this was going to be a different kind of war.

Another Egyptian commando battalion had landed by boat just before dark Saturday a few miles northwest of Baluza on the sandspit leading to Budapest. The two-hundred-man force placed mines and waited for Israeli reinforcements to try to reach the outpost. Close to midnight, eight Israeli tanks started up the road. When the first hit a mine, the Egyptians sent up flares and unleashed a volley of Saggers, hitting two more tanks. The Israelis pulled back. They resumed movement at first light but were again stopped by mines and Saggers, losing another tank.

The commandos were well dug in overlooking the road and were difficult to see in their foxholes. A belt of mines and the narrowness of the sandspit prevented flanking. The Egyptian scouts whose footprints Motti Ashkenazi had evidently seen had chosen the ambush site well. An Israeli force made another attempt at 9 A.M. after shelling the area with mortars, this time infantrymen moving ahead of the tanks. The foot soldiers were exposed as they moved along the shore, and in the ensuing battle fifteen were killed and thirty wounded. Budapest remained cut off.

On the coastal road, Adan's division was tied up in traffic jams all the way back to El Arish, ninety miles from the canal. The deep sand alongside the road made it difficult to push stalled vehicles off. An order was finally given for tanks and APCs to be offloaded from transporters so that they could continue forward on their own tracks through the sand. Fighter planes circling overhead guarded against air attacks.

The approach of Sharon's division to the front went smoothly. The Egyptians had intended commando ambushes along this route as well, but Israeli planes had downed most of the force's helicopters. Sharon himself had left for the front at 2 A.M. Sunday in a mobilized pickup truck painted with the sign "Ray of Light Solar Heaters." The owner of the vehicle had chosen to stay with it as driver. With Sharon was an old friend from his paratroop days, Zeev Amit, who had decided to join him for the war. Sharon's wife found a pair of her husband's old boots to lend him. Reaching Refidim, the main IDF base in Sinai, Sharon entered the underground war room. The officers and men inside instinctively rose, as if he were still front commander.

General Mendler was relieved to see Sharon and to hear that the lead elements of his division were not far behind. Mendler was visibly weary. The situation on the front was unclear, he said. What remained of Reshef's brigade was confronting the forward elements of the entire Second Army. Shomron's brigade was opposite the Third Army. Amir's brigade barely existed. Tank losses were heavy. So were casualties. The Egyptians were now three to five miles east of the canal, and their forces were streaming across the waterway without hindrance.

For Sharon, this succinct account was a consummation of his worst fears about the Bar-Lev Line. Arriving at Tasa, he moved forward in a jeep to a point overlooking the canal area. Smoke from artillery fire rose all along the front in the distance. Sharon flagged down several withdrawing tanks and talked to their commanders. "I saw something strange on their faces," he would write. "Not fear but bewilderment." For the first time in the soldiers' lifetimes, an Israeli army was being driven back, and they could not fathom what was happening.

It was clear to Sharon what had to be done—a swift and concentrated blow by at least two divisions before the Egyptians fortified their bridgeheads. The attack could be launched the next day, Monday, when his and Adan's divisions would be in place. It was vital, Sharon believed, that the Egyptians be denied the feeling of success. The psychological factor was critical in war, and the Egyptians had to be thrown off balance by a swift counterattack. His aim, he would write, was "to create in the Arabs a psychology of defeat, to beat them every time and to beat them so decisively that they would develop the conviction that they would never win."

Another thought taking shape as he looked out over the battlefield was the need to rescue the men in the forts. Returning to Tasa, he asked to be put in radio contact with the forts in his sector. Identifying himself only by his radio code number, 40, he sought to get a feel for the tactical situation and the mood.

In Purkan, radio operator Avi Yaffe, who had brought a tape recorder to reserve duty from his Jerusalem recording studio, recorded Sharon as he spoke with Major Weisel, the fort commander.

"Do the Egyptians seem tired or do they have momentum?" asked Sharon. He himself sounded tired and was plainly unclear about the situation. "How many tanks do you see? Are they moving towards Tasa?"

Weisel, sounding unruffled, even jaunty, said the Egyptian tanks were deployed on Lexicon, the road paralleling the canal. "They seem to be waiting for our tanks to attack," he said.

Weisel noted that Israeli planes had attacked the Egyptians in his area earlier. "It reminded me of six years ago," he said, referring to the Six Day War.

"Were you in that war?" asked Sharon.

"I've been in four, well, three," said Weisel. "You're talking to an old man of almost forty-one."

Sharon laughed politely but his voice remained deadly serious. "I just got here. I'm going to try to get you out. What vehicles do you have?"

"Two half-tracks and a truck."

The radioman at Fort Hizayon, Max Maimon, a Jerusalem bank clerk, cut into the conversation. He had been issuing desperate calls for assistance since the day before and he recognized Sharon's voice.

"Forty, forty. We know you. We know you will get us out of here. Please come to us."

As a twenty-year-old lieutenant in Israel's War of Independence, Sharon had been badly wounded and barely managed to crawl to the rear after his platoon had been forgotten on the battlefield by withdrawing Israeli forces. Most of his men had not made it back. That experience made for his ready identification with the men cut off on the Bar-Lev Line. A soldier on his staff saw his eyes grow moist. Contacting Gonen, Sharon said it was a moral duty to try to rescue the men trapped in the forts. He proposed that tanks move forward after dark on a narrow front with a heavy artillery bombardment creating a "firebox" on their flanks and front to keep off the RPG teams.

Simultaneously, the men in the forts would emerge under the cover of darkness in vehicles or on foot to meet the tanks at predetermined points. Sharon believed it was still possible to rescue them because the bulk of the Egyptian army, particularly the tanks, had not yet crossed. The menace, however, lay with the infantry, which was already deployed in force. Gonen, whose sangfroid had given way after seeing most of Mendler's division dissolve in fruitless attacks, rejected Sharon's proposal. The men in the forts would have to wait for a general counterattack, which he was planning for the next day.

Sharon had no hesitation about going over Gonen's head and calling Dayan directly to ask for his intervention. The defense minister said the subject of the forts would be discussed with Elazar at a meeting that night at Gonen's headquarters. Sharon and the other division commanders would also be attending.

Mitzna's battalion, holding the high ground five miles east of Hizayon, had watched the Egyptians flowing across a bridge just south of the fort since dawn. After the enemy units formed up, they moved across the sandy plain and climbed the hills towards the Artillery Road. Mitzna's battalion blocked their way in this sector, destroying dozens of tanks in daylong skirmishing. Like the units that had encountered Saggers for the first time the day before, Mitzna's tank crews improvised responses to the new threat—firing directly in front of their own tanks to create dust, moving back and forth and firing towards the presumed location of the Sagger operator. Such techniques, improvised by troops in the field in the opening hours of the Yom Kippur War, would subsequently be adopted by NATO forces adjusting to the newly perceived threat of Warsaw Pact Saggers.

By late afternoon, ammunition and fuel were nearly exhausted and many of Mitzna's tanks had been hit. Company commander Rami Matan climbed out of his turret to smoke a cigarette during a pause in the firing as he watched another Egyptian wave forming up. Reconciled to death, the twenty-two-year-old captain reckoned that he would be able to fire off his last few shells before being overrun. The Egyptians had not yet attacked, however, when a dust cloud to his rear indicated tanks approaching. Matan was ordered to prepare to pull back.

The conscript soldiers of the standing army who had borne the brunt of the Arab attack for two days were being joined by their older brothers, as it were; in some cases, even by their fathers. The reserves were moving into the line.

With darkness, the fighting tapered off and there was time for the men to listen to Israel Radio and try to make sense of what was happening. The situation was unclear but fighting appeared to be heavy everywhere. It would have been no consolation to the Israeli soldiers in Sinai to know that as bad as things seemed for them, the situation on the Golan front, three hundred miles to the northeast, was far worse.

Fourteen

SYRIAN BREAKTHROUGH

S YRIA EXPECTED TO REGAIN THE GOLAN HEIGHTS in the course of a single day, and with good reason. Opposite the 177 tanks Israel had on the heights Yom Kippur morning, Syria had 1,400. Opposite Israel's 11 artillery batteries, Syria had 115. Opposite 200 Israeli infantrymen manning ten strongpoints along the forty-mile-long front were three Syrian infantry divisions with 40,000 men.

That the Israeli command was willing to accept this dizzying disparity reflected a contempt for Syrian arms even more than it reflected Israel's limited manpower. As Elazar had said a few days before, 100 tanks on the Golan should be sufficient to deal with 800 Syrian tanks. Had it not been for the arrival of Ben-Gal's brigade over the past ten days, the ratio of tanks would not have been 8 to 1 but 18 to 1.

The Syrians assumed it would take the Israeli reserves twenty-four hours to reach the front. They intended to conquer the Golan before then. The broad outlines of the Syrian plan had been known to Israeli intelligence for at least two months, and an updated version was acquired a week before Yom Kippur. The three Syrian infantry divisions on the line—the Seventh in the north, Ninth in the center, and Fifth in the south—would attack simultaneously. Despite their infantry designation, the divisions numbered 900 tanks among them, including an independent armored brigade attached to each on the eve of the war. Two armored divisions with another 470 tanks were deployed to the rear, a few hours' drive from the front.

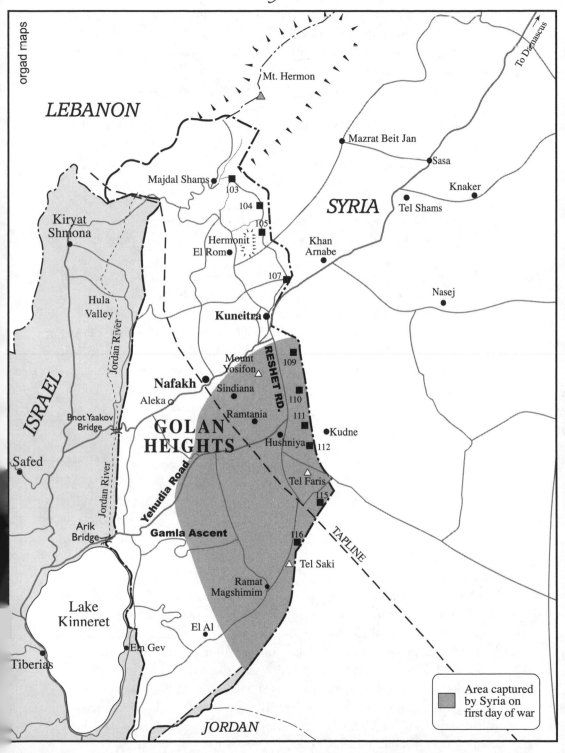

orgad maps

LEBANON

Mt. Hermon

Mazrat Beit Jan

Sasa

To Damascus

SYRIA

Majdal Shams

103

104

105

Knaker

Tel Shams

Kiryat
Shmona

Hermonit
El Rom

Khan
Arnabe

107

Nasej

Hula
Valley

Kuneitra

Jordan River

Mount
Yosifon

RESHET RD.

109

ISRAEL

Nafakh

Sindiana

110

Aleka

Ramtania

111

Kudne

Bnot Yaakov
Bridge

GOLAN
HEIGHTS

112

Hushniya

Safed

Jordan River

Tel Faris

115

Yehudia Road

Arik
Bridge

Gamla Ascent

116

Tel Saki

TAPLINE

Lake
Kinneret

Ramat
Magshimim

El Al

Tiberias

En Gev

JORDAN

Area captured
by Syria on
first day of war

Engineering units were given three hours to bridge or fill in the tank ditch and clear the minefields. Infantry would then move through to capture the Israeli frontline strongpoints and the *tels*—dormant volcanic cones—which served as observation points behind the Israeli front line. The tank formations would follow and overwhelm the Israeli armor within three to four hours.

A key element in the Syrian plan was the landing of commandos by helicopter at the Jordan River bridges ten hours after zero hour. They would block, or at least delay, the reserve armored divisions that would try to reach the heights. By dawn, less than sixteen hours after zero hour, the entire Golan would be in Syrian hands and the major approaches across the Jordan would be cut. There were no operational plans for continuing on into Israel itself, but the option of continuing on to the Arab city of Nazareth was left open.

If all went well, the conquest of the Golan would be achieved without even calling on the most powerful element in the Syrian army, its two armored divisions. These would remain to the rear, blocking Israel's way to Damascus in case something went wrong. The divisions—the Third in the northern sector and the First in the southern—would support the attack if it stalled and would anchor the defenses against the anticipated Israeli counterattack after the heights were captured. The Israeli counterattack would be of limited strength, Damascus believed, because the bulk of Israel's reserves and the bulk of its air force would be occupied on the Egyptian front.

The Israeli military hierarchy was divided as to where the main Syrian thrust would come. AMAN believed it would be in the southern Golan where the terrain was relatively flat. Northern Command believed it would come in the northern sector near the abandoned town of Kuneitra. The terrain here was more difficult but a breakthrough would swiftly bring the Syrian forces to Nafakh, the main Israeli base on the Golan, and to the Bnot Yaacov Bridge over the Jordan, the main gateway between the Golan and Israel proper.

A valley winding through the hills just north of Kuneitra—the Kuneitra Gap—was considered by Northern Command the most likely avenue for a Syrian thrust. General Hofi had in the summer ordered tank ramps built on the hills overlooking the valley. The ramps permitted defending tanks to fire with only their turret and gun exposed, giving them a substantial advantage over fully exposed tanks in the valley. Tank ramps already existed near the infantry strongpoints on the front line. Kuneitra itself, which had been the district capital of the Golan before its capture by Israel in 1967, was a ghost town except for a limited Israeli military presence on its periphery.

The Israeli line was held by two tank battalions, totaling 77 tanks, from the 188th Brigade commanded by Col. Yitzhak Ben-Shoham, an amiable Turkish-born officer who had taken command only two months before. His two battalion commanders on the front were Lieutenant Colonel Nafshi, whose unit manned the northern half of the line, and Lt. Col. Oded Erez, who had recently taken over the southern battalion. Nafshi's unit had won the armored corps proficiency citation and had hosted the corps' Passover seder.

As with the Bar-Lev forts, the main purpose of the frontline infantry outposts, each garrisoned by twelve to twenty men, was observation, artillery spotting, and warding off minor probes. The northern outposts were manned by the Golani Brigade, and the southern by men from the Fiftieth Paratroop Battalion. In the event of a Syrian ground attack, it would be upon the tanks that the main burden of defense would fall. The arrival of the Seventh Brigade, dispatched piecemeal to the Golan following Dayan's intervention on Rosh Hashana eve, more than doubled Israeli armor strength on the Golan. The last of the brigade's 105 tanks arrived on Yom Kippur morning and joined the others in holding areas in the northern part of the heights.

Unlike in Sinai, where an intercepted message from a UN outpost had alerted the Israeli forces to an impending Egyptian artillery strike, the opening barrage on the Golan came without warning. Lt. Oded Beckman, a platoon commander in Oded Erez's battalion, was trying to persuade a crew member to break his fast when the barrage hit with a deafening roar. He could see the ground rippling as the Syrian guns methodically worked their way across preplanned target areas. His tanks managed to scramble out of the way just in time.

Smoke blanketed every crossroad, military camp, strongpoint, command center, tank park, and communications facility on the heights. The battalion commanders from the Seventh Brigade were just arriving at Nafakh for their scheduled 2 P.M. meeting with Colonel Ben-Gal when four MiGs dropped bombs. "Everyone to your tanks," the brigade commander shouted. A sentry already lay dead at the gateway.

As he moved off in his half-track, Ben-Gal was contacted by Ben-Shoham and told to move two of his battalions to the nearby Wasset junction and await further orders. General Hofi, before flying to Tel Aviv at noon for his second meeting of the day with Elazar, had given Ben-Shoham temporary command of the Golan. Unaware of this, Ben-Gal balked at receiving orders from someone equivalent to him in rank and position and decided to return to Nafakh to straighten out the chain of command. Entering the underground command bunker, he found that so many men had crowded in to shelter from the shelling that he could not push through to Ben-Shoham at the far end. Spotting the Northern Command operations officer, Lt. Col. Uri Simhoni, Ben-Gal shouted above the noise, "I'm moving the brigade towards Kuneitra," and hurried out to his half-track.

Although Simhoni was of lower rank than the two brigade commanders, who were full colonels, he was the channel through which orders were normally passed from General Hofi. Ben-Gal did not hesitate to accept orders from Simhoni, who did not mention their source. In a curious command transformation, the source quickly became Simhoni himself.

The surprise attack had created a command vacuum. Not only was Hofi absent from the Golan; so were his deputy, his chief of staff, and his division commanders. Ben-Shoham had nominal command, but apart from the problem of giving orders to Ben-Gal, he had his hands full commanding his own brigade now that the battle had begun. He sat with earphones in front of radio sets communicating with his two battalion commanders, who were engaging Syrian forces all along the line. As Simhoni saw it, this left the reins in his own hands. It was a responsibility he embraced. He chose not to seek instructions from his superiors by radio. He knew more about the swiftly changing situation than they, and he felt more competent in the circumstances than they to exercise command. Thus it was that a lieutenant colonel effectively took upon himself the role of a major general commanding the most sensitive front in the critical opening hours of Israel's most difficult war.

Simhoni's first order would be one of the most important issued in the war. Military analysts would still be debating years later whether it was the right one. Barely half an hour after the opening barrage, he directed Ben-Gal to send one of his three tank battalions to the southern Golan and to deploy the other two battalions north of Kuneitra. These forces would back up the two tank battalions from Ben-Shoham's brigade which were holding the line—Yair Nafshi's in the north and Oded Erez's in the south. Ben-Gal's earlier decision to head for Kuneitra on his own had no legitimacy and could readily have been revoked. It was Simhoni's order, delivered under the mantle of Northern Command, that committed the bulk of Israel's reserves on the Golan Heights to the northern sector.

His decision was based in part on information coming in from the front. The southern sector reported that it was keeping the Syrians at bay. Reports from the northern sector were more alarming because observers there had a better view of the approaching Syrian masses from high ground, including Mount Hermon. But the major factor influencing Simhoni was past war games by Northern Command which had concluded that the Syrian main effort would be in the Kuneitra area.

The battalion taken from Ben-Gal to reinforce the southern sector was commanded by Maj. Haim Barak. Simhoni briefly considered keeping back one of Ben-Gal's two remaining tank battalions as a reserve in case the situation in the southern sector deteriorated, but decided against it. His decision to deploy three tank battalions in the northern sector and two in the southern, with nothing held in reserve, dictated the course of the coming battle, for better or worse. By committing all his reserves in the opening hour, before the battle had truly been joined, he was violating one of the basic principles of warfare. He feared that failure to commit all available forces might lead to a Syrian breakthrough; and of the two sectors, he viewed the northern as more critical.

In a curious dichotomy, half the Israeli forces on the Golan were braced for war and the other half only for a battle day. Ben-Gal had told his battalion commanders that war would break out this day on two fronts. He had so been briefed by division commander Eitan, who heard it from Hofi. The deployment of Ben-Gal's forces would reflect this assessment. His units operated at no less than company strength, the better to deal with large-scale incursions. But Ben-Shoham, in passing on Hofi's alert, had not mentioned war. "Something's going to happen today," he told his officers. The brigade's tanks were thus dispersed thinly for a battle day, which usually involved static exchanges of fire across the front line. Ben-Shoham believed that "war" was an imprecise designation for what could be expected. Indeed, Hofi himself did not anticipate an attempt to drive Israel from the Golan even though he had dutifully passed on the war alert.

Ben-Gal's tanks were positioned two miles behind the front line, overlooking it from high ground. One battalion was deployed at the southern end of the sector, near Kuneitra, and the other at the northern end, just beneath the slopes of Mount Hermon. Between the two, on a ridge called Hermonit, Ben-Gal created a new force with tanks taken from the other battalions. Thus he once again had three tank formations to maneuver even after Haim Barak's battalion had been sent south.

Nafshi was near Kuneitra when the Syrian barrage struck. Even inside his tank, he could feel the ground trembling. "This is 10," he said on the battalion radio net, giving his identity number. "Capital. Repeat, Capital. Good luck." Capital was the code word for the battle day they had been awaiting. As his units headed for their predetermined positions, Nafshi drove to Booster Ridge near the southern edge of the sector. His tank ran over the mess kits of tankers who had been breaking their fast when the shells hit. Syrian planes returning from bombing runs roared low overhead. One flew so close that Nafshi could see the pilot grinning.

Ben-Gal drove along the front in his half-track to see if the Syrians were attacking, but dust and smoke reduced visibility to virtually zero. Near Kuneitra he ordered his driver to stop. From across the line he detected a distant clanking and the sound of engines. Abruptly, the shelling ceased, and from the settling dust cloud emerged a mass of Syrian tanks.

In Nafshi's tank, his operations officer had taken out a notebook to record reports from the unit's tanks of hits on enemy tanks and positions. This was the routine record-keeping of a battle day. However, what Nafshi was looking at as the dust settled was like no battle day he had ever seen. All along the broad front, hundreds of Syrian tanks and APCs were advancing. Leading them were bridging tanks capable of throwing a span across the tank ditch. At his order, his tanks opened up on the bridging tanks at long range, as much as 3,500 yards.

At Strongpoint 107, two miles north of Kuneitra, Lt. Elimelekh could not see through the smoke and dust. His men had taken shelter in a bunker, as called for, but Elimelekh and his radioman remained outside, in a sheltered observation position. The Golani officer asked his battalion headquarters, atop a hill to his rear, whether the Syrians were moving. But artillery was hitting the hill as well, obscuring the view. However, Lt. Shmuel Yakhin, commander of the tank platoon moving forward to 107, reported to Elimelekh that Syrian vehicles were advancing towards him.

When the bombardment ceased, Elimelekh could see through binoculars a mass of tanks and trucks coming down the Damascus road. Infantrymen aboard the trucks held their rifles in the air and pumped them up and down in exultation. Yakhin's three tanks took positions on two firing ramps several hundred yards on either side of the strongpoint and opened fire at a range of 2,000 yards. The tank gunners methodically worked their way down the line of Syrian vehicles. After the first ranging shots, the second shots almost always hit. Elimelekh pinpointed for Yakhin enemy tanks the tank officer couldn't see from his position because of folds in the ground.

At one point, Yakhin pulled back to load shells from the belly of his tank into the turret. The loader was outside the tank when Yakhin looked up to see a column of enemy tanks 400 yards away, the lead tank pointing its gun at him. He lowered his head to await the blow. However, the loader managed to scramble back into the tank and get a shell into the breech. Yakhin's gunner fired, holing the Syrian tank before it got off a shot. The swift reaction time of Israeli crews compared to that of Syrian crews would prove a major factor offsetting the disparity of forces, the Israelis getting off two or more rounds in the time it took for the Syrians to fire once.

Seven other tanks under company commander Zvi Rak took positions alongside Yakhin's platoon, adding to the burning tanks along the Damascus Road. To the Israelis' astonishment, Syrian tanks kept coming, swerving around those which had been hit. It was not until some thirty tanks were knocked out that the column turned south out of range.

When Strongpoint 109, a mile south of Kuneitra, reported Syrian tanks approaching, Major Rak dispatched his deputy, Capt. Oded Yisraeli, with three tanks. Following a narrow track along the border, Yisraeli came upon a company of Syrian tanks crossing the tank ditch on two spans laid by bridging tanks. Yisraeli's tanks had caught the Syrians on their flank and within minutes destroyed them all. A mile further on, he saw a second company crossing. These tanks were accompanied by a bulldozer which had filled in the tank ditch in their sector. Alerted by the fight with their sister company, the Syrian tanks were waiting for Yisraeli. He called on Rak to send him reinforcements. "It's like a movie out here," he said.

Leaving Yakhin's three tanks at 107, the company commander started south with his remaining four tanks in Yisraeli's wake. As they skirted the border, Rak heard an explosion and found himself covered with blood. It was a moment before he realized the blood was not his. His loader had been standing with his head out of the loader's hatch when an RPG decapitated him. While the other three tanks continued on to join in the fight, Rak returned to Kuneitra to extricate the body and change tanks. His gunner and driver became hysterical at the sight of their comrade's body. Rak slapped them and threw water on them and they calmed down.

Yisraeli's force, meanwhile, had destroyed the second Syrian company; an Israeli officer was killed in the fight. As Yisraeli continued on, he hit two more tanks coming up a small wadi from the border. These were the spearhead of a third company. The Syrian tanks had crossed in dead ground not visible from the Israeli strongpoints and were attempting to filter up wadis running between a series of low hillocks.

Taking position near 109, one of Rak's platoon leaders, Lt. David Eiland, noticed antennas behind trees alongside the border. He took his tank down the nearest wadi. Fifty yards to his front was a Syrian tank with its gun pointing in his direction. Just behind it was a second, and a hundred yards beyond, a third, facing in the other direction. Eiland's gunner hit all three. In the distance, other tanks could be seen pulling back, the remnants of the Syrian battalion that Yisraeli and his handful of tanks had virtually destroyed.

————

As with the Egyptians, the Syrian strategy was to stretch the limited Israeli defenses by attacking on as broad a front as possible and exploiting weak points. The Ninth Division in the center of the Syrian line sent forces against Kuneitra in the northern sector and also attacked in the south. When the latter proved more porous, the division shifted its weight there, further tilting the balance against Ben-Shohan's undermanned sector.

Maj. Shmuel Askarov, the deputy commander of Oded Erez's battalion, holding the southern part of the line, was the officer who had predicted war to Dayan and Zeira during their visit to the Golan ten days before. At twenty-four, he was the youngest deputy battalion commander in the IDF. Awaiting the Syrian attack, he had driven at noon to battalion headquarters at Hushniya and left his tank parked a few feet from his office door, like a favorite sports car.

A few minutes before 2 P.M., the Yom Kippur stillness gave way to the roar of aircraft and explosions. As MiGs pulled away, artillery shells tore into the base. Askarov and his crew mounted their tank and, with half a dozen others, headed through the barrage to join the tank platoon posted at Strongpoint 111 opposite the Syrian fortifications at Kudne.

Moving onto one of the tank ramps, Askarov could at first see nothing because of the smoke. As the Syrians lifted their barrage, a mass of tanks loomed into view. Five bridging tanks were the first to reach the Israeli ditch. Askarov managed to hit the three within range.

He noticed for the first time that the tanks he had come with had not mounted the ramp. He called on their commanders by radio to move up but got no clear response. Askarov told his driver to reverse down the slope. They braked alongside the nearest tank and Askarov climbed aboard. Pulling out his pistol, he pointed it at the commander's head. "Get up there or I shoot," he said.

Within a minute, all the tanks were on the ramps firing. Given the number of tanks and APCs passing under the Israeli tank guns, it was like shooting fish in a barrel. Except that some of the fish were shooting back. For the most part, the Syrians simply swerved around crippled tanks and pressed on, ignoring the Israeli fire. Some, however, detached themselves to engage the tanks on the ramps.

Askarov could not help admiring the Syrians' determination. They kept pushing forward, as if indifferent to their losses. One after another, the tanks on the ramps alongside him were hit and most of their commanders killed.

Askarov's tank was hit four times but remained operational. He moved from ramp to ramp in order to throw up dust and create the impression of a large force. He had no illusions about surviving the day intact.

Askarov's gunner, Yitzhak Hemo, from the outlying town of Kiryat Shmona, was regarded as the finest tank sniper in the brigade. Askarov would pick the target and turn the turret, roughly aligning the gun. Hemo did the rest. Within two hours, Askarov would claim thirty-five tank kills, in addition to APCs.

At 4 P.M., Hemo hit a tank fifty yards away which had come up from the Kudne track to the left of the ramp. Looking to the right, Askarov saw another tank thirty yards away. He swung the turret and shouted to Hemo, who fired the same instant as did the Syrian gunner. Askarov was blown out of the turret by the Syrian shell. Retrieved by men from the strongpoint, he was carried into a bunker. A few tanks remained on the ramp but the Syrians passed out of range to the south. With darkness, they would pour through unhindered into the southern Golan.

As the tanks of Capt. Uzi Arieli's company sped from Hushniya at 2 P.M. towards their preassigned positions on the front line, Lieutenant Beckman found himself unable to control the shaking of his limbs, even though his mind functioned clearly. The tanks were to support a platoon at Juhader, where the 1,200-mile-long Tapline oil pipeline entered Israeli-held territory. The pipeline stretched from Saudi Arabia to Lebanon, cutting diagonally across the Golan Heights. The tank platoon at Juhader had been pushed back from the firing ramps by the time Arieli's tanks arrived. Pressure was unrelenting. Beckman saw a Syrian column led by a bridging tank approaching the tank ditch. He let the bridge be laid and then hit the first tank to mount it when it was halfway across. When a second tank came onto the bridge in order to push the first across, he hit that too, thus effectively blocking passage. A second bridging tank approached and Beckman hit this one before it reached the ditch.

Towards dusk, he was dispatched by Arieli to Strongpoint 115, where a high ramp offered a good view along the front. Beckman approached the lip of the ramp on foot. Below were four stationary Syrian tanks and two APCs with mounted Saggers waiting to cross the cease-fire line. Lying down, the platoon commander beckoned his gunner forward and showed him their prey. Beckman said they would undertake rapid fire, with the loader assembling shells for quick insertion and the gunner shifting swiftly from target to target. Beckman's tank moved forward and in less than half a minute the six Syrian vehicles were burning. The last in line managed to get off a Sagger that missed, leaving Beckman covered with a length of its guide wire.

Second Lt. Yossi Gur, commanding Strongpoint 116 at the southern end of the line, had arrived only the day before to fill in for the regular commander, who had gone home for the holiday. He found the strongpoint insufficiently prepared for serious fighting. There was little small-arms ammunition and only five bazooka shells. The fort had been built 200 yards on the Syrian side of the cease-fire line because of the site's elevation. The Syrians had swallowed this intrusion, but it meant that the fort lay forward of the tank ditch. There was thus no barrier separating the strongpoint and its fourteen defenders from the Syrian army except for mines and barbed wire surrounding the position itself.

The opening Syrian barrage hit the position dead center. Gur ordered the men to the bunkers while he kept watch from a "rabbit hole." The view through the periscope was limited and he periodically ducked out into a trench to scan the surrounding terrain. On one such foray in the late afternoon, he saw two long columns of Syrian tanks approaching the tank ditch 400 yards away. Bridging tanks were already laying spans. He reported his sighting to Lt. Yoav Yakir, who commanded the three tanks assigned to the defense of 116.

Yakir was several miles away. With the opening barrage, he had led his platoon south to stop twenty-five Syrian tanks crossing the cease-fire line along an old Roman roadway that had once led to Damascus. The accuracy of the platoon's fire reflected the fact that the gunners in both Yakir's tank and that of his first sergeant, Nir Atir, had won a number of battalion gunnery contests. Firing from the ramps overlooking the ancient roadway, they hit the bulk of the Syrian tanks during a two-hour exchange.

With Gur's report, Yakir led his tanks back towards 116. Dozens of Syrian APCs and tanks were already on the Israeli side of the ditch. Yakir's platoon fired from open terrain at distances ranging from 200 to 1,000 yards, sometimes not stopping to aim. Two tanks from a neighboring platoon joined them but both were soon knocked out. When darkness fell, Yakir asked Gur to fire flares from a mortar. In their light, the platoon continued to score hits.

At 9 P.M., Yakir informed Gur that he was out of ammunition and would have to pull back to rearm. Two of the tanks had fired all the shells they had—seventy-two each—and only five shells remained to the third tank. The two lieutenants, both aged twenty, realized that withdrawal of the tanks put the outpost's survival in serious question. Yakir's platoon had hit dozens of tanks and APCs but the Syrians were still pouring across. When he requested permission from his company commander to pull back, the reply was negative. So desperate was the hour that Yakir was told to use his machine guns against the Syrian tanks in the hope that this sign of an Israeli presence, however pathetic, would give the enemy pause before advancing.

Shortly afterwards, Yakir was killed by machine-gun fire. Sergeant Atir, assuming command of the platoon, ordered Yakir's gunner to tie the fallen officer to the gunner's chair and to take command of the tank. At this point, brigade commander Ben-Shoham cut into the radio net to talk directly to Atir. He ordered the sergeant to fall back for ammunition. Strongpoint 116 would have to hold out on its own.

The Syrians, although pressing home a bold plan, were beginning to display telling deficiencies in tactics, training, and command. Time and again, the Israeli tanks would whittle down the odds by engaging larger formations and shooting faster, straighter, and at longer range. The professionalism of the Israeli tank crews—their tactics, gunnery, and coolness in action—was compensating in good measure for the failures of the Israeli political and military command that had exposed them to the surprise Arab assault. But they could not compensate entirely.

Haim Barak's battalion, sent south by Ben-Gal, theoretically doubled Israeli strength in the southern Golan. In fact, however, the battalion would go largely to waste this night. Even as Erez's battalion was fighting a desperate war of survival nearby, Barak's saw limited action.

Erez's thirty-six tanks could not hold a twenty-mile-wide front when the Syrians were attacking in strength along its entire length. Instead of splitting the southern sector between the two battalions, Ben-Shoham kept Barak's tanks in reserve, to be fed into the battle as needed. The piecemeal way this was done would prove highly inefficient. Barak, whose Seventh Brigade tanks had arrived on the Golan only this morning, had no idea of what was happening on the front line, a mile or so away, and he was receiving orders directly from both Simhoni at Northern Command and Ben-Shoham. Erez, for his part, did not even know there was another tank battalion in his sector.

Barak's battalion was an odd mix. Two of its companies were only halfway through their basic four-month armor training course. The third, commanded by Capt. Eli Geva, was a veteran unit considered one of the best companies in the armored corps. One of the trainee companies ended

up at Strongpoint 111, but only after the Syrians had completed their penetration there. The other was dispatched to Strongpoint 116 and was
ambushed along the way, losing most of its tanks. The one effective battle
waged by the battalion this day was when Geva's company, moving at dusk
along the main north–south road half a mile from the Purple Line, was fired
on by tanks that had infiltrated. Geva's tanks quickly deployed and engaged
the Syrians. Air photos the next day would show that Geva's gunners
destroyed some thirty tanks while losing only one.

To observers on the Israeli-held spur of Mount Hermon, 6,600 feet above
sea level, the battle on the Golan was grand opera viewed from the upper
balcony. Although there were Syrian troops higher up the crest—the Syrian
Hermon, as it was known—the Israeli position seemed detached both from
them and from whatever was happening on the plateau below.

The Hermon spur had been occupied as an afterthought in the Six Day
War when it was realized that it made a superb intelligence platform and
early warning station. A large outpost was built atop the mountain, much of
it underground. Its electronic equipment monitored Syrian activity along the
front line and as far as the Syrian capital forty miles to the east.

There were fifty-five men in the Hermon outpost on Yom Kippur. The
bulk were army and air force intelligence personnel and technicians. The
outpost was in the final stages of extensive reconstruction, and the defensive
positions around it had been temporarily stripped away. The security detail
consisted only of a dozen infantrymen from the Golani Brigade, three of
whom were detached to man an observation post a mile away. The fact that
such a valuable installation would be without defense positions, even temporarily, and its security left to a single squad of soldiers reflected a belief
that the Syrians, so easily routed in the Six Day War, could not muster the
will or capacity to attack it.

The Syrians had in fact placed the Israeli Hermon at the top of their target list. Lt. Ahmed Rifai al-Joju, a company commander in the Eighty-
second Paratroop Battalion, the elite combat unit of the Syrian army, was
given a final briefing on his mission Saturday morning. He and his men
would be landed by helicopters half a mile from the Israeli structure and
would take positions covering the outpost and the single road leading up to it
from the Golan. The rest of the battalion, some two hundred men, would set
out on foot from the Syrian Hermon. This force would attack the outpost,
with al-Joju's men providing covering fire.

Four Syrian helicopters lifted off at 2 P.M. and headed towards the Israeli position. One of the craft crashed when its rotor struck a slope, but the others delivered their troops safely, the men leaping down from the craft hovering just above the ground. Artillery fire was placed on the Israeli outpost to keep the defenders' heads down. By 2:45 P.M., the attack force from the Syrian Hermon reached the outpost. In the absence of trenches or firing positions, the Golani soldiers could only fire from the narrow entranceways to the structure. After an exchange of fire lasting forty-five minutes, the surviving defenders pulled back into the building and slammed shut the metal door. By 5 P.M. the attackers, dropping grenades and smoke canisters through air ducts, had forced their way in.

Eleven men managed to escape, but thirteen were killed and thirty-one would be taken prisoner, four of them after hiding in a basement for seven days. Soviet experts who arrived to dismantle the electronic equipment were exultant to discover most of it intact. For the Syrians, the information elicited from Israeli intelligence personnel in interrogation would prove an even greater windfall.

The fall of the Hermon was for Israel the single most humiliating episode of the Yom Kippur War. From the Golani Brigade to the General Staff, a grim determination took shape to regain it at any price.

General Hofi returned to Nafakh from General Staff headquarters at 4:30 P.M., bringing with him as air force liaison Gen. Motti Hod (res.), who had commanded the air force until a few months before. Hofi did not take exception to Simhoni's earlier decision to commit all the reserves, and to send most of them to the northern sector. He divided the front into two separate commands. The Seventh Brigade was given responsibility for the northern half of the line, taking Nafshi's battalion under its command. Ben-Shoham's brigade would be left with responsibility only for the southern sector. This force was now made up of Oded Erez's battalion and Haim Barak's, transferred from the Seventh Brigade.

By late afternoon, the Syrian offensive appeared to have ebbed and Israeli commanders were reporting that they were in control all along the front. This soothing assessment would not last long.

Just before darkness, the Syrians threw two brigades against the northern sector and four against the southern. Erez's battalion had lost twelve tanks during the afternoon's fighting—a third of its strength. Two of his three company commanders were dead and his deputy, Major Askarov, wounded.

As dusk descended and the Syrians began to press their attack more vigorously, Erez called futilely for air and artillery support. The situation in the northern sector, by contrast, was under control. Nafshi's battalion had lost seven of its thirty-three tanks but had blocked Syrian penetration. Ben-Gal's brigade to the rear had yet to be hit.

At Strongpoint 109 just before darkness, Major Rak asked his officers to join him at his tank during a lull in the shelling. "There's a war going on," said the company commander. It was not a jest or an inanity. Despite the company's destruction of some fifty Syrian tanks and the intensive artillery bombardment they had experienced for the past hours, the general assumption was that this was a battle day—more intensive by far than any they had ever experienced, but a one-day event. What made Rak realize that it was something more were the reports on Israel Radio he had heard now for the first time on a crewman's transistor radio about the battles in Sinai. A two-front war was raging and it was not going to end with nightfall.

Late in the afternoon, Lieutenant Colonel Kahalani led his Centurion battalion through the shell-pocked fields of Kibbutz Ein Zivan near Kuneitra towards Booster Ridge. The drivers, still with a peacetime mindset, attempted to avoid irrigation equipment left by the kibbutz farmers. The Booster, behind Strongpoint 107, was the southernmost of the ridges on which Ben-Gal deployed his units. Kahalani saw clouds of dust being thrown up by Syrian armor far to the east moving down the Damascus–Kuneitra road.

All afternoon, the attackers in the northern sector had been kept at bay by Nafshi's frontline battalion. With darkness, Syrian tanks began to infiltrate between the strongpoints towards Ben-Gal's brigade on the ridges beyond. When they struck, it was in the center of the line—the Hermonit ridge defended by a force commanded by Lt. Col. Yos Eldar. He called for flares but the supply was soon exhausted. In planning for a battle day, which always ended by nightfall, the Israelis had failed to prepare for combat that would continue after dark. The seemingly trivial logistic oversight would prove a major handicap.

Kahalani could make out additional Syrian tanks moving towards Eldar's position. He ordered his men to fire on them but the range was too great.

"Brigade commander," he called to Ben-Gal on the radio, "this is Kahalani. I'm firing at the tanks attacking Yos but I'm afraid it's a waste of ammunition. I suggest that I move up to join him."

Ben-Gal assented but ordered him to leave a small force on Booster. As

Kahalani approached Eldar's position, he heard him addressing Ben-Gal on the radio net in a strained voice.

"Brigade commander, this is Yos. Over."

"This is the brigade commander," replied Ben-Gal. "Over."

"I'm wounded. I'm evacuating myself to the rear."

Eldar had been hit over an eye by shrapnel. Kahalani reached Eldar's position and took command. The Syrians had for the first time that day penetrated the sector in some strength. The attack on Eldar's position appeared to have been repulsed, but the Syrians were now hitting the battalion at the northern end of the line, commanded by Lt. Col. Meshulam Rattes. They were also attacking in the vicinity of Kuneitra where Nafshi's tanks were positioned. Kahalani ordered his men to fire two of the few mortar flares available. As these slowly descended he could see no enemy tanks to his front.

"Battalion commander, this is Emi." It was Captain Palant, a company commander who was positioned on Kahalani's northern flank. "About fifteen tanks moving in my direction. I'm waiting for them."

Through infrared binoculars, Kahalani could make out a line of infrared headlights in the distance, still inside Syrian territory. When he looked in the same direction with his naked eye, he could see nothing.

Some of the Israeli tank commanders had similar binoculars, but the tanks themselves were not equipped for night fighting. The Syrian drivers could navigate with infrared headlights illuminating the road and infrared projectors could light up targets for the gunners without the Israelis even being aware that they were being illuminated. No special importance had been given by the Israeli military to the infrared equipment in Arab hands since it was assumed that they would not initiate night fighting. The Arabs were now doing a lot of things the Israelis had not expected.

The moon had risen higher and was offering a misty light. Bushes moving in the wind downslope and the ruins of an abandoned village took on menacing aspects. At one point, Kahalani thought he could make out a pair of infrared lights moving in his direction and ordered his gunner to fire. But it proved another night mirage. As he raised his infrared binoculars to check on the Syrian tanks to the north, he saw his own tank as if in daylight. When he lowered the binoculars he could see nothing, but when he put them back to his eyes, there it was again. He raised the binoculars higher and, with a chill, found himself staring straight into an infrared projector a few dozen yards away.

"Driver, back up," he shouted. "Quickly." The tank shot backwards down the slope, not stopping until it reached bottom.

Kahalani took it back up the ridge to a different position. As he scanned the other tanks on the line, he saw that one had its rear lights on. By radio, he ordered officers to make sure their tanks had their lights out. All reported back to confirm. But Kahalani could still see the taillights. He ordered engines cut, but the lights of the single tank stayed on and he could hear its engines working.

It was mad to think that an enemy tank had deployed among them. It was possible that a tank from a neighboring unit, not on their radio frequency, had blundered in. But Israeli tanks did not have infrared projectors. If it was a Syrian tank, its commander must realize by now, after having studied Kahalani's tank, that he had wandered into an Israeli position. But the intruder had taken his place in line, his gun facing towards the Syrian lines. Kahalani told an officer near the intruder to have one of his tanks prepare to flash a projector on it. If it was Syrian, said Kahalani, his own tank would fire. He ordered his gunner, Sgt. David Kilion, to be prepared. The commander of the tank with the projector reported himself ready.

"Light," said Kahalani.

The white shaft that broke the darkness illuminated a Syrian T-55 fifty yards away.

"Fire," barked Kahalani.

The Syrian tank burst into flames.

"Battalion commander, a suspicious tank in my area," called an officer on the right flank.

"Confirm that it's an enemy tank before firing," replied Kahalani.

In the light of the burning tank, Kahalani made out another Syrian tank backing away into the darkness. He ordered Kilion to fire, but another tank hit it first.

Kahalani ordered his men to keep their motors off in order to be able to hear the sound of approaching tanks. Captain Palant said the enemy column had reached the tank ditch to his front. Scanning his map inside the turret, Kahalani told his artillery officer to call down fire on the crossing point.

Things quieted down after midnight and Kahalani permitted the men to take turns sleeping.

Despite the ferocity of the Syrian attack, and despite having passed on the warning of war, Hofi still saw it in terms of a limited territorial grab. His objective remained the one Elazar had outlined before the war—to deny the enemy any territorial gain. This meant spreading his forces so as to prevent any incursion. At 9 P.M. Hofi was still telling his commanders that "we must make an effort to block every attack, even the smallest." The cherished principle of armor—concentration of force—was being ignored here, as it had been in Sinai, in order to cling to territory.

In the command bunker at Nafakh, the chief intelligence officer of General Eitan's division, Lt. Col. Dennie Agmon, was becoming increasingly convinced that this was more than a limited attack. Listening to Simhoni directing the frontline commanders on the radio, it sounded to Agmon as if the Syrian attack was not slackening. Opposite him at a long table sat General Hofi. Agmon permitted himself to make an operational suggestion directly to the front commander. The Syrians, he said, might be attempting to recapture the entire heights, not just a settlement or strongpoint. If so, they would try to seize the Bnot Yaacov Bridge. Hofi doubted that but he ordered that an engineering unit near the bridge be alerted to deal with the possibility.

At the far end of the table, General Eitan had been standing for hours, his back against the wall and one foot propped up on a chair, saying little. From a farming village in northern Israel, Eitan was an earthy, taciturn paratrooper who had a colorful turn of phrase when he did speak. One hand was wrapped in a bandage. He had a few days before lost the tips of two fingers to an electric saw in his workshop at home. As long as Hofi and his senior officers remained in Nafakh directly running the war, division commander Eitan was outside the loop. But he did order Colonel Ben-Shoham to join his brigade in the field. Ben-Shoham still considered this to be a battle day, run from the command bunker, not a full-scale war. Eitan believed otherwise.

Ben-Shoham left Nafakh at 6:30 P.M., heading south on the Tapline road in an APC serving as a mobile command post. It passed a mile from Hushniya without incident but was halted shortly afterwards by heavy artillery fire. Pulling back to a sheltered wadi, Ben-Shoham asked that his tank be sent to him from Hushniya. When it arrived, the driver reported passing many tanks in the darkness. It was a puzzling remark since Ben-Shoham knew that all his tanks were deployed four miles to the east along the Purple Line. The Syrians had learned from observation on battle days where the Israeli tanks would be deployed and were now infiltrating those positions.

For hours after nightfall, reports of Syrian penetration in the southern sector were dismissed at Northern Command because the tank forces on the line were reporting that the Syrians had not gotten past them. But the Syrians were infiltrating massively between the strong points. A shortage of flares and night-sight devices meant that the Israeli forces were blind to what was going on beyond their immediate front. When a radio monitor heard a Syrian brigade commander reporting that he was in Hushniya, Ben-Shoham was asked by Northern Command if that could be true. Having passed near Hushniya himself not long before, Ben-Shoham said the Syrian commander must be confused.

However, Maj. Yoram Yair, commanding the paratroop force manning the southern strongpoints, was getting reports from his men that said otherwise. A five-man paratroop observation team atop Tel Saki, just behind the line near Strongpoint 116, reported Syrian tanks on the Israeli side of the line heading south towards the settlement of Ramat Magshimim. Yair learned from Strongpoint 111 that Syrian tanks had penetrated the line there. Another report spoke of a penetration between 115 and 116. When the paratroop officer passed on these reports to Ben-Shoham, the brigade commander was dismissive. "You don't know what you're talking about," Yair would remember him saying. When Major Barak had earlier informed Ben-Shoham that his men heard Syrian tank engines from the area of Hushniya, the brigade commander said that it was probably the tank he had summoned from the Hushniya camp.

The collapse of the southern sector stemmed in part from the relatively flat topography, which made it easier to penetrate, and in part because there were fewer Israeli tanks defending there and far more Syrian tanks than in the northern sector. But disjointed command also played a key role. In the north, Ben-Gal was positioned just behind the front. Ben-Shoham, by contrast, conducted the battle in the critical opening hours of the war from the bunker at Nafakh. It was initially the logical place to be since he had overall command on the Golan while Hofi was in Tel Aviv. But when Hofi returned at 4:30, Ben-Shoham remained in Nafakh for another two hours. Prevented later from reaching the front by artillery fire, he maintained radio contact with his units from his isolated APC off the Tapline but was unable to properly read the flow of the battle from there. In dismissing reports of massive Syrian penetration, Ben-Shoham failed to grasp the major development in his sector. And despite the dire situation, Barak's battalion—half the brigade's force—was underutilized.

The first undeniable confirmation of Syrian penetration came from the commander of a supply convoy dispatched down the Tapline road with ammunition and fuel. When the convoy came abreast of Ben-Shoham's personnel carrier, its commander alighted from his jeep to speak to him. Ben-Shoham said it was too dangerous to take the trucks forward because of the shelling. Only tanks could navigate the area safely. Raising Erez on the radio, Ben-Shoham asked him to send his tanks back one at a time to rearm and refuel at the convoy's present location. Erez said he could not release even a single tank without risking a Syrian breakthrough.

As they talked, two tanks approached Ben-Shoham from the south and stopped twenty yards away. The brigade commander asked Erez if in fact some tanks had not pulled back. Erez, sounding surprised, said he would check. A few moments later, he said no tanks had been sent to the rear. Ben-Shoham concluded that the crews had fled the front. He asked the convoy commander to walk over and order the tank commanders to get their carcasses back to the line. The officer approached the tanks and began shouting at the nearest commander whose outline he could make out in the turret. The figure dropped into the tank without a word, pulling the hatch closed, and the tanks roared off. As they did, the officer distinguished the silhouettes of Syrian T-55s.

Ben-Shoham ordered the supply convoy to return immediately to Nafakh. A few minutes after setting off, the convoy commander radioed that he had just passed the intersection with the Hushniya road and found himself driving through a mass of Syrian tanks. "I don't know how I got through," he said.

Hofi ordered Ben-Gal, whose sector was relatively calm at the moment, to send another battalion to Erez's aid. The Seventh Brigade commander dispatched a battalion but recalled it before it got far. He told Hofi that his brigade was coming under attack and that he could now spare no one. Hofi did not argue the point. Ben-Gal's sector was not in fact under heavy attack, but the brigade commander had lost confidence that his superiors were in control of the battle and was determined to keep his force intact. "If I don't look after myself," he would explain later, "who will?" Ben-Gal had already displayed an unwillingness to part with assets, regardless of orders. In transferring his brigade to the Golan he had disregarded instructions to leave behind in Sinai the company commanded by Eli Geva. The unit had been trained in towing a bridge to the Suez Canal, a task more complex than it might seem and critical if war came. Ben-Gal believed that a fight with Syria was likely but did not think war with Egypt was in the offing. In bringing Geva north, in defiance of orders, he left behind a serious operational vacuum on the Egyptian front. He was now leaving the defender of the Golan's southern sector to make do with what they had.

For Lieutenant Gur in Strongpoint 116, that meant having to hold out without tank support. An hour after Yakir's tank platoon had pulled back, Gur saw the dark shapes of three Syrian tanks approaching down the narrow track linking the fort to the Israeli border road to his rear. The tanks moved slowly, one behind the other, but did not fire, as if the commanders were uncertain whether the position had been captured. Gur had earlier ordered a soldier to place two rows of mines on the surface of the track. A soldier with a bazooka crouched alongside Gur in a trench. As they watched, the lead tank went over the mines but there was no explosion. Powder from the crushed mine spilled into the roadway and Gur realized that the soldier who had placed the mine had failed to arm it. He could see a red light emanating from somewhere inside the tank as it crashed through the gateway ten yards from him and entered the fort's courtyard. The tank commander, who had not opened his hatch, had a limited range of vision and his tank ran into an inclined basalt wall surrounding the fort's mortar position. The tank rose up at a 30 degree angle, as if trying to climb it. Gur told the bazookist to fire. The soldier had difficulty making out the odd silhouette in the darkness. "Fire in the general direction," said Gur. A moment passed and the bazookist shouted, "Misfire." Following the drill for such a situation, Gur told the soldier to take his hand off the firing mechanism. The lieutenant removed the defective shell from the back end of the weapon and inserted a new one. The bazooka fired, striking the tank in the turret. As the Syrian crew leaped out, Gur fired at them, hitting two of the four crewmen.

The second tank had now reached the entrance, and the bazookist, without prompting, set it aflame. This time Gur hit all four of the crewmen as they emerged. The third tank turned and made off as Israeli artillery shells, called down by Gur, struck the area. Fearing that crewmen from the first tank might still be inside the compound, he ordered his men to stay inside their positions. Together with one of his soldiers, he ran through the trenches firing to his front, but encountered no enemy soldiers.

The area outside the strongpoint was alive with Syrians on foot, many of them crewmen from disabled tanks. Gur's fear was that Syrians would infiltrate the strongpoint in the darkness. The operator of the garrison's heavy machine gun—the one weapon with ample ammunition—cut down enemy soldiers in the immediate vicinity. Wounded Syrians cried out on the barbed-wire fence surrounding the strongpoint. One of them near the gate could be heard weeping all night.

About 2 A.M., a large Syrian supply convoy approached the tank ditch and halted. Gur called for artillery but the overtaxed batteries could provide only a few shells. With first light, the convoy crossed over the ditch. As it did so, ten soldiers detached themselves and approached the strongpoint. They appeared to believe that the position had been captured. Gur prayed they would turn away but they kept coming. The garrison opened fire at thirty yards, cutting them down.

As Gur feared, the firing stirred the hornet's nest. APCs disgorged infantrymen; some provided covering fire while others crawled forward. The strongpoint's machine gun raked the vehicles in the convoy and the strongpoint's mortar fired on APCs attempting to approach. With rifle ammunition low, Gur ordered his men to hold fire until the Syrian infantrymen reached the fence.

After a protracted battle, the attackers pulled back. Three of Gur's men were wounded, one of them seriously. But there were no Israeli fatalities. The garrison had won this round.

At Tel Saki, two miles to the south, the paratroop observation team was joined by three tanks from Haim Barak's battalion, survivors of the ambush which had destroyed the rest of their company, and by Sergeant Atir's three tanks, which had fallen back from 116 without ammunition. During the night, the men on the *tel* hit Syrian tanks and APCs below. But most of the Israeli tanks were knocked out by RPGs. Half an hour before dawn, the paratroop commander on Tel Saki, Lt. Menahem Ansbacher, reported to Major Yair that a large Syrian force was preparing to attack. There were now thirty men on the *tel*, mostly crews of disabled tanks.

In a desperate move, Yair dispatched three half-tracks from his command post at the settlement of El Al just before dawn to evacuate the position, despite the Syrian forces besieging it. The vehicles were ambushed as they neared the *tel* and most of their occupants killed. With first light, Syrian tanks and infantry attacked up the slopes. Ammunition exhausted, the defenders fell back towards a bunker near the summit. At 6:30 A.M., Yair received his last message from Ansbacher. "This is Menahem. The Syrians are at the entrance to the bunker. This is the end. Say good-bye to the guys. We won't be seeing each other again."

Although now recognizing the danger in the southern sector, Northern Command was still misreading the battle. A Syrian mechanized brigade had reached the religious settlement of Ramat Magshimim less than an hour after students at a yeshiva there had been evacuated. Unaccountably, the Syrian force halted. Except for the handful of men with Major Yair five miles down the road at El Al, there was nothing to prevent them from driving south another twenty miles into Israel's Jordan Valley. Alternatively, the Syrians could continue ten miles west and descend to the shore of Lake Kinneret, the biblical Sea of Galilee.

These, however, were not the scenarios the Syrians had in mind. Their primary objective was the main Israeli base at Nafakh and the Bnot Yaacov

Bridge. The direct approach through the Kuneitra gap was blocked by Naf-shi and the Seventh Brigade, but the Syrian plan had a built-in alternative—breaking through into the southern Golan and then turning north. The Fifty-first Brigade, with one hundred tanks, was to reach Hushniya and then turn north along the Tapline straight to Nafakh. A parallel thrust would be made by the Forty-third Brigade, which would turn north as soon as it crossed the Purple Line and proceed on the main north–south road, code-named Reshet. Only seven Israeli tanks guarded the Reshet road. There were no tanks at all on the Tapline road.

Enter Zvika Greengold. Waiting to begin a course for tank company commanders, Lieutenant Greengold, twenty-one, was unattached to any unit when the war began. When the sirens sounded, he was at home in Lokhamai Hagetaot (Fighters of the Ghettos), a kibbutz founded by Holo-caust survivors, including his parents. Donning a dress uniform, the only one he had at home, he hitchhiked to Nafakh, which he reached in late after-noon. There were no tanks immediately available, but when three damaged Centurions arrived from Kuneitra, Greengold was told to lead them back to the front as soon as they were repaired.

He oversaw the removal of dead crewmen and helped wash the tanks of blood. At 9 P.M., with two tanks ready, Greengold was ordered to move out and take command of the scattered tanks remaining near Strongpoints 111 and 112. All officers there were casualties, he was told, and a sergeant was in command. On the way, Greengold was to pass through Hushniya. There were unconfirmed reports of a Syrian presence there. Greengold was to destroy any enemy he encountered.

The mission seemed straightforward enough to the lieutenant. He was given the frequency of Ben-Shohan's radio net and was assigned a code name, "Force Zvika." It was a designation that would enter Israeli military lore.

The two tanks set off down the Tapline road. It took a while to adjust to the darkness, but Greengold knew the area well. The Tapline was a service road, not an artery. Until a few years before there had only been a narrow dirt track marking the route of the oil pipeline buried below. After Palestin-ian guerrillas blew a hole in the line in the early 1970s, the American owners of the Tapline built a ten-foot-high chain-link fence on either side of the track at Israel's request, creating a fifteen-yard-wide corridor, and laid a nar-row asphalt patrol road just outside the fence. It was down this patrol road that Greengold proceeded. He kept one tank track on the dirt shoulder to minimize damage to the asphalt, a constraint reflecting the lingering civilities of peacetime. Given the boulders strewn about the area, tanks generally stuck to the roadway, particularly at night, rather than venture cross-country. The Tapline ran arrow-straight between Nafakh and the Hushniya turnoff for fifteen miles, but through a landscape of dips and rises.

Greengold proceeded cautiously, halting every time he topped a rise to examine the landscape. He ordered his gunner to load a shell into the breech and keep the gun off safety. Greengold kept watch to the front and left. The other tank commander, thirty yards behind him, was responsible for the rear and right.

The two tanks had proceeded only three miles when Greengold saw a column of vehicles approaching with headlights on. The jeep in front stopped when its lights illuminated the tanks and an officer ran forward. It was the convoy commander whom Ben-Shoham had sent back to Nafakh. He told Greengold of having just passed among many Syrian tanks at the Hushniya intersection.

Proceeding even more cautiously, Greengold had passed the halfway point to the intersection when he topped a rise and saw a tank speeding towards him.

"Fire," he shouted.

The gunner squeezed the trigger and the approaching tank exploded, barely twenty yards in front of them. Greengold had not had time to identify the tank before firing, relying on the convoy commander's information that any tank to the front was hostile. In the light of the burning vehicle, he saw with relief that it was a T-55. His driver pulled back into the darkness. The vibration from the firing had knocked out the electricity in the tank turret. Greengold switched tanks, telling the other commander to return to Nafakh for repairs.

Beyond the burning Syrian tank, the night was swarming with "cat's eyes"—tiny running lights the Syrians placed on the edges of their tanks. The impression Greengold had was that the Syrian formation was organizing, perhaps refueling, rather than in movement. The tank he had encountered could have been a forward picket. From time to time, the Syrians sent signal rockets skyward. Taking his tank up a low hill, Greengold came upon three Syrian tanks with their lights on. He destroyed them before they could return fire. Half an hour later, he opened fire on a convoy of some thirty tanks and trucks. Their running lights and the signal rockets they periodically sent up provided him with illumination. He could sense that fire was being returned but it was ineffective, as he kept shifting position. In this cat-and-mouse game he had one advantage. Every tank he saw was a target. The Syrians, on the other hand, had difficulty identifying him, even with night sights. Greengold took care to keep his tank on rear slopes, only the gun and turret top projecting over the crest. He plowed back and forth through the chain-link fence as he shifted from position to position. Parts of the fence caught on the tank treads and he was soon dragging a long train of fencing, including fence poles, wherever he turned. He would not be able to remember how many tanks he hit in this skirmishing.

Listening to the radio net during lulls in the fighting, he began for the first time to grasp the enormity of the situation. Tanks in Erez's battalion were reporting that they were almost out of ammunition and fuel. Supplies were not getting through and desperate calls for reinforcement were met by replies that no tanks were available.

Colonel Ben-Shoham made contact with "Force Zvika" and attempted to ascertain its strength. Aware that the Syrians were probably monitoring communications, Greengold evaded a direct answer so as not to reveal that his was the only tank between the Syrian force and Nafakh. Ben-Shoham, believing the Syrians to be a small raiding party, ordered Force Zvika, which he assumed to be of at least company strength, to press forward to the western end of the Hushniya road. Battalion commander Haim Barak was told to position himself at its eastern end. When Force Zvika pushed the Syrian force back, Barak would be waiting for them. Greengold attempted to signal his inability to undertake offensive action by saying, "The situation isn't good." After an hour of solitary skirmishing, Greengold, to his relief, was informed that another force was on its way to join him.

Ten tanks belonging to a "rapid reaction" reserve battalion commanded by Lt. Col. Uzi Mor had begun moving from their base camp at the foot of the Golan at 8 P.M. towards Nafakh. At Hofi's orders, the tanks had not been stripped of their equipment after their last mobilization exercise a few days before and were thus ready to move out as soon as crews were organized. They were directed down the Tapline road, where they linked up with Force Zvika. At 10:30 P.M., little more than twelve hours after mobilization began, Mor's force became the first reservist unit on either front to enter into battle.

It would be a devastating baptism of fire. Greengold briefed Mor on the situation and the battalion commander ordered an immediate advance. Mor's tanks moved in column on the asphalted road. Greengold moved parallel to them on the dirt track between the fences. As the tanks descended the first deep dip in the road, a waiting Syrian force unleashed tank fire and RPGs.

All eight tanks that had begun the descent were hit. Mor was blinded and lost an arm but his men managed to extricate him under fire and carry him back up the hill. Some men who managed to escape their burning tanks, including a badly wounded company commander, were captured by Syrian infantrymen. Greengold's tank was hit too, apparently by friendly fire, but he did not feel it. The gunner, whose clothing was afire, lunged for the turret, and for an absurd and terrifying moment he and Greengold filled the narrow aperture and were unable to move. Greengold finally forced his way back down into the tank as the gunner scrambled out. Something inside the tank exploded, peppering Greengold's face, and his clothes caught fire. He leaped out and rolled on the ground to extinguish the flames. Fearing that the tank was about to explode, he clambered over the fence and found himself lying among boulders alongside his gunner and loader. The driver had been killed.

The three men made their way back up the hill shouting, "We're Israelis, we're Jews, don't shoot." Wounded and dead were being loaded aboard two of the three tanks in Mor's force that had not been hit. Greengold himself climbed onto the deck of the third tank and sat there while he slowly regained touch with himself. The pain from his wounds was now registering but he did not feel incapacitated. He signaled to the commander of the tank to take off his helmet with its earphones so that he could talk to him. "My name is Zvika," he said. "I've been fighting here all night. I know the area. Let me take your tank." The reservist looked at him for a moment and then handed him his helmet, climbing out of the turret to find a place on another tank.

Greengold introduced himself in the darkness to the crew. "I'm Zvika," he said. "What are your names?" When they had told him, he said, "I've been fighting here since the beginning of the night. I'm now your commander."

The two other tanks pulled back with the casualties, leaving Greengold alone once again on the Tapline. He put the tank's radio onto Ben-Shoham's wavelength. "This is Zvika," he said. The brigade commander's sigh of relief was audible. All Ben-Shoham had known was that the relief force had been pummeled. He had not been sure that anyone was left on the Tapline to stop a Syrian drive towards Nafakh. He asked Greengold for a status report. The lieutenant declined once again to go into details beyond reiterating that the situation was not good. This time, however, he added, "We need a general here." The remark was intended to indicate both the scale of the challenge and the paucity of resources to deal with it.

Ben-Shoham got his drift. He told Greengold to assume a secure firing position. "Don't initiate any firing. Shoot only at tanks that try to move up the road towards Nafakh. Wait for reinforcements."

It was now 2 A.M. Greengold pulled back a few hundred yards. It would be another hour before reinforcements arrived. Among the things that

passed through his mind, he would later say, was an awareness that the Holocaust his parents had survived was suddenly relevant again, a sense that he
stood between an enemy and the prospect of his people's annihilation.

At 3 A.M., the commander of a disabled Israeli tank reported a large number
of Syrian tanks moving north past him on Reshet Road. Maj. Meir Zamir,
commander of Tiger Company, posted in the vicinity, was ordered to stop
them. He hastily organized an ambush, deploying his deputy with four tanks
800 yards east of the road and taking up position with his four remaining
tanks 1,200 yards to the north, two on each side of the road. He told a platoon commander near him to be ready to throw on his projector.

They soon heard the sound of tanks. In the moonlight, Zamir could
make out a long column approaching. He waited until the bulk of the column was between him and his deputy. "Light," he commanded. The projector lit up the column and Zamir's tanks opened fire, setting a dozen tanks
and APCs aflame. The projector was shut after the opening salvos and
Zamir's tanks closed to "bayonet range," in tanker parlance, on a battlefield
illuminated now by burning Syrian tanks. The Syrian force was the spearhead of the Forty-third Armored Brigade, numbering 100 tanks and heading
towards Nafakh. Most of the force fled back to Syrian territory but part of it
scattered on the Israeli side. Zamir's reduced company had stopped a major
brigade movement without any losses.

It was not until midnight that Hofi began to grasp the scale of the Syrian
penetration. Three hundred Syrian tanks had broken through in the southern Golan and there were fewer than thirty Israeli tanks left to oppose
them—almost out of ammunition and fuel after ten hours of battle. Substantial reserve forces would not arrive until the afternoon. Hofi expressed
doubts to Elazar that the heights could be held. "Only the air force can stop
them," he said. Disturbed by Hofi's tone, Dayan told Elazar he was flying up
to Northern Command in the morning "to see if we're going to lose the
Golan."

At the forward command bunker in Nafakh, radios crackled with reports
from the embattled units along the front. Hunched over maps, Hofi and his
staff officers issued orders as they tried to read the enemy's moves.

Motti Hod was a relatively detached observer. He had himself directed numerous operations from bunkers when he was commander of the air force but never from one where he could hear artillery shells exploding outside. Just six years before, he had sat in the air force war room in Tel Aviv consuming jugs of water as he orchestrated the strikes that destroyed the Egyptian air force in three hours and determined the outcome of the Six Day War. What alarmed him now more than the explosions outside or the dismaying reports from the front was what was going on in the bunker itself. Everybody was reacting—to events, to each other—but it was plain that nobody, from the tank commanders in the field to Hofi and his staff, had time to think. How can you conduct a war without thinking? Hod asked himself.

Shortly after midnight, the airman's unpracticed ear detected what he took to be direct Syrian tank fire on the Nafakh camp. Turning to Hofi, he said, "Khaka [Hofi's nickname], the army's going to need you tomorrow. I suggest we get out of here." Hod was wrong about Nafakh being attacked by Syrian tanks. But only by a few hours.

Close to 1 A.M., Hofi handed over command of the Golan to General Eitan and drove back into Israel in a jeep with Hod. Crossing the Hula Valley, they drove up to Northern Command headquarters on Mount Canaan outside Safed, a city which had been the center of Jewish kabbala in the Middle Ages. Hod looked back across the valley and saw the Golan covered with bonfires. Some were brushfires but others were burning tanks. Barely twelve hours into the war, the Syrian army was already deep inside the Golan Heights.

Fifteen

DARKEST AT DAWN

R EPORTS FLOWING INTO THE PIT from the Syrian and Egyptian fronts this first night of war competed with each other in their unrelenting bleakness. "The worst thing is the reporting from the field," Elazar told the cabinet Saturday night. "It keeps changing all the time. First they say the enemy is here, then they say he isn't. We're trying to grope our way through the fog of war."

The chief of staff would have to decide before dawn which front was more needy of the two powerful instruments that were his to allocate—the air force and a reserve armored division commanded by Gen. Moshe (Moussa) Peled. The impression gained during the early part of the night was that the Syrian drive had slowed while the Egyptians were making rapid headway. It was thus decided to unleash the air force against the Egyptian missiles in the morning.

Elazar had planned to send Moussa Peled's division to Sinai as well before Hofi began signaling distress. The division constituted the main General Staff reserve. Its assignment affected not just the Egyptian and Syrian fronts but the Jordanian front as well. The division was assembling in camps on the West Bank and was the principal force that could meet an attack from Jordan if King Hussein decided to join in the war. Elazar summoned Lieutenant Colonel Keniezer, the head of AMAN's Jordanian desk, to ask his appraisal of the king's intentions. Keniezer believed the king would not attack across the Jordan River and thereby open his kingdom, undefended by SAMs, to the wrath of the Israeli air force. Accepting this appraisal, which echoed his own, Elazar ordered Peled's division north, leaving the Jordanian front virtually naked. It was, he acknowledged, a high-risk gamble, but in the circumstances every move was a gamble. Meanwhile, he ordered Hofi to evacuate endangered infantry strongpoints and to prepare a fallback line near the edge of the Golan plateau.

Summoned Saturday night to a meeting of the full cabinet, the chief of staff attempted to calm the ministers' nerves. This was the first time, he said, that the IDF was undertaking a defensive battle. "We know how to do it from the books but we've never actually done it before. We have to simultaneously block and mass forces and only afterwards go over to the attack." The blocking stage was going "reasonably well," he said. Dayan also tried to be optimistic. The crisis should have bottomed out by the next day, when the reserves began to reach the battlefield, he said. But he could not avoid pointing to a danger that lay beyond the horizon. If Syria and Egypt appear to be winning, he said, Iraq, Jordan, and Lebanon might enter the war.

Commanding a reserve tank brigade assembling at the foot of the Golan was Col. Ori Orr, who had returned from a year's study in the United States just two months before. The thirty-four-year-old colonel had never before commanded reservists and had not been enthusiastic about the prospect of leading a collection of paunchy soldiers with civilian mind-sets into battle. However, he had received a young brigade, most of whose members had finished regular service only two or three years before.

The brigade's mobilization base had been moved during the summer from the opposite end of the Galilee, a shift that saved precious hours now. As buses arrived with reservists, officers conducted shotgun weddings— matching up tank commanders, drivers, gunners, and loaders arbitrarily into tank crews even though they had never worked with each other before. The brigade contained a relatively large number of yeshiva students. A tank commander who found that his three crewmen wore skullcaps said, "Fellows, I want you to know who you're going to war with. I'm an atheist." The commander, who had recently returned from six years in Los Angeles, acknowledged to the younger crewmen that he had forgotten how to run a tank. "By the time we get up to the heights," he said, "I'll remember how to close the hatch and how the radio works. Meanwhile, check the firing system and load as many shells as you can."

Orr had been surprised during his stay in the United States to learn that the American army, instead of rotating entire tank units to Vietnam, rotated tank crewmen individually. It was gospel in the IDF that men fought best in the company of comrades whose good opinion they valued. Now Orr found himself forced to scrap that important principle precisely in a war situation.

Shortly after midnight, the brigade dispatched a platoon up to the southern Golan, the only reserve tank formation that would be directed there this night. Lt. Nitzan Yotser was arbitrarily chosen from the milling crowd of reservists as platoon commander. He was told to ascend the Yehudia road and proceed to its intersection with the Tapline, where he was to block any enemy force attempting to advance. The whereabouts and strength of the Syrians were not known. One of Yotser's four tanks broke down before even exiting the camp. A reconnaissance jeep guided the remaining three to Arik Bridge, just north of Lake Kinneret, and took leave of them. Crossing the bridge, the tanks continued straight for two miles before the foot of the heights.

As the tanks ascended, Yotser was gripped by the surreality of the situation. Only twelve hours before, he had been spending a leisurely Yom Kippur afternoon with his girlfriend in his student apartment in posh north Tel Aviv, remote from any thought of war. Drafted two months after the Six Day War, he had been convinced that he would never see war in his lifetime except in the cinema. Israel's army was so demonstrably powerful that the Arabs, so demonstrably ineffective, would never dare take up arms against it again. Since completing his three years of military service in 1970, he had studied economics at Tel Aviv University and faithfully done his annual reserve duty. But he had grown his hair long and permitted himself the hedonistic fancies of the sixties generation that had belatedly reached Israel. This Yom Kippur afternoon, he had not even bothered opening the radio or making a phone call when the sirens sounded. When his mother telephoned to inform him of war on two fronts, he was certain she had misunderstood the radio announcement. On the bus carrying him to base, he admitted to himself that he had misgauged the Arabs. But he was certain too that they had misgauged their own strength and that "we'll soon show them."

Leading a tank platoon now up the Golan Heights, he was no longer sure it would be easy. The pandemonium in the camp, the hasty arming of the tanks, and the formation of nonorganic crews suggested to him that the IDF was not entirely prepared for this war, and not just because it had been surprised. He had not had time to take on a full load of shells or to be issued an Uzi before being sent off. Only as his tank had begun to move did someone throw him an extra box of ammunition for his machine gun. This was not the way to be going to war. There had not even been time for the crew to learn each other's names. He addressed his men by their job designations— "Driver, straight ahead."

He had no idea that his three tanks were the spearhead of the Israeli counterattack in the southern Golan—in fact, for the next few hours, the entire counterattack. Nor did he know that hundreds of Syrian tanks had broken through to his front. His immediate concern was to remember how to command a tank. His three tours of annual reserve duty as a deputy company commander had been spent dealing with logistics and he had forgotten basic skills. Almost any of the officers in the teeming camp below had more recent experience handling a tank than he. He was not sure, for instance, which way to push the radio switch in his helmet if he wished to speak only to his crew and which way if he also wished to speak to the other tanks. He had forgotten the proper way of issuing orders, a basic requirement if he wanted the crews of three tanks to act in coordination. Unlike in the Six Day War, when the reserves had three weeks in which to hone their skills, prepare equipment, and prepare themselves psychologically, the reserves were going into this war stone-cold.

As he looked at the road in the moonlight and listened to the sound of the tank engines, he found himself undergoing a strange metamorphosis. Imperceptibly disconnecting from his "make love, not war" mind-set, he began to focus on the task at hand—namely, making war. He was a civilian wearing a uniform at the bottom of the heights. When the tank reached the top he was a soldier.

Cresting the plateau, Yotser saw a large fire in the distance and assumed it was a brushfire touched off by artillery shells. The road carried the tanks in the direction of the fire. Drawing close, Yotser saw that the fire was on the road itself—a column of burning ammunition trucks. The trucks were facing east, which meant they were Israeli vehicles which had been on their way to the front. As Yotser's tanks drew close enough to the fire to be visible in its glow, shells exploded around them. The Syrian tanks that had ambushed the trucks were still out there.

The instincts drilled into Yotser during his army service now kicked in. He barked a litany of commands directing the tanks to pull back into the darkness and take up defensive positions. For the next three hours, Yotser and his men exchanged sporadic fire with the Syrian tanks, aiming at gun flashes. They could not see the Syrians but had the feeling that the Syrians could see them. A shell hit Yotser's tank a glancing blow at one point but caused little damage.

Meanwhile, Orr was dispatching other tanks to the northern Golan as fast as they could be readied. Tanks that had even half an ammunition load were sent up, via the Bnot Yaacov Bridge, in groups of three without regard to unit affiliation. Before first light, Orr himself set out, leading twenty tanks.

Even as the reservists were beginning to mount the heights, Northern Command was preparing for the Golan's evacuation should the defenses crumble. At 4:30 A.M., it ordered documents evacuated from army bases. Trucks began bringing down ammunition from a large depot at Snobar above the Bnot Yaacov Bridge. Engineers prepared a cache of antitank mines on the southern shore of Lake Kinneret in the event that tank obstacles had to be created at the edge of the Golan escarpment and bulldozers were ordered to stand by to cut the roads leading down from the heights.

Meanwhile, in the southern Golan, the remnants of Erez's battalion continued their lonely battle. Four tanks under Captain Arieli had been holding off enemy tanks at Tel Juhader since dusk. As the night wore on, the men began seeing green flares to their rear. These were used by Syrian tank commanders to signal their location to their units. The Syrians, it was clear, were filtering through. At 1 A.M., Ben-Shoham ordered Arieli to pull back half a mile to a small army camp where the tanks would be better protected behind earthen barriers. The camp controlled the intersection of the main north–south road, Reshet, and the Tapline. The crossroad was soon lit with burning Syrian tanks and APCs.

In the predawn hours, fighting tapered off all along the line. Syrian forces continued to flow through unguarded sectors into the Golan, but there was no dash for the Jordan River and no commando landings at the bridges. At some places, tanks continued for a while to exchange desultory fire, but gradually the situation became static. Both sides were waiting for the new day.

Arriving at Northern Command by helicopter at dawn, Dayan was taken aback by the gloom. Hofi told the defense minister bluntly that the heights might have to be abandoned. There were no forces capable of preventing the Syrians from pushing south from Ramat Magshimim to the Jordan Valley. One of the first settlements the Syrians would encounter in that direction was Kibbutz Degania, where Dayan was born. The kibbutz still preserved a Syrian tank stopped on its perimeter fence during the War of Independence in 1948. Degania had also been Motti Hod's home. "We can't let it happen," said the former air force commander, who joined the conversation.

"Only the air force can stop them," said Hofi.

Gen. Dan Laner, commander of a reserve division, shared Hofi's pessimism. "The fighting is over in the southern Golan and we've lost," he told Dayan. "We don't have anything to stop them with."

The grim picture confronting the defense minister touched an apocalyptic chord which would resonate in him through the coming days. But it did not impede his ability to make quick, and generally insightful, tactical and strategic proposals. As defense minister, it was not in his authority to issue operational orders to officers—except the chief of staff. But he would do so frequently, generally offering it as nonobligatory "ministerial advice" if he encountered raised eyebrows, but sometimes skipping that legal nicety. He told Hofi to prepare the bridges across the Jordan for detonation and to ensure that all roads descending the heights were well defended. Sappers were to be posted alongside the bridges with orders to blow them up on command, and antitank guns were to be positioned there as well. Dayan asked Hofi to send a senior officer to organize defense of settlements in the Jordan Valley.

Unable to get Elazar on the phone, Dayan had himself patched through to Benny Peled at 5 A.M. What are your plans for this morning? asked Dayan. Peled told him of the pending attack on the Egyptian missiles. Forget it, said Dayan. There's only sand in Sinai and the Suez Canal is 150 miles from Tel Aviv. The situation on the Golan is critical and only the air force can hold the Syrians off until the reserves arrive. If planes are not attacking by noon, said Dayan, the Syrians would reach the Jordan Valley. For the first time, Dayan used a phrase that he would repeat in the coming days to the dismay of all who heard him. The Third Temple, he told Peled, is in danger.

The First Temple, built by Solomon, was razed by the Babylonians in 586 B.C., and the Second Temple, built by Herod, was destroyed by the Romans in A.D. 70. The Third Temple was a metaphor for the modern state of Israel.

Final squadron briefings on Operation Tagar began at air force bases at 6 A.M. The air crews were given files containing the latest air photos of their targets, radio frequencies, code words, navigation instructions, and updated intelligence.

The four-stage attack was aimed at the sixty-two SAM bases in the canal zone. The first wave would target not the missile batteries themselves but the antiaircraft guns defending them. Seven Egyptian air bases whose planes might attempt to interfere with the Israeli blitz would also be hit. The missiles themselves were to be dealt with in three follow-up attacks during the day.

Almost all the planes in the IAF were to be involved in the spectacular operation—hundreds of planes coming in just over the desert floor at high speed, then attacking in precisely orchestrated sequence. The heart of the plan was the low-level approach. The planes would skim the ground below radar range until almost upon their targets. At a precise point, they would pull up steeply to 6,000 feet and dive directly into the attack. The few seconds during which they would be exposed to the SAM batteries were too brief, theoretically at least, for the missiles to lock on. The flying had to be so finely calibrated that when the planes rose up and dove, the targets would be right in front of them, since there would be no time for adjustments.

The attack was to be augmented by an elaborate assault on the enemy radar screens, which were to be flooded with false targets. Chaff—aluminum strips that can be taken for airplanes on radar screens—would be fired into the missile zone with rockets. Similar images would be sent electronically from dozens of helicopters and other aircraft on the fringe of the missile zone. Unmanned drones would further clutter the radar screens. In among this multitude of false targets would be the Israeli warplanes. If the radars were activated, planes would drop American-made Shrike bombs, which home in on radars. If the radars remained dormant so as to foil the Shrikes, low-flying planes would sweep in and hit them with "dumb" bombs. The operation demanded clockwork choreography and precision flying.

It was a brilliant plan with two problematic aspects. One was the mobility of the SAM-6s. Half a day would probably elapse between the last air photo mission and the attack. The cumbersome SAM-2 and SAM-3 batteries could not be transferred to a new site in that span of time. The SAM-6s, however, mounted on tracked vehicles, could easily be moved. This was somewhat less worrying in Sinai, where only ten of the sixty-two batteries were SAM-6s. On the Syrian front, fifteen of the twenty-five missile batteries were SAM-6s.

The second problem was the low-level approach itself. It protected the planes from missiles but exposed them to the masses of conventional antiaircraft guns deployed by both Arab armies. There was also danger, in flying over an area dense with troops, from thousands of rifles, machine guns, and tank guns firing into their flight paths. As random as this kind of shooting was, it threw up a curtain of fire that was not infrequently lethal to low-flying aircraft. For this reason, Tagar called for a preliminary attack on the antiaircraft guns guarding the missile batteries and on troop concentrations in the

Israeli soldiers look across the Suez Canal at Ismailiya shortly after the Six Day War. Israel and Egypt had not begun to fortify their respective banks.
Photograph courtesy of Israeli Government Press Office

The narrow Jordan River, with the Golan Heights in the background.
Photograph courtesy of Israeli Government Press Office

Syrian tanks at Israeli antitank ditch on the Golan. A tank, hit by Israeli fire, has fallen off one of the two bridges the Syrians laid across the ditch. Another knocked-out tank lies in the ditch. To the left is the roadway the Syrians later succeeded in opening through the barrier.
Photograph courtesy of Israel Defense Forces Archive

Israeli long-range artillery piece firing on the Golan.
Photograph courtesy of Israel Defense Forces Archive

Reservists arriving on the Golan in half-tracks.
Photograph courtesy of Israel Defense Forces Archive

Gen. Yitzhak Hofi (seated at center of table), head of Northern Command, on the second night of the war. Sitting next to Hofi is Gen. Haim Bar-Lev. Between the two men, looking over their shoulders, is Gen. Motti Hod, former commander of the Israeli air force.
Photograph courtesy of Israel Defense Forces Archive

Israeli Centurion tanks attacking on the Golan early in the war.
Photograph courtesy of Israel Defense Forces Archive

Israeli tanks moving to the front in the Sinai.
Photograph courtesy of Israeli Government Press Office

Lt. Cols. Avigdor Kahalani (right) and Yossi Ben-Hanan
after the battle for Kuneitra Gap.
Photograph courtesy of Israel Defense Forces Archive

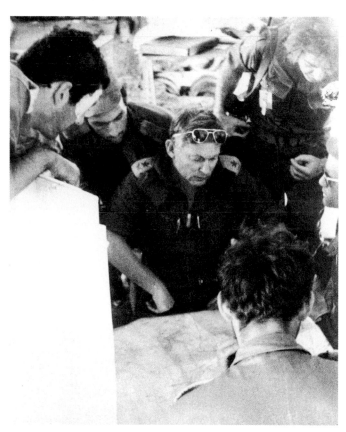

Gen. Avraham Adan studies a map with staff officers.
Photograph courtesy of Israel Defense Forces Archive

Lt. Zvika Greengold,
six months before the war.
He would receive Israel's
highest medal.
*Photograph courtesy of
Israel Defense Forces Archive*

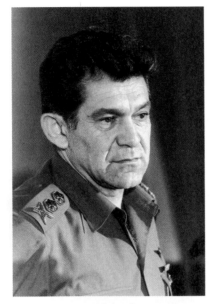

Israeli chief of staff
Gen. David Elazar.
*Photograph courtesy of
Israeli Government Press Office*

Israeli air force commander
Gen. Benny Peled.
*Photograph courtesy of
Israeli Government Press Office*

Col. Amnon Reshef. The brigade he commanded during the war was the only Israeli armored unit on the Bar-Lev Line when the Egyptians attacked.
Photograph courtesy of Israel Defense Forces Archive

Gen. Shmuel Gonen, head of Southern Command.
Photograph courtesy of Israeli Government Press Office

Motti Ashkenazi.
Photograph courtesy of Motti Ashkenazi

Gen. Gonen (with glasses, second from left) sitting alongside Gen. Uri Ben-Ari (face towards the camera) in Southern Command headquarters.
Photograph courtesy of Israeli Government Press Office

Gen. Elazar (seated, center, with hands touching) at a briefing in Southern Command headquarters. Behind him, holding a cigarette, is Yitzhak Rabin.
Photograph courtesy of Israeli Government Press Office

area. This was to be done by tossing cluster bombs from several miles away rather than diving on the targets directly.

General Peled decided that the first stage of Tagar was too far advanced to halt. Col. Ron Pekker, commander of Tel Nof Air Base, flew with the first wave of Phantoms. As his flight approached the canal zone, Pekker saw a cloud of dust rising. With a start, he realized that it was being churned up by tank battles and that the Egyptians must have crossed the canal in strength. He had never thought he would see such battles being waged on Israeli-held territory.

The navigators in the rear seats of the Phantoms pressed their stop-watches as the planes passed over white "exit towers"—stacks of painted drums—serving as markers. The aircraft roared low across the canal at 540 knots as the navigators counted down. At a precise second, the pilots pulled their sticks back and hit the afterburners, sending the planes thrusting sky-ward at 60 degrees. The bombs were released at a predetermined height and flew towards their distant targets as the planes themselves looped in the opposite direction and headed back towards Sinai. Toss bombing lacked accuracy but it reduced exposure to ground fire. Two planes were neverthe-less lost in the attack.

Arriving back at their bases, the squadrons were to be quickly refueled and rearmed and turned around for the first attack on the missile batteries themselves. But a major surprise awaited them. Peled himself had called to notify base commanders that Tagar was being called off. Phantom squadrons were to prepare instead to carry out Dougman 5—the attack on the Syrian missiles—before noon.

Independently of Dayan's reaction, Elazar had also ordered Peled to cancel Tagar and go to Northern Command's aid after a phone conversation with Hofi. These directives to Peled, and his swift acquiescence, would affect the course of the war in a fundamental way.

The order appalled senior officers in the air force war room. Peled had passed it on in a brief phone call from the Pit, and he was unavailable when staff officers tried to get back to him. The officers were incensed that two years of intensive preparations were being thrown out the window just as the operation had gotten under way. More energy and creativity had gone into formulating Tagar than had gone into the preemptive strike in 1967 that accounted for Israel's victory. Intelligence on the Egyptian missile sites was freshly updated. All the devices that had been prepared to deceive the SAM radars were in place. The air crews, at their fighting edge, were ready to go.

When Peled returned from the Pit, he assembled senior staff around a table and explained that the northern front was crumbling. Operations chief Col. Giora Furman and others pointed out that a squadron of Skyhawks at Ramat David Air Base in the north had been deliberately excluded from the Tagar operation in order to be available on the Golan Heights for such contingencies. This, they argued, was sufficient to provide the ground forces there with any close support needed. In addition, there was simply no room over the narrow Golan for the entire air force. There was therefore no logic in calling off an attack that promised to destabilize the Egyptian armed forces, Israel's principal enemy, before sundown. Colonel Furman engaged Peled in a heated argument in which, as he would recall it years later, they almost came to blows.

Col. Avihu Bin-Nun, heading the team planning air strikes and a future commander of the IAF, was the primary architect of Tagar. He believed Peled had made a snap judgment in response to Dayan's call. If he had only asked for ten minutes to consult with his staff, Bin-Nun believed, they would have convinced him that the availability of the Skyhawk squadron in the north fulfilled Northern Command's needs. Col. Amos Amir, Furman's deputy and a future deputy commander of the air force, was among those at the table who believed that brilliant though Peled was, he lacked the operational experience to grasp the inappropriateness of the order.

Logic may have been on the side of the staff officers, but Peled was the only man in the room who had heard Dayan's voice that morning. He forcefully closed off the debate. "I understand you all," he said, smacking the table. "The air force goes north."

So great was the sense of urgency that the operational orders for Dougman were a travesty of the carefully structured plan that had been exercised so diligently. The helicopters bearing the electronic equipment needed to deceive the Syrian radars had been flown to Sinai for Tagar and there was no time to bring them north. There was no time, either, for a softening-up attack on the Syrian antiaircraft guns and the ground forces in the path of the attacking squadrons, like the one just carried out in Sinai. Worst of all, there was no time for a photo mission to ascertain that the SAMs were still where they were when last seen the previous afternoon. Weather conditions did not permit photo reconnaissance early in the morning. Given that the Syrian army had moved forward, there was a good chance that the mobile SAM-6s had as well.

In late morning, sixty Phantoms raced eastward over the Galilee and thundered low over the Golan Heights. The advancing Syrian troops were now massed on both sides of the Purple Line. When the planes flew over their heads at 100 feet, the infantrymen and tanks joined the antiaircraft guns in throwing up a wall of small-arms and machine-gun fire. The planes pulled sharply up as they neared the presumed battery sites. Gaining altitude, the pilots saw that almost all the SAMs were gone. Only one battery was destroyed. Six of the low-flying Phantoms were shot down, all by ground fire rather than missiles.

The day's results were calamitous for the air force and for Israel's entire defense posture. Tagar had been aborted and Dougman had failed miserably. The IAF, normally so meticulous and decisive, had been jarred into sloppy haste. In a single day, its reputation for invincibility had been shaken, a startling turn of events that affected the self-confidence of the decision makers and the air force itself.

Of all the what-ifs of the war, the decision to call off Tagar is perhaps the most weighty. If the operation had been successfully executed, stripping the Egyptian army of its missile shield, it would clearly have been a different war. Without the missiles to worry about, the IAF could easily have eliminated the conventional antiaircraft batteries from altitude. The planes would then have been free to hover over the canal and hit the bridges and ferries, and they would have been able to methodically attack the ground forces that had already crossed.

Not all air force officers were certain about how Tagar would have played out given the mobility of the SAM-6s and uncertainty about suppressing conventional antiaircraft fire by toss bombing. But Bin-Nun, Furman, Amir, and other senior air force officers would remain convinced that Tagar's cancellation denied Israel an early and decisive victory. There was no question that the Egyptian missiles would have been eliminated, Amos Amir would say years later. The only question was how many planes would have been lost. This, he expected, would have been in the dozens.

As for Dougman, Gen. David Ivri, Peled's successor, would later say that if it had only been delayed by two hours, there would have been time to complete a photo reconnaissance mission to determine the location of the SAM-6s and time to bring up the helicopters with the electronic equipment from Sinai.

Peled had warned his senior commanders two days before that they might have to "go into the fire" if the SAMs could not be destroyed. They had gone into the fire and were rapidly being consumed. In the first two days of war, thirty-five planes had been lost and there was little to show for it. The Arab missile defenses remained intact. Their ground forces had hardly been impacted from the air except for the helicopter-borne commando forces destroyed on the first day.

The air force was not without impressive successes. By persistent attacks on the enemy's airfields, it kept the Egyptian and Syrian air forces busy defending their airspace. Air force cover permitted the reserves to reach the fronts without enemy interdiction, and the skies over Israel would be kept almost totally clear of enemy planes. (Three Syrian planes that attempted to attack a radar station on Mount Meron in the Galilee on the first day of the war were shot down and a fourth crashed trying to evade the Israeli planes. Two Syrian planes would likewise be downed trying to attack the Haifa oil refineries later in the war.) In dogfights, the IAF was shooting down enemy aircraft by the bushel.

These successes, however, meant little to the beleaguered Israeli ground troops on both fronts who kept looking skyward and asking, "Where's the air force?"

General Peled would note that the air force controlled the skies over all of Syria and Egypt—indeed, anywhere it chose in the Middle East—except for the narrow strips over the battle zones dominated by missiles. But it was there that the Yom Kippur War would be won or lost.

Sixteen

THE FALL OF THE
SOUTHERN GOLAN

Refreshed by a few hours' sleep in his tank on the Hermonit ridge, Avigdor Kahalani rose in the turret at first light Sunday to breathe deeply of the chill morning air. A rumbling emanating from the landscape sounded to him like the distant roar of lions preparing to feed. It was the sound of tank engines revving up. Dark smoke rose from vehicles on both sides of the line. In the distance, clouds of dust were already being thrown up by Syrian tank columns on the move. Raising his company commanders on the radio, Kahalani wished them good morning and told them to prepare for a Syrian attack.

One hundred yards to his front were two earthen ramps which had been prepared for tanks defending this sector. He had not seen them in the darkness. He ordered his force to occupy them.

"Move carefully," he cautioned. "There are Syrian tanks on the other side."

The tanks descended in a broad line, the commanders standing in the turrets. Kahalani stayed behind to check their deployment. A moment after the first tank reached the top of the main ramp, it began firing.

"Battalion commander, this is Yair," came a call from the right flank. "A number of enemy tanks heading in my direction. I'm moving into position and opening fire."

Kahalani ordered his driver to move forward. "Kilion," he called to his gunner, "be prepared to fire." As his tank edged up the ramp, Kahalani braced. "Stop," he called. Before him was a brown, barren vale. This was the Kuneitra Gap, through which the Syrian tanks in this sector would have to advance if they wished to proceed towards Nafakh and the Jordan River. At first Kahalani could detect no movement. Then he noticed a single tank throwing up black smoke. In a moment, other tanks could be seen detaching themselves from the landscape and moving forward. The Syrians were commencing their attack.

"Our sector," he called to his tank commanders in a litany straight from a training exercise. "Range 500 to 1,500 meters. A large number of enemy tanks moving in our direction. Take your positions and open fire. Out."

The tank guns began barking almost immediately. Kahalani's own tank joined in, his operations officer, Gidi Peled, directing the fire. Unlike the other tanks, which had four-man crews, command tanks shoehorned in an operations officer as well.

Syrian tanks began to burn and Kahalani called encouragement to his men. "We caught them with their pants down," he cried. "We've got good positions and they're in the open. Finish them off."

"Kahalani, this is Yanosh." The voice of the brigade commander, who had been monitoring the radio net, was crisp. "Report."

"I'm in contact with Syrian tanks moving towards me from the east."

"Do you need help?"

"Not for the moment. I'll report later. I'm personally in contact."

Ben-Gal did not intrude further.

The large bowl below Kahalani was now aswarm with tanks. The Syrian tank commanders were buttoned up inside with hatches closed. Periodically, they halted and fired two shells at the Israeli turrets on the skyline before starting forward again.

Exultant cries were coming from Centurion commanders along the line. "Battalion commander, this is Emi. We're pounding them. They're burning like torches. I'm being heavily pressed." It was company commander Emi Palant. Syrian tanks were burning all over the slopes. Sometimes an internal explosion sent a Syrian turret flying skyward.

The Israelis were taking hits too. Kahalani could see burning Centurions and the radio brought first reports of casualties. One of his company commanders was already dead.

"This is the battalion commander," said Kahalani. "You're doing great work. This valley is beginning to look like Lab B'Omer," a reference to the bonfires lit on that Jewish holiday. "Keep firing. We've got to stop them." Accurate Syrian artillery fire struck the ramps.

From time to time, tanks backed off to permit crewmen to load ammunition into the turret from the belly of the Centurion. Kahalani watched the tank commanders move unhesitatingly back up into the firing line. Palant, on the left, reported more of his tanks knocked out. Kahalani ordered two platoons from the opposite flank to go to his assistance.

"Brigade commander, this is Rattes." It was the battalion commander on the brigade's left flank talking to Ben-Gal. "It looks like a lot of tanks attacking Kahalani."

Ben-Gal raised Kahalani. "Do you see anything?"

"It's not clear to me what he's talking about," said Kahalani.

The report worried him. He did not know if Rattes was referring to the tanks already attacking or to yet another force he did not see.

"There are a lot of Syrians coming at me, Yanosh. I'll manage."

Ben-Gal sent Kahalani the three tanks which protected his mobile command post, the brigade's only reserve. Moving constantly around the battlefield, the brigade commander fine-tuned the defense as he shifted companies and even platoons from one sector to another in anticipation of shifting Syrian pressure. It was his principal task, as Ben-Gal saw it, not to react to specific Syrian moves—his commanders on the ground would attend to that—but to imagine what the problems were likely to be in another fifteen minutes or two hours. To effectively command, it was important to be near the heart of the action. Only thus could he detect weak spots on both sides and understand the flow of the battle.

Like Askarov in the southern sector, Kahalani was struck by the courage of the Syrians. They kept on coming, passing around their burned-out tanks and pressing on. But it appeared to him a mindless courage. If he were attacking, thought Kahalani, he would have slowed the pace and attempted to find another opening. The Syrians just continued banging their heads against the same wall. However, with a wall as thin as the Israeli line and a force as large as the Syrians', there was no telling how the story would end.

From Booster Ridge overlooking Kuneitra, the officer in command said he wished to send one of his tanks back to bring up ammunition. Kahalani could see Syrian personnel carriers moving in that direction. "I don't want any tank leaving the line now," he said.

Palant, on Kahalani's left flank, cut into the radio net. "The Syrians are trying to break through my company."

"Are there any points you don't control?" asked Kahalani.

"I'm controlling everything. I just wanted you to know. Over."

The message being passed on to him by his commanders was the same that he was passing on to Ben-Gal—the situation was serious but not desperate.

As his own tank pulled back for a few moments to load shells into the turret, Kahalani glanced along the line. The tanks were no longer the neat fighting machines they had been in the morning. Pieces of equipment had been knocked ajar by shell fire, and the sleeping bags and other personal accoutrements lashed to the exterior of the tanks were riddled with shrapnel. He could see one of Palant's tanks burning. The gun of another tank that had been hit hung askew. The faces in the turrets were dark with powder and dust. He could sense, however, an easing of the pressure. Here and there, enemy tanks continued to fire, but when he mounted the rampart he could see that the great armored wave had broken.

"Kahalani. This is Yanosh. What's happening?"

"We've managed to stop them. The valley below me is full of burning and abandoned tanks."

Ben-Gal asked if he could estimate their numbers. "Eighty or ninety," said Kahalani.

"Well done. Well done." Coming from a hard case like Ben-Gal, the warm words were not a compliment Kahalani took lightly.

The fight was not yet over. MiGs appeared overhead and dropped bombs. The explosions were deafening but the bombs hit one hundred yards behind the rampart. "Where's our air force?" Kahalani asked Ben-Gal. Neither had any idea of the desperate situation on the southern Golan or Sinai.

By noon the Syrian artillery had abated. For the first time in twenty-four hours, men got out of the tanks, one at a time, to relieve themselves. The tanks pulled back in rotation a mile to the rear for fuel and ammunition. Kahalani drove to Ben-Gal's command post.

"I've lost a lot of men," he reported. He sensed that the brigade commander did not want to talk about it.

"I want you to know," said Ben-Gal, "that the Syrians are not stopping. They've got enough tanks and they'll try to break through again."

Kahalani was taken aback by the thought that they might have to go through this once more. As he started back to his vehicle, the brigade operations officer, who had followed the progress of the battle on the radio net, embraced him. "You were great, brother," he said.

As grim as was the prospect of another round, Kahalani and Ben-Gal had less cause for anxiety than did General Hofi. The front commander knew that the grueling but controlled battle the Seventh Brigade had put up this day was the one bright spot in Israel's entire military picture, on the ground and in the air. The battle for the southern Golan had been lost. In

Sinai, the Egyptians had destroyed the Bar-Lev Line and were pushing inland. In the air, Israeli planes were being knocked down with frightening frequency by Soviet missiles. Something had gone terribly wrong.

Skyhawks had begun flying over the southern Golan at 7 A.M., despite their vulnerability to the SAMs, in a desperate bid to slow the Syrian tanks. Ben-Shoham's intelligence officer, Maj. Moshe Zurich, saw the first four Skyhawks come in low from the southwest. Within seconds, a volley of missiles rushed at them and all four appeared to be hit. A few minutes later another foursome approached and two were downed. It was apparent to Zurich that salvation would not be coming from the skies.

Skyhawk pilot Shlomo Kalish circled over Lake Kinneret with the other three planes in his flight, waiting for the foursome which had gone in ahead of them to vacate the area. It was still unclear to the young pilot why the mission in Egypt they had trained so extensively for had been abruptly called off and why they had been hastily dispatched, with virtually no briefing, to the north. Whatever was happening on the Golan was obviously serious. Just how serious became apparent when the flight leader told them as they started in to stay low to avoid missiles and to "hit anything you see." Kalish realized this meant there were no more Israeli forces in the southern Golan. As they swept in over Ramat Magshimim he saw a large number of tanks parked in rectangular formation. He started to dive when a shoulder-held Strella missile exploded near his tail. A light on his instrument panel indicated an engine fire. Lieutenant Kalish continued his dive and unloaded his bombs. He managed to land his plane at the Ramat David air base a few minutes later. Instead of receiving kudos when debriefed, he was rebuked for not having headed immediately for base when the warning signal went on. Six Skyhawks had been downed in the desperate bid to halt the Syrian tanks, and eleven planes, like Kalish's, were hit but managed to get back. The effect of the air attacks on the Syrian tide was marginal.

Major Yair, commanding the paratroop contingent manning the southern strongpoints, had also seen the Skyhawks devoured by the Syrian missiles. When he reported that the Syrian tanks at Ramat Magshimim, five miles to his north, were starting to move in his direction, he was ordered to leave El Al immediately. He told the men at his command post to descend to the Kinneret and to take all the vehicles with them. Unwilling to leave while he still had men cut off on the front line, Yair told headquarters he was remaining to report on Syrian movement. If he had to escape he would be better off on foot. Two of the men volunteered to stay with him. The Syrian tanks reached seven hundred yards from El Al and halted.

General Hofi ordered the evacuation of the frontline strongpoints as

Elazar had directed, and Yair passed the order on to the commanders of the strongpoints manned by his paratroop unit. Col. Amir Drori, commander of the Golani Brigade, which manned the five northern strongpoints, objected to the order. He told Hofi that his men were holding their own and inflicting heavy losses. Hofi relented. A similar protest was made by AMAN chief Zeira when he learned of the order to evacuate an important intelligence post overlooking the Syrian lines near Kuneitra. Reinforce it with tanks and protect it with planes, said Zeira. Here, too, the evacuation order was rescinded.

At Strongpoint 111, a radioman at dawn picked up a transmission from the commander of a Syrian unit. "I see the whole Galilee in front of me. Request permission to proceed." The answer that came back was "Negative." The paratroopers manning the strongpoint had beaten off infantry attacks and developed a measure of fatalism after hours of numbing shelling. During a lull in the firing, they heard the sound of a vehicle approaching from the rear. An Israeli APC swung into the compound. "We're getting out," shouted the platoon commander. "Leave everything. You have one minute to get in." The bodies of two dead paratroopers were placed on the vehicle floor. Sgt. Yoram Krivine tried not to step on them as eighteen men crowded in. The APC commander stood with his head out of the turret so that he could guide the driver cross-country, well away from roads. At some points, the men had to get out to enable the APC to cross steep wadis. Krivine was so put off by the crowding that he asked his officer for permission to find his way back to the Israeli lines on foot. The request was denied.

The APC commander calmly described to the men inside what he was seeing, including occasional Syrian tanks in the distance. At one point, the vehicle turned a sharp bend and the men heard tank engines very close. "Two Syrian tanks," said the officer. No one was visible in their hatches, and the crews, after a day and night of battle, may have been asleep. The officer's body twisted as he flung a grenade. The men could hear a muffled explosion. "Got it into the turret," said the officer. "The other tank's taking off." When the APC finally stopped and the men tumbled out, they found themselves in the Nafakh camp. Although he had never before been claustrophobic, Krivine, a future high-tech executive, would be ever after.

Dawn brought the end to an agonizing night for Colonel Ben-Shoham. Cut off in a remote wadi, he had attempted to conduct the battle by radio without a coherent picture of what was happening. Daylight had made his personal situation precarious. A large dust cloud indicated that Syrian units were beginning to get under way in his area. The dust trail moved westward towards the Gamla Ascent, Ben-Shoham's only escape route. He requested permission from Northern Command to descend the heights into Israel in order to come back up to Nafakh via the Bnot Yaacov Bridge. Permission was granted. Syrian tanks came into view two miles to the rear as Ben-Shoham's tank and APC crested the escarpment and began the descent.

His last order to Erez before departing was to fall back with all his remaining tanks on Tel Fares, the highest mound in the southern Golan. "All we can do now is hang on until the reserves come up," said Ben-Shoham. "We've done our bit."

Seventeen

THE BEANSTALK

To the reservists approaching the Golan Heights Sunday morning, the Hula Valley at its foot was mocking in its serenity. Cotton fields tufted the valley floor in festive white, but the men who should have been harvesting them were fighting on the heights above or in far-off Sinai. Except for wisps of smoke seeping over the edge of the escarpment from brushfires, there was hardly a hint of war—no enemy planes, no bombs, no sound of artillery except for a few long-range shells which hit the town of Rosh Pinna. To those familiar with Jack and the Beanstalk, it was easy to imagine the winding roads climbing the escarpment as ascents from an innocent garden to the high place where the ogre dwelt.

It was beginning to dawn when Col. Ran Sarig and twenty-five tanks crossed Arik Bridge and began to climb the Yehudia road. The force was the first to be dispatched to the southern Golan since Lieutenant Yotser's platoon had gone up in the early hours of the morning. Contact had been lost with Yotser and his fate was unknown. "There's no Jew responding to radio calls south of the Tapline," General Eitan radioed to Sarig in his picturesque style. "Find the Syrians and start fighting."

The ogre was waiting for Sarig ten miles up the road, masked by the rising sun. The Israeli column topped the Katsbiya ridge and came upon an open area teeming with one hundred tanks and scores of APCs, trucks, jeeps, and fuel tankers. The burned-out remains of an Israeli supply convoy showed that the Syrian force had been there for hours. This was the convoy which Yotser had seen burning the previous night. Had the Syrian force, the Forty-sixth Armored Brigade, moved just a few hundred yards further west, they would have dominated the Yehudia road and could easily have blocked any Israeli force ascending. Lieutenant Yotser and his three tanks from Orr's brigade descended from the positions they had taken during the night and joined the column. Before the Israelis could go into action, two of Sarig's tanks were hit from the side and set aflame. The lead company pivoted to confront the attackers.

The hurried mobilization had left no time to boresight the tank guns, a procedure in which the gunner's sights are aligned with the barrel of the gun so that what he sees through his sights is what the gun is pointing at. The deficiency became immediately evident to Sarig when his gunner fired at a Syrian tank only two hundred yards away and missed. Backing briefly out of the fray, Sarig conducted an abbreviated form of boresighting that provided a rough alignment. Returning to the battle, he found the tank he had previously missed and his gunner set it alight. A flanking force sent by Sarig reached high ground overlooking the Syrian ambushers and took them under fire. Sarig could see hatches on the Syrian tanks being raised one after the other as the crews escaped. General Hofi, anxious to avoid further erosion, ordered Sarig to proceed cautiously.

Riding in Sarig's tank was his operations officer, Maj. Giora Bierman, who had the day before checked himself out of the hospital where he was being treated for a severe case of jaundice. His illness did not prevent him from carrying out his duties, but as smoke and the smell of cordite filled the tank he felt himself losing consciousness. Telling Sarig that he needed air, Bierman climbed out of the tank and lay down in a ditch alongside the road. There, with shells exploding about him, he passed out.

When he woke an hour later, the battle was still going on over his head—tank shells, artillery, machine-gun fire. The brigade had moved forward slightly. He ran to the nearest tank and looked inside. It was empty but blood spattering the tank's innards told its tale.

The next tank he climbed was commanded by Sgt. Dan Meridor, a Jerusalem lawyer who would, in a few years, become cabinet secretary under Menahem Begin and then a minister. Bierman could make out the brigade commander's tank two hundred yards away, but Sarig was not in the turret. Borrowing Meridor's binoculars, Bierman focused on the flat surface projecting from Sarig's turret, a map rest installed on brigade commanders' tanks. There was no map there but Bierman could see blood. He ran to the tank and learned from the crew that Sarig had been seriously wounded in his neck and shoulder by shrapnel. Bierman climbed into the tank and, in the absence of any other senior officer, took temporary command of the brigade.

The advance of Sarig's force marked the reopening of the battle for the southern Golan. The only Israeli forces left were in enclaves cut off along the Purple Line. The area south of Ramat Magshimim had not fallen only because the Syrians had not chosen to move in that direction, which was devoid of Israeli forces except for Major Yair and two paratroopers at El Al. The Syrians had stopped near the edge of the escarpment above Arik Bridge, where Sarig met them, and on a parallel road, the Gamla Ascent, within sight of the Kinneret.

The task of reconquering the southern Golan was delegated to Dan Laner, a veteran armor general who had retired in February from the regular army to his home kibbutz in the Galilee. He had been asked in the spring to form a reserve division to supplement General Eitan's division on the Golan in time of war. The framework of the new division had been only partially completed. On Yom Kippur morning, one of Laner's first orders to staff officers was to find six half-tracks to serve as a mobile command post and to provide them with radios and maps. Thus equipped, he set off for the Golan approaches.

Positioning himself early Sunday near Arik Bridge, he channeled the units streaming in from camps around northern Israel towards the southern Golan. All units were arriving understrength because they had hurried towards the front before their mobilization was completed and because of tank breakdowns along the way. Almost all went into battle lacking equipment, from maps to machine guns. Pressed to make all possible speed, virtually none took time to boresight their guns before reaching the battlefield, a procedure that normally takes up to half an hour. Commanders assumed there would be time to do so before going into battle, but there almost never was.

The movements resembled less those of an organized army going to war than of a militia responding to a clanging alarm bell. Laner laid his hands on a tank battalion assigned to Eitan's division when it passed through his area and sent it up the Yehudia road to support Sarig. Sometimes Laner fleshed out understrength forces by attaching other units to them. Sometimes he split units in order to plug dangerous holes. The fluidity with which the Israeli tank forces, from companies to divisions, changed their organizational shape in battle permitted them to reorganize themselves instantaneously, according to shifting operational needs.

A brigade led by Col. Yaacov Hadar was directed up the Gamla Ascent. Nearing the top, Centurion commanders in the lead were startled to see T-55 tanks silhouetted against the skyline. The Syrians had reached the edge of the escarpment and were reveling in the splendid view of the Kinneret and the Galilee. Although the Syrian tanks occupied the higher ground, they were at a disadvantage since they could not lower their guns sufficiently to hit the Israeli tanks coming up the steep road and had to come forward on the slope, exposing themselves. The Israeli force pushed the Syrians back three miles, knocking out a dozen tanks without loss.

Major Yair was on the roof of his command bunker at 9 A.M. watching the Syrian tanks to his north through binoculars when his sergeant shouted, "Tanks behind you." The paratroop commander instinctively threw himself flat and rolled off the low roof. The tanks were Israeli, a column of Centurions approaching from the south. Yair flagged them down and ran to the officer in the lead tank. There were men trapped at Strongpoint 116, said Yair, and he wanted a platoon of tanks with which to skirt the Syrian force up the road and rescue them. But the tank officer, Lt. Col. Yossi Amir, a battalion commander in Sarig's brigade, had explicit orders from Laner to take up blocking positions at El Al. The terrain here formed a narrow waist, only a mile wide, between two ravines. For the first time since the war began, there was a force in place to block Syrian movement south towards the Jordan Valley. Amir's nineteen tanks moved forward and engaged the Syrians just north of El Al.

In the early afternoon, a second force of reservists arrived at El Al, a brigade led by Col. Mordecai Ben-Porat. The trip from the mobilization base near Haifa had taken nine hours. Of forty-four tanks which started, eighteen broke down on the way. The tanks were Korean War–vintage Shermans which had been upgraded. Half had been fitted with 105 mm guns capable of penetrating Syrian tank armor. The other half had 75 mm guns which could not penetrate but could disable with a well-placed hit. It had been a brigade joke that if war came they would be posted with their old Shermans to guard the Haifa oil refinery. But they were about to take their hoary tanks into a real war. Colonel Ben-Porat took Amir's Centurion battalion under his command. By dusk the combined force had advanced two miles.

Fearful that the Syrians pushing up the Tapline would soon reach Nafakh, Hofi suggested to Eitan shortly before 8 A.M. that he evacuate the camp. Maps were hastily pulled off the walls of the command bunker and burned. Eitan and his staff left on a half-track for the Aleka base, a mile closer to the Bnot Yaacov Bridge. They returned to Nafakh within an hour, and directed Ori Orr, who had arrived with twenty-two of his brigade's tanks, to the Kuneitra area to protect the southern flank of Ben-Gal's brigade. From there, Orr's tanks sparred with Syrian forces across the Purple Line, but the brigade commander was surprised at the relative tranquillity of the area. He had, during the night, conjured up a desperate picture from monitoring Ben-Shoshan's radio net. From this vantage point, it did not seem so bad.

Reservists were slowly taking over the fight in the southern and central Golan, but the standing army units which had been fighting since Saturday afternoon remained in action. Major Zamir set out with Tiger Company in pursuit of elements of the Forty-third Syrian Brigade which had remained on the Golan after the previous night's ambush on Reshet Road. In a series of running battles, he knocked out ten more tanks as well as APCs and trucks, again without loss.

On the Tapline, Lieutenant Greengold's lone vigil had been reinforced during the early morning by tanks from Lieutenant Colonel Mor's rapid-reaction battalion. At 3 A.M., Colonel Ben-Shoham ordered his deputy, Lt. Col. David Yisraeli, to leave the war room at Nafakh and take command of the force. When Yisraeli arrived, Greengold descended from his tank to brief him. Although no longer under Greengold's command, the force, which now numbered sixteen tanks, was still designated on the radio net "Force Zvika." With first light, Yisraeli led the tanks forward. They had topped two rises when they saw Syrian tanks coming towards them over the next one, a mile away. The Syrian advance on Nafakh had resumed.

In the ensuing clash, the Israelis benefited from the shape of their tanks. The British Centurion and the American Patton had higher profiles than the Soviet tanks used by the Arabs. On flat ground this made them more prominent targets, but in a rolling landscape it offered a decided advantage. The Western tanks could position themselves hull down on rear slopes—that is, with only the turret and gun projecting over a hilltop or embankment. The Soviet tanks, on the other hand, could not depress their guns sufficiently and had to fire from the forward slope, exposing themselves completely, as had happened at the Gamla Ascent.

Arriving at Nafakh after his escape from the southern Golan, Ben-Shoham dropped off his intelligence and communications officers who had been with him during the night and picked up the brigade operations officer. "The brigade doesn't exist anymore," Ben-Shoham said to him. "Let's go fight." He turned down the Tapline to take command of Force Zvika.

In the course of a brisk battle, the Israeli tanks drove the Syrians back a mile. The tanks dropped back in rotation to refuel and rearm. When it was Greengold's turn, he and the crew dismounted to stretch their limbs. It was the first time they had a chance to see each other in daylight. One of the reservists was still in civilian clothing. The crewmen were shocked at Greengold's appearance. His face was covered with burns, cuts, and soot, and he looked as if he'd escaped from a hospital bed. He had indeed almost passed out during the night. The crewmen insisted that he sit and leave the loading of shells to them. One man climbed onto the tank and extracted from his knapsack an apple he had brought from home the day before. He handed it to Greengold, who accepted it gratefully.

Meanwhile, Golani troops in the frontline strongpoints repulsed repeated attacks. At Strongpoint 107, the defenders watched Syrian infantrymen descend from trucks a mile away and advance towards them in skirmish lines. When Lieutenant Elimelekh reported the advance to his battalion commander he was told to let them reach the outpost fence before opening fire. However, Lieutenant Yakhin, still riding herd on the outpost with his three tanks, did not want RPGs getting that close and opened fire at five hundred yards. The strongpoint's machine guns joined in. The forward line of Syrian infantrymen was cut down. Those behind went flat and after a few minutes began to pull back. There had been no attempt by the Syrian infantry at fire and maneuver and no coordination with their tanks, which would soon mount a failed attack from another direction.

At Strongpoint 104 beneath the Hermon, Syrian troops succeeded in occupying an empty Israeli firing position. Colonel Drori summoned a platoon from the Golani's reconnaissance company, which retook it. Watching the fight from an adjacent ramp, Drori saw enemy troops counterattacking. There was something odd about their appearance. Their glistening helmets and their uniforms were not anything he had seen on Syrian troops before. Their attack was also oddly unprofessional. The soldiers ran in a straight line up a path and were easily shot by the defenders. A few of the attackers were captured and identified as Moroccans by some of Drori's men who were themselves Moroccan-born. The attackers were from a Moroccan brigade which was operating on the Syrian northern flank. Israel would discover in the coming days that it was up against more of the Arab world than it had expected.

Eighteen

THE BATTLE FOR NAFAKH

THE SYRIAN COMMAND RECEIVED TWO unexpected reports from its forces in the southern Golan early on this second day of battle. Part of the Forty-seventh Brigade had erred in navigation and, instead of reaching Ramat Magshimim, found itself on the upper switchbacks of the Gamla Ascent. Turning a bend, the Syrians saw below them to their left in the early morning light the bright expanse of Lake Kinneret, with the city of Tiberias clinging to the slopes on the far shore. This was the force Ben-Shoham had seen before he descended the heights. The glittering sighting, however, was overshadowed by a message from the commander of the Forty-sixth Brigade on the Yehudia road. Israeli reserves had reached the battlefield, reported the officer.

It was this brigade that had encountered Sarig's tanks shortly after sunrise, well short of the twenty-four hours that the Syrians had believed a minimum for the arrival of Israeli reserves. Uzi Mor, one of Sarig's battalion commanders, had in fact entered battle on the Tapline nine hours after the war began, although the Syrians had no reason to suspect that this was a reserve force. Yotser's platoon had encountered the Forty-sixth Brigade's tanks on the Yehudia road three hours later and likewise was not distinguishable as a reserve force. But the appearance of Sarig's tanks moving in column on the road leading up from Arik Bridge clearly meant the arrival of reserves after only fifteen hours.

The Battle for Nafakh

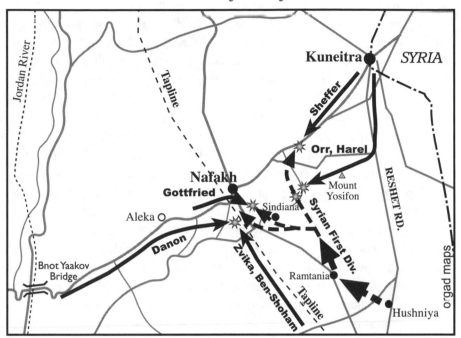

In midmorning, the Forty-seventh Brigade had the same unpleasant surprise when its view of the Galilee and Lake Kinneret was interrupted by Hadar's brigade moving up the Gamla Ascent.

If the Israelis were ahead of schedule, the Syrians were far behind. They had not yet descended the plateau, let alone seized the bridges over the Jordan as their plan called for by zero plus ten. The consequence of their failure to press home their advantage at night when all lay open before them would become steadily more apparent as the day progressed.

It is not clear whether the Syrians would have attempted to continue towards the river during the night if they had not encountered Israeli forces. The Forty-third Brigade was indeed in movement towards the Nafakh area when it was stopped by Tiger Company after midnight, but the Fifty-first Brigade on the Tapline and the Forty-sixth Brigade on the Yehudia road both appeared to be stationary when Lieutenant Greengold and Lieutenant Yotser, respectively, made contact with them. The units may have only paused for refueling or reorganization—or they may have been waiting for daylight. The Syrian brigade at Ramat Magshimim stopped about 4 A.M.

without encountering any Israeli opposition, and the supply column near Strongpoint 116 likewise halted until dawn of its own accord.

In the absence of any account of the war by authoritative Syrian sources, the reason they did not continue their attack at night after breaking through in the southern Golan is one of the major remaining mysteries of the war. The northern axis, on which they had hoped to quickly seize the Golan jugular—Nafakh and the Bnot Yaacov Bridge—was blocked by Nafshi and Ben-Gal. But in the southern sector, despite fierce resistance which threw their schedule off by hours and shattered several battalions, the Syrians had nevertheless succeeded in inserting hundreds of tanks capable of reaching the Jordan bridges virtually unopposed. Yet they had not done so.

A possible factor was the change in zero hour, after the attack plan had been completed, from 7 A.M. to 2 P.M. as a compromise with Egypt. This meant that the bulk of the Syrian fighting had to be done at night, which they had not counted on. Although their possession of tanks with night sights appeared to give them a major advantage over the Israelis, they had not trained extensively in night fighting and avoided it if they could. Their gunnery at night, all along the line, had proven grossly deficient. On the Seventh Brigade's northern flank, tanks from Rattes's battalion were positioned on the edge of the Druze village of Bukata and in its vineyards when they came under fire from a sizable Syrian force attempting to cross the border. Rattes had no flares and could not see the Syrian tanks, but from the shells that hit nearby it was clear to him that they could see his tanks. Nevertheless, the Syrians failed to score hits. Rattes's tanks, firing at the flare of the Syrian tank guns, managed to hit several, and the light from the burning tanks permitted them to hit several more. In the southern sector, Major Barak, whose tanks engaged the Syrians in the darkness, was surprised to find the Syrians missing by a wide margin. Greengold, too, had managed to avoid being hit in duels on the Tapline and so had Tiger Company in the Reshet road ambush. In all these cases, the Israeli tanks, even without night sights, managed to score numerous hits. The only clash in which the Syrian gunnery had proven effective was in the ambush of Uzi Mor's force on the Tapline, where the Israeli tanks were confined to a narrow roadway and the Syrians to their front had had ample time to prepare. Even here, however, RPGs appeared to play a major role.

If the Syrians' original zero hour had been adhered to, they would have gotten in more than ten hours of fighting before darkness. The commandos would have been landed by helicopter near the Jordan bridges at dusk, which would have given them just enough time to locate their landing sites and secure the area before being cloaked by darkness. With the revised schedule, the Syrian tanks had only three hours of daylight fighting before night descended—barely time enough to get across the antitank ditch and mine-fields—and the commandos would have had to be landed in difficult terrain near the river at midnight. But Syrian helicopter pilots had little or no train-ing in navigation at night.

A map found later in a captured tank on the Tapline included a written order stipulating that the Fifty-first Brigade would make its way to the aban-doned customshouse, above the Bnot Yaacov Bridge, where it would link up with a unit that would be waiting there. This was almost certainly a com-mando unit that was to have blown the bridge. Defense minister Mustafa Tlass would say after the war that Syria had agreed to the postponement of zero hour in order to permit the Egyptians to cross the canal under cover of night. Noting that the afternoon start time meant that Syria would be enter-ing the war with the sun in their troops' eyes, he said, "We paid a price." The price, however, may have been much higher than poor visibility.

By midmorning Sunday, the beginning of stabilization in the southern Golan measurably improved the mood at Northern Command. But not for long. The Syrians had thrown 720 tanks into the battle as of Sunday morn-ing, including the tanks blocked by the Seventh Brigade in the northern sec-tor. Israeli tanks numbered only 250, including the first of the reserve units to arrive. As the morning wore on, dust clouds in the Hushniya area attested to a further buildup of Syrian armor in the heart of the Golan.

At Northern Command it was still assumed that the Syrians were preparing to push south past El Al and west towards the Jordan River. The first reservist forces had been thrown across these routes. But the main Syrian objective lay to the northwest—Nafakh and the Bnot Yaacov Bridge. Blocked by Force Zvika on the Tapline, now led by Ben-Shoham himself, and on Reshet Road by Tiger Company, the Syrian command chose a route between the two, passing through the abandoned villages of Ramtania and Sindiana, a mile east of the Tapline.

Battalion commander Haim Barak, riding with Eli Geva's company, would make contact with this force in midmorning. After Geva's company destroyed a Syrian battalion at dusk Saturday, it had been skirted for the rest of the night by the furies sweeping the area. Barak's second company, com-manded by Capt. Yaacov Chessner, had spent the night at Strongpoint 111, exchanging desultory fire with enemy tanks in the darkness. Geva's and Chessner's companies were only two miles apart, but unknown to them, large Syrian forces had passed between them in the darkness and entered the Golan.

Before dawn, Geva's company moved north to Mount Yosifon to meet a logistics convoy from Nafakh. When the tanks had been fueled and armed, Barak was ordered to proceed to the Sindiana road, where part of Mor's rapid-reaction battalion was reported to be in trouble. While most of the force had been directed to the Tapline during the night, a few tanks had been dispatched down the Sindiana road towards Hushniya. At first light, these had found themselves facing a mass of Syrian tanks. There had been no time to boresight their guns and their fire was ineffective. The Syrians destroyed two tanks and the Israeli force hastily withdrew. Barak found the reservist commander disoriented by the encounter.

Large dust clouds could be seen moving towards Hushniya, four miles south, and Barak could see the two Israeli tanks burning in that direction. He obtained Ben-Shoham's permission to move to Ramtania, overlooking the large base. The boulder-strewn terrain confined passage at points to a single navigable track. The battalion commander led the way, pausing at every rise to scan the terrain ahead. After three miles, he crested a ridge and saw below him in the Hashniya camp a mass of tanks—some fueling, some in defensive positions, some preparing to move out. There seemed to be hundreds. Syria's First Armored Division had arrived, joining units that had been in the area since the previous day. Barak ordered his tanks to take position on the ridge and open fire.

"Just point the gun anywhere and shoot," he said to his gunner. "You're sure to hit something." Barak's tank managed to get off two rounds, setting a Syrian tank afire, before itself being hit. Barak was blown out of the turret and temporarily blinded. His operations officer alongside him and two crewmen were killed.

Captain Geva had the casualties lifted into a half-track and ordered his tanks to fall back as an angry swarm of Syrian tanks began to climb towards them. Fighting a delaying action, he peppered the pursuing Syrians with long-range fire and attempted unsuccessfully to raise Ben-Shoham. With no one else to turn to for instructions, he switched to the radio frequency of his home brigade, the Seventh, and relayed his predicament to Ben-Gal. The brigade commander was immersed in his own battle and had no idea of what was happening elsewhere. He told Geva to fall back on the Seventh.

Meanwhile, Chessner had also been ordered to pull back to Yosifon to rearm and refuel. Moving north on Reshet Road, his company destroyed four Syrian tanks and dispersed an infantry concentration. The surprise Chessner detected in Ben-Shoham's voice when he reported his arrival at Yosifon, and the heartfelt "Well done," made him realize that the area he had passed through was now effectively under Syrian control.

He had not yet loaded ammunition when Geva notified him of the clash at Ramtania and the wounding of their battalion commander. Setting out to join Geva, Chessner saw to his south a chilling mass of enemy tanks heading in his direction. His tanks opened fire at long range and began to fall back towards Nafakh. Two of Chessner's tanks were knocked out by Saggers fired by Syrian infantrymen who had already reached Mount Yosifon. Down to his last shells, he told his tank commanders not to fire except at his order. He tried to raise Ben-Shoham or any other voice of authority but no one responded. When Geva told him that Ben-Gal had instructed him to fall back on the Seventh Brigade's logistics depot at Wasset, Chessner decided to do the same. Without ammunition it was impossible to continue the battle. Chessner and Geva, with seventeen tanks remaining between them, joined up near Nafakh and headed northwest.

The Syrians were striking at precisely the right place and the right time to splinter the Israeli defenses. If Nafakh and the high ground to its northeast were seized, the Israeli position in the northern and central Golan was doomed. Besides capturing the Golan command center at Nafakh itself, the Syrians would be in position to turn right and strike the embattled Seventh Brigade from the rear and to turn left and swoop down on the Bnot Yaacov Bridge. The departure of Geva and Chessner left no Israeli force in the Syrians' path. The Israeli command at Nafakh had received a report of Barak's sighting from Ramtania but was not aware that an armored division was racing in its direction and was only minutes away.

As Chessner passed Nafakh, he saw a newly arrived reservist artillery battalion parked at the side of the road, its men leisurely sprawled on the ground. He fired a machine gun into the air to get their attention. "Start shooting or get out," he shouted. "The Syrians are right behind us." Encountering his own battalion's logistics officer at the head of an ammunition convoy, Chessner told him to turn around. As far as he knew, there were no other Israeli tanks in the central Golan.

He was mistaken. Besides Force Zvika on the Tapline, Ori Orr and a score of his tanks were five miles east, near Kuneitra. Other tanks from Orr's brigade with ad hoc crews were drifting up from the Bnot Yaacov Bridge ten miles to the west. One such group, twelve tanks led by Lt. Col. Ron Gottfried, had reached the outskirts of Nafakh when Chessner's and Geva's tanks darted across the road to their front. Startled by the sight, Gottfried halted the column. Before he had a chance to call Orr, he was contacted by division headquarters inside Nafakh and told to halt. A jeep emerged from the camp and took him to the command bunker.

General Eitan seemed relaxed when Gottfried entered and even greeted the tank commander with a smile. Personnel were milling about in apparent confusion, and the blare of military radios made it difficult to hear anyone. Eitan told Gottfried he was detaching his force from Orr's command and sending it down the Sindiana road. "Ben-Shoham's in trouble," he said. Gottfried asked about the general situation but got no clear reply. From the atmosphere in the bunker, he guessed that Eitan didn't really know. In order to test the general's sense of urgency, Gottfried asked whether he should proceed in column—the fastest way—or move with his tanks deployed for possible combat. In column, said Eitan. "Get there fast." This suggested that Eitan did not believe enemy tanks were anywhere in proximity. However, Gottfried's glimpse of the apparently retreating Israeli tanks and his sense of the confusion at division headquarters made him opt for caution.

Turning into the Sindiana road, he deployed his tanks to either side of him and told the commanders that they would pause at every rise to survey the terrain before advancing. Topping the very first rise, they saw the spearhead of the First Syrian Division bearing down on them. The T-62s were only a thousand yards away and closing fast. "Fire," Gottfried barked. Syrian tanks began to burst into flame but dozens of others kept coming, returning fire without pausing to aim. The range was too short and the Syrian advance too swift and massive for the dozen Israeli tanks to stop them. Gottfried counted eight or nine Syrian tanks burning before his turret was blown off and he was flung unconscious into the air.

When he woke, his face was so puffed by burns that he could barely see. His driver lay nearby, with similar injuries. The two other crewmen were dead. It was not clear how much time had passed. Half a dozen of his tanks lay gutted around him. There were Syrian hulks as well. Gottfried took the stunned driver by the hand and walked back to the Nafakh–Kuneitra road. As they turned left towards Nafakh, a mile away, Gottfried heard tanks approaching from that direction. He planted himself in the middle of the road and raised his hand, palm outward. The lead tank stopped just in front of him. Gottfried's vision was blurred but he could make out the officer in the turret, a man of about thirty with a mustache. He appeared to be smiling at the sight of the two soot-covered tankers hitchhiking so imperiously. It was a moment before Gottfried realized that the tank he was leaning on was a T-62. Grabbing the driver, he scrambled into a ditch. The Syrians recovered from their own surprise and began spraying machine-gun bullets in their direction, but the two men were not hit and the tanks moved on.

Other tanks from Orr's brigade were meanwhile arriving at Nafakh from the direction of the bridge, finding themselves without warning in the middle of the war. Since they were not yet in the framework of organized units, tank commanders reacted according to their individual temperament. Some leaped into the swirling fight, which by this time had reached the perimeter of the camp. Others pulled back to await orders.

Lt. Hanan Anderson had found the mood lighthearted among the men in his makeshift platoon as they ascended the heights at 12:30 P.M. But columns of smoke, artillery explosions, and the roar of warplanes dissolved assumptions of a victory romp. At the edge of the Nafakh base, the platoon was flagged down by an officer. "You're in a battle zone," he said. "Don't go any further." He was Maj. Hanan Schwartz, communications officer of Ben-Shoham's brigade. Schwartz told the tank commanders from Orr's brigade to switch to Ben-Shoham's frequency.

Through the trees, Anderson could make out Syrian tanks five hundred yards to the east, two of them burning at the camp gateway. On the radio net came an order to enter the camp's garage area and stop tanks approaching from the Tapline to the south. Anderson was not sure for whom the order was intended, but he was familiar with the base and climbed a steep road to the garage area with another tank. Six to eight Syrian tanks were approaching from the direction of the Tapline. He hit one. The others took cover and exchanged fire. Next to the camp's perimeter fence was a guard dog attached to a long wire leash. Anderson, a farmer's son with an eye for dogs, noticed that every time his tank fired, the dog—a beautiful shepherd—was propelled by the blast into a somersault. After a lengthy exchange, the last of the Syrian tanks to Anderson's front was knocked out. The tank alongside him had been hit and its commander killed. The dog was still on its feet, its barking inaudible in the battle din.

In the command bunker, the air conditioner had stopped functioning and the air was stifling. Periodically, intelligence officer Dennie Agmon made his way to the entrance for a breath of fresh air. As he mounted the steps about noon, the sound of incoming artillery gave way to a sharp new sound—the explosion of tank shells. Venturing out, Agmon saw a score of Syrian tanks outside the camp fence, some as close as fifty yards, the furthest five hundred yards away. As he watched, a tank at the fence swiveled its gun and hit one of two half-tracks parked outside the command bunker. It was his own half-track. The other was that of division commander Eitan. The only Israeli tank in the vicinity, immobilized by a broken tread, was parked next to a helicopter pad. Its crew was aboard and the gunner destroyed the Syrian tank. Another Syrian tank destroyed the Israeli tank.

Agmon hurried back into the bunker and described to Eitan what he saw. "It's a minute before midnight," said Agmon. "We've got to get out." The general thought otherwise. "From what you tell me," he said, "it's a minute after midnight. We can't go out now."

Eitan raised Orr on the radio. Soviet advisers were known to be handling radio intercepts for Syrian intelligence, and it was assumed that they recognized the voices of Israeli commanders. Eitan therefore kept his message elliptical so as not to let the enemy know that the Israeli divisional commander was trapped inside Nafakh. "I've got lice in my hair. Maybe you can help me scratch." Orr had already been ordered to Nafakh by Northern Command, which was closely monitoring the radio nets and had a better view of the battle than Eitan or Ben-Shoham. Orr got the message and started his tanks towards Nafakh.

Orr dispatched three tanks under a battalion commander, Lt. Col. Rafael Sheffer, down the road from Kuneitra towards Nafakh to block any Syrian force that might attempt to turn east and hit the Seventh Brigade from the rear. His main force, fifteen tanks under Lt. Col. Moshe Harel, proceeded with Orr himself along a roundabout route on high ground to the south. From there they had a view of the terrain which the Syrians had to cross to get to Nafakh. They spotted forty Syrian tanks heading in its direction. The tanks were a shiny green and looked as if they were fresh off the factory floor. The Israeli force split into two groups under Orr and Havel. Attacking from the flank and rear, they knocked out most of the Syrian tanks.

The void through which the First Division had begun its drive for Nafakh was being filled by Israeli units converging from different directions. Gottfried's force and scattered tanks like Anderson's met the Syrians head-on from the north. Orr's tanks struck from the east. Now, Ben-Shoham, summoned by Eitan, headed towards Nafakh from the south with Zvika Greengold falling in close behind. Most of the other tanks of Force Zvika remained to block the Fifty-first Syrian brigade on the Tapline. From high points on the undulating road, Ben-Shoham and Greengold could see Syrian tanks outside Nafakh's fence firing into the camp. Abandoning the road, they cut cross-country together with a reservist lieutenant who joined them, pausing at every rise to fire. As they drew closer to the camp, they passed burned-out Syrian vehicles—tanks and APCs—as well as Israeli hulks. Dead and wounded from both sides were scattered on the ground. These were remnants of the battle by Gottfried's tanks.

At one point, Ben-Shoham disappeared from Greengold's view. On the radio net, the brigade commander could be heard calling for support. "I'm in the lead alone. Close up on my right and left." When Greengold regained the road a mile from the camp, he saw Ben-Shoham's tank lying on its side. The brigade commander and his operations officer had been cut down by machine-gun fire from a disabled Syrian tank at the side of the road as they stood with their heads out of the turret. The distraught driver had driven off the road and turned the tank over. Not far behind, Ben-Shoham's deputy, Lieutenant Colonel Yisraeli, lay dead alongside his tank. With the Syrians at the gates of Nafakh, Greengold had no time to pause.

By now, another Israeli force was converging on the battlefield, this time from the west. Three tanks led by Maj. Haim Danon were the last of Orr's brigade to cross the bridge. Danon was unable to make radio contact with Orr as he started to climb the heights, but the sight of half-tracks and trucks heading down towards the river gave him an uneasy feeling. A senior division officer in a jeep stopped alongside. "Get up there fast," he shouted. "The Syrians are in Nafakh."

Danon left the main road before he reached the camp and headed east cross-country. Beyond the Tapline two miles south of Nafakh, he saw Syrian tanks near Sindiana and engaged them at long range, hitting eight. Spying a group of Israeli tanks on the Tapline—the remains of Force Zvika—he took them under his command.

Meanwhile, Greengold and the reservist lieutenant reached Nafakh's perimeter. They fired on the Syrian tanks outside the fence until there were no more targets.

Absorbing the silence for a moment, Greengold called the command bunker. It was all right to come out, he said. Soldiers began appearing from different corners of the camp. Eitan's staff piled into his half-track, which had been spared, and headed down to the bridge with documents they had scooped up. The division commander himself drove off in a jeep, together with his intelligence officer, and headed north on the Golan to set up a command post in an open field a few miles north of Nafakh. Eitan had had a reputation as a fighter since pre-state days when he helped drown one of two armed Arabs who had intercepted a group hiking through the Galilee. At the battle for San Simon Monastery in Jerusalem in 1948, he insisted on remaining in the fight after being shot in the head. His comrades propped him up on a chair set on a table, from where he fired through a window at Arabs trying to come over the compound wall. In the Six Day War, leading a brigade of paratroopers on the Egyptian front, he had been shot in the head again. The surgeons extracting the bullet also removed fragments from the 1948 bullet. Eitan was not accustomed to withdrawals but he had evacuated

Nafakh twice in one day. The base was clearly too unsafe to serve as a divisional command post. But Eitan resolved in his own mind that, come what may, he himself would not retreat from the Golan.

Greengold got through to Uri Simhoni at Northern Command and informed him that there were "no live Syrian tanks" in the immediate proximity of Nafakh. Believing that the rest of Force Zvika had been destroyed, he said there were also no Israeli forces any longer on the Tapline. "And I think number one was killed." Shocked at the report of Ben-Shoham's demise, Hofi's operations officer asked Greengold to verify it by checking the overturned tank. Greengold, his strength gone, passed the request on to the reservist lieutenant.

Tank commanders, unable to raise Ben-Shoham, started calling Zvika, a name they had been hearing since the previous night, to ask for orders. The lieutenant asked them to call Major Zurich, the brigade intelligence officer, in Camp Aleka.

On his tank intercom, Greengold suddenly heard strangled breathing. "What's wrong?" he asked. The sounds were coming from the driver's compartment. With the assistance of the other crewmen, Greengold lifted the driver out. There were tears in the reservist's eyes and he was breathing with difficulty. Nothing was physically wrong with him, it was soon apparent, but the stress of the past hours had finally overcome him. Without a word, the soldier climbed out of the tank, climbed aboard a half-track evacuating wounded, and sat down.

Stranded, Greengold radioed Zurich and requested a driver. An officer drove up from Aleka with a young soldier who had volunteered for the job. Faint from his wounds and emotionally drained after twenty hours of continuous battle, Greengold asked the newcomer to drive to Aleka. The lieutenant was unaware of any other Israeli forces in the vicinity. It was clear to him after the death of Ben-Shoham that the fall of Nafakh and of the Golan was imminent and that there was nothing more he could do about it.

Seven members of the Golani Brigade armed with two bazookas had decided on their own to stay on at Nafakh after their unit pulled out. They fired five shells—all they had—at the Syrian tanks but scored no hits. As Greengold drove out of the camp, he saw several of these infantrymen at the entrance. An officer among them signaled to Greengold. Above the noise of the tank, he mouthed the words "Don't leave us." But Greengold could no longer carry on.

The scene along the road to Aleka reminded him of films of the Second World War—burned-out vehicles, wounded men walking towards the rear supporting each other, trucks filled with soldiers escaping the Syrian onslaught. His new driver's volunteering spirit proved greater than his driving skills. Wildly weaving, he bumped into almost everything in their path but finally managed to brake awkwardly at a roadblock outside Aleka. Zurich was waiting there. Greengold descended from the tank and collapsed but Zurich caught him. "I can't anymore," said Greengold. He was placed in a jeep and driven to a hospital in Safed.

Some officers involved in the battle would later maintain that Greengold had single-handedly prevented the capture of Nafakh by blocking the Syrian drive up the Tapline Saturday night and that in saving Nafakh he had saved the Golan Heights. Had the Syrians reached Nafakh, they would have trapped Hofi, Eitan, and their staffs in the command bunker. It is not clear, however, whether the Syrians on the Tapline in fact stopped because of the unexpected encounter with Greengold on the narrow roadway or for other reasons. In any event, Greengold's performance would deservedly win him the country's highest medal.

In approaching Aleka earlier on his way back from Nafakh, Major Zurich was dismayed at the sight of vehicles continuing down the road towards the bridge, including tanks. The pungent smell of panic hung in the air. The tanks were apparently manned by makeshift crews and not part of coherent units. In addition, the death of Ben-Shoham and the next two most senior officers of his brigade and the departure of the divisional staff from Nafakh had left a command vacuum. The retreat had come to look dangerously like a rout.

Zurich ordered his driver to swerve their armored personnel carrier across the road. Old Syrian minefields on either side made this a perfect choke point. A Golani mortar platoon was waiting at the roadside and Zurich ordered its commander to have his men flag down all vehicles approaching from Nafakh. "From here, no one retreats," Zurich said. "If anyone tries, we shoot." The lieutenant responded enthusiastically, and within an hour a dozen tanks, including the one Greengold left behind, were deployed with guns pointing up the road towards Nafakh. But no Syrian tanks appeared.

Towards evening, Zurich returned to Nafakh and found that some men had remained in the camp. Syrian tanks with hatches open were scattered outside the perimeter fence. Some were intact, their engines running, but the crews had fled. As with Greengold's driver, they had reached the end of their tether.

The main Syrian force had pulled back under the pressure of Orr's tanks, although not far. By the time darkness fell, Orr, bolstered by stray tanks from other units, succeeded in establishing a thin, four-mile-long defense line on high ground parallel to the Nafakh–Kuneitra road, the first semblance of a line in the central Golan since the war's start.

The Israeli forces on the Golan had been staggered by the Syrian attack, whose scope was beyond anything they had imagined. Unlike on the Egyptian front, however, the type of battle they had engaged in was the kind they had trained for—tank versus tank. The Egyptians had resorted to Saggers and RPGs in massive numbers in the opening battles in Sinai because their own tanks were not able to cross the canal in time to meet the initial rush of Israeli armor. But not even they had expected Israel to lose two-thirds of an armored division in half a day in a battle against infantrymen. The Syrians were no less well supplied with RPGs and Saggers but had not resorted to them en masse because they did not need the infantry as a stopgap. They were able to cross the physical barriers separating them from the Israeli line—the antitank ditch and minefields—with relative ease and meet the Israeli tanks with their own tanks. Saggers and RPGs were used in small numbers, but for the most part the Israeli tank crews on the Golan had to contend only with crushing odds, not a new form of warfare.

The battle at Nafakh exemplified the characteristics that would permit the Israeli forces to regain their balance despite the awesome nature of the blow they had been struck. Small groups, operating independently of each other with pick-up crews in a situation of imminent chaos, had displayed high motivation—instinctively lunging at a far more powerful enemy—and exemplary professionalism—shooting faster, straighter, and at longer range and making better use of the terrain. The battle had crescendoed in the spontaneous convergence of tank forces at Nafakh in which Ori Orr and his reservists had lifted the sword from Colonel Ben-Shoham even as he fell.

At a staff meeting that night at Northern Command, General Hofi gave his terse appraisal of the battle. "Ori saved us today."

Nineteen

CUT OFF

From tel faris, lieutenant colonel erez could see Syrian tanks flowing freely into the Golan Sunday morning. Apart from his twelve remaining tanks, there were no other intact Israeli tanks along the southern half of the line Sunday morning. Since war's outbreak the previous afternoon, Erez had lost two-thirds of his battalion. Also on the *tel* were sixty unmounted personnel—paratroopers evacuated from nearby strongpoints, crews of disabled tanks, and intelligence personnel who had been manning the lookout post atop the *tel*. They were now cut off behind Syrian lines. From time to time, Israeli Skyhawks dove on Syrian tanks. Erez saw a few tanks hit, but it made no impact on the armored tide. He counted five Skyhawks shot down.

The Syrians mounted several disconnected attacks on the *tel* during the day by platoons of tanks and by infantry-bearing APCs, which were easily driven off. At 2 p.m., six helicopters bearing commandos approached from the north. Tanks and paratroopers downed three with machine-gun fire and drove off the rest. With the fate of the Golan in doubt, Northern Command ordered Erez to try to make his way back to Israeli lines as soon as darkness set in.

Elazar spoke with Hofi in the late afternoon and urged him again to form a second line of defense at the edge of the plateau. It was vital, he stressed, to maintain a foothold on the heights until Moussa Peled's division reached it in the morning. Hofi was not certain he could do it. The Syrians had almost overrun Nafakh and they had still not committed all of their armor.

The conversation disturbed Elazar. He respected the northern front commander and was aware that without his warning about the Syrian buildup the heights might have fallen by now. But Hofi, he told his aides, was exhausted and needed a senior officer at his side to share the burden. Dayan had expressed uneasiness about Hofi's mood when he returned from Northern Command in the morning and Elazar had already decided to send up Gen. Yekutiel Adam, a former commander of the Golani Infantry Brigade, to serve as Hofi's deputy. He now had another idea as well—to send up Haim Bar-Lev, his predecessor as IDF chief of staff, to assess the situation.

Bar-Lev, now commerce minister, was a boyhood friend of Elazar's in Yugoslavia, where they were both born. His famously slow drawl enhanced his reputation for unflappability, a characteristic sorely needed in these hours. When Elazar put the idea to Dayan, the defense minister responded enthusiastically. So did Golda Meir. Bar-Lev accepted the proposal immediately. Meeting with Dayan before setting out, he asked what was wanted of him. Dayan said that the original intention was for him to replace Hofi, who, he said, was "collapsing, tired, worn out." Elazar had in the end ruled that out. "But in practice," said Dayan, "the intention is that you do replace him, with an official appointment or without." Dayan repeated his principal directive—no descent from the Golan.

At Northern Command headquarters, the situation seemed only marginally less fluid with the arrival of the reserves. These units too were beginning to be ground down by the unending flow of Syrian armor. As the day progressed, a question increasingly being asked was "Where's Moussa?"

Gen. Moussa Peled had taken leave of his reserve division the day before Yom Kippur for a year's study at university. He was at home the following morning when the deputy division commander, Brig. Gen. Avraham Rotem, telephoned. "You might want to get here," suggested Rotem. Peled stepped back into harness without further ado.

As a strategic reserve, the division had the luxury of a more thorough mobilization process than other units since the General Staff needed time to decide which front to send it to. It was not until 10 A.M. Sunday that Peled was summoned by Elazar, who told him the division was to go north. "The Syrians have broken through," he said. "Get up there quickly." Peled ordered Rotem by phone to start the division moving. Peled himself drove ahead with staff officers in two jeeps.

Northern Command's war room on Mount Canaan had been hastily set up the previous night in a movie theater whose seats had been removed. Cubicles and soundproofing had not yet been installed and the din from military radios echoing in the large space was grating. Peled was unable to get a clear briefing from anybody. He found Hofi lying on a cot in a darkened side room, trying to get some rest.

"My division arrives tonight," said Peled. "Where do you want me?"

As Peled would remember it, Hofi asked him to form a defense line along the Jordan. Peled was shocked by the order, which implied abandonment of the Golan. He was even more shocked to learn that engineers had already prepared the bridges for demolition. Hofi looked calm but Peled presumed him to be laboring under the strain of the apocalyptic events of the past day. Peled himself was fresh and untraumatized and he had an armored division at his back.

"I don't believe in defense," he said. "I believe we have to attack." Hofi asked him to return in the evening to participate in a meeting of senior commanders.

With a few hours at his disposal, Peled drove across Arik Bridge and climbed towards the southern heights. A veteran warhorse, he wanted to smell battle once again as he attuned himself to the task ahead. He found what he was looking for after just a few miles—the familiar low profile of Syrian tanks in the distance and the sound of artillery and tank fire.

The division was meanwhile straggling into Tsemach, at the southern end of Lake Kinneret. Almost half the tanks had broken down along the way and maintenance crews had gone out to repair them. No fuel trucks were waiting, but officers persuaded the proprietor of a gas station to fuel the tanks in return for IOUs. Instead of holidaymakers who normally lined up at the pumps on weekends, tank crews now patiently waited their turn.

When Bar-Lev arrived at Northern Command headquarters he was appalled at the din and sense of confusion. He ordered all radios shut off, then asked anyone whose task did not require them to be there, like drivers, to leave. The radios were then turned back on.

It was dark when Peled returned to Hofi's headquarters. Bar-Lev wanted to hear his thoughts. Peled proposed pushing straight north from El Al towards Rafid, twenty miles northeast. This move would cut across the main Syrian points of entry into the southern Golan. Once their logistic lines were threatened, the Syrian command would be obliged to withdraw their forces or risk their annihilation. It would be a terrible mistake to waste the division by having it form a defensive line along the river, he argued. It would also be a mistake to have it continue north to the Bnot Yaacov Bridge in order to counterattack from the central Golan, as was also being proposed. It would mean losing at least eight hours in transit and risk additional tank break-downs along the way.

Bar-Lev favored Peled's approach and called Elazar. After the chief of staff questioned Peled on the phone, he gave the plan his blessing. Hofi received the news as he conferred outside the building with his officers. "The plan is approved," said Bar-Lev. "We're going to counterattack." He handed Peled a cigar. "Smoke it when the time is right," he said.

At Tel Faris as darkness fell, the tanks formed into column and foot soldiers climbed atop them—five or six per tank. The dead and severely wounded were placed in a half-track. Company commander Uzi Arieli took the lead, followed by Lieutenant Beckman. With hundreds of Syrian tanks and tank hunters between them and the Israeli lines, they proceeded with extreme caution, avoiding roads and making use of their intimate knowledge of the terrain. Stopping before every rise, the drivers shut their engines to permit Captain Arieli to listen for enemy tanks. He and Beckman would then walk forward to look over the top of the rise. The way proved clear until they reached the last rise before the Tapline. Straddling the dirt track ahead, just short of the Tapline fence, were four Syrian tanks, facing in their direction.

"What do we do?" asked Beckman.

"We go quietly," said Arieli.

He called the tank commanders forward to explain the situation. They would pass between the Syrian tanks without firing but keep guns trained on them. In the darkness, the Syrians might not identify them. They would then plunge through the Tapline fence and proceed west cross-country. It was wild, trackless terrain but Arieli knew it well.

Moving slowly, Arieli and Beckman's tanks reached the Syrian tanks and passed between them, with just a few yards' clearance. It was as if the Syrian crews in the buttoned-up tanks were sleeping. Or perhaps they preferred avoiding a firefight they would clearly lose. As the third Israeli tank approached, however, one of the Syrian tanks fired. It had not raised its gun to aim and the shot hit low, damaging the Israeli tank but not disabling it. The twelve Israeli tanks responded with a volley that set the Syrian tanks aflame. Arieli smashed through the Tapline fence and led the tanks into a wadi beyond as Syrian tank formations nearby sent up flares.

Arieli navigated cautiously through the rough, boulder-strewn terrain. As the wadis began to deepen towards the edge of the Golan plateau, precipices appeared. Regaining high ground, the column was confronted by a mile-deep stretch of brushfires. Arieli could have gone around the flames but feared that if he did the tanks would offer a perfect silhouette to any Syrian tanks in the area. It would be safest, he decided, to pass through the fire.

Lieutenant Beckman could smell the scorched earth as they plunged into the flames. Soon he could smell scorched rubber from the tank bogies, near the treads. Between patches of fire, the charred earth glowed. The soot-covered riflemen clinging to his tank's superstructure were invisible except for the whites of their eyes and the orange light of the flames reflected by the ammunition bandoliers draped across their chests. Looking back, Beckman saw the tanks forming a half crescent—a line of armored behemoths plunging through a field of fire like the Horsemen of the Apocalypse. It was a scene that would remain vivid decades later.

With their frequent pauses to look and listen, it took close to ten hours to cross the narrow width of the Golan. Nearing the escarpment, they fired on the silhouettes of four Syrian tanks which proved to have been knocked out earlier in the day, apparently by aircraft. Finally they reached the last rise before the descent to Arik Bridge. Arieli and Beckman went forward on foot again and, seeing nothing, returned to their tanks. As Arieli led the column over the rise, his tank was hit. The shell killed the battalion operations officer riding alongside him and wounded the company commander himself. The driver hastily pulled back.

The column had reached the outskirts of the night encampment of Colonel Hadar's brigade at the upper stretch of the Gamla Ascent. The forward pickets of Hadar's force had positioned themselves with only their guns projecting above a rise and were virtually invisible. Hadar himself had heard the tanks approaching and notified General Laner, saying that they sounded like Centurions. Laner had not been informed of the breakout from Tel Faris. He asked Hadar to try to raise the tanks on the emergency radio wavelength to which all tanks were supposed to be tuned. When there was no response, Laner told him to open fire. Northern Front command, monitoring both sides, realized what was happening and ordered everyone to cease fire. Lieutenant Beckman told Northern Command he was switching on his headlights and moving forward. He topped the rise and friendly lights flashed back at him.

The abandonment of Tel Faris left Strongpoint 116 as the only Israeli position along the southern part of the cease-fire line still manned. Heavy artillery fire had resumed with darkness. Feeling the evening chill, Lieutenant

Gur donned a flak jacket for warmth. It was the first time he had worn one since the fighting began. At 8 P.M., five Syrian tanks turned off the border road towards the strongpoint. The lead tank pushed aside disabled vehicles and stopped to fire at the position. After every round, it moved forward a few yards and fired again, showering the trench with bits of sharp basalt. With only two bazooka shells left, Gur decided to try a rifle grenade, about whose efficacy he was uncertain. He told the bazookist to be prepared to back him up. When the lead tank reached the entrance to the compound, Gur rose and fired. He could not tell what physical impact it had but the tank stopped moving and stopped firing. He hit the second tank in line with another rifle grenade. It too stopped but the other three tanks opened fire.

Gur called down artillery on the strongpoint and its surroundings. One shell exploded directly behind him. The flak jacket absorbed most of the impact but shrapnel gouged a deep hole in his right shoulder where the jacket ended. The lieutenant lost feeling in his arm and then passed out. Soldiers carried him to a bunker where a medic bandaged the wound and Gur regained consciousness. He had already decided that if he was to be hit he would pass command to a private who had been fighting alongside him since the battle began. The young soldier was outranked by almost everyone else but he had shown the stuff of a natural leader—courage, a sharp eye, and the ability to analyze a situation quickly. Gur wanted to say "Take command" but the phrase struck him as too theatrical. "Go back up and make order," he said.

During the night, Gur felt himself floating near the tempting shores of death, but towards dawn his mind began to clear. From time to time, the private and others would come down to see how he was and to seek advice. They reported driving off several attacks by Syrian infantrymen. There were only ten men still on their feet. Haunted by the thought that Syrians might penetrate the outpost, Gur told the three other wounded men with him that they had best place their weapons alongside them. One man eased the safety on the grenades so that those who had the use of only one hand, like Gur, could detach the pin easily with their teeth if need be.

In midmorning, Syrian tanks began methodically pounding the fort. Dust coming in through the air vents filled the bunker and stone chips fell from the ceiling. The shelling was interminable but, released from responsibility, Gur felt strangely calm until he heard what he feared most—shouts in Arabic. The Syrians were inside the strongpoint.

The lieutenant pulled himself to his feet and, together with one other wounded soldier who could walk, moved to the bunker exit, gripping his rifle in his left hand. It was drizzling outside and the sky was gray. In the court-yard to his front, near a basketball hoop, were three Syrian soldiers. One, a tall, mustachioed figure with a bandolier of bullets across his chest, held a machine gun in both hands and sprayed bullets in a random arc. None of the men in the garrison could be seen. Propping his left leg up on a jerrican of water just inside the entrance, Gur rested the rifle on it and fired on auto-matic with his left hand. The Syrians were not hit but disappeared from view. At the fort gateway, he saw Syrians with RPGs. One fired in Gur's direction and basalt splinters from the bunker wall hit him in the back. Suddenly there was the sound of exploding grenades and small-arms fire. The other soldiers in the garrison had been sheltering in the deep trenches from the pounding of the Syrian tanks and were unaware that there had been a penetration until they heard the gunfire in the courtyard. They now counterattacked, killing some of the attackers and driving off the remainder. With his adrena-line flowing, Gur resumed his post at the gate.

Shortly after dark Sunday, Major Yair at El Al heard a muted voice on the radio. "Everyone's dead or wounded. Hurry and get us out." The caller identified himself as a tank commander on Tel Saki. It was Sgt. Nir Atir. He was calling from a disabled tank near the bunker in which the Israeli sur-vivors on the *tel* had taken shelter. He kept his voice low so as not to be over-heard if Syrian soldiers were still in the area. Yair had given up hope of anyone remaining alive on Tel Saki after Lieutenant Ansbacher had made his farewells more than twelve hours before.

Close to thirty men had taken shelter in the inner room of the unfinished bunker near the top of Tel Saki Sunday morning. The Syrians fired a shell through the wall of the bunker, then tossed two grenades inside. Almost all the men were hit, some fatally. But the Syrians did not enter for fear of armed survivors. Ansbacher was among the badly wounded. "Somebody go out and surrender," he said. A tank crewman took off his white undershirt and held it aloft as he left the bunker. Two bursts of automatic fire outside were heard. "The bastards aren't taking prisoners," said someone. But the soldier had not been hit. Taken prisoner, he told his captors that he was the last one alive in the bunker. They chose not to check.

The Israelis lay all day where they had fallen. One man shouted for a while in pain. The others tried to silence him. However, he had been deaf-ened by the explosions and could not hear them. One of the soldiers said the shouter would have to be killed or else they would all die. A soldier wrote a note on a cigarette pack and held it in front of the wounded man, who read it by the light of a match held for him. "You must keep quiet," it said. He stopped shouting. Spirits rose after Sergeant Atir returned with half a jerrican of water and a message from Yair about the coming counterattack.

As darkness approached on Sunday, the battle in the central sector tapered off. Ori Orr asked a contingent of Golani infantry to scour the battlefield for disabled tanks and to check them for wounded and dead. There were many missing, including two battalion commanders. The infantrymen found Colonel Sheffer and his crew lying wounded next to their tank on the road from Nafakh to Kuneitra. The officer had been blinded in one eye. The second battalion commander, Harel, whose disabled tank had been found earlier, arrived on foot after eluding Syrian troops. He too was wounded.

In view of the heavy casualties, it was necessary to rebuild the brigade from scratch. Orr appointed virtually all officers to new tasks. Apart from the wounded battalion commanders, two of his company commanders were dead and two others wounded. Some officers whom he had not regarded highly had performed superbly under fire and others had disappointed him. Altogether, the men had fought well despite the psychological wrench of being thrown into battle straight from civilian life and despite the random way the crews had been formed. They had gone into battle unbonded, which made the unnatural deed of moving into the way of death even more harrowing. Orr decided not to reorganize the crews into their original prewar configurations but to leave them as they were, now that they had fought together.

General Eitan, operating from his command half-track north of Nafakh, ordered Orr to attack in the morning on the Sindiana road. With his tanks deployed on full alert, Orr could not summon his officers for a briefing and he spent much of the night moving along the line to talk to them individually. Sometimes he paused in the darkness to listen to the conversations of the men on the tanks. It was apparent from what he heard that the one rallying point all had in common was Orr himself. His voice on the radio net and his status as an authority figure were central factors in the brigade's functioning.

In a book written by Chaim Sabbato, a yeshiva student who served as a gunner in Orr's brigade, the author describes Orr climbing onto his tank in the darkness after the first day of battle. Introducing himself—"I'm your brigade commander"—the colonel pulls a bar of chocolate from his shirt pocket and distributes it among the crewmen. "I know it's difficult for you.

You're young. It's difficult for me too. I've fought in a tough war [the Six Day War, in which Orr had been commander of a reconnaissance company under Gonen] but this is something else altogether. We've lost a lot of tanks. You're without a battalion commander and company commander. But we're going to win. Whoever hangs on longer wins. We've got no choice. Before dawn we're going to attack towards Hushniya. Your company will provide covering fire." Taking his leave, the brigade commander says, "It's going to be a tough day tomorrow. Get some rest."

It was still dark when Avraham Rotem started up the Gamla Ascent Sunday night with two half-tracks and a jeep. The vehicles traveled without lights. Moussa Peled had ordered Rotem, his deputy, to take command of the left wing of the counterattack that would get under way in the morning. Hadar's brigade, which had been incorporated into Peled's division, constituted the left wing. Hadar was not responding to Rotem's radio calls, adding to the sense of unease about what was happening up there. The brigade commander was maintaining radio silence so as not to risk his unit's presence being picked up by Syrian directional finders.

As they rounded a bend, Rotem heard the sound of approaching tanks. He ordered the drivers to pull over and cut engines. In a few moments he detected with relief the familiar sound of Centurions. Dark shapes loomed ahead and he flashed a recognition signal. It was the tanks from Tel Faris. As they came abreast Rotem saw that they were covered with soldiers, some of them wounded. He had the disturbing impression of an army in flight.

It was dawning when the Tel Faris convoy approached Arik Bridge. Reservists heading towards the Golan waved and called out to the men returning from the front. They fell silent when they drew closer and saw the exhausted, soot-covered faces. After unloading their passengers, the tankers were ordered to refuel, rearm, and return to the battalion's rear base, Camp Jordan, on the heights. Their war was not over.

In two days of battle, the young conscripts posted on the Golan had succeeded, with the help of the first reserve units, in blunting the enemy onrush. The Syrian attack had not yet peaked, but a thin line of reserve units was beginning to form around the enormous hole gouged in the Israeli lines. Northern Command, which had Sunday morning made preparations for withdrawal from the Golan, was preparing by evening for a counterattack.

After midnight, Moussa Peled briefed his officers in a eucalyptus grove at the southern end of Lake Kinneret. There was no intelligence available about the Syrian disposition. The fall of the Hermon had deprived AMAN of its eyes on the Golan, and the antennas on forward listening posts had been shot away, depriving it of its ears. However, the division's attack was not dependent on intelligence. It would drive north regardless of what lay in its path and cut the entrance points into the Golan south of Kuneitra. By concentrating on a narrow front, said Peled, they would offer a clenched fist powerful enough to smash through anything the Syrians put in their way. And they would be surprising the enemy by striking his flank.

By the light of a pocket flashlight, the division intelligence officer showed on a map what their line of attack would be. They would be going into battle, he said, against three Syrian divisions. General Peled advised the officers to get a few hours of sleep. As they started to move off, Peled called them back. "Just a moment. We have a guest who wants to say a few words."

The officers could not make out the figure standing alongside the division commander in the darkness, but they immediately recognized his voice. "You're Israel's last hope," said Haim Bar-Lev. "The eyes of the nation are upon you. Get up there and good luck."

Twenty

HAND ON THE TILLER

F OR GOLDA MEIR, THE DESCENT into the General Staff "Pit" Sunday
morning for a briefing could have served as a metaphor for what she
would experience this day—a descent into a trough of despair deeper and
more charged than any she had ever imagined.

The visit itself was less devastating than it might have been, thanks to the
positive twist put by General Elazar on reports from the battlefield. He made
it sound like the situation, while serious, was in the process of being resolved,
or at least stabilized.

Moshe Dayan knew otherwise. His visit to Northern Command at dawn
had colored his mood darkly. With his visit to Southern Command later
in the morning, concern turned to despondency. The war room at Umm
Hashiba was better organized than Northern Command's, and Gonen was
far more confident than Hofi, his northern counterpart. That, however, was
part of the problem. "He was too sure of himself," Dayan would write,
"about knowing what was happening and understanding the situation as it
really was." With the arrival of the reserve divisions, Gonen told him, it
would be possible to drive the Egyptians out of Sinai and perhaps to cross to
the west bank as well.

Annoyed at Gonen's easy optimism, Dayan told him that top priority
must be given to forming a fallback line that could be held if the current
front crumbled. The Bar-Lev forts must be given up, he said; enough forces

had been eroded trying to reach them. Garrisons that were surrounded should attempt to make their way out on foot after dark, and there must be no more attempts to break through to them with tanks. Immobile wounded would be left behind to be taken prisoner. The defense minister recommended that the new line be set up along the Artillery Road, six miles from the canal. Gonen said that that line could not be held because of the topography. "It is within my authority," said Dayan, adopting an uncharacteristic formality, "to order you to form a line that you can hold. Otherwise we will end up on Israel's [pre–Six Day War] border. Let the line be on the Artillery Road or the Lateral Road." The defense minister advised Gonen to consult with Elazar on where the line should be drawn.

On the helicopter ride back to Tel Aviv, Dayan pondered the implications of what he had seen on his visits to the two fronts. Like everyone else, he had been shocked by the Arab attack. Unlike anyone else, except Elazar, the major burden of responsibility for what had to be done fell upon him. His colleagues knew him to possess a personal courage that seemed to reflect indifference to death. What he sensed now was Israel's mortality and it shook him. He was gripped, he would later write, by an anxiety he had never before known.

An unspoken premise on which Israel had built its defense strategy—and he its prime architect—was that the Arabs they would face in the next war were the same Arabs they had so handily defeated in the Six Day War and the Sinai Campaign of 1956. It was a premise that permitted strategic corner-cutting, such as maintaining outlandishly small forces along the front lines. A single day's battle had now demonstrated that these were not the same Arabs. Both the Egyptians and the Syrians were attacking according to a well-thought-out plan—better thought out, clearly, than Israel's own. They had been massively supplied with modern weapons by the Soviets, including weapons Israel had no answer for, like the SAM-6 and the Sagger. More troubling still, they were infused with a fighting spirit they had never before shown. They were not running, even when hit hard. Israel had not calculated the vital psychological boost the Arabs would derive from having seized the initiative.

What concerned Dayan most was not the immediate battle, troubling as that was. Beyond the front lines, beyond Egypt and Syria, lay the rest of the Arab world. Israel's three million Jews were facing eighty million Arabs. Syria and Egypt might accept a UN-imposed cease-fire, but they could renew the fighting at any time with expeditionary forces from other Arab countries and fresh arms from the Soviet Union. Israel would be steadily worn down.

The breadth of Dayan's strategic vision had become the depth of his despair. Before the helicopter landed at Sde Dov Airport on the Tel Aviv seafront, he determined to share his nightmare with Elazar and Mrs. Meir.

Most Israelis had little doubt that while the situation was difficult, the country had the resilience to recover and win the field. The day before, with the war only two hours old, Dayan himself had spoken optimistically at a meeting with Israeli newspaper editors. "The Egyptians have embarked on a very big adventure they haven't thought through. After tomorrow afternoon [when the reserves begin to reach the front] I wouldn't want to be in their place." Now it *was* tomorrow afternoon and it was Israel that was in trouble, not the Arabs. "Do you know what I fear most in my heart?" he said to Elazar and other senior officers in the Pit upon returning to Tel Aviv from Umm Hashiba. "That Israel will be left without sufficient arms to defend itself, regardless of where the new line is drawn. That there won't be enough tanks and planes, that there won't be enough trained personnel." The war was not against Egypt and Syria, he said. "This is the war of Israel against the Arabs"—that is, the entire Arab world. This was the message he intended to transmit in the coming hour to Mrs. Meir. "If you take exception to anything," he said to Elazar, "tell me now." He was not advocating an immediate retreat, said Dayan, but a fallback line had to be prepared, perhaps along the Lateral Road, and a second fallback line as well, perhaps from Sharm el-Sheikh to the Sinai passes.

Elazar did not address Dayan's apocalyptic visions, only his operational recommendations. The chief of staff agreed that efforts to reach the Bar-Lev forts should be abandoned and that a second line of defense should be established along the Lateral Road where Sharon's and Adan's divisions were already forming up. However, Elazar favored a counterattack once the reserves were ready. The difference between him and Dayan, he said, was that he, Elazar, believed it possible to block the Egyptians.

Dayan departed for his meeting with Mrs. Meir and her inner cabinet, leaving behind a cavernous gloom among the officers who had heard him. For them as for the general public, Dayan was a military icon embodying the nation's self-confidence and its ability to meet any challenge. He was now probably the most depressed man in the country, certainly the most depressing.

The impact of Dayan's words on Mrs. Meir was predictable. She heard them "in horror," she would write, and the thought of suicide crossed her mind. Her longtime assistant, Lou Kedar, was at her desk in the room next to the prime minister's when Mrs. Meir rang after Dayan's departure. "Meet me in the corridor," she said. There were other people in Mrs. Meir's office and she wanted a private space. Although she had the country's top military and political advisers on call, she could share her deepest feelings only with an old friend. When Kedar emerged into the corridor, Mrs. Meir was already waiting for her. Kedar was shocked at her pallor, which matched the gray jacket she was wearing. There was despair in her face. Kedar would remember the prime minister leaning heavily against a wall and saying in a low and terrible voice, "Dayan is speaking of surrender."

If Dayan had used that word, it is inconceivable that he used it in the conventional sense. But he *had* spoken of surrendering territory—pulling back from the Bar-Lev Line—and of his belief that it would be impossible to force the Egyptians back across the canal. He had offered his resignation, which Mrs. Meir refused. When she asked what his reaction would be if the UN ordered an immediate cease-fire, he said he would grab it, even if this meant the Egyptian army remaining on the east bank of the canal.

Mrs. Meir stared hollowly at Kedar, her mind elsewhere. The moment seemed interminable. Slowly, the expression on Mrs. Meir's face began to change and color seeped back into her cheeks. "Get Simha," she said. Kedar heard the familiar determination once again in her voice. Through Ambassador Simha Dinitz in Washington, Mrs. Meir intended to start putting pressure on the American administration for arms. Many excruciating days still lay ahead, but psychologically the prime minister had touched bottom and had begun to regain her balance.

Many in Israel would be going through similar emotional plunges as the country reeled from the war's opening blows. Senior officers realized with a stab that they had prepared for the wrong war, that basic assumptions on which their confidence had rested were illusions. The Arab soldiers were not running—they were attacking and they were fighting well with new weapons and new spirit. The Israeli air force was hardly being felt on the battlefield and it was losing planes at an alarming rate. Israeli tank forces had been unable to hold the line on either front except on the northern Golan. Israeli intelligence was not all-knowing; it had been responsible for an astounding glitch that threatened to bring disaster on the country. Everything was coming apart and the war was hardly a day old. If the Arabs had succeeded in accomplishing so much in this span of time, what else lay in store?

The soldiers on the front line were generally too busy fighting to spare thoughts about national survival. Sometimes, however, they too were gripped by dark thoughts, particularly airmen who had a broader view. A Phantom pilot who returned to base from a mission over the Golan on Sunday was asked by an operations clerk what it had been like. He described to her columns of dark Syrian tanks rolling slowly across the Golan Heights like hordes of giant ants, with nothing to stop them. Alarmed by his description, the clerk said that her brother, a tank crewman, "is up there." She wanted the pilot to tell her that things would be all right. Instead, he said absently, "*Was* up there," as if nothing could survive the Syrian juggernaut. In the briefing room of a Phantom squadron, the acting commander said to the assembled pilots after a day of flying over SAMs, "Take a good look at each other. When this war is over, a lot us won't be here."

For civilians too, the abrupt switch from tranquillity and national self-confidence on Yom Kippur afternoon to all-encompassing war and existential alarm—without what psychologists would call "the positive process of anticipatory fear"—was a shock that would not quickly heal. The distress was amplified by realization that the battle lines were not holding.

In this, the most perilous period in Israel's history, the effort to avoid national disaster hinged in good measure on the steady nerves of one man. Given the gloom all about him, given the debacle on the battlefield and the abrupt collapse of the military doctrine on which Israel had rested its security, given too the appalling prospect of national annihilation that was suddenly perceived, David Elazar merits a niche in history's pantheon of military leadership just by virtue of not losing his head.

He was hardly without sin. He had accepted and propagated a doctrine that left the IDF unprepared for this war, a doctrine resting on scorn for the enemy. He bore responsibility as chief of staff for deferring to AMAN and not seeking partial mobilization in the days before Yom Kippur. He advocated a static defense on the canal in all circumstances, against basic military sense, and it was he who appointed Gonen head of Southern Command. Nor would he be without occasional error in the conduct of the war itself, although the great bulk of his decisions would prove sound. But in the cruel testing, with basic concepts giving way and strong men about him faltering, his was the stable hand on the tiller. Examination of the protocols of his meetings shows the steadiness, and even good humor, with which he directed operations, although there were moments when he too was close to despair. Around his firm presence a calm space emerged where issues could be objectively analyzed and sensible decisions made. In the circumstances, it was not a foregone conclusion that Israel's center would hold, but it did hold and David Elazar was the center. "He was a rock," Golda Meir would later say. It would be on him, rather than Dayan, that she would primarily rely for the difficult decisions that had to be made.

Elazar's coolness in crisis had been noted in 1948, when, as a junior officer in the elite Palmach strike force, he took part in the battle of San Simon Monastery in Jerusalem against hundreds of Arab militiamen. In the battle, which lasted sixteen hours, Elazar moved from breach to breach to drive off attackers. "He had a special tone of voice during a battle," recounted an officer who was there, Mordecai Ben-Porat, "quiet-like, as if he were singing, as if he were having a friendly chat or explaining something. I didn't know him before, but I remember saying to myself then: 'What a character that one is.' "

Towards the end of the battle, he was among only 20 of the 120 Palmach fighters still on their feet—40 were dead and 60 wounded. A decision was made for the walking wounded and able-bodied to retreat when night fell. Instead of leaving the remaining wounded to the mercies of the Arabs, it was decided to bring the structure down on them by blowing it up. Elazar and two other officers were to remain behind and detonate the explosives. Before that happened, the Arabs pulled back.

The harrowing battle helped shape all who survived it. Several were now senior officers serving under Elazar—among them Raful Eitan, commanding a division on the Golan; Uri Ben-Ari, now assistant to Gonen; and Ben-Porat, leading a mechanized brigade on the Golan. Elazar was still blessed with a calm temperament, and his upbeat assessments would provide encouragement and guidance to the embattled front commanders and to the cabinet with which he met almost every day. Unlike Dayan, who served up the cruel truth cold, Elazar warmed it to digestibility with an innate optimism. Things, after all, had looked much worse at San Simon and they had come through.

After Dayan left the Pit, an important decision had to be made regarding the two reserve divisions now forming up behind the front in Sinai. Dayan had demanded preparation of a fallback line. Sharon, on the other hand, called Elazar to urge an immediate crossing of the canal. So did Gonen. Elazar's instincts placed him somewhere between the two approaches—it was too early to attempt a canal crossing but he did not want to pull back so far that it would be difficult to reach the canal in a counterattack. Adding to his disinclination to pull back was a report from Zeira that Egypt's two armored divisions, which were supposed to cross the canal in the wake of the five infantry divisions, showed no signs yet of doing so. Elazar hoped that they would cross to the Sinai bank and be whittled down in a major tank battle before the IDF crossed.

Dayan was still conferring with Mrs. Meir when Elazar arrived to outline the three alternatives he saw. The army could fall back to the Lateral Road to create a stable line for a day or two and then counterattack in an attempt to win back the territory inside Sinai captured by Egypt. Or the army could fall even further back, to the passes, and dig in, a suggestion Dayan himself had raised. But that would mean abandoning two major installations—the air base and logistics center at Refidim and the Umm Hashiba command and intelligence post. The third possibility was to try to cross the canal, as Sharon and Gonen were proposing.

Dayan responded a bit less gloomily than he had in the Pit. His visit to the front, he said, left him skeptical about the prospects of a counterattack. But he agreed that Elazar should fly to Southern Command and explore the possibilities. If the chief of staff concluded that a counterattack within Sinai was realistic—not Sharon's cross-canal gamble, Dayan stressed—the cabinet would authorize him to carry it out.

After Elazar's departure for Mrs. Meir's office, the mooted pullback was discussed by the officers who remained in the Pit. The talk angered air force commander Benny Peled, who regarded any pullback as a grievous error. Returning to the air force war room, he ordered an immediate air attack on the canal bridges "at all costs." When Elazar returned, he was informed by Peled that seven of the fourteen bridges on the canal had been knocked out. The report caused a wave of elation, but in fact the bombing had little impact on the Egyptians because the damaged bridge sections were swiftly replaced. Nevertheless, the attack had an impact on the Israeli command, giving them the impression that the Egyptian crossing was being contained. This permitted them to think more boldly in terms of counterattack.

Elazar set off in late afternoon by helicopter on his flight to Sinai accompanied by Yitzhak Rabin. The latter had no official standing but provided a sympathetic ear for the chief of staff, whose relations with his deputy, General Tal, were becoming increasingly strained by differences of view—Tal consistently urging caution while Elazar was prepared for a bold stroke that would shift the tide of battle.

Most of the southern front's senior commanders were waiting for Elazar in the war room at Umm Hashiba when he arrived at 6:45 P.M., but it was so noisy with the blare of military radios that they repaired to Gonen's office, a small room with a map covering one wall. The only person missing was Sharon. Gonen said there had been a misunderstanding about where he was to be picked up by helicopter. Adan was struck by Elazar's seeming serenity. Gonen and Ben-Ari looked weary. So did Mendler, whose division had borne the brunt of the fighting for the past two days. In response to Elazar's question, Adan said the Egyptian commandos he encountered on the coast road that morning had fought surprisingly well. They had held their fire until the Israeli troops were almost upon them and they did not flee when they came under mortar fire or even from a head-on tank attack. Their commander had been taken prisoner, still feisty. He cursed his superiors for failing to reinforce him as promised.

After waiting awhile for Sharon, Elazar started the meeting without him. He presented an overview of the situation on both fronts and asked those present for their thoughts. Gonen proposed that Sharon and Adan cross the canal the next night at Suez City and Kantara, in the southern and northern sectors, respectively, on captured bridges. Mendler proposed that the two divisions attack together in the central sector. Sharon, according to Gonen, wanted to send his forces that night to rescue the men in the forts in his sector. Adan said that any rescue attempts would be costly and probably not succeed. He recommended a limited counterattack whose purpose would be only to break the Egyptian momentum. There should be no attempt to reach the canal, he said, until sufficient strength had been built up. Ben-Ari said that no canal crossing should be attempted at this point and that an effort should be made instead to prevent the Egyptians from deepening their bridgehead.

Agreeing with the cautious approach voiced by Adan and Ben-Ari, Elazar decided on a limited counterattack the next day. Adan, in the northern sector, would start the operation by sweeping southward parallel to the canal. He would keep at least two miles from it so as to stay out of range of the tank guns and Sagger missiles on the canal-side embankments. The force should by noon reach a point inland from Fort Matsmed, halfway down the canal. If all went well, Adan would then halt and Sharon's division would move out, executing a similar sweep parallel to the canal from Matsmed to a point opposite Suez City at the canal's southern extremity. Both attacks would be supported by artillery and planes. Mendler's battered division would hold fast in the southern sector.

A basic element of the plan, which Elazar stressed repeatedly, was that it must be carried out "with two feet on the ground"—that is, only one division would move at a time while the other two would remain in place, ready to support it if necessary. Gonen was told he would have to request approval before unleashing Sharon's division after Adan completed his sweep. The object was not to uproot the Egyptian bridgeheads or to cross the canal, Elazar said, but to seize the initiative and blunt any Egyptian attempt to push further into Sinai. The IDF's counterattack would come later, preferably after the Egyptian armored divisions attacked. He left open the possibility of reaching, or even crossing, the canal the next day if the Egyptian army should suddenly collapse, as happened in 1967. But that was not part of the plan, only a contingency to be kept in mind. On the other hand, if some catastrophe should strike, it would be possible to pull back to a secondary defense line along the Lateral Road.

It was now 10 P.M. and Elazar had to return to the Pit to monitor developments on the northern front. He told Gonen that he wanted to receive from him during the night his detailed operational order for tomorrow's attack. As Elazar, Rabin, and Adan emerged from the command bunker, they ran into Sharon, who was hurrying from the helicopter that had finally brought him. Furious at having missed the meeting, Sharon hurriedly made his pitch to Elazar. He had been in radio contact with the men in the forts and they were waiting for rescue. The IDF never abandoned its men, he said, and he had a plan for breaking through to some of the forts this night.

As Elazar would remember the meeting, he asked Sharon whether, if the rescue effort were made this night, his division could mount an attack in the morning. Sharon replied in the negative, and Elazar said there could therefore be no rescue attempt. As Sharon would remember the meeting, he told Elazar that a concentrated attack was needed against the Second Army bridgehead. The Egyptians were heady from the scent of success, and only the shock of a combined attack by at least two divisions could restore a psychological balance.

"I can't risk the only two divisions I have between Sinai and Tel Aviv," said Elazar. He did not refer to Mendler's depleted division.

"The Egyptians aren't heading for Tel Aviv," replied Sharon. "That's beyond them. Their target is the canal and the line of hills. They can't afford to go beyond their missile cover."

Sharon had precisely read the thinking of the Egyptian command, but Elazar was unwilling to risk an all-out attack in view of the heavy losses and unpleasant surprises of the past two days. He told Sharon that Gonen would brief him on the plan that had been decided on.

Sharon had missed the meeting because the airstrip near Tasa, where he would normally have boarded the helicopter, was a potential target of Egyptian commandos believed to be prowling the area. He had given Gonen's headquarters the coordinates of a site in the dunes some distance away where the helicopter should pick him up. He waited for close to two hours before it arrived. Sharon was convinced that the delay had been ordered by Gonen to keep him from presenting his plan for the rescue of the garrisons.

Ever the tactician, Sharon did not show his anger when he entered the bunker. Instead, he took Gonen aside and attempted to persuade him that he was not trying to usurp his authority. "Look, Shmulik," he said, using the diminutive of Gonen's first name, "I've left the army already. My life is going in an entirely different direction. I'm not coming back to take your place here. The only aim I have is to defeat the Egyptians. Once we're finished with them, I'm gone. Shmulik, you can win this war. You can come out a winner. All you have to do is to concentrate your forces against them. You don't have an enemy in me. You don't have to deal with me at all. Just deal with the Egyptians." His words seemed to touch a chord in Gonen, who nodded his head.

Adan believed that Sharon, whose division had not yet been seriously engaged, did not realize the nature of what they were up against and that he had been overly influenced by his radio contact with the men in the forts. It was clear to Adan that the only solution for the beleaguered garrisons was for them to try to get out on their own.

At Orkal, the northernmost outpost, permission for a breakout was received this night. The Egyptians had captured the entrance to the sprawling compound, and only the presence of the three tanks stationed at Orkal had prevented the rest of the fort from being overrun. One tank had been knocked out. As soon as darkness set in, the garrison survivors climbed onto a half-track sandwiched between the two remaining tanks and into the rearmost tank. The three vehicles charged towards the exit and broke through the surprised Egyptians. But they still had to travel five miles on the causeway before reaching the road through the lagoon. Commanding the lead tank was Sgt. Shlomo Arman, who had been leading the platoon since his officer was killed at the opening of the war. The convoy stopped after two miles to pick up several men from observation posts who had been cut off when the fighting broke out. They had found shelter in the lagoon, just off the road, while maintaining radio contact.

One of them, Yitzhak Levy, a thirty-three-year-old reservist, climbed into Arman's tank. The twenty-one-year-old tank commander patted Levy on the shoulder and said, "Soldier, you're saved. There's nothing that can stop this tank." Levy recognized the confident voice as that of the tank commander he had heard on the radio conducting the battle in Orkal for the past two days. Shortly after the convoy started forward again, the half-track and rear tank were hit by RPGs. Arman reported the ambush by radio to a company officer and said he was going to their assistance. "Negative," came the response. "Keep moving." Arman protested, but the officer said, "Negative. They'll kill you all. Move out of there fast. Out."

The tank resumed movement, but after four hundred yards it too was hit. The crew leaped out to the left and Levy, their passenger, jumped to the right. He landed among a group of Egyptian soldiers. They struck at him with rifles and he punched back. Suddenly he heard Arman's voice: "Reservist, where are you?" Levy managed to get away in the dark and joined the tank crew plunging through the waist-high waters. Levy's strength gave way and the young tank crewmen supported him. But Levy felt he could no longer go on. Leave me, he said. I'll continue later by myself. "No one stays in this swamp," said Arman. "If we make it, we'll all make it. If we don't, it'll be all of us." As they continued on, Arman asked Levy to talk about his wife and children. "We'll soon be there," he said.

It was close to midnight when they saw the outline of Israeli tanks to their front. "Hey, tankers," shouted Arman. "We're from the forts."

"Don't move," came the reply. "Who are you?"

"We're from Orkal."

"Who knows you?"

Arman gave them the names of his battalion and brigade commanders. "Where in Israel are you from?" A series of other questions followed. And then: "What company are you from?" L Company, said Arman. There seemed to be a consultation among the dimly visible figures to their front, who were braced for Egyptian commandos. "What company did you say?"

"L Company."

A tank fired a shell which exploded alongside the five men, killing Arman and another crewman. Levy, who survived, would never know why the gunner fired.

Another reservist, Yeshayahu Mor, was escaping alone through the lagoon when a voice asked in Arabic, "Who's there?"

"Me," replied Mor.

"Who are you?"

"A soldier."

Mor, of Yemenite origin, had come on an Egyptian outpost on a dry elevation in the lagoon. The Egyptians could not make out his uniform in the dark and took him for one of their own. They saw that he had been shot in the arm and dressed the wound. Lying on the roadside after the ambush, Mor had pretended to be dead when the ambushers closed in. One had shot him twice in the arm to see if he was faking and he had not moved. The Egyptian soldiers in the lagoon offered him coffee, the first hot drink he'd had since the onset of Yom Kippur. Mor, who spoke perfect Arabic, managed to avoid saying anything during the night that would indicate his identity. With dawn, however, the Egyptians discovered that the congenial brother-in-arms with whom they had spent the night was the enemy. He was taken prisoner.

At Fort Milano, the war had settled into routine for Captain Trostler by Sunday night. His men had fought well, beating off several attacks. The garrison had been reinforced by eight crewmen from Gabi Amir's brigade whose tanks had been disabled nearby during the previous night. The young tankers manned gun positions inside the fort with enthusiasm. The crew of a tank which had thrown a tread 150 yards from the front gate was asked by Trostler to remain in the tank in case its gun was needed. A few hours later, two Egyptian APCs loaded with infantry approached the gate. Trostler's deputy, Lt. Micha Kostiga, knocked one out with a bazooka. The disabled Israeli tank, which the Egyptian APCs had ignored as battlefield litter, destroyed the second from behind. With darkness, the Egyptian attacks ceased, but Trostler could see in adjacent East Kantara lanterns, flashlights, even the glowing ends of cigarettes. The ghost city had come to life.

The company commander had adjusted to the idea that they might have to hold out for days before being rescued. At 10 P.M., however, brigade headquarters in Baluza ordered the garrison to try to reach the Israeli lines on foot this night. Trostler was given map coordinates of a site seven miles to the southeast where tank forces would meet him. The garrison would have to start within the hour in order to reach the rendezvous point before dawn. Trostler wanted to take the four dead with him, but headquarters ruled that out.

The garrison organized for departure, checking weapons and filling canteens. When someone called, "What about the wounded?" the answer that came back was, "Whoever wants to live, assemble here now." There were six wounded, three of them seriously. All insisted on walking, rather than being carried on a stretcher.

The men, forty-two in all, formed up inside the main gate. The wounded were put in the middle of the column. Trostler said they would move through the town itself, rather than around it, since it offered cover. Leading his men out of the fort gate, Trostler entered East Kantara. Voices in Arabic came from buildings they passed. The town was serving as a divisional headquarters, and the raspy blare of military radios accompanied them. If any

Egyptian soldier saw the men moving through the side streets, he could presume they were Egyptian.

Passing through the town without incident, they entered the open desert, whitish in the light of the moon. After only a few hundred yards, Trostler saw dark shapes to the front, tanks or artillery pieces. As he tried to find an opening, his group was spotted. Flares lifted into the air and there were random shots. Trostler pulled back and led his men due east, where passage seemed clear. But fire was opened on them again and everybody went flat. Lieutenant Kostiga, who knew Arabic, shouted, "Are you crazy? Why are you shooting at us? We're Egyptian."

After a pause, a voice shouted, "They're not Egyptian." Kostiga had pronounced the Arabic word for crazy, *majnoon,* as it is pronounced by Palestinians, with a soft *j;* in Egypt, however, it is pronounced with a hard *g.* Fire was opened again, this time more intensely. The Israelis responded in kind. Several men were wounded. Trostler looked back at the town and saw the treeline broken by the silhouette of a large house. "Everybody back to Kantara," he shouted. "To that house we can see."

Reaching it, he raised Baluza on the radio and described their situation. Headquarters gave him a new rendezvous point, this time to the northeast. He told the men crouched around him that they would move through the town to the cemetery at the other end before striking off into the desert again. As they went, they could hear vehicles moving on nearby streets as if search parties were out. In the seclusion of the cemetery, Trostler counted the men. To his dismay, there were only twenty-four, including all four officers. Eighteen men were missing. He had to decide quickly whether to go back and search for them. To do so, he decided, would be to risk the lives of all. He announced his decision and they set off into the desert. With his group were several of the wounded. There was little more than two hours left before first light and they would have to move fast. Kostiga and the tank crewmen formed a rear guard. They helped the wounded and some of the older reservists winded by the forced march.

Meanwhile, the missing men were trying to assess their options. The last man to leave the ambush site, Sgt. Shalom Chala, who fired a light machine gun to cover the retreat, found the other seventeen men taking cover in a bomb crater. At twenty-one, Chala was one of the youngest men in the unit, which included men well into their thirties. But as a product of the Golani Brigade, he was one of the few with serious combat training. As he listened to the men around him discussing what to do next, he saw it becoming a pointless symposium. In the absence of any officer, he said he was taking command. No one argued the point. The group included several who had just been wounded as well as several who had been wounded in the fort. It was apparent that they could not get far walking. Chala led them into a one-story house just inside the city, and the wounded were put into an inner room.

With first light, a lookout at one of the windows spotted Egyptian trackers following their footprints in the sand. Shortly afterwards, bullets were fired in through the windows. An Egyptian officer appeared in the doorway holding a pistol. "Throw your weapons down," he said in Arabic, and ordered the men outside. Some left the building; others, including the wounded, didn't. The Egyptians threw grenades inside, killing all who were there. Chala and seven others were taken into captivity.

When dawn came, Trostler and his men had not yet reached the site where the tanks were to pick them up. An Egyptian artillery battery was firing not far away and the ground was pocked with footprints. The area around them was a sandy plain offering no cover. Trostler led the men towards a marshy zone indicated on the map. A dark shape that looked like an Egyptian tank loomed ahead of them. Through binoculars, it proved to be a patch of brush which had taken root in the marsh. They took shelter there, hoping to remain undiscovered until nightfall. In midmorning, two tank shells exploded nearby. Tank crewmen in the group listened to the sound of engines and treads in the distance. "They're our tanks," they said. An Israeli tank commander had fired at the brush because it had looked to him too like an Egyptian tank. The men did not rush from cover. Any Israeli tanks in the area would presume that foot soldiers approaching from the direction of the canal were Egyptian. One of the tankers said he had an idea. Borrowing a prayer shawl from a religious soldier, he said he would wave it at the tanks from a distance. "If it works, we'll be back soon," he said before disappearing down a dune with a comrade. "If not, so long." Not long after, a tank came roaring up the dune, with the two men sitting atop it, one of them holding the prayer shawl.

In Tel Aviv, when the cabinet met at 9 P.M. Sunday night, Mrs. Meir regretfully noted that Elazar had not yet returned from Sinai. She had come to rely on his positiveness as a balm against the gloom projected by Dayan. However, the defense minister, aware of the demoralizing impact his words had had on his colleagues, made a supreme effort to sound optimistic as he outlined the military picture. His own mood had improved considerably since his difficult meeting with Mrs. Meir in the afternoon. He was no longer talking about the Third Temple. He had not abandoned his demand for a fallback line in Sinai in the event that the front line gave way, but he now advocated a quick counterattack across the canal. "The chief of staff's optimism about a counterattack has gotten to me," Dayan acknowledged to the ministers. "We've got to smash the Egyptian armor as soon as possible and also [smash] the new legend that's beginning to be woven about the Arabs having become phenomenal warriors. There may be some narrowing of the gap but a nation doesn't change in six years. Individuals change. Not nations. This is not just a war of armor but a serious war of nerves." He seemed to be regaining his own nerve, offering constructive proposals and avoiding doomsday warnings. On the northern front, he said, he was looking for a breakthrough that would put the IDF on the road to Damascus. "We won't capture Damascus but we want to oblige the Syrians to dance to our tune."

A colleague who had worked with Dayan for many years knew him to be an instinctive pessimist, despite the cavalier, self-confident air he generally projected. However, the colleague would say, Dayan was a "constructive" pessimist. "Instead of saying 'Everything will be all right,' he would say 'Everything won't be all right unless we do something, so let's figure out what we're going to do.'" Even though he had lost his composure, Dayan had in fact been in constructive mode from the beginning of the war, rationally trying to identify the holes in the dam and determine the ways best to plug them.

The change in the Arabs' war-making ability was indeed not due to an overnight change in national character. In 1967 they had seemed totally inept because they had been stunned by Israel's opening blow and were ordered by their high command into a catastrophic headlong retreat. Now, they were executing a meticulous plan that they had been exercising regularly for three years. They had seized the initiative, they were well prepared operationally to meet the Israeli counterattack, and psychologically the wind was at their back. It was Israel that had taken the opening blow this time, one even more stunning than the air strike inflicted on Egypt in 1967, and it was still struggling to find its footing. But it had not broken.

At midnight, Dayan stopped by the Pit to hear Elazar brief his staff after his return from Sinai. The atmosphere was taut with anticipation and Elazar addressed his officers as if they were about to set off into battle themselves. There would be counterattacks tomorrow morning on both the northern and southern fronts, he said. This was the turning point they had all been waiting for. He outlined Moussa Peled's battle plan in the north and the plan he himself had dictated to Gonen in the south. There should be six hundred battle-ready tanks on the southern front by morning. In a clerical oversight that would prove telling, Elazar's battle plan, as outlined by him to his head-quarters staff, was not written down by the operations branch and transmitted to Southern Command as a formal order, which was standard procedure.

Dayan was swept up in the enthusiasm pervading the war room. "From tomorrow we would begin to lift our head out of the water," he would write later, in recalling his own thoughts. "The initiative was ours and we could pick the battleground and assemble our forces accordingly. Why shouldn't we win? The divisional and brigade commanders were the best of our sol-diers. Arik [Sharon], Bren [Adan], Albert [Mendler]—the major league of the IDF. The entire chain of command up to the chief of staff was from the armored corps. All of them are experienced in combat, all of them know the Sinai well. Tomorrow will be the day of armor."

Tomorrow, however, would be the day of Shmuel Gonen. Despite the blows his forces had suffered over the past two days, the front commander nurtured the thought that he would repeat, on an even grander scale, the rout of the Six Day War he had helped inflict on the Egyptians as a brigade commander. Elazar had repeatedly told him, in the presence of the other senior commanders, that the counterattack must be a limited one, that his forces should not get closer than two miles from the canal, that only one divi-sion was to move at a time, and that there would be no canal crossing or attempt to rescue the Bar-Lev garrisons except in the unlikely event of a sud-den Egyptian collapse. Gonen would proceed to act as if Elazar had said exactly the opposite.

He had gone to sleep without sending off to Tel Aviv the detailed opera-tional plan for the attack that Elazar had requested. Ben-Ari woke him half an hour later after headquarters called to ask for it. It took only thirty-five minutes for Gonen to complete a plan—consisting of a sketch and a brief text. It was dispatched by air to Tel Aviv with a liaison officer from the General Staff at 2:45 A.M. "The objective," read the text, "is to clear the area between the canal and Artillery Road, destroy enemy forces, rescue of men in the forts, retrieval of disabled tanks, and preparation for crossing to the other side of the canal." Instead of distancing the attack forces two miles from the canal, Gonen was proposing rescue of the men in the canal-side forts, which Elazar had specifically ruled out. In addition, the forces were to prepare themselves for crossing the canal, which Elazar had also ruled out.

In conversations with Sharon and Adan by radio later in the morning, Gonen would spell out his thoughts in greater detail. Sharon was to destroy the Third Army in the southern sector, then cross over on an Egyptian bridge and establish a defense line twelve miles further west, towards Cairo. Adan would do more or less the same in the northern sector. One proposal called for the day's operations to begin not with a north–south sweep by Adan, as Elazar had stipulated, but with an east–west thrust by Sharon's division to the waterline to rescue the men in the forts. At 6:17 A.M., Gonen dropped this plan and reverted to the north–south sweep.

His optimism was untempered by the fact that the Egyptian army had less than forty-eight hours before put five divisions across the canal, destroying two-thirds of General Mendler's crack tank division, with no significant losses to itself. Gonen also gave little weight to the fact that Egypt had two powerful armored divisions and other forces on the west bank which had not yet come into action. Nor did he take into consideration his paucity of artillery, which was more essential than ever now because of the need to suppress the Egyptian infantry wielding antitank weapons. Artillery had lower priority than tanks on the roads into Sinai, and the bulk of the guns would not reach the front till late in the day.

Staff officers in the Pit noticed that Gonen's plan deviated from the plan as outlined to them by the chief of staff in his midnight briefing, but they did not raise an alarm, perhaps because of the press of events a few hours before counterattacks were to be launched on two fronts. Elazar was shown the attack plans submitted by both front commanders. He made changes to the plan submitted by Hofi regarding the attack by Moussa Peled's division, but he made no changes to Gonen's plan, assuming that it reflected what he himself had dictated to Gonen the night before at Umm Hashiba. Elazar would later testify that he had no recollection of having seen Gonen's plan; that he did not have time to read all the papers laid on his desk during battle. One way or another, he had permitted Gonen's plan to get past him. An Israeli analyst would conclude that while the IDF was blessed with improvisation, it would have been better served by sound staff work.

Shortly after 6 A.M., Gonen informed Elazar by telephone that Adan would launch his attack in two hours. He requested permission for the division commander to cross the canal after he had completed his north–south sweep. Elazar was less dismissive of the possibility than he had been the night before. He was exultant over the early arrival of the reserves on the battlefield and over the fact that a counterattack was to be launched on both fronts less than two days after the Arab surprise attack. With some six hundred Israeli tanks expected to join battle during the day, the possibility of an Egyptian collapse may have seemed less remote to him now than it had the previous evening. He discussed the possibility of a canal crossing this time with Gonen as a reasonable possibility. If a crossing is undertaken, he said, it should be at Matsmed, where one flank would be protected by the Bitter Lake. Only one brigade should be sent across and it would take up defensive positions five miles to the west. Elazar expressed doubt, however, that the Egyptians would leave an intact bridge for Gonen to capture. The Israelis were not aware that even if bridges were captured, they could probably not support their Western tanks, which were fifteen to twenty tons heavier than the Soviet tanks for which the Soviet-made bridges were intended.

This matter-of-fact discussion of a possible crossing operation with the chief of staff reinforced Gonen's fixation on the subject. But Elazar had not changed his position from the previous night that a crossing would be considered only if there was a general collapse of the Egyptian forces. The chances of that happening seemed a little less unlikely now, but it was hardly certain. Elazar's objective at this stage was not relief of the forts or crossing the canal but destruction of Egyptian tanks believed to be moving inland from the Sinai bank. Whether or not there would be a crossing, he said to Gonen, depended on the results of Adan's sweep. And only the General Staff, he reminded him, could authorize a crossing.

"Shmulik, be careful not to go too close to the ramparts," cautioned Elazar again. "Good luck."

Twenty-one

FAILED COUNTERATTACK

ADAN'S DIVISION BEGAN ROLLING WESTWARD at 2 A.M. Monday from the Lateral Road, thirty miles from the canal. The launching of a counterattack by Israeli reservists only thirty-six hours after the war's start, and on the most remote battlefront, boded well.

The tanks moved slowly in broad deployment, uncertain where they might encounter the enemy. A single tank platoon had been posted since sundown on a ridge near the Artillery Road, six miles from the canal, as a forward listening post. Its commander reported hearing intense vehicular activity to the west where tanks were crossing the canal, but the Egyptians had not pushed appreciably inland.

Only two of Adan's brigades were involved in the advance, the third having not yet freed itself from the traffic jam on the coastal road. The two, Gabi Amir's battered brigade from the standing army and a reservist force commanded by Lt. Col. Natan (Natke) Nir, had 120 tanks between them, just over half their allotted strength. The clashes at Kantara and Mifreket and with the commandos on the coastal road had induced caution as they moved towards the coming encounter.

At Gonen's headquarters, however, caution was on indefinite leave. The southern front commander had, like everyone else, been shocked by the surprise attack and by the determination displayed by the Egyptians. He had quickly recovered, reverting overnight to the bravura mind-set of the Six

Day War. General Elazar's careful, two-feet-on-the-ground attack plan—appropriate to the uncertain circumstances—was dropped by Gonen, who was planning to kick the enemy with both feet. Adan, feeling his way westward, still believed that his mission was the one outlined by Elazar the night before at Umm Hashiba—to sweep south some thirty miles from Kantara to Fort Matsmed while approaching no closer to the canal than two miles in order to keep clear of Saggers.

At 4 A.M., Adan was contacted by Gen. Kalman Magen, who had taken command of the Baluza sector, with new orders transmitted from Gonen, who was unable to make direct radio contact with Adan, at least in part because of Egyptian jamming. He was to head for the canal, after all, and link up with Forts Hizayon and Purkan. If he found an Egyptian bridge intact, he would send a brigade across and have it take up defensive positions twelve miles to the west on a twelve-mile-wide front. If there was no bridge available, he would continue south to Matsmed and cross there on a captured bridge, likewise sending a brigade westward twelve miles.

This gross deviation from Elazar's plan—and from reality—was enough to alert Adan to a major problem at Southern Command. But that was only the start. Fifteen minutes later, Gonen sent a correction via Magen: Adan would link up with Hizayon and Purkan but would not attempt to cross there, only at Matsmed. And the defense line would be established six miles west of the canal, not twelve. When Magen ventured that Adan would have difficulty effecting a linkup with the forts since he had made no preparations for it, Gonen immediately changed his instructions. The linkup, he said, would be carried out by Sharon. Adan would pause in his southerly progress to permit Sharon to dash in and rescue the two garrisons. Sharon would then pull back to get out of Adan's way.

At 4:30 A.M. Gonen was finally able to make direct contact with Adan. This time he put both options to the division commander: Either link up with the two forts on the way down to Matsmed or let Sharon carry out the rescue operation. Adan said he would not be able to answer until daylight, when he could assess the opposition confronting him.

"Prepare for both options," said Gonen crisply.

By dawn, Amir's and Nir's brigades had descended the low hills overlooking the plain fringing the Suez Canal. Here they turned left and halted to await the order to begin the southward sweep. At 8 A.M., Adan gave the order. Amir's brigade took the lead, with Nir following several miles behind.

The division had encountered no Egyptian tanks on the way west and encountered none now as it headed south, parallel to the canal, although several teams of Egyptian artillery spotters along the way were killed or captured. The third brigade, commanded by Lt. Col. Arye Keren, had arrived with sixty-two tanks during the night and moved parallel to the rest of the division on Artillery Road, four miles east, as a reserve force.

As Nir's brigade came abreast of Kantara, he was ordered to halt. Photo interpreters examining the results of a fresh reconnaissance flight had identified a brigade of Egyptian T-62s under camouflage netting at the edge of the city. Unable to ignore the threat to his rear, Adan ordered Nir to remain in place.

It was Nir's men who would pick up the escapees from Milano. Major Brik, who had been involved in the clash on the coastal road the day before, spotted two men approaching from the direction of the canal and prepared to fire. Looking again through his binoculars, he saw them waving something white and recognized it as a prayer shawl. One of the pair was Lt. Ilan Gidron, a tank platoon commander and, like Lieutenant Vardi, who was killed at Mifreket, the son of a general. He asked for command of a tank, declining Brik's suggestion that he rest from his ordeal for a day or two before going back into battle. The officer was sent to the brigade's maintenance unit in the rear and would join Brik's company later in the day with a repaired tank.

Adan's swift advance was taken both in Umm Hashiba and the Tel Aviv Pit as a portent of Egyptian collapse. In fact, the Egyptians had not sent forces forward from the canal in this sector and Adan was merely punching air. The mood in the Pit became even jauntier when Gonen asked the air force to stop bombing the Egyptian bridges so that his forces could cross on them. Gen. Rehavam Ze'evi, assistant to Elazar, suggested that tank transporters stand by to shift a division from Sinai to the Golan front as soon as the Egyptians had been driven back across the canal. The chief of staff accepted the proposal. Elazar had no desire to seize territory across the canal except perhaps for small bridgeheads for tactical purposes. But on the Syrian front, he saw room for territorial games. "If Gorodish can get back to the canal, I don't need more. But there, in the north, 'the sky's the limit,'" he said to his staff, using the English phrase. "It could be that I bring a division from the canal and go with it to Jebel Druze [a Druze enclave which some Israeli strategists saw as ripe for breaking away from Syria] and with another division to Damascus and I don't know where else. Listen, if there's a place to exploit success, it's there."

Elazar realized, however, that he was indulging in fantasy. Talking with several former chiefs of staff, including Rabin, who had become an almost permanent presence in his office since the war's start, he said, "Listen, fellows. This army has launched a counterattack on two fronts thirty-six hours after the war began. Nice? That's first of all. Second of all is 'Why isn't it nice enough?' Because the attacks haven't sufficiently developed yet. All it takes is a phone call from Northern Command or Southern saying that their attack has bogged down and we'll be in deeper trouble than we were yesterday."

Dayan urged the seizure of territory across the canal as a deterrent and a bargaining chip. He pressed Elazar to recommend to the cabinet the capture of Port Said at the northern end of the canal. Dayan planned to do so himself, but the recommendation would bear more weight if it also came from the army. Elazar was reluctant. "It's too early to talk to the government about this," he said. "If I speak about Port Said, I'm committed. We're now beginning the counterattack. I hope our two divisions cave in their bridgeheads. But they haven't done it yet."

Elazar's caution was more warranted than he imagined. The counterattack by Adan's division that was supposed to begin turning the tide had taken on an oddly static, aimless character. His three brigades were widely separated and were not acting in coordination against any specific target. By ordering Nir to halt with his entire brigade opposite Kantara in case the T-62s emerged, Adan had left Amir's depleted brigade alone at the cutting edge of his southerly attack, with Keren's reserve brigade miles away to the east. Adan agreed to Gonen's request to link up with Hizayon, but in the absence of artillery he wanted massive air support. Gonen assured him that it would be forthcoming.

Even though Adan had encountered no Egyptian tanks thus far, Gonen was already relating to the destruction of the Egyptian bridgeheads in Sinai as a done deed. With every passing hour, his focus was increasingly shifting to an attack across the canal. Intelligence had passed on an unclear report that an Egyptian brigade commander in the Third Army sector was pulling back. This, combined with the untroubled progress of Adan's division, had dispelled for Gonen any doubts that he would, on this very day, smash the Egyptian army. (The report from the Third Army of a pullback might have been connected to the difficulty in cutting openings through the clay soil of the Israeli ramparts in that sector. Units had shifted northward to other crossing points.)

It was impossible for Adan to fully grasp Gonen's intentions because his orders were unclear and constantly changing. At 9:20, Adan asked Gonen if he was just to evacuate the garrison at Hizayon or to cross the canal there.

"Before crossing, I want you to destroy all enemy forces that have pene-trated," said Gonen, without responding to the question about evacuation.

"The process of reaching Hizayon will *be* a process of destroying forces," noted Adan dryly.

"I mean that you should destroy all enemy forces from Milano [the Kan-tara area] to the end of your sector at Matsmed [a thirty-mile stretch]. After you've destroyed all these forces, cross over."

"I understand," said Adan. What he understood was that he was to break through to the beleaguered garrison at Hizayon but was not to cross the canal until he had reached Matsmed, fifteen miles further south.

"It's very important that the movement south flows like a stream without a break," said Gonen. "When you get to Matsmed, that's where I intend for you to cross and form up on the Havit line," six miles west of the canal.

Adan said that his third brigade, under Arye Keren, was moving south on the Artillery Road towards the Matsmed area and would execute that part of the mission. "Do you want me to evacuate the men from Hizayon?" he asked again. It was not an idle question since on Saturday there had been an order not to evacuate the garrisons.

"Affirmative."

Gonen summed up the conversation: "So, two important things. To take small footholds, one or two, on the other side, and to head south very quickly and cross at Matsmed. Out."

Within the space of a minute, Gonen had given Adan two conflicting orders—the first, to complete his drive south to Matsmed "like a stream" before crossing the canal, and the second, to cross at Hizayon and seize "one or two" footholds across the canal before continuing to Matsmed.

Gonen was behaving as if this were a sand table exercise, with a virtual enemy whose movements could be dictated and an endless array of options for the home side to try out. His most far-reaching option was still to be played. Elazar's plan had called for Sharon to undertake his own north–south sweep only after Adan had reached the canal's midway point. Sharon would roll up the forward elements of the Third Army, as Adan had done with the Second Army. Gonen, however, feared that the Egyptians would pull in their bridges as Sharon advanced south, making it impossible to cross the canal to Suez City at the end of his sweep. To avoid this, he proposed that Sharon pull back and travel inland around the Third Army bridgehead in order to strike it on its southern flank directly opposite Suez City. This, he believed, would surprise the Egyptians and enable Sharon to find a bridge intact. Sharon would then send a brigade across to capture the city while his other two brigades rolled up the Third Army bridgehead on the Sinai bank from south to north, rather than the other way around. The problem was that it would take at least four hours to make the roundabout movement, leaving little more than an hour of daylight at best in which to fight.

Gonen had not internalized the revolutionary nature of what had been happening on the battlefield, something the soldiers in the field understood very well. He was aiming to have the Second Army for lunch, as it were, and the Third Army for dinner this very day. His nightcap he would enjoy on the road to Cairo.

When Gonen outlined his new plan to Elazar, the chief of staff tried to talk him out of it. He noted that Sharon would be wasting a whole afternoon in movement instead of engaging the main body of the enemy. Finally, however, he bowed to Gonen's enthusiasm. In the Pit, Rabin expressed surprise at Elazar agreeing to such a far-reaching change to the plan he had spelled out only the night before. "Since it's a borderline case," said Elazar, "let [Gonen] do what he wants."

It was, however, very far from borderline, and Elazar's waiving of his own strong instincts out of deference to the commander in the field was a glaring error. Dayan was upset when he heard of the change and called Southern Command for an explanation. The reason offered by Gonen was that a large Egyptian force had crossed the southern end of the canal and was preparing to attack down the eastern coast of the Gulf of Suez towards the oil fields at Abu Rodeis. Speeding Sharon south would permit him to deal with this force, said Gonen, before carrying out the rest of his mission. Gonen's grand design—breaking the back of the Egyptian army and getting across the canal this day—was thus portrayed to Dayan as a spin-off of a mission connected to the marginal Suez Gulf area.

Dayan had already begun to have an uneasy sense that the day's counterattack would achieve no significant results. "You don't get the feeling that [the Egyptians] are pulling back," he said. "They're still pushing across forces." Elazar shared with his staff his own discomfort about the way the battle was developing. He was unable to get a clear picture of the situation from Gonen and had no idea what was happening with Adan's division. Nothing much, in fact, was happening to it. Adan was just marking time in the desert, waiting vainly for the air force to strike at the Egyptian forces blocking the way to Hizayon, in lieu of artillery, before sending his tanks forward.

At 10:45 A.M. Gonen ordered Sharon to prepare to disengage and move south as a follow-up to "Adan's success." Sharon was flabbergasted. He had been observing Adan's forces from high ground and had witnessed no success, only stalled movement. More to the point, the dominant ridges he him-self was holding were critical both for blocking an Egyptian advance and as a jumping off point for an Israeli counterattack towards the canal. The chances of finding an intact Egyptian bridge after a lengthy detour to the southern end of the canal, he believed, were close to nil. He protested in what he would describe as "the strongest terms" and urged Gonen to come forward to see the situation in the field. Gonen, however, insisted on Sharon carrying out his order. "If I didn't obey," Sharon would recall in his memoirs, "I would be dismissed immediately. Immediately. 'Then come down here and see for yourself,' I repeated. 'No,' Gonen shouted. 'You will be dis-missed. I will dismiss you right now.'"

Gritting his teeth, Sharon ordered his staff to get the division moving. Unlike in Adan's sector, the Egyptians opposite Sharon's division had moved massive amounts of armor and infantry inland from the canal. Staff officers protested moving out before Adan's forces took over their positions. At their urging, Sharon left behind the division's reconnaissance battalion to defend two key ridges.

Gonen began urging Adan to proceed in haste to Missouri, where large enemy concentrations were reported. He did not explain the reason—namely, that he was pulling Sharon's division out of its positions opposite Missouri. "I'm not interested in stretching my forces too thin," replied Adan unhappily. "But if this is very important, I can do it."

"It's important," said Gonen. "And another thing, when you get to Hiza-yon, grab the other side [of the canal] with a small force. It's very important to me. Afterwards, carry out the main mission at Matsmed." A few minutes later, he informed Adan that he was drawing up plans to have him seize "many small footholds" west of the canal.

Thus, in a bewildering series of orders and counterorders, Adan had been told in succession to roll up Egyptian forces in a thirty-mile-long swath but to keep two miles away from the canal, to reach the canal in order to cross either at Hizayon or Matsmed or both on captured bridges, to post forces twelve miles west of the canal, then six miles, to send entire brigades across, to send small forces across, to capture Matsmed first, to capture Hizayon first, to put "one or two" bridgeheads across near Hizayon, to seize "many" bridge-heads, and to proceed south to meet a major Egyptian tank force at Missouri. All of this presumed that Adan had won the field, whereas he had not yet had his first encounter of the day. Worst of all, Gonen left out of this war game the other player—namely, the Egyptian army with its new spirit, its new compe-tence, its masses of armor and artillery, and its suddenly devastating infantry.

Adan, with a half-strength division and virtually no artillery or air support, was being asked to subdue the better part of three fully intact Egyptian divisions which had already demonstrated surprising fighting ability. He would then cross the canal on bridges the Egyptians would conveniently leave for him and deal with at least one of the two powerful armored divisions waiting on the west bank. And all this before nightfall.

Although he was only a short helicopter trip from the front, Gonen remained in his command bunker at Umm Hashiba, oblivious to the true situation in the field and the perceptions of his field commanders. As an Israeli analyst would put it, Gonen was commanding from a bunker, rather than from the saddle.

With the war having just started, he had built-in credit which accounted for veteran warhorses like Elazar and Adan going along with his decisions despite rapidly deepening reservations. Even if Gonen's orders seemed absurd or quixotic, not to say fantastical, Adan assumed the front commander knew something he didn't, like possible signs of an Egyptian collapse. Gonen, indeed, had seized on such dubious "signs." In addition, Adan did not care to begin the war by challenging the decisions of his nominal superior, regardless of what he thought of him, or to say he was unable to carry out an order. He had performed with distinction as a commander in all of Israel's wars and did not wish to end his military career as someone pleading inability to carry out a mission. He chose to signal his discomfiture indirectly by refraining from expressions of optimism and by repeatedly noting that he had no infantry or artillery. It was a subtlety lost on Gonen. One of Adan's major failings this day was in not having vigorously stated his reservations about the missions given him. His laconic attitude permitted Gonen to continue building on his illusion that Adan's division was controlling the battlefield, an illusion the General Staff came to share. Adan's reticence about speaking his mind fed Gonen's fantasies.

Elazar, for his part, was distracted by the Golan front, where Moussa Peled had started his counterattack. He had also spent an hour and a half with the cabinet in the morning during the most critical period of Gonen's decision making. Elazar was kept informed by notes passed into the cabinet room. It was a poor way to understand Gonen's thinking and the chief of staff was in any case inclined to give Gonen the benefit of the doubt as the commander in the field. Elazar still thought of him as a tough, competent commander of armor.

Colonel Ben-Ari called Adan shortly after 10 A.M. to report "slight indications" that the enemy had begun to collapse and to direct him to complete his sweep of Egyptian forces down to Matsmed at maximum speed. "Otherwise they're liable to get away." Half an hour later, Ben-Ari called back with Gonen's latest order. "After finishing with Missouri, we want you to cross at three places." At this point Adan, still a long way from Missouri, moderately balked for the first time. "I wonder what reports you've been getting. Here in the field it looks completely different."

The slack provided to Gonen by his fellow generals would soon disappear, but not before October 8 would register as the most ignominious day in Israel's military history, a day in which the IDF in Sinai defeated itself in a dreamlike succession of errors that dashed whatever chance it had of smashing the Egyptian bridgeheads. The day had only begun.

The movement of Gabi Amir's brigade towards Hizayon was more drift than purposeful march. While waiting for air support, the force bided its time for close to two hours under heavy artillery fire, constantly moving to avoid presenting a stationary target on the open plain. One of Amir's two battalions, commanded by Lieutenant Colonel Yoffe, had been savaged Saturday night at Mifreket and Kantara. It came under long-range fire now from tanks and Sagger teams positioned around a palm grove near the canal, two miles north of Hizayon, the brigade's first direct contact with enemy forces this day. The other battalion, a reservist unit commanded by Lt. Col. Haim Adini, a lawyer in civilian life, slowly moved closer to Hizayon. The fort had inscribed itself on the consciousness of those listening to the radio net because of the desperate pleas by its radioman for rescue. The Egyptians had erected two bridges adjacent to Hizayon and the area was a major crossing point.

With the trauma of Saturday night's battles still fresh, Colonel Amir was uneasy about the prospect of trying to break through to a canal-side fort again with his depleted brigade. He asked Adan to arrange for a tank battalion from Sharon's division, visible on an adjacent hilltop, to be attached to him for the attack. Adan passed on the request to Gonen, who approved. However, when Amir approached the battalion commander, Ami Morag, the latter checked with his superiors and was told that Sharon refused. The division was moving south and Sharon wanted to retain all his units.

Accompanying Adini's battalion as it hovered on the Hizayon approaches was the deputy brigade commander, Lt. Col. Shilo Sasson, who was growing increasingly frustrated at marking time when there was a war to be fought. He sensed an opportunity to lunge eastward and capture a bridge. It was, he would later say, a commander's duty to take initiatives. Brigade commander Amir had gone off to search for high ground from which he could see the broad battlefield. In his absence, at 11 A.M., Sasson ordered both battalion commanders—Yoffe and Adini—to move towards the canal. Yoffe, however, broke off and led his tanks to the rear, saying he was out of ammunition and almost out of fuel.

For Adini, Sasson's order was a trumpet blast. He ordered his twenty-one tanks to advance in broad deployment, two companies forward, one to the rear. Dust clouds lifted up around them as they picked up speed. It was a textbook charge and it looked for a while as if it was going to succeed. Adini would compare the experience of a tank charge to an orgasm. There was nothing, he would say, like the smell—a mixture of gunpowder, sweat, and grease—and the sight from a tank turret of an enemy fleeing before you. He saw them fleeing now, hundreds of Egyptian infantrymen bolting towards the canal.

As the tanks raced across the sandy plain, missile and tank fire erupted from the rampart across the canal and from the rampart on the Israeli side. Four tanks were hit by Saggers and began to burn, but the others continued forward. Suddenly, from the seemingly empty terrain to the front, Egyptian infantrymen rose out of shallow foxholes and unleashed RPGs at the charging tanks.

Just five hundred yards to his front, Adini could see the canal. That was as close as he got. An Egyptian soldier five yards in front of his tank hit the turret with an RPG before he was run down. Adini, wounded, ordered the battalion to pull back. Seven disabled tanks were left behind on the battlefield. Of the fourteen that returned, only seven were still fit for battle. Nineteen men were dead, and many wounded.

Neither the division commander nor the brigade commander had ordered the attack. There had been no artillery or air preparation except for bombs tossed from a distance without visible effect by two aircraft.

Stunned when he learned what had happened, Colonel Amir appealed again to Morag to "rescue us." Morag's battalion had already begun to pull out in order to join Sharon. He halted and once again contacted his own brigade commander. Amir cut into their conversation to say, "You people are arguing and my people are being slaughtered." Morag's tank commanders, who could hear the exchange on the radio, began to turn their tanks back in order to go to Amir's assistance. But the order that came down to Morag was firm—disengage and join the rest of Sharon's division on the Lateral Road.

When Morag caught up with the division, he saw Sharon on the roadside and descended from his tank. The abandonment of Amir, Morag told the division commander, weighed heavily on his conscience. Sharon replied that he took the responsibility entirely upon himself. There was a "holocaust" at the Mitla Pass and the division was needed there in all its strength, he said. Reports of some kind of massive Egyptian incursion were indeed circulating within the division to explain its sudden movement south.

From the hill on which Adan had positioned himself, he could not see the site of the failed attack, and he heard only fragmentary radio reports. What he heard did not adequately reflect the blow Adini's battalion had received. Adan's reports to Southern Front command thus did little to upset its sense of complacency.

Determined now to attack Hizayon with two brigades, Adan ordered Nir to come down from Kantara, leaving one of his three battalions behind to guard against the T-62 tanks. He ordered Nir and Amir to meet in order to coordinate their efforts but did not join them himself. The brief meeting between the two brigade commanders would only be a prelude to further misunderstanding. For reasons not clear, Amir did not mention Adini's failed charge even though Nir was about to attack in the same sector. Nir thought that Amir's brigade would be attacking too. Amir believed his role was only to provide covering fire. The absence of Adan's coordination was critical.

Sharon's division had by this time disengaged and pulled back twelve miles to the Lateral Road, where it turned south for its planned sixty-mile run around the Third Army bridgehead. At 2:15 P.M., with the division strung out over thirty miles, Ben-Ari called the division's operations officer. "All units are to halt in place until further orders," he said. A helicopter from Umm Hashiba landed alongside Sharon's mobile command post shortly afterwards and an emissary from Gonen emerged to inform him that he was to return to the positions he had abandoned little more than three hours before.

Gonen had received a warning from AMAN that the Egyptians were about to push forward all along the line. At the same time, the reality of Adan's situation was beginning to be grasped for the first time at front headquarters. The division was not killing Egyptian tanks but was in fact bogged down.

Controlling his rage, Sharon ordered the division to execute an about-face, to the bewilderment of all. Gonen, for his part, had a new request for the air force—bomb the bridges. He would not be using them.

Meanwhile, Act Two at Hizayon was about to begin, an uncanny repeat of Act One, except worse. Gabi Amir's force now consisted solely of a newly arrived battalion under Lt. Col. Eliashiv Shimshi, which took position two miles southeast of Hizayon. Yoffe's battalion had been sent to another sector and the remnants of Adini's were reorganizing at the rear.

Looking towards Hizayon through binoculars, Shimshi saw masses of Egyptian tanks. He could make out numerous infantry as well. The Egyptians had seen the dust cloud marking the arrival of Nir's tanks and deduced correctly that the Jews were about to try for Hizayon again. This time the Egyptians would be waiting in even greater strength.

Shimshi was startled when Colonel Amir told him to be prepared to provide covering fire for a battalion that would soon be attacking Hizayon. How could a single battalion attack an enemy concentration as massive as this? thought Shimshi. And without artillery or air preparation. Shimshi consoled himself with the thought that the forces in the field had already been fighting, some of them since Saturday, and presumably knew things he did not. Perhaps they had learned that the Egyptians would collapse at the sight of charging tanks. It was not very convincing but he tried to hang on to the thought.

Battalion commander Assaf Yaguri and his officers had no such comfort. They had been at the spearhead of the division since its arrival yesterday morning and knew that the Egyptians were not running at the sight of tanks. Yaguri did not know that Adini's battalion had only a few hours earlier failed in an attempt to break through to Hizayon. Yaguri's battalion had in fact passed the survivors heading for the rear. They did not respond to Yaguri's gestures to stop, but the look on their faces was enough to alert Yaguri and his men to trouble ahead.

As they waited for Nir to return from his meeting with Amir, Yaguri and his company commanders scanned the Hizayon area through binoculars from atop Havraga Ridge six miles away. It was difficult to make out details because of the glare. "I see something but I'm not sure what," said Yaguri. Over the radio, he heard Nir order the battalion to be prepared to send a platoon across the canal to "join up" with forces already on the other side, an order that had come down from Gonen. "Well, at least we won't be the first this time," said Yaguri's deputy, referring to their spearhead role until now. A report that Israeli forces had crossed the canal had been gaining increasing circulation. It apparently originated with a radio monitor at General Staff headquarters in Tel Aviv who misunderstood a remark on Adan's radio net. Elazar was informed of the alleged crossing as he was briefing the cabinet and passed it on, to the delight of all present.

The report, however, did not diminish the apprehension of Yaguri and his men. They could make out large clouds of dust near the canal. If a small Israeli force had indeed broken through to the other bank, the Egyptians seemed to have sealed off the passage. A group of Yaguri's officers approached him and said the battalion was being asked to carry out an unreasonable mission. "If you're going, I'm going with you," said a company commander. "But this is suicide." Yaguri believed so too and did not attempt to argue the point. He had urged that more forces be assembled and more information obtained on the enemy disposition before an attack was launched. But the front command was pressing for speedy action.

Returning from his meeting with Gabi Amir, Nir did not assemble his officers again to brief them but ordered everyone to board their tanks. To his operations officer, he yelled, "Bring a lot of cigarettes and get on the tank." For Nir, getting on a tank was an unnatural act. Badly wounded in both legs in the Six Day War while commanding a battalion at Abu Agheila under Sharon, he had undergone numerous operations in Israel and abroad. He had lost his right kneecap and moved the leg in a stiff, semicircular motion. His left leg was sustained by a metal pin. Climbing into a tank turret was an effort and he sometimes needed help, but he had pressed for a return to field command and it had finally been granted.

Adan would later maintain that he had not, in fact, ordered Nir to attack, only to prepare for it. Without artillery, Adan was still waiting for the air force to provide effective close support, not just two planes tossing bombs from a distance. Nir believed he had heard Adan order him and Amir to launch a two-brigade attack towards Hizayon. Once again, as in a bad dream, there was a fatal disconnect between the division commander and his forces in the field. Once again, a planned two-brigade attack would become a one-battalion attack—one-sixth the intended strength. Once again, the division commander would be surprised that one of his forces was attacking.

Nir had intended to carry out a two-battalion attack but one of his battalions had been dueling with forces in the palm grove, as Yoffe had done in the morning, and had lost two tanks and a half-track. Nir told the battalion commander to remain in place and provide covering fire for Yaguri from behind the hillocks in his area.

Yaguri's tanks descended from the hills and deployed, three companies abreast. Several tanks with mechanical problems fell behind as the force picked up speed. Yaguri told his men to maintain wide dispersal, to move fast, and to keep up constant fire when they closed range with the enemy. Brik's company was on the left flank with Yaguri between it and the middle company. Colonel Nir, bringing up the rear, noticed that Shimshi's battalion was not joining the attack and protested angrily to Amir on the radio.

Shells began to hit among the tanks and the dust swirled up around them. Yaguri glanced at his deputy in the turret of the tank alongside him. The officer smiled back. Whatever their reservations, they were launched into the attack. Almost a mile from the canal, Egyptian soldiers rose out of foxholes around them. Sunday's ambush on the coastal road flashed across Brik's mind. With a deafening crash, tank and artillery shells, Sagger missiles, and RPGs exploded around the tanks and a dense cloud of smoke and dust closed in. From what Brik had been able to see, they were plunging into the center of a tight defensive deployment with fire coming from three sides.

To battalion commander Shimshi, providing covering fire from the south, the scene looked like a Soviet propaganda film from the Second World War—tanks racing heroically at the enemy across a broad front and spewing fire. A more apt comparison would have been to the Crimean War's "Valley of Death," into which the Light Brigade—"theirs but to do and die"—charged to its doom. In the lead were the tanks of Yaguri, his deputy, and one of the company commanders.

Shilo Sasson, Amir's deputy, who had ridden into the "valley" with Adini that morning, followed a mile behind Yaguri's force out of curiosity even though this was not his brigade. He saw the battalion moving forward at high speed, well deployed, slightly north of the route that Adini had taken. The ambush this time was sprung eight hundred yards short of Lexicon Road, which Adini had crossed, and the fire was much heavier than that which hit Adini. Tank after tank was struck.

Yaguri survived the opening salvos, but when he called his commanders on the radio, only Brik responded. The battalion commander realized that his worst apprehensions had come true. His tanks were attacking the main bridgehead of the Second Army with no artillery or air cover and were absolutely alone. "Pull back," he called on the radio. "Keep on firing and pull back." Amidst the smoke and noise he didn't know who besides Brik was left to hear him. His own tank lurched and stopped as it was hit in the treads. He ordered the crew to get out. With his operations officer, they were five. They raced towards a large bomb crater nearby. Three of them made it. They were joined by a crewman from another tank. Egyptian APCs sped towards the crater, machine guns firing, but an Egyptian officer ran forward and signaled for them to stop. He took Yaguri and the others prisoner and placed them in an APC.

Brik had been confronting the most difficult dilemma of his life. On the one hand, he believed they were going to the aid of a force cut off across the canal and he was impelled to push through. On the other hand, it was absolutely clear that they could not make it. A battalion of tanks was not going to provide the "armor shock" to stampede an entrenched divisional bridgehead. A shell had hit Brik's gun early in the charge, rendering it inoperable, but he continued forward. It was with relief that he heard Yaguri's pullback order. He ordered his driver to go back in reverse gear in order not to waste time turning. Through openings in the drifting smoke, he saw two men abandoning a disabled tank and took them aboard. Of the eighteen tanks that had charged, only four returned.

Pulling further back, Brik came upon Nir's tank. The brigade commander was trying futilely to raise Yaguri on the radio. Brik asked for permission to go forward again to see if he could pick up more crewmen. "It's suicide," said Nir. He finally relented and Brik moved forward in his tank about a mile, sheltering in a depression from which he could scan the landscape. The central feature in the panorama before him was burning Israeli tanks surrounded by hundreds of Egyptian soldiers. Beyond them he saw one hundred Egyptian tanks as well as APCs being formed into line for an attack. Brik hurried back to Havraga Ridge, where he rounded up four tanks and descended again to the edge of the plain to meet the Egyptians. The seven tanks which had survived Adini's charge intact returned now to the battlefield under a company commander and took up positions nearby.

Nir and Amir had meanwhile been summoned by Adan, who descended from his hilltop position this time to meet with them. For Adan, this was his worst crisis in four wars. Apart from the two disastrous attacks at Hizayon, his third brigade, under Arye Keren, had lost a strategic plateau called Hamutal five miles to the south to a large Egyptian force and was now staging a counterattack which was running into trouble. Looming ever larger in Adan's mind was the possibility of issuing an order he had never given in his long military career—retreat.

With Nir and Amir, he was bending over a map laid on the sand when the deputies of both brigade commanders called to report that the Egyptians were attacking. "Get back to your brigades fast," said Adan.

The Egyptians were moving forward with two mechanized brigades—a mass of infantrymen, many armed with Saggers and RPGs, flanked by tanks and supported by heavy artillery fire. It was the kind of combined arms operation that Israel had hitherto been unable to muster. But the advance was slow and not well coordinated. The Israeli tanks opened fire at long range to keep the infantrymen at bay.

The reports Adan began receiving from his brigade commanders were alarming. "They're coming on a very broad front in huge numbers," said Amir. Nir called urgently for air support. "They're coming in masses," he said. "In masses. We don't have enough strength." The most effective weapon for dealing with the advancing infantry was artillery but there was none.

Nir feared that the Egyptians would overwhelm them and then reach the supply and maintenance units a few miles to the rear, effectively destroying the division. His fear went beyond that prospect; in view of the way the war had been going for the past two days, he feared now for the survival of the country.

Adan, in his command half-track, saw his staff looking at him as he weighed the options. In the end, there seemed to be only one. "We've got to pull back," he said. Raising Amir and Nir on the radio, he gave the order. In the heat of action, there was no immediate response. Nir switched off his radio to avoid hearing the order repeated.

The impromptu defense line thickened as Shimshi's battalion, stray tanks, and Nir's second battalion joined it. Some fifty tanks from different units, mixed in with each other, were now engaging the approaching Egyptians. The setting sun in the Israelis' eyes made aiming difficult. At one point, Shimshi made out three figures approaching his sector on foot. They were shouting and waving their arms. He thought he heard Hebrew and told his men to cease fire. The three were survivors from Yaguri's battalion.

When Nir switched his radio back on after ten minutes, he heard Adan, surprised that they had not pulled back, asking him and Amir if they could hold on a bit longer. Both responded affirmatively and said that the Egyptian pressure appeared to be easing. Some Israeli tanks had pulled back on their own but were now returning to the line.

The moment the sun slipped below the horizon and out of the gunners' eyes, Israeli tank fire accelerated and became more precise. Nir saw the tank next to his—that of Shilo Sasson, Gabi Amir's deputy—scoring many hits. Columns of smoke marked burning Egyptian vehicles all along the front. Israeli tanks were burning too, but in much lesser numbers. In the last remaining light, scores of Egyptian APCs weaved their way around their knocked-out tanks and approached the Israeli line. Many were hit and infantrymen could be seen leaping from the burning vehicles. The Israeli commanders braced for an attack with Saggers and RPGs. But the Egyptians had had enough. Infantrymen could be seen fleeing to the rear, dark figures receding into a darkening desert.

Elazar had flown to Northern Command immediately after the morning's cabinet meeting and found the mood still depressed despite the relative successes of the day's battles on the Golan. The Syrians were preparing to throw in more armor and senior officers were not certain how it would all end. Returning to the Pit at 3:30 P.M., Elazar was startled to hear what had been happening on the southern front. He had authorized Gonen's changes to his plan on the basis of the front commander's optimistic reports. He realized now that he had permitted his solid plan to be gutted for naught.

"No, no, I don't want him to get near the rampart," he shouted over the phone at Gonen in a rare display of anger, when Gonen spoke of a renewal of the attack by Adan on Hizayon. Both were unaware of the attack by Yaguri that had occurred shortly before. Adan must stay out of range of the missiles on the ramparts, said Elazar, and confine himself to destroying tanks that had penetrated inland. "He [Adan] should not reach the canal at any point." Hanging up, he vented his anger to aides at the fact that Sharon's division had been sent on a futile runaround. "We've wasted a day," he said. "We've wasted a day." Elazar took comfort in the mistaken understanding that Adan had destroyed much Egyptian armor during his sweep south. As for Gonen, "I don't understand him," he said.

The battle at Hamutal had been no less desperate than that at Hizayon. The plateau sat astride an important road leading from Tasa to the canal, opposite Ismailiya. Lieutenant Colonel Keren had sent eight tanks there in the early afternoon under battalion commander Dan Sapir. Sapir reported 1,500 Egyptian infantrymen approaching from the direction of Missouri to the south. He fired at them but they kept coming and were joined by tanks. As the infantrymen began firing Saggers, several of the Israeli tanks pulled back without orders. Sapir told the officer commanding them that he had no permission to withdraw. The officer said he was on the verge of being overrun and that his tank commanders had begun to pull back on their own. "I'm not staying here by myself," he said. With his defenses compromised, Sapir received permission from Keren to pull back.

Half an hour before sunset, at Adan's order, Keren launched a counterattack. The force consisted of Sapir's battalion, numbering fifteen tanks, and Yoffe's battalion—comprising twelve tanks—now attached to Keren's reservist brigade. Sapir was killed at the start of the attack and his disheartened force pulled back. Yoffe's tanks raced across the plateau, cutting their way through Egyptian tank formations and infantry. Yoffe's own tank was hit three times and his overheated gun barrel exploded but he continued to lead his men, wielding his machine gun. When only five of his tanks remained operational, he too pulled back.

With darkness, Adan's brigades left screening forces behind and fell back. It had been a long and desperate day marred by excruciating errors of judgment and abysmal battlefield management. The surprise this day was not the newfound capacity of the Egyptian soldiery but the bewildering incoherence of the Israeli command. There had been no field intelligence to provide basic information on the enemy deployment, accounting for Adan's uncontested north–south sweep and the false optimism that arose from his swift progress. The principal cause of the debacle was the confusing and unrealistic orders issued by Gonen. These had thrown both Adan's and Sharon's divisions off stride and resulted in grievous tactical mistakes. Gonen was the day's choreographer, but Adan's performance had been marked by a disastrous absence of control. There had been puzzling performances as well at brigade levels. The shock of the war's outbreak and the unexpected aggressiveness of the Egyptians had thrown individual and collective mind-sets out of sync. Adan would recover. His performance as division commander after this day would be regarded both by the high command and by his own senior officers as superb. But the day's events had first to be internalized. It was apparent now to the Israeli command that this would not be a quick war.

The division had lost some fifty tanks. More grievous was the profound blow to self-confidence. In this first attack initiated by the IDF in Sinai, failure had been total, except for the desperate blocking action at sunset. At times during the battle Adan had wondered if he would still have a division when the day ended. Watching his tanks now moving through the darkness to rear assembly points in orderly columns, the silhouettes of their commanders erect in the turrets, he was touched beyond words. The division had been whipped but it had not broken.

It was clear to all that there were lessons to be derived from this agonizing day. The outcome of the war depended on it.

Twenty-two

BOMB DAMASCUS

Mounting the podium of the Journalists Association in Tel Aviv Monday night for his first press conference of the war, Elazar sought to offer an anxious nation a measure of reassurance even if he had to stretch the parameters of reality. He also intended to send a signal to the enemy. The IDF had launched counterattacks this day on both fronts, he announced, and was meeting with success. "This war is a serious one, but I am happy to say we are already at the turning point." In response to a question about the war's likely length, he declined to commit himself, but added: "I can foresee one thing: that we'll continue attacking and striking back at them and that we'll break their bones."

It was a remark that would, when the truth about the day's events emerged, draw criticism as baseless braggadocio that demeaned the chief of staff's credibility. However, his words were aimed primarily at discouraging the leaders of Jordan and Iraq from throwing in their lot with Syria by depicting the dire fate that awaited that country.

Given the swift pace of events and the slow ascent of information from the field, the picture Elazar had of the two fronts much of the day was the reverse of reality. Still unaware of what had happened to Adan's division, he saw a wasted day on the southern front, not a calamity. His concern was focused on the north. The picture Hofi had presented during Elazar's visit to Northern Command was a desperate one when in reality the troops had

found a tenuous footing and were beginning to push the Syrians back. Referring to reports that Syrian tanks had almost reached the Upper Customs
House, above the Bnot Yaacov Bridge, Elazar told aides: "There isn't a single [Israeli] tank from there to Haifa. And it's a quick enough drive from
Haifa to Tel Aviv." It was urgent, he said, to create a fallback line at the edge
of the heights and to direct all available resources to the north. The canal, he
noted, was far from Israel's border, leaving ample room for tactical withdrawals. "As long as I have a few hundred tanks there, I trust the boys to
maneuver their way back to the canal. But I don't have any breathing space
on the Golan."

The only place where Israeli troops this day had in fact fared badly in the
north was on the Hermon. Soldiers who had escaped from the outpost on
Saturday reached the bottom of the mountain Monday morning, after hiding the previous day. They told Golani commander Amir Drori that the bulk
of the men were still holed up inside the outpost when they got away and
that the position was besieged by the Syrians. Their sense of time was distorted, however, and they said that they had escaped the day before, instead
of two days before.

Believing that men were still holding out, the Israeli command decided
on an immediate rescue operation. Colonel Drori ascended the mountain on
its one road with a force of Golani infantrymen in half-tracks, accompanied
by several tanks and a bulldozer to clear obstructions. Another force, led by
battalion commander Yudke Peled, ascended on foot. Peled's force was
stopped by a Syrian commando battalion a third of the way up, firing from
behind boulders. Golani rifle fire at two hundred yards proved ineffective,
the curve of the tracer bullets showing Peled how their flight was being bent
by the powerful wind. Seeking to close range, he ordered his light mortars to
fire smoke shells. Clouds scudding along the slope provided additional cover
as the troops bounded up from boulder to boulder. At fifty meters, Uzis
proved effective. The Syrian battalion finally pulled back, leaving the field to
Peled's force, which suffered two dead and eight wounded. However, the
vehicular force was ambushed on the road and badly mauled. With a total of
twenty-five dead and fifty-seven wounded, Drori ordered a withdrawal.

In the Tel Aviv war room, General Tal suggested dropping plans for a canal
crossing and instead sending an amphibious force across the Gulf of Suez.
Such a move would outflank the Egyptian army along the canal and threaten
Egypt's major oil fields and even the Nile Valley. This was a long-standing

contingency plan and the navy had tank-landing ships at Sharm el-Sheikh capable of ferrying an amphibious force across. Dayan was willing to consider it but still favored attacking at the other end of the Egyptian line and capturing Port Said at the mouth of the canal. One way or the other, he said, it was important to seize territory to offset the Egyptian gains in Sinai. Dayan had regained something of his wry humor. When Tal said that Sharon was determined to cross the canal, the defense minister said, "If I know Arik, he'll head straight for Cairo and try to get votes for Likud."

Sharon himself was in no mood for levity. He was convinced that an opportunity to turn the war around had been lost this day by the failure to launch his and Adan's divisions against the Second Army bridgehead in a combined attack before the Egyptians had had a chance to fortify their positions. Once the Second Army bridgehead was disposed of, they would have dealt with the Third Army bridgehead. It was still possible, he believed, to collapse the Egyptians by bold action, but he no longer had confidence that those running the war were capable of it. He viewed the caution of the General Staff and Southern Command as reflecting a debilitating loss of self-confidence. The Egyptians, he pointed out, were digging in and laying minefields, not advancing. If they were broken at one point, he was confident that their whole line would collapse. But every passing day would make that more difficult.

Adan did not share Sharon's evaluation. The understrength and still unorganized Israeli divisions would have suffered even greater disaster if they had undertaken an all-out attack, he believed. He would argue that on October 8 the IDF should have attacked only those Egyptian forces which had penetrated inland. It would then have held the line until sufficient forces were organized for a counterattack and a canal crossing.

Close to midnight Monday, Elazar flew south to discuss the day's events and determine immediate strategy. Dayan joined him, as did Gen. Aharon Yariv (ret.), Zeira's predecessor as head of AMAN. Yariv had agreed to unofficially assume the duties of army spokesman, a post made critical by the tenuous state of the nation's morale. Meeting with his staff before departure, Elazar had spoken angrily about Gonen's performance. "I was taken in because I was fed overoptimistic information. If my plan had been carried out, I would be sitting with Arik in Suez now." He was still unaware of the full extent of the day's failures.

The atmosphere in Gonen's headquarters as the commanders assembled for the meeting was heavy with unspoken anger. Adan was the last of the divisional commanders to arrive. The burden of the day's failure had fallen on him and he felt that he had been put in an intolerable position. He was angry over the deviations by Gonen from the agreed-upon plan and over the fact that his forces had to mark time for hours under heavy shelling while waiting for promised air support that never came. He was bitter too at being kept in the dark about the pullout of Sharon's division that had endangered his own flank and about the contradictory orders he had received throughout the day. In his one angry aside, he told Gonen that he would wait until after the war before asking for an investigation into why he had been given false information about the Egyptians fleeing and why he had been pressured to cross the canal. Gonen, for his part, felt he had been misled by overconfident reporting by Adan. Sharon was furious beyond words over his division's runaround and the fact that it had been prevented from coming to grips with the enemy on this critical day.

The participants had not slept for three days except for brief catnaps. Despite their exhausted state, all recognized the urgent need for quick decisions. Gonen wisely kept the discussion from deteriorating into an angry analysis of what went wrong. Inept though his performance had been, he had not lost his nerve. He began with a terse review of the day's events and a report on current strength: 590 tanks. Sharon urged an attack across the canal. He said the crossing could not depend on the capture of Egyptian bridges, which he regarded as unlikely. The IDF must bring forward its own bridges. While avoiding direct criticism of Gonen, he said that if a two-division attack had been carried out this day, no Egyptian would have been left east of the canal. "Sometimes you've got to gamble," he said.

General Mendler agreed with Sharon's call for a cross-canal attack. Adan, however, said the IDF would have to build up its strength before attacking again. In addition, the use of the Israeli bridges was problematic. He pointed out that they would have to be towed some five miles through the Egyptian bridgehead before reaching the canal. Gonen had been sobered by the day's events. "It may not sound popular, but I'm against crossing the canal with our present strength," he said. Like General Tal, he now proposed attacking across the Gulf of Suez.

Elazar learned for the first time at the meeting that Adan had hardly met Egyptian tanks during his southward sweep, had suffered considerable losses at Hizayon, and at the end of the day had been forced to withdraw. Sharon's division had been run in circles. The battle, in short, had been totally bungled. After hearing out his generals, Elazar said that Southern Command would restrict itself in the coming days to defensive action and keep its losses to a minimum while building up its strength. The IDF would meanwhile focus on knocking Syria out of the war. Elazar left open the option of resuming the offensive in Sinai later in the week, perhaps with the capture of Port Said. Sharon objected that Port Said, isolated on the marshy northern flank, was a sideshow that would have no impact on the outcome of the war. Victory, he said, could only be achieved by crossing the canal on the main part of the battlefield. Unlike Dayan, who wanted the port city as a diplomatic bargaining chip in postwar negotiations, Sharon was intent on going for the enemy's jugular—plunging into the center of his line and throttling him until he surrendered. He asked for permission to cross at Kantara in two days with his division. Elazar said he would keep that option open.

On the flight back to Tel Aviv, Dayan and Elazar lost themselves in their own thoughts, freed by the noise of the helicopter from any obligation to converse. The grievous failure of the counterattack in Sinai, whose full extent they had only now learned, together with the failure of the Golani Brigade to retake the Hermon earlier in the day, made it apparent that the strategy of the war had to be rethought. The high command had been thrown badly off balance. Facing it now was the likelihood of a prolonged conflict. Dayan had returned to his back-to-the-wall mode, but this time it was as a clearheaded war leader with a pragmatic agenda, not as a demoralizing prophet of doom. He spelled out his thoughts upon their return to the Pit before dawn Tuesday.

The nation was facing a major crisis, the defense minister said to the officers who gathered in Elazar's room, and it had to make painful adjustments. Large nations like Britain and the Soviet Union had undergone similar crises in war, he noted. The Israeli public would take it hard when it learned that the IDF could not throw the Egyptians back across the canal, but there was no way around it. "We have to tell the nation the truth."

In order to knock Syria out of the war before Jordan and Iraq joined in, Dayan said, extreme measures were justified. The war had disproven many of the IDF's basic assumptions. "We thought our tanks could stop the Egyptians from putting up bridges but we didn't imagine the forest of antitank missiles. The air force had plans for eliminating the antiaircraft missiles but they didn't work. We have to learn life anew. The Arab world has gone to war. They have much power and we must understand that there is no magic formula."

To cope with the possibility of a protracted conflict, the IDF had to build up its strength swiftly, said Dayan. The mobilization pool had to be expanded to include men in higher age brackets. In addition, the IDF should explore the possibility of giving seventeen-year-olds advanced training, particularly those youths qualified for pilot courses and those destined for the armored corps, so that when they were drafted at eighteen they would be ready for actual service. Additional armaments on a large scale were essential and request lists must be prepared for Washington. More immediately, antitank weapons similar to those which had proven so effective in the hands of the Egyptian infantry must be distributed to "the whole country" in the event that enemy armor reached Israel's heartland. This startling proposal indicated the magnitude of the danger Dayan saw confronting the nation.

As for the battlefronts, a suitable fallback position had to be prepared in Sinai, a line which could be held under any circumstances. This might be well to the rear of the Gidi and Mitla Passes, hitherto considered the ultimate fallback line—perhaps a line running from Sharm el-Sheikh to El Arish, two-thirds of the way back to the Israeli border. "It may be that I'm more pessimistic than Dado [Elazar]," said Dayan of his fallback proposal. "Maybe it's the age difference." (At fifty-eight, Dayan was ten years older than Elazar.) On the Golan there was no room to pull back, he said. "We fight there until the last man and we don't fall back a centimeter. If we lose all our tanks there, we'll lose them, but the Syrian force will be destroyed too." He would repeat this later. "Even if we lose all our armor we must bring the battle in the north to a decision."

Commanders—at all levels—who cannot carry out this mission must be replaced, Dayan said. After his visit to Northern Command Sunday morning, he had told Elazar that Hofi was "tired and depressed" and that part of the problem was that he was a foot soldier, not a tank officer. Dayan had proposed that veteran commanders be sent north to bolster him. He now suggested that Elazar consider replacing Hofi—not dismissing him, but placing someone else alongside him in effective command.

Gonen clearly had to be replaced. Command of the southern front, said Dayan, was simply beyond him. One possibility was to have Sharon take over the post, which he had vacated only three months before. Dayan proposed another possible candidate—Bar-Lev.

It was of paramount importance to knock Syria out of the war, the minister said, both because of the threat to northern Israel and because of the IDF's need to quickly subdue one of its enemies so that it could concentrate on the other. It was easier to get Syria out of the way first. To bring the war in the north to an end, all possibilities must be examined, "even the wildest, including the bombing of Damascus. . . . My recommendation is to make a maximum effort—I permit myself to say brutal effort—till we force them to end the war. It is within our capacity to do this, which is not the case on the Egyptian front."

Although Dayan would in decision-making forums push for the army to reach within fifteen miles of Damascus so as to put the city within range of its long guns, he would indicate more than once in conversations with Elazar that he would not be averse to reaching Damascus itself if that was possible. "If there's a possibility of entering Damascus . . . I don't dismiss it out of hand," he wrote in a note to Elazar. "Entry to Damascus would offset our retreat from the canal." (Kissinger was also encouraging Israel to move towards the Syrian capital in order to give it more muscle at the negotiating table. "When you reach the suburbs you can use public transportation," he quipped to Dinitz.)

Dayan's unsparing remarks challenged any lingering illusions within the General Staff that the initial Arab successes were an unfortunate fluke that would soon be set right as the IDF regained its stride. This was a new kind of war and Israel would have to quickly refocus if it was to save itself.

After Dayan's departure, Elazar picked up on the theme of attacking the Syrian hinterland. The air force, he told his staff, should halt its attacks on Syrian air bases and instead go after four major cities—Damascus, Homs, Aleppo, and Latakia. "To destroy them. I need something effective and dramatic that will make the Syrians cry '*gevalt*' [woe, in Yiddish] and stop shooting. To hit their power stations, everything." Despite the ferocious-sounding remarks, Elazar did not speak of attacking civilian quarters, and in fact none would be attacked.

Air force commander Peled, who had been scornful of the depressed mood among many in the Pit—the Holocaust Basement, as he would bitingly refer to it—was himself jarred by the report of the failed counterattack in the south. His colleagues in the air force war room found him pale when he returned from the meeting with Dayan and they shared his shock when he told them what had happened. Just as the ground forces expected the air force to sweep the skies clean and provide close support, the air force never doubted that the tanks, once unleashed, would demolish the Egyptians. The air force was now as disappointed, and shaken, by the failure of the armored corps—normally its rival for budgets and glory—as the latter was by the air force's suddenly revealed inability to provide close support.

The hard truth about the country's military situation was presented to Prime Minister Meir by Dayan at a 7:30 A.M. meeting. Also present were Elazar, Yariv, and Meir's closest advisers, ministers Israel Galili and Yigal Allon. Dayan began by saying that there was at present no possibility of approaching the canal, let alone crossing it. The IDF's immediate emphasis must be on persuading Syria to seek a cease-fire. Towards this end, he proposed bombing military targets in Damascus. Dayan noted that the Syrians had fired close to a score of Frog ground-to-ground missiles at the Ramat David air base over the past three nights. Frogs had hit the air base and killed a pilot in a dormitory. But the missiles had also hit nearby civilian settlements—Kibbutz Gvat and the town of Migdal Haemek—and wounded a score of people. This was enough to justify an Israeli attack on Syrian urban areas and infrastructure. "Our targets are military but we can't rule out the possibility that civilians will be hurt."

As for Sinai, a fallback position must be prepared, said Dayan, but he was not recommending that the IDF retreat to it unless it became necessary. The defense minister said he believed it would be possible at a later stage to push the Egyptians back across the canal but the IDF must first reorganize. He proposed bringing back into service members of the "old guard," retired generals with battle experience, to shore up the IDF command structure. Victory, in short, was not around the corner.

The prime minister raised what she called "a crazy thought"—that she travel incognito to Washington to make a personal appeal to President Nixon to meet Israel's arms requests swiftly and in full. Not even the Israeli cabinet need know of her visit. Dayan supported the idea, but Washington would prove decidedly unenthusiastic. Before the meeting ended, Dayan suggested that he appear on television that night, the fourth of the war, to address the Israeli public.

Elazar, as usual, was not as gloomy as the defense minister. Instead of focusing on the possibility of retreat in Sinai, he concerned himself with how to hold firm on the present line. Nevertheless, he authorized preparation of a fallback line at the passes if retreat became necessary. A general would be dispatched to Sinai to oversee the work. Elazar intended to wait for the Egyptian armor to attack, an encounter he was certain would significantly erode enemy tank strength. At that point—and not before, as Sharon was urging—the IDF would cross the canal. There would be no more attempts, he said, to rescue garrisons holding out on the Bar-Lev Line. Elazar was not aware of details, but more than a score of tanks and scores of men had already been lost in the attempts to reach Hizayon with its twenty-one-man garrison.

Mrs. Meir objected to hitting targets in Damascus. If there were civilian casualties, she said, the Americans might hold up arms shipments. But when she put the question to minister Galili, her veteran counselor, he said, "We have to do it." Meir bowed to his judgment and had a message sent to Dinitz requesting him to explain to Kissinger that the object was to knock Syria out of the war and dissuade Jordan and Iraq from joining in.

Returning from an early bombing run on the Egyptian front Tuesday morning, Maj. Arnon Lapidot stopped in at the Phantom squadron's operations room at Tel Nof Air Base to check the teleprinter. As deputy squadron commander, it was Lapidot's task this day to assign crews to the missions received from air force headquarters. The mission list had arrived and Lapidot was jolted to see that it included Damascus. Eight planes were to attack Syrian General Staff headquarters and the adjacent air defense headquarters in the heart of the city. Why us? was his first thought. The war until now had been brutal enough. But the air defenses around the Syrian capital would be more murderous than anything they'd yet seen. Even during the Six Day War the approaches to Damascus had been a rough ride.

There were only two pilots available in the squadron with the experience to lead a raid as hazardous as this and one of them was Lapidot. Loath to dump it on his mate, the twenty-seven-year-old kibbutznik assigned himself the task.

In selecting pilots and navigators for the mission, Lapidot chose men not only for their skill but also for their nerve. By now, everyone felt fear, unlike on the first day of the war when it had been tallyho and an eager rush for action. One-eighth of the entire air force—forty-nine planes—had been shot down in just four days. Every time they went up—which they did three to five times a day—the airmen were narrowing their own odds for survival. Some men coped with these odds better than others.

One of the pilots Lapidot chose was American-born Joel Aronoff, a graduate of the U.S. Air Force Academy who had flown more than two hundred combat missions with Phantoms in Vietnam before mustering out in 1969 and immigrating to Israel. With the air force just beginning to absorb Phantoms, his application to join was accepted in a rare departure from normal practice. The Israeli pilots had listened with interest to his experiences evading SAMs over North Vietnam, but he was the first to admit that they were far better pilots than he, particularly in air-to-air combat. Aronoff was the one pilot in the world able to compare firsthand the Soviet-made Arab air defenses with those fielded by the North Vietnamese. After his first foray over the Suez Canal on Yom Kippur afternoon, he reported that ground fire was "much more than anything I ever saw in Vietnam." Lapidot chose him because the cheerful American had demonstrated his coolness in combat over the past few days.

Examining the latest air photos showing the deployment of Syrian antiaircraft guns, Lapidot sharpened a pencil and drew a flight path that would avoid most of them. It would be impossible to avoid all. The planes would hug the ground all the way to target to avoid revealing themselves to enemy radar. The main hazard would thus be conventional antiaircraft guns, which were effective up to 4,500 feet. Lapidot decided that he would lead the planes in over the mountains north of Damascus, which meant a wide swing through Lebanon.

In case they went off course for whatever reason and had to take new bearings, Lapidot chose a landmark recognizable from low level that would permit them to continue towards target without breaking stride. Otherwise, they would have to climb to see where they were and thus expose themselves. The landmark he picked on the map was a disused British airfield from the Second World War at Ya'at in the Bekaa Valley.

Lapidot completed the plan in forty-five minutes and briefed the crews. Their faces were somber and there were few questions. Before moving out to the aircraft, Lapidot left a little time as he always did for the men to commune with themselves. Some would be running through the attack plan in their heads, some might want to make a phone call, others would have to make closure with themselves. From the time they climbed into their cockpits, there would be little time for thoughts beyond the business at hand.

Heading out to sea, the flight turned north. Off the coast of Lebanon, Lapidot saw a ship with large white containers on the deck, apparently a spy ship top-heavy with electronic equipment. He could not distinguish its nationality but had to make a worst-case assumption—that it was Soviet and that the Syrians already knew that eight planes would soon be penetrating their airspace. However, they could not know where the planes were headed.

Half an hour after takeoff the planes turned inland at Jounieh, a Lebanese Christian resort city just north of Beirut. From an altitude of 3,000 feet, its hotels and casinos were clearly visible. As they crossed the coast, Lapidot saw in his mirror one of the planes turn back. Radio silence was being maintained and he assumed, correctly, that the plane had experienced a malfunction.

Lapidot led the planes eastward up a broad wadi cutting through the Lebanon Mountains. Villas were perched on wooded slopes on either side, as in a Swiss postcard. Roaring up the canyon at 500 knots, the planes passed below high-tension lines spanning the tops of the mountains. Clouds were piling up, Lapidot noticed, leaving little clearance above the mountaintops. As rain began to fall, visibility became difficult. Partway through the mountain barrier, the wadi lost its eastward orientation and turned north. Lapidot had planned to rise over the mountains at this point in order to continue fly-ing eastward towards the Damascus basin. By skimming the mountaintops, he could avoid being picked up by Syrian radar. However, he would now have to rise above the clouds, which would put him on the Syrian screens.

The pilots behind him wordlessly took a formation aimed at avoiding collisions when passing through clouds. They had often drilled for this even-tuality and needed no radio command. They broke into pairs, a mile between each pair. Within each pair, the planes took position two hundred yards apart, one above the other.

Lapidot, however, decided to stick with the wadi, even though it was now taking them off course. The other planes dutifully followed. The wadi debouched into the Bekaa Valley, still inside Lebanon, and the planes dove down to hug the valley floor. They were now well off course but Lapidot spotted the fading gray runways of the old Ya'at airport almost indiscernible amidst the green and brown fields worked by Lebanese farmers. He turned gently and headed southeast towards Damascus on his new bearings.

One more mountain range lay between the Israeli planes and the Syrian capital—the so-called Anti-Lebanon. As they raced towards it, Lapidot saw that the mountains were completely covered with clouds. There was no wadi that would take them through the barrier, and not even a squirrel hole between the mountaintops and the clouds through which they might squeeze.

To fly into a missile zone above clouds meant near-certain death. In a cloudless environment, a warplane—particularly an agile and powerful plane like the Phantom—has a reasonable chance of dodging a missile, if the pilot begins maneuvering when he spots the missile far below. But in heavy overcast, the missile will burst from the midst of the clouds, too close for the pilot to react.

For the first time, Lapidot thought about aborting the mission. But he suddenly recalled a lecture from a meteorologist during his pilot training course. Humid air coming off the sea is pushed upwards when it encounters a mountain mass and forms clouds, he had said. However, where the other side of the mountain falls away into desert, the relative humidity is lowered and the clouds on that side will soon dissipate. Lapidot also knew this from Mount Gilboa in northern Israel—the desert-edge mount on which King Saul died in battle against the Philistines and which subsequently bore David's curse, "Let there be no rain or dew upon you." On the other side of the Anti-Lebanon range, just beyond Damascus, was the Syrian desert. Might not the clouds on that side of the mountains be thinner than on this side? Making a quick calculation, Lapidot reckoned that if he went above the clouds he would have a minute's flying time before the missile radars picked him up. If the clouds didn't disappear in that time, he would turn back. He hoped at least to encounter some MiGs on the way home so that it would not have been a totally wasted mission.

Pulling his stick back, he climbed above the clouds and leveled off at 12,000 feet. The six other planes tagged behind. The cloud cover was thin— only some 2,000 feet—but it was full, offering no holes to dive through. Within half a minute, however, the clouds grew ragged and then disappeared, just as the meteorology lecturer had suggested. The planes dove, leveling off at 1,000 feet over the ground.

In going above the clouds they had been picked up by regional Syrian radar but not by the missile radars. Lapidot could see on his sensors that a SAM radar was groping for them, but they were too low for it to lock on. According to the flight plan, a conventional antiaircraft battery still lay in their path. There was no way to avoid it if they wished to remain on course. Approaching it, the pilots could see the crews hastily swiveling the gun barrels and firing, but the shots missed. The planes swayed upwards slightly behind Lapidot to pass over a high-tension line.

Damascus now lay dead ahead. There was no longer need for radio silence.

"Pull up," said Lapidot. In air force headquarters in Tel Aviv, where the flight's radio frequency was being closely monitored, it was the first sign of life.

As the nose of his plane rose, Damascus appeared below. The city was densely built, as ancient cities are, most of the buildings only three or four stories high. It was not a large city and it was surrounded by orchards and palm trees. Lapidot was enchanted. Asphalted streets glistened from a recent shower that had washed the city clean. Damascus, he would recall, glowed "like a bride in a church."

He had decided that the attack would be made from 10,000 feet, in order to keep well above the range of the antiaircraft guns. He had ten seconds in which to climb, pick out his target in the midst of the city, align his sights, and release his bombs.

"One going in," he said. Each plane would announce itself in numerical order as it began its run in order to ensure that they kept out of each other's way. As he climbed, Lapidot scanned the cityscape for the landmarks he had taken note of in drawing up his plan. He saw the stadiums he had circled on his map, Mazeh Air Base just west of the city, and then, in the midst of the urban matrix, his target, the V-shaped General Staff headquarters. Even though it was only seven stories high, it projected distinctly above the surrounding buildings. Antiaircraft guns opened on him as he entered his dive.

Buffeting from a strong side wind made it difficult for him to align on the base of the V as he intended. Heading towards the building at a slant angle of 30 degrees—an angle chosen to ensure that the bombs penetrate their target instead of bouncing off like pebbles thrown into a pond—he pressed the bomb release button on his control stick a mile from target. Eight 500-pound bombs fell away, giving the plane a slight bounce as it freed itself of their weight. Lowering a wing to clear his line of sight, Lapidot saw smoke blossoming on the northern wing of the building. There was smoke too in the street beyond, indicating that the wind had carried some bombs wide of the target. The detonators had been set so that the bombs exploded deep inside the building, down to the second floor where the main offices were believed to be.

"Two going in." The other planes were beginning their attack. Once their bombs were released, each plane would have to wend its own way through the curtain of antiaircraft fire until the flight could re-form.

The exit route Lapidot had chosen followed the Damascus–Beirut highway. The antiaircraft guns had gone wild, attempting to make up for having been outflanked. Wherever Lapidot looked below, he saw the feverish sparkle of guns, all being fired at him. Unlike the antiaircraft ordnance of the Second World War, which dotted the sky with dark puffs, these guns left few marks in the sky, but their deadly outpouring was far more prodigious. Like a cornered animal fighting for its life, Lapidot hurled his plane, flying now at 4,500 feet, in wild gyrations, undertaking pendulum swings a mile wide.

From the start of his climb on the approach to Damascus to the point where he finally outran the gunfire on his exit, only forty seconds had passed. But they had taxed every physical and moral fiber of his being. Dry-mouthed, he headed into the calmer skies of Lebanon to catch his breath and await the others. The radio, however, left him no respite. "Parachute": The report was at once bad news and worse news. Parachute meant that a plane was down. Parachute in the singular meant that one of its two crewmen had gone down with it.

Lapidot asked the planes to report. Number Three was missing. In addition, the pilot of Number Five, Omri Afek, reported both engines aflame. Lapidot could hear Afek's wing mate, Joel Aronoff, describing the damage to Afek in his mangled Hebrew—"Small fire left engine, big fire right engine." Afek closed the engines down in succession and then, despite considerable risk of explosion from leaking fuel, restarted one. Shepherded by Aronoff, Afek took the direct route back to Israel, risking ground fire along the way, rather than follow Lapidot and the others the long way around through Lebanon. Afek skillfully nursed the plane over the Hermon and descended towards Ramat David, Israel's northernmost airfield. The Phantom's hydraulic system and steering mechanism were defunct, and so were the rear parachute that could have slowed the plane down and the emergency hook that could have grappled restraining wires. The burning plane hurtled down the runway, only partially slowed by the failing brakes. It was finally stopped by a net raised at the end of the runway.

In debriefing, it emerged that damage to the buildings in Damascus had been moderate. All the bombs that struck army headquarters had hit the northern wing. Of the two planes which attacked air defense headquarters, one had had a malfunction and its bombs fell short by thirty yards, damaging a Soviet cultural center, where a number of Soviet personnel were killed and wounded. A television station was also hit accidentally.

However, the attack on the military nerve center in the heart of Damascus helped reestablish Israel's deterrent image. It mattered little that damage was limited and that the Syrian military hierarchy was in underground war rooms elsewhere. There would be no more Frog missiles fired at Israel.

In the basement of Syrian army headquarters, Lt. Avraham Barber, a Phantom pilot downed in the Dougman operation two days before, was being interrogated when the bombs hit. The lights went out and dust filled the room. Barber was blindfolded and rushed outside. He knew there were other pilots in the basement and assumed they were being led out too. Rubble crunched under his feet before he was thrust into a vehicle.

According to information Israel later received, the Syrians believed that Israeli intelligence had known of the pilots' presence in the basement—which was not true—and had aimed their bombs so as to spare them. Barber also believed that Israeli intelligence must have known the airmen were in the building, but he believed the mission planners were trying to kill them, not spare them. It was a dark thought based on what he had seen so far of the war. First had come the surprise of the Arab attack, then the sudden cancellation of Tagar, and then the squadron's hasty dispatch north to execute an improperly prepared Dougman. The first Syrian intelligence officer to question Barber after he parachuted said he had been listening to Israel Radio's Arabic service and it was clear that Israel was going under. You're lucky you're here, said the Syrian, not unsympathetically. Barber had arrived in Damascus blindfolded and did not know what building he was being taken to. But of all the buildings in Syria, it was the one the air force had chosen to bomb. He assumed that the desperate Israeli leadership had decided that the pilots must be killed to prevent them from talking. "Things must be in a bad way at home," he mused. The thought would dissipate within a few days. Unknown to Barber, the bombing had been carried out by his own squadron.

Returning to base, Lapidot and his crews had little time to dwell on the Damascus mission since they were scheduled to set out for other missions in a couple of hours. He learned for the first time that his was one of three squadrons that were supposed to attack Damascus this day. One flight had taken a different route and encountered the storm system that had just washed Damascus. Unable to find a chink in the clouds, the flight leader aborted. On his way back, he was directed to the Golan Heights, where he dumped his bombs on Syrian positions. The third flight was canceled before taking off because of the weather.

The attack on Syrian army headquarters would win Lapidot and his navigator the country's second-highest decoration. It was not, however, the pilot's most trying experience of the war. This would come two days later when he led a second attack in the area of Damascus, this time on the Syrian air force's wartime operations center, hidden beneath an orchard on the city's outskirts.

As they neared the area, Lapidot identified the target amidst a sea of orchards. All that was visible aboveground was eight air vents, each a square meter in size. As Lapidot was going into his attack, two SAM missiles were fired in the distance. Still dogged by the loss of his comrades over Damascus two days before, he turned to see if the SAMs were endangering the rear planes in the flight. When he turned back to his targeted air vent, he could not find it and dropped his bombs aimlessly on the orchard. The only pilot to score a direct hit was the one who had aborted over Lebanon during the previous attack.

The attacks on the Syrian capital would be followed by 130 sorties against ports, refineries, power stations, bridges, and other infrastructure. These were only a tiny fraction of 6,000 sorties the IAF would carry out on the Syrian front. The infrastructure attacks were painful for Syria, but not enough for it to cry woe. They deprived it of half its fuel capacity, but replacement fuel was trucked in from Lebanon and Iraq. Roads and bridges were destroyed but alternative routes were organized. The worst damage was caused by the bombing of two power stations near Damascus, which knocked out 80 percent of the country's electricity supply. Although they presumably had a psychological impact on the Syrian leadership, these strategic strikes would fail to knock Syria out of the war. The bombing brought home the cost of the war to the Syrian population at large—something that might be borne in mind in the future—but had no visible impact on the battlefield. In a relatively brief war, it would be developments on the front line, not limited strategic bombing, that would decide the outcome.

Twenty-three

TOUCHING BOTTOM

Tuesday would be for many in the Israeli hierarchy the worst day of all. It was the day they learned the dimensions of the failed counterattack in Sinai and realized that their expectations of a quick turnaround in the war were illusion. As General Tal would describe it later, "We didn't have any reserves left, there was nothing left. The war was perceived not just as at a critical, almost hopeless, stage but as a struggle for our very physical survival."

According to an account published abroad, the inner cabinet met on Monday, October 8, and decided to arm Israel's nuclear arsenal for fear the army might collapse. But the dimensions of the October 8 failure were still not known in Tel Aviv Monday evening. The low point of the war for the high command was reached only the following day after the return of Dayan and Elazar from Umm Hashiba. If there was a time to contemplate desperate measures it was this day when the cabinet indeed decided to send the air force against Syrian infrastructure in a bid to drive Damascus out of the war.

According to a report on the Israeli press thirty years after the war, General Tal told a secret forum in 1974 that the General Staff had recommended that Tuesday morning, October 9, taking "extreme measures" against the Arabs. After the meeting, according to this account, a senior officer approached Tal in tears and said, "You've got to save Israel from those madmen," a reference to those who had approved the "extreme measures."

Egypt was aware of Israel's nuclear potential, but Sadat's limited operational goals in Sinai did not threaten Israel's borders and therefore were not seen as risking a doomsday response. Syria's war plan, however, did call for reaching Israel's border, and perhaps beyond, and for the first two days it seemed they might succeed. Damascus's perception of Israel's nuclear policy is not known.

The editors in chief of Israel's daily newspapers were offered a glimpse of Dayan's dark vision Tuesday evening. His off-the-record talk with them was part of his decision to "level with the nation." The IDF, he said, was doing well on the Golan and would soon regain the territory it had lost. But on the southern front, Israel did not at present have the strength to throw the Egyptians back across the canal. Nowhere in the world, said Dayan, including the Soviet Union and Vietnam, was there such a dense deployment of modern Soviet weaponry. The war was against Soviet weaponry more than against the Arabs. Israel might have to withdraw deep into Sinai, and this carried far-reaching implications. "The world has seen that we are not stronger than the Egyptians. The aura, and the political and military advantage of it being known that Israel is stronger than the Arabs and that it would beat them if they go to war, this has not been proven here."

Dayan's harsh appraisal stunned his listeners. An editor asked whether the assumption shared by Israelis that the country could cope with any Arab attack, even one involving all the Arab states, was no longer true. "On the contrary," Dayan hastened to respond, recognizing the implications of his words. "We can stand against all the Arab states, against all the Soviet armaments."

Nevertheless, the editors were aghast when Dayan said he intended to address the nation on television this night. Even though he said he would speak in less stark terms than he had to them, they feared that his appearance would demoralize an already shaken nation. An editor passed on his concern to Mrs. Meir, who had already experienced the demoralizing effect of Dayan's unvarnished truth. She agreed with the editor and asked Dayan to step aside for General Yariv. In a much praised television appearance that night, Yariv doled out the truth to the Israeli public in measures that could be swallowed. He offset the bitter taste not by fabrication but by offering hope.

Inside Hizayon, hope had evaporated by Monday afternoon. Egyptian commandos penetrated the fort several times and were driven off only after the garrison had taken cover in the bunkers and called down artillery on the fort itself. At 5:15 P.M. the acting commander notified his superiors that they could hold out no longer.

Radioman Maimon passed the word to the men in the bunkers on the intercom: "We're going to surrender." In the medical bunker, Dr. Ohri turned to the others with him and said, "Not yet." From the courtyard outside, Maimon could be heard calling in Arabic, "We surrender." In Sergeant Strolovitz's bunker, he and the four men with him likewise decided not to go out. One of his men suggested suicide, another that they go out shooting. The sergeant said that they would wait until night and try to get back to the Israeli lines.

With darkness, Strolovitz led his men out. But as they approached the gate, they heard the voices of Egyptian sentries and returned to the bunker. In the morning, Strolovitz left the bunker to surrender and was shot at. He tried again and this time he and the others were taken prisoner. As they were led away, they saw the bodies of eleven men from the command bunker lying in the courtyard, their hands tied behind their backs. Unaware of the fate of the others, Dr. Ohri remained in the medical bunker with the wounded commander of Hizayon, Lieutenant Bareli, and three other soldiers.

Many other forts had by this time been abandoned or captured. The thirteen-man garrison at Fort Lakekan on the northern end of the Bitter Lake had been ordered Sunday afternoon to pull back. When night fell, they and seven crewmen from disabled tanks who had joined them climbed aboard the post's solitary half-track and headed east. Avoiding roads, they climbed with difficulty through the dunes. Nearing the Artillery Road, they stopped and moved forward on foot until they heard Hebrew being spoken. The tankers who received them were astonished that they had made their way through the Egyptian lines safely.

At Fort Matsmed, five miles north of Lakekan, hundreds of Egyptian infantrymen attacked on Monday afternoon, reaching the fences before being driven back. The defenders hit two tanks with bazookas. The fort commander, Capt. Gideon Gur, called for artillery but few shells fell. This was the third day of battle and the thirty-five-man garrison had only one bazooka shell left. With night coming on, Gur thinned out his outposts to let as many men as possible get some sleep.

Thick fog covered the area Tuesday morning when the sound of tanks was heard again. Gur sounded the alarm and the men rushed to their posts. The tanks were only twenty yards from the main gate when they loomed out of the fog. Infantry followed close behind. This time the attack could not be stopped. Gur called for artillery but there was none. He ordered the men into the bunkers. The Egyptians poured into the compound, throwing fragmentation grenades and smoke grenades into the bunker entrances. The defenders managed to throw some back but men began to choke. At 8 A.M. Tuesday, Matsmed surrendered.

Fort Purkan had been spared attacks since Yom Kippur afternoon except for occasional rounds from heavy mortars. With the Egyptians steadily building up strength, rescue was becoming increasingly unlikely. Major Weisel spent much of Monday scanning the desert through binoculars to search for gaps in the Egyptian deployment. In the late afternoon, he assembled all men who could be spared from their posts. The gathering resembled the Saturday night communal meetings at his kibbutz where issues of the day were decided on by majority vote.

"Fellows, we're leaving here tonight on foot," said Weisel. He spelled out the situation as he saw it and asked the men whether they were prepared to risk making their way through the Egyptian lines. His deputy objected. Without orders to abandon the fort, he said, he himself would not leave. Weisel said headquarters would be asked for approval but that meanwhile he wanted to know how the men felt about it. The overwhelming sentiment was to go. The garrison had been lucky so far. They could not expect their luck to hold out much longer.

With darkness, Weisel contacted brigade headquarters and announced his intention of bringing the men out. Displaying a caution that even senior officers were neglecting, he assumed the conversation was being monitored by the Egyptians and used Yiddish for the more sensitive parts. Brigade's reaction was hesitant. Weisel sensed that the officers there were reluctant to authorize passage through the heart of the Second Army. "If you don't make a decision," he said, "I'll make it myself." When brigade continued to hesitate, he said, "OK, we're going." The officer responding said, "No," then "Wait."

The next voice Weisel heard was that of Ariel Sharon. Weisel outlined his intentions. "You haven't got much of a chance," said Sharon. "We can't come to help you."

"We're leaving anyway," said Weisel.

"If you think it will work, go ahead," said Sharon. He advised Weisel not to start out until the moon went down at 2:45 A.M. A rendezvous point was fixed at the foot of Hamutal Ridge, six miles east, where tanks would meet them.

"Take care of yourselves," said Sharon.

Arrow-straight Tapline Road, where Lt. Greengold met a Syrian brigade.
Photograph courtesy of Israel Defense Forces Archive

Gen. Moshe (Moussa) Peled (with mustache), division commander,
leading the drive to recapture the southern Golan.
Photograph courtesy of Israel Defense Forces Archive

Defense minister Moshe Dayan (with eye patch) and Gen. Ariel Sharon (with white bandage) on the west bank of the Suez Canal. Dayan visited both fronts regularly during the war. On the left is an armored personnel carrier.

Photograph courtesy of Israel Defense Forces Archive

Col. Ori Orr (right), whose brigade blocked the Syrian attack on Nafakh, and Lt. Col. Moshe Harel, a battalion commander who was wounded twice.

Photograph courtesy of Israel Defense Forces Archive

Maj. Arnon Lapidot led the air attack on Syrian military headquarters in Damascus. *Photograph courtesy of Israeli Government Press Office*

Lt. Col. Ami Morag (left), tank battalion commander.
Photograph courtesy of Ami Morag

Soldiers from the Golani Brigade atop Mount Hermon after its recapture.
Photograph courtesy of Israeli Government Press Office

Israeli intelligence outpost on Mount Hermon after its recapture.
Photograph courtesy of Israel Defense Forces Archive

Israeli soldiers on the bank of the Sweetwater Canal.
Photograph courtesy of Israeli Government Press Office

Gen. Bar-Lev (left), the former chief of staff who assumed command of the southern front. On the right is Gen. Rehavam Ze'evi.
Photograph courtesy of Israel Defense Forces Archive

Col. Danny Matt, commander of the reserve Israeli para-troop brigade that established the Israeli bridgehead on the west bank of the canal.
Photograph courtesy of Israeli Government Press Office

Egyptian president Anwar Sadat.
*Photograph courtesy of
Israeli Government Press Office*

Col. Ran Sarig in the Sinai. His
armored brigade was the only
one to be shifted from the Syrian
front to the Egyptian front during the war. *Photograph courtesy of
Israel Defense Forces Archive*

Israeli paratroopers breaking through an Egyptian commando ambush on a sandspit
leading to Fort Budapest on the Sinai front. *Photograph courtesy of Israel Defense Forces*

Israeli forces moving through the Sinai towards the Suez Canal.
Photograph courtesy of Israel Defense Forces Archive

The "Yard" from which Israel launched its attack across the Suez Canal. The bulldozer in the foreground had helped open the breach in the ramp where the first bridge would be built. *Photograph courtesy of Israel Defense Forces Archive*

Crossing the canal on the pontoon bridge.
Photograph courtesy of Israeli Government Press Office

Pontoon being towed in the Sinai. *Photograph courtesy of Israel Defense Forces Archive*

Israeli-made "roller bridge" on the Suez Canal.
Photograph courtesy of Israel Defense Forces Archive

Weisel assembled the soldiers in the courtyard to outline the plan. They would burn documents but would not blow up anything so as not to alert the Egyptians. If they found their way blocked, they might have to return and would want the radio and other equipment intact. To be less conspicuous, they would split into two groups—one under command of his deputy—and meet at designated map coordinates near Hamutal. Weisel told the men to eat and to fill their canteens.

As he spoke, a guard at the main gate announced the arrival of a soldier. "He says he's a tank driver." A thin young soldier appeared. He related that his tank had thrown a tread while battling Egyptian tanks during the day and that the other three crewmen had been shot as they climbed out. The Egyptians had tried to kill him too, but he closed his hatch and they couldn't get at him. They finally booby-trapped the exterior of the hatch and left. He had escaped through the emergency exit at the bottom of his compartment and had hidden until darkness. He was told to get some sleep before they set out.

After calling down artillery on the surrounding area, Weisel led the way out the front gate moments after the moon went down. They were thirty-two men in all. Crossing Lexicon Road, they found themselves in an Egyptian bivouac area. It was empty but sleeping bags on the ground were still warm. Less than one hundred yards away, men were hammering stakes into the ground for a tent encampment. Weisel and his deputy split up and the two groups hurried forward in the darkness.

Dawn revealed a desert glistening with gossamer sheen. Thin, silvery guide wires from Sagger missiles lay across the sand like spiderwebs. As they approached the foot of Hamutal, a fierce tank battle broke out above. They could hear the bark of guns and occasionally see tanks topping a rise. Weisel halted and reported his arrival on the radio.

Although Colonel Reshef's brigade had been shifted to another sector, he asked Sharon's permission to bring in Weisel and his men. He admired Weisel's courage in coming out on foot through the Egyptian army. The commander of another fort to whom Reshef had suggested a similar escape had declined, even though there had been no enemy forces in his vicinity. That garrison had been taken prisoner after a battle. Reshef gave the rescue assignment to battalion commander Shaul Shalev, who set out himself, accompanied by one other tank containing an artillery liaison. Weisel's precise location was not clear and the area was swarming with enemy tanks and Sagger teams. When Shalev reported that he did not see any sign of the Purkan garrison, Reshef ordered him to return.

Raising Weisel on the radio from a hilltop, Reshef asked him to fire a green flare, despite the risk that this might betray his position to the Egyptians. A flare rose above the dunes two miles away. This time, Reshef in his tank joined Shalev and the artillery officer. The three split up to widen the search area as they drove through the dunes. Following Shalev were several half-tracks bearing infantry.

Reshef was close to the approximate area of the flare when he saw thirty soldiers on a hill two hundred yards away. He halved that distance before he saw that they were Egyptians. Ordering his driver to charge, the brigade commander raked the enemy soldiers with machine-gun fire. The Egyptians returned fire as Reshef fed a new ammunition belt into his gun. Sagger missiles fired from somewhere to the side passed overhead. The driver ran down surviving enemy soldiers.

Shalev also encountered Egyptian infantry dug in on a hill and charged. As he did so, his operations officer pointed to the left where the top of an antenna could be seen projecting over a low dune. Shalev changed direction, leaving the Egyptians to be dealt with by the infantry following behind. Sweeping around the dune, he found Weisel and his men. The garrison's three wounded soldiers were lowered through the turret into the tank itself, and the remaining twenty-nine clambered aboard the exterior, somehow finding handholds. Shortly afterwards, Reshef saw a bizarre apparition approaching across the sand. It was a moment before he recognized it as Shalev's tank covered with the Purkan garrison.

Two of the Israeli infantrymen in the accompanying half-tracks were killed, but the report of the rescue on the radio nets sent a surge of satisfaction through the Israeli lines, hungry for good news.

In the morning, the Egyptians discovered Purkan evacuated. General Shazly, who was touring the front, asked to be taken to the fort, which he had viewed from the opposite bank only four days before. Entering the gate through which Weisel and his men had passed a few hours earlier, Shazly said, "Alhamdu lillahi, allahu akbar"—Thanks be to God, God is the greatest."

Lt. Col. Zussia Keniezer, the head of AMAN's Jordanian desk, was summoned Monday night to the office of Arye Shalev, Zeira's deputy. Shalev was standing before a large wall map of Sinai with the head of the Egyptian desk, Yona Bandman. Placing his hand on Keniezer's shoulder, Shalev said Keniezer would be taking over Bandman's job. "Dado [Elazar] doesn't want to see us anymore," Keniezer would recall him saying. The chief of staff would henceforth ask to get intelligence briefings on the Egyptian and Syrian fronts directly from the heads of the respective desks.

Emerging cautiously from his bunker in Hizayon Tuesday afternoon, almost a day after the fort's surrender, Dr. Ohri could see no sign of life. He searched the skies vainly for Israeli planes. The only things moving were Egyptian tanks heading east into Sinai. There was not even the sound of distant battle to indicate that Israeli forces were still out there. It seemed to the doctor as if Israel itself might already have fallen.

Nevertheless, he returned to the bunker, determined to put off surrender as long as possible. Apart from Lieutenant Bareli, whose arm had been severed, there were two lightly wounded soldiers. Another soldier had been with them but his nerves had snapped that morning. He had suddenly run into the compound, firing his Uzi. He was not killed but taken prisoner. The Egyptians had not come into the bunker afterwards.

With nightfall, the bunker was totally dark except for faint starlight coming through the entrance. One of the soldiers pulled the pin of a grenade and called on the others to stand with him around Bareli so that they could die together. Ohri firmly rejected the proposal. He had been trained in saving life, not taking it. "We'll get out of this," he said. The soldier did not reinsert the pin, but sat on a cot gripping the grenade. Over the past three days Ohri had gotten close to Bareli, the son of a Jerusalem judge. They were both twenty-five and found that they had a lot in common, even mutual acquaintances. The morphine Ohri had been giving Bareli had run out. Given the pain and the unlikeliness of rescue, the wounded man asked the doctor to kill him. Ohri refused. "We'll get out of this," he repeated.

Ohri had hardly slept since the war began. He was slumped on a cot at the far end of the banana-shaped bunker at 7 P.M. when the outline of an Egyptian soldier appeared in the entranceway. The soldier lit a piece of paper which he used as a torch. He saw a helmet and lifted it. Turning his head, the Egyptian found himself looking into a pair of eyes a few feet away staring wildly back at him. With a shout, the Egyptian bolted from the bunker. The Israeli who had been holding the live grenade leaped after him. Ohri heard the grenade explode and then the sound of guns. A few moments later a smoke grenade was tossed into the bunker and then a long tongue of fire from a flamethrower penetrated the narrow space. Ohri passed out.

When he woke, he thought himself in hell. The heat was unbearable and it was difficult to breathe. He could smell burned flesh. With a pocket flashlight, he glanced at his watch and saw that it was midnight. He crawled out of the bunker, past Bareli's body, and reached the narrow trench outside. There he sat all night, his back against the trench wall, gripping his ankles and gulping the cold night air. There was something seriously wrong with his lungs. He heard Arabic, and when he raised his head, he could see soldiers moving about the courtyard but they did not notice him. After a while, there were no more voices.

With dawn, he could see that his skin was pinched, a sign of dehydration. Craving water, he rose and saw the men from the command bunker lying dead in the courtyard. There were no Egyptian soldiers. Almost all the bunkers had collapsed under the pounding of the heavy mortars, and all freestanding structures, including the kitchen, had been flattened. Amidst its ruins was a jerrican of water. It was, he feared, too good to be true. Ohri remembered a warning that Egyptian raiders sometimes poisoned water supplies. His will to live overcoming his thirst, he turned away and continued out the fort entrance, hoping to find someone to whom to surrender.

As he staggered up the road, an armored personnel carrier approached. It stopped fifty yards away and a squad of Egyptian soldiers descended. Forming a line, the soldiers took magazines out of their pouches and slammed them into their Kalashnikovs. Ohri tried to shout that he was a doctor but no words came out of his burned throat. He felt like a gasping fish. Suddenly a jeep dashed up the road and stopped between him and the soldiers. An Egyptian officer emerged. He approached Ohri, who slid to the ground, his legs no longer able to support him. The officer tossed a canteen to the Israeli, who gulped down its contents and asked for another, then another. The officer came forward and offered him a biscuit but Ohri could not get it down his throat. "More water," he whispered.

Meanwhile, the soldiers from the personnel carrier had approached. One kicked Ohri, then a second. Others were about to join in when shells exploded around them. Everyone ran into the fort and took shelter in the trenches. Ohri was with the officer and his driver, the others some distance away. With his mouth close to the officer's ear, Ohri managed to whisper in English that he was a doctor.

"They want to kill you," replied the officer. "They may kill me too."

"But you're an officer," said Ohri. "They're just fellahin [peasants]."

The officer nodded. Then, signaling to his driver, he yanked Ohri to his feet and the three ran to the jeep amidst the falling shells. As they sped off, the officer, sitting in the rear, blindfolded Ohri, who was sitting next to the driver, and tied his hands behind him. They reached a place where, by the sounds, there were a lot of soldiers. The officer took leave of Ohri, who was led to a shell hole and told to sit. From time to time he was given water. Finally the blindfold was removed. Hundreds of soldiers, it seemed, stood around him. His face was blackened and his clothes covered with blood from the men he had treated.

Someone asked Ohri his name, rank, and serial number. When he said he was a doctor, a soldier was called forward, apparently a medic. The soldier, who spoke English well, said he would ask some questions to test Ohri's medical knowledge. "What do you take for heartburn?" he began. Ohri signaled that he could not speak and asked for a pencil and paper. These were supplied and he was able to furnish answers to the medic's satisfaction.

They were near the canal and Ohri was led on foot to a boat which ferried him across. As he was being lifted out on the other side, he fell into the water, his hands still bound. Someone reached down and pulled him back up by his hair.

In a prison hospital in Cairo a few hours later, the Egyptian doctor examining him, a Christian Copt, correctly diagnosed bronchitis. An Israeli prisoner doctor was also summoned to the bedside. After examining Ohri, he said to the Egyptian in English: "He's not going to make it."

Forcing the words out of his mouth, Ohri said, "I'm going to live."

Television cameraman Mohammed Gohar was probably the first Egyptian civilian to cross the canal. He had been hastily dispatched from Cairo Tuesday morning to film Israeli POWs in Sinai before they were carried off to prison. The results were to be rushed to Jordan for showing on television in the evening. Israelis could not pick up Egyptian television, but many did view television from Amman. Seeing their soldiers as humbled prisoners would clearly be a devastating blow to Israeli morale.

The twenty-one-year-old cameraman crossed at Kantara and was led to a group of prisoners near the canal. They sat in rows—unshaven, heads bowed, with the vacant look of men who have surrendered to their fate. Egyptian soldiers were milling about watching the scene. Gohar told his military escort to have the soldiers moved away. Scanning the prisoners, he saw that some were wounded. He asked that they too be shifted out of camera range.

That done, he examined those remaining. There were sixteen in all and he made his calculations regarding light and camera angle. Before beginning to shoot, he looked at the prisoners again, this time not with the camera's eye but his own. It was, he realized, the first time he had ever seen Israelis. He had never even seen a photograph or a television image of one. All he knew of them were the grotesque cartoons in Cairo newspapers of Dayan and

Golda Meir. He was surprised to see that the soldiers looked perfectly normal—in fact, like himself. They were about his age and many of them—Sephardi Jews—had olive skin like his and the expression they wore was what he expected his would be in their situation. All he had heard about Israelis, all he had learned about them in school, had not prepared him for this. As he studied them, he saw some raise their heads and look at him quizzically. They took in his stare, trying to understand what it meant. And they took in the camera he was pointing at them. Having their picture taken—and shown on television—meant that they were likely to survive captivity. He understood what they were thinking, and from the eye contact he believed they were beginning to understand something of what he was thinking. Gohar would in time become the official photographer of President Sadat. But from that brief encounter on the bank of the Suez Canal at the high point of Egyptian military achievement, he became a believer in peace with Israel.

Elazar ordered Southern Command this day to deploy defensively while it built up strength. Tanks were to do no more than snipe at the Egyptian tanks from long range. Several times during the day, he repeated his warning to Gonen not to erode his forces. "We're sticking to the principle of a defensive battle, without too much maneuvering. [The Egyptians] are the ones who should get worn out while advancing."

Sharon, however, did not want to spend another day without confrontation. "This was not the time to sit back and allow the Egyptians to build up their bridgeheads and their defenses," he would write. "We should be pushing them, probing for their weak points."

He duly interpreted the order to conduct a defensive battle in his own fashion. It would be a "mobile defense" that involved movement—forward movement. His opportunity came when the Egyptians opened an attack all along the line which was repelled in sharp skirmishing. One of Sharon's brigades, commanded by Col. Tuvia Raviv, destroyed thirty Egyptian tanks with hardly a loss.

At that point, one of Raviv's battalions was ordered to attack a hill on which Egyptian infantry was digging in. A crewman aboard Maj. Haim Elkan's tank, hearing an argument on the radio about the attack, recognized one voice as that of Sharon. When Elkan said that Sharon was commander of the division they were now part of, the crewman was reassured. "If Arik is in charge, then everything will be all right," he said.

The brigade had rushed to the front without machine guns and the crews had to make do with Uzis and grenades in attacking infantry. Tankers would wield these infantry weapons on the Egyptian front more than did infantrymen as Israeli armor charged repeatedly into masses of Egyptian infantry. Elkan's gunner passed loaded Uzi magazines to him as the officer fired the submachine gun with one hand and flung grenades with the other, pulling their pins with his teeth. The gunner fired the tank gun into troop concentrations as close as fifty yards away.

The tank was hit by a missile but the crew doused the ensuing fire with an extinguisher and the driver succeeded in restarting the engine. Elkan ordered him to run down enemy infantrymen in their path, but the driver swerved at the last moment. The war was still young, and for some, crushing people to death was still an unnatural act. In face of the stiff resistance, Raviv recalled the battalion. Sixteen tanks had been hit, more than half the force. Most made it back to the Israeli lines but six had to be left behind.

Another one of Sharon's units, a battalion under Maj. Ami Morag, ascended Hamutal in midmorning and found the three-mile-long plateau seemingly empty. "Hamutal is in our hands," Morag reported. A moment later, his tank was hit by a Sagger and Morag was knocked to the bottom of the tank. Regaining consciousness, he slapped his face to convince himself he was not dead. All three of his crew were wounded but said they could carry on.

Climbing back into the turret, Morag saw that a fold in the ground divided the plateau in two. His side was empty of enemy soldiers, but on the other side, sand was flying, indicating that troops there were digging in. In the absence of machine guns, Morag ordered one of his companies to crush the infantrymen while another company provided covering fire with tank guns. The attack force raced over the foxholes, the commanders firing their Uzis and throwing grenades. To Morag's astonishment, when the tanks had passed, Egyptian soldiers rose up from those foxholes which had not collapsed and resumed firing RPGs.

The second company was sent in, with similar results. This time, the company commander turned around and made a run along the edges of the excavations so that the treads were better able to crush those inside. Even now, surviving infantrymen fought back. Egyptian artillery fire on the plateau was so dense that the smoke made it difficult for the tank commanders to see each other.

The Israelis could now make out an extensive deployment of tanks and infantry at the far end of the plateau. Morag's men quickly dealt with the

Egyptian tanks—sixteen were destroyed—but infantry was another matter. The swirling battle was often face-to-face, sometimes even hand-to-hand. An Egyptian soldier climbed onto a tank and with his rifle butt broke the jaw of the loader, whose head was projecting from his hatch. The loader succeeded in toppling him from the tank.

Morag pulled out of the battle to transfer his wounded driver, who could no longer carry on, to a tank evacuating casualties. When he returned, he found that in the five minutes he was gone all his company commanders had been wounded and almost all the platoon commanders. Morag contacted brigade commander Haim Erez and obtained permission to pull back.

Morag asked one of the company commanders to lead the battalion back down. The officer had been wounded twice during the half-hour skirmish. His tank was burning, although not in apparent danger of exploding. Morag called on tank commanders to "follow the burning tank." He himself meanwhile swept across the plateau to make sure no one had been left behind. He found a tank whose commander had not heard the pullback order and led it down. It was under cover of this battle that the Purkan garrison was rescued at the foot of Hamutal.

Of the twenty-four tanks that had begun the battle, three were destroyed on Hamutal and fourteen were damaged but managed to descend from the ridge. The twenty-seven-year-old Morag, a regular army officer in his first battalion command, was distraught as he looked at the casualties laid out along the roadside. Of the men whom he had led into battle for the first time barely an hour before, more than a quarter were casualties—eight dead and twenty wounded, including almost all his officers. Morag asked Colonel Erez to send the brigade's best doctors. "They fought too well for us to let them die," he said. As he watched, a doctor performed a tracheotomy to save the life of a company commander who was struggling to breathe.

Only seven tanks were still operational. "What do we do?" Morag asked his deputy, Maj. Yehuda Tal, an older reservist. Tal suggested that Morag go off by himself a bit while the wounded were being tended to.

Recovering his composure after a few moments, Morag assembled his men. They were all stunned by the violence of the encounter. "We took a beating on Hamutal," Morag began. "We didn't expect that infantry, especially Egyptian infantry, would stand their ground against charging tanks and that they would fire back with antitank weapons instead of running. We've taken casualties but we have no alternative. This is a battle for our existence. We'll screw them yet."

He ordered that those tanks still intact take under tow those which had difficulty moving. With that, he led the battalion back to Tasa, where the damaged tanks would be repaired and crew losses made up from the replacement pool.

In the Pit, Elazar explained to his staff that it was imperative to conserve strength in order to be able to meet the two Egyptian armored divisions which might cross at any time and strike for the passes. "I can't risk erosion of our forces."

Although this decision was passed on to Sharon, he attempted persistently from midmorning to cajole Gonen into permitting him to undertake a major divisional attack on Missouri and the Chinese Farm where the Egyptians were massing. "If I succeed, then we'll reach Matsmed today . . . You didn't let me do it yesterday. Let me do it now." Fort Matsmed was a jumping-off point for a canal crossing.

When Gonen informed Elazar of Sharon's request at noon, the chief of staff repeated his order: "No fight that can lead to loss of tanks, no movement in the direction of Matsmed."

At 1 P.M., Sharon informed Gonen that he was moving forward and repeated his request to attack Missouri. Alarmed, Gonen told him to keep his distance from the Egyptians. "That's all right," said Sharon soothingly. "We're with you." From monitoring Sharon's radio net, Gonen grew increasingly suspicious that he was still moving forward. Gonen helicoptered to Tasa and drove forward in a jeep to find Sharon in an advanced position. "Break contact," Gonen ordered him. Sharon agreed. By the time Gonen returned to his headquarters, he learned that one of Sharon's battalions had attacked and retaken the Televisia staging area.

The initiative for this move had come from brigade commander Reshef, who had been informed that an Israeli tank crew had found shelter in one of the buildings there. Obtaining Sharon's permission, he sent forward the battalion of Shaul Shalev, who had rescued the Purkan garrison that morning. The crew was rescued but there was one Israeli fatality in the attack—Shalev himself.

Earlier in the day, a newly arrived officer had presented himself to Reshef for assignment. Lt. Col. Yoav Brom had been traveling in Europe when the war broke out and had hurried home on the first available plane. The boyish-looking officer had given up a coveted position as school principal in his kibbutz in order to return to the regular army two years before. Reshef suggested to Sharon that Brom replace the commander of the divisional reconnaissance battalion who had been killed the day before fighting for the vital ridges in Sharon's sector after the division had been sent off on its pointless run. Reshef also suggested that the battalion be attached to his brigade. Sharon, as accommodating to subordinates as he was willful towards superiors, accepted both suggestions.

Lookouts reported that the area between Forts Lakekan and Botzer on the shore of the Bitter Lake appeared to be empty. Reshef asked Brom to check it out, avoiding contact with the enemy if possible. If the area indeed was undefended, Reshef intended to seek permission to move forces into it and attack the southern flank of the Egyptian Sixteenth Division opposite him.

The reconnaissance force set out at dusk across the dunes which had been crossed two days before by the Lakekan garrison. The deep ditches of the Chinese Farm extended this far south and the vehicles had to navigate around them. It was dark when the battalion descended onto Lexicon Road. Brom sent a patrol to nearby Lakekan. After turning off their engines and hearing no sounds of life, the tankers entered and found the fort empty. Sending one company south to patrol partway down the shore of the Bitter Lake, and Brom started north with his other two companies along Lexicon. After they proceeded five miles, the sound of outgoing artillery grew loud, and Brom detected movement to his front. The battalion had been provided with the latest Patton tanks, which were fitted with night sights. Through them, Brom saw Egyptian soldiers eight hundred yards to his front digging foxholes at the junction of Lexicon and Tirtur Roads. Beyond, an Egyptian artillery battery was firing eastward. Brom summoned his deputy and one of his company commanders, Capt. Rafi Bar-Lev, nephew of General Bar-Lev. They could barely see each other in the darkness as they stood atop Brom's tank. Despite their distance from the Egyptian soldiers they talked in whispers. Brom decided to pull back a bit and notify Reshef of the situation.

The Egyptian Second Army had crossed the canal north of the Bitter Lake and the Third Army south of the lake. But the Egyptians had not deployed along the twenty-five-mile-long shore of the lake itself, too wide to be crossed except by amphibious vehicles. The Egyptian command chose to concentrate its available forces as compactly as possible along the canal itself in order to confront the Israelis with an impenetrable line. But the Second Army had negligently rested its southern flank not on the edge of the lake but on Tirtur Road to its north, which formed a convenient boundary. This left almost a mile of the Suez Canal, between Tirtur and the lake, unguarded. It was as if the army's ankles had been exposed to mosquitoes by a blanket pulled up too tight. With Brom's radio report to Reshef, the mosquitoes had started to buzz.

The news of Brom's whereabouts electrified Sharon. He realized that the reconnaissance battalion had stumbled on the "seam" between the Second and Third Armies, a gap of still uncertain dimensions but wide enough perhaps to permit his division to shoulder its way through to the canal without having to fight its way through the Egyptian bridgehead. Instead of attacking the flank of the Second Army, as Reshef envisioned, Sharon saw an opportunity to continue straight across the waterway into the Egyptian rear. This was the move, he believed, that would change the course of the war. Furthermore, the seam reached as far as Fort Matsmed, where Sharon had prepared a staging area for a crossing when he was front commander.

Sharon called Gonen. "Shmulik, we're near the canal. We can touch the water." Describing the patrol's location, Sharon said, "The canal bank's in our hand. Request permission to cross." Sharon would in later years maintain that he was only indicating a desire to cross after adequate preparations had been made, not that night. But that is not the way the transcripts read. As his superiors understood it, Sharon was proposing this very night to attack the Egyptian division north of Matsmed and then to cross the canal without any preplanning or logistical arrangements, including the preparation of bridging equipment.

"Get him out of there," shouted Elazar, when General Tal called from Southern Command to inform him of Sharon's whereabouts and intentions. "Get him out of there." The chief of staff was beside himself with anger as his clear directives were once again being flouted in Southern Command. "I tell you he is not to cross," he said when Gonen came on the line. "Not to cross. Not to cross."

Sharon was not put off when Gonen got back to him with Elazar's message. A bridge, he said, could be moved up in a few hours. "I'm already here. The moment we cross, the whole situation will change." If they had reached the canal yesterday during Adan's failed attack it would have been considered a major achievement, he said. Why not exploit it now? What if the Egyptians close the seam? Gonen remained adamant. Sharon tried unsuccessfully to reach General Tal, then called back to Southern Command but Gonen "couldn't be reached." With no other recourse, Sharon told Reshef to pull the battalion back in the morning.

At the same hour that the newspaper editors in Tel Aviv were being cast into a funk by Dayan's remarks and Dr. Ohri was sitting in the gloom of his bunker contemplating the unthinkable—little more than twenty-four hours after the debacle of October 8—the key had been found for reversing the course of the war on the southern front. But it was not yet time to turn it.

Twenty-four

GOLAN COUNTERATTACK

The Syrian divisions occupying a bulge in the heart of the Golan Monday morning were ideally placed to punch a hole through the thin Israeli cordon around them wherever they chose to concentrate their forces. But the momentum had gone out of the Syrian attack. They had failed to push for the Jordan River Saturday night when only a handful of tanks stood in their way, and they had failed to crack the hastily formed Israeli line on Sunday when the odds were still overwhelmingly in their favor. Those odds would narrow today when Moussa Peled's division joined the battle.

A quiet night on Sunday had given the Israeli reserve units their first opportunity to organize. Tanks which had been thrown randomly into the battle in desperate bids to plug holes rejoined their organic units, casualties were replaced, and damaged tanks repaired.

Moussa Peled's division began climbing the heights before first light. It consisted of a single tank brigade commanded by Col. Yossi Peled (no relation), a reconnaissance battalion, and a brigade of infantry in half-tracks. Northern Command doubled the division's tank strength by attaching to it the brigades of Ben-Porat and Hadar already on the southern heights—each a mixture of Centurions and old Shermans.

On Sunday, while the division was making its way northward from the center of the country, Yossi Peled had driven ahead in a jeep to view the fighting zone. He was afraid the war would be over before he could get to it.

This feeling abated when he reached Kibbutz Ein Gev on the eastern shore of Lake Kinneret and saw antitank guns being set up on its perimeter. When his jeep turned up the Gamla Ascent, he was fired on from the heights by Syrian tanks at the edge of the escarpment. A survivor of the Holocaust as a boy in Belgium, the colonel found himself thinking existential thoughts he had believed long behind him.

On Monday morning, when his brigade reached El Al, he was briefed by Colonel Ben-Porat, whose tanks had resumed fighting at first light. Despite the Shermans' age and their penetrability, their upgraded guns were getting the better of the Soviet-made tanks opposite. Colonel Peled's brigade passed through Ben-Porat's formation and began driving the Syrians northward.

The Israelis trapped in the bunker atop Tel Saki deduced from the sound of Syrian tanks pulling back that a counterattack had begun. At noon, an artillery barrage hit the *tel* and the men heard the voices of two Syrian soldiers who had taken shelter in the outer room. A moment later a grenade exploded in the bunker. Virtually everybody was peppered with shrapnel again but no one made a sound. The Syrians chose not to enter. An hour later the scene was repeated by other Syrian soldiers sheltering from another barrage. This time, two grenades were thrown into the room, but again the Syrians did not enter.

Shortly afterwards, the men heard footsteps, then a cry in Hebrew: "Is anyone alive?" At the response from the bunker, two officers entered. To one of the tank crewmen, the reservists seemed old enough to be his father. He could see tears in their eyes at the sight that greeted them. All but five of the thirty men in the bunker were still alive, all of them wounded.

At Strongpoint 116, Lieutenant Gur led soldiers out of the fort in the morning to collect Kalashnikov rifles and ammunition from dead Syrians. The approaches were strewn with tanks, APCs, and some seventy bodies—testimony to two days of battle by the tiny garrison. Gur had no idea of what was happening elsewhere on the Golan. The young officer, who had resumed command despite his wound, was determined to gather enough ammunition to hold out for as long as it took.

There was no movement in their vicinity until close to noon, when Syrians, recognizable by their overalls as tank crewmen, were seen fleeing eastward on foot. It was the first indication of an Israeli counterattack. In late afternoon a jeep turned down the track towards the fort. As the men readied their weapons, someone shouted, "It's ours." Two reconnaissance personnel from Moussa Peled's division stepped out of the vehicle to tell Gur and his men that half-tracks would arrive in half an hour to evacuate them.

———

The conquest of Tel Juhadar near Strongpoint 116 provided the Israelis with a view of the landscape north towards Tel Faris, from where Erez's battalion had pulled back the night before. Hunkered down in the folds of ground between the two volcanic cones were two battalions of Syrian infantry armed with Saggers and RPGs. The Golan battles had thus far been largely tank versus tank, but the Syrians had now deployed large numbers of tank-killing infantry to guard their endangered southern flank.

General Peled ordered artillery to lay down a rolling barrage just ahead of the tanks. This was the effective response to enemy tank hunters that had been missing in Sinai. Artillery was far more effective on the rock-strewn Golan, where the shells were shattered into lethal splinters, than in the Sinai, where shellfire was muffled by the sand.

The Syrians had established dense antitank positions—concentrations of antitank guns and Saggers—on main axes. Ben-Porat's brigade succeeded in overcoming the first one encountered. While one battalion provided covering fire, another swept in from the flank and destroyed twenty-four antitank guns as well as numerous Sagger teams. However, an attack on another position was repulsed.

Maj. David Caspi, a deputy battalion commander, was shepherding a convoy of trucks to a forward logistics depot when a shell exploded alongside his half-track. Two Syrian tanks and three armored personnel carriers broke into the open to his right front at six hundred yards. Caspi, an elementary school principal in civilian life, ordered the men on the trucks to dismount. His half-track and the one behind him turned towards the Syrians, now two hundred yards distant, and opened fire with their heavy machine guns. Caspi told the gunners to fire long bursts at the tank turrets. The effect was immediate. Machine-gun fire could not harm the tanks, but the heavy hammering of the .50 caliber bullets unnerved the tank commanders, whose view was limited by the closed hatches. The armored vehicles stopped and the crews bolted.

The advance of Peled's division from the south did not ease pressure on Ori Orr's brigade in the central Golan. The First Syrian Armored Division had resumed its drive on Nafakh at dawn along the Sindiana axis. Orr's brigade, which began the day with sixty tanks, little more than half its full strength, blocked the advance in a brutal slugging match.

Erosion of personnel was merciless. Two more of Orr's company commanders—appointed only the day before to replace fatalities—were killed. The brigade was under heavy artillery and Katyusha attack, the Katyushas recognizable by their distinctive howl. During one barrage, everyone in Orr's command half-track ducked for cover as shrapnel rattled off the vehicle's sides. When they rose, the communications officer remained crouched on his seat. "You can get up now," said Orr, who had been sitting alongside him. "It's over." When the officer did not rise, Orr touched his neck and his hand came away with blood. The wounded officer was evacuated.

The Syrians pushed hardest on Orr's right flank, anchored on a quarry near Nafakh. The battalion commander there, a replacement appointed the night before, had questioned his own fitness for the job, but Orr said there was no one else. At one point, the officer said his men could not hold on any longer. "I've got to pull back."

"Negative," replied Orr. "The Syrians don't know it's tough for you. They'll break soon." But the Syrians overwhelmed the battalion, killing the commander, and broke through. Major Danon, who had taken command of the battalion in the center of the line, found himself under fire from the rear as the Syrians swept around his right flank. He shifted his tanks to meet the new threat. Orr ordered Lieutenant Colonel Harel, on the left flank, to rush to Nafakh with his twelve remaining tanks. Wounded the day before, Harel had returned to action. He stopped the Syrians once again at the edge of Nafakh.

Receiving six tanks as reinforcement, Orr counterattacked and reached Sindiana, a mile southeast of the quarry. Division commander Eitan, still operating from a field north of Nafakh, ordered Orr to continue south and take the abandoned village of Ramtania, which overlooked Hushniya, the main Syrian hub. Danon, in the lead, reached the village with one other tank and opened fire on several dozen Syrian tanks in Hushniya below, hitting six. The Syrians returned fire, setting both Israeli tanks aflame. Danon carried his seriously wounded loader on his back through the village until he was picked up by another tank. Orr pulled his tanks back to Sindiana to form a line protecting Nafakh.

Sarig's brigade, on the western edge of the Syrian bulge, did not push far forward in order not to get between Peled's division advancing northward and Orr's brigade driving south. But Sarig advanced a mile to the Tapline in heavy fighting.

By evening, the Syrian enclave had shrunk but the Syrian divisions remained aggressive despite their heavy losses. It was clear to both sides that the next day, Tuesday, October 9, would be decisive.

In Safed Hospital, Barukh Askarov, a high school senior from Tel Aviv, had found his brother Shmuel lying in bed Sunday with his forehead and throat bandaged. Shmuel's vocal cords had been damaged by the Syrian shell which propelled him from his tank at Strongpoint 111 and he could only whisper. In the next bed lay an officer whose face and blond hair were blackened by burns and soot. He seemed to be sleeping but kept tossing and muttering, "What a mess, what a mess." Shmuel identified him to his brother as Lt. Zvika Greengold, with whom he had served in the past.

When Greengold opened his eyes he was astonished to see his girlfriend sitting by the bedside. She was from a kibbutz in the Jordan Valley and he was certain that the Syrians had by now descended into the valley. "How did you get here?" he asked.

During the day, Major Askarov received reports from visitors of an unending series of disasters. The brigade had in effect been wiped out. Colonel Ben-Shoham was dead. So were his deputy and the brigade operations officer. The remnants of Erez's battalion—Askarov's unit—were cut off behind enemy lines with almost no ammunition. Soldiers had begun to retreat on their own. Divisional headquarters at Nafakh had been captured by the Syrians. This last was incorrect—the Syrians had reached Nafakh but not captured it.

Askarov had been told Saturday that he would have to remain hospitalized for two weeks. Early Monday morning, together with Yos Eldar, the wounded battalion commander from the Seventh Brigade, he slipped out and headed for the Golan in Eldar's jeep.

Askarov got off at a tank base at the foot of the Golan. With his brigade no longer functioning, he had decided to organize a new tank force and lead it into battle. Rounding up four trucks, he assembled everyone he found at the base. There were 150 men, including crewmen from disabled tanks. Speaking as loudly as his vocal cords permitted, Askarov said he was going back up the heights and wanted to take them with him. Every man was needed and he had trucks outside to transport them.

It seemed for a moment that they would all join him, but then an officer spoke up. "I'm a major and I ran away. You can put me in prison but I'm not going back to that hell." In the circumstances, that sounded to the others more like the voice of reason than Askarov's plea for heroics. He drove off to the Golan alone.

At Camp Jordan, he found the tanks that had returned from Tel Faris. Most of them were damaged. Oded Erez was there too. The battalion commander was emotionally drained after losing two-thirds of his tanks trying to hold off two Syrian divisions and after the excruciating escape through the

Syrian lines. The men were visibly dispirited, not just from the ordeal of the battle itself but from a sense that they had been exposed to impossible odds by the powers that be and abandoned to their fate.

Askarov called them together. The situation was desperate, he said, and the tanks must be prepared for battle by morning. Despite his raspy whisper, his purposefulness came through. The response this time was enthusiastic. Mechanics were soon swarming over the damaged tanks, cannibalizing some in order to repair others. Work went on intensively through the night. Askarov's call for volunteers to replace dead and injured crewmen drew a ready response.

At one point, a colonel from Northern Command arrived. Shocked at Askarov's appearance, he ordered him to return to the hospital. "I'm commanding the brigade now," replied the young major, "and I'm giving orders here." The colonel relented.

Shortly before dawn, someone tapped Askarov on the shoulder. It was Lt. Col. Yossi Ben-Hanan, who had been commander of the battalion until a month before. He had left for a course at the U.S. armored school at Fort Leavenworth but had taken leave first to get married. On Yom Kippur, Ben-Hanan was in Nepal on his honeymoon when he learned from the BBC of the outbreak of war. He and his bride caught a plane to Delhi in the morning and made a connecting flight to Greece. From Athens, Ben-Hanan telephoned his parents and arranged to have his uniform and personal equipment, including binoculars and pistol, waiting for him at Ben-Gurion Airport. After stopping at Northern Command headquarters for a briefing from Hofi, he continued on to the Golan. Askarov readily handed over command of the force—eleven tanks and crews—to Ben-Hanan. Their old battalion was emerging from the ashes.

At Strongpoint 107 alongside the Damascus road, Lieutenant Elimelekh took shelter with his radioman when Syrian artillery opened up once again. As the barrage continued without letup, the twenty-year-old officer decided to see how his men were faring in the bunker. Running thirty yards from his observation post to the bunker entrance was a terrifying experience. The ground heaved and shrapnel whistled all about. Pausing in the bunker's sheltered entranceway, his shirt soaked with sweat, Elimelekh drank a canteenful of water and smoked a cigarette. Only then did he enter with a casual "How you doing?" He found that his first sergeant had organized a strict regimen in order to keep discipline intact. One-third of the men were preparing for inspection—cleaning weapons, polishing boots, shaving. Another third were on alert status, prepared to rush to their positions if the alarm was sounded. The remainder were sleeping.

When the barrage lifted, Elimelekh deployed the men in a 360-degree defense. Syrian commandos and armored vehicles had penetrated in large numbers between the strongpoints, and an attack could come from any direction. On Sunday night, a Syrian half-track had darted from the rear and skirted the strongpoint when it ran over a mine which killed all aboard. On Monday, a Syrian tank heading back on the same path hit a mine 150 yards away. The explosion threw the tank commander from the turret and killed the others aboard. Instead of fleeing, the survivor ran towards the strongpoint waving a white undershirt. He passed through a minefield but the Syrian artillery fire had detonated the mines and he reached the strong-point unhurt. The garrison's astonishment at his safe passage turned to amazement when he shouted in Arabic, "Ana Shmuel [I am Shmuel]." The Israelis understood him to be indicating that he was a Jew from Damascus who had been drafted into the Syrian army. He was taken prisoner and eventually sent to the rear, but the garrison never learned whether he was who they thought he was.

Monday night, the commander of the tank platoon that had been guarding 107, Lieutenant Yakhin, informed Elimelekh that he had been ordered to pull back. In three days, Yakhin's platoon and other tanks from Major Rak's company had knocked out at least forty Syrian tanks on the approaches to the strongpoint. Elimelekh called battalion to protest at being left without tank support. Do the best you can, he was told. I don't have air support or artillery either, said Elimelekh. "The nation is behind you," battalion assured him. It was a phrase Elimelekh would grow accustomed to hearing.

The next morning, a single Syrian tank was stopped by mechanical problems four hundred yards from the strongpoint, just out of bazooka range. The tank commander took advantage of the situation to methodically shell the firing positions within the strongpoint, destroying all of its four mounted machine guns. When the tank finally made off, the garrison was left with only Uzis and two rifles. Elimelekh sent men out to the destroyed Syrian half-track. It was filled with dead soldiers but also an abundance of weaponry. The men brought back machine guns, Kalashnikov rifles, and RPGs.

For the Seventh Brigade, Monday was relatively quiet. Kahalani's battalion was ordered forward in the morning to ensure that manned Syrian tanks were not lurking among the knocked-out tanks littering the landscape. They found that many tanks had been abandoned while still intact.

Ben-Gal ordered Yos Eldar to take command of the ramps in the center of the line, shifting Kahalani to the southern flank. A few officers who had served in Kahalani's battalion in the past and had no current combat assignment joined him after making their way to the Golan on their own. He assigned them to tanks whose commanders had been hit. As Monday night fell, Kahalani heard Eldar on the radio calling for flares. Something was stirring out there. When will it end? Kahalani asked himself. Where were the Syrians drawing their strength from?

Before dawn, Tuesday, Moussa Peled briefed his brigade commanders. They would push northeast this day, cutting the main Syrian routes into the southern Golan. Strong resistance could be expected. Peled deployed his division on a narrow front to meet the aroused Syrians with a concentration of force. At first light they moved out. Yossi Peled's brigade, in the lead, proceeded cautiously, braced for the Syrian counterblow. In midmorning, clouds of dust signaled the approach of two tank columns, one from across the cease-fire line to the east and one from Hushniya to the west. The Syrians, recognizing the threat to their lifeline, were responding in force. For three hours, the two sides battled at close range. When the fight was over, fifty-five Syrian tanks lay inert on the battlefield and the remainder pulled back.

In late morning, Yossi Peled was notified that eight Phantoms were approaching his sector with bombs to spare. This was the flight which had aborted the mission to Damascus because of heavy cloud cover. The air force offered to have them deposit their bomb load wherever desired. Colonel Peled's satisfaction turned to horror when he saw the first bombs falling towards his own brigade. No damage was done and the planes, duly corrected, dropped the rest of their bombs on Tel Kudne, the heart of the Syrian defenses across the Purple Line.

Ben-Porat's Shermans attacked Hushniya frontally and were repelled. Shifting to the left flank, they swept through the large base as dusk descended, knocking out armored vehicles and supply trucks. The Syrians re-formed, and when the Israeli tanks tried to make a return sweep they were stopped.

Only seventy tanks were still operational when Moussa Peled's division compiled its status report Tuesday night. Maintenance crews working through the night would permit the division to begin the next day with two hundred. On both fronts, the work of the maintenance teams was critical. The fact that the Israeli side was now advancing meant that tanks that had malfunctions or were damaged in battle could be reached by repair crews. Each night, the armored corps would go to bed a cripple, and each morning it would be born anew, shrunken only by a relatively small number of tanks beyond repair.

In the central sector Tuesday morning, Ori Orr braced for a renewed attack on Nafakh by deploying two battalions on rear slopes astride the anticipated Syrian route. In a make-or-break effort, the Syrians added elements of a third armored brigade to the two brigades that had been fighting in this sector for the past two days. The force included bridging tanks, indicating expectations of crossing the Jordan River.

The sun was in the Israelis' eyes, diminishing the effect of the ambush when it was sprung. But the Syrian attack was driven back in fierce fighting. The awkwardness of the first day when tank crews were randomly thrown together had been smoothed by three days of intensive fighting. Basic tank skills had been polished; the crews had bonded and so had the brigade. Orr drew comfort about the country's prospects from the performance of this collection of reservists who only a few days before were virtual strangers to each other. The yeshiva students, he was pleased to hear, had performed very well in combat.

On Sunday, Orr had seen a lieutenant standing in the middle of the battlefield in a state of shock, apparently the sole survivor of a tank. Instead of having him sent to the rear, Orr took him into his half-track. For the first day, the lieutenant sat in a corner saying nothing and staring blankly as the war raged around him. The second day, he began to display an interest in his surroundings and helped prepare food for the brigade staff. On the third day, he asked to be given command of a tank. Orr sent him back into battle.

After beating off the Syrian attack Tuesday morning, the brigade pushed south again towards Ramtania. Major Danon took the lead. The boulder-strewn slopes made for slow going. In a battle sometimes fought at ranges of fifty yards, Danon conquered the village. His orders were to wait for another battalion to join up with him before attacking an adjacent *tel*, where defenses were strongest. But dusk was descending and Orr ordered him not to wait. Danon's tanks were in secure firing positions and the tank commanders were reluctant to emerge once again in the face of heavy Sagger and tank fire. Danon, however, led the way out, and in a final rush, his tanks took the *tel*, the last defenders fleeing down the slopes towards Hushniya.

In the north, the tanks of the Seventh Brigade had been engaged in their own war for three days now, detached from what was happening elsewhere on the Golan. Theirs was a classic defensive battle, the kind that IDF doctrine virtually ignored in favor of offense. The brigade had already filled the

Kuneitra Gap with masses of destroyed Syrian armor. In doing so, it had lost more than half its tanks, but the critical juncture was only now at hand.

The Syrian high command, in a final effort, had assembled the largest force yet mustered in this sector. In addition to elements of the Seventh and Ninth Divisions that had been engaged there since the start of the war, a fresh brigade from the Third Armored Division, guarding the road to Damascus, was sent forward. So were seventy tanks from the Presidential Guard commanded by Rifat Assad, President Assad's brother. Syrian tanks in this sector now numbered 160, four times Ben-Gal's strength. From the underground bunker of the Syrian General Staff, President Assad followed the climactic battle and personally exhorted the division commanders by radio.

Ben-Gal's men were physically exhausted and emotionally numb on this fourth day of battle. A brigade staff officer fell asleep as Ben-Gal was talking to him. Here and there tanks were beginning to pull back without authorization. Seeing two tanks heading towards the rear, Ben-Gal asked their commanders on the radio where they were going. To refuel and rearm, they said. Ben-Gal ordered them back to the line. The contending armies had reached the endgame. One final effort, one minute more of endurance, could make the difference.

The day began with the most massive Syrian barrage the brigade had yet experienced. It was so fierce that Ben-Gal ordered the tanks on the ramparts, the focus of the Syrian shelling, to pull back a few hundred yards.

Lieutenant Elimelekh at Strongpoint 107 was the first to see the enemy tanks. They came through a breach in an earth barrier two miles to the east—two long columns heading for the Kuneitra Gap to his left rear. The tanks passed within three hundred yards of the outpost, their hatches closed. Elimelekh ordered the bazookist on the side of the outpost to fire at them. The soldier, Sgt. Yossi Tsadok, had knocked out a Syrian tank two days before. He now hit five more. Ignoring the Israeli position, the other tanks thundered west towards the Hermonit ridge, a mile away.

Ben-Gal called his battalion commander on the southern flank.

"Kahalani, this is Yanosh."

"This is Kahalani. Good morning." It was still quiet at his end of the line.

"Move out immediately and position yourself in my area. You will be my reserve."

"On my way."

Ben-Gal had taken up position near Kibbutz El-Rom on a hill two miles behind the tank ramps. When Kahalani deployed alongside him, Ben-Gal told him he would serve as a second line. The battalion commander was surprised. Was Ben-Gal expecting the front line to break? Kahalani could see heavy artillery fire in the area of the ramps. Eldar's commanders were reporting that their ammunition was running out. There could be no more than a dozen or so tanks left intact there.

Four Syrian helicopters passed directly overhead. Four others followed. One was shot down by ground fire, but the others landed near Nafakh, disgorging commandos. Ben-Gal could not spare tanks to deal with them because his front was at this very moment cracking.

Lead elements of the Syrian tank force were approaching the empty ramps. Unable to make contact with the tanks that had pulled back from the ramps, Ben-Gal ordered battalion commander Rattes on the northern flank to move south to fill the gap.

After four days of hands-on direction, Ben-Gal's control was unraveling as officers were hit and orders were not passed on. There appeared to be no alternative but to have the tanks fall back. Even if they managed to outrace the Syrians to the new line, however, they would not be able to hold it for more than half an hour, he estimated.

Ben-Gal decided on a last desperate bid to shore up the collapsing front.

"Kahalani, this is Yanosh. Move out. Fast. Over."

The battalion commander had been waiting impatiently for the order. Uncertain whether the front was still where he had left it the day before, he ordered his men to be prepared to fire without warning. The ramp came into view straight ahead. It was empty except for the hulks of knocked-out tanks, Israeli and Syrian. The remaining Israeli tanks were now scattered five hundred yards to the rear.

Ignoring them for the moment, Kahalani cut across a plowed field towards a wadi to the left. It was through this gully, with its navigable incline, that Syrian tanks had penetrated onto the Israeli high ground from the valley on Sunday. Kahalani wanted to make sure it was empty before reoccupying the ramp. A fifteen-foot-high pile of dark basalt stones, cleared by kibbutz farmers, stretched across much of the field. As Kahalani's tank turned the corner of the stone pile, he came upon three Syrian tanks. Two were static, the third was moving beyond them.

"Stop," he shouted.

His driver braked so sharply that everyone was thrown forward. Kahalani swung the gun at the nearest tank, just twenty yards away.

"Fire," Kahalani ordered.

"What range?" asked Kilion, the gunner. They were so close he did not realize the dark object filling his scope was a Syrian tank.

"It doesn't matter. Just fire."

Kilion fired, holing the tank. Kahalani shifted the gun towards the second standing tank. "Do you see it?" he asked.

"Yes," said the gunner.

"Then fire. Quickly."

A hole appeared in the Syrian tank's turret.

Kahalani looked for the third tank. It had stopped and was pointing its gun straight at him. As he looked down the barrel, black and enormous, "T-62" registered in his mind. He had never encountered one before. "Fire, fire," he called.

"Misfire," shouted Kilion.

The casing of the previous shell was stuck in the breech. As the loader lunged at the shell to extricate it, Kahalani lowered his head into the tank and placed his hands on the lip of the turret in order to extricate himself if possible when the tank was hit. As company commander in the Six Day War, Kahalani had been gravely burned when his tank was hit. He had barely been able to pull himself out of the turret and had spent a year in the hospital.

When the explosion came, it was the comforting one of an outgoing shell. Raising his head, he saw the T-62 aflame. A fourth Syrian tank was now racing towards them. Kahalani moved the gun slightly to the right and Kilion fired. The tank was hit but continued to charge like an enraged bull. Before Kilion could get off a second round, another Israeli tank which had moved forward delivered the coup de grâce. The vaunted T-62 was proving to be as vulnerable as the T-55s.

Kahalani reported the encounter to Ben-Gal, who told him to take command of the sector, including the tanks of Rattes's battalion, which were on their way. Yos Eldar, who was operating from a personnel carrier rather than a tank, had had to pull back because the APC was too vulnerable to the intense artillery fire.

It was critical to regain the ramp if the Syrians were to be stopped. As Kahalani weighed the situation, another Syrian tank came up out of the wadi. He turned the turret and Kilion punched a hole in it. A few seconds later still another T-62 emerged and Kilion stopped it too. Kahalani looked around for a tank he could position at the head of the wadi. Seeing none, he ordered his driver forward to a knoll overlooking the length of the wadi. Within minutes, Kilion had notched up five more kills. This cleared the wadi, but from his position Kahalani could see into the valley beyond. Heading towards the Israeli line was a mass of tanks.

The Israeli tanks behind the ramp were scattered like lost sheep, their commanders unaware of the approaching danger. If they were to survive, it was essential to pull them together and get them up the ramp before the Syrians reached it. Only from there could the vast disparity in numbers be offset by superior firing position. When Kahalani called them on his radio he got little response. The tanks were from several units and operating on different frequencies. At his request, the brigade communications officer cut into every company's radio net to order the tank commanders to switch to Kahalani's frequency. When his calls continued to draw little response, Kahalani understood that most of the tank commanders preferred not to hear him. This was the fourth straight day of intensive battle. They had been under constant artillery bombardment and the Syrian air force had had several goes at them. Half their comrades were dead or wounded, they had hardly slept since the battle started, and they could no longer bring themselves to face the curtain of fire on the ramp. They had reached their breaking point.

Four miles away, Lieutenant Colonel Nafshi was monitoring a battle between Major Rak's company and a Syrian tank force trying to cross the cease-fire line south of Kuneitra when Ben-Gal asked if he could see what was happening in the Kuneitra Gap. Nafshi could not. He gathered five other tanks, including Yakhin's platoon, and headed towards the Hermonit. On the radio, he could hear Ben-Gal giving Kahalani command of the area and imploring him to hang on. On the way, he turned up a slope for a look at what was happening in the valley beyond. As his six tanks started up abreast, Nafshi saw faint smoke rising above the ridgeline. He recognized it as exhaust smoke from tanks climbing from the other side. They could only be Syrian and they were plainly closer to the summit than he. He stopped and waited for them to come over the top. In the ensuing shoot-out, half a dozen Syrian tanks were knocked out. Three Israeli tanks were hit and two of their commanders killed. Nafshi's was the third tank hit but he was unhurt. He shifted to another tank and moved up to the summit. The valley below was aswarm with tanks heading towards the Hermonit, intent on breaking through the battered center of the Seventh Brigade line.

In the tank with Kahalani, Lieutenant Peled had since the start of the war felt fear knotted in his stomach. The operations officer had seen fear in Kahalani's face as well and knew that everyone was gripped by it. But until now the battalion had operated like a well-tuned racing car with fear along only as a silent passenger. Now, as he monitored the nonresponse to Kahalani's calls and noted that tank commanders were keeping their hatches closed, it seemed that the passenger had moved into the driver's seat. Like many others, Peled had reconciled himself to the certainty that he would not survive this day intact. He permitted himself only to hope that he would come out of it with no more than injury to an arm or leg.

A Syrian tank topped the ramp, rising high to crest the front edge and then dropping down onto the firing position. As its gun swiveled in search of prey, Kilion set the tank aflame. When another tank from the Syrian spearhead force came over the top, it was knocked out by one of the Israeli tanks to the rear of the ramp.

Hope flared when Rattes arrived with his seven remaining tanks. The battalion commander's voice was weary. Kahalani had once served under him as a crewman and he sought to cushion the fact that Rattes had now been placed under his command by framing his directives as requests rather than orders. The sound of explosions was constant. Syrian and Israeli crews who had escaped from damaged tanks could be seen scrambling over the terrain, ignoring each other as they tried to make it back to their respective lines. Suddenly Rattes's tanks bolted for the rear. It was several minutes before Kahalani learned that Rattes had been killed by a direct hit. His deputy was also killed. The unit had gone through its own hellish days and the now leaderless tank commanders had panicked.

A nightmarish dilemma gripped Kahalani. Only he could see the approaching danger in the valley and only he could muster the crews to regain the ramp. Nothing but the personal example of the senior commander on the spot would get the paralyzed tank commanders, most of them nineteen- and twenty-year-old conscripts, to move. But he could neither abandon the wadi, through which Syrian tanks could debouch at any moment, nor make radio contact with most of the tanks. Ten of the spearhead Syrian tanks had already topped the ramparts and been hit. In a little while, twenty or thirty would come over and there would be no stopping them. Kahalani weighed the possibility of ordering the men to fall back on the second line, but he feared they would be swarmed over before they made it.

The same thought was occurring to Ben-Gal. He took the radio microphone in hand to issue the pullback order but then called instead to General Eitan to report his intentions. Eitan was watching the battle from a ridge just south of the Hermonit. He could see the small number of Israeli tanks sheltering behind the ridge and the mass of Syrian tanks surging across the valley towards them. Behind the Syrian tanks a line of APCs and supply vehicles stretched two miles east to the Syrian village of Ufana.

"Hang on five minutes more," said Eitan. "Reinforcements will be moving up to you." They both knew that the minutes Eitan asked for were not measured by the clock but by calculations of life and death, personal and communal.

The division commander told Ben-Gal that a new unit was being put together under Lieutenant Colonel Ben-Hanan. The latter's father, a physical education instructor, delivered early morning wakeup exercises on the radio, hence the patchwork unit's code name—Morning Exercise. Ben-Hanan's force was almost ready, said Eitan.

Calling Capt. Emi Palant, the senior officer behind the ramps, Kahalani told him to use a signal flag to get the tank commanders' attention and to lead them up the ramp. The company commander waved his flag but got no response. Seizing his machine gun, he fired at the side of the nearest tank. When the startled commander looked out, Palant passed on the message. He then ran from tank to tank, rapping on turrets to get the commanders' attention. Remounting his own tank, he started forward. When no tank followed, he returned to his starting point.

On the radio net, Kahalani heard a new voice addressing him, a tank commander from Rattes's unit introducing himself as "sergeant, Platoon Four." It was a cool voice and Kahalani ordered the sergeant to come alongside. A solution to his dilemma seemed at hand. "Sergeant, Platoon Four, take my position and guard the wadi opening. Destroy any Syrian tank that tries to come up."

"This is sergeant, Platoon Four. All right, but I don't have any shells left."

Kahalani tried to review his options but there didn't seem to be any. On the radio net he heard Major Zamir, flanking his position to the south, reporting a massive Syrian attack. Zamir asked permission to shift the few tanks remaining to Tiger Company to a better position slightly south. "Negative," said Ben-Gal, aware of the gap this would open because of the unmanned ramp. "Stay where you are. Kahalani, report."

"This is Kahalani. Not all the tanks here have made contact with me. I'm not managing to control them and they're constantly drifting to the rear." In his reports to Ben-Gal since the war started, he had tried to avoid sounding alarmist in order not to add to the brigade commander's burden. Even this report was phrased moderately, but the facts were stark. Ben-Gal said he would try to get more tanks up to him.

"Sergeant, Platoon Four," said Kahalani into his mouthpiece. He had made a decision. "I know your situation. Stay here in my place and don't let anyone up from the wadi. Clear?"

"This is sergeant, Platoon Four. I remind you that—"

"I know," he said. "Stand high in the position so that they see you. If they see you well, they won't enter."

Starting towards the tanks behind the rampart, Kahalani addressed their commanders. "This is the battalion commander. Whoever hears me, raise your flag." There were ten tanks that he could see. Most of their commanders raised flags. "We must regain the ramp. Otherwise—" His remarks were interrupted by two planes diving on the cluster of tanks and dropping bombs. The explosions were powerful but none of the tanks were hit. As the second plane pulled up, Kahalani saw a Star of David on its tail.

Despair threatened to overwhelm him. On the right flank, Zamir reported that he had only three tanks left and almost no ammunition. "Help is on the way," said Ben-Gal. "Just fifteen minutes."

"I don't know if I can hold on fifteen minutes," said Zamir.

Kahalani reached the tanks behind the ramps. "This is the battalion commander," he began again. "A large enemy force is on the other side of the ramp. We are going to move forward to regain the ramp. Move."

His tank started forward and a few others began moving, but with agonizing slowness. Two Syrian tanks came over the top of the ramp. Kilion fired along with other tanks, setting the Syrians aflame. The Centurions that had moved forward behind Kahalani now pulled back to the more sheltered position from which they had started. Seeing how his own tank was exposed to any Syrian tank coming over the ramp, Kahalani now understood better the reluctance of the tank commanders to cross the open space.

Ben-Gal came on the radio to inform him that he was sending him a number of tanks under the command of Eli Geva. "Morning Exercise" was on its way to relieve Tiger Company on the southern flank. Looking behind him, Kahalani could see the dust cloud of Geva's tanks in the distance. For the first time since the battle began this morning, points of light were beginning to appear.

"This is the battalion commander." Addressing his men, Kahalani realized that straightforward commands would no longer work. "Look at the courage of the enemy mounting the position in front of us. I don't know what's happening to us. They are only the Arab enemy we have always known. We are stronger than them. Start moving forward and form a line with me. I am waving my flag. Move." He had spoken in an even tone but shouted the last word.

A platoon commander two hundred yards to the rear had been sitting in his buttoned-up tank literally shivering from fear. The rest of his crew were in the same condition, their nerves shattered. He had not fled to the rear, the lieutenant told himself repeatedly, he had not fled. But he was unable to force himself to move forward or to stop shaking. To his front he could identify the battalion commander's tank by the number painted on its turret. He had heard Kahalani's calls on the radio but had not responded. This time the battalion commander's words stung. Was he suggesting they were cowards?

"Move," the lieutenant said to his driver. The other tanks had already started forward.

"Don't stop," Kahalani called as he watched the tanks form into line. "Keep moving. Keep moving."

A Syrian tank came over the ramp and Kahalani swiveled his turret, but the tank next to him fired first. Kahalani was exhilarated as he glanced at the formation.

"You're moving fine," he called. "Don't stop. Be prepared to fire."

The hatches were open now but the tank commanders kept low in their turrets, their eyes just above the edges. Everyone was fearful of what awaited them. As they climbed abreast they had to make their way between burning Syrian and Israeli tanks. Not until they pushed up the final yards into the firing positions could the commanders see the valley.

The Kuneitra Gap was dark with armor. In among the mass of tanks, personnel carriers, and trucks knocked out during the previous fighting, scores of tanks were moving doggedly forward. The furthest were a thousand yards distant, the closest only fifty.

The Centurions opened fire. Each tank commander now fought his own battle, unleashing his pent-up fury and fear on the approaching enemy.

"Aim only at moving tanks," called Kahalani. He was afraid they would waste scarce ammunition shooting at tanks which had already been knocked out. Syrian crews could be seen jumping from damaged tanks and running to the rear. Geva's Centurions now reached the ramp and joined in the shoot. For the first time, the Syrian tanks seemed to waver and search for a more protected approach, but they kept coming. Finally, there were no more targets for the Israeli gunners.

A heavy Syrian artillery barrage descended on the ramps and the tank commanders pulled back into the turrets. When the shelling subsided, Kahalani put his head back out. Nothing was moving to his front except flames.

The Syrian attack on Ben-Gal's right flank was likewise heading towards its climax. Major Zamir, who had ambushed the Forty-third Brigade the first night of the war, was down to two tanks and again requested permission to withdraw. But Ben-Gal ordered him to stay. Help was on the way, he said. Just hang on a few minutes more.

But Zamir, his ammunition exhausted, could wait no longer. The force led by Ben-Hanan arrived at precisely the moment that Zamir was pulling back. Ben-Hanan waved a nonchalant "shalom" to Zamir as they passed each other. Topping a small rise just ahead, Ben-Hanan saw a T-55 heading towards him just fifty yards away.

"Stop," he called to his crew. "Fire." His war had begun.

Askarov took up position alongside Ben-Hanan as the rest of the unit formed a battle line. Shell splinters cut Ben-Hanan's face and broke his eyeglasses. He passed command to Askarov and retired briefly to be treated by a medic. Askarov set ablaze a tank just forty yards from him but he himself was struck in the head by a bullet and seriously wounded. Once again, he was carried to the rear.

As Eitan watched the battle from the adjacent ridge, his intelligence officer, Dennie Agmon, suddenly said, "The Syrian General Staff has decided to retreat." Eitan looked at him askance. Agmon had not been listening to any radio net and had no visible source for that far-reaching pronouncement. "Look there," said Agmon, pointing with his binoculars. Vehicles which had been in the column streaming past Ufana had stopped and were turning around. This was not a panicky retreat from the battlefield but an orderly pullback, beginning with vehicles at the rear, plainly a command decision. After a while, Strongpoint 107 reported Syrian tank crewmen in gray coveralls running towards the rear from the Kuneitra Gap. Finally, the last tanks still intact on the battlefield turned as well.

Ben-Gal came forward to watch from a ridgetop as the Syrian wave ebbed. In the valley lay 260 Syrian tanks as well as numerous armored personnel carriers, trucks, and other vehicles which his brigade, and Nafshi's tanks, had stopped during the past four days. Many of the tanks were still intact but had been abandoned by their crews.

In the afternoon, Ben-Gal's tanks pulled back a few at a time for ammunition and fuel. Kahalani drove to the brigade command post to talk with Ben-Gal, who had not slept for four days except for brief catnaps. In an upbeat tone that sounded forced, the brigade commander said, "We've been ordered to counterattack into Syria." Lieutenant Peled, the operations officer accompanying Kahalani, was horrified. After having survived the nightmare of the past four days, how could they be asked to undertake a counterattack? Were there no other units available?

Eitan wanted Ben-Gal to attack the next day, Wednesday, in order not to give the Syrians respite. But Ben-Gal asked for a day to permit the exhausted men to rest and to fill the enormous gaps in his ranks. "Phase One is over for us," he told Kahalani. "Phase Two is about to start."

Syrian commandos staged a successful ambush this day of a reconnaissance company at Bukata in the northernmost part of the Golan. Five Israeli APCs were hit by RPGs and twenty-four men killed. The commando force which had overflown Ben-Gal fared less well. Elements of Israel's elite commando force, the General Staff Reconnaissance Unit, had been impatiently waiting at Nafakh for a role in the fighting. In a swift charge, its men killed forty of the Syrians, at a cost of two dead. Other Syrian commandos who landed nearby were overcome by Golani troops.

Close to noon, Ben-Gal informed Nafshi that Strongpoint 107 was not responding to radio messages and had apparently fallen. Nafshi headed there through Kuneitra, accompanied by two other tanks. As he passed the town's cinema, the most prominent structure in Kuneitra, RPGs hit his tank and the one behind. The commander of the second tank was killed but Nafshi again escaped unhurt except for temporary deafness. Picking up a contingent of Golani infantrymen in two half-tracks, he drove through the part of town closest to the Syrian lines in the belief that the Syrian troops who had penetrated the town would not be expecting an Israeli approach from that direction. Syrian soldiers appeared from side streets and waved at the dust-covered vehicles, assuming they were Syrian. Nafshi, dust-covered himself, waved back. Emerging from the built-up area, he took a cleared path through an Israeli minefield that permitted an indirect approach to the strongpoint. Cautiously driving into the compound, he saw that the exhausted soldiers were sound asleep at their posts.

Since the war's start, the Israelis had been struck by what they saw as a zombie-like implacability with which the Syrians were hurling themselves at the Israeli defenses. But on Wednesday morning, electronic monitors picked up an order from the commander of the First Armored Division, Gen. Tewfik Jehani, to shell one of his own units, the Ninety-first Brigade, which had spearheaded the division's attacks. The order appeared aimed at stopping men from abandoning their tanks and fleeing on foot. In the end the order was canceled but it pointed to a crisis in the Syrian ranks.

On Wednesday morning, Israeli tanks in the central sector pushed the last Syrian units back across the Purple Line. Climbing a ridge overlooking Strongpoint 110, Major Bierman of Sarig's brigade saw hundreds of Syrian infantrymen besieging the post. A few tank shells dispersed them. The tanks also fired at Syrian vehicles snaking back across the cease-fire line.

At the sight of the withdrawing enemy, the tankers on the ridge cheered and fired their weapons into the air. When they descended to the strongpoint, the Golani troops, under siege for four days, climbed the tanks to embrace them. Moussa Peled lit up the cigar Haim Bar-Lev had given him with the injunction to smoke it "when the time is right."

General Jehani had refused to leave the Golan until all his units had exited. When he finally started back with members of his staff, he found that Israeli units were already between him and the Syrian lines. Israeli intelligence would learn later that he had lain up in a culvert until nightfall, with Israeli units passing within yards, before escaping across the line in the dark.

For Israel, the nightmare glimpsed on the Golan the first night of the war had given way in four days to stunning victory. The Syrians had left more than eight hundred tanks behind, the bulk of their armored strength. The scenario Elazar had once daydreamed about for Sinai—falling back from the canal and luring the Egyptian armor into a killing ground—had inadvertently transpired on the Golan. The Israeli fallback on the Golan had not been deliberate—it was in fact a collapse—but the results were the same. The area had become an enormous tank trap which snapped shut with Moussa Peled's drive from the south. Only the Hermon remained to be reconquered.

The return to the Purple Line was the first measure of consolation afforded Elazar since the war began. It also posed a major dilemma—what next? Should the IDF deploy again along the Purple Line or should it push towards Damascus? A strategic choice had to be made quickly, and it would be one of the most important in the war.

Nine hours of continuous discussion began with a meeting in the Pit Wednesday afternoon conducted by Elazar. The chief of staff first spelled out the situation on the ground. For all their losses, the Syrians had retreated in good order. Probes across the Purple Line from the southern sector this morning showed that their defense line was intact. Fresh Syrian troops manning the line had been reinforced by those retreating from the Golan. As for the Israeli forces, they were in a state of exhaustion. Officers reported that entire battalions were falling asleep whenever their tanks halted. Men were not responding to radioed orders because they were dozing off. Elazar ordered all operations halted so that the troops could rest in the coming hours.

Remaining on the Purple Line, he said, would permit the IDF to send one of the three northern divisions, with 200 to 250 tanks, to Sinai. Another argument for halting was that the line was already fortified with an antitank ditch, minefields, and strongpoints. It would be more defensible, after some improvements, than any line they were likely to halt on along the road to Damascus.

The other alternative—an attack towards Damascus—offered the prospect of knocking Syria out of the war. At the least, it would leave Israel in possession of territory that would serve as a political counterweight to Sinai territory remaining in Egyptian hands.

At this stage of the thinking-through process, Elazar favored halting on the Purple Line.

The discussion moved to Dayan's office, where the participants explored the military and political implications. If the IDF drew close to Damascus, it might lead Moscow to push for a cease-fire. Or it might provoke Soviet military intervention. Would a swift attack encourage the Iraqis and Jordanians to rush to the aid of the Syrians, or would it deter them?

At night, all repaired to the prime minister's office, where Mrs. Meir awaited them, along with her closest advisers, ministers Galili and Allon. The discussion began again with Elazar spelling out the options. He had by now reversed himself and was in favor of crossing the Purple Line. His major reason was a desire to restore the IDF's deterrent image by seizing enemy territory before the war ended. The possibility of a swift and successful counterattack existed only on the Syrian front.

General Tal took exception. For a counterattack to be meaningful it had to be on the Egyptian front, he said. But the Egyptians had first to be lured out from under their SAM umbrella. Dayan, who had expressed reservations about attacking into Syria during the earlier discussions, supported it now. Air force commander Peled drew everyone's attention to the prospect of a substantial Iraqi expeditionary force joining the Syrians. It was important, he said, to hit the Syrians before the Iraqis arrived.

Mrs. Meir grasped the cardinal point raised by the generals. It would take four days to shift a division to Sinai. If a cease-fire were imposed during this period, the war would end with territorial loss for Israel in Sinai and no gain in the north—an unmitigated defeat. This was a political matter and her decision was unhesitating—to cross the Purple Line. At the very least, she wanted Syrian territory to bring to the bargaining table. The attack would be launched tomorrow, Thursday, October 11.

At Poriya Hospital outside Tiberias, where his life had been saved in an operation on Sunday, Colonel Sarig was feeling well enough by Wednesday for doctors to permit him a one-day visit to his nearby kibbutz, Bait Hashita. Anticipating that an Israeli attack into Syria was imminent, he joined the "escapees" fleeing hospitals for the front. He stopped home to don a fresh uniform and headed for the Golan. He had no feeling in his left arm and would need help getting on and off a tank. He had also been warned by the doctors not to cough lest his neck stitches open. It was dark when he reached General Laner's command post on Mount Yosifon. Vehicles were burning from a Katyusha barrage moments before. One of the men killed in that barrage, he learned, was a member of his kibbutz. No one told him that a few hours earlier his younger brother, a company commander in Hadar's brigade, had been killed in the final push to the Purple Line.

Elazar called Hofi after midnight to notify him of the government's decision to cross the line. The chief of staff came north at dawn on a helicopter flight that afforded him a blessed hour of sleep. After reviewing the attack plans with Hofi, he continued on to Nafakh to talk to the divisional and brigade commanders. It was his first meeting with them since the start of the war. The sight of the unshaven, bone-weary faces touched him deeply, particularly Ben-Gal's haunted visage. The coming battle would be a turning point, he told them. It was doubtful that they could reach Damascus, but their aim would be to get close enough to threaten it.

Unlike the Syrians, who had attacked on Yom Kippur all along the line, the Israeli counterattack would be concentrated in the sector north of Kuneitra. Raful Eitan's division would advance along the foot of Mount Hermon, whose slopes would secure the left flank. Kahalani's battalion would lead this effort. A second force, under Ben-Hanan, would move on a parallel route a mile south. The attack had been set for 7 A.M. but Ben-Gal persuaded Northern Command to postpone it to 11 A.M. so that the sun would not be in their eyes.

Dan Laner's division would attack up the Kuneitra–Damascus road, code-named America. This was the obvious attack route, so obvious that the Syrians had long since made it the most heavily defended sector on their borders. The road was under the guns of a major fortification at the village of Khan Arnabe. The IDF had not even prepared a contingency plan for an attack along this route since it never intended a head-on assault. But Hofi believed Syrian morale was at the breaking point and that an attack up America would work. The Syrians had crumbled in the Six Day War once the Israeli attackers had gained a foothold on the Golan. However, Elazar, who had commanded the 1967 attack, admitted that the staying power of the Syrian forces now was an unknown factor. Eitan vainly urged that Laner's division follow him through the northern break-in point and then capture Khan Arnabe from the rear rather than try to break through the formidable defenses on America.

Ben-Gal summoned his battalion commanders to a preattack briefing. Three-quarters of the brigade's tank crewmen at the start of the battle five days before were dead or wounded. But replacements overnight had brought the brigade back up to one hundred tanks. When the briefing was over, Ben-Gal called Kahalani aside. "Listen," he said, placing a hand on Kahalani's shoulder. "I met the chief of staff this morning and I wanted you to know that I told him what you did." Ben-Gal seemed to have difficulty expressing himself. "I told him you were a Hero of Israel [the name of Israel's highest medal for valor]. I wanted you to know this." Backing away from his emotion, Ben-Gal shook Kahalani's hand and said awkwardly, "It'll be all right. See you."

Lieutenant Peled, Kahalani's operations officer, watched the scene with bemusement. He had not heard the conversation but it was plain from Ben-Gal's body language and from the comradely hand placed on Kahalani's shoulder that the brigade commander was moved and was making personal contact. It was a view of Yanosh Ben-Gal the lieutenant had never expected to see.

Back at his battalion's staging area, Kahalani asked for the officers to be assembled. He scanned their faces as they sat on the ground in front of him. Most were new. "First, for all those who have just joined us and still don't know where they are, this is the Seventy-seventh Battalion of the Seventh Brigade. Battalion commander Kahalani stands by chance before you." A hesitant smile appeared on the tense faces. "Before I explain our mission, I want to know who you are and what your tasks are."

Each new man was asked to tell which company he had been assigned to, what he had done since the beginning of the war, and from what organic unit he came. A number were reservists. Kahalani asked each of the latter personal questions—what part of the country they were from, what they did in civilian life, whether they were married, how many children they had. Lieutenant Peled, accustomed to the spartan tone of briefings in the standing army, found these personal questions puzzling. What have they to do with the business at hand? Only later would he understand that Kahalani was spinning a human web, creating of this disparate group of strangers thrown together on a remote battlefield a cohesive team willing, in moments of danger that would shortly be upon them, to risk death because he asked them to.

Only when this bonding was done did Kahalani turn to his operations officer and ask him to unroll the map. "The brigade has been ordered to break through the Syrian lines," said Kahalani. "Our battalion will spearhead the attack." He pointed out their route and spelled out the order in which the units would move. "I wish you all success. And, the main thing, fight like lions. We're moving out in twenty minutes. On your tanks."

Twenty-five

IRAQI INTERVENTION

T HE MINEFIELDS CONFRONTING KAHALANI'S FORCE lay behind a broad swath of agricultural land inside Syrian territory. The Syrian army had left openings in the minefields to enable Syrian farmers to access the fields. The Israeli force passed unscathed by following these paths.

In Ben-Hanan's area a mile south, engineers cleared paths through the minefield with bangalore torpedoes. With artillery providing a rolling barrage five hundred yards to their front, the two tank forces moved eastward on parallel routes, encountering no opposition except for artillery fire.

The easy success of the northern break-in encouraged the belief that the Syrian defenses on the Damascus road would quickly collapse. That confidence was not shared by the man who would be at the spearhead of Laner's force. Maj. Giora Bierman, who had passed out from jaundice on the battlefield five days before, was to lead a battalion against the Khan Arnabe fortification, which lay across two miles of flat terrain, by racing as fast as he could straight up the road with his sixteen tanks. A reconnaissance battalion commanded by Lt. Col. Hanani Tavori would attack to the left of the road with nineteen tanks across an open field.

Bierman regarded the mission as suicidal and said so to Colonel Sarig. But the brigade commander shared the belief that the Syrians were too dispirited to put up effective resistance. The tanks would rely on shock and speed, firing as they went. Most were bound to get through, he said.

The Israeli Enclave

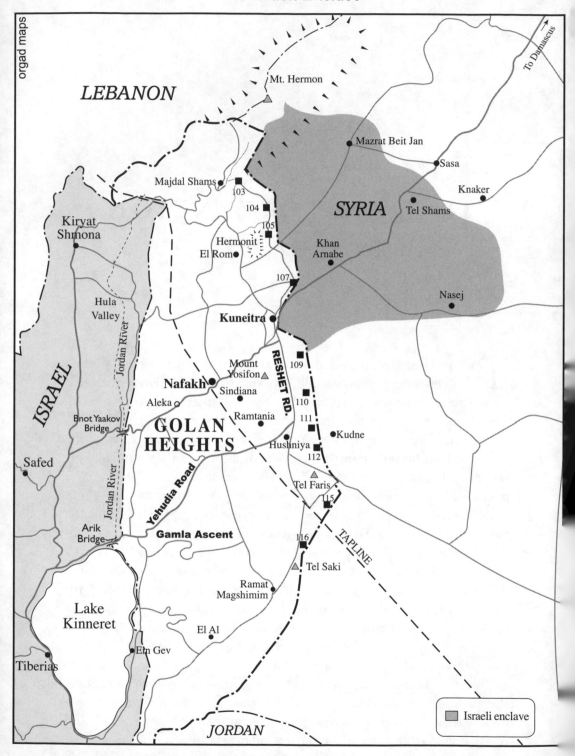

orgad maps

LEBANON

Mt. Hermon

To Damascus

Mazrat Beit Jan

Sasa

Majdal Shams

103

104

105

SYRIA

Knaker

Tel Shams

Kiryat
Shmona

Hermonit

El Rom

Khan
Arnabe

107

Nasej

Hula
Valley

Kuneitra

Jordan River

ISRAEL

Mount
Yosifon

RESHET RD.

109

Nafakh

Sindiana

110

Aleka

Ramtania

111

GOLAN
HEIGHTS

Bnot Yaakov
Bridge

Hushniya

Kudne

112

Safed

Tel Faris

115

Jordan River

Yehudia Road

TAPLINE

Arik
Bridge

116

Gamla Ascent

Tel Saki

Ramat
Magshimim

Lake
Kinneret

El Al

Ein Gev

Tiberias

JORDAN

Israeli enclave

Resigning himself to his fate, Bierman positioned his tank close to the head of his column and waited for the signal to advance. Sarig, traveling in a thin-skinned personnel carrier, took position further back.

The attack commenced under withering Syrian fire. Bierman's column started up the road but passage was soon blocked by knocked-out tanks. The sound of mine explosions marked the progress of Tavori's battalion across the field. All of Tavori's tanks had treads blown off except for a few which escaped by gaining the road. But all of these were soon hit by missiles. The road became a cauldron of smoke and burning tanks. Instead of making a swift dash up the road, those tanks still operational exchanged fire with the fortification, shielding behind tanks that had been knocked out.

Finally, Bierman and a few other tank commanders managed to extricate themselves and charged the Syrian position. Bierman's tank was hit as it reached Khan Arnabe's outer trench. The gunner was killed and Bierman and his loader wounded. As he extricated himself from the turret, Bierman saw fire beginning to lick at the tank's innards. He and his loader sheltered behind the tank as Syrian infantrymen in a trench five yards away tried to shoot them. Other tanks had made it inside the fortification and were firing machine guns into the trenches. Looking back, Bierman was relieved to see a fresh force starting up the road. He knew these would be Ori Orr's tanks. Swift exploitation of the breakthrough was essential if the Syrians were not to slam the door shut again. Orr had in fact been told to wait until evacuation of the casualties from the road and minefield. However, he feared that the sight was having a dispiriting effect on his men and received permission to begin his attack immediately.

Bierman and his loader climbed onto the front deck of the tank, keeping the turret between them and the Syrian trench. The major called on the driver, who had remained in his compartment, to begin driving in reverse. Unable to move one wounded arm, Bierman held on to the tank with the other and guided the driver towards the open field. After half a mile, Bierman called on the driver to stop and to get out before the fire touched off an explosion. As the driver emerged, artillery struck, killing him and wounding Bierman again—this time in the head, stomach, and lungs. Bierman would be retrieved unconscious by medics and helicoptered to a hospital.

Twenty-five tanks—two-thirds of Sarig's force—were knocked out. But the six tanks that made it to Khan Arnabe had opened the way for Orr, who was followed by Mordecai Ben-Porat. The two reduced brigades moved off to the east and south, and a force of paratroopers was sent in to clear the Khan Arnabe trenches of remaining Syrians. During the night, Sarig received reinforcements and tanks that had been repaired. He would be able to notify Laner in the morning that his brigade was ready to continue.

On the northernmost axis, Kahalani's task force had by late Thursday afternoon reached a hill overlooking its objective, the village of Mazraat Bet Jaan, without a single casualty. Abandoned Syrian tanks and damaged fortifications along the way showed the effect of three hours of artillery and air softening up, the kind Adan had futilely called for at Hizayon three days before.

In contrast to the stony landscape and bleak mud-hut hamlets to the south, Mazraat Bet Jann was a picturesque village in a well-wooded setting nestling at the foot of the Hermon. The thick vegetation could hide an ambush and Kahalani carefully studied the surroundings from the hilltop. Residents were fleeing the village on donkeys and on foot. Kahalani decided to give them time to get well clear before descending. But as he watched, Syrian tanks moved into the village from the east and four helicopters landed to disgorge troops. The Syrians were not giving up. With night almost upon him, Kahalani obtained Ben-Gal's permission to wait until morning before attacking.

Ben-Hanan's force was also just short of its objective, Tel Shams, when night fell. The fortified hill dominated the Kuneitra–Damascus road and was "the cork in the bottle," as Elazar put it, on the approach to Sasa. Hofi's mission was to reach at least as far as Sasa. From there, artillery would be able to shell Damascus's suburbs. Only if Israeli shells fell close to Damascus would the Soviets, on Syria's behalf, ask for a cease-fire in the UN, Dayan had told the front commander.

Hofi was uneasy, however, about ordering a head-on attack on Tel Shams after the grim results of his order to attack at Khan Arnabe. Studying the war map in the Pit, Elazar expressed concern that a handful of Syrian tanks on Tel Shams would be sufficient to repel an attack. "Our force has to climb up the valley. It won't get past it." Ben-Gal was also uneasy and was inclined to call off the attack. He acceded, however, to Ben-Hanan's request to let him go ahead with it in the morning.

Ben-Hanan moved out at first light Friday with eight tanks. The road passed through the Leja, a dark plain covered with basalt boulders that severely impeded off-road movement. As they approached the *tel*, a volley of Sagger missiles was fired at them and Syrian planes attacked the formation. A rocket hit Ben-Hanan's tank, tearing off a piece of his ear and bursting his right eardrum. Remaining in action, he led his tanks back, but when out of sight of the *tel* he turned into the Leja itself on a tortuous route. Reaching the rear of the fortification in late afternoon, Ben-Hanan's tanks surprised the

Syrians and destroyed more than a score of vehicles, including tanks. As Ben-Hanan began to ascend the rear of the mound, two Saggers hit his tank, propelling him from the turret and killing two of his crewmen. The rest of the tanks were either hit or pulled back.

As he lay beside his burning tank, Ben-Hanan saw that his left leg was dangling. On a radio retrieved from the tank by his driver, Ben-Hanan contacted Ben-Gal. "This is Yossi," he said. "My leg's gone. I'm lying beside my tank. Get me out of here." The driver pulled Ben-Hanan to a pit that offered some shelter. Following a doctor's radioed instructions, he tied the officer's shattered leg with a tourniquet.

Brigade urged the survivors of Ben-Hanan's force, who had pulled back into the Leja, to return to the hill. The radio exchange was overheard by Maj. Yoni Netanyahu, deputy commander of the General Staff reconnaissance unit, who cut into the transmission to offer his services. Ben-Gal gratefully accepted. Within three hours, Netanyahu and a small commando force reached the *tel* on foot and extricated Ben-Hanan and his driver.

Elazar urged Hofi to avoid attacking Tel Shams with tanks and instead to use infantry at night. If they got close enough to Damascus to shell its suburbs, Elazar believed, the Syrians would ask for a cease-fire. Dayan visited Generals Eitan and Laner at their command posts bearing the same message. There was no intention to conquer the city or shell it, he said, as long as the Arabs did not bomb or shell Israeli cities. But it was important to impress on the Syrians that their attempt to capture the Golan would end with Israel on the approaches to Damascus. The generals replied with what seemed to the defense minister a pro forma "We'll try." After a week of constant combat, the brigades were well under half strength and the men were exhausted. No less important, the existential threat to Israel had clearly passed, reducing readiness to take excessive risks.

At a mobile listening post attached to Eitan's division, a radio monitor turning the knob as he scanned Syrian radio traffic suddenly sat upright. The radioman he had come upon was talking with an Iraqi accent.

"Are you sure?" asked the unit commander, Capt. David Harman.

"I can tell you what village he's from," said the monitor, himself an Iraqi-born Israeli. The radioman was talking about taking tanks off their transporters.

When Harman passed the report up to division, the reaction was skeptical. The Iraqis were known to be sending forces to Syria's aid, but they were not expected yet. An intelligence officer suggested that the intercept was the result of a freak atmospheric bounce of radio waves from somewhere near the Iraqi border.

Iraq had not been made privy to the war beforehand by Sadat or Assad. But with its outbreak, Baghdad immediately notified Syria of its readiness to send an expeditionary force despite the uneasy relations between the two countries. Iraq simultaneously obtained Iran's agreement to keep their volatile border calm so that Iraqi troops could move to Syria's aid. A similar agreement was struck between Baghdad and the Kurds of northern Iraq. Israeli operatives had been training Kurdish guerrillas for years precisely in order to have them keep Iraqi troops tied down in the event of an Israeli-Arab war. But the Kurdish leadership decided at this moment of truth not to engage in a military adventure on Israel's behalf. The Iraqis started a division on the road to Damascus the next day, with a second armored division to follow. AMAN was aware of the Iraqi move and on Tuesday reported that the lead Iraqi brigade would reach Damascus that evening after a trip of eight hundred miles. However, AMAN subsequently lost track of the Iraqi force.

Resuming movement Friday morning, Orr's brigade was reinforced by a tank battalion made up of reservists who had returned from abroad after the war started. He let the unit take the lead, warning its commander not to be deceived by the seemingly empty landscape. "Move slowly," he said. "This isn't the Six Day War." An hour later, the battalion was ambushed and mauled. Orr sent forward one of his veteran battalions, which drove back the Syrians.

Sarig's tank commanders had been traumatized by the Khan Arnabe battle. In the first skirmish Friday, only tanks commanded by officers responded when he gave the order to move into firing positions. When the battalion resumed forward movement, Sarig took the lead in his personnel carrier to set an example. The men settled down and the going became increasingly easy. Sarig felt for the first time the way he had in the breakthrough stage of the Six Day War. Moving parallel to him was Ben-Porat's brigade. Their joint objective was Knaker, the last fortified position before the Damascus region. From Knaker, they could proceed either north towards Sasa or east towards Damascus itself, only some twenty miles distant.

Monitoring their progress from atop Tel Sha'ar in the center of his divisional sector, General Laner could make out the dust trails of the two brigades moving northeast. They were to be joined at Knaker by Orr's brigade, presently refueling at Nasej village to their rear. Another brigade, Col. Yossi Peled's, which had remained behind on the Golan, was on its way across the Purple Line to join Laner's division in kicking open this outer gateway to Damascus.

As Laner idly shifted his gaze to the southeast, he was startled to see dust clouds there as well. A sizable tank force was moving swiftly towards his exposed flank. Intelligence had given no indication that the Syrians had forces capable of attacking from that direction. He thought at first that Moussa Peled's division, which was holding the line in the southern Golan, might have made a wide swing to join him. But when he checked with Northern Command he was told that Peled had not moved.

Sarig and Ben-Porat were only three miles from Knaker when they were ordered by Laner to halt immediately and return south. He did not say why. Both brigade commanders protested at being stopped just as the enemy was crumbling. "You're not listening to what I'm saying," countered Laner. "Stop and return with all your tanks."

Orr was told to halt refueling and prepare to meet enemy forces heading in his direction. His tanks deployed around the Nasej crossroads. The lead tank had just taken position when its crew saw two columns of tanks and APCs approaching from the southeast. They bore an unfamiliar color but they were T-55s and thus clearly enemy. The tanks appeared to be moving uncertainly, as if their commanders were not sure where they were. Orr's opening volley at four hundred yards took them by surprise and set the lead tanks aflame. The remainder pulled back.

The Iraqis had arrived on the battlefield.

Laner drew up plans that night to hit them in the morning before they had gained their bearings. As he conferred with his staff atop Tel Sha'ar, an officer came in from an observation post to report dust clouds in the distance moving in their direction. The officer ventured that the Iraqis were resuming their attack. Laner was skeptical. The Syrians had not initiated a serious night attack since the first night of the war, and it was unlikely that the Iraqis would do so only a few hours after having reached the battlefield, particularly after the bloody nose they had received from Orr. Laner asked the officer to take another look. The officer returned ten minutes later and repeated his finding. This time Laner asked his deputy, Brig. Gen. Moshe Bar-Kochba, to have a look.

It was a bright moonlit night, enabling visibility far across the landscape. Through his binoculars, Bar-Kochba could make out seven or eight parallel dust clouds, indicating a large tank formation moving in broad and deep deployment, four to five miles distant. The clouds appeared to be heading straight towards Tel Sha'ar. Upon receiving Bar-Kochba's report, Laner ordered the division to prepare immediately to meet an attack.

Ben-Porat's and Yossi Peled's brigades deployed from Tel Sha'ar westward. Orr's and Sarig's brigades took position several miles to the east. The units thus formed a box with the southern end open towards the Iraqis. If the Iraqis moved into the center, both wings would converge on it. If they attacked either one of the wings, the other would hit the attackers in the flank or rear.

At 9 P.M., lookouts reported that the dust clouds had disappeared. The division's tanks remained in position but tank crewmen took turns dozing off. At 3:30 A.M., the men of a Sherman battalion heard engines approaching from the south. Lt. Col. Benzion Padan, the battalion commander, called for flares. In their light, the low silhouettes of Soviet-made tanks could be seen in the distance. Padan's tanks opened fire and the Iraqis fired back. The Israelis could detect no sign that the enemy shells were hitting anywhere near them.

"Fellows, these are rookies," said an officer on the radio net. "They're shooting at the sky." Colonel Padan told his men to stop firing in order to encourage the enemy tanks to resume their advance. When the Iraqis did, the Sherman knocked out the six tanks in the lead and the rest of the formation halted out of range.

When dawn came, the Iraqis found Orr's brigade on their eastern flank and the Sherman battalion, reinforced by a Centurion battalion, to their front. In a battle that lasted an hour and a half, twenty-five more Iraqi tanks were knocked out. Sarig's brigade was meanwhile sent on a wide sweep into the enemy rear and destroyed twenty more tanks. The Israeli units reported no losses to themselves.

Despite the blow inflicted on the Iraqis, their swift arrival on the battlefield had changed the strategic situation in a fundamental way. The Israelis, instead of continuing northeast towards Damascus with their newly gained momentum, had now to deal with the challenge to their southern flank. The Iraqis' fighting ability did not impress the Israelis—Eitan would reckon them far inferior to the Syrians—but their numbers could not be ignored. Their swift arrival on the battlefield, without any preplanning, was an impressive accomplishment that neutralized the Israeli threat to Damascus.

In the coming days, the Iraqi expeditionary force would come to number 500 tanks, 700 APCs, and 30,000 men, including commando units. It was a force that by itself matched Israel's strength on the northern front. Unlike the bruised Syrians, the Iraqi forces were fresh and eager to do battle. Confrontation with the Israelis would cool their ardor but their massive presence tied Israel's forces down.

At the same hour that Bar-Kochba was watching the approach of the Iraqi brigade in the moonlight, Maj. Shaul Mofaz was looking down from a helicopter at the Syrian landscape one hundred miles northeast of Damascus. The Teheran-born officer commanded a twenty-five-man paratroop team whose mission was to ambush Iraqi reinforcements at a bridge leading from the Iraqi border. Reaching the ambush site, the force waited for more than an hour but no convoy appeared, only occasional pairs of trucks. The paratroopers prepared to blow the bridge and call it a night when a solitary tank trailer lumbered out of the gloom carrying a T-55. When it mounted the bridge, explosives sent bridge and tank crashing into the wadi. The paratroopers had been supplied with newly arrived LAW missiles but there had been no time to practice. Some of the men had read the training manual and succeeded in hitting the upended tank with two missiles. To their astonishment, the missiles, instead of exploding, covered the tank with a white substance. They would later learn that these were training devices filled with plaster. The force was back in Israel before first light.

The following night Mofaz was dispatched again behind Syrian lines, this time to blow a bridge on the road between Damascus and the northern city of Homs. The road was used to transfer SAMs to the battle zone. Forty paratroopers participated.

The helicopter pilot, Lt. Col. Yuval Efrat, set the men down several miles from the bridge and lifted off for Israel to await Mofaz's call for evacuation after the mission's completion. As the paratroopers were moving through a wadi an hour later, a truck traveling without lights stopped on the road above. Thirty soldiers alighted and opened fire at a distance of two hundred yards. The paratroopers fired LAW missiles, this time real ones, which exploded among the Syrians and sent them to cover. Mofaz led his men up into the hills and prepared to call for a rescue mission. From the heights, however, he could make out the bridge in the moonlight, not far away. Conferring with his officers, he decided to complete the mission.

As they started to move off, the paratroopers saw that the road below was filling with vehicles and soldiers. A plane circling overhead dropped flares, and the paratroopers froze in place until the orange light died. There were by now some five hundred soldiers below scouring the terrain with the aid of floodlights. The barking of search dogs could be heard. The bridge, Mofaz assumed, was probably swarming with soldiers as well. He led his men higher and called for rescue.

Efrat was more than halfway back to base when he heard the call. His gauge showed that he did not have enough fuel to return for the men and make it back to Israel. He continued to the Ramat David air base where he, his copilot, and the flight engineer hastily transferred to an already fueled helicopter that had been kept in reserve for an emergency rescue. Exhausted after seven days of intensive action, Efrat fell asleep as soon as he was airborne. Snapping awake, he removed his helmet and emptied a canteen over his head, letting the water soak his uniform and run down his back. With that, he was able to focus. The mission they were about to undertake, he told the two crewmen, would be a difficult one, probably conducted under fire.

The Syrians on the Homs road, certain that they had the Israeli intruders trapped but uncertain exactly where they were, moved cautiously. At one point, soldiers began to climb in the direction of Mofaz's force and some of the paratroopers prepared to fire. Mofaz stopped them. No one was to fire, he said, without explicit orders. The Syrians still didn't know where they were. Two hours had passed since his call for evacuation and the prospect of rescue before dawn was rapidly receding. Mofaz was thinking of breaking the force up and hiding out until a rescue attempt could be made the next night—a desperate plan with virtually no chance of success—when the radio came alive. It was Efrat. "I'll be with you in fifteen minutes." Mofaz set off with one of his officers to search for a flat landing surface shielded from view of the Syrians. The best he could find was a moderate slope with rocks.

The moon offered Efrat a good view of the landscape below—a gray, lifeless expanse he found depressing. It offered neither the greenery of Israel nor the golden sheen of the Sinai desert. One of his gauges flickered as Mofaz activated an electronic signal beacon. They were a few kilometers apart now but the beacon provided only a general direction. Approaching closer, Efrat asked Mofaz to flash a light but the paratroop commander said he could not. The Syrians were only eight hundred yards away. Suddenly, Mofaz shouted, "They're firing at you." Efrat saw nothing but a moment later he heard a thud of bullets and thought he smelled gunpowder.

Below he could see the Homs road and beyond it a line of low hills. Mofaz was up there somewhere. Efrat took his craft on a wide swing so as to approach the hills from the other side, away from the Syrians. Slowing down and lowering his wheels, he headed towards the back of a hill where he thought Mofaz might be, given the location from which the Syrians had fired.

"Give me a light just for a second," said Efrat.

Mofaz flashed a hooded light that projected a narrow beam not visible from the sides. Efrat was looking right at it when it went on a mile away. "I see you," he said. Keeping his eyes fixed on the spot, he asked his copilot to read the gauges and give him a running account of speed and altitude. Reaching the hill, Efrat saw the paratroopers one hundred feet below. He set the helicopter straight down, without taking the time to check whether the site was clear of men. "Count them as they come in," he said to his engineer. The paratroopers swiftly entered the craft, officers last.

"Forty," said the engineer.

"Close it," said Efrat. "We're lifting off."

As they rose, one of the officers yelped. A bullet penetrating the floor had hit him in the backside. A paratrooper looking out a side window saw a mortar barrage blossoming on the hilltop they had just left seconds before.

After making an emergency landing an hour and a half later at Ramat David air base, Efrat found the helicopter's rotor and skin peppered with bullets. (Mofaz would in time become IDF chief of staff and then defense minister. Efrat would become an El Al pilot.)

This same night, October 13, a paratroop unit attacked Tel Shams on foot in accordance with Elazar's instructions and succeeded in capturing it, a five-hour battle, with only four wounded.

The commander of the only long-range artillery battalion on the Golan, Lt. Col. Aldo Zohar, had been ordered to hit Mazeh Airport outside Damascus this very night without waiting for the breakthrough at Tel Shams.

Since the beginning of the war, the 175 mm guns had been striking targets deep behind Syrian lines. But in the tumultuous battles they had also approached within a mile of the front line to fire over open sights in direct support of ground troops. Surveying his map, Zohar saw that to hit Mazeh he would have to move even further forward—to the front line itself and perhaps across it. With the road to Sasa still blocked, the only way to approach firing range was through the Leja. Examination of air photos had revealed a path wide enough for tracked vehicles to weave their way deep into the boulder-strewn volcanic field. Ben-Hanan had followed a similar path in his foray through the Leja the day before.

Colonel Zohar—whose first name, Aldo, reflected the Italian influence that had prevailed in his native Libya—moved forward with two guns after darkness. A Golani squad led the way into the Leja on foot, marking the route with small fluorescent lights and maintaining a lookout for Syrian commandos who might have penetrated the Leja from the other end. Reaching their predetermined firing position after five miles, Zohar deployed the guns but ordered that motors be kept running in case a commando attack or Syrian counterbattery fire necessitated a quick getaway. The guns fired twenty-three shells before Zohar was ordered to pull back. Air photos the next day would show hits on the runways and terminal buildings at the airport. Far more important than the physical damage, however, was the lingering sound of the artillery explosions wafting into Damascus's western suburbs.

The next night, Zohar was ordered to hit targets in Damascus itself. Eitan's forces had been blocked several miles short of Sasa by hastily erected antitank defenses. To reach firing range, Zohar entered the Leja once again. A reconnaissance team headed by Yoni Netanyahu led the way this time. Five military and government structures were designated as targets but Zohar dropped one because of its proximity to the city's Jewish quarter. The guns had just reached firing position when an order was received to abort the mission. The political level in Tel Aviv, reportedly Golda Meir herself, had ruled it out, whether for fear of Soviet reaction or of retaliatory Syrian rocket attacks on Israel's cities.

It was clear by now that the attack into Syria had played itself out. With the arrival of the Iraqis, Israel did not have sufficient strength on the northern front to force Syria out of the war. In addition, Moscow had let Washington know it was uneasy about Israel's proximity to Damascus and the Soviets had reportedly put airborne divisions on alert. Dayan did not take the implicit Soviet threat lightly. "We must be as careful as we can not to bring the bear out of the forest," he said. He was willing to halt along the present lines in the north, he said, if the army found them tactically acceptable.

There would be room in coming days to improve positions in the Syrian "enclave," as the captured area had come to be called, and a major effort was still in the offing to recapture the Hermon. But it was time now, eight days into the war, to focus on the Egyptian front. If there was to be a strategic turning, it would be there, against Israel's most formidable foe.

Twenty-six

POWERS THAT BE

I N HIGH-CEILINGED OFFICES FAR from the battlefields of the Middle East, a parallel confrontation, no less fateful, was under way between the superpowers.

The attitudes of decision makers in Washington and Moscow had been almost identical when the war broke out. Both sides were convinced that Israel would quickly defeat the Arab armies. The Americans reveled at the prospect and so did top Soviet officials, peeved at Sadat and Assad for ignoring their urgings to avoid war. Both in Washington and in Moscow there was determination that the détente they had worked so hard to achieve would not be undermined by their unruly clients. However, realpolitik and developments on the battlefield steadily shifted the two powers' stand from shoulder-to-shoulder to face-to-face.

They could not stand aloof because the success or failure of their clients reflected directly on their status as superpowers. Already on Yom Kippur, Kissinger proposed that the U.S. Sixth Fleet in the Mediterranean move closer to the war zone in case the Soviet Union felt called upon to flex its muscles on behalf of the Arabs. But from the beginning, it was clear to him that the war could open the way to a peace process. Support for this view came from Sadat's security adviser, Hafez Ismail, in a message delivered through intelligence channels on the second day of the war. On the face of it, there was nothing new in the Cairo note. It reiterated Sadat's call for total

Israeli withdrawal from territories occupied in 1967 and rejected any interim agreements. Kissinger recognized that this was only an opening position.

One sentence bore particular resonance. "We do not intend to deepen the engagements or widen the dispute." To Kissinger, this meant that Sadat did not intend to pursue his offensive into the depths of Sinai or to "widen the dispute" by attacking the United States verbally. Capable of sniffing diplomatic subtlety halfway around the globe, Kissinger sensed that something momentous was afoot. By not depicting America as the cause of his woes, as Nasser had done, Sadat was leaving open the possibility of Washington serving as a mediator following the war, rather than seeing itself primarily as Israel's patron. Kissinger now understood for the first time Sadat's dramatic expulsion of Soviet advisers as a move aimed at clearing the way both for war and for American involvement after the war. The message from Cairo also offered a revealing, almost touching glimpse of the psychological impulse behind Egypt's bold move. "[We want] to show we are not afraid or helpless."

"Until this message," Kissinger would write, "I had not taken Sadat seriously. [His] ability from the very first hours of the war never to lose sight of the heart of the problem convinced me that we were dealing with a statesman of the first order." Kissinger would come to understand that Sadat's objective was to shock Israel into greater flexibility and restore Egypt's self-respect so that he, Sadat, could be more flexible as well in order to achieve an agreement. "Our definition of rationality did not take seriously the notion of starting an unwinnable war to restore self-respect," Kissinger would write.

The Soviet leadership was mustering far less empathy for the Egyptian leader. At a Kremlin meeting three hours after the war's outbreak, Chairman Brezhnev predicted speedy defeat for the Arabs. They would soon be sorry they had not followed Moscow's advice, he said. Nevertheless, the Soviet leader saw no option but to offer "our Arab friends" Moscow's support.

Foreign minister Gromyko brought up Assad's request on October 4 that the Soviets seek a cease-fire in the Security Council forty-eight hours after the outbreak of war so as to secure Arab gains before the Israeli reserves could counterattack. In the circumstances, this was seen as a reasonable way out, and Moscow's ambassador in Cairo, Vinogradov, was asked to obtain Sadat's consent. But the Egyptian leader adamantly rejected the idea. Moscow expected Sadat to reverse himself as soon as the tide of battle turned. But to general amazement, the tide was not turning, at least in Sinai.

Matters were different on the Syrian front. On Sunday night, October 7,

Assad summoned Ambassador Mukhitdinov and described the situation as critical, with the Israelis about to counterattack. Looking anxious, the Syrian leader asked that the Soviets move immediately for a cease-fire. When Vinogradov approached Sadat the next day with Assad's renewed request, the Egyptian leader remained dismissive. If Assad wants to end the war, he said, that was his business. Egypt intended to carry on. When Vinogradov asked what Egypt's goals were, Sadat said that its strategic goal was to exhaust Israel, its territorial goal was the Gidi and Mitla Passes, and its political goal was a peaceful settlement of the Middle East conflict. The military situation on both fronts was excellent, he said, and he wanted no Soviet proposal for a cease-fire placed on the UN's agenda. Moscow had expected Sadat to be wringing his hands by now at having blundered into a war he could not win. Kremlin leaders expressed anger at his "stubbornness." Said Brezhnev: "His position is ridiculous."

The Soviets had, in truth, distorted Assad's request in depicting it to Sadat. The Syrian leader had linked a cease-fire to Israeli withdrawal to the 1967 lines, but the Soviets had failed to mention that since they knew it would be a nonstarter if presented at the UN that way. When the omission was mentioned to Gromyko by an aide, he replied, "Don't make our life more complicated, please." A simple cease-fire held no charm at all for Sadat. When Vinogradov tried again the next day to persuade him, the Egyptian leader spoke of Arab military momentum. The Syrian situation, he said, would resolve itself as soon as Iraqi forces reached the front line. As for Egypt, it would shortly begin moving forward in Sinai.

The Arab successes had astonished military observers in both superpower capitals. The chief of the Soviet General Staff, Marshal Victor Kulikov, had not believed the Egyptians capable of crossing the Suez Canal without the direct participation of Soviet advisers. Irritated at Sadat's expulsion of the advisers, he was looking forward with undisguised glee to the debacle he believed awaited Egypt. But three days after the outbreak of the war he acknowledged the Arab successes in an analysis he offered the Politburo. The Israelis had been surprised, he said, and had not put up the expected resistance. He pointed out with pride the central role played by Soviet weaponry, particularly the SAMs and antitank weapons, in the Arab advances. However, the veteran tank warrior who had fought in the Second World War denied that the success of the RPGs and Saggers meant the demise of the tank. Assisted by infantry and planes, he said, the tank would continue to rule the battlefield. It was the sort of encouragement Israeli generals could have used at the moment.

Kulikov complained that the Arabs had no clear-cut military doctrine and had failed to exploit the success of their initial tank attacks by using airborne troops against the Israeli rear. The Arab air forces had failed to gain control of the air, he said, and strategic cooperation between Egypt and Syria had not outlived their opening strike. For reasons he could not explain, said Kulikov, the Syrians had stopped their opening attack in midstride. When asked why Soviet advisers had not improved the Syrian performance, Kulikov said, "They don't listen to us. They pretend to be their own military strategists." As for the Egyptians, he said, they had made a fatal mistake by entrenching themselves on the Sinai bank and failing to move inland. The Soviet chief of staff cited enormous Arab losses thus far in weapons, ammunition, and personnel as reported by Soviet attachés in Cairo and Damascus. He had no information about Israel's losses.

The Arab success was likewise mystifying Washington. At the initial meeting of top policy makers on Saturday, most participants presumed that Israel had started the war. When the initial Arab successes were verified, Pentagon experts predicted that Israel would seize the initiative within seventy-two hours, when its reserves were in place. But as time passed, Kissinger was increasingly puzzled by Sadat's refusal to consider a cease-fire. The secretary appreciated that the Egyptian attack had a political objective but believed that Sadat understood that he could not stand up for long against Israel and would want to quickly lock in his gains with a cease-fire. But it was not happening.

On Monday evening, Israeli ambassador Dinitz relayed to Kissinger an upbeat assessment of the war situation as seen in Tel Aviv. It did not incorporate what Elazar would learn during his late night visit to Southern Command about Monday's failure in Sinai. Kissinger was thus totally unprepared when he was wakened at 1:45 A.M. by a call from Dinitz. The ambassador wanted to know whether arms shipments to Israel could be speeded up. The urgency made no sense, given Dinitz's assessment a few hours earlier and given that almost all of Israel's arms requests thus far were in the process of being met. Kissinger told the ambassador they would talk about it in the morning. An hour later, the phone rang again. It was Dinitz once more, with essentially the same request. "Unless he wanted to prove to the [Israeli] cabinet that he could get me out of bed at will," Kissinger would write, "something was wrong."

Dinitz had been ordered to make the calls by Golda Meir—"I don't care what time it is," she said when he demurred. "Call Kissinger now. Tomorrow may be too late." Her demand reflected the alarm, not to say panic, that seized her following the briefing Tuesday morning from Dayan on Monday's failure in Sinai. At 8:20 A.M., Kissinger and aides met in the White House Map Room with an apologetic Dinitz, who was accompanied by the Israeli military attaché, Gen. Mordecai Gur. The Americans were stunned when Gur spelled out Israel's losses in the first four days of battle. They included forty-nine warplanes and five hundred tanks—one-eighth of its air force and a quarter of its armor. How did it happen? asked a flabbergasted Kissinger. Dinitz said he did not know. "Obviously something went wrong."

Kissinger ordered his aides to provide Israel with intelligence information Gur had asked for and told Dinitz he would see what could be done about increasing arms shipments. For the first time Kissinger understood the reason for Sadat's cockiness—his armed forces were doing amazingly well. It was agreed that planes from Israel's national airline, El Al, with their identifying markers painted out, could land at American air bases and load the ammunition, electronic equipment, and other items Israel was now requesting. However, the seven El Al planes available were inadequate to meet Israel's needs and Kissinger said he would consult with his colleagues about ways to increase shipments.

At the end of the meeting, Dinitz asked Kissinger to see him alone for five minutes. The ambassador passed on Mrs. Meir's request for a visit with Nixon to plea for stepped-up arms aid. Kissinger flatly rejected the request. Her visit could not be kept secret and it would be interpreted as panic. In addition, the United States would be forced to publicly announce massive arms shipments to Israel, destroying its future standing as a mediator.

Meeting with top administration leaders later in the morning, Kissinger found them skeptical about Israel's reported emergency. Some saw it as an attempt by Israel to gain more weapons just before it turned the war around. CIA chief William Colby said that Israel had ammunition for at least two more weeks. (The ammunition shortage, which baffled Israel's own logistics officers, turned out to be largely a function of faulty management. Ammunition in the pipeline between the center of the country and the battlefronts had been lost track of by the logistical command. The only real shortage was in long-range artillery shells.) Secretary of defense James Schlesinger, unenthusiastic about rushing aid to Israel, said a distinction should be made between ensuring Israel's survival within its borders and helping it maintain its conquest of Arab lands. This view was shared by others at the meeting. Kissinger said that such calculations were now irrelevant. A defeat of American arms by Soviet arms wielded by Egypt and Syria would be a geopolitical disaster for America, he said. American assistance was essential, he believed, for Israel to pull itself together. Assurance of resupply from Washington would itself enable the Israelis to use their existing weaponry more freely.

Later in the day, Kissinger met with President Nixon to discuss the situation. The Watergate scandal was at its height and, in a separate episode, the resignation of Vice President Spiro Agnew was to be announced the next day. Nevertheless, the president proved as focused and decisive as ever in foreign affairs, welcoming the opportunity to deal with matters of state rather than his own sorry affairs. His decision on Israel's arms request was sweeping. Israel, he told Kissinger, was to be assured that its battlefield losses would be replaced. Everything on Israel's wish list was to be supplied except for laser-guided bombs, too new in the American inventory to be shared. Most importantly, all aircraft and tank losses were to be replaced. "The Israelis must not be allowed to lose," said Nixon. In his memoirs, Kissinger would describe the scandal-beset president as having "the composure of someone who had seen the worst and to whom there were no further terrors."

Anxious to avoid unduly angering America's friends in the Arab world, like Saudi Arabia, the administration sought to augment the El Al planes by arranging for private air charter companies to carry the supplies to Israel rather than American military aircraft. The companies, however, were unwilling to fly into a war zone or to risk an Arab boycott. Three days were spent in fruitless negotiations. On Saturday, October 13, Nixon ordered that supplies be flown directly to Israel in American military transports. The airlift, which got under way the next day, would soon come to be seen in Washington as serving America's own interests, apart from supporting an ally in trouble. The Soviets had begun an airlift to their Arab clients on October 10. It would not do, particularly after the failures of Vietnam, for the United States to be outdone in logistical muscle-flexing. Abandoning his former discreet approach, Kissinger now wanted the American airlift to be visible as a "demonstrative counter" to the Soviet airlift.

European nations, alert to the threats of an oil embargo beginning to be heard from the Arab world, refused to permit the planes to refuel on their territory. Portugal was persuaded to extend landing rights in the Azores only after Kissinger sent its prime minister a scathing letter over President Nixon's signature that "threatened to leave Portugal to its fate in a hostile world," in Kissinger's words. Even aircraft sent from American bases in Germany had to be routed through the Azores because of the refusal of European countries to permit overflights on the way to Israel. U.S. aircraft carriers were spaced across the Atlantic and Mediterranean as fueling stops for Skyhawks destined for the IAF. The American warplanes were escorted on the final leg from Crete by Israeli fighters.

The change in political mood in the Kremlin was almost a mirror image of that in Washington. A request by Egypt and Syria for arms was initially greeted with skepticism by Gromyko and other officials, who said the Arabs had sufficient weaponry and that additional supplies would only prolong the war. The military too was ambivalent, fearing that advanced weapons might fall into Israeli hands. Within two or three days, however, the Kremlin came to see its own prestige and interests inextricably tied to the side wielding Soviet arms. In addition, the surprising spirit of the Arab armies elicited a new respect. The sinking of a Soviet merchant ship by Israeli missile boats during an attack on a Syrian port and the bombing of the Soviet cultural center in Damascus infuriated the Soviets, who claimed that thirty Soviet citizens had been killed in the bombing. Some Soviet officials advocated retaliation, but Brezhnev ruled out direct Soviet involvement. Threats, however, were another matter. "The continuation of criminal acts by Israel will lead to grave consequences for Israel itself," the Kremlin warned.

Soviet technicians provided direct support for the Syrian military effort. They repaired tanks and equipment damaged on the battlefield, assembled fighter aircraft that arrived by sea, and drove tanks from ports to Damascus. On both the Golan and Sinai fronts, Soviet military personnel retrieved American equipment left on the battlefield by the Israelis for shipment to Moscow.

As the war continued, the superpowers became increasingly militant patrons. Even as Kissinger was urging Israel to recapture the territory it had lost, Marshal Kulikov, the Soviet chief of staff, was pressing Sadat to attack towards the Gidi and Mitla Passes. When the Soviets warned after the Damascus bombing that Israeli population centers would not remain immune, Kissinger let Dobrynin know that "any Soviet involvement would be met by American force." Both nations reinforced their Mediterranean fleets. The Soviets placed seven airborne divisions on alert, knowing that the move would be picked up by American intelligence. Ambassador Dobrynin hinted broadly to Kissinger over lunch that the alert was connected to the proximity of Israeli troops to Damascus.

Kissinger was willing to risk the collapse of détente if that was the price of maintaining America's position in the Middle East. "Once a great nation commits itself," he would write, "it must prevail." If Soviet proxies won the war, he argued, it would be Moscow that controlled postwar diplomacy in the region. He was looking ahead to a postwar American role as the one mediator acceptable to both sides. In a message to Hafez Ismail, he said, "The U.S. side will make a major effort . . . to assist in bringing a just and lasting peace to the Middle East."

Even as they were rushing armaments to their clients and thereby feeding the flames of war, the powers realized that they might be caught up in the conflagration if it continued unabated. Moscow was the first to acknowledge this by informing Washington in cumbersome diplomatic language on Wednesday morning, the fifth day of the war, that it was "ready not to block adoption of a cease-fire resolution" at the UN. The Soviets were less prepared than Kissinger to risk the collapse of détente. Kissinger found the timing awkward for a cease-fire because it would leave Israel the clear loser. He told Ambassador Dobrynin that the proposal was "constructive" but that the administration needed some time to think about it.

Consulting with Dinitz, he said he would stall a cease-fire resolution in the UN as long as he could but urged Israel to fight its way back quickly to the prewar lines or beyond them, at least on one front. After Israel recovered the Golan, Dinitz told Kissinger that the government had not yet decided whether to cross the cease-fire line. "Why don't you?" was the response reported back to Tel Aviv.

"Our aim was to slow down diplomacy without appearing obstructionist," Kissinger would write in his memoirs, "to urge a speedup of military operations without seeming to intervene, and then to force a cease-fire before . . . impatience . . . or unforeseeable events could rip the whole finely spun fabric to smithereens."

This possibility was also heavy on Moscow's mind. Fearful of being drawn into a clash with the United States or of seeing its Arab clients suddenly collapse, Moscow had since the beginning of the war been encouraging Sadat to accept a cease-fire, even as arms shipments were stepped up. But the Egyptian leader had no intention of halting the war. His army was solidly entrenched in Sinai and the Israelis were unable to budge it. The vaunted Israeli air force was helpless before his SAMs and their armored forces had been stopped dead by his antitank weapons. It was now a war of attrition in which numbers would tell.

Twenty-seven

ISRAEL SEEKS
A CEASE-FIRE

For the first time since the telephone woke him on Yom Kippur morning eighty-three hours before, General Elazar lay down to nap Tuesday afternoon on a cot in his office. Until now he had been getting by on adrenaline and on catnaps during helicopter flights to and from the fronts. When he woke three hours later, it was to an unpleasant task—displacing Gonen as head of Southern Command. He discussed the matter with Dayan after asking everyone else to clear the room. Gonen, he said, was an able field commander but could not look beyond the battle in progress and prepare for the next day's battle. In addition, he was totally unable to control Sharon. This day, in defiance of explicit orders, Sharon had sent his division forward again in a series of skirmishes. Fifty of his tanks had been hit, eighteen of them left behind in enemy territory beyond the reach of repair teams. The division had actually reached the canal, said Elazar—a reference to the reconnaissance probe sent by Amnon Reshef.

"What does Arik want there?" asked Dayan.

"What does he want? He wants to cross."

"Cross how? How is he going to cross?" Israeli bridging equipment was still well to the rear and the prospects of capturing an Egyptian bridge were slight.

Sharon wanted this very night to attack the Chinese Farm, held by an Egyptian infantry division, and cross the canal before dawn, said Elazar. "It borders on madness. I'm being sucked into a reckless adventure, a gamble I can't afford to risk." Dayan chuckled at Sharon's audacity but agreed that such insubordination could not be tolerated. During their visit to Southern Command the night before, he said, he had looked over at Sharon and wondered what was going on in his head. "He would be asking himself," said Dayan, " 'What will I get out of this business? That I should remain here in a blocking position? Together with Kalman [Magen], Albert [Mendler]? Gorodish? What about Arik moving up to the canal and putting things in order? So, let's go. If we succeed, great. If we don't, so the Jewish people have lost two hundred tanks but Arik will have made a Rommel-type breakthrough.' He really thinks this is the way to go. He has a personal problem and it's called Ariel Sharon. It won't do for him to be sitting in a bunker like other commanders." This acerbic insight came from Sharon's major supporter— perhaps sole supporter—in the high command. "All this isn't to say that he isn't making a contribution," Dayan added. The minister wholeheartedly accepted Elazar's suggestion that Bar-Lev take over Southern Command and that Gonen be moved sideways, not down. Dismissal would be an acknowledgment of command failure and a blow to morale. Bar-Lev would be posted "alongside" Gonen, rather than in his stead, but it would be made clear at Southern Command headquarters that Bar-Lev gave the orders.

The raspy blare of radio sets and the shouts of staff officers trying to make themselves heard provided appropriate aural accompaniment to the sense of disorder and tension prevailing in Southern Command headquarters. General Gonen sat at a long table filled with military radios and telephones. The front commander was seething at Sharon's disobedience in sending his tanks forward. From time to time he would throw something to vent his frustration.

But paratroop brigade commander Danny Matt, who arrived at Umm Hashiba during the day, was surprised to receive a fatherly embrace from Gonen. Colonel Matt's reserve brigade had been designated to seize the bridgehead in any canal crossing. Gonen said he had a special mission for him before then.

Leading him to a wall map, Gonen pointed at the area code-named Missouri and the adjacent Chinese Farm. Information was sketchy about the Egyptian presence there. Gonen wanted Matt to send out "silent patrols" this night consisting of officers to determine the Egyptian positions. The phrase "silent patrol"—scouting rather than fighting—struck Matt as something out of the First World War. On the basis of what the patrols found, said

Gonen, Matt would attack the next night with his entire brigade. Using the paratroopers would permit Gonen to keep up pressure on the Egyptians while obeying Elazar's injunction against further erosion of tank forces.

Gonen radioed to Sharon and informed him that his bearded friend had arrived. Sharon understood that he meant Matt. Continuing to use elliptical language to confound Egyptian radio monitors, Gonen hinted at the mission he had asked Matt to carry out in Sharon's sector. Sharon's voice came booming out of the loudspeaker. "Do you know what you're talking about? There are ten thousand Egyptian soldiers there and at least one hundred tanks." Gonen dropped the idea.

Gonen did not attempt to hide his dismay when Elazar called to inform him of his changed status. Had he run things badly? Gonen asked plaintively. "Not badly," said Elazar, anxious to minimize the pain, "but we're mobilizing all our talent so that things will go even better." Bar-Lev, he pointed out, was a former chief of staff who outranked Gonen, so it would be no disgrace to serve under him. Gonen would retain his title, O/C Southern Command. The public announcement would simply say that Bar-Lev was assuming special duties as representative of the chief of staff and that this assignment was presently bringing him down to the southern front. "But he is the commander," Elazar made clear.

Bar-Lev's visit to Northern Command on Sunday had been unofficial and he had retained his civilian status, even though he had made the key recommendation to have Moussa Peled's division attack from the south. But he was now formally mobilized so that he could exercise command in Sinai. This meant he had to give up his ministerial portfolio since the law did not permit a serving officer to be a member of the cabinet. Visiting the Pit in his army uniform before heading south Wednesday morning, October 10, he was told by Elazar that his first task would be to assess the situation and recommend a course of action. Sending his childhood friend to take command of the most problematic front, Elazar felt his own load measurably lightened. If Sharon refused to obey orders, Elazar told Bar-Lev, he should be dismissed and Gonen named in his place as division commander.

Arriving at Umm Hashiba, Bar-Lev closeted himself with Gonen and made sure that the front commander understood that he, Bar-Lev, held ultimate command despite his amorphous title. "If we look around it seems I'm the only one here who is a former chief of staff," he said. "So to make life easier for everyone, let's agree that I'm in command." To soften the blow, he noted that Elazar, who had been his subordinate, was now his, Bar-Lev's, commander. For that matter, Motti Hod was serving under his former deputy,

Benny Peled, and Sharon himself was now serving under Gonen, who had once served under him.

Gonen was not mollified. "I've got my own private chief of staff," he said sardonically. As soon as the war was over, he said, he would quit the army. In a telephone conversation with Elazar later in the day, Bar-Lev said Gonen had accepted the new arrangement, albeit "with a kvetch."

After spending much of the day in intensive reorganization of his headquarters, Bar-Lev announced that he was going to sleep. "A tired general is a dumb general," he told his staff. "Wake me only if Arik makes trouble."

When he woke three hours later, Sharon was waiting for him. The replacement of Gonen by Bar-Lev was not glad tidings for Sharon. The two men had not gotten along when Bar-Lev was chief of staff and it required an effort for both to remain civil in their current incarnation. The relationship closely paralleled that of Shazly and Ismail. Following rejection of his plea the day before for a canal crossing, Sharon had requested permission to attack the Third Army bridgehead on the Sinai bank. He had flown up with his brigade commanders to try to persuade Gonen. When Gonen deferred to Bar-Lev, Sharon waited for him to waken. Bar-Lev heard him out and then asked Sharon's brigade commanders what they thought. They disagreed with Sharon. Reshef said they had to avoid further head-on attacks and find a better way to throw the Egyptians off balance—like crossing the canal. Haim Erez agreed. So did Bar-Lev. Sharon's relations with Gonen had become strained almost to the breaking point since the war started. His relations with Bar-Lev would not be any happier.

Bar-Lev's arrival was for Colonel Ben-Ari an act of grace. Discussions at headquarters were now calm and decisions carefully calculated. No less important, there was now effective control of the forces in the field, instead of organizational chaos. Each division was assigned a separate section of the war room with its own maps, logbook, and staff for follow-up and control. Gonen himself would settle down and perform competently as chief of staff to Bar-Lev. A visitor to Southern Command headquarters in Bar-Lev's absence might have thought that Gonen was still in charge. But his orders now were within a framework fixed by Bar-Lev. At the personal level, Gonen remained abusive but would no longer throw things or dismiss officers at whim.

At 8 P.M. the division commanders gathered at front headquarters for a review with Bar-Lev of the options. Almost all had already changed their minds about the best course of action more than once since the battle started. They would do so again as conditions on the ground changed and their own perceptions of Israeli and Egyptian stamina shifted. Sharon repeated his call for a divisional attack against the Third Army bridgehead. Adan suggested that one brigade be committed to such an operation. Mendler proposed crossing the canal south of the Bitter Lake. Others favored the capture of Port Said.

General Tal was known to vigorously oppose a crossing of the canal as too risky and was now advocating instead elimination of the Egyptian bridgehead in Sinai. Other options included an amphibious operation across the Gulf of Suez or pulling back into Sinai to lure the Egyptians out from under their SAM umbrella. Gonen and Ben-Ari proposed that no offensive action at all be undertaken until Southern Command had built up its strength. Gonen, no longer dismissive of the Egyptians, said the command had only six hundred tanks and needed one thousand for a major assault.

It was the latter approach that Bar-Lev adopted. The Egyptians, he believed, would continue to attack and erode their forces. Meanwhile, Southern Command would build its strength, gather intelligence, and prepare detailed offensive plans.

A parallel debate was going on this Wednesday evening in Tel Aviv, where Elazar was wrestling with monumental decisions. For the first time, he was showing signs of fatigue and his optimism was in retreat. On the northern front, the troops had that morning pushed the Syrians out of the Golan. But during his visit to Northern Command, Elazar had been disappointed to learn that probes across the cease-fire line had met stiff resistance. He did not think it would be possible to push the Syrians back from the line with the forces available. As for the southern front, "every day we're doing the same thing, killing a lot of Egyptians and losing a bit of territory." Within five days, he said, the army might be pushed back deep into Sinai.

The logic of events was leading Elazar to a far-reaching conclusion: Israel could not win this war and must prepare instead for the next one. "I'm in a black mood if we're not heading for a cease-fire," he said to Dayan when the two conversed in the Pit. "I'm only thinking out loud, and it may well be that I exaggerate. But I'm saying what I think right now. The goal is to reach a cease-fire in place. Things won't get better than they are now. Therefore we need a cease-fire so that we can rebuild the army." The new army Elazar was contemplating would be twice as big and would have thought through the strategic and tactical implications of the current war.

In a reversal of roles, it was Dayan who took an optimistic tone. The tide was turning in Israel's favor in the north, he said, and would do so in the south as well as long as the IDF did not try to do what Sharon had earlier advocated—cross the canal. (Dayan did, however, favor crossing it on a limited scale to capture Port Said.) If the Egyptians tried to advance out of their present bridgehead, they would be trounced, he said. In that case, countered Elazar, the Egyptians would stay put and engage in a costly war of attrition.

"Excuse me, Dado, but that's not the model," said Dayan. "If the Egyptians start a war of attrition, we send the air force on deep penetration raids. The Egyptians won't be able to conduct a war of attrition." This is what had happened during the War of Attrition in 1969–70 when deep raids led to Egyptian acquiescence to a cease-fire. The Scuds would now give the Egyptians the ability to retaliate if the Soviets handed over operational control to them, but Dayan was prepared to risk it. He suggested putting Egyptian economic targets even now on the air force target list.

When Dayan left the Pit, one of Elazar's staff said the defense minister had been on an "up." Said Elazar: "His downs are too low and his ups are too high." Nevertheless, within a few hours, Elazar would come out of his own down and recommend to the government that Northern Command cross the cease-fire line into Syria. There was still a day or two to decide about the Sinai front.

Following the failed counterattack of Monday, the ground war in Sinai had tapered off. The Egyptians skirmished vigorously eastward every day, making incremental gains up to points on the Artillery Road. But there was no attempt to push towards the Sinai passes. Both sides were waiting for the other to stage a major attack. The main Egyptian effort went into consolidating their bridgehead, now five to six miles deep. On the Israeli side, tanks knocked out in the first days of fighting were repaired and most equipment shortages remedied.

Elazar had decided on the war's second day to relieve Southern Command of responsibility for South Sinai so that it could focus on the canal front. Gen. Yeshayahu Gavish (res.), who headed Southern Command in the Six Day War, was asked to assume command of the southern area. Gavish, who had found Gonen uninterested when he offered his services, now had an independent command which stretched for two hundred miles to Sharm el-Sheikh, at the southern tip of the peninsula. The area included the mountain regarded by tradition as Mount Sinai, where Moses had received the Ten Commandments. Thou Shalt Not Kill had been suspended for the duration of the war, but the mountain was too remote from the battlefield to serve even as an observation post.

To assemble a staff, Gavish rounded up several neighbors in his Tel Aviv suburb, where many retired officers lived. Flying down to Sharm el-Sheikh, he first took stock of his assets. To defend the vast area, he had only two battalions of second-line troops, a score of old tanks, a battery of heavy mortars, and two understrength battalions of paratroopers.

Hundreds of Egyptian commandos had been landed in South Sinai by helicopters on the first day of the war, scattering into the mountainous areas just inland from the coast. The downing of many helicopters had thrown their operational plans out of kilter and demoralized the survivors. Thanks to the Israeli navy, supplies and reinforcements had not crossed the Gulf. Gavish put two helicopters at the disposal of a paratroop force which hunted the surviving commandos down with the assistance of Bedouin trackers. Within three days almost all of the commandos had been killed (196) or captured (310), at the cost of two Israeli dead.

What worried Gavish most was the possibility that the Egyptians would send armored forces south from the Third Army bridgehead. The only place he had a chance of stopping them was at Abu Rodeis, fifty miles from the canal, where a narrow passage between the mountains and the gulf created a natural defensive position. The paratroopers were ordered to dig in there with antitank weapons. Gavish ordered the evacuation of a small naval base and a Hawk antiaircraft battery at Abu Zneima, halfway between the canal and Abu Rodeis.

Air force commander Peled protested the pullback of the Hawks, which were under control of the air force, and an angry-sounding Dayan was soon on the phone to Gavish. Did you order the evacuation of Abu Zneima? he asked. Gavish said he had. Dayan said he was flying down to Sharm to talk with him. Three hours later, a light plane landed at the Sharm air base. The pilot was General Peled himself, taking a break from the underground war room. The one passenger was Dayan. On what authority, he demanded of Gavish, did you order a retreat? Gavish explained his strategy on a wall map. He was not retreating; he was falling back in order to be able to fight on his own terms. Dayan studied the map with his one good eye and, with no further ado, turned back to the plane. Gavish's strategy not only made sense; it was a microcosm of what could have been done on the Suez battlefront if the army had pulled back from the canal.

Peled had designated a squadron of Super-Mystères to attack the Egyptians if they ventured down the Gulf of Suez coast beyond the SAM umbrella. A few hours after Dayan's visit to Gavish, an Egyptian infantry brigade supported by tanks peeled off from the Suez Canal front and started towards Abu Rodeis, just as Gavish feared and the air force hoped. The brigade had orders to move only at night, but its commander chose to get a head start several hours before sunset. It was the IAF's first chance to get at enemy ground forces without worrying about SAMs. Warplanes swooped in and knocked out dozens of vehicles, including tanks. The remnants scuttled back north. It was a pointed reminder to Shazly of the dangers of abandoning the missile umbrella.

The Egyptians were having more success at the other end of the battlefront, where a tenacious commando unit had been blocking the road to Budapest since the first night of the war. On Wednesday, an Israeli paratroop battalion under Lt. Col. Yossi Yoffe, cousin of tanker Amir Yoffe, was ordered to break through to the beleaguered fort. Moving forward after calling down artillery, they found that the Egyptians had pulled back through the lagoon. Lt. Shaul Moses, the tank officer who had driven off the attack on Budapest Yom Kippur afternoon, could see them moving through chest-high water about half a mile away, holding their weapons over their heads. Since they were not attacking the outpost, he did not expend his scarce ammunition on them.

With the road opened, a paratroop unit arrived to replace the Jerusalem Brigade reservists commanded by Motti Ashkenazi. Ashkenazi's four-month-old German shepherd, which he had taken with him to reserve duty, had not only survived but contributed to the post's defense. He could hear the sound of outgoing Egyptian artillery and mortar fire before the soldiers could, and his barking had provided them timely warning to take cover.

After dark, the new unit's sentries at Budapest reported hearing noises. Flares were sent up and the sentries said they could see figures moving outside the fence. The outpost commander called for artillery fire. Moses, who had remained at Budapest with his two tanks, thought that the young conscript soldiers were jumpy or just spoiling for a fight. The commander of his other tank, however, said he also thought he saw something outside the front gate. "All right," said Moses. "Fire." After the crack of the gun, there was silence for a few moments and then an RPG was fired back from the darkness. Artillery fire was brought in tight around the outpost. With first light, Moses saw eight pairs of Egyptians lying dead outside the fort—RPG teams caught by the shelling, the closest only twenty yards from the gateway.

In the morning, a sentry on the western side of the fort reported tanks advancing from the direction of Port Fuad. Almost out of armor-piercing shells, Moses sent the two tank crews into an ammunition bunker to get some. He was alone in his tank when an Egyptian half-track swung past the front gate. Behind it were three others. The vehicles, not waiting for their tank escort, had raced to the fort and come around the narrow strand between the fort and the sea to the gateway on the eastern side of Budapest. The Egyptian half-tracks unloaded infantrymen who passed through holes blasted in the fence by artillery. Moses called the garrison commander on the radio. "Egyptians inside the fort. Get your men out." The paratroopers scrambled out of the bunker and engaged the Egyptians with grenades and small arms. Moses's crewmen, meanwhile, rushed back with shells. The tanks destroyed the four half-tracks and joined in the fire on the intruders. Examining the body-strewn landscape after the battle, Moses deduced that the task of the RPG teams, which had come via the lagoon, had been to eliminate the two tanks at first light, before the infantry arrived. The well-planned attack had been thwarted by the alertness of the garrison and the precision of the artillery.

Four days later, a commando force would filter back through the lagoon and ambush an Israeli convoy heading for Budapest, setting several half-tracks afire. Yoffe's paratroopers were summoned back. This time the Egyptians did battle before pulling back, leaving forty-five bodies behind. Others were killed as artillery fire followed them into the lagoon.

In a crisis of confidence that overtook the air force after the failure of Dougman, squadrons increasingly adopted their own tactics rather than rely blindly on directives from air force headquarters. A Phantom squadron leader addressing his pilots said that in the uncertain new circumstances flight leaders should rely on their own good sense in deciding how to carry out their assigned missions. Some squadrons employed low-level attacks. Others preferred to attack from high altitude and risk the SAMs—which they could attempt to evade—rather than run the murderous gauntlet of conventional antiaircraft fire. The powerful Phantoms, by turning on their afterburners, had a better chance of outmaneuvering missiles than did the Skyhawks. Each dodge, however, slowed the planes down, and if the first few missiles missed, later ones often didn't. IAF improvisations at squadron level in response to the SAM threat were a mirror image of the way tank battalions were independently improvising methods for dealing with the Saggers.

As the fighting raged in Sinai and on the Syrian front and skeleton forces deployed opposite Jordan, the high command was alert to the possibility of other fronts opening up, as well. Forty Katyusha rockets fired Tuesday by

Palestinian guerrillas from Lebanese territory at villages on Israel's northern border marked the apparent opening of one. Elazar requested permission to send forces into Lebanon to confront the Palestinians, but Dayan refused to siphon off strength from the Syrian front. The threat tapered off to border skirmishes in which twenty-three Palestinians would be killed. A small number of Israeli civilians on the border would be wounded by shelling.

Another concern was that the Palestinians of the occupied West Bank and Gaza Strip might rise up. Small forces, particularly border police, were assigned to deal with such an eventuality, but there were no incidents. Israel's own Arabs demonstrated remarkable loyalty to the state, given their natural sympathy for their fellow Arabs across the border. A reporter driving past the Arab city of Nazareth found Arab women at the main road intersection handing out soft drinks and cakes to soldiers on their way to the Golan front just like Jewish women were doing on roadsides around the country. Scores of Arab men volunteered for farm work at kibbutzim where the adult males were almost all on the battlefronts, and Arabs donated blood for the war wounded. The mayors of Arab Nazareth and neighboring Jewish Upper Nazareth maintained daily telephone contact to deal with emergencies arising from the war situation. Such cooperation would succumb in a few years to rising tensions stemming from the Israeli-Palestinian confrontation.

Parallel to Israel's grinding land and air battles, a war was being fought at sea that in its brilliance, though not its impact, matched the air force strike that wiped out the Arab air forces in the opening hours of the Six Day War. On the first night of the war, missile boat squadron commander Michael Barkai led five boats north to the Syrian coast. Their objective, he told his captains, was to draw Syrian missile boats out of their main harbor, Latakia. "If they don't come out," he said, "I mean to sail into the harbor and destroy them. We're going to go in close enough to heave our docking lines if we have to."

The Israeli craft sank a torpedo boat and minesweeper on picket duty off the Syrian port. The Syrian vessels had reported the approach of the Israeli vessels before going down, and three Syrian missile boats emerged to challenge them. The range of the Soviets' Styx missile, thirty miles, was twice that of the Israeli Gabriel. Barkai's boats switched on their antimissile electronic umbrella and raced at full speed towards the Syrian vessels in the first duel of missile boats in naval history. At naval headquarters, Admiral Telem listened tensely as Barkai reported enemy missiles launched. It was two minutes before the Styx completed their flight and Barkai was heard again. "They missed." It was now the turn of the Israeli boats as the Syrian boats ran for harbor. The volley of Gabriels sank two; to avoid the same fate, the captain of the third boat deliberately ran it onto a beach, where it was destroyed by gunfire.

The success was repeated two nights later off the Egyptian coast. Three pairs of Israeli missile boats and two pairs of Egyptian missile boats charged towards each other. The Egyptians fired at maximum range and kept coming, firing three more salvos while still out of range of the Gabriels. On the Israeli boats, crewmen on deck could see red balls of fire descending in their direction. The Israeli electronic devices sent out false images, and the missiles, with their half-ton warheads, exploded in the sea, sending up huge geysers. With the last salvo, the Egyptian boats turned and ran for Alexandria. The faster Israeli boats closed to Gabriel range and sank three of them.

From this point on, neither the Egyptian nor the Syrian fleets, both far larger than Israel's, would venture beyond the mouth of their harbors, leaving Israel's Mediterranean coastline unthreatened and its vital sea routes open. The Egyptians succeeded in closing off maritime access to Eilat by blockading the Straits of Bab el-Mandeb between the Horn of Africa and the Arabian Peninsula, more than 1,000 miles to the south.

Meanwhile, a different kind of naval war was being waged in the Gulf of Suez and Red Sea—old-fashioned cut-and-thrust raids by patrol boats and naval commandos. A week into the war, intelligence reported that the Egyptians were again building up a fleet of fishing boats—this time at Ras Arib, midway on the Gulf shore—for a commando landing in South Sinai. Five Israeli patrol boats commanded by Lt. Commander Ami Ayalon entered the anchorage after darkness. When they withdrew, they left behind nineteen sunk or sinking fishing boats loaded with supplies and ammunition.

The Israeli high command had since the beginning of the war contemplated sending an armored brigade westward across the gulf on LSTs which were stationed at Sharm el-Sheikh. The option, however, was endangered by the presence of two Egyptian missile boats based at Ardaka, on the Red Sea coast.

SAM batteries at Ardaka protected the boats from Israeli aircraft, but Captain Almog, commanding naval forces in South Sinai, believed that naval commandos could do the job. It would mean crossing sixty miles of rough waters in rubber boats at night and locating the anchorage on the dark coast using only simple navigational devices. Once they reached Ardaka, the commandos would have to penetrate a narrow, two-mile-long channel before reaching the boat anchorage.

Lt. Commander Gadi Kroll, a burly commando veteran, volunteered for the mission. He set out in late afternoon with two boats, each with two frog-men and two backups. After a rough six-hour crossing, the boats reached Ardaka but found a patrol boat barring the way halfway up the channel. Kroll returned to base but two nights later tried again. This time the channel was unguarded. Swimming underwater, he and his partner found one missile boat in the anchorage and attached their mines. The second frogman team failed to locate the other missile boat and came under fire. Kroll, who had already swum back with his partner to their boat, dashed back with it to res-cue them. They had reached open waters when the missile boat blew up.

In naval warfare, at least, Israel was demonstrating its old military mas-tery.

Twenty-eight

DECISION TO CROSS

CLOSE TO MIDNIGHT THURSDAY, OCTOBER 11, after another briefing to the cabinet and before another helicopter flight to the front, the unrelenting stress of running two wars simultaneously for six days caught up with Elazar. He was discussing the next day's battle plans with two generals and leafing through a batch of fresh reports on his desk when he turned pale and seemed about to faint. Alarmed aides brought him something to drink. "I don't want any pills," he hastily said. He would need his wits for a major decision that had to be made in the coming hours.

Southern Command had been marking time since Tuesday as Northern Command drove the Syrians back across the Purple Line. It was time now to decide about the next step in Sinai. Instinct was irrelevant in matters as ramified as this and there was no textbook solution. But with an orderly breakdown of the issues and a readiness to follow logic wherever it led, Elazar would work his way through the problem. As with Wednesday's decision to cross the cease-fire line in the north, the process would involve a daylong exercise in thinking aloud and challenging his peers to react. In the end, after sharp changes in position, the way forward would emerge.

The process began in the early hours of Friday morning, October 12, at a meeting of Elazar and senior officers. Bar-Lev was due up from Sinai in a few hours to present the recommendations he had arrived at after consultation with the generals on the southern front. Elazar wanted to informally examine the underlying factors before then.

Zeira opened the discussion by noting that the UN Security Council was expected to pass a cease-fire resolution within forty-eight hours. He and Benny Peled believed that the IDF should move swiftly to cross the canal before then. "You don't have to convince me that we have to attack by tomorrow night," said Elazar. "The question is what happens afterwards."

Expanding on the motif he had sounded in his talk with Dayan two days before, Elazar made it clear that his goal was no longer victory but a stable cease-fire that would permit Israel to rebuild its armed forces. His hope was for a cease-fire that would go into effect on Monday, three days hence, leaving the IDF just enough time for a final lunge that would help restore the strategic balance.

Defeating Egypt was no longer a near-term option, said Elazar. This was a painful admission for the commander of an army which until a few days before had been considered unbeatable by any combination of armies in the Middle East—an assumption he himself heartily shared. It was to Elazar's credit that he was not reduced to denial or paralysis by this startling turn of events. He accepted the new reality as a given and attempted to formulate a rational response.

Elazar was convinced that Sadat would not accept a cease-fire unless shaken by some dramatic military move, like Israel's crossing of the canal. But he was not sure that even a crossing would do it. Dayan in fact argued that the Egyptians would never agree to a cease-fire if Israel gained a foothold on the west bank, with Cairo no longer protected by the waterway. There was also the possibility that if the IDF did cross the canal and achieved a cease-fire, the situation would deteriorate swiftly into a war of attrition. In that event, the army would find itself in a dangerously vulnerable deployment with thin extended lines on both sides of the canal.

Despite these concerns, Elazar inclined towards a canal crossing because he could think of no other possibility, however remote, of jarring Sadat into a cease-fire. "I would be happy, and you don't know how happy, if you have any better ideas," he said to the officers.

They didn't. Peled expressed confidence that a crossing would bring about a swift Egyptian collapse. Elazar did not share that optimism. Northern Command had thrown all it had at the Syrians and made good progress at first, but its offensive had run out of steam. The army in the north would not be getting appreciably closer to Damascus and there was little hope that the Syrians would be prodded into requesting a cease-fire. Elazar saw no reason to believe it would be much different on the Egyptian front even though he expected the crossing itself to succeed. Nevertheless, he saw no better alternative.

If a crossing, then where? Two formidable armored divisions remained on the other side of the canal, as well as other forces. Together they fielded twice as many tanks as Israel could send across. Such odds were no longer dismissed as irrelevant.

A possible solution lay in the Egyptian war plans in Israel's possession. Having them had not helped the IDF stave off the surprise Egyptian crossing and had proved useless once the war began imposing its own dynamic. But it might help now. According to the plan's "Phase Two," the two armored divisions were to be dispatched across the canal after the bridgehead was secured and would attack towards the Sinai passes. Unknown to the Israelis, this plan had been rendered irrelevant by Shazly's more limited Badr plan, but events were about to make it relevant again.

It was best to await the Egyptian attack, the generals agreed. For one thing, it would avoid having the Israeli crossing contested on the west bank by the armored divisions. For another, it would permit the IDF to engage the Egyptian armor inside Sinai from defensive positions of its own choosing. If the armored divisions crossed into Sinai this day, Friday, or even the next day, there would still be time to defeat them and cross to the west bank before the anticipated cease-fire came into effect.

But would the armored divisions cross? According to the Egyptian plan, they were to have crossed already, but it had not happened yet and intelligence was picking up no signs of movement. Elazar asked the air force to stop bombing the bridges in case they did intend to cross. If, however, they remained on the west bank, the IDF must undertake "a maximal, hazardous offensive" by tomorrow night, he said.

Three crossing proposals drawn up before the war were on the table: a limited one aimed at seizing Port Said; a two-divisional attack at Deversoir, opposite Fort Matsmed in the central sector; and a split attack by two divisions—one at Kantara in the northern sector and one at Deversoir.

Zeira, whose operational insights during the war would prove far more realistic than his intelligence assessments before the war, supported a two-divisional crossing at Deversoir, which would necessitate breaking through to the canal only at one point. The Israeli forces, he said, would probably come up against the soft underbelly of the Egyptian army—supply depots, artillery batteries, missile sites. The crossing offered a chance of cutting off much of the Egyptian army in Sinai by severing its supply lines.

A Deversoir crossing was opposed by others who noted that SAM missiles in the central sector would prevent air support. The air force enjoyed open skies to the north, where it had knocked out the Port Said SAM batteries. General Tal said an attack in the Deversoir sector was more likely to encounter an armored fist than a soft underbelly. Elazar himself inclined towards a major attack at Deversoir because he doubted that a lesser attack would be sufficient to make Sadat seek a cease-fire. But he suspended judgment until Bar-Lev had had his say.

The newly appointed southern commander arrived at 9:30 A.M. The tense atmosphere he found in the Pit reflected the fateful nature of the decision they were being asked to make. Bar-Lev had come to the same conclusion as Elazar. Only a canal crossing, he believed, had a chance of salvaging something from the war. He had arrived at this by a process of elimination. It was possible to destroy the entrenched Egyptian bridgeheads in Sinai, but the IDF would exhaust its strength doing so. Standing still and not attacking was a futile option that would keep the entire army mobilized indefinitely. The only viable choice was an attack across the canal that would throw the Egyptians off balance and exploit Israeli mobility. He favored sending two divisions—with about 300 to 350 tanks, at current strength—across the canal at Deversoir, where their left flank during the crossing would be protected by the Bitter Lake. "Regretfully," he said to Elazar, "I don't have another solution."

Tal protested that Bar-Lev's proposal to plunge through the center of the Egyptian line rested dangerously on improvisation. It was not at all certain that the bridging equipment could be brought safely to the canal bank through the Egyptian lines. Even if the crossing was successful, the Israeli tanks on the west bank could find themselves facing overwhelming odds without the protective barrier of the canal itself. If the crossing was inconclusive, the army would have to remain fully mobilized and would be subject to constant attrition. Bar-Lev said he agreed with Tal's assessment. "But I see no alternative."

The dominant view favored a crossing. But a crossing in itself would not resolve Elazar's dilemma. The key element in his calculations was the assumption that a crossing would induce a cease-fire. This was basically a political assessment and he wanted the political level to take responsibility for the final decision. Dayan, who was visiting Northern Command, had told Elazar to bring the matter before the inner cabinet himself if he, Dayan, had not yet returned. Elazar declined that option because he wanted the defense minister to be involved in the decision. At the chief of staff's insistence, Dayan flew back from Northern Command to join the meeting in late morning. Elazar reviewed for him the discussion, which had been going on for several hours now. The major objective of a crossing, he said, was to achieve a cease-fire in order to rebuild the army "for a hundred years." This could not be done in conditions of war, with hundreds of thousands of men under arms. Did Dayan believe that a crossing would make a cease-fire more likely? he asked. Or did he not?

Dayan was uncomfortable with the chief of staff's formulation. It was for Elazar to decide, he said, whether a crossing would be a good military move. If Elazar recommended it, Dayan would support it in the cabinet. But the minister thought a crossing made the possibility of Egypt accepting a cease-fire less likely rather than more likely. The best way of achieving a cease-fire, he said, was to order Northern Command to advance "at all costs" to within artillery range of Damascus. That would prompt the Soviet Union to move for a cease-fire. Dayan's line appeared to contradict the cancellation on Sunday of the planned shelling of Damascus by Aldo Zohar's two guns. Benny Peled said the air force could easily bomb Damascus. "There's a difference," said Dayan. "They know that planes don't conquer [territory]." Artillery, on the other hand, suggested an army at the gates.

In the middle of the discussion, the defense minister rose and said that he was going to report to Mrs. Meir. Elazar was upset at Dayan's sudden departure since no decision had yet been made. The minister left behind his military aide-de-camp, Gen. Yehoshua Raviv. Angry at what he took to be Dayan's evasiveness on this central issue, Elazar told Raviv to convey to him that he wanted the matter resolved this day. "This is a decision of tremendous military-political importance," he said, "and the chief of staff will do whatever the defense minister decides." Elazar proposed through Raviv that the matter be put to the inner cabinet. If the consensus was that a cease-fire was improbable, he would not recommend crossing the canal. If the cabinet believed a cease-fire was possible, he would formulate a battle plan. "I want clearance from the political echelon today."

The chief of staff's blunt message brought swift results—an invitation to a meeting at 2:30 P.M. in Golda Meir's office.

For General Shazly too, this was a day for excruciating decisions. The satisfaction he had permitted himself at the way the war was going had been badly jarred Thursday when he returned to Center Ten from a tour of the front. He had found his divisions well dug in and officers and men confident they could meet anything the Israelis could muster. The armed forces had given Sadat exactly what he had asked for, a firm foothold from which he could begin leveraging Israel out of the rest of Sinai through political means. A message was waiting in the operations room for Shazly from war minister Ismail asking him to stop by. The question put by Ismail was one Shazly had been dreading—could the army continue eastward to the passes?

A major reason the Badr plan had succeeded was that it did not permit the army to go beyond the protective umbrella of the SAMs. The destruction of the brigade that had proceeded down the Gulf of Suez shore demonstrated what could happen when caution was abandoned. Shazly vigorously objected to the proposal and Ismail did not press the point. By Friday morning, however, the suggestion had become an order. "It's a political decision," said the war minister. "We must develop our attack by tomorrow morning."

The decision had been made by Sadat in response to a plea by Assad. The Syrian leader had sent an emissary to ask him to attack in order to ease Israeli pressure on Damascus. Although Sadat had thus far declined to honor his prewar pledge to attack towards the passes, he could ignore Assad no longer.

The IDF counterattack in the north had failed to force Syria out of the war, but it had succeeded strategically in an unexpected way by forcing Assad to call on Egypt for help. In responding, Sadat would provide Israel with what it was waiting for—a major tank battle.

The Egyptians had until now successfully tailored Soviet doctrine to their own needs. Soviet advisers had helped draw up the initial plan for a canal crossing and a drive to the passes. In downsizing this plan to Badr, the Egyptians showed a healthy respect for Israeli capabilities and awareness of their own limitations. They had built compact bridgeheads just inland of the canal and secured them with mines and antitank weapons. This cautious approach, which included the infusion of Saggers and RPGs to frontline units in numbers well beyond what Soviet doctrine called for, had served them well. Soviet doctrine also called for quick insertion of armored divisions to follow up a successful crossing of a water barrier with a powerful advance, but the Egyptian high command had until now avoided doing so. Against Shazly's better judgment, this caution was now to be abandoned.

When he passed the attack order on to the commanders of the Second and Third Armies, Generals Saad Mamoun and Abdel Muneim Wasel, both protested. Mamoun offered his resignation, which was rejected. Shazly summoned both generals to Cairo for a meeting with Ismail at 6 P.M. Friday. The war minister heard them out but was in no position to revoke Sadat's order. The most he could do was agree to Mamoun's request to postpone the attack until Sunday morning.

Not all Egyptian officers opposed an eastward drive. General Gamasy, chief of operations, had been pressing for such a move. He believed it vital to push the Israelis back to the passes while they were still off balance. As for the danger of advancing beyond SAM coverage, he argued that the proximity of the Egyptian and Israeli tank formations to each other in battle would make it difficult for Israeli pilots to distinguish between them. He also believed that the Egyptian air force could acquit itself reasonably well against the Israeli pilots. Meanwhile, SAM batteries could be shifted eastward into Sinai to extend the missile umbrella. When he put his case to Ismail earlier, Gamasy found the defense minister still influenced by the trauma of 1967. Voicing his concern over Israeli air power, Ismail had said, "We have to keep our armed forces intact." Now, however, Sadat had decided to advance eastward and there was nothing Ismail could do but obey and pray.

To the critical meeting of the inner cabinet in Tel Aviv Friday afternoon, October 12, Elazar brought Bar-Lev and members of the General Staff. Also present at the prime minister's invitation was Mossad chief Zvi Zamir. The inner cabinet itself consisted of Mrs. Meir, Dayan, and ministers Galili and Allon. Once more, Elazar reviewed the need for a cease-fire and said he wanted the government to determine whether a canal crossing might bring a cease-fire closer before he made his operational recommendation.

Bar-Lev spoke in optimistic terms of what a crossing could accomplish—the severing of supply lines to the Egyptian bridgeheads and the destruction of SAM missile batteries by ground forces. There were serious risks, he acknowledged, principally the possibility that the bridge link might be severed after forces had already crossed. He spoke to his former cabinet colleagues of the high spirits of the men on the front and of the superb quality of their officers. "Our boys are fighting, bless them, with cool heads, a dash of humor, without panic. And they're *fighting*." But continuation of the status quo would erode the army's strength, he said. He noted that while his own spirits had been uplifted at the front, ever since returning to Tel Aviv he felt himself sinking into the pervasive gloom.

Peled told the ministers that the air force was almost at its "red line," beyond which it would not have enough aircraft to provide ground support for a major attack. Therefore, he said, it was critical that a canal crossing be executed quickly while the air force could still participate. Peled would relate decades after the war that he lied to the cabinet about the red line in order to prod it into approving an immediate canal crossing. The air force strength he cited referred only to planes capable of providing ground support, which was about 80 percent of actual operational strength. Peled asked permission to create sonic booms over Cairo "so that when Sadat agrees to a cease-fire they won't butcher him in the presidential palace." (Permission was not granted.)

In the midst of the discussion, an aide entered the room and whispered to Mossad chief Zamir. He excused himself and the discussion marked time. When Zamir returned, he held a written message. It was a radioed report just received from an agent in Egypt informing the Mossad that Egyptian paratroop forces would attack the Mitla Pass and the Refidim base either tomorrow night, Saturday, October 13, or on Sunday. The message made no mention of the armored divisions, but according to the known Egyptian war plan, the insertion of paratroopers was prelude to the armor crossing.

The atmosphere in the room was suddenly electric. Elazar could not have hoped for better news. He had been prepared to send his forces across the canal Saturday night despite the high risk of battling for a bridgehead in the face of two armored divisions. Now, Zamir's report meant that the IDF would have a chance to first significantly erode Egyptian tank strength inside Sinai. Whatever traumas the Saggers and RPGs had inflicted, the IDF had not lost confidence in its ability to deal with enemy tanks. The cabinet agreed to put off a decision on an Israeli crossing until after the armored push had been dealt with. Elazar and his officers hastened back to the Pit, buoyed by the prospect of the upcoming Egyptian attack, which they saw changing the direction of the war.

An hour later, Shazly and his army commanders left their meeting with Ismail in Cairo with an identical assessment—the attack imposed on them would turn the war in Israel's favor. They would have been appalled had they been aware that the Israelis knew of the planned attack and were already preparing to meet it.

Although the Mossad was not part of the country's military structure, Zamir's warning was the second piece of information he had provided that would have a critical operational impact—the first being the all-important warning on Yom Kippur morning about the pending Arab attack.

After Elazar and the other generals had left, Dayan drew the cabinet's attention to the political dimension. Kissinger had been telling Ambassador Dinitz that he could not put off a cease-fire resolution in the UN much longer. The Soviets were pressing for it. Under no circumstances, said Dayan, should Israel request a cease-fire. But, he suggested, Ambassador Dinitz should be instructed to tell Kissinger that Israel was withdrawing its objections to a cease-fire. Dayan did not believe that Egypt would accept one at present—certainly not before it had launched Phase Two, the drive to the passes. But that would give time for the Israeli counterblow. In addition, withdrawing objections to a cease-fire would position Israel better for further arms requests to the United States by avoiding the appearance of recalcitrance. Dayan, who had been sitting on the fence regarding a canal crossing, was still ambivalent about it, but he looked forward to the upcoming clash of armor in Sinai. The IDF would prepare itself now for battle and the government would prepare the diplomatic context. The initiative on the Sinai front, which for the past eight days had lain with Egypt, was finally being seized by Israel.

Twenty-nine

STOUTHEARTED MEN

IT WAS QUIETER ALONG THE CANAL FRONT Saturday than it had been since the Egyptian crossing a week before but in both Cairo and Tel Aviv mindsets were being shaped this day that would determine the war's direction.

Sadat was wakened shortly before dawn and informed that the British ambassador had arrived with an urgent message. Kissinger had asked the British to submit a cease-fire resolution in the Security Council. He had been assured by Dobrynin that Sadat would welcome it. The British, dubious, asked their envoy to verify Egypt's position. Sadat rejected the proposal out of hand. There would be no cease-fire, he said, until Israel agreed to withdraw from all of Sinai.

Acceptance would have achieved for Sadat the goals he had set before the war—a firm Egyptian foothold in Sinai and international involvement in a peace process, thus sealing a brilliant Egyptian victory. But Sadat hoped now to do even better.

Egypt, he believed, was controlling the battlefield. The Israelis had not attempted to advance since Sharon's attacks on Tuesday while the Egyptians had been making small-scale pushes eastward towards the Artillery Road every day, with some success. SAM batteries were being sent across the bridges at night to extend the missile umbrella eastward towards the passes. Overall, Arab strength was steadily increasing as the Soviet airlift hit its stride and the Arab world dispatched reinforcements to the two battlefronts.

Israel's forces, on the other hand, were eroding every day and it was not receiving supplies from abroad except for what its small El Al fleet could carry. (The American airlift would not begin until the next day.) Israel's agreement to a cease-fire without regaining the canal was itself confirmation of its weakness.

Sadat's assessment was not far from Israel's own. Elazar's perception of Israel's weak hand was still the motivation for the planned crossing of the canal. But the looming tank battle in Sinai, regarded as certain now in the wake of the warning Zamir had received, held out for the first time the tangible prospect of a reversal of fortune, perhaps on a major scale. A large tank battle, which had eluded them so far, could significantly erode Egyptian strength. If it did, the Israeli crossing could be more than a desperate lunge aimed at persuading Sadat to stop the war. It could be the key to winning the war. This line of thought was not yet being articulated by Elazar but was beginning to work its way into his consciousness, as imperceptibly but inexorably as a tide turning.

Saturday, October 13, was Sergeant Nadeh's twenty-fourth birthday. The Egyptian soldier had survived a week of war, which was reason enough to celebrate. His unit was in Fort Botzer, midway on the Sinai shore of the Bitter Lake, from which the Israeli garrison had escaped Monday night. Nadeh and his comrades found it an amazing oasis—a veritable underground city with a trove of canned goods and water, toilets, pinups, and cigarettes. "The Jewish cigarettes are really good," he wrote in his diary. A birthday, like the war itself, was occasion for reflection—the kind common to young men gone to war. "I've achieved many things which I had thought impossible. I've reached the third year in humanities. Fate brought me to situations I could not have imagined. I used to be afraid and miserable. I became someone with strength. I tried to love and I passed through all the stages of love, from the pleasures of the flesh to real love, in which I failed. Now that I am in war I feel I need someone who would appreciate me."

Apart from Budapest, only one fort on the Bar-Lev line continued to hold out after Tuesday—Fort Mezakh at the southernmost end of the line. The garrison had been augmented by the crews of several disabled tanks. Egyptian commandos and tanks had made repeated attempts to break in but were driven off. With land approaches sealed off, Southern Command proposed rescuing the garrison by water. The fort lay on a spit projecting into the Gulf of Suez near the mouth of the canal. Naval officers were dispatched to General Mendler's headquarters Friday to examine the possibility of extricating the men in rubber boats. The officers concluded that any such attempt was doomed. The closest point from which boats could be launched was six miles away. It would be a moonlit night and the Egyptians had the entire area covered by radar-controlled artillery. If the boats weren't spotted on the way to the fort, they certainly would be as they made their way back after what was bound to be a noisy shoot-out.

"I can't oblige you to do it," said General Mendler. "But you're their last chance."

The naval officers bowed to his words. The plan they drew up called for six rubber boats to set out shortly after dark from the Gulf of Suez coast. They would halt offshore eight hundred yards from the outpost while a small commando team swam ashore. Only at that point would radio silence be broken to inform the garrison of the rescue attempt. As the boats closed on the shore, the commandos would eliminate any Egyptians between the fort and the landing point and the garrison would rush to the boats, carrying their wounded while artillery provided covering fire. The boats set out that night but were spotted before reaching the fort and forced to pull back under heavy artillery fire. The fate of the garrison was now sealed.

Of the forty-two men who had been trapped in Mezakh, five were dead and sixteen wounded. In Southern Command, surrender was seen now as the only way out. Moshe Dayan objected to ordering the garrison to surrender and insisted that the fort's commander, Lt. Shlomo Ardinest, be given "permission" to surrender if he so chose. General Mendler was furious at the decision. If the high command had come to the conclusion that the men couldn't be rescued, then they should be ordered to surrender, he told his staff, and not be left to make the decision themselves. By now, however, Ardinest had been persuaded that there was no alternative. There was not even enough ammunition to resist another determined attack.

In its final radio report Saturday morning, the garrison passed on the names and health status of the men. Any sudden deterioration would be attributable to their captors.

"Is our situation known to you?" an officer at division headquarters asked Ardinest.

"Negative."

"Our situation is good. The deed [the surrender] is being done because it would be too late by the time we reached you" (an attempt to indicate that a counterattack would be coming).

"We've taken it in good spirits. Give our regards home."

"This [the surrender] is approved by higher authority."

"Otherwise," said Ardinest, "it would have been another Massada" (meaning the deaths of the entire garrison).

"We'll see you on the [television] screen. Keep your heads up. There will be Red Cross representatives."

"We're transferring the wounded and dead."

"Brief your men. Tell them to keep their heads up and smile. Anything to add?"

"Ask the fellows to see to our parents. Console them. I'm feeling fine. See you. We're doing it for the wounded."

As thousands of Egyptian soldiers on both banks watched, the garrison emerged, one man holding a Torah scroll.

The fall of Mezakh effectively concluded the saga of the Bar-Lev Line. Of 441 men in sixteen forts, 126 had been killed and 161 taken prisoner. The remaining 154, including 60 men at Budapest, which would hold out through the war, made it back.

Distressed by the surrender, General Mendler left division headquarters, where the conversations with Ardinest were being conducted, to visit units in the field. He was talking on the radio with General Gonen when an Egyptian tank shell hit his half-track, killing him, an aide, and an Israel Radio reporter.

Mendler's death would be blamed on a lack of radio discipline. According to military historian Chaim Herzog in his account of the war, Gonen asked to be driven the next day to the site where Mendler was killed. A lieutenant who had been with Mendler accompanied him. When the junior officer attributed Mendler's death to his having broadcast his location, Gonen asked how long afterwards the shell had hit. Thirty seconds, said the lieutenant. Gonen stopped the jeep, called his headquarters, and gave his name in the clear, together with his location. They sat for ten minutes but no shells fell. "Have I proved my point?" asked Gonen.

Flying over the Israeli lines in a helicopter Saturday afternoon, Elazar had a view of the vibrant army that had sprouted on the dunes of western Sinai—thousands of vehicles, endless encampments, figures moving purposefully. Egypt had staggered the IDF but it had expended its bag of surprises. Arrayed against it now was an army with its fighting ability honed and its psychological balance restored. The scene Elazar witnessed radiated an energy and optimism that became even more tangible when he landed. Maintenance units were swarming over damaged tanks. Adan's division, pulled off the line, was taking up position behind Sharon's division in order to cross the canal once the anticipated Egyptian attack had been repulsed and a bridgehead established.

In Sharon's headquarters at Tasa, there was general agreement that the Egyptian armor would strike hardest in the center of the line, but it was not clear when they would attack. Sharon proposed not waiting. A cease-fire could be declared at any time, he argued, and it was best to begin biting into the Egyptian lines immediately. He was overruled by Elazar. The chief of staff said the IDF would cross the canal within the next two days even if the Egyptians did not attack. But he believed they would.

Confirmation had come during the night that the Egyptian armored divisions had begun to move. Elements of the Fourth Division were crossing over in the Third Army sector and the Twenty-first Division was crossing in the Second Army sector. "It's about time," Elazar said to Bar-Lev. "We need a big, beautiful offensive with lots of Egyptian tanks—to wipe them out east of the canal and then to cross. That's today's program."

Bar-Lev termed the limited bridging equipment available to him "a joke" and the crossing itself brazen. A few shells hitting the bridges, and the army would find itself stranded west of the canal with no way to get back— at least, not the tanks. The Egyptians had a dozen bridges along the length of the canal; Israel would be lucky to have two and they would be close together, within the range of hundreds of Egyptian guns and mortars. But, Bar-Lev reiterated, it was a risk he was ready to run.

Returning to Tel Aviv and the dour confines of the Pit, Elazar shared his uplift with his staff. "Whoever feels depressed in these dark corridors should go into the field and see the boys. You'll come back in a grand mood. We're eight days into the war, but when you meet the tankers they talk as if this is the third year of World War II. They're on top of things. They know what the Egyptians are up to and have an answer for everything. The repair shops are working, the tanks are fine, there's ammunition. The best of our people are down there."

That night, Sharon tried to reach Dayan in order to win his support for an immediate attack. Unable to track him down, he telephoned Dayan's daughter, Yael, who had served as a soldier in Sharon's divisional headquarters in the Six Day War. She didn't think her father would return home before morning. "What, he's not sleeping at home again?" joked Sharon, a reference to Dayan's once notorious reputation for one-night stands. Yael took umbrage. "Come on, Yael, what happened to your sense of humor?" asked Sharon. Dropping his jolliness, he asked her to pass on a message to her father if she spoke with him this night. "Tell him that the whole division

Gen. David Elazar, Israeli chief of staff (center), arriving by helicopter on the Golan. To the left, in civilian clothes, is Yitzhak Rabin.
Photograph courtesy of Israel Defense Forces Archive

Col. Avigdor Ben-Gal, brigade commander on the Golan.
Photograph courtesy of Israel Defense Forces Archive

Gen. Rafael (Raful) Eitan, division commander on the northern Golan.
Photograph courtesy of Israel Defense Forces Archive

Syrian tank knocked out in night battle by paratroopers at Strongpoint 116 on the Golan. In the background are other knocked-out tanks.
Photograph courtesy of Israel Defense Forces Archive

Lt. Yossi Gur, commander of Strongpoint 116 on the Golan Heights (with sling), shortly after an Israeli counterattack broke through to his beleaguered position. One of his men is being treated by medics. *Photo by David Rubinger/Yedioth Archive*

Lt. Col. Yitzhak Mordecai, who led a paratroop battalion in the battle for the Chinese Farm.
Photograph courtesy of Israeli Government Press Office

Israeli paratroopers west of the canal.
Photograph courtesy of Israeli Government Press Office

Israeli vehicles rushing to retrieve an Egyptian pilot on the west bank of the Suez Canal.
Photograph courtesy of Israeli Government Press Office

Israeli soldiers in Sinai foxholes.
Photograph courtesy of Israel Defense Forces Archive

Exhausted artillerymen take advantage
of a lull in the battle.
Photograph courtesy of Israel Defense Forces Archive

Dayan being briefed by division commander
Avraham Adan in the Sinai.
Photograph courtesy of Israeli Government Press Office

Tense meeting in the dunes. Sharon (with white bandage) leans on map. Looking over his shoulder is Dayan. Facing him is Bar-Lev. In left foreground is Adan. It was at this meeting that Sharon thought of striking Bar-Lev.
Photograph courtesy of Israeli Government Press Office

SAM at captured base.
Photograph courtesy of Israeli Government Press Office

Egyptian soldiers loading jerricans of water onto boats on the Israeli-held west bank of the Suez Canal for transfer to the surrounded Third Army on the Sinai bank. On the opposite bank is one of the openings that was cut through the Israeli ramp on the first day of the war.
Photograph courtesy of Israeli Government Press Office

Gen. Ariel Sharon and troops after the battle.
Photograph courtesy of Israeli Government Press Office

Egyptian general Abdel Ghani el-Gamasy, chief of operations (in khaki uniform) and Israeli chief of staff David Elazar being saluted by UN guards as they emerge from the tent at Kilometer 101, where negotiations were held for the separation of forces.
Photograph courtesy of Israeli Government Press Office

Prime Minister Meir and Defense Minister Dayan meeting with troops during the cease-fire.
Photograph courtesy of Israeli Government Press Office

President Sadat and former Israeli prime minister Meir enjoy a joke during Sadat's visit to Jerusalem. On the right is Shimon Peres.
Photograph courtesy of Israeli Government Press Office

here is stamping its feet. The horses are ready for battle. You remember the picture—like the eve of the Six Day War. Explain this to him. He must understand that there's enough initiative here to break the Egyptians. Otherwise, we'll enter a cease-fire in the present miserable situation." In a telephone conversation with retired air force commander Ezer Weizman the day before, Sharon had complained of the mood at the rear—"as if this is the final battle of the Warsaw Ghetto." To his right, said Sharon, was Adan. To his left, Mendler. The troops on the front line were ready. "Believe me, we can finish everything quickly."

In Cairo, General Shazly contemplated the coming battle with trepidation. For five days, ever since Israel's failed attack of October 8, both sides had been hoping for the other to attack and break against its defenses. It was the Egyptians who would now take the offensive. The Twenty-first Armored Division, which had already sent one of its two tank brigades to Sinai, was to send the other as well. The Fourth Armored Division was to leave one of its brigades with 100 tanks behind on the west bank and cross with the rest. Also west of the canal were 250 other tanks in strategic reserve, including 120 of the Presidential Guard in Cairo. The Egyptian command believed this strength, 350 tanks, ample to cope with any likely Israeli incursion.

The attack plan for Sunday, October 14, was devised by war minister Ismail himself. Two armored brigades would push separately towards Tasa in the center. In the north, an armored brigade would drive towards Baluza and another would attack between Baluza and Tasa. In the south, an armored brigade would push towards the Mitla Pass and a mechanized brigade towards the Gidi Pass. In all, 400 to 500 tanks would participate in the six thrusts. Israel had 700 tanks in Sinai, half deployed on the line, half in reserve. The Israelis would be waiting for the most part on high ground.

Replacing Adan's division on the line was a reserve brigade commanded by Col. Yoel Gonen, younger brother of General Gonen. The unit, made up of captured Soviet T-55s, had not yet been in combat and Southern Command placed one of Adan's brigades behind it in case of need.

Preparatory to the tank attack, Egyptian helicopters set down one hundred commandos near the Lateral Road shortly after 3 A.M. Sunday to disrupt the Israeli rear. An Israeli reconnaissance unit backed by tanks quickly subdued them, killing sixty before they could overrun the artillery battery that was their target. Still bruised by the extensive losses their commandos had suffered on the opening day of the war, the Egyptians were unable or unwilling to implement further commando operations that were planned in conjunction with the armor attack.

(Of 1,700 commandos inserted behind Israeli lines during the war, 740 would be killed—many in downed helicopters—and 330 captured. Of the commando units landed behind Israeli lines, only those near Baluza and those blocking the road to Budapest succeeded in inflicting measurable damage. However, commandos who fought on the front line as tank hunters on Yom Kippur were highly effective.)

At 6 A.M. Egyptian aircraft darted across the canal for a bombing run. There were no reports of damage. Colonel Reshef, whose brigade was deployed in the center, kept his tanks on the rear slopes of the Hamadiya and Kishuf ridges. He and his battalion commanders moved up to observation positions, their tanks edging up the slopes until only the heads of the officers, standing in their turrets, protruded above the ridgeline. The Egyptians opened a fifteen-minute artillery barrage so heavy that for the first time since the war began, Reshef was obliged to close his hatch.

At 6:30, tanks of the Twenty-first Division appeared to his front, an enormous flow of fast-moving armor that reminded Reshef of the flash floods that erupt in the Negev after a rain and sweep everything before them. For a moment he wondered whether he too would be swept away. At first, the Egyptians could see nothing on the ridges to their front. When the tanks were 3,000 yards away, Reshef ordered his men to move up into firing positions. The ridges began to be dotted with dark shapes as company commanders moved up to stake out their sectors, then platoon commanders, and then the rest. The ridgelines in Reshef's sector now bristled with one hundred tanks. As they opened fire, Egyptian tanks began burning. Some managed to cross the killing ground safely and reach the foot of Hamadiya, where they were hidden from the Israeli tanks on the ridge above. The Egyptians lunged upwards and engaged from as close as a few dozen yards. Reshef ordered tanks on Kishuf Ridge to his left to descend and hit the attackers on their flank. He called down artillery on the Egyptian rear, to impede their retreat. Within half an hour the battle on his front was over. Scores of enemy tanks were burning. Five of his own tanks had been hit. The brigade's casualties were six dead and a few wounded. At 7 A.M. Reshef radioed Sharon's deputy: "I broke their attack. Improving positions to the west." However, that innocently phrased proposal for an advance westward was rejected by Southern Command, monitoring the radio net of Sharon's division.

Reshef's neighboring brigade commander, Col. Haim Erez, had raised his turret hatch with the end of the Egyptian barrage to find a tank coming at him through the shell smoke barely twenty yards to his front. His gunner stopped it. The Egyptian attack here was clumsily executed, the tanks getting in each other's way and firing little before being hit. An Israeli tank com-

mander spotted Sagger teams and reported "tourists with suitcases" deploying in the sands. Erez sent a battalion to outflank the enemy force, which was
soon in retreat.

On the northern end of the front, near Baluza, a small force commanded by Col. Aharon Peled watched as a T-62 brigade advanced from the
direction of Kantara. Two miles from the Israeli line, Egyptian infantrymen
who had hidden in the sands during the night rose to join the attack. They
walked between the tanks, which reduced the tanks' speed to the pace of the
foot soldiers. Peled waited until they were at 1,200 yards before opening fire.
Nine Egyptian tanks were hit and the attackers pulled back to reorganize.
When they came again, twenty-one more tanks were hit and the Egyptian
commander called it a day. Peled's losses consisted of a single tank hit by a
Sagger.

Colonel Gonen's still unbloodied brigade, deployed between Aharon
Peled and Erez, fared less well. An assault by Egyptian Sagger teams and
tanks cost him a dozen tanks—a loss greater than that suffered by all other
Israeli units combined.

At the southern end of the line, where the Egyptians were trying to
reach the Gidi and Mitla Passes, an armored brigade pushed up a broad
undefended wadi. Sighted by Israeli lookouts, the spearhead was stopped by
small groups of hastily deployed tanks and by paratroopers firing jeep-
mounted recoilless rifles. The thrust carried the Egyptian tanks beyond the
SAM umbrella and Israeli warplanes were soon taking a toll.

By late afternoon, the surviving Egyptian tanks all along the line had
pulled back. The attack, the most massive since the initial Egyptian assault
on Yom Kippur, was a total failure, the first major Egyptian reversal of the
war. Instead of concentrating forces or maneuvering, except for the wadi
thrust, they had expended them in a head-on attack against the waiting
Israeli brigades. Egyptian losses for the day were estimated at between 150
and 250 tanks. A score of Israeli tanks were hit, but most were soon repaired.
For the first time since the start of the war on the southern front, the inherent strength of Israel's armor had come into play.

Since the beginning of the war, the Egyptian field commanders—and to
a large extent even the Egyptian media—had been sticking to more or less
reliable reporting, a far cry from the "oriental imagination" Israel had chor-
tled at in previous wars. This ability to deal with reality worried Israel since it
made Egypt a more formidable opponent. Now, however, towards the end of
the day, wishful thinking once again could be heard on the Egyptian radio
net, including reports of the capture of the Mitla Pass and other imagined

successes. Bar-Lev would sum the situation up succinctly in a telephone conversation with Golda Meir: "We've returned to ourselves and the Egyptians have returned to themselves."

Sharon would put it even more pointedly as he tried to cajole Bar-Lev into letting him take up pursuit of the retreating enemy. "I saw the Twenty-first Division today," he said, "and if I may use a crude expression in a conversation with a minister [a lighthearted reference to Bar-Lev's just vacated position as minister of commerce], they're the same old shits. They came, they were hit, and they started to run." He himself would be reminded soon enough that the Egyptians were not to be dismissed so lightly. But after the most difficult week in the country's history, Israel had cause to celebrate.

At Center Ten, Shazly tried to reach the commander of the Second Army, General Mamoun, by phone in late morning but was told that he was resting. Shazly found it odd that Mamoun would be resting at 11 A.M. in the middle of a major battle and that his aides would not summon him when the chief of staff called. But he did not press. Two hours later, Sadat asked him to visit the front. Shazly reached Second Army headquarters in Ismailiya in the late afternoon. This time when he asked to see Mamoun he was told the truth—the general had had a breakdown and was lying on a cot. A doctor told Shazly that Mamoun should be hospitalized, but at Mamoun's request Shazly delayed the evacuation by a day. Shazly continued on, with the intention of crossing into Sinai. He found that of the two bridges in the sector, one had been knocked out by artillery and the other had been pulled in to avoid the same fate.

Returning to Cairo near midnight, he reported to Ismail and Sadat on "our most calamitous day." The decision to engage in battle this day was not only militarily disastrous, to his mind, but purposeless. The Egyptian attack was not going to draw off Israeli forces from the Golan Heights to Sinai, as Assad hoped, because the Egyptian army did not pose the kind of threat to Israel's heartland that Syria did. In any case, Israeli air power was sufficient by itself to prevent a crossing of Sinai by the Egyptian army once it moved beyond the protection of the SAMs. Furthermore, the Iraqis had already taken the field and the situation on the Golan front had stabilized. Shazly's analysis was perceptive. He would have been even more upset had he known that Sadat had the day before turned down a cease-fire which would have nailed down Egypt's gains on the Sinai bank.

Despite their success, Israeli commanders were left with a feeling of a meal only half eaten. They had hoped to destroy more tanks but the Egyptians had not pressed home their attack. Dayan expressed doubt that this was Phase Two of the Egyptian war plan—the push by the armored divisions for the passes. Elazar believed it was, although more limited than originally planned. In order to encourage the Egyptians to try harder, Elazar held a radio conversation with Bar-Lev for the benefit of Egyptian radio monitors in which the two generals referred to the day's battle as a defeat. Sharon came up with his own ploy. He told Reshef to lay down a heavy smoke screen, as if to protect his forces, and report on the radio that he was under heavy pressure and had to pull back. His battalion commanders would join in with cries for assistance. The bait was duly dangled but the Egyptians were not in the mood for amateur theatrics.

The day's events had converted Dayan into an enthusiastic advocate of a canal crossing. When he returned to the Pit Sunday evening, Elazar told him that he had ordered the air force to halt most of its activity in order to prepare for the crossing operation. As always, Elazar was thinking a couple of days ahead. "I'm concentrating on the main effort," he said. "Tomorrow night the breakthrough. The day after tomorrow, a day of battle. Not until we've established ourselves on the other side will we come down on the Egyptians with all our might." Dayan again criticized the senior command on the northern front for not showing sufficient aggressiveness. Elazar noted that unlike on the southern front, where there had been a relative lull for several days and a rotation of units on the front line, the troops on the northern front had been engaged in almost constant combat for eight days. "The boys have been fighting day and night. They're bone tired."

After briefing the editors of the nation's daily newspapers, Elazar appeared Sunday night before the cabinet, which had yet to give its approval for a canal crossing. He attempted to reassure ministers who feared that the crossing was a high-risk gamble. "We've built our plans on sound military thinking. If I thought there was a risk of disaster, I wouldn't propose it. The plan is not built on luck. We're not going to all this trouble so that if a bridge is hit, the show is over." Nevertheless, he did not deny there was risk. "The outcome of a battle can only be presumed. It can't be divined with absolute certainty." The operation would be carried out in stages and it could be decided at any point to call it off. In a worst-case situation, where the bridges were demolished after a small force had already crossed, the men could be brought back in rubber boats even if tanks had to be left behind. "I believe that the chances of failing are pretty meager and the odds of success are good. How great the success will be I can't say, but it may be very great."

It was not an easy decision for the cabinet. The worst-case situation Elazar described was not the worst case imaginable—instead of a small force being cut off, it could be a substantial part of the army. But Mrs. Meir trusted Elazar's judgment. The cabinet in turn relied on hers. She had recovered her composure and become a source of strength for the ministers. Half an hour after midnight the crossing was approved.

Elazar had not troubled the cabinet with his own nightmare—crossing the canal and getting bogged down in a war of attrition. He had ordered his staff to prepare for such an eventuality by drawing up plans for training new recruits, returning wounded men to their units, repairing damaged tanks and acquiring new ones.

The pending operation was named Stouthearted Men. Gonen had drawn up its broad outlines before the war, adding it to several existing contingency plans for a canal crossing more limited in scope. The plan involved not only the crossing itself but also a breakthrough on the west bank. Bar-Lev had reworked it to fit present circumstances and intensive staff work was now under way in Southern Command to flesh it out.

The plan called for laying two bridges across the canal. They would be crossed by two divisions which would capture a fifty-mile-wide area between Mount Ataka, south of Suez City, and the outskirts of Ismailiya in the north. Suez was to be taken within forty-eight hours of zero hour, after which "the forces will be prepared to continue the attack west towards Cairo." The tank forces which remained behind in Sinai would bring about the "surrender and destruction" of the Egyptian bridgeheads.

The crossing would be from Fort Matsmed. A major advantage of the site was that it lay just inside the seam between the Second and Third Armies. Despite the ambitious formulation, Elazar and Dayan were uncertain how far the army could get. The crossing force would thus avoid a costly plunge through the Egyptian bridgehead, bristling with antitank weapons and minefields. However, Matsmed lay only eight hundred yards south of the Chinese Farm where the Egyptians were entrenched. Once the waterline was reached, therefore, a major effort would have to be made to push the Egyptians back in order to create a safe corridor. Another advantage of Matsmed was that the opposite bank was apparently empty of enemy forces. Sharon, during his term as front commander, had prepared a staging area for a crossing alongside the fort. Known as the Yard, it was surrounded by earthen ramps to provide a measure of protection for the forces waiting to cross.

Sharon's division, already deployed in the sector, was assigned the breakthrough. Its task was to establish a bridgehead, lay the bridges, and push back enemy forces in the Chinese Farm at least two and a half miles to form a corridor. Bridgeheads are not considered secure unless they are out of enemy artillery range, but in the circumstances this was not a possibility. The attack force would be plunging through a hole in the very center of the Egyptian lines and the crossing point would be covered by guns and mortars on both banks. The best that could be hoped for was to secure its approaches from direct-fire weapons like tanks and Saggers.

Once the bridges were up and the corridor secured, Adan's division would cross the canal and turn south. It would eliminate SAM batteries as it went, opening the sky for the Israeli air force, which could then begin providing support to the ground forces.

At a final conference at Umm Hashiba Sunday night with the division commanders, Bar-Lev made a point of spelling out Sharon's role in a way intended to prevent him from interpreting orders as he saw fit. "We must expand the bridgehead [on the Sinai bank] to the north at least four kilometers to secure it and this task, Arik, remains yours until the end."

"It remains what?" asked Sharon.

"Your responsibility. Securing the bridgehead remains your responsibility." Before he gets to the Cairo Hilton, Bar-Lev told Sharon, he would have to be released from his assignment at the bridgehead.

Concluding the meeting, Bar-Lev said the operation they were about to undertake was intricate. "But we will demonstrate that we can do it with improvisation and that we can do it right. On condition that everything agreed upon here is executed precisely. If we begin shoving one another, it will become a mess." He appeared to be warning against any competition to get across the bridge out of turn.

Crossing the Suez Canal had been on the IDF's mind since it came to an abrupt halt at the waterway in the Six Day War. Western countries sought to discourage such thoughts by refusing to sell Israel bridging equipment. The best that could be acquired was a British system consisting of floatable iron cubes which could be linked together into pontoons. The system, known as Unifloat, was intended for civilian use in harbors. Israeli army engineers scouring Europe recognized that nine such cubes linked together would create a pontoon capable of carrying a tank. Eight pontoons linked front-to-end would be sufficient to span the Suez Canal. To make them war-ready, the pontoons were preassembled by the engineering corps on land and filled with polyethylene to help keep them afloat if hit by shells.

Also acquired in Europe, as scrap, were amphibious rafts called Gilowas after the French general who developed them. Their main advantage was that they could travel on their own to the water's edge. Three Gilowas linked together could carry a tank. Their disadvantage—and the reason they had been abandoned by all armies that tried them, including NATO forces—was their vulnerability. They were kept afloat with inflatable rubber belts that could be punctured by shrapnel. There was a heated debate within the IDF about investing in them and only half the junked rafts acquired were refurbished.

Not content with either of these options, the IDF decided to develop its own bridge. It was the venerable David Lascov who conceived it—a preassembled "assault bridge" that could be thrust intact into the canal and pushed across the 180-yard waterway to the opposite bank. Deputy chief of staff Tal, himself a technical innovator, was enthusiastic about the idea and the two men developed a 200-yard-long construction, called the roller bridge, that could be towed on floatable iron rollers.

Completed shortly before the war, the bridge sections were transported to a storage area in Sinai code-named Yukon, fifteen miles east of the canal. In the event of war, the sections were to be transported to a point five miles from the canal for assembly—far enough to be out of sight of the Egyptians but close enough for the bridge to be easily towed to the canal overnight across flat terrain.

Because the unwieldy structure had to be towed in a straight line, a dirt road, code-named Tirtur, was built from the planned assembly point to the canal edge just north of Matsmed. However, the assembly site fell into Egyptian hands at the beginning of the war and the bridge was assembled at Yukon itself. To reach the canal, the 400-ton structure would now have to be pulled three times the planned distance and over dunes. More problematic still, Tirtur now lay inside Egyptian lines, forming the southern perimeter of the Second Army. Its dual role—Egyptian defense line and would-be Israeli artery—would turn this nondescript desert road into a major strategic pivot.

By Saturday, October 13, assembly at Yukon was completed. On the same day, eight Unifloat pontoons began to be towed towards Tasa, rear headquarters for the crossing operation. Twelve other pontoons at Baluza on the Mediterranean coast would start out two days later. The Gilowa battalion was training on Lake Kinneret when the war broke out and the crewmen watched occasional Syrian shells exploding in the lake for two days before transporters arrived to carry the rafts to Refidim.

The company of Eli Geva, which had been specially trained for the towing of the roller bridge, was fighting now on the Golan. The towing was assigned instead to a battalion commanded by Lt. Col. Shimon Ben-

Shoshan of Erez's brigade. It reported to the bridge assembly area Sunday night after participating in the day's battle against the Egyptian armor. The men were astonished at the sight of the 200-yard-long span in the midst of the dunes. Engineering officers warned the tankers that the heavy structure could run away from them when descending slopes if not properly braked. The engineers had never envisioned the bridge being towed up and down steep dunes and were not sure of the outcome.

In addition to ten tanks pulling from the side and one in front, a tank was positioned at the rear to act as a brake. Waiting for the preparations to be completed, the tankers tried to fight off their accumulated exhaustion. As he prepared to start, Ben-Shoshan asked each tank commander in turn to report readiness. By the time the last had responded, crews in the first tanks had fallen asleep. This happened several times. Finally, they got under way, moving with painstaking slowness. On one of the first descents, the bridge partially overran several tanks but there was no serious damage. After a fitful few hours of stops and starts, they had managed to move less than two miles. The convoy halted at first light and the bridge was covered with camouflage netting. They were not to move by day because of the bridge's vulnerability to air attack. Mobile antiaircraft guns guarded it and from this morning, Monday, October 15, the air force would maintain a continuous presence overhead.

Sharon had asked brigade commanders to assemble at his headquarters shortly after dawn Monday, to be briefed on the canal crossing this night. It was still dark when paratroop commander Danny Matt started out for Tasa from the Mitla Pass, where his brigade was deployed against the expected Egyptian airborne attack, which had been called off.

The brigade had been assigned the task of establishing the bridgehead. Matt had fought in every one of Israel's wars and in numerous skirmishes in between, but never had he felt the weight of responsibility he did now. The battlefield was still fitfully slumbering. Jagged flashes pierced the darkness and slowly falling flares decorated the night sky like lanterns. From the distance came an occasional rumble of artillery. Sitting in the commander's chair of his half-track, a small light illuminating a reading surface in front of him, Matt set aside the map he was studying and removed from his breast pocket a tiny book of Psalms given to him the day before by the chief army chaplain. Although no longer observant, Matt had had a religious upbringing and still drew solace from the Psalms. Turning to the first page, he read,

"Happy is the man that hath not walked in the counsel of the wicked. . . . [H]e shall be like a tree planted by streams of water, that bringeth forth its fruit in its season." As always, the words calmed him.

Matt's sense of destiny was shared by the other commanders who assembled at Tasa, an awareness that the turning point was at hand. Rarely in history had a nation recovered from so massive a blow so swiftly and attempted to seize the initiative. The United States after Pearl Harbor and the Soviet Union after Barbarossa had had the depth and the time to fall back on their resources and prepare the counterblow. Israel did not have resources to fall back on and was pushing the conflict to a swift decision. The swings of fortune that in great wars often take place over months or years as nations muster their resources or exhaust them were taking place along the Suez Canal in days.

The operation, Sharon told them, would begin at dusk with a diversionary attack by Tuvia Raviv's brigade. The bulk of the fighting would fall to Amnon Reshef's brigade in the Chinese Farm. Under its cover, Matt's paratroopers would cross the canal and Haim Erez's brigade would tow the bridges to the canal.

It was a monumental operation in which the division would be engaging the Egyptians in the darkness simultaneously from front, rear, and flank. Sharon had executed a night attack of similar complexity at Abu Agheila during the Six Day War, but the stakes now—and the odds—were far higher. "I looked at the faces of the commanders and wondered if, after all that had happened, they believed we could pull this off tonight," he would write. "They believed."

The paratroopers were to start crossing the canal in rubber boats at 8 P.M. If all went well, both bridges would be ready for Adan's division to cross by 5 A.M. Elazar liked the plan even though the timetable seemed overly optimistic. He would be happy, he said, if even one bridge was up by morning. Sharon appointed his deputy, Col. Yehuda (Jackie) Even, to command the bridging operation.

Bar-Lev, appreciating the enormity of the task, asked Sharon Monday afternoon if he wished to delay the attack by a day in order to organize. Sharon said he would stick to the schedule. He had his own doubts about being able to get the bridges to the canal on time. But he feared that if the attack was delayed, either the Egyptians might discover what was afoot or the Israeli high command might have second thoughts about undertaking the crossing at all.

As he moved towards the front with his mobile command post, Sharon passed encampments embellished with wooden huts made from ammunition boxes and covered with palm fronds. The feast of Succot had arrived and the troops had found time to build the traditional holiday huts evoking the wandering of the Israelites in this very desert more than three thousand years before.

At Southern Command headquarters, there was a brief pause in the afternoon for a ceremony bestowing upon Colonel Ben-Ari the rank of brigadier general. The field promotion was acknowledgment of the key role he had been playing in Southern Command as a stable anchor, particularly during the hectic opening days of the war. Bar-Lev also named him deputy front commander. For Elazar, it was a touching moment as he pinned the badge of rank on the shoulder of the man with whom he had fought, literally back-to-back, at the battle of San Simon.

Matt's paratroop brigade had arrived in Sinai in civilian buses which were too vulnerable to carry the men forward into the combat zone. For this, the brigade had received thirty half-tracks upon arrival in Sinai; sixty more were supposed to be waiting Monday morning at an assembly area along with the rubber boats they would need to cross the canal this night. But neither half-tracks nor boats were there. Capt. Hanan Erez was ordered by a battalion commander to take drivers with him in buses and rustle up half-tracks wherever he could find them. Otherwise the brigade would not be able to get to the canal, which meant no bridgehead. Erez was told to be back by 2 P.M., four hours' time. "Don't come back without them," said the commander.

Erez headed for Refidim where he had seen rows of new half-tracks lined up two days before. They were still there. His drivers were getting into the vehicles when Erez was hailed by a white-haired lieutenant colonel who asked him what he was doing. The captain was struck by how clean and well-pressed the officer's uniform was. The vehicles were urgently needed by Matt's brigade, he explained.

No problem, said the logistics officer. Just show me your orders.

We're the force crossing the canal, said Erez. I don't have written orders.

No orders, no vehicles, said the colonel.

The paratroop captain, a kibbutznik, attempted unsuccessfully to persuade the colonel. Running out of arguments, he cocked his Uzi. "Enough nonsense," he said. "If you try to stop me, I'll shoot you."

Persuaded, the colonel stepped aside. "Onto the half-tracks and follow me," shouted Erez to the drivers.

A long line of vehicles were waiting at the base's fueling station. Erez took aside the officer in charge and explained that the half-tracks were designated for the canal crossing. The officer immediately gave them priority at the pumps. Senior officers were posted now at every crossroad, holding up traffic while they sorted it out according to priority. At each such stop, Erez descended to explain his unit's mission and was waved on through. He asked all the officers to whom he mentioned the pending crossing to keep the information confidential. At 1:45, he led the half-tracks into the brigade assembly area and handed them over to the battalion commander with fifteen minutes to spare.

The half-tracks were still not enough for the entire brigade. It was decided that one of the two battalions would continue forward in buses to a point just out of Egyptian artillery range. The men would remain there until the half-tracks carrying the first battalion returned from the canal to fetch them. There were still no rubber boats but Matt was told they would be waiting at a rendezvous point closer to the canal.

At 4:30 P.M., the brigade moved out. It was soon caught up in the stream of vehicles making their way towards the front. An asphalt road code-named Akavish, which ran southwest from Tasa to the northern end of the Bitter Lake, some twenty miles, was the main approach to the crossing zone. Traffic converging on it was already backed up for miles. It took an hour and a half for the paratroop convoy just to make the turning into Akavish.

Periodically, traffic had to pull to the side to make way for vehicles bringing wounded back from the front. The excitement was palpable. Armored units which had been engaged for the past week on isolated missions along the battlefront now saw themselves part of a powerful army moving up for the decisive battle as they joined the flow. Vehicles bore freshly painted slogans like "Cairo Express." A chaplain appeared on the roadside distributing copies of the Psalms, which were snatched up even by avowed agnostics.

The Gilowas moved up to Yukon to position themselves closer to the canal. Soldiers along the road looked quizzically at the amphibious vehicles, folded into their mobile mode. Upon grasping their purpose, they raised their fingers in V's and cheered the crews on.

Colonel Reshef spent the day going over maps and air photos with his officers and designing the complex choreography of the coming battle. The vast Chinese Farm, his prime objective, was an agricultural development site on which work began in the 1960s with UN participation. Israelis who came upon it in the Six Day War had mistaken the Japanese writing on irrigation equipment for Chinese. Cutting the area were deep irrigation ditches, presently dry, which could double as trenches or tank traps.

Reshef's brigade, which had lost the bulk of its tanks on Yom Kippur, had been substantially reinforced and now had ninety-seven tanks as well as three paratroop and commando detachments. Late Monday afternoon, the brigade formed up by battalions off the Artillery Road near the point where they would cross the dunes.

Making the rounds of his units, Reshef first visited Brom's reconnaissance battalion, which would lead the force. The battalion had been under Reshef's command for almost a week but he had not yet had a chance to meet the men. Addressing them now, he emphasized the importance of the coming encounter and the key role that was theirs. Taking leave of Brom, he said, "What matters is stubbornness. *Stubbornness.* Do you understand what I mean?" Brom said he did.

In the adjoining battalion, Amram Mitzna outlined the mission to his officers, trying to sound as matter-of-fact as he could. After ten days of combat, however, they understood that a brigade plunge into the heart of an Egyptian army was an adventure from which few were likely to return intact, if at all. A radio-telephone had been made available and Mitzna asked every man to call his family. Mitzna himself wrote a farewell letter to his wife which he left with his jeep driver, who would not be coming on the attack. The men sat quietly on the tanks waiting for darkness.

Not far away, Adan visited his three brigades in turn as night fell. At each encampment, two thousand men rose at the shout of "Attention" and then sat back down on the ground as the division commander mounted a tank. In the light of vehicle headlamps, Adan told the men that he had often wondered how the younger generation, which had known only quick wars, would bear up to the kind of setbacks he and his generation had known in the War of Independence twenty-five years before. In the past nine days, he said, the men of the division had demonstrated their grit in a series of engagements more intensive than any experienced in 1948. It would be incumbent upon them in the coming battle to fight not only bravely but intelligently in order to overcome the disparity in numbers, he said. They would wait for Sharon to establish the bridgehead and then cross the canal to rip through the enemy rear in the final campaign of the war.

At 5 P.M., artillery opened up on the entire Egyptian line, so as not to give away the point of attack. Raviv began his diversionary attack on Missouri in the last light. The brigade managed to penetrate the Egyptian defenses and inflict substantial casualties. Even after it withdrew, leaving behind four tanks in a minefield, the rattled defenders would keep firing for hours.

At 6:05 P.M., Reshef ordered Brom to move out. Following the reconnaissance battalion at fixed intervals were Reshef himself with his forward command post, then three tank battalions. At the rear were the reconnaissance troops and paratroopers in half-tracks. In the light of a large moon, the armored vehicles moved in line over the pristine dunes towards the canal, six miles to the west, like a necklace undulating across the white sands. Following their movement from a distance, Sharon was held by the beauty of the scene. To help orientation, Reshef called for phosphorous shells to be fired at Fort Lakekan, the point where they were to emerge onto Lexicon Road.

In the crowded war room at Southern Command headquarters, Gonen, the former yeshiva student, quoted to those around him an obscure phrase from the Talmud that contrasted the sweetly scented world of the spice merchant with the malodorous leather trade: "The world cannot function without perfumes and without tanneries. Happy is he who works as a spice merchant and woe to him who works in a tannery." Reflecting a sense of the momentous nature of the enterprise they were embarking upon and his gratitude for being part of it, Gonen added, "As for me, I consider myself a spice merchant."

General Yariv shared the sense of magnitude. "I don't remember a night this fateful in all our wars."

Elazar, studying the large wall map, was moved to a reflection of his own. "If the history of how we pulled this off is ever written," he said, "it will be seen as the height of chutzpa."

Thirty

THE CHINESE FARM

EXCEPT FOR THE PHOSPHOROUS SHELLS bursting with a brilliant white light around Fort Lakekan, all was quiet when Reshef's brigade emerged onto Lexicon Road. Five miles to the north lay Tirtur. Just beyond it was the Chinese Farm where the Egyptian Sixteenth Infantry Division was entrenched. Reshef's mission was to crush it before dawn.

He needed surprise on his side because the numbers weren't. The Twenty-first Armored Division, positioned just beyond the Sixteenth, could be expected to join in the battle. The Twenty-first had taken a beating in the armored attack the day before, but the two Egyptian divisions together still had half again as many tanks as Reshef did. Of greater concern were the hundreds of Saggers and RPGs in the hands of the Egyptian infantry who would be fighting from the cover of the irrigation ditches. Military doctrine calls for an attacking force to have at least a 3-to-1 numerical advantage if it is to have a reasonable chance of overcoming an entrenched defense. Reshef estimated that the overall odds in the Chinese Farm were on the side of the defenders, and by at least 5 to 1.

Intelligence reported the Tirtur intersection with Lexicon undefended. In crossing it, the brigade would be slipping through a side door in the Egyptian deployment, four miles behind their front line. Reshef intended to penetrate as deeply as he could before opening fire. He wanted to explode in the very heart of the Egyptian disposition like a grenade, with units bursting

The Israeli Crossing of the Suez Canal

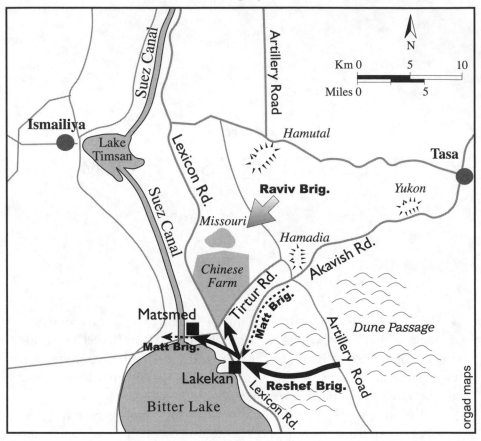

in every direction. The sudden eruption of Israeli armor in the Egyptian rear in the darkness could possibly stampede them. If it didn't, it would be a bloody affair.

Two units peeled off from the column before the intersection in opposite directions. Yoav Brom's reconnaissance battalion, turning west for a mile, reached the canal and secured a two-mile strip along the waterway straddling Fort Matsmed without encountering resistance. A company from one of the tank battalions was dispatched east to clear Akavish Road. It encountered no enemy on Akavish itself but two tanks were damaged by Saggers fired from Tirtur. The two roads, and Lexicon at their base, formed a near triangle. Akavish and Tirtur didn't quite touch, but where they came close Akavish was within easy Sagger range of Tirtur, less than a mile.

With Brom's departure, Mitzna's battalion moved to the head of the column. It crossed the Tirtur intersection without drawing fire. So did Reshef with his mobile command post, consisting of his tank and two half-tracks. Mitzna's mission was to reach a point on the canal five miles to the northwest of the intersection. This was well beyond the two and a half miles decided on for the bridgehead corridor, but the battalion had been asked to seize a bridge that intelligence had located. Next in line was a battalion under Lt. Col. Avraham Almog, who had replaced Shaul Shalev, killed a few days before. The rear of the tank column was brought up by a battalion under Maj. Shaya Beitel. He had taken command earlier in the day from an officer who had been sent home after his brother was killed in action and his brother-in-law went missing.

As Almog came abreast of the intersection, he saw the silhouettes of tanks projecting above an earthen barrier to the right. The intersection was not undefended. Since the last Israeli photo reconnaissance, the Egyptians had deployed heavy forces there but they did not at first identify the tanks passing them. Half of Almog's battalion had crossed when the intersection erupted with tank shells and RPGs. Ten of Almog's tanks were hit or ran onto roadside mines as they tried to bypass those disabled. Tanks from the following battalion, Beitel's, which were supposed to turn up Tirtur could not see the intersection because of burning tanks blocking it. Most of Beitel's tanks were knocked out and he himself was wounded.

Half the brigade had been stopped but the truncated head of the column, plunging into the enemy rear, was sowing havoc. Mitzna's battalion found itself in the midst of a divisional logistical center—ammunition dumps, jeeps, tanks, trucks, personnel carriers, fuel tankers, artillery batteries, and SAM batteries. The tanks fired in every direction. SAM missiles, hit by shells, took off in wild gyrations and ammunition dumps exploded. Hundreds of Egyptian soldiers could be seen running in the reddish yellow light of burning vehicles and the flare of explosions. Some came out of foxholes wrapped in blankets against the cold desert night. The Israeli tank commanders hurled grenades and used their Uzis against close-in targets, but it was the machine guns and tank guns that carried the fight. The commanders took to crushing ammunition crates under tank treads instead of shooting at them in order to avoid the explosions and glare that would expose them to RPG teams.

Recovering from their surprise, Egyptian tank units and infantrymen began to challenge the intruders. It was difficult in the darkness to distinguish friend from foe. Company commander Rami Matan halted after knocking out an Egyptian tank at fifty yards to search for others when a figure climbed onto his tank. It was an Egyptian soldier, a rifle slung casually over his shoulder. "Do you have a cigarette?" he asked. Matan, who understood Arabic, bent down into the turret and tossed a live grenade. An Israeli medic made the same mistake when he climbed onto a tank to ask its commander to take aboard wounded from a disabled tank. The Egyptian tank commander fired a pistol at him but the medic managed to leap off in time.

An Israeli tank commander, fearful of losing touch with the rest of the battalion in the darkness, was happy to be moving between two other tanks. At almost the same moment, the tanks on either side of him were set aflame.

Opposition dwindled as the tanks left the encampment behind but intelligence reported an imminent counterattack by the Twenty-first Division to the north. Mitzna pulled back a short distance to form a defensive line. As he did, three Egyptian tanks passed twenty yards away. Mitzna set one aflame, but as he turned his gun towards a second his own tank was hit. Two crewmen were killed and Mitzna was hurled from the turret. His knee shattered, he attempted to pull himself onto another tank just as it fired. The blast sent him sprawling, but he finally managed to climb aboard. Command passed to his deputy, who succeeded in repelling the Egyptian attack.

Almog had been knocked unconscious by an explosion after passing the intersection. Recovering, he found his tank alone. The tank that had been following was blocking the road several hundred yards to the rear, and the tanks beyond could not pass it because of roadside mines. Descending from Almog's tank, his operations officer, Lt. Zeev Lichtman, ran back down Lexicon, passing scores of Egyptian soldiers likewise running in the dark. Climbing on the immobilized tank, he saw that the machine gun atop the turret was smashed. Lying mortally wounded inside was Maj. Eliezer Caspi, the company commander who had attempted to reach Hizayon the first night of the war. The other crew members were in shock. Lichtman ordered the driver to close up behind the battalion commander.

Almog turned east, into the heart of the Chinese Farm. The tanks sprayed the trenches with machine-gun fire and the commanders tossed grenades. When Almog halted, he discovered that only four tanks had kept up with him. They set ammunition dumps aflame and turned a radar station into an enormous torch. Infantrymen drawing close with RPGs were cut down. After an hour, six of the strayed tanks joined Almog. He posted some facing north, others facing east. The force engaged Egyptian tanks which came forward to challenge them at ranges of less than four hundred yards. Sometimes, Egyptian tanks unaware of their identity were dispatched at closer range.

At one point, an Israeli tank commander glanced at a tank pulling into line alongside him and saw that it was a T-55. Its commander, believing he had attached himself to an Egyptian unit, was scanning the landscape for Israeli tanks in the light of burning vehicles. The Israeli commander turned his tank gun on his neighbor and told the gunner to fire. The gunner squeezed the trigger but nothing happened. "Misfire," he shouted.

For the first time, the Egyptian glanced over. He found himself looking down the barrel of a tank gun a few feet from his head. Realizing his mistake, he began swiveling his own gun towards the Israeli tank. By this time, the commander of the Israeli tank on the other side of the T-55 grasped the situation and backed off sufficiently to put a shell into it.

Reshef had halted across Lexicon Road from Almog's force. The brigade was scattered now in pockets over several miles and units were reporting heavy casualties. Reshef ordered the foot soldiers in the half-tracks to dismount and retrieve the wounded, no simple task on the chaotic nighttime battlefield. He asked that the tank carrying Mitzna be positioned alongside his own together with the battalion doctor. An aid station was set up in the shelter of the two tanks and two command half-tracks. Reshef called on Brom at Matsmed to send one of his companies north to reinforce what was left of Mitzna's battalion. The company that arrived was Rafi Bar-Lev's. Within minutes of arriving, Haim Bar-Lev's nephew was killed by a tank shell.

As Reshef was talking on the radio, the brigade intelligence officer cut in with an urgent report from radio monitors. "We are now firing at the headquarters of an Egyptian brigade. The shots that have just been fired were fired at the headquarters of an Egyptian brigade."

Reshef looked over at Almog's tanks and saw them firing machine guns to the east. He raised the battalion commander. "It's you," said Reshef, his normally calm voice rising in pitch. "You're firing at enemy headquarters. Pour it on. Use your tank guns. Call down artillery."

Even as he was maneuvering his units by radio, Reshef was engaged in a personal battle for survival as Egyptian infantrymen surged at him out of the darkness. He fired his machine gun so relentlessly that his hands were cut from the grip and from cocking the weapon. He and the two depleted battalions which had passed the intersection—Mitzna's and Almog's—had created separate fire bases miles deep inside the Second Army's bridgehead. They had penetrated a hornet's nest and the hornets were swarming, angry but disoriented.

The scene was lurid. Burning vehicles lit the landscape. Egyptian vehicles and infantrymen moved in every direction, some fleeing, some fighting.

Five Egyptian tanks lumbered out of the darkness near Reshef. Ordering his gunner to prepare for rapid fire, Reshef hit four. He raised Sharon on the radio net and said, "Forty, this is Four," their respective code designations. "I've just destroyed four tanks." It was not customary to report tank kills on the radio, but his men would be listening and Reshef wanted them to know that the brigade commander was fighting alongside them. His voice on the radio net was important reassurance in a world that had lost recognizable shape. When he told Sharon of Mitzna's wounding, Sharon said that Reshef's counterpart—the commander of the Egyptian Fourteenth Armored Brigade opposite him—had no such worries. Intelligence had just reported him dead, probably the result of Almog's fire.

As the battle progressed, Reshef found himself, for the first time since the beginning of the war, freed of fear. It was not denial of death that liberated him but acceptance of its certainty. The chances of emerging alive from the Chinese Farm were so remote that he bowed to his fate, leaving nothing more to be afraid of.

That did not mean abandoning civilities. At one point, he would be reinforced by a unit whose commander spoke crudely. Reshef brought him up short. "We don't talk like that here," he said. "If you do again, you'll be dismissed."

Sustaining Reshef and his men was the understanding that they were changing the course of the war, that a bridgehead was being created behind them even as they reaped the bitter harvest of the Chinese Farm. But there was no bridgehead and with every passing hour the likelihood of one was decreasing. The Israeli high command was in fact turning its mind to calling off the operation.

The optimism that suffused Southern Command when Stouthearted Men got under way at sundown had eroded as the hours passed. Dayan was the first to express fear that the crossing might have to be aborted. Elazar said more time was needed before such a decision but he too had reconciled himself to the possibility. At 8 P.M., when Colonel Matt's paratroopers were supposed to be putting their rubber boats into the water, they were still trapped in a miles-long traffic jam far from the canal. It had taken them three hours to cover just two miles. The pontoons were spread out even further back. As for the roller bridge, tank crews untrained for the mission were having difficulties simply towing it. It was still a long way from Tirtur, which, in any case, was in Egyptian hands.

Given the problems with the roller bridge in particular, Elazar wondered aloud whether the paratroopers should be permitted to cross the canal, presuming they reached it at all. The roller bridge was intended as the main span, with the pontoons serving as a secondary bridge. The Gilowas were merely supplementary rafts. Coming to terms with a possible worst case scenario, Elazar said that if the crossing were aborted the IDF would expand the foothold it had gained on the Sinai bank around Matsmed. If a cease-fire were declared, Israel would thus at least have regained a portion of the waterline.

Bar-Lev, however, did not reconcile himself to the possibility of failure. If Sharon's division continued to have difficulties opening Tirtur and bringing the bridges forward, he said, Adan's division should be sent in to help. Committing it to the battle for the roads would mean eroding the division's strength before it crossed the canal. But otherwise there might be no crossing at all. Adan himself had suggested that his division undertake the diversion, thereby permitting Raviv's brigade to assist in the Chinese Farm. For the moment, Bar-Lev's proposal was left hanging while all waited to hear what tidings issued from the radios. A dollop of good news came from intelligence intercepts which indicated that the Egyptians were viewing Reshef's attack as an attempt to roll up the Sixteenth Division's flank northward, not as a prelude to a canal crossing westward. The diversionary attack by Raviv at Missouri to the northeast had encouraged that perception.

Gonen repeatedly urged Matt to move faster. The hapless paratroop commander not only was trapped in gridlock but still had no boats. He had been told that an engineering unit would meet him with the boats, but one rendezvous had already been missed. Matt had been assigned the code word "Acapulco" to pronounce when he secured the bridgehead. That prospect was beginning to seem as remote as the Mexican resort itself.

At 9 P.M., Matt finally linked up with the engineers waiting at the side of upper Akavish, just out of Egyptian artillery range. It took an hour and a half to inflate the thirty-six boats and lift them atop the half-tracks. The vehicles, which normally carried no more than twelve soldiers, were crammed with twenty-two or more. Two more men were now added to each—combat engineers who would ferry the boats across the canal. The engineers distributed life jackets and explained how to carry the boats to the water and how to get in and out of them.

At 10:30, the paratroopers, escorted now by a tank company, started forward again. The road ahead was empty now. When they reached the stretch of Akavish exposed to Tirtur, a few Saggers sailed overhead and bullets hit some of the boats atop the half-tracks without causing serious damage. Akavish was clearly not yet secure, and would be even less so in daylight. As the convoy reached Lexicon close to midnight, the paratroopers glimpsed evidence of the battle that had been raging for hours around the Tirtur intersection—scattered bodies and burning tanks. In a torn Israeli half-track, twelve flaming corpses were still sitting upright. Paratroop pathfinder teams in the lead were dropped off to stake out the route with small signal lamps for the half-tracks following.

Matt ordered the artillery batteries assigned to him to begin softening up the opposite bank. He told the commander of the tank escort to position his company at the Tirtur intersection, which he presumed had already been cleared by Reshef. "Secure towards the north and keep an eye out to the east," said Matt.

Reaching the Yard—the staging compound at Matsmed—paratroopers in the lead company leaped from their vehicles and swept through the area, firing short bursts from Uzis into dark corners. After depositing the paratroopers, the half-tracks started back to pick up the second battalion. At Lexicon, the drivers saw some of the tanks that only minutes before had escorted them burning at the Tirtur intersection a few hundred yards to the north. In the light of the flames, Egyptian tanks were visible.

Meanwhile, engineers cleared the canal embankment of barbed-wire concertinas with explosives. Six rubber boats filled with equipment were dragged with difficulty up the embankment and eased into the water. Outboard motors carried the lead paratroop company swiftly across the canal. Platoon commander Eli Cohen was the first man to climb ashore. A few steps inland was a five-foot-high concrete wall, topped by a barbed-wire concertina. Lieutenant Cohen tossed a sack of TNT with a timing device atop the wire and leaped back into the boat. It pulled out into the canal and the men lowered their heads. With the explosion, the boat returned.

Climbing through the hole opened in the fence, Cohen surveyed the terrain beyond. To his left, barbed wire appeared to enclose a minefield. Straight ahead was a dirt path. There were no Egyptians in sight. One of the men inserted a stake with a green light into the canal bank to indicate a landing point. Another squad which crossed a hundred yards north placed a red light. A company commander monitoring the operation from a boat in the middle of the canal radioed Matt on the Sinai embankment that the landing points were secured. "Acapulco," said Matt into his mouthpiece. It was 1:35 A.M. The one-word message was heard not just in Sharon's division headquarters, to which it was addressed, but in Southern Front headquarters at Umm Hashiba and the Pit in Tel Aviv, where anxious officers, monitoring the division's radio network, had been awaiting it for hours.

The crossing by the 750 paratroopers in the first battalion proceeded rapidly, the men embarking from red and green "beaches" on the Sinai bank to their counterpart landing points across the canal. Once across, they moved swiftly inland to stake out a perimeter three miles wide and one mile deep.

Sharon reported to Umm Hashiba that Matt's force had met no opposition. "How's it going elsewhere?" he asked.

Dayan, gripped by the enormous gamble to which they were now committed, took the microphone. "Arik," he said, "there is no elsewhere."

Tirtur remained a bone in the throat. Not only was the road itself blocked to the roller bridge, but Sagger teams at its upper end were able to interdict Akavish, which the pontoons were to take. A brigade of Egyptian infantry was deployed in the deep trenches abutting Tirtur, armed to the teeth with antitank weaponry. Without secure roads, no canal crossing could be sustained. Determined to pry Tirtur open, Reshef ordered Brom to attack it with his two remaining companies. The reconnaissance commander led the attack himself at 3 A.M. Heavy fire was opened on his force as it drew near the intersection. Brom managed to hit two Egyptian tanks. A sergeant commanding a tank dashed forward and destroyed another T-55 at point-blank range. But Brom's tank was hit by an RPG thirty yards from the intersection and the attack halted. The reconnaissance commander who had discovered the seam between the Second and Third Armies was dead.

Reshef called forward a reserve paratroop unit under Maj. Natan Shunari. The unit, one of the most unusual in the IDF, was an "old boys' " unit, made up of men who had served at one time or another in the same elite paratroop reconnaissance battalion. Although most were recent veterans in their twenties, almost half were over thirty and at least one was over forty. Among them were men whose names were legend to Reshef himself. Many were personal friends of the country's military leaders, alongside whom they had fought in past wars. The unit had been dispatched on Yom Kippur to the foot of the Golan Heights. Shunari called division commander Raful Eitan and asked him to "give us work."

"What color are your boots?" asked Eitan.

"Red," replied Shunari, the color of paratroop footgear.

"I need black," said Eitan, meaning tank crews.

Shunari prevailed on Eitan to bring the unit up to the heights, but after a couple of days the army dispatched it to Sinai, where Egyptian commando operations were beginning to put a high premium on special forces. After conducting patrols for Mendler's division for several days, Shunari called his old friend Ariel Sharon to ask if he had more interesting work to offer. Sharon immediately had Shunari's unit transferred to his division. It was placed under Reshef's command just as Stouthearted Men was getting under way. Within hours, Shunari and his men, who had feared being left out of the war, would be approaching the most dangerous strip of ground on either front.

Reshef gave Shunari's paratroopers the task of opening Tirtur Road and placed the tanks of Capt. Gideon Giladi under his command. Giladi had taken over what remained of Major Beitel's battalion. He had been involved for hours in the melee around the Tirtur intersection, and had already had one tank shot out from under him after losing one earlier in a ditch crossing the dunes. The wildness of battle was upon him. His tank constantly moved back and forth to avoid presenting a sitting target. When the commander of another tank company who had just arrived climbed on Giladi's tank for a briefing, he found Giladi impatient. I have no time to talk, he said. I have to open the road. Giladi started his tank forward even before the other officer leaped off.

Giladi had earlier spotted the opening to Tirtur Road, barely visible in the darkness beyond the wrecked armored vehicles that littered the intersection. But he had been ordered not to enter until sufficient forces had been assembled. Now he was told to lead the six half-tracks bearing Shunari's paratroopers up the road.

Giladi, a former paratrooper, had switched to the armored corps after his brother was killed commanding a tank in the Six Day War, and had served in his brother's unit. Approaching Tirtur, he had only two tanks, his own and his deputy's. The pair wove their way between the smoldering wrecks and entered the road without being fired on, the first time it had been penetrated since the battle began. "The intersection's open," Giladi reported to Shunari, who followed a few hundred yards behind. The veteran paratroopers could smell war—scorched rubber, cordite, smoke. The smell was familiar but not the intensity. A tank crewman ran towards them out of the darkness. His face was blackened with soot and he was weeping. All the other crewmen in his tank had been killed, he said. The young tanker vainly implored the men in the half-tracks to turn back.

On the radio, Giladi reported that he had encountered masses of infantry but was coping. Then silence. His deputy radioed that he was turning back but then his radio, too, went dead. Continuing forward, Shunari found Giladi's tank burning and the other disabled. Dead tankers were sprawled on the ground. Shunari reported the scene to Reshef, who told him to dismount and proceed on foot, for fear that the half-tracks would likewise be hit.

Shunari, however, preferred to keep his men inside the half-tracks which offered a measure of protection against small-arms fire. Within moments, Saggers and RPGs were exploding around them and gunfire raked the vehicles. Shunari managed to break through, together with the vehicle behind him, but the rear half-tracks were all hit. The men in the trapped vehicles returned fire but their situation was hopeless. Shunari called on Reshef for artillery support. "They're slaughtering my unit," he shouted. The brigade commander said no artillery was available. "I'm in the same situation you are."

Shunari ordered his men to abandon the vehicles and head south on foot towards Akavish Road. By this time no one was alive in the rearmost half-track. Some of its occupants had attempted to charge the Egyptian positions but got only a few paces. The rest were hit as they fired from the vehicle or from positions they took alongside it. Some men managed to escape the other burning half-tracks and began pulling back. The Egyptians took up pursuit. A group of Shunari's men including the unit doctor heard the treads of an approaching Egyptian tank as they made their way through the sands, carrying wounded. Dawn was breaking and there was nowhere to hide, but as they prepared for death fog draped itself over the desert with the suddenness of a shade being drawn. The tank passed within a few dozen yards. The men could not see it but they could hear its engine growing louder and then more distant.

Another group of Shunari's men took cover at the sound of incoming mortars. Three were killed by the explosions. The fourth, at forty-one the oldest man in the unit, turned to see a line of infantrymen heading for him. He fired the antitank missile he was carrying into their midst and succeeded in escaping. Of Shunari's seventy men, twenty-four were killed, including his younger brother, and sixteen wounded.

While Reshef's brigade was fighting its desperate battle in the Chinese Farm and Raviv was creating a diversion at Missouri, Sharon's third brigade, commanded by Haim Erez, was attempting to tow the bridging equipment to the canal. The seemingly pedestrian chore proved far more onerous than had been imagined. The roller bridge was once again harnessed to the tanks of

Shimon Ben-Shoshan's battalion in the expectation that Tirtur was about to be opened. The men had caught up on their sleep during the day. "Ready," said Ben-Shoshan. "Ready. Engage gears. Move." The giant structure began undulating across the dunes like a monumental caterpillar. On one of the first descents, the bridge ran up on one of the tow tanks. There were no injuries but it took so long to extricate the tank that hopes of reaching the canal before dawn faded. As the dunes became steeper, more tanks were put in harness. There were frequent stops and Ben-Shoshan's voice grew increasingly hoarse as he barked commands. "Ready. Ready. Engage gears. Move." In the distance, Israeli artillery could be heard pounding the Egyptian lines. It was 5 A.M. when they ascended the steepest slope yet. There were sixteen tanks pulling now. Two bulldozers braked from behind on the downslope.

Suddenly a tank commander shouted, "Stop."

The noise of the engines abated and the officer said, "It's snapped."

"Then change the towline," said Ben-Shoshan.

"It's not the towline. It's the bridge."

Engineers rushed forward and saw that the bridge had indeed broken under the strain. They estimated that it would take twenty-four hours to repair. Informed of the breakdown, Sharon ordered Ben-Shoshan to disengage and move up to the canal. Another unit would take over when the bridge was ready.

A reconnaissance officer was dispatched by Sharon to report on the bridge's status. At its inception, the bridge had been called the Lascov Bridge after its originator. When General Tal provided his input and pushed the project through to completion, it came to be called the Tal Bridge. When the reconnaissance officer returned to Sharon, he said, "You can call it the Lascov Bridge again," a hint that it was something a senior officer would no longer care to be associated with.

The tanks assigned to towing the Unifloat pontoons found their task no less excruciating. Jammed roads made passage virtually impossible. A tank officer towing a pontoon from Refidim asked the driver of an empty bus blocking his way to drive into the sands at the side of the road until he could get past. "I'll pull you out afterwards," he said.

The bus driver balked. "If I go into the sands no one will pull me out."

After a fruitless exchange, the tank commander said he was going through. "Just do me a favor; don't stay inside."

With that, he brusquely pushed the bus off the road, not before seeing the driver bolt. But the roads soon became too jammed even for such measures. Pontoons coming from the Baluza area on the Mediterranean coast encountered the same problems. Uri Ben-Ari, overflying the road in a light plane, used a loud hailer in an effort to have vehicles make way. Another officer, however, ordered the pontoons off the road so that other vehicles could get through.

With the pontoons stranded and the roller bridge disabled, Sharon contacted bridgemaster Jackie Even. Only the alternative remained. Are the Gilowa rafts ready? he asked. They were. Then get them moving, said Sharon. Perhaps these retreads from a junkyard would be able to get through.

Apart from being slimmer than the pontoons and not requiring towing, the amphibious Gilowas had a major advantage in that they traveled in convoy while the pontoons were towed separately, each one having to make its own way through traffic. The rafts were also starting out from a point closer to the canal. As they progressed westward, they picked up a tank battalion escort commanded by Maj. Giora Lev. When they reached upper Akavish, Sharon and the five APCs constituting his mobile command post joined them. Small-arms fire was directed at the convoy when it moved into the stretch exposed to Tirtur, but no missiles. Sharon told Lev not to respond and to keep moving. Lev's mission, said Sharon, was to get across the canal "even with one tank."

A bulldozer loomed out of the darkness and the driver flagged Lev down. "How do I get to Tasa?" he asked. The tank officer had no idea how a bulldozer could have reached this remote part of the battlefield, but it occurred to him that he would need one. "Follow me," he said. The bulldozer driver obligingly turned his vehicle around, unaware that he was being led in the opposite direction from Tasa.

The Gilowas reached the Yard before dawn. Lev told the bulldozer driver to break through the canal-side rampart in order to open it for the rafts. Sharon, during his term as head of Southern Command, had placed red bricks to mark a ramp section hollowed out for this very purpose. In his memoirs, he would write that he led the bulldozer to that spot. As Lev would remember it, the first opening was made randomly at his—Lev's—order, not at the hollowed-out section, which was breached later.

Fifteen Gilowas lined up abreast and on command the drivers inflated the rubber floats by pumping in air from the engines, a process that took ten minutes. It was a pretty sight and the tankers watched bemused in the blissful silence. Sharon's intelligence officer, who on Akavish had been listening to the startling, staccato firing of tank guns emanating from the Chinese Farm, was bemused to hear morning birdsong on the banks of the canal.

At 6:30 A.M., the Gilowas passed through the breach and descended into the water, where they were linked up by the engineers to form five rafts, each capable of carrying a tank. Through the breach, Sharon could see palm trees and lush growth on the far bank, like some desert mirage. In the command APC, a sergeant watched Sharon, sitting in the commander's chair, fastidiously straighten out the red paratrooper's beret tucked into his shoulder strap and brush back his hair with his hand before calling his wife on a radio-telephone. Lily, he said with excitement, we're here. We're the first. Sharon asked the sergeant to make sure the men in the command vehicles were shaved. The crossing of the Suez Canal was an occasion that merited a bit of primping.

There was still no bridge but there was now a way to get tanks across the canal. Israel's major strategic move in the war, on the verge of being abandoned, was literally being kept afloat by recycled junk.

In the Chinese Farm, dawn wrapped itself in thick fog as if reluctant to reveal what had transpired in the darkness. Two armies which had hacked unrelentingly at each other for ten hours had fallen silent, resting for the moment on their swords. It had been a surreal night, given up to combat without lines that separate "us" from "them." Death had become so familiar that it was meted out with a weary offhandedness. An Egyptian tank hurrying down Lexicon Road was followed by hollow eyes until someone, at less than fifty yards, put a shell into it almost as an afterthought.

The air was heavy with the smell of cordite and acrid smoke. Orange pulses in the mist hinted at fires all about. Were it not for the morning cold that set teeth chattering, the curtain seemed about to go up on a scene from hell. As the fog dissipated, hell revealed itself. Hundreds of gutted vehicles were strewn over the desert floor, many still burning. Shattered jeeps and trucks were scattered like chaff. But it was the remains of the heavy tanks that most bespoke the violence of the night. Some had their turrets blown off. Some were upended like toys, their gun barrels embedded in the sand. Charred Israeli and Egyptian tanks lay alongside each other. Corpses were strewn on the sand. There were many more inside the vehicles and in the ditches. There was no hint of the orderly lines of a divisional encampment, which this had been, or of the orientation of enemy formations facing each other on a battlefield. This was the all-around chaos of a murderous street brawl that left only an exhausted few still standing.

There had been madness here and no one sensed it in the quiet of dawn more keenly than Lt. Yuval Neria. The twenty-one-year-old officer had been in combat since Yom Kippur afternoon. The battalion he had served with had been destroyed that day and he ended up joining another in one of the hopeless battles at Hizayon on October 8. In the ensuing days, Neria drifted like a vagabond warrior across the battlefield. Three times, the tank he was in was hit and he climbed out to take over other tanks. After his tank was hit in the battle for Hamutal, he hitchhiked to Tasa. Finding three tanks outside brigade headquarters awaiting assignment, he told the crews he was their new commander and moved with them towards the front until he encountered Mitzna's battalion. Mitzna, whom he had not met before, assigned him three more tanks and made him a company commander.

Approaching the Tirtur junction at the opening of the battle, Neria's tank ran onto a mine. He saw to the evacuation of his crew and decided to rejoin the battalion, which had meanwhile advanced into the Chinese Farm. Holding his Uzi close to his body to mask its distinctive profile, he set off on foot in the darkness through the Egyptian lines. He passed within a few dozen yards of Egyptian soldiers in foxholes, chatting or eating, seemingly oblivious to the battle raging a few hundred yards from them. Anyone noticing him would have taken him for someone bearing a message or obeying nature's call. To his front after a while he saw a line of tanks firing towards the north. As he drew close he could see that they were Israeli Pattons. He managed to climb aboard one from the rear without getting shot and discovered that the tanks were from Almog's battalion. The tank commander was not welcoming and Neria boarded another whose commander was happy to let Neria take over as gunner. For the next few hours, he fired as if in a trance, as the Egyptians staged local counterattacks. Ranges were so close that the tank sometimes had to back away from burning vehicles because of the heat. At dawn, Neria was surprised to find himself still alive. But the world itself seemed to have reached its end, reduced to charred metal, a shell-pocked desert, and numbed men at the limit of their endurance.

For Reshef too, dawn offered no balm. Tirtur remained blocked, Akavish was too dangerous for use, and the Egyptians were still stubbornly clinging to the Chinese Farm. He had lost 56 of his 97 tanks. The brigade would lose 128 dead and 62 wounded in the Chinese Farm—tank crewmen and foot soldiers—without causing a significant dent in the Egyptian defenses. By objective standards, the attack was a failure, a bold enterprise that had come undone. Reshef, however, had no intention of writing it off. As he had told Brom the day before, the battle would go to whichever side was more stubborn. If he was hurting, so were the Egyptians.

At 5:50 A.M. Reshef reported his situation to Sharon. His men were

exhausted, he said, but he intended to renew the attack on the Tirtur intersection. He had called down artillery fire on it after Brom's failed attack with
no visible effect. The infantry in the deep ditches were too well protected.
Reshef asked that units from the division's two other brigades—those of
Erez and Raviv—be temporarily assigned to him in order to try to force the
road simultaneously from its eastern end, where elements of those brigades
were positioned. Sharon put a battalion from each of the other brigades at
his disposal.

Daylight would have left Mitzna and Almog exposed on an open plain,
so Reshef ordered them to fall back to a high dune closer to the canal. The
two battalions, which had had forty-three tanks between them when they set
out the night before—little more than half strength—now had ten. As he
started down Lexicon in the heavy fog, with Almog following some distance
behind, Reshef's tank almost collided head-on with an Egyptian tank traveling at high speed. Before he could react, the tank swerved past him and disappeared into the fog. Reshef warned Almog, "T-55 coming straight at you."
The battalion commander had barely absorbed the message when the tank
burst out of the fog to his front. Its hatches were closed and two commandos
with submachine guns were sitting atop it. Almog grabbed his machine gun
but his operations officer had his head out of the loader's hatch, blocking his
line of fire. The Egyptian tank veered off the road and brushed past them on
the left. Before pulling his head back into the turret, Almog had time to see
the commandos cocking and raising their weapons. His operations officer,
who had ducked inside, came back up with his Uzi and sprayed it in an arc.
Almog put his head out in time to see the commandos toppling from the
tank. As the T-55 disappeared into the fog, Almog turned his turret and
pegged a shot in its direction. He was turning the turret back when a jeep
mounted with Saggers darted out of the fog and almost ran into his tank.
"Back up," Almog shouted at his driver. The tank went into reverse and
crushed the vehicle.

Meanwhile, an attack was launched on the intersection by a company
led by Maj. Gabriel Vardi, the first attack undertaken in daylight. Vardi had
approached the crossroad on his own initiative with three tanks, while four
others provided covering fire. He could see the Egyptian disposition that had
been hidden at night, including the ditches sheltering the infantry and
earthen mounds behind which tanks were positioned five hundred yards to
the northeast. His force sheltered behind knocked-out Israeli tanks and
dueled with the enemy tanks, hitting eight without suffering a loss. When a
vehicle mounted with Sagger missiles appeared in one of the broad ditches,

Vardi put a shell into it. A soldier ran from the burning vehicle, stopped, hesitated, and then ran back to lift out a wounded man. The tank commander swung his gun towards the two Egyptians. He too hesitated, then turned the gun away. He proceeded north for a mile, pumping shells into the Egyptian positions, clearly visible at last. With ammunition exhausted, he pulled back.

Reshef meanwhile had gathered the remnants of the reconnaissance battalion and personally led another attack on the crossroad, passing Vardi's force. This time, the defenders, who had stood all night against repeated attacks, raised a white flag. The battle for the Tirtur-Lexicon intersection was over. But not the battle for the rest of Tirtur or for the Chinese Farm itself.

Thirty-one

THE BRIDGES

AMI MORAG'S BATTALION HAD BEEN SERVING since Monday night as outrider for the roller bridge, guarding it against commando attack. Keeping up with the bridge's snail-like pace grated on the tankers' nerves but Tuesday morning, October 16, Morag received a new assignment. The battalion had drawn the short straw as one of the units that would attack the Chinese Farm from its eastern end at Reshef's behest. It was to proceed down the length of Tirtur to its intersection with Lexicon. Morag had little idea of the fierce battles that had raged around Tirtur all night. It was his understanding from Reshef that he would be encountering random bands of tank hunters. He was also to evacuate survivors of Shunari's unit, believed to be sheltering in ditches.

Fog limited visibility to a few yards as Morag approached the upper end of Tirtur. He told his deputy, Yehuda Tal, to stay on high ground to the rear with one company to provide covering fire. As Morag moved forward with his second company, two men emerged from the fog—Shunari and one of his officers. They told Morag where they believed their comrades to be. As they conversed, the fog began to lift like a theater curtain. On the vast stage that revealed itself was the Chinese Farm, veined with ditches. Two miles to the northwest were two large buildings housing pumping equipment, the major structures in the farm. Out of the gray landscape, red balls of fire began to waft in their direction. "Missiles," shouted Morag.

He knew the area from years of service in Sinai and led his tanks into the shelter of an adjacent shallow quarry. As the last tank entered, the missiles passed overhead. To Morag's surprise, Saggers continued to overfly them. The missiles even appeared to be dipping downwards, as if searching the tanks out in the quarry. Morag realized that the Sagger operators were firing at the tank antennas projecting above the depression and were attempting to guide the missiles down into the quarry with their joysticks even though they could not see the tanks themselves. He had his men lower the antennas and the firing ceased.

Morag remounted the road and led his tanks forward, but a torrent of missiles sent them scurrying back. The battalion from Raviv's brigade assigned to Reshef moved into position a mile north to provide covering fire. Morag was concerned about friendly fire and asked the commander of the tank behind him to keep his eye on the nearest tank in the covering force. As he moved up to the road, the tank commander behind him said, "He's swiveling his gun." Morag ordered his driver to pull back. As he did, a shell exploded where he had just been. Morag asked Reshef to have Raviv's battalion withdraw. "I have troubles enough with the Egyptians," he said.

To his left, he could see Ben-Shoshan's battalion, which had disengaged from the roller bridge, heading down Akavish towards the canal. It was escorting half-tracks bearing the second half of Matt's paratroop brigade. Morag warned Ben-Shoshan to beware of Saggers. "Thanks, I see them," came the reply. A moment later, a missile hit Ben-Shoshan's tank, wounding him. The tanks continued forward but the half-tracks were ordered back.

Morag tried to move forward once again, but the rate of enemy missile fire had not slackened, and he pulled back. Raising Reshef, he said it was suicidal to try to force Tirtur. We're not up against tank hunters, said Morag. There's an army out there. With the entire crossing operation dependent on opening the road, Reshef was unyielding. If Morag did not push down Tirtur, Reshef warned, he would face charges of disobeying an order. He promised that when the tanks moved forward this time, artillery support would be heavier.

Major Tal, who heard Reshef's order, could see a multitude of Egyptian infantrymen carrying Sagger suitcases and RPGs moving into positions paralleling the length of Tirtur. He told Morag to refuse the order. It was madness to move down that road, he said. Unaware of the importance of their assignment and of the battle for Tirtur that had raged during the night, Morag's officers believed that Reshef was ordering them to undertake a doomed mission only because they were not part of his organic brigade. The battalion had still not fully recovered from the trauma of its baptism by fire at Hamutal, even though it had been in numerous skirmishes since. It had suffered another grievous blow the previous night when its third company, detached to escort Matt's paratroopers to the canal, lost four of its seven tanks at the Tirtur intersection. The dead included the company commander—a platoon commander appointed to the post after all of the company commanders had been wounded at Hamutal.

Morag understood now that his mission was do-or-die. He would carry out Reshef's order but save what he could of the battalion. Tal's force would stay where it was. Of the eight tanks with Morag, three commanded by sergeants would remain behind at the edge of the quarry to provide covering fire in relative safety. The remaining five, all commanded by officers, would follow him down Tirtur. Morag told the officers they would move fast, firing everything they had, and keep advancing "at all costs."

As soon as Morag's force emerged into the open, a tank was hit by a missile but managed to limp back to the safety of the quarry. The remainder continued forward under an astonishing barrage of missiles. The unit had encountered Saggers on Hamutal and since, but nothing like this. To one officer, it seemed as if some enormous machine gun were spraying missiles rather than bullets. From the heart of the Chinese Farm, Saggers were lifting off like fireworks.

Morag, in the lead, saw the ditches intersecting the road dark with infantrymen. The tank commanders were exposed in the turrets but the Egyptian infantrymen in the trenches were too stunned by the armor thundering by to shoot straight. The tank guns fired into the trenches and the tank commanders raked them with machine-gun fire. The loaders worked like railroad firemen, feeding shells into the guns as fast as they could, pausing only to hand up machine-gun ammunition boxes to the commanders in the turrets. There was no time to throw the casings of the expended shells out of the loader's hatch, so the hot metal tubes began to pile up inside the tanks.

The drivers weaved as they sped along the narrow road to throw off the aim of the Sagger operators. Guide wires from near misses wrapped themselves around antennas. Morag had given up any thought of emerging alive. He called for artillery to be fired at the tanks as they moved so that shells straddling them would impact on the enemy infantry. In less than two miles, Morag's gunner fired thirty shells. Morag himself, flinging grenades and firing his machine gun, went through three ammunition belts and resorted finally to his Uzi. "Wherever we fired, we hit," he would report. "There was infantry everywhere."

One tank was stopped by a Sagger. Major Tal could see the commander—who happened to be Amnon Reshef's brother-in-law—emerge from the smoking vehicle, carrying a wounded crewman on his back. The other two crewmen followed. An APC manned by paratroopers dashed in from the south. It too was hit and its commander seriously wounded, but it managed to reach the tankers and make it back with them to Akavish.

Two-thirds of the way to the Tirtur-Lexicon intersection, Morag found the road blocked by the two disabled tanks of Major Giladi and his deputy and by the skeletons of Shunari's half-tracks. Deep trenches barred any way forward. Missiles were now also being fired at them from somewhere between Tirtur and Akavish. "Left," Morag shouted to his driver. They turned off Tirtur and found themselves racing alongside a ditch filled with Egyptian soldiers. Until now the ditches had intersected the road at an angle, but this one was parallel. Morag could see the frightened faces in the ditch. He also saw the RPGs. His tank gun fired point-blank at the soldiers and the machine guns wreaked havoc. They were so close that Egyptians in the ditch were being burned by the flare from the tank gun, which was almost touching them. Morag kept using an override device to take control of the gun from the gunner in order to fire at RPG holders in the trench ahead. The gunner, feeling naked, kept calling for him to give him the gun back.

To his immediate front, Morag saw a ditch cutting across their path. "Stop," he shouted.

The driver, however, had, from his seat lower in the tank, been looking straight into the faces of the infantrymen they were passing. "I'm not stopping for anything," he shouted back. He hit the near lip of the ditch at top speed and the tank spanned the void. Morag could hear the treads trying to grip the ground on the other side of the ditch and then find purchase. The other tanks all managed to get across or around.

For the first time since they had started out, there was no enemy in sight and no Saggers. To their front was a low hill. Morag halted alongside it and the other tanks pulled abreast of him in a swirl of dust. Silence descended. From their turrets, the tank commanders looked at each other in amazement. It made no sense but they were all still alive. Everyone's shirt was soaked with sweat. Someone let out a whoop. Then all began to cheer. The crews descended from the tanks to urinate and to let their frayed nerves settle. As they luxuriated in a long pee, Morag heard shouts in Arabic on the other side of the hill, but it made little impression on him. As he would later describe his feeling, he was "beyond reality."

Climbing back onto his tank, Morag was contacted by Major Tal. "I see your tanks," he said. "Don't get off them. There are Arabs near you." Tal guided Morag, steering him away from the Egyptian forces scattered between Tirtur and Akavish. The route took them through a wide ditch—wide enough for tanks. They had not proceeded far in it when they came upon twenty soldiers. Morag recognized them as remnants of Shunari's force. The paratroopers were exhausted and without water. They climbed on the tanks and within moments had drunk dry the jerricans of water stored on the outside of the turrets.

When the tanks reached upper Akavish, Morag reported his position to his organic brigade, that of Haim Erez. He did not want to get any more orders from Reshef, he said. He did not want to talk to him; he did not want to see him. If he saw him, he said, he would shoot him. (The two men would work together amicably in the future when Reshef was head of the armored corps and Morag served as his deputy.)

The tanks had penetrated almost the length of Tirtur, through the heart of an infantry brigade armed with antitank weaponry, and made it back without a fatality. They had rescued the paratroopers and had inflicted heavy casualties. But the bottom line remained unchanged. Tirtur was blocked and Akavish too dangerous for use.

Matt's paratroopers across the canal found themselves in an unreal world—green and tranquil. The west bank of the canal was a lush agricultural strip, dotted with palm trees and mud-hut villages—a striking contrast to the barren wastes of Sinai. The strip was irrigated by Nile water fed by the Sweetwater Canal, which ran down its center. The troops were beginning to call the territory west of the canal "Africa." Like the Bosporus, which separated Asia from Europe on the other side of the Mediterranean, the canal in effect separated Asia from Africa.

The paratroopers were prepared to hold out alone against armor, if necessary. Equipped with three hundred LAW antitank missiles, newly arrived in the American airlift, as well as the forty bazookas organic to the unit and a number of recoilless rifles, they were prepared to do to Egyptian tanks what the Egyptian infantry had been doing for the past ten days to Israeli tanks. The paratroopers did not remain alone for long. The Gilowas which Giora Lev had escorted returned the courtesy by ferrying his fourteen tanks across the canal at dawn together with a company of infantry in APCs.

The Egyptians still had no idea what the Israelis were up to; not a shell had been fired at either bank. In this bucolic interlude, soldiers could imagine that they had left the war behind. A tank officer being ferried across, in a lighthearted gesture to the tank commander on the raft following, bent the antenna of his tank towards the water as if it were a fishing rod. But Matt told his men to dig foxholes in anticipation of what was bound to come.

Major Lev led two tanks, each carrying a paratroop officer in the turret, to a former airfield housing Egyptian logistics units a mile from the landing point. A sentry at the gate, assuming they were Egyptian, saluted as they approached. The tanks rolled down the runway, shooting up a score of vehicles and antiaircraft guns. Returning to the crossing point, Lev received a call from someone who identified himself with a code number he did not recognize.

"Who are you?" asked Lev.

"Do you know my voice?" asked the caller. This time Lev recognized the drawl of Haim Bar-Lev. "Yes sir," said the major.

"I'm putting you under the command of the air force commander," said Bar-Lev.

A new voice now addressed Lev. It sounded like Benny Peled.

"Do you see the flowers on your map?"

If the sudden transfer of his tank battalion to the air force was strange, this question was stranger still.

"What flowers?" Lev asked.

"Do you see numbers in red?"

On his map, Lev saw groupings of four red numbers in many locations on the west side of the canal. Now that he looked, he noticed that alongside each was a sketch of a daisy.

"Yes, I see them."

"Destroy all those in your area. Out."

Lev decided to wait for brigade commander Erez, who was accompanying Ben-Shoshan's battalion. They were ferried across at 10 A.M. Erez was as puzzled as Lev about what the flowers designated.

Setting out on the mission with twenty-one tanks and the infantry company, Erez left seven tanks to protect the bridgehead. When they reached a bridge over the Sweetwater Canal, they encountered Egyptian tanks. The Israeli column had to remain in single file because of bogs straddling the road. Only the tank in the lead, commanded by Capt. Yossi Regev, could engage. In an hour-long cat-and-mouse duel through the shrubbery, Regev destroyed four tanks. Urged by Lev to move forward, Regev said he believed a fifth tank was lying in ambush. He spotted it at last, through the window of a hut. The tank had entered by breaking through the back wall. Regev put a shell through the front wall.

The tanks set off across a flat, flinty plain unsoftened by the dunes familiar from Sinai. Egyptian trucks which appeared randomly on the road, some of them carrying Frog missiles, were destroyed. At a desert encampment, the raiders came on half a dozen tanks and a score of personnel carriers fitted with antitank recoilless rifles, a configuration the Israelis had never seen before. Erez's tanks destroyed them at a mile's range.

After half an hour, they approached the map coordinates of the first "flower." A mound appeared in the distance. As they got closer, they could see earthen ramps, an antenna, a van, and the sleek outline of SAM missiles pointing skyward. A reserve officer who was an engineering student at the Technion told Lev that the van was the brain center that controlled the system. As the tanks fired, the missiles ignited, cavorting wildly before exploding in a puff of yellow-orange smoke. Two other SAM sites would be hit, the tankers looking forward each time to the pyrotechnic display. The tanks fired from a distance but entered one installation to top up from drums of diesel fuel.

The raid took the force twenty miles west of the canal. Asked by Sharon how he was faring, Erez said, "I can go on to Cairo," about fifty miles distant. When an Egyptian truck convoy was spotted far to the west, Erez sent the infantry company to deal with them. The APCs reached ten miles closer to Cairo before overtaking and destroying the convoy.

In late afternoon, Erez asked division whether he should remain where he was in order to intercept enemy forces heading towards the bridgehead. He was told to come back; his force was not big enough for such a mission. The tanks returned to the bridgehead before dusk after having completed a sixty-mile circuit, leaving behind them a small hole in the skies free of the threat of SAMs.

Although Erez's brigade was part of Sharon's division and constituted the first tank force to operate west of the canal, this activity was considered part of the establishment of the bridgehead itself. It was Adan's division that was designated for the breakout from the bridgehead, a decision that Sharon found hard to swallow. When Gonen had earlier reminded him in a radio conversation that Adan's division would cross first, Sharon had not replied.

"Do you hear me, Arik?" asked Gonen.

"I hear you," Sharon had finally responded. "No problem here. I can also cross. No problem."

"I'm ordering Bren to prepare to cross."

"He can cross first," said Sharon. "He can cross second. It's not important."

Matt's paratroopers had during the day destroyed seven trucks filled with Egyptian troops at the northern end of the perimeter. But overall, the bridgehead remained the calmest place on the southern front. With no one shooting at them, the paratroopers and tankers had the leisure to get small fires going for coffee and to enjoy the tranquillity, well aware that their oasis holiday would not last long. In this relaxed atmosphere, the ebullient Lev, a future mayor of the city of Petakh Tikva, did a stand-up routine for Erez and Matt in which he portrayed an angry Sadat upbraiding an apologetic Shazly for not knowing about the Israeli crossing. As a group of soldiers nearby looked out at the waters of the Bitter Lake, into which the canal opened, one of them noted that some scholars believed this to be the area where the waters had parted for the Israelites more than three thousand years before on their way out of Egypt. "If they don't get a bridge up soon," said another, "we'll have to do it again, in the other direction."

The 890th Paratroop Battalion had thus far taken only a marginal part in the war. Israel's first paratroop unit, it had set combat standards for the IDF in the 1950s under its first commander, Ariel Sharon. With the onset of the war, most of the battalion was flown down to the Gulf of Suez, where it hunted down an Egyptian commando battalion and skirmished with Egyptian forces descending south from the Suez Canal front. But the battalion, part of the standing army, was still waiting for a mission appropriate to its potential.

On Tuesday morning, battalion commander Yitzhak Mordecai was told to prepare his men for an amphibious operation. Landing craft would carry his unit across the Gulf of Suez for a deep penetration raid with half-tracks and tanks. The battalion was already at its embarkation point when Col. Uzi Ya'ari, commander of the brigade to which the 890th belonged, arrived to announce a mission change. Lieutenant Colonel Mordecai's battalion was to board planes immediately for Refidim.

Although the Gilowas were performing nobly, headquarters was unwilling to rest a two-division attack across the Suez Canal on a handful of rafts. Apart from their limited capacity, the Gilowas could easily be sunk once shelling started. Construction of at least one bridge was imperative. Southern Command began pressing Sharon late Tuesday morning, when the dimensions of the problem became apparent. There was a growing feeling at headquarters that in his eagerness to cross the canal, Sharon had not applied himself sufficiently to opening the roads and bringing up the bridges. It was an issue that would bring to the fore the latent antagonism between Sharon and other generals, particularly Bar-Lev.

"What we need," said Bar-Lev to Sharon on the radio, "is a bridge and a road. To my regret we have neither. Can you do this with your own forces or should we send in someone else [a reference to Adan's division]?" Sharon said he had no need of help. "Aha," said Bar-Lev, not hiding his skepticism. "You don't need anyone else right now. Arik, as long as there is no real bridge, we can't cross."

The warning was repeated to Sharon by Gonen. Without a bridge, he said, the operation would have to be canceled. Telephoning the Pit, Gonen said, "I'm calling so that the mood where you are doesn't become too optimistic. What happened is that Sharon dashed for the canal and left behind unopened roads." Bar-Lev barred further transfer of tanks across the canal.

The order struck Sharon as madness. "In war," Napoleon had written, "there is but one favorable moment. The great art is to seize it." This was the time, Sharon argued, to send over as many tanks as possible and turn them loose upon the enemy's SAMs and supply lines while the Egyptians still didn't realize what was happening. If the breakout was delayed, he argued, the Egyptians would have time to seal off the bridgehead. George Patton was described by Erwin Rommel's chief of staff as the only Allied general in the Second World War who dared to exceed safety limits in an attempt to win a decision, a description that applied to Sharon. He disagreed with Southern Command's contention that the forces across the canal were in danger of being cut off. We're not surrounded, he said. It's the Egyptians who are surrounded.

Southern Command was not persuaded. Gonen warned again that unless a bridge was put up soon, the forces west of the canal might have to be withdrawn. Bar-Lev put it differently to Dayan later in the day. If the roads were not opened, the APCs would be brought back but the paratroopers and the twenty-eight tanks already there would remain. In a worst-case situation, the men could be brought back by rubber boats and perhaps even the tanks could be evacuated if the Gilowas were still afloat. As for now, the bridgehead would remain.

Sharon was not thinking in terms of Dunkirk but of blitzkrieg. He wanted to send one hundred to two hundred tanks across on the Gilowas and strike before the Egyptians grasped the situation. Elazar agreed with Bar-Lev that such a large force could not be risked without a bridge, although he agreed to a slight increase in the existing force. The dispute stemmed from a basic difference in temperament that would mark the dissonant relations between Sharon and his superiors throughout the war—the difference, as Bar-Lev would see it, between calculated risk and irresponsible gamble. As Sharon would see it, this was the opportunity they had been seeking since Yom Kippur to unhinge the Egyptian army and it was being thrown away by timidity.

But Stouthearted Men was hardly conservative. The IDF was taking an enormous risk in attempting to infiltrate the bulk of the army through the middle of the enemy line, across a water barrier, with a single pontoon bridge and a handful of rafts and with only a narrow, still unsecured, corridor to the rear. To attempt it without any bridge at all was a risk of a totally different magnitude.

The situation was complicated by a major security slip perpetrated by none other than Mrs. Meir. Unable to contain herself after eleven grim days of war, she decided to share the good news with the nation without first consulting the military hierarchy. "Right now," she said in a speech to the Knesset late Tuesday, "as we convene in the Knesset, an IDF task force is operating on the west bank of the Suez Canal." She assumed that she would not be telling the Egyptians anything they didn't know. But she was mistaken. Dayan was furious but said nothing to her. Elazar was upset too. He was planning to evacuate the forces which had crossed the canal unless Akavish and Tirtur were opened soon. After Mrs. Meir's upbeat remarks, evacuation would be a severe blow to national morale.

Fortunately for Israel, the Egyptians didn't believe her. President Sadat was quick to dismiss Mrs. Meir's remarks as "psychological warfare." Reports of skirmishes west of the canal were filtering in but they did not add up in Cairo to a major crossing, only a showcase raid.

With Sharon's division near exhaustion, Bar-Lev decided to transfer responsibility for opening the roads and bringing up the bridging equipment to Adan.

The arduous task of extricating the pontoons from the twelve-mile-long, bumper-to-bumper traffic jam they had been stuck in since the day before was undertaken by Adan's deputy, Brig. Gen. Dov Tamari, who was assisted by reconnaissance teams and bulldozers. Vehicles blocking the pontoons were pushed into the sands and then pushed back onto the road when the pontoons had passed. It was an excruciating job, but by nightfall a dozen pontoons had reached upper Akavish.

Until the rest of Akavish was safe, there could be no pontoon bridge. Until Tirtur was opened, there could be no roller bridge. If neither was opened, there could be no crossing. The prospect of the roads being opened seemed no closer after a day of heavy fighting.

Adan deployed tanks north of Akavish facing Tirtur, but after a few probes he concluded that the only way to get at the Egyptians in the ditches was with foot soldiers. Southern Command had come to the same conclusion. Colonel Ya'ari was ordered to put one of his battalions at Adan's disposal. The 890th Battalion would go into action this night.

After dark, ammunition and fuel for the Israeli force across the canal were dispatched over the dunes on the route pioneered by Brom. The convoy included Matt's second paratroop battalion, which had been turned back on Akavish that morning. The convoy commanders oriented themselves this time not by phosphorous shells on Fort Lakekan, now occupied again by Israeli forces, but by the lights of ships anchored in the Bitter Lake. The vessels had been stranded when the canal was closed in the Six Day War and foreign shipowners had been maintaining skeleton crews aboard them ever since.

Adan asked his chief ordnance officer, Lt. Col. Haim Razon, to examine the roller bridge, which engineers had estimated would take at least a day to repair. Razon decided it could be done in three hours. Instead of repairing the broken section, he simply cut it away and welded the span back together. This shortened it by five meters but it was still long enough to comfortably bridge the canal. Razon was in the midst of the task when he was informed that his son, a tank officer, had been seriously wounded three miles away. He wanted to rush to him but the doctor tending his son told him by radio that he would be all right and was being evacuated to the rear.

Many senior officers were fighting the war with one ear cocked for news of their own sons on the battlefield. Uri Ben-Ari at Southern Command headquarters periodically had himself patched through to his two sons, who were officers in tank formations on the front line. General Tal took leave of the Pit early in the war to visit his seriously injured son, a tank crewman, in the hospital. Air force commander Peled learned of his pilot son being shot down over the canal when a note was handed to him while he was giving a press conference. He learned of his rescue from a note handed to him a few minutes later, while still answering questions from reporters.

Danny Matt's son was a tank commander in Amir Yoffe's battalion. When he arrived at southern front headquarters, Colonel Matt was jolted to hear that only a handful of Yoffe's tanks had returned from their battles at Mifreket and Milano. He asked the chief medical officer at Umm Hashiba for a list of dead on the southern front. His son was not on it. He did not ask for the list of wounded and would never again during the war inquire about his son's status for fear that his own functioning might be impaired by bad news. (His son would be wounded towards the end of the war.) At the Yard, where Sharon had positioned his forward command post, a crewman descended from a tank and ran to Sharon's APC to embrace his father, the division's signal officer. An hour later, word was received that the youth's tank had been hit and that he was in critical condition, paralyzed in both legs. Sharon urged the officer to take a brief leave to console his wife, but he refused to leave the front.

With Ben-Shoshan's tanks having crossed the canal, the task of towing the repaired roller bridge fell to a battalion commanded by Yehuda Geller. Pulled off the battle line, he found nobody who could issue clear instructions about towing. The engineers seemed to have lost their confidence after the previous failure. Geller had seen a training film about the bridge and tried to remember the towing methods used there. The bridge at least had reached flat terrain. Geller was astonished when told it had been towed over dunes to this point. He and his deputy designed their own drill litany—"Prepare to move—one, two, three—move." With darkness, the towing began. The bridge had progressed less than a mile when Geller was ordered to halt. His tanks remained in harness and the men drowsed off in their seats. About 3 A.M., those who were awake could hear the sounds of heavy firing to their front—infantry weapons, not tank guns. A battle was raging in the vicinity of Tirtur Road.

Colonel Ya'ari had landed by helicopter near Adan's command post off upper Akavish at 10 P.M. and was briefed by the division commander. Tirtur had to be cleared of Egyptian tank-hunting teams before dawn. Otherwise, the bridges would not get through. In short, the paratroopers' mission was critical.

Mordecai and his battalion had been on the go since early morning, when they had prepared for the amphibious operation. At Refidim Air Base, while waiting three hours beside the runways, they had had to take cover from an Egyptian air attack. Buses finally arrived to carry them to Tasa. Mordecai descended repeatedly to talk the convoy through road jams. At Tasa, helicopters lifted them to upper Akavish close to midnight.

Mordecai made his way to Adan's tent to receive his assignment. The

Egyptians were moving about in deep trenches, he was told, so he could not be given specific targets. No air photos were available and there was no time to bring forward an artillery liaison officer. The paratroopers would simply move forward in broad deployment until they made contact. They had to begin moving immediately, Adan said, if the mission was to be completed by dawn, only five hours away. Foot soldiers moving across the terrain in daylight would have no chance.

This was not the way paratroopers were accustomed to work—no hard intelligence, no air photos, no detailed plan, no artillery support. The battalion would be following the route of Morag's run that morning, although no one in Adan's command post knew anything about it since Morag was part of Sharon's division. No one was aware of the masses of infantry Morag had seen in the trenches.

The battalion began moving after midnight. A young paratroop sergeant was elated as he set out in the moonlight on his first combat operation. Three companies, each with eighty to ninety men, moved abreast with a fourth company following in reserve. Attached to the latter were fifty officers who had formerly served in the battalion and had obtained Mordecai's permission to join him for the war.

First contact was made at 2:45 A.M. by the company on the right flank, commanded by Lt. Yaaki Levy. When Mordecai asked what he was up against, Levy, sounding his usual confident self, said he could deal with it. He ordered a platoon to flank the enemy on the right. The platoon commander had not gone far when he caught a glimpse of the Egyptian forces opposite. He went to ground and called Levy. "These aren't just tank-hunting teams. The area's full of troops." There was no reply. Levy, who had charged the Egyptian position, was already dead. His deputy too had been hit. The company was caught on flat terrain immediately to the Egyptians' front. The Egyptians were backed by tanks and supported by artillery and they had night sights, which left the Israelis totally exposed.

Mordecai ordered the company in the center of the line to outflank the enemy position on the left, but it too was caught in the open and its commander killed. The paratroopers in the lead companies were two hundred yards from the Egyptian line, some as close as fifty yards. Almost all officers had been hit. Mordecai called forward officers who had attached themselves to his battalion to replace them.

Maj. Yehuda Duvdevani, one of the volunteers, was ordered to take over the company in the center. As he ran forward, shells exploded around him. The concussions jarred him from side to side but the sand absorbed the shrapnel. Reaching the company, he heard cries from wounded paratroopers lying in no-man's-land. He ordered men to bring them in but no one moved. The young soldiers did not know Duvdevani and would not respond to the gruff voice shouting at them above the din.

He grabbed a stretcher and shouted, "Give me cover." The men did respond to this, and laid down covering fire as Duvdevani started forward, sometimes crawling, sometimes on all fours. Three wounded men were lying fifty yards from the forward Egyptian trench. Duvdevani placed the most seriously wounded man on the stretcher and began sliding it towards the rear as he crawled backwards. Periodically, he would leave him and pull the other two by their arms. "Help me," he said to them. The two managed to propel themselves a bit as bullets hit the sand around them, but Duvdevani had to pull them much of the way. A bullet clanged off a smoke grenade on his pouch, another nicked his belt. At one point, the sand rippled from a machine-gun burst that hit the stretcher. Duvdevani pulled the men one hundred yards before reaching a ditch serving as an aid station. Medics pronounced the man on the stretcher dead. The other two were rushed to the rear. Duvdevani reported to Mordecai on the radio. "I've brought in the wounded. I'm taking command."

The men now responded to his orders. Hearing the sound of tanks just behind the Egyptian lines, he divided his men into teams armed with LAW missiles. As the Egyptian tanks started forward, the first team rose and set the lead tank ablaze. The other tanks pulled back.

Meanwhile, the reserve company came forward to evacuate casualties from Levy's company. With dawn not far off, their commander told them not to waste time crawling. What mattered was speed. Every time he made his way back carrying wounded, the officer saw the trail to the evacuation point marked by more dead and wounded.

Mordecai set up a base of fire with machine guns to cover the rescuers. The man next to him was killed and he himself was cut in the chest by a ricochet but he covered the wound with sand so that his men would not see.

At dawn, a tank battalion commanded by Lt. Col. Ehud Barak, future prime minister of Israel, was sent in. The battalion was made up of men, like Barak himself, who had been studying abroad and had hurried home with the outbreak of the war. Seven tanks advanced—not to rescue the paratroopers but to lead them against the Egyptian positions. Duvdevani told his men to prepare to charge. The tanks lined up abreast of the paratroopers, but a barrage of Sagger missiles erupted from the Egyptian lines and five tanks were knocked out. The other two pulled back.

Lt. Shimon Maliach found himself at first light hugging the ground with casualties all about him and no cover. He and others began stacking the bodies of dead men to shelter behind. The brigade intelligence officer, lying nearby, addressed Maliach by his nickname. "Blackie, look at the mess we've gotten ourselves into." He didn't quite finish the last word. Maliach crawled closer and saw a bullet in his forehead. Men clawed at the sand in an attempt to dig holes.

"Blackie, what's up?" said someone conversationally. It was one of the attached officers, a redhead whom Maliach knew only by his family name, Rabinowitz. As they spoke, Rabinowitz was hit in the back. Maliach put two fingers into the wound to stanch the flow of blood. Rabinowitz gripped Maliach's shirt and said, "Blackie, my wife's about to give birth. Don't let me die." Maliach said, "I'm staying with you. Nothing's going to happen to you."

An APC appeared behind them and a doctor leaped out. Ignoring the fire, he lay on his side alongside Rabinowitz and treated his wound. When one of Barak's tanks was hit nearby and crewmen emerged with their clothes aflame, Maliach and others ran out to roll them in the sand and drag them behind the wall of bodies. The Egyptians spotted them and opened fire with mortars, killing several, including the doctor. Everyone still alive crawled back except Rabinowitz, still groggy from morphine, and Maliach, who stayed with him. Maliach saw Egyptian troops coming out of their trenches and beginning to move forward. To remain was to die. Slapping Rabinowitz to waken him from his stupor, Maliach explained the situation. He was going back for help, he said. Egyptians were advancing. If they reached him before help came, he should play dead.

Wounded by a mortar shell, Maliach kept crawling until he reached a deep trench. Seeing Mordecai there, he begged him to send an APC forward to collect Rabinowitz. None were available. Maliach was evacuated to the hospital. Afflicted with guilt, he would be treated for severe mental stress.

Even before Mordecai's paratroopers made contact with the enemy, Adan had dispatched APCs down Akavish to test Egyptian reaction. The vehicles reached Lexicon without drawing fire. Adan weighed the chances of the pontoons getting through. They were huge, lumbering targets—easy marks for the Saggers—and their destruction would virtually eliminate the chance of a canal crossing, given the difficulties the roller bridge was encountering. But the battle around Tirtur had now begun and the attention of the Egyptians was fixed there.

Adan decided to take the risk. He ordered his deputy, Dov Tamari, to lead the pontoons forward. No fire came from Tirtur, where the paratroopers' fight was raging, as the pontoons were towed down Akavish. The first pontoon arrived at Matsmed at 6:30 A.M., a full day after the Gilowas. The rest would follow over the course of several hours.

Groups of paratroopers would remain pinned down in the Chinese Farm until late afternoon. Seventeen hours after the battle had begun, APCs managed to dash in, with tank and artillery support, and extricate the last men known to be alive. Most of the dead had to be left on the battlefield.

A third of the battalion were casualties—forty-one dead and more than one hundred wounded. Grieving over their losses and angered at having had to fight in such conditions, the paratroopers viewed the battle as an unmitigated disaster. But by loosening the Egyptian grip on Akavish, Mordecai's battalion had opened the way to Africa.

Thirty-two

CROSSING INTO AFRICA

I NITIAL REPORTS TUESDAY MORNING about an Israeli incursion at Deversoir raised little alarm in Cairo. By midafternoon, there were puzzling reports of SAM bases being attacked by a small number of tanks but there was no idea where they had come from. When newspaper editor Heikal passed on to Sadat an account from the wire services of Mrs. Meir's speech in the evening, the president telephoned war minister Ismail, who said there were only "three infiltrating Israeli tanks." Later there were reports of a handful of amphibious tanks which had crossed the Bitter Lake. Still later, the force was said to constitute a raiding party of seven to ten tanks.

Chief of staff Shazly contacted the acting commander of the Second Army, Brig. Taysir al-Aqqad, who said the intrusion was negligible and would be dealt with promptly. Nevertheless, Shazly ordered an armored brigade near Cairo to begin moving towards the canal.

Shazly proposed to Ismail that the Twenty-fifth Armored Brigade be pulled back to the west bank from the Third Army bridgehead in Sinai to deal with the intruders. He also proposed that the Twenty-first Armored Division, in the Second Army bridgehead, send a brigade south along the Sinai bank to close the gap in the Egyptian line through which the Israeli tanks had evidently passed. Given the blow the Israelis had received at the start of the war and the fact that they were heavily engaged on the Syrian front, the Egyptians were thinking in terms of a raid, not a major canal crossing.

Ismail refused to withdraw the Twenty-fifth Brigade from Sinai. Any such withdrawal, he feared, might trigger a catastrophic stampede as in 1967. In order to avoid panic, the Egyptian command had refrained from issuing an alert about the Israeli incursion. Erez had thus been able to pounce on unsuspecting convoys and bases. There had been a number of clashes involving Erez's tanks and the paratroopers but no one in Cairo—or Second Army headquarters—was fitting the pieces together.

Instead of pulling the Twenty-fifth Brigade back, Ismail wanted it to attack northward on the Sinai bank and link up with the tanks from the Twenty-first Division pressing south. Shazly vehemently objected. Such a move, he argued, would place the Twenty-fifth in a death trap. It would have to proceed north for twenty-five miles with its left flank confined by the Bitter Lake and its right flank exposed to possible Israeli attack. Ismail was unmoved. When Shazly raised his point with Sadat during a visit by the president to Center Ten, Sadat turned nasty. "Why do you always propose withdrawing troops from the east bank?" he asked. "You ought to be court-martialed. If you persist in these proposals, I *will* court-martial you." Stung by Sadat's words, Shazly did not argue the point. But he saw to it that a number of antitank infantry battalions in Sinai were sent back quietly to their mother units west of the canal. AMAN picked up on the goings-on at Center Ten. At 8 P.M. it reported that Sadat had taken personal command at army headquarters.

The commander of the Third Army, General Wasel, was deeply distressed by the Twenty-fifth Brigade's marching orders. He telephoned Shazly at 3 A.M. to say that technical difficulties would prevent it from attacking at first light. Although sharing Wasel's fears, Shazly told him the operation would have to get under way as planned. In that case, said Wasel, the brigade was doomed. He pronounced a Moslem prayer signifying resignation to one's fate—"Man has strength for nothing without the strength of God." The brigade, made up of T-62 tanks, started north shortly after 7 A.M.

Adan, meanwhile, began cautiously pressing north from Akavish towards the Chinese Farm with four tank battalions. Egyptian tanks came forward as if to engage but then veered off to lure the Israeli tanks into range of infantry armed with Saggers and RPGs. The advance was slow and contact with enemy tanks mostly at long range.

The attack by Mordecai's paratroopers, in addition to opening the way for the pontoons, had severed a final thread of fortitude among the defenders of Tirtur, who had been subject to attacks for more than twenty-four hours from every direction. They had stood their ground but the pain was cumulative and Adan sensed that they were beginning to buckle. With Akavish still free of enemy fire after the passage of the pontoons, he permitted armored vehicles to proceed down the road from 7:30 A.M. At 11 A.M., the road was opened to nonarmored vehicles as well. Supply and fuel trucks which had been backed up on Akavish for more than a day began finally to stream towards the Matsmed crossing, where construction of the pontoon bridge was under way.

Adan notified Gonen that he intended to send the survivors of Mordecai's battalion to the rear. Gonen objected. The paratroopers, he said, would be needed to keep the Egyptians from infiltrating back into the ditches around Tirtur. Adan said the battalion had been savaged and needed to be pulled off the line to reorganize. There was no point, he said, in prolonging its suffering, particularly now that four tank battalions were involved in the battle. Gonen, however, insisted that the paratroopers remain.

One of Mordecai's officers found him sitting on the ground in the afternoon eating battle rations. Hesitantly, the officer asked, "What happens now?"

The answer was the one he feared. "What happens now? We go in again tonight. Isn't that obvious?"

If he had reservations, Mordecai did not show it. He intended to insist this time on artillery and tank support. And now that he knew the Egyptian disposition, he would attack from a flank rather than head-on.

The battalion commander ordered the men assembled. The ordeal they had passed through was unmistakable on the faces of the young conscripts who sat on the ground in front of him. "We paid a heavy price," said Mordecai, "but the war isn't over. I tell you, soldier to soldier, that whoever doesn't have the spiritual resources to go on can opt out. I will not hold it against him. Whoever fought last night has done his share in this war. But I intend to fight until the war is over. Whoever wants to, can fight with me. It may be that we will have to fight in the same place we did last night. Now, look to your ammunition, have something to eat and drink. Be prepared to move out in two hours."

No soldier backed out even though the thought of going in again to the Chinese Farm was appalling. When Bar-Lev arrived at Adan's command post shortly afterwards, he overrode Gonen and agreed to the paratroopers' withdrawal.

Ferrying vehicles and supplies westward and bringing back casualties, the Gilowas continued to link the two banks. With the onset of Egyptian shelling

Wednesday morning, one raft was hit. It did not immediately sink because its ramp was resting on the western bank, but it was no longer usable. To limit casualties, the crews of each Gilowa were reduced from twelve men to five. The others were ordered to remain in foxholes until summoned to take their turn on the rafts.

In midmorning, Wednesday, October 17, a flight of MiGs attacked the Yard where Sharon had positioned himself. The Egyptians had finally pinpointed the crossing point, some thirty hours after the paratroopers landed on the west bank. Sharon grabbed one of his APC's three machine guns and joined in firing at the aircraft. An artillery barrage descended, turning the Yard into an inferno. Anyone not in an armored vehicle or foxhole was hit. Sharon's best friend, Zeev Amit, who had come down from Beersheva with him as a volunteer wearing a pair of Sharon's boots, was fatally wounded as he leaped from Sharon's APC to return to his own personnel carrier.

Sharon ordered his command vehicles out of the compound as shells burst around them. On the way, his APC fell into a crater and everyone was thrown. Sharon, riding with his head outside a hatch, suffered a gash on his forehead. The crewman who bandaged it concluded that the wound was from shrapnel. Emerging from the Yard, the APCs encountered a tank towing a burning pontoon. Half a mile away were Egyptian tanks. They were facing the other way but Sharon was afraid that they might turn and enter the Yard, where they could in minutes destroy the Gilowas, the pontoons, and the rubber boats, bringing the enterprise to a close. There were no Israeli tanks in the immediate vicinity. Sharon called on Reshef to send help immediately and ordered his APCs to fire their machine guns at the Egyptians. The sergeant manning the heavy machine gun in the command APC hesitated. "But they're tanks," he said.

"Fire," repeated Sharon. The bullets would do no harm to the tanks but would distract their commanders.

The APCs opened fire and managed to scurry behind nearby dunes before the Egyptians turned their guns on them. Reshef's tanks arrived within a few moments and destroyed the intruders. Another pontoon had been hit but the remainder trundled into the Yard intact.

Protecting the bridgehead from the north was Amir Yoffe's battalion, with fifteen tanks. During the night, Yoffe had reported Egyptian infantry withdrawing from the Chinese Farm, in the wake of the paratroop attack on Tirtur. He was told not to interfere with the pullback.

The day began for the battalion with an attack by infantrymen firing Saggers. Well positioned behind the crest of a large dune, Yoffe's tanks dispersed the attackers with a single volley. Soon after, a warning was received of an imminent assault by sixty tanks from the Twenty-first Division. When an hour passed without their appearance, tensions eased.

The only Egyptian vehicle to appear was a fuel truck which had apparently lost its way. Several tanks fired at it and missed. Instead of trying to get away, the driver stopped as if perplexed by the shots. Sgt. Eliezer Barnea, the gunner in the tank nearest the road, was ordered to hit it. Looking through his sights, he saw five men descend from the vehicle. They lined up alongside the truck and faced in his direction as if posing for a photograph. The men apparently took the Israeli tanks for Egyptian. This, Barnea said to himself, is an execution. He took aim and paused—"to give them another second to live"—before squeezing the trigger. He saw the man in the center disintegrate before all disappeared in a ball of flame.

The gunner was acutely aware that death on the battlefield was a capricious reaper and that he was as much its quarry as its instrument. Moving across the battlefield two nights before, he and the other crewmen had told the driver to look through his periscope for the moon, newly risen in the east, if they were hit. Drivers stood the best chance of surviving a hit, and the crewmen wanted to be sure that theirs would carry them back towards the Israeli lines. This morning, the sergeant and his comrades had laughed when Egyptian MiGs attacked an Egyptian tank formation. Not long after, Israeli Mirages attacked Yoffe's battalion, wounding a tank commander. Barnea himself had fired the tank's machine gun at low-flying Mirages someone said were Libyan. They turned out to be Israeli. In approaching the position to relieve another battalion the day before, they had been fired on by one of the latter's tanks and a tank commander was killed. It turned out that both tank commanders—the one who fired and the one who died—were friends who had participated in the same tank course.

After hitting the fuel truck, Barnea climbed into the tank turret and lit a cigarette to steady his nerves. As he did so, he noticed on the ridge opposite dark objects that had not been there before. The objects took on the shape of tank turrets and were joined by many others. The box of matches dropped from his hand. There were flashes from the ridge and pillars of smoke and sand began erupting near the Israeli tanks. The Twenty-first Division tanks had arrived.

The Egyptian tanks descended and closed range. Yoffe ordered his men to commence firing at 1,500 yards. Barnea fired at the tank closest to him. He saw a flash on its skin and shouted "Hit." His comrades cheered but the tank kept coming. He hit it again but the tank came on. Feeling the edge of panic, he wondered if the Egyptians were using some new kind of armor. He hit the tank a third time. It continued for twenty yards and stopped. No one emerged.

Barnea took aim at another tank, but when he squeezed the trigger nothing happened. "Misfire," he shouted. Looking through his sights, he saw an Egyptian tank aiming at his. He touched the Uzi at his feet. If he was trapped in a burning tank, he had decided, he would shoot himself. He saw the flash of the Egyptian gun and shut his eyes. It would take only two seconds for the shell to hit. He counted, "One, two." There was an explosion nearby. The tank commander shouted "Reverse" and the driver took them to the safety of the rear slope, where the loader cleared the breech and inserted a new shell. When they came back up, the tank commander ordered the driver to move forward of the battalion line to a better firing position. Colonel Yoffe ordered them back into line. The tank commander was a sergeant who had started the war as a loader. Barnea and the other crewmen chided him for bucking for a medal.

The Egyptian formation pulled back, leaving dozens of knocked-out tanks. No Israeli tank had been hit. On the radio net, Yoffe asked the tank commanders to report the number of tanks they had knocked out. Such reckonings were generally inaccurate, sometimes wildly so. Apart from the human tendency to exaggerate, two or more tanks often hit the same target and each counted it in its own toll. But the estimate offered at least a rough idea of enemy losses. One crew, commanded by a sergeant named Avi, claimed twelve tanks, an astonishing figure. The total for the battalion came to forty-eight. To general laughter, Yoffe noted dryly that if Avi raised his estimate by two, the battalion could claim an even fifty.

Meanwhile, Adan's forces were preparing to receive the Egyptian attack from the south. The night before, Uri Ben-Ari—now General Ben-Ari—had passed on to Adan an intelligence report that the Egyptians were planning to send the Twenty-fifth Brigade north. With the brigade's line of march apparent, Adan saw the makings of a classic ambush. Tank ambushes are rare because tanks are not easy to hide, particularly in a naked desert. When staged, it is usually by small formations. But Adan intended now to stake out an ambush involving almost an entire division.

On the African shore this day, Matt's paratroopers, reinforced by their second battalion, expanded the bridgehead. A half-track-borne company led by battalion commander Dan Ziv approached the village of Serafeum, site of a major logistics center, and came under heavy fire from the village and wooded areas around it. Despite uneasiness expressed by his officers at the large disparity in forces, Ziv pushed ahead. It seemed to a tank commander accompanying the force that the paratroopers had not yet learned what the tankers had learned: the Egyptians in this war were not to be taken lightly.

The lead half-track, containing fourteen soldiers including Ziv and company commander Asa Kadmoni, was cut off in the middle of the village by an Egyptian counterattack. The fight was led by Kadmoni, who took a position which covered approaches from several directions. Using grenades and ammunition passed to him by the others, he held off attackers at ranges as close as twenty yards for three hours. Several times he scored hits on Egyptian positions with LAW missiles. Kadmoni, who would be awarded the country's highest medal for his stand that day, was down to his last bullets when he heard the sound of tanks. A paratroop combat team using smoke grenades to cover its approach dashed in to retrieve the stranded men. The patrol suffered twelve dead.

While this skirmishing was going on, another front was opening that Israelis would come to call "the war of the generals." It had been in the making since Sharon's arrival in Sinai. No one projected greater charisma among the troops than he. They would paint "Arik, king of Israel" on their vehicles when there would be time for such things. An intelligence sergeant at Umm Hashiba noted the way the body language even of the other generals in the war room changed when Sharon entered—a big man, with a heavy walk and a smile that exuded confidence and a forceful personality. No one ignored him.

Sharon was fed up with Gonen and believed that Elazar and Bar-Lev were behaving timidly when risk taking was called for. The three were unaware of the situation on the ground, he maintained, because they did not visit the front. A formative experience for Sharon had been the battle for Latrun on the road to Jerusalem in 1948. Of the thirty-five men in his platoon, fifteen were killed, eleven wounded, and five captured. Sharon himself was seriously wounded. He would later say that the battle had gone amiss because no senior officer was in the field to make critical decisions. His criticism of his superiors now was outspoken, and he increasingly interpreted orders as he saw fit. Nor was he always generous with his comrades-in-arms. Twice on October 8 he had declined to send forces when Adan had asked for help. When the situation would later be reversed, Adan did not hesitate to send him one of his own battalions.

What particularly infuriated Elazar were the attacks Sharon had staged on October 9 after being ordered not to risk the loss of more tanks. When

Sharon's superiors suspected him of deviating from orders and tried to reach him in the field, he was often unreachable because of "communications failure." More than once he told the commander of his mobile command post not to answer when Gonen, his direct superior, tried to reach him by radio. Elazar was angered during the night of the canal crossing at "the sloppy reports coming in from the crossing site [where Sharon was], like nothing I've heard in all my years of warfare." The reports from Sharon's headquarters about the Tirtur crossroads had referred to an "obstacle" or an "ambush," without making it clear to higher headquarters that it was a major impediment endangering the entire operation. Sharon avoided terminology that might discourage the high command from continuing the attack.

His periodic assertions that the Egyptians were about to break were not supported by events. The IDF was able to deal handily with Egyptian tanks but it had not developed tactics for breaking through entrenched infantry armed with antitank weapons. Since the Egyptian defenses in Sinai were based on entrenched infantry, talk of imminent collapse was unwarranted.

Exacerbating the professional differences and the conflicts stemming from Sharon's assertive personality was the bizarre intrusion of party politics. In the three months since leaving the army, Sharon had embarked on a full-blown career in politics and was managing the Likud's election campaign. From the battlefield, he did not hesitate to telephone Likud leader Menahem Begin to express his frustrations over the way the war was being run and to ask for his intervention. He periodically called the defense minister himself, blatantly bypassing the chain of command.

There was suspicion among his fellow generals that, apart from professional considerations and natural pugnaciousness, Sharon was motivated by a desire for personal glory that would help him in his political career after the war, in particular the glory that would come from being the general who led the attack across the canal. The suspicion was deepened by the fact that Sharon warmly welcomed reporters who visited his division headquarters. Sharon supporters pointed out that he did not solicit these visits and that reporters sought him out because he was optimistic, friendly, colorful, and accessible. (Adan's command post was generally in the dunes.) Even the bandage around Sharon's forehead came to be seen as a contrived image enhancer. When Sharon was reported to have tossed oranges from his APC to troops as they waited to cross the canal, an officer who had served with him in the early days of the commandos smiled at what he saw as the populist gesture of a newborn politician. "It's not like him," the officer said. "He used to act like a general even when he was a major."

When Bar-Lev took over Southern Command, the political aspect took

on added resonance. Bar-Lev was a politician now too, and from the opposite camp at that. He had temporarily given up his post as commerce minister in the Labor government in order to return to uniform. When the war
was over, he and Sharon would be on contending lists for the Knesset. At
first, the two "politician-generals" joked about it with each other, despite
their personal antipathy. There was lighthearted talk of a "Likud division,"
Sharon's, and a "Labor division," Adan's. Although Adan was not a political
figure, he was, like Bar-Lev and Elazar, a veteran of the prestate Palmach
strike force, which was identified with the Labor Party. As differences over
the conduct of the war deepened between Sharon and Bar-Lev, lightheart-
edness gave way. "He's a divisional commander who's a politician," said Bar-
Lev on October 14, after Sharon sought to pursue the Egyptian tanks, falling
back on their well-defended lines, instead of waiting for implementation of
the canal crossing operation that was to begin the next night.

   "It's not the insubordination that's so astounding," Elazar had complained to Dayan of Sharon's positioning himself for a canal crossing on
October 9 in defiance of orders. "It's the logic of his plan." Dayan also heard
from Bar-Lev that Sharon was not obeying orders. "Whatever I ask for is not
executed. I don't know what he's doing."

   Elazar seriously considered dismissing Sharon for insubordination—
Ben-Ari was one of the officers mooted as a replacement—but he knew that
Dayan would oppose it. Although Dayan was also upset by Sharon's insubordination, he could not help admiring his battlefield flair and boundless
energy. Some officers feared the adverse effect of Sharon's dismissal on
morale, both in the country and among the troops. Sharon was adulated
by his men and respected by his officers. Many of his key personnel were
members of kibbutzim whose left-leaning political views differed sharply
from his. Even when these political differences deepened in later years, they
would still count it a blessing that Sharon had led the division in war. Reshef,
who had not known Sharon well before the war, found him a superb field
commander—able to read a battle, decisive, cool under fire, and able to del-
egate authority. His subordinates would credit his firm leadership with the
crossing's success.

   The tensions surrounding Sharon came to a head during an impromptu
conference at Adan's forward command post at noon Wednesday. Dayan
had helicoptered in to be briefed by Adan on the upcoming battle with the
Twenty-fifth Brigade and his division's pending crossing of the canal. The
minister invited Sharon to come up from the Yard to meet with him. Bar-Lev
dropped in on his own and Elazar would soon arrive as well. Sharon had a
few hours earlier come through the air attack on the crossing point in which

he had lost his close friend. He had not seen the other generals since the grueling battle for the bridgehead began two days before and he could have anticipated congratulations at having executed the crossing and good wishes for what lay ahead. But when he descended from his APC, no one extended a hand and Dayan was the only one to greet him. Bar-Lev's first words were: "Any resemblance between what you promised and what you've done is purely coincidental." Bar-Lev was speaking of the failure to open the roads or secure a corridor. In his autobiography, Sharon would write: "At that moment I felt tired to death. After all those terrible battles and casualties . . . when I saw this group of neatly dressed, washed, clean-shaven people and I heard that sentence, I knew there was only one thing to do. I had to smack Bar-Lev's face. I don't know how I kept myself from hitting him."

Adan, who had his own grudge against Sharon for having refused him assistance on October 8, spread a map out on the sand. The others sat down alongside it to discuss the coming moves. When a journalist Sharon had brought along tried to get close, Adan waved him back. Elazar arrived by helicopter and joined the circle. Tones were restrained but the tension was palpable. Sharon said the pontoon bridge would be completed by late afternoon. He urged that four brigades, two from each division, be sent across the canal this night. The Egyptians were already building up a sizable force west of the bridgehead and it was important to smash them quickly, he said. This proposal upset Adan, whose division had been designated to execute the breakout into Africa. It would be a mistake, he said, to send four brigades across since substantial forces were needed on the Sinai bank to expand the corridor. Sharon argued that if the IDF pressed hard enough on the west bank, the Egyptians on both banks would collapse.

"I've been hearing about this collapse for the past week," said Bar-Lev. Sharon's expectations had not been fulfilled, said Bar-Lev—neither the creation of a broad corridor nor the collapse of the enemy.

"Soon you'll be saying I wasn't even in this war," said Sharon.

Bar-Lev decided that two brigades would cross this night, one from each division. The division commanders would cross with them, he said, leaving the bridgehead on the Sinai bank under the command of the deputy division commanders. It seemed like a generous gesture towards Sharon, who was supposed to establish and secure the bridgehead, not participate in the breakout, according to the original plan. But Bar-Lev would later tell Dayan that he preferred having Sharon cross because he believed that Adan's efficient deputy, Dov Tamari, would do a better job of securing the corridor on the Sinai bank.

However, Elazar, who had been listening quietly to the debate, overruled

Bar-Lev on the dual crossing. Stouthearted Men would be executed as planned, he said, and there would be no splitting of the divisions. That meant that Sharon would remain to expand the corridor and Adan's division would pass through to attack on the west bank. Turning to Sharon, Elazar said, "Complete the task assigned to you and then you can cross too." With that, Adan left to monitor the ambush of the Twenty-fifth Brigade. It was time to put the war of the generals aside, if only for a little while, and get back to war with the Arabs.

The killing ground Adan had chosen for the Twenty-fifth Brigade was the sandy plain bordering the northern end of the Bitter Lake. The desert might not have trees to shelter behind but it had dunes. Two of his brigades would hide among them east of Lexicon Road, along which the Egyptians were proceeding. One brigade would be near the head of the column when the trap was sprung. The other would be at the rear, to cut off retreat. Four tanks from Reshef's brigade, already posted on Lexicon several miles south of Matsmed, would block the lead Egyptian tanks, at which point Adan's brigade would strike from the flank. In all, the Israeli tanks involved in the ambush outnumbered the Egyptians by 2 to 1.

It took time to get all Adan's units into position because of the distances involved and the deep sands, which made for slow movement. But the Egyptian brigade commander, Col. Ahmed Badawi Hassan, uneasy about his mission, halted frequently. When he reached Fort Botser, midway up the lakeshore, where Sergeant Nadeh was posted, he paused for three hours. The Israelis were unsure whether he was contemplating going back or waiting for air cover.

Col. Natke Nir's brigade was to attack the main part of the column. His brigade, which had been involved in the failed battle of October 8, included the reconstituted remnants of Assaf Yaguri's battalion. Approaching the ambush site, company commander Yitzhak Brik, a survivor of Yaguri's charge, looked out at the barren landscape with trepidation. He was reminded of that terrible day when he stood on Havraga with Yaguri and the other officers, uneasy about what awaited them in the distant haze. Once again, there were telltale clouds of dust from vehicular movement in the distance. As at Hizayon, the Israeli tanks would have to descend into the plain in order to reach firing range. When Nir ordered the tanks forward, Brik prayed that there would not be Saggers and RPGs this time. Crossing over dunes, unlike traveling on the desert floor, the tanks did not throw up dust that could be visible to the Egyptians in the distance. The tanks halted in an area of low dunes two miles east of Lexicon. The brigade's reconnaissance unit, which had scouted the area in jeeps, ushered them into places where they would be hidden from the road.

At 1:30 P.M. the spearhead of the Twenty-fifth Brigade encountered Reshef's small force on Lexicon. The Israeli tanks opened fire at long range and scored hits. This was the signal for Adan's tanks to spring. Brik led his company out into the open. The Egyptian column, which had not put out a screening force on its flank, continued north for a few moments, unaware of the tanks coming at them out of the dunes to their east. Only when the Israeli force was a mile away did the Egyptians halt and turn towards it. The Israeli tanks likewise halted. The Egyptian tanks were T-62s but Brik was relieved to see that there was no infantry. Facing each other in two long lines like mythic gunslingers on a dusty mile-wide street, the two sides went for their guns. The Egyptian crews, shaken at the sudden apparition of enemy tanks on their flank, fired wildly. Brik could see his own tanks hitting with almost every shot. Egyptian crews began abandoning burning tanks, sometimes even tanks that were still intact. In a short time, the battle in Brik's sector was over without an Israeli loss. Egyptian tanks charged the adjacent Israeli battalion and reached within eight hundred yards before being stopped.

Several miles to the south, a battalion commanded by Elyashiv Shimshi topped a high dune after a thirty-mile dash. Two miles to its front, rear elements of the Egyptian brigade were proceeding northward with a strange nonchalance. "Enemy armor to the front, three thousand to six thousand meters," called Shimshi. "We will close range and destroy it." Designating the order of attack to his company commanders, he led the way forward. Most of the Egyptian force was spread out between Lexicon and the lake, two miles beyond the road. While some of Shimshi's tanks dealt with the vehicles on Lexicon itself, the battalion commander rushed across the road with the rest of his force to hit the main enemy body before it recovered from the surprise. The plain was soon covered with burning Egyptian tanks and APCs.

Shimshi halted near the shore of the Bitter Lake. The sun was about to set and visibility had become difficult because of the dust glare and the smoke of burning vehicles. The Egyptians had recovered sufficiently to call down accurate artillery fire. Egyptian MiGs attacked as well. The commander of Shimshi's southernmost company reported destroying numerous Egyptian trucks and other vehicles, including APCs bearing infantry, at the tail of the

Egyptian column. Shimshi could see dozens of fires in that direction. As the sun went down on a burning desert, the battalion commander pulled his forces back. Some twenty Egyptian tanks, including that of the brigade commander, found shelter in Fort Botzer.

The Egyptian brigade lost an estimated fifty to sixty tanks in the battle as well as artillery and scores of APCs and supply vehicles. Israeli losses amounted to four tanks, two of them to mines, and two dead crewmen. Together with the losses suffered by the Twenty-first Division in the clash with Yoffe's battalion north of the crossing point, the ambush added to the significant erosion of Egyptian tank strength in Sinai—250 to 350 tanks—that began with Sunday's tank battle. As darkness descended, a jubilant Adan ordered his commanders to refuel and rearm before they headed for the crossing point.

Dayan had accompanied Sharon back to the canal after the conference at Adan's command post. Army engineers were putting the pontoon bridge together and bulldozers were leveling ground at both ends of the bridge-head. The two men crossed on a raft and Sharon offered to take Dayan on a tour in an armored vehicle, but Dayan preferred to feel Africa under his feet. When he returned to the canal at 4 P.M. he was able to cross on the bridge. It had taken eight hours for its construction, four times longer than in training. Tides, damage inflicted to the pontoons in transit, and periodic shelling had confounded the timetable. But it made no difference since Adan's forces were engaged with the Twenty-fifth Brigade and were not ready for crossing.

In Tel Aviv that evening, Dayan reported to Mrs. Meir and mentioned in passing his visit across the canal.

The prime minister was astonished. "You were there?"

"Yes," said Dayan. "There are a thousand soldiers there now. Tomorrow morning the whole state of Israel will be there."

Satellite pictures had been laid on the desks of decision makers in Washington and Moscow the day before showing a patch of desert with a score or so of antlike dots. The foray of Haim Erez's tanks beyond the agricultural strip at Deversoir had been spotted. Analysts in both capitals saw this as a raid. Israel described it as such to the Americans. Kissinger hoped it would prove to be more. Movement on a cease-fire had been in abeyance since Sadat rejected the proposal forwarded to him by the British ambassador on the thirteenth. But there had meanwhile been an extraordinary diplomatic development. Kissinger had sent a message to Hafez Ismail in Cairo in the hope that this back channel to Sadat which he had come to value would remain open despite the launching of the American airlift to Israel. "The United States . . . recognizes the unacceptability to the Egyptian side of the conditions which existed prior to the outbreak of recent hostilities," said the message. "The U.S. side will make a major effort as soon as hostilities are terminated to assist in bringing a just and lasting peace to the Middle East."

Ismail's reaction to this measured flash of empathy was an invitation to Kissinger to visit Egypt—this in the midst of a war in which the United States was supplying arms to Egypt's enemy and providing it with its political backing. Sadat was making his move, a political move no less audacious than his military move—turning from the embrace of the Soviets, on whose weapons he was dependent, towards an amicable relationship with the United States, the entity best positioned to pressure Israel. As Sadat had hoped, the war had provided him with the wedge he needed to begin shifting political realities that had seemed as immovable as the Pyramids.

Upon receiving the invitation, Kissinger understood that an endgame was in the offing. But before he joined in he wanted Sadat's hand weakened a bit. Those dots on the satellite photos held the promise of sobering the Egyptian leader, heady from his early victories, more effectively than any amount of diplomatic nimbleness.

The Soviets were frantically trying to keep up with the game, unaware that Sadat had invited in a new player with whom he intended to replace them. American intelligence had learned this day, October 16, that a Soviet VIP plane was en route to Cairo. Premier Alexei Kosygin had abruptly canceled a meeting in the morning with the visiting Danish prime minister and it was believed that Kosygin might be the passenger. It was indeed him. He had been charged by the Politburo, after a seven-hour meeting ending at 4 A.M., with flying immediately to Cairo and persuading Sadat to accept a cease-fire.

Moscow's concern was that the Middle East war not bring it into direct conflict with the United States. For this, a speedy end was mandatory. Chairman Brezhnev noted at the Politburo meeting that the Soviet military was warning that an Israeli counterthrust was imminent. "Remind him [Sadat] that Cairo is not far from the canal," he said to Kosygin. The Soviet premier was to make it clear that Soviet troops would not become involved in the fighting. Foreign minister Gromyko said that without an immediate cease-fire, prospects were dire. "The Arabs would be defeated, Sadat himself would be dismissed, and the Soviet Union's relations with the United States, as well as the Arabs, would deteriorate." President Nikolai Podgorny objected to Kosygin's argument that the Americans would not let Israel lose—which the flaunting of the American airlift was specifically designed to hammer home. To acknowledge that, said Podgorny, "would be a recognition of our weakness." It was too good an argument, however, for Kosygin to abandon.

Before meeting with Sadat the following morning, Kosygin was briefed by the head of the Soviet military mission in Cairo, just back from the front, on the Israeli incursion. Sadat greeted his guest courteously and listened patiently as Kosygin transmitted the Soviet leadership's congratulations on his military achievements. When Kosygin broached the subject of a cease-fire, Sadat said there would be none until he had received international guarantees that all territories captured by Israel in the Six Day War—not just Egyptian territory—would be liberated. Kosygin mentioned Israel's cross-canal operation and warned that Egypt's military situation might worsen if the war went on. Sadat dismissed the penetration as an insignificant event, an Israeli "political maneuver."

The talks continued over three days without making progress. Kosygin said that the Soviets could not continue resupplying Egypt and Syria when their losses came to a thousand tanks a week. The Egyptians themselves had lost six hundred thus far, he noted. "Our resources are not unlimited." The Soviet military attaché told Kosygin that the best Egyptian troops were in Sinai and that Cairo, which had no defensive fortifications, lay open to Israeli attack. At the final meeting, on Thursday, October 18, Kosygin showed Sadat photographs of the battlefield taken by MiG-25 reconnaissance planes. The photos revealed the seriousness of the Israeli penetration but Sadat professed to be indifferent. The "tactical" situation around the Bitter Lake, he said, would have no impact on the war.

The coin, however, had finally dropped. With Kosygin's departure, Sadat hastened to Center Ten and authorized withdrawal of a limited number of armored units from Sinai in order to meet the Israeli threat. The IDF spokesman's office had been instructed by Elazar not to use the term "bridgehead" or "offensive" in talking about events west of the canal. Mrs. Meir's revelation could hardly be refuted but spokesmen would only confirm what she had already said, that troops were fighting west of the canal. Sadat, however, could no longer delude himself that this was merely a raid.

While maneuvering between the Soviets and the Americans, the Egyptian leader also had to work his way around his Syrian ally. A speech Sadat had given in the National Assembly on October 16, a few hours before Mrs. Meir's speech in the Knesset, deeply upset President Assad. The Egyptian leader had said that he was prepared to accept a ccase-fire if Israel agreed to withdraw to all its pre–Six Day War borders. Once the withdrawals were completed, Egypt would be prepared to attend a peace conference convened by the UN and would do its best to persuade other Arab states and Palestinian representatives to attend as well. Assad, who had no intention of ever making peace with Israel, sent Sadat a message expressing sorrow that he had not been informed beforehand of the nature of the speech. Sadat replied to "Brother Hafez" that there was nothing new in his remarks that required consultation. Despite the soft wording, the exchange was a reminder that the Egyptian-Syrian alliance was a marriage of convenience that might not survive changed conditions.

Sadat's speech to the National Assembly had included a warning to Israel that if it struck at Egypt's cities he would retaliate against Israel's cities with Al Kahir missiles. The Al Kahir was a highly inaccurate descendant of missiles Nasser had tried to develop with the help of German scientists in the early 1960s. But there were far more effective missiles in Egypt that could indeed reach Tel Aviv—two brigades of Scuds in the Port Said area. It was these that Sadat had in mind even though they were still under the full control of Soviet crews in the process of training their Egyptian counterparts.

The day after Sadat's speech, an American satellite photographed the uncamouflaged missiles and the pictures were passed on to Israeli intelligence. The Scuds were clearly intended to be seen by U.S. satellites. Mutual deterrence would prove effective. Sadat had publicly threatened to fire Scuds into Israel if his cities and economic infrastructure were attacked. Israel, in turn, warned Egypt via the United States not to fire missiles into Israel or to use poison gas, which it had used a few years before when it sent its army into Yemen. Except for the Kelt air-to-ground missile launched in the opening hour of the war at central Israel and intercepted, Egypt did not fire missiles into Israel. Israel in turn abstained almost entirely from attacking Egyptian infrastructure. The one exception was an attack carried out against underground communication cables at Banha in the Nile Delta. Destruction of the cables obliged the Egyptians to transmit sensitive messages by radio, which could be intercepted. Sadat ignored a request from Assad to send his planes against Israeli cities in retaliation for the Israeli raid on Damascus.

———

Sergeant Nadeh, who had witnessed the ambush of the Twenty-fifth Brigade close-up from Fort Botzer, was filling his diary now with battle scenes. "We saw the attack of the enemy, which pursued the remnants of our brigade that had been well ambushed. But with God's help we managed to silence the enemy and opened our gates to the ambushed tanks." Nadeh was asked the next day to clear a path in the minefield where two of Shimshi's tanks had blown off treads. He climbed into the tanks and found small El Al bags and canned food. He also found an Israeli army jacket which he wore on the way back. When a sentry challenged him, Nadeh responded in German for the fun of it. Before the sentry overreacted, Nadeh laughed and whipped off the jacket.

Listening to Sadat's speech, the Egyptian sergeant had found the president sounding quite confident. "We understood that we have won a victory but that the war will go on," he wrote. Nadeh visited his friend from Alexandria, Adel Halad, in his foxhole next to the canal to discuss the speech. Adel thought they would get a bonus for being in the first wave to cross the canal. "I wondered what I would do with the money. Adel told me, 'Nadeh, you're going to be a great man and you'll achieve all your desires.' I thought of buying a ring for my girlfriend. But I'll get that from my civilian salary when I'm released. With the bonus I'll buy a ring for my mother."

After one of his friends predicted that the war would soon be over and that they would be returning to Alexandria, Nadeh dreamt that he was returning home. "Father ran to me, even though he has suffered in his leg for years. I burst out crying and realized that we have to avoid such thoughts."

His platoon commander, wrote Nadeh, "sleeps all day and gives us hair-raising missions at night." Nadeh was ordered to plant mines in the dark.

Mood swings were wide. "I feel that we are facing great days. We've gotten used to the war and aren't afraid of anything."

The next day he wrote: "An hour doesn't pass without the soldiers arguing among themselves. The war is making us nervous."

Nadeh was asked by his battalion commander to throw grenades into the canal and bring in fish for dinner. "I feel like hearing Beethoven's symphony on courage—the Third, *Eroica*. Today we celebrated Muhsan's birthday. He's twenty-seven. We're fighting all the time with Mahmoud Rezek.

"Every time a shell explodes, I want to explode with it. God preserve us. War is the dirtiest word I know."

Thirty-three

BREAKOUT

A DARK SHAPE LAY ACROSS THE SHIMMERING WATERS of the Suez Canal when General Adan approached close to midnight Wednesday at the head of his division. "The bridge is a magnificent sight," he said to his brigade commanders on the radio. "It's waiting for you."

The way to Africa had been open for seven hours but the battle with the Twenty-fifth Brigade had delayed the crossing. Adan's driver handed him a bottle of whiskey he had been saving for this moment. The general raised a toast to his staff. "Friends, we've come a long way. It won't be much longer before we break the enemy. *L'haim.*"

Shortly after Adan's tanks started to trundle onto the bridge, Egyptian artillery unleashed a furious bombardment. Shells exploded on both banks and straddled the bridge. A tank driver hurrying to cross the bridge drew too close to the tank in front of him, causing one of the pontoon sections to break from the combined weight of the tanks. A bridging tank was summoned to lay its span across the broken section as a temporary measure.

The patch slowed movement but passage continued simultaneously on the faithful Gilowas. The four remaining rafts had been linked into two double rafts, capable of ferrying two tanks on each trip. The raft hulls had been punctured in numerous places by shrapnel, but crewmen managed to plug the holes and pumps worked constantly to remove water. The multilayered rubber floats had thus far absorbed shrapnel without deflating. Tank crews

crossing on the rafts were ordered to keep their hatches open and to be prepared to evacuate instantly in case the raft was hit. Because of the heavy
shelling, however, two tank crews on one of the rafts had closed their
hatches. The raft was hit in mid-canal and immediately capsized, sending
the tanks and their crews to the canal bottom, forty feet down. The Gilowa
crewmen were picked up by rubber boats but the tank crews perished. The
remaining raft remained in use until the damaged pontoon on the bridge was
replaced. The "junk" rafts had constituted the sole vehicular link to the
bridgehead for the better part of two days, ferrying across 120 tanks as well as
APCs and supply vehicles.

Despite the intensive shelling, engineers remained in the open throughout to keep traffic moving and the bridge repaired. When the bridge was hit,
they ran out to fill the hole with sand and cover it with wooden planks. Also
remaining in the open were paratroopers lying along the edge of the bridge
to guard against Egyptian frogmen, periodically throwing grenades into the
water. All duties at the bridgehead were assigned to pairs of men so that if
one was hit there would be a replacement on call. After the initial barrage, in
which some paratroopers were buried alive in collapsed foxholes, Colonel
Matt ordered the men to fill them in and make do with shallow holes. If
tanks were parked in the vicinity, the troops preferred sheltering beneath
them.

Bar-Lev decided that Adan's division would bivouac for the night within
the western bridgehead and get a few hours' sleep before breaking out in the
morning. Sharon's division would meanwhile remain on the Sinai bank and
broaden the corridor. Sharon protested that the existing corridor was sufficient and asked permission to bring over at least one of the two brigades he
had in Sinai to join Erez's brigade, which had been securing the bridgehead
west of the canal. Bar-Lev, who had lost patience with Sharon's constant
challenging of orders, urged Elazar to replace him. "If you go back north
without solving the Arik problem," Bar-Lev grimly joked, "I'm going with
you." Elazar, however, had decided to leave Sharon in place.

Erez's battalion commanders, who had already spent a day in Africa,
briefed Adan's brigade commanders about what to expect. They noted that,
unlike in Sinai, the fog did not come with first light but an hour later and
could last until 9 A.M. They recommended waiting for the fog to provide
cover before moving out in the morning.

Unable to form a defense line at the outer edge of the greenbelt when he
returned from his raid Tuesday because of his limited number of tanks, Erez
had pulled back behind the protective barrier of the twenty-yard-wide

Sweetwater Canal inside the greenbelt. By dawn Wednesday, Egyptian tanks and infantry had penetrated the outer edge of the greenbelt and were skirmishing with the Israeli forces. Egyptian artillery observers, some of them in treetops, were ranging in guns on the bridgehead. An unhampered foray like Erez's was no longer possible. To get out of the bridgehead now, Adan would have to fight his way out.

Unaware of the extent of the enemy buildup, Adan planned to exit the bridgehead Thursday morning on two axes. Gabi Amir's brigade would move out of the southern end and head for the Geneifa Hills, where numerous SAM batteries were located. Natke Nir's brigade would head west across the Sweetwater Canal before swinging south into the open desert in a parallel drive. The division's objective was Suez City, thirty-five miles south, where the supply routes to the Third Army converged. Adan's third brigade, Arye Keren's, was meanwhile being retained in Sinai by Southern Command as a general reserve.

Not waiting for the fog, Nir and Amir pushed off at 6 A.M. and encountered resistance immediately. Egyptian tanks as well as Sagger and RPG teams had taken cover in the foliage and were blocking the narrow exits from the greenbelt. The Israeli armored units, no longer presuming to win the war by themselves, called for foot soldiers. A paratroop company went to the aid of Amir's brigade, which was held up by a fortified position. The paratroopers swiftly cleared the enemy trenches, killing forty-five commandos while losing three men. As at Tel Shams on the Golan, infantry proved capable of rapidly overcoming resistance that had stopped armor. The paratroopers discovered that the Egyptians had thirteen RPGs, or one for almost every three men, which accounted for their tank-stopping capacity. Israeli platoons of almost similar size were issued only one bazooka. Many Israeli units not yet supplied with LAWs had begun equipping themselves with captured RPGs in addition to captured Kalashnikov rifles, which the soldiers preferred to the Belgian FNs which often had stoppages.

After advancing a few miles, Amir's column encountered a formidable Egyptian position, with dug-in tanks, at a crossroad code-named Tsach. Once beyond it, the Israelis would be in open desert. Adan decided to wait for Nir's brigade to join in a coordinated assault. The division commander would avoid dissipating his strength as he had in the failed counterattack on October 8.

As Nir's tanks were passing through the seemingly abandoned Abu Sultan army camp to the north, Major Brik, the survivor of Yaguri's charge, was fourth in line. Without warning, the three tanks in front of him were hit and burst into flame. Brik's tank was hit too but not disabled. Scanning the sur-roundings, he saw tank guns protruding from the windows of mud huts six hundred yards away. Egyptian tanks had broken in through the rear walls. They were swiftly destroyed.

Beyond the camp, at a fortified crossroad, the column encountered a tenacious commando battalion wielding antitank weapons. Here, too, infantry—the brigade's own armored infantry company—was summoned forward to clear the way for the tanks. Capt. Benny Carmel was in a person-nel carrier when an RPG exploded through its side. The company first sergeant, sitting next to Carmel, said, "I've had it," and fell over dead. An officer fell dead out the back door. Carmel was the only person still alive, though wounded. He threw grenades at a nearby enemy position from a hatch until another RPG hit his vehicle, setting it ablaze. Leaping out, Carmel ran towards a small knoll with a bush on it, the only cover in the vicinity. He reached it together with an Egyptian soldier coming from the opposite direction. Carmel fired first and lay down behind the Egyptian's body.

The officer could see men from his company sixty yards away, also pinned down. Between them and him was English-born Max Geller, firing a light machine gun. From time to time Egyptian soldiers tried to move towards Carmel but Sergeant Geller's fire stopped them. The other men kept throwing Geller loaded magazines. Finally, an APC dashed up and stopped next to Carmel. The back door opened and someone pulled him in. As they moved off, a machine gunner firing out of a hatch fell on Carmel with a bullet in his head and an RPG set the vehicle afire. Carmel once again managed to extricate himself, despite his loss of blood and dehydration. There was a building nearby where he had seen men from his company tak-ing shelter, but the entrance was blocked by a damaged APC. Carmel dove through the window. Among the men inside was a lieutenant who had been wounded ten days before in the battle against the commandos near Baluza. He had returned even though not completely recovered and had now been hit again. Outside, a wounded tank crewman saw three Egyptian com-mandos running towards the building. He shot them dead with his Uzi and fell unconscious. Carmel and the others were retrieved later in the day but the unconscious tanker, lying among the dead Egyptians, was not noticed. He woke at night, not knowing where he was, and walked until he found an Israeli unit.

The two-brigade assault on the Tsach crossroad was launched at noon but fire from the Egyptian position quickly took a toll. Adan stopped the attack and called for air support. Informed that SAMs prevented air activity in the area, he sent two battalions on raids twelve miles into enemy territory to destroy three missile bases. The SAM bases had adopted a new tactic to defend themselves. As the tanks approached, the antiaircraft missiles were lowered and fired in a flat trajectory at them. In the first such encounter, the missiles overflew the tanks and exploded miles to their rear. At another base, a missile struck within ten yards of the command APC but did not cause injuries. Fifteen minutes after the last SAM base was destroyed, Israeli Mirages appeared overhead and engaged a flight of MiGs that rose to meet them, shooting down six in the last light. Their mission completed, the raiders returned as the sun was setting, towing one tank which had run out of fuel. In the first day's battle by Adan's division west of the canal, it had moved out of the agricultural strip but had not yet broken loose into the enemy rear because of stubborn resistance.

In an ironic turning, it was the ground forces that were now providing support for the air force by knocking out SAM batteries. But the air force had also begun helping itself, chipping away at the edges of the Egyptian SAM array. Over the course of several days, the air force worked its way southward from Port Said, methodically opening up missile-free sky, although not without cost. The Egyptian air force attempted to make up for the rapidly receding SAM umbrella by tripling its sorties. The IAF welcomed this opportunity to take on the Egyptian pilots without missiles getting in the way.

Avihu Bin-Nun emerged from the air force's subterranean headquarters in Tel Aviv once every three days to return to a Phantom cockpit. As the chief planner of attack operations, the colonel would on these days issue mission orders in Tel Aviv early in the morning, drive to an air base where he would be briefed along with other pilots on the mission he himself had assigned, participate in the attack, take part in the subsequent debriefing at the base, then return to air force headquarters, where he would receive the debriefing reports in the evening.

Staff officers at headquarters included many of the best pilots in the air force and they welcomed any opportunity to get back into the air. Col. Gad Eldar, who had been working out of a basement office in Tel Aviv, managed to return full-time to his old Mirage squadron, where in two weeks he downed twelve planes, four of them during one sortie.

With the crossing of the canal, the Israeli high command had begun to think about the finish line. As General Tal put it at a meeting in the Pit Thursday morning, October 18, the war-of-survival stage had ended for Israel. The IDF now had to determine where it wanted to be when the shooting stopped. A basic consideration was that Egypt pay a price for having gone to war. On the Syrian front, this had already been achieved by pushing the Syrians well beyond the former line. The idea of advancing towards Cairo was dismissed by Elazar. Apart from concern about Soviet intervention, he wanted to avoid a cease-fire with the IDF overextended on long, vulnerable lines. It was agreed that the encirclement of the Third Army would be the appropriate finale. To achieve this, the Israeli salient in Africa would be bolstered with all forces that could be spared.

General Magen, who had been holding the southern part of the line in Sinai, was ordered to take half his truncated division, some eighty tanks, and cross the bridge. Adan's third brigade was released from the general reserve in Sinai to join him in Africa. A reduced brigade was ordered south from the Golan Heights and tanks were brought up from Eilat. Sharon was told that he could bring over Reshef's brigade from Sinai. Tuvia Raviv's brigade, however, was to remain there to expand the bridgehead corridor northward.

A reporter visiting a tank company behind the front lines in Sinai this day found the men eager to cross the canal. The company commander said his crews were supposed to have been rotated days before but refused to come off the line. "As long as they want to stay, we'll let them." The unit had been engaged in combat since Yom Kippur and had learned to cope with the Saggers, the captain said. "We worked out a system in the course of the battle. The percentage of missile hits is just a fraction now of what it was at the beginning." The officer praised the Egyptian infantry—"They fought like men"—and said their artillery had improved as well but not their tank corps.

While the tanks were being refueled, a group of young platoon leaders with stubbly beards knelt in the shade of a Patton tank listening to an information officer with a map describe what was happening on the Syrian front.

The company commander introduced a lieutenant attached to the unit as an artillery observer. A cast covered the lieutenant's right forearm. The son of a Beverly Hills psychiatrist, he had emigrated from the United States four years before. He had not been in contact with his family since arriving in Israel, he said, but his tour of duty was up in a few weeks and he intended to fly back for a visit. "I feel fulfilled," he said. Crossing the canal a few hours later, the lieutenant would be killed by shellfire.

Stouthearted Men called for Sharon's division, once it crossed, to drive south parallel to Adan's division. Sharon requested, however, to attack north towards Ismailiya. Permission was granted on the condition that he press north on the Sinai bank as well to widen the bridgehead corridor. Sharon argued again that if supply routes on the west bank were severed, the Egyptian army in Sinai would collapse. Elazar rejected this approach. Tirtur, he said, still needed to be secured so that the roller bridge could pass. In addition, the Egyptian forces on Missouri remained a threat to the corridor.

The tension between Sharon and Southern Command continued unabated as he attempted to sideslip his orders to keep two brigades on the Sinai bank. "He's back to his games," Gonen complained at Umm Hashiba after a sharp exchange with him. For his part, Sharon believed he was being arbitrarily kept on a short leash by commanders who were ignorant of the battlefield realities because they had not once visited his forward positions and because some of them had personal grudges against him. Akavish, he argued, was secure enough to permit traffic. Even General Tal, the officer on the general staff whom Sharon respected most, had lost patience with him. "Arik is ready to expose the northern flank of the bridgehead in order to cross the canal," he said. Elazar was at Umm Hashiba a few hours after the charged meeting at Adan's field headquarters when he heard Sharon once again on the radio trying to persuade Gonen that there was no need to keep his division in Sinai. "My intention is to move tonight," said Sharon, "and tomorrow to leave one element [brigade] here and to move forward [across the bridge]."

Elazar took the microphone.

"Sharon," he said, pointedly avoiding use of his first name. "This is Dado. Do you hear me?"

"I hear."

"Your plan is totally unacceptable. It is not suited to the mission I've given you. I want you to hold the bridgehead. We will talk about crossing afterwards. This is the mission now and it is to be carried out completely." Elazar stretched the last word for emphasis.

"Listen, Dado," said Sharon. "I've carried out every mission until now completely."

"I'm not dealing with history," replied Elazar. "I'm giving orders for now."

"I accept them."

This accommodating line changed when Elazar insisted that Tirtur be opened.

"It is not needed for the bridgehead," Sharon shouted. "Not needed." Changing his tone, he said, "But if you want it opened, I'll open it."

"Yes, I want."

"Okay. If I have this bridgehead, I understand that tomorrow you'll let me cross."

"Sharon," said Elazar, "tomorrow we'll do what has to be done. For now, execute [this mission]. Good luck."

"All right," said Sharon. "Thanks."

In his memoirs, Sharon would bitterly attack Elazar and Bar-Lev for ordering him to expand the corridor on the Sinai bank, implying that they deliberately intended to prevent him from sharing in the laurels of the break-out. "I cannot free myself from the feeling that one of the reasons they were pressing me to attack the Sixteenth and Twenty-first Divisions [in Sinai] was not because they considered the corridor too narrow but because they wanted to keep my troops on the eastern side. My strong impression was that the antagonisms of years between myself and those in command [Bar-Lev and Elazar], augmented now by political considerations, played a consider-able role in the military decisions that were made at the time." Bar-Lev and Elazar in turn believed Sharon to be motivated by politics and a desire for personal glory.

President Sadat, increasingly concerned by the Israeli incursion, con-ferred Thursday with war minister Ismail at Center Ten and agreed to trans-fer an armored brigade from the Third Army bridgehead to the west bank. To Shazly, this was a hopelessly inadequate response to the Israeli threat. Sadat did not ask his opinion. Instead, he instructed him to proceed to the Second Army to assess the situation and shore up the front as best he could. The chief of staff set off from Cairo at 2:45 P.M. and arrived at Second Army headquarters at 5:30. He found that in addition to Adan's southward thrust from the bridgehead, Sharon's division had begun to advance northward. The only forces in position to stop the move towards Ismailiya were two commando battalions and a brigade of paratroopers.

Maj. Gen. Abdel Munim Khalil, who had taken over command of the Second Army from General Aqqad, who had failed to perceive the serious-ness of the Israeli incursion, presented Shazly with a plan for dealing with the threat. It called for destroying all bridges across the Sweetwater Canal, which formed a barrier south of Ismailiya. Inside the agricultural belt, Sharon's advance would be resisted by the commandos and paratroopers. The Fifteenth Armored Brigade, with its T-62 tanks, would be withdrawn from Sinai to Ismailiya. Commando raids and artillery fire would meanwhile harass the Israeli crossing point at Deversoir. Shazly gave his blessing to Khalil's plan. He remained at Second Army headquarters for the next twenty-four hours.

Dayan visited Adan's forward command post in the agricultural belt Thursday morning. Like many other Israeli soldiers with a farming background, he was intrigued by the ancient wells, primitive duck coops, date palms, citrus groves, and peanut fields. When Dayan strolled away from the command post to study the vegetation, Adan said to the minister's aide-de-camp, "Keep an eye on your boss. There may still be Egyptian soldiers around." Two Egyptian helicopters appeared at treetop level and large drums filled with napalm were pushed out of their open doorways, exploding about fifty yards from Dayan in a dense cloud of black smoke. Machine-gun fire downed both craft. The helicopters had been dispatched on a desperate mission to knock out the bridge. Others would succeed in getting closer but they were shot down by antiaircraft guns posted at the bridgehead. Dayan was impressed by the bravery of the fliers as well as that of the numerous Egyptian infantrymen who had chosen to confront the Israeli tanks and whose bodies were now scattered about the area alongside their RPGs.

The defense minister went on to visit Sharon, who offered to show him "something special." They drove back across the canal and turned left to the outskirts of the Chinese Farm. Dayan was stunned by the tableau—hundreds of blasted vehicles covering the landscape as far as the eye could see. He had been involved in every one of Israel's wars and had spent time with the American army in Vietnam as an observer. But he had never seen evidence of such fierce battle, not even in photographs or movies. In addition to the 56 Israeli tanks knocked out were 118 Egyptian tanks that had been disabled and another 15 abandoned intact. There were also scores, if not hundreds, of destroyed APCs, trucks, and other vehicles. Colonel Reshef, who joined them when they crossed the bridge, surveyed the scene as if seeing it for the first time. "Only now," he said, "do I understand what went on here."

As the personnel carrier carrying Dayan and Sharon started back towards the bridge, a solitary MiG appeared overhead and dropped a bomb that rocked the vehicle. Dayan was sitting with his head out of a hatch and a sergeant grabbed his leg to pull him back inside. The defense minister told him not to worry. "Do you know how many people are lined up for my job?"

Mordecai's paratroopers had returned to Tasa drained emotionally and physically. The two companies most heavily engaged in the Chinese Farm had suffered more than 50 percent casualties. The men's soot-covered faces bore the vacant gaze of shock. Major Duvdevani, serving now as Mordecai's deputy, assembled the battalion and announced an inspection within an hour. He wanted, he said, to see shaved faces, polished boots, and cleaned rifles. He was greeted with looks of incomprehension. When a soldier protested, Duvdevani slapped him. He did the same to a second soldier who complained. The men drifted off to prepare. Duvdevani could hear the mutterings: "He's crazy," "What does he think he's doing?" He strolled through the encampment periodically, providing a countdown. "Forty minutes." "Twenty minutes." The men washed the dirt and blood off their faces, cleaned the sand from the FNs with brushes, and cleaned their boots. They lined up in formation after precisely an hour and Duvdevani walked down the ranks. He did not look closely at their boots or their shave but he saw what he wanted to in most of their eyes, the vacant stare giving way to a semblance of focus. They were coming back to life.

The battalion was dropped off near the bridge and crossed on foot between artillery bombardments. The veteran reservists of Matt's paratroop brigade who received them on the other side were touched by the faces of the young conscripts. Apart from the shock of the battle and the loss of their comrades, the men of the 890th Paratroop Battalion believed they had totally failed in their mission. They did not yet grasp that the very bridge they had crossed had been erected, in large part, because of their sacrifice.

Brigade commander Raviv began Thursday morning to push north into the Chinese Farm from Akavish. He reached Tirtur without firing a shot. There he found the bodies of thirty of Mordecai's paratroopers left behind after the previous day's battle because they lay under the Egyptian guns. Among them was a wounded paratrooper still alive. The tankers were surprised at the extent of the defenses the Egyptians had managed to build along Tirtur.

With the road clear at last, battalion commander Geller, who had detached from the roller bridge during the paratroopers' battle, was ordered to reharness his tanks. The towing resumed, this time in daylight, with bulldozers moving ahead to clear a thirty-yard-wide path—pushing aside destroyed tanks, evening out slopes, and filling in ditches. Israeli planes patrolling overhead intercepted Egyptian aircraft trying to reach the tempting target crawling slowly across the desert. Seven MiGs fell to earth during the day around the convoy. Egyptian artillery also groped for it. The bridge reached the canal bank a mile north of the pontoon bridge in the last light of day. By 6 A.M. Friday, October 19, it was anchored to both banks. The Israeli bridgehead, established three days before with rubber boats and rafts, luxuriated now in two stable bridges.

Before crossing to join Sharon west of the canal, Reshef requested permission for a final attack on the Chinese Farm. The Egyptians were reeling after three days of incessant pounding. According to radio intercepts, the situation was desperate enough for the Sixteenth Division commander, Gen. Abcd Rabb al-Nabi, to have personally led a company in a counterattack on Tirtur Road. But Saggers were still keeping Raviv's brigade at bay whenever it tried to move north from Tirtur.

Attacking from the west, Reshef's tanks fired into the heart of the Chinese Farm. Infantrymen cautiously entered the area and found that the Egyptian defenses had almost melted away. A reconnaissance company rushed the pumping station and captured it with the loss of two men. Another unit moved in the last light of day into the center of the farm without casualties and formed a defensive perimeter, together with tanks. All night long, it called down artillery on Egyptian units pulling back.

Reshef handed over the newly won positions to Raviv's brigade Friday morning and led his unit across the roller bridge, the first to cross it. After three and a half days of battle, the Chinese Farm had fallen except for scattered pockets. But Missouri, on slightly higher ground to the north, was intact. It had, in fact, been substantially reinforced by the troops pulling back from the Chinese Farm.

In Africa, Adan's division prepared for the breakout into the Egyptian rear. Thursday's tank raids on SAM sites had persuaded the Egyptians to pull back other SAM bases in the vicinity as well, opening the adjacent skies to the IAF. An air attack on the Tsach crossroads cleared the way Friday morning for Adan's tanks, the first time in the war that close air support had opened a hole for the ground forces to exploit.

Breaking through into the open desert beyond, the division moved southward on two axes, with battalions splitting off to attack missile sites and army camps and rejoining to do battle with Egyptian tank formations. Spirits soared as the tanks sprinted across the desert. A battalion commander in Nir's brigade, noting the name of their location on the map—the Aida Plains—serenaded his men with a rendition of the victory march from Verdi's opera. Adan was thrilled at the sight of his division racing across the flat expanse, the first time in the war that Israeli armor had shaken loose. This was the vision that Israeli tank officers had conjured up for years. The featureless terrain, the immense clouds of dust thrown up by the fast-moving tanks, and the smoke rising from burning SAM bases and dummy missile sites obliged periodic halts and radio identity checks in order to enable commanders to establish their position and ensure that they did not fire on each other.

The rendering of the victory march had been premature. The battalion commander who sang it was himself wounded half an hour later by Saggers fired by defenders at a SAM site. A second battalion commander in Nir's brigade had lost an eye the day before, but insisted on staying with his unit on a stretcher in a personnel carrier, offering guidance to his deputy. Ten miles west of the Bitter Lake, Nir's tanks came on an Egyptian artillery brigade which had been participating in the massive shelling of the bridgehead. At the approach of the tanks, the Egyptian guns were lowered and opened direct fire. Because of his difficulty moving his legs, Nir had tried to avoid thinking about the problem of getting out of his tank quickly if it was hit. It was hit now but he was spared the effort of a quick exit, the explosion propelling him from the turret onto the desert floor. Recovering, he ordered his tanks to charge. The Egyptians fired until the tanks were two hundred yards away and then broke. The tanks overran the position. Scores of artillerymen were killed in the fight and many more taken prisoner. Two Israelis were killed. One was 2d Lt. Ilan Gidron, the general's son who had been among the escapees from Fort Milano. It had been Gidron and another soldier who held up the borrowed prayer shawl that identified them to Israeli tankers.

Adan's division covered twenty-two miles this day, reaching the Geneifa Hills. Magen's division, following behind, cleared pockets of resistance that had been bypassed. The tank forces had reverted to form, employing maneuver, smoke, superior gunnery, and verve to overcome the Egyptain forces encountered.

Sharon's advance northward was largely within the agricultural strip, which made for slow going. Reshef, whose tanks were augmented by an infantry reconnaissance unit, attacked a logistics center defended by an Egyptian commando battalion. Moving methodically, Reshef's force was spared the kind of shapeless fight that characterized the battle for the Chinese Farm. For the first time since the war began, the numerical odds were on Reshef's side. Surveying the enemy positions in daylight, Reshef prepared a plan that gave foot soldiers the major role. The infantrymen worked their way down the trenches, supported by tanks which moved alongside them and raked the trench sections to their front. An infantry commander reported the trenches packed so tight that he inflicted casualties every time he threw a grenade. The position was conquered before nightfall at a cost of eighteen Israeli infantrymen dead, seventeen of whom were killed when a Sagger struck a packed personnel carrier. When a search was made of the trenches and bunkers the next morning, more than three hundred Egyptian bodies were found. Fifty Egyptians hiding in bunkers were taken prisoner.

Mordecai's paratroopers, participating in Sharon's drive, pushed enemy forces back this day far enough so that the bridges were for the first time out of sight of Egyptian artillery observers perched atop palm trees. But Egyptian artillery would continue to pound away massively at the crossing point. As the troops moved north along the canal, they placed Israeli flags on the ramparts to undermine the morale of the Egyptian forces in Sinai who could see themselves being cut off.

Elazar visited Sharon Friday near the Abu Sultan camp. Sharon had been in the thick of battle and was beaming. Imagine, he told Elazar, "you're commanding a division and suddenly there you are, you yourself, standing with your machine gun facing Egyptian tanks. I've fought in wars over twenty-five years but this is the first *real* war." One of his men had earlier given him a captured Kalashnikov rifle for firing at artillery observers in tree-tops.

Elazar's message wiped away Sharon's smile. The chief of staff wanted Missouri. He had fixated on it. The entire crossing, he feared, could turn into a disaster if the Egyptians, attacking from Missouri, closed off the corridor and stranded the forces on the west bank without ammunition or fuel. The Egyptian forces in Sinai vastly outnumbered the skeleton forces Israel had left behind. "I'm worried about Asia [the Sinai bank], not Africa," Elazar said to the General Staff. Sharon argued again that Missouri would collapse once the Second Army was cut off. But Elazar did not believe Sharon had sufficient strength to cut off the Second Army. Elazar studied the faces of the frontline soldiers. They had been in almost constant combat now for two weeks. Their weariness was plain, but spirits were high.

On the way back, the pilot of Elazar's helicopter mistakenly took them over an Egyptian position in Sinai. The Egyptians opened fire, hitting the craft's hydraulic system, but the pilot managed a safe landing at Umm Hashiba. There, Elazar told Bar-Lev and Gonen that the army's main priority was to expand the bridgehead northward on both sides of the canal, but particularly towards Missouri. So worried was he about the potential threat to the bridgehead that he gave only secondary priority to surrounding the Third Army. Top priority went to Missouri.

In the evening, in areas where the battle had tapered off, the men gathered to hear the Sabbath ushered in by the kiddush prayer over wine, a poignant reminder of home and other days. Giora Lev's battalion was posted on the northern edge of Sharon's division. During the day it had reached a point from which Ismailiya was clearly visible to the northeast, including the Hilton Hotel and the Tomb of the Unknown Soldier. With darkness, the battalion organized a night laager, the tanks lining up in a rectangle, guns pointing outward on all four sides, and the infantry APCs sheltering between the tank columns. Lev was in his turret close to midnight when an infantry officer called up to him softly. The officer commanded the detail guarding the encampment and was equipped with a captured SLS night-viewing instrument that magnified starlight. Egyptian commandos, he said, were approaching from the front. Looking through his own SLS, Lev saw a force of Egyptian soldiers two hundred yards away moving towards them. Lev told the officer to have his men alert the rest of the battalion, but not by radio, which the approaching enemy might hear.

Repelling an infantry attack on a night laager was an exercise tank units were trained in. It called for a massive response aimed at shocking the attackers. The tanks would throw on headlights and projectors, and charge, guns firing. Lev had never experienced such an attack and did not expect that he ever would. But here it was. The Egyptians halted fifty yards away and began to deploy. Lev could see RPGs and machine guns. "Charge," he called. Projectors flashed on, and the tanks and APCs sprang forward, guns firing. The ensuing carnage was mercifully hidden by the darkness. But in the morning, the tankers could see what they had wrought. An Israeli officer came on an Egyptian major, apparently the commander of the force, his legs gone but still clutching a map and a pistol.

During Elazar's visit to Sharon, he had been only a few miles from his counterpart, General Shazly, who was at Second Army headquarters in Ismailiya. The two chiefs of staff started back to their respective headquarters in Tel Aviv and Cairo at about the same time late Friday afternoon, Elazar buoyed by his visit and Shazly shaken by the ominous turn the battle had taken. Shazly was convinced that only a massive pullback of Egyptian armor from Sinai could save the day. At Center Ten, he reported to Ismail on the dire condition of the Second Army and learned that the condition of the Third Army was even worse, with Israeli forces racing to cut it off. Shazly urged that four armored brigades in Sinai, presently sitting idle, be withdrawn to the west bank lest both armies be surrounded. Ismail refused. Shazly pressed him to invite Sadat to Center Ten to discuss the matter. It was 10 P.M. and Ismail was reluctant to call the president but he finally acquiesced.

Newspaper editor Heikal, a friend and adviser of Sadat, was with the president in his apartment in the Al-Tahira Palace. Heikal had found Sadat sitting alone on a balcony in the darkness. As they talked, the telephone rang. An aide said it was war minister Ismail. "Do you want me to come over to Number Ten?" Heikal heard Sadat say. "Well, all right then, I'll come." When Heikal asked what was happening, Sadat said that General Shazly had returned from the front with a full picture of the situation.

When Sadat arrived, he closeted himself with Ismail in the latter's office for half an hour. The minister relayed Shazly's request to bring back four brigades. According to Heikal, Ismail believed that any further withdrawal of forces from Sinai would, at best, severely undermine morale and, at worst, trigger a total collapse as in 1967. Sadat agreed. Furthermore, he believed that a reduction in Egypt's strength in Sinai would weaken its position in the eventual political negotiations. He had gone to war in order to seize a foothold in Sinai and nothing must be done to endanger that.

Shazly had assembled five senior generals for the meeting, including Hosni Mubarak, commander of the air force and future leader of Egypt. When Sadat and Ismail joined them, the president asked each man to give his opinion in turn. General Gamasy opposed withdrawal of any forces from the Sinai bank on the grounds that it would be psychologically harmful to the army and because it was operationally unnecessary. When all present except Shazly had spoken, Sadat said, "We will not withdraw a single soldier from the east to the west." An officer next to Shazly whispered, "Say something." But the chief of staff saw no point in arguing his case after the president had already stated his position with such finality.

When the meeting was over, Ismail asked to have a word with Sadat in another room. He was now speaking for history, he said, and as a patriot. If the president saw a way open for a cease-fire on acceptable terms, he would support his decision. "I'm not pessimistic," said Ismail. "Our army is still intact. But in no circumstances should we get involved in any military development which will again face our armed forces with the threat of destruction." A week before, it had been Elazar who eagerly sought a cease-fire. It was now the turn of Egypt's senior command.

Sadat, in his autobiography, describes Shazly as having returned from the front "a nervous wreck." In the meeting at Center Ten, he writes, all the other generals present "were of my opinion—that there was nothing to worry about." After the meeting, he ordered Ismail to replace Shazly as chief of staff with Gamasy, but not to announce it publicly so as not to harm morale. Gamasy, to his credit, would in his own account of the war refute Sadat's description of Shazly that night and indicate his respect for him as a soldier. "He was not dispirited, as President Sadat has described." Adan, who would have the opportunity to examine some of Shazly's operational orders which fell into Israeli hands, would describe him as "a very capable officer indeed." Sadat, for his part, understood now, despite his seemingly unruffled air, that there *was* something to worry about and that a cease-fire could no longer be put off if the scenario he had so artfully constructed was not to explode in his face.

Hardly twenty-four hours before, in his final meeting with Kosygin, he had rejected the Soviet pitch for a cease-fire as he had rejected, five days before that, the U.S.-Soviet cease-fire initiative to which Israel had agreed. But there was now no more room for posturing. Returning to Al-Tahira Palace close to midnight, he asked that the Soviet ambassador be summoned. Vinogradov was startled when Sadat told him that after conferring with his military commanders he had decided to ask the Soviets to seek an immediate cease-fire at the Security Council. "What are the conditions?" asked Vinogradov. Sadat said he would accept a cease-fire on existing lines, an about-face from his previous insistence that a cease-fire be linked to Israeli withdrawal to the 1967 border. Hafez Ismail, Sadat's security adviser, who was also present, described the Israeli incursion as a serious threat to Cairo.

Vinogradov wakened Brezhnev at 4 A.M. to inform him of the meeting. Brezhnev told him to return to Sadat despite the hour and clarify several points, including the attitude of other Arab leaders, particularly Assad, to a cease-fire in place. Brezhnev would describe Sadat's request as "a desperate appeal." He told his colleagues in the Kremlin, "He [Sadat] got what was coming to him," a reversion to the prevailing attitude in the Kremlin at the beginning of the war.

At 5 A.M., Vinogradov, who had just wakened the leader of the Soviet Union, appeared at the palace to waken Sadat. The Egyptian leader greeted him in pajamas, refreshed after a short sleep. He told the ambassador that he had just sent a message to Assad informing him of his decision. In any case, he noted defensively, Assad himself had sought a cease-fire at the beginning of the war. As for other Arab nations, said Sadat, their positions could be ignored.

Sadat's message to Assad was firm. "We have fought Israel to the fifteenth day," he wrote. "In the first four days, Israel was alone, so we were able to expose her position on both fronts. . . . But during the last ten days I have been fighting the United States as well, through the arms it is sending. To put it bluntly, I cannot fight the United States or accept the responsibility before history for the destruction of our armed forces for a second time." He was therefore prepared to accept a cease-fire subject to guarantees from the Soviet Union and the United States. He would insist, he said, on the convening of a peace conference to achieve an overall settlement. "My heart bleeds to tell you this, but I feel that my office compels me to take this decision. I am ready to face our nation at a suitable moment and am prepared to give a full account to it."

Assad was dismayed. If Egypt pulled out of the war, Israel would concentrate its forces on the Syrian front. Israeli artillery had already been heard in the suburbs of Damascus. In his reply to Sadat, Assad wrote: "I received your message with deep emotion. I beg you to look again at the military situation on the northern front and on both sides of the canal. We see no cause for pessimism. . . . My brother Sadat, for the sake of the morale of the fighting troops it is necessary to emphasize that although the enemy has as a result of an accident been able to break our front this does not mean that they will be able to achieve victory. . . . My dear brother President, I am sure you appreciate that I have weighed my words with the utmost care and with full realization that we now face the most difficult period of our history. God be with you." There would be no reply from Sadat.

Of all the Arab leaders, the most nuanced role was demanded of King Hussein. He had hoped to stay out of the conflict and Egypt and Syria had initially indulged him. The mere presence of the Jordanian army along the Jordan River was sufficient, they believed, to pin down substantial Israeli forces in defensive positions. Israel, however, had left only a flimsy skeleton force opposite Jordan. As a worst-case contingency, explosives had been placed beneath the roads to Jerusalem to be detonated in case the Jordanians did cross the river, so as to delay them until reinforcements arrived.

As the Arab position on the battlefields deteriorated, pressure on Hussein mounted to send his army into action. He found a way to meet these demands without opening his kingdom to Israeli air attack. Instead of attacking Israel from their common border, he would send an expeditionary force to Syria. He let Israel know of his intentions, through U.S. intermediaries, in the hope that it would accept that this was not a casus belli justifying an attack into Jordan. Dayan declined to offer any such assurance, but Israel had no intention of opening another front.

Dayan had, in fact, ordered the bridges between Jordan and the West Bank kept open. A reporter visiting Allenby Bridge, near Jericho, on the fourth day of the war saw the captain in command of the Israeli end walk out onto the span and call on his Jordanian counterpart by his first name to ask when the next bus was coming.

Jordan's Fortieth Armored Brigade crossed the border into Syria on October 13 and went into action three days later. Unlike the other Arab armies, Jordan used Western tanks—Centurions and Pattons—and American APCs, identical to those used by Israel. Only when Israeli officers looking through binoculars spotted small green pennants flying from antennas did they realize that the armored vehicles approaching less than two miles away in two columns were an enemy force. Fire from Ran Sarig's brigade stopped one column. The other was hit by Ori Orr's brigade. It was not only the Israelis who were confused about the identity of the tanks; Syrian tanks and Iraqi artillery also fired at them. The brigade pulled back, leaving twenty tanks and APCs on the battlefield.

The Syrian high command planned a major counterattack on October 19, together with the Iraqi and Jordanian forces. However, on the night of October 18–19, Israeli forces just east of Kuneitra captured the village of Um Butna in an effort to improve local defensive positions. The move inadvertently disrupted the Arab counterattack, which called for the Syrian Ninth Division to push northward at dawn from Um Butna. A fierce fight broke out for the village between the Syrian division and Yaacov Hadar's brigade, with heavy losses on both sides. In view of the unexpected development, the Syrians pulled the Ninth Division back into reserve and asked the Iraqi division and Jordanian brigade to launch a combined attack earlier than planned.

Due to lack of coordination, the Iraqis attacked first, with several thrusts across a broad front. In the ensuing tank battles, Yossi Peled's outnumbered brigade inflicted heavy losses on the attackers. At a critical moment, Peled ordered his reserve of seven tanks to move out into the open on the Iraqi flank. Within five minutes, the exposed flanking force destroyed nine tanks without loss to itself and the Iraqis pulled back.

The Jordanian attack began more than an hour after the Iraqi attack had been stopped. The recurring difficulty in identifying the Jordanian Centurions led to a Jordanian force passing unchallenged between two Israeli Centurion companies deployed on the line. When the Jordanians were finally recognized, a slugging match broke out at close range and the Jordanians were driven back.

The Soviets, meanwhile, were wasting no time in following up Sadat's plea for a cease-fire. Ambassador Dobrynin in Washington called Henry Kissinger Friday morning to read an urgent message from Brezhnev for transmission to President Nixon. It proposed the speedy dispatch of Kissinger to Moscow, noting that every hour counted, given the fast-moving pace of events. "It would be good," said the message, "if he could come tomorrow, October 20."

It had been Dobrynin who suggested the invitation to his superiors. The idea was eagerly grasped by Brezhnev. Gromyko suspected that it was in fact Kissinger himself who suggested the idea to Dobrynin, with whom he enjoyed an amicable relationship. The foreign minister believed Dobrynin would not have dared make such a proposal to Moscow—and expose Brezhnev to the possibility of an embarrassing rejection—unless he was certain the invitation would be accepted. In his memoirs, Kissinger offered no hint of such collusion but expressed delight at the invitation. "I felt it solved most of our problems."

The Arabs had unsheathed the oil weapon by announcing cutbacks in oil production and raising prices. Saudi Arabia declared a total embargo on the sale of oil to the United States a day after President Nixon announced a $2.2 billion supplemental appropriation to pay for the military aid being sent to Israel. Europe was panicking—distancing itself from American policy and demanding an immediate cease-fire.

American interests required an end to the conflict on terms that did not undermine its client, exacerbate U.S. relations with the Arab world, or endanger détente with the Soviets. A cease-fire was plainly in Israel's interests too, but it was important for Washington's standing that its client emerge from the conflict looking like a winner, not a loser. The Soviets had so far been reasonable, but it was easy to see how the clash between the client states, if not halted, could lead to a direct confrontation between the superpowers.

This craggy political landscape was the kind of terrain in which Kissinger moved with the deftness of an Indian scout. He saw the importance of stopping the war, but not before Israel had advanced far enough to at least even the score with the Arabs strategically. On the other hand, it would not do to let the Israelis advance so far as to humiliate the Arabs. Moscow would have to be engaged in a constructive partnership so as not to leave the Russian bear feeling vengeful. But the Middle East war presented the United States with an exceptional opportunity to lure away Moscow's Arab clients by demonstrating the superiority of American arms, as wielded by Israel, and by showing that Washington alone had the ability to make Israel toe the line.

After consulting with Nixon and the president's other senior advisers,

Kissinger called Dobrynin to accept the invitation. He would leave the next morning, Saturday, October 20, and arrive in the evening, Moscow time. With the Israeli counterattack across the canal threatening to bring about an Egyptian collapse, turgid diplomacy had suddenly acquired winged feet. Kissinger informed Dinitz of his upcoming journey and asked the Israeli ambassador to furnish him detailed reports of the military situation three times a day during his stay in Moscow. He estimated it would be four days before the cease-fire took hold. In discussions that night among Dayan, Mrs. Meir, and Dinitz, it was reckoned more realistically that military operations might have to be concluded as early as Monday evening, October 22—that is, another three days.

Elazar was uncertain about what could be achieved on the battlefront in that time, given the fight the Egyptians were putting up. "What's troubling me about this war," he said in the Pit to Yigael Yadin, a former chief of staff, "is that nowhere are we pushing them to the point of complete collapse."

"Because the IDF doesn't have enough strength," said Yadin.

The IDF had achieved what it had by nimbly massing forces. To establish the bridgehead it concentrated two divisions at one narrow point in the Egyptian line. Now, by posting skeleton forces in Sinai opposite the static Egyptian bridgeheads—at ratios of 1 to 4 in Egypt's favor—the bulk of Israeli armor could cross to the west bank and achieve a ratio of about 1 to 1 for the crucial battles there. But there were no armored reserves left to throw into the battle.

At 9:15 Friday night, Elazar met with the war cabinet in Mrs. Meir's office. The main subject was Kissinger's trip and the options left to Israel before the fighting stopped. Elazar hoped the Soviets hadn't grasped the extent of the Israeli advance and thus wouldn't press for an immediate cease-fire. The Soviet military, however, had a clear picture from their satellites and were warning the Kremlin that if the Israeli momentum kept up, it could lead to the military and political collapse of Egypt.

Elazar's mistaken belief that the IDF was almost out of ammunition left him uncertain about how much longer the IDF could keep up its drive. Casualties were another limiting factor. When it was suggested that the IDF's main effort be directed at the Egyptian bridgeheads in Sinai, Elazar ruled it out because it meant attacking entrenched infantry. Confrontation would be sought only with enemy tanks. He had curbed commando operations behind enemy lines in order to keep down casualties, a policy also urged by Dayan. A daring commando raid deep behind Egyptian lines before the Israeli crossing of the canal was called off after four helicopters had already landed the jeep-borne teams near the Cairo–Ismailiya road. At Dayan's insistence, the chief paratroop and infantry officer, Brig. Gen. Emanuel Shaked, recalled the men, who were only ten minutes away from striking. Raids planned near Cairo and in the Nile delta were canceled. But two operations were carried out atop Mount Ataka southwest of Suez City. However, on the fifth night of the war two helicopters landed two light howitzers atop Mount Ataka behind Egyptian lines. For fifty minutes, artillerymen shelled vehicles on the Suez–Cairo road and a communications center. The helicopters returning to pick them up found the site clouded over. Only squadron commander Yuval Efrat managed to land but he extracted the men and guns.

Elazar was not sure whether the IDF would be able to complete the encirclement of the Third Army in the time available. There was one target besides Missouri whose conquest he regarded as essential. "I want the Hermon within forty-eight hours." Dayan called Bar-Lev close to midnight to inform him of Kissinger's trip and of the cease-fire countdown. What are the chances of reaching Suez City in the next two days? Dayan asked. Fifty-fifty, said Bar-Lev.

Egyptian commandos this night attacked one of Matt's companies guarding the northern approaches to the Suez bridges. They were driven back after a battle in which the defenders were assisted by effective artillery fire. Three paratroopers died in the fight. In the morning, the bodies of thirty commandos were found in front of the position. Brigade commander Matt arrived shortly afterwards. Unlike his own troops, who came in all sizes, the Egyptian commandos were all strapping fellows, as if physical build was a criterion for the Egyptian special forces. As he looked down at them, he saw one of the Egyptians moving. Thinking about the possibility of his own son lying wounded on the battlefield, he ordered that the man be carried to an aid station.

The next day, Saturday, October 20, Adan advanced southward thirteen miles against stiffening resistance. His division cut the Suez–Cairo railway line, brought one of the two main Suez–Cairo highways under fire, and destroyed more missile bases. Much of the Egyptian logistical echelon had begun fleeing towards Cairo, but fighting units were remaining in place. Egyptian troops, urged on by the commander of the Third Army, General Wasel, staged repeated counterattacks.

Dayan made a point of visiting the battlefront every day. A senior officer who had witnessed the minister's depression during the early days of the war was convinced that his frequent passage through the heavily shelled bridgehead reflected a death wish. Dayan's public mood, however, was jaunty and his self-confidence appeared to have returned. On Saturday, he managed to visit all three divisional headquarters west of the canal. Sharon was optimistic and attack-minded as usual. He intended, he said, to seize bridges across the Sweetwater Canal and cut Ismailiya and the Second Army off from Cairo. Dayan did not believe that Sharon had the strength for that but he was nevertheless buoyed by Sharon's upbeat spirit, which seemed to have imprinted itself on his whole division. Dayan found Magen's division, which had been spared the breakthrough battle, fresh and eager to go.

Adan too was in a buoyant mood. They discussed Kissinger's visit to Moscow. More than ever, the political dimension now guided Dayan in weighing military moves. He wanted the IDF to be holding a solid line on the African side of the canal from Ismailiya to Suez when the fighting stopped. This would offset the Egyptian gains on the Sinai bank.

He urged Adan to turn east and capture the flat strip between the Geneifa Hills and the Suez Canal. This area, the immediate rear of the Third Army, was full of fresh Egyptian forces, well entrenched. There were also Arab expeditionary units, including a Palestinian brigade and a Kuwaiti battalion. Much of the area was covered with vegetation, marshes, military camps, and villages, which made it ideal for defense. Until now, Adan had chosen to avoid it for precisely that reason. He told Dayan he wanted to keep going south through the desert so as to close off the last escape routes of the Third Army and only then turn towards the canal. Dayan was not sure there was enough time to do both.

"It's a good deed [mitzvah] to eliminate the Egyptian army," Adan said.

"You do good deeds after you've done necessary deeds," Dayan responded. But he did not attempt to impose his will.

Meanwhile, Raviv's brigade was eliminating the last holdouts in the Chinese Farm and closing in on Missouri. The area was covered with fire, smoke, and burned-out vehicles and suffused with the smell of death. The only thing missing, thought tank gunner Avi Weiss, was devils prancing about with pitchforks. His energetic platoon commander, Capt. Mendi Feibush, in whose tank Sergeant Weiss served, stopped alongside a truck filled with dead Egyptian infantrymen and brought back three Kalashnikov rifles which would provide better range than the tankers' Uzis. Both Feibush and Weiss were officers of the Student Union at the Technion in Haifa. Feibush had been on a visit to the United States with his wife when the war broke out. His readiness to volunteer his tank for dangerous missions sometimes upset his crew, but they could not help admiring his spirit.

As the brigade pressed northward, Feibush had to scrounge shells from other tanks after using up all of his ammunition in two hours. He asked

Weiss to keep a list of targets hit. At the end of the day, the list included nine tanks, fifteen trucks, some of them filled with troops, six APCs, and numerous infantry positions. Hundreds of Egyptian soldiers near the canal took shelter behind the Israeli canal-side rampart, but on the side exposed to the west bank. They were taken under fire by Israeli forces there. According to Col. Yehoshua Sagui, Sharon's chief intelligence officer, Sharon ordered the fire halted on the grounds that it was too much like a massacre. Sharon, according to Sagui, ordered that the Egyptians be taken prisoner by Raviv's forces east of the canal.

Many Egyptians on Missouri were indeed surrendering. Israeli planes were carrying out bombing runs now over the position. They also dropped leaflets promising good treatment to prisoners. In the afternoon, enemy soldiers began to approach Raviv's forces with leaflets clutched in raised hands. An Egyptian officer who surrendered was sent back in a captured truck to bring out others willing to lay down their arms. The officer returned with thirty men.

Three Israeli artillery officers who made a wrong turn in Sinai south of the bridges were themselves taken prisoner at a Third Army outpost and brought to Fort Botzer for interrogation. An Egyptian intelligence officer introduced himself as Major Suleiman. He spoke a reasonable Hebrew and also spoke Russian, having studied in a military academy in the Soviet Union. Another officer spoke a faultless Hebrew. If this is the quality of their officers, one of the prisoners, Lt. Allon Kaplan, said to himself, Israel's in trouble.

The atmosphere was relaxed enough for Kaplan to remark to his captors that life often takes strange turns. "You know, Major Suleiman, we're in your hands at the moment, but tomorrow you might be captured by our soldiers." The Egyptian laughed. "You never can tell," he said. "But it's not going to happen. Your army has received a blow."

With darkness, the Israelis were taken across the canal by Suleiman and guards in a rubber boat to a waiting vehicle. "I'm taking you to Africa without a passport," joked the Egyptian officer, adopting the Israeli geographical usage. They had driven only a short distance when they were taken under fire. Everyone leaped from the vehicle, the Egyptians running back towards the canal and the prisoners running forward, shouting, "We're Israelis." Kaplan and his colleagues reached the Israeli patrol safely. Their captivity had lasted six hours.

At the cabinet meeting Saturday night, Dayan said the end of the two-week-old war was approaching. He permitted himself a note of congratulations. "A war that began with us being pushed back from the eastern bank of the Suez Canal and ends with us sitting on the west bank is a tremendous victory." Elazar said the Israeli salient west of the canal now stretched thirty-five miles north–south and up to twenty miles to the west. Resistance remained stiff and it was not clear whether there would be time to complete encirclement of the Third Army. The outcome of the war depended now more on Henry Kissinger than on the IDF.

Thirty-four

KISSINGER TO THE FORE

K ISSINGER HAD STIPULATED BEFORE HIS ARRIVAL in Moscow that he would not enter into negotiations until he had had a good night's sleep. Apart from the need to rest after a fifteen-hour flight, he reckoned that the delay would add half a day to Israel's military timetable. Shortly after their arrival, however, Kissinger and his party were invited to dinner at the Kremlin. The evening's conversation consisted of diplomatic foreplay that managed to keep just short of negotiations. Brezhnev tried to win Kissinger's assent to a comprehensive peace settlement that would oblige Israel's return to the pre–Six Day War boundaries. Kissinger pointed out that he had come to discuss a cease-fire, not a peace settlement. The dinner, which Brezhnev spiced with his usual hearty anecdotes, ended close to midnight.

Before Kissinger went to bed, he conversed with Alexander Haig, White House chief of staff, and learned that Washington, normally somnolent on weekends, was in turmoil, and for reasons unconnected to the Middle East. President Nixon had just fired special prosecutor Archibald Cox. Attorney General Elliot Richardson and his deputy had then resigned. It was the Saturday Night Massacre and the climax to Watergate was fast approaching. Kissinger hoped that Brezhnev would not interpret this news as a sign of American weakness and toughen his position.

Brezhnev, however, had other things on his mind. Early the next morning, Sunday, October 21, he assembled his advisers to talk through the Soviet position before his meeting with Kissinger. Defense minister Grechko and chief of staff Kulikov warned that if the Israeli attack continued, the Egyptian army would be completely surrounded and the war lost. On the northern front, they said, the Syrians, together with Iraqi and Jordanian forces, were planning a major counterattack, but it would not succeed. Their assessment increased Brezhnev's determination to reach a cease-fire quickly. He was prepared now to waive the linkage of a cease-fire with Israel's return to the pre–Six Day War borders, a position Sadat himself had already abandoned.

The Soviets, whose men were on the scene, had a starker view of the plight of the Arab armies than did the Americans. A report received from Dinitz while Kissinger was still airborne offered little indication of the IDF's progress and no hint about its strategic objectives or timetable. A second report from the envoy said that Israeli forces had cut the Suez–Cairo road but that the Egyptians were expected to counterattack. There was no request for Kissinger to stall. There would be no further reports from Dinitz, which Kissinger took to mean that the Israelis themselves were not sure how the battle was developing.

When negotiations began at noon Sunday, Kissinger was surprised at Brezhnev's readiness to deal. It took only four hours to arrive at an agreement, one which met every one of Kissinger's demands. A major achievement was the agreement's call for negotiations "between the parties concerned"—that is, Israel on the one hand and its Arab adversaries on the other. Since Israel's establishment in 1948, the Arabs had refused to negotiate with it directly.

Kissinger understood the Soviet eagerness for a cease-fire to reflect the desperation of the Arabs' situation. But the absence of haggling meant that the clock would start running sooner than expected towards a cease-fire that might well bring the IDF to a halt before it had attained its objectives. Kissinger was able to slow the clock down a bit by proposing to Brezhnev that they allow nine hours for their governments to consult with their respective clients and allies before the UN debate. The cease-fire would go into effect twelve hours after the Security Council adopted its resolution. Brezhnev grudgingly accepted the timetable.

In a letter to be dispatched to Mrs. Meir in Nixon's name, Kissinger informed her of the agreement. He then lay down to nap. When he woke, he found that all transmission channels from Moscow were garbled and that the message had not gone out. He suspected the Soviets were playing electronic games. Four hours had been lost in informing the Israelis that the cease-fire countdown had already begun.

On the battlefield, both sides attempted to improve their positions before the looming cease-fire went into effect. Sharon sought permission to swing out of the agricultural belt and drive north through the open desert in an attempt to cut off the Second Army. He had planned to launch such an attack the previous night but had been stopped by Southern Command, which was monitoring his division's radio net down to battalion level to keep track of what Sharon was doing.

To his dismay, he was ordered instead to mount an attack on Missouri. When his protests were rejected, he summoned brigade commander Raviv and told him that he must expand the corridor northward through Missouri at all costs. Raviv pointed out that he had only forty-six tanks, less than half his brigade strength. Missouri was a formidable position which had withstood Israeli attacks since the beginning of the war, and it had been augmented now by forces retreating from the Chinese Farm. The order, however, stood. Sharon did not mention that he himself adamantly opposed the attack but Raviv sensed the absence of his usual enthusiasm. Returning to his brigade, Raviv summoned the commanders of the two battalions remaining to him. In a replay of his meeting with Sharon, he passed on the attack order, without acknowledging his own strong reservations. The battalion commanders protested too, but, as one of them, Yehuda Geller, would later say, "not strongly enough."

Geller, whose battalion had towed the roller bridge to the canal, knew that his men would regard the order as suicidal, a view he shared. He knew too that they would carry it out. There were many ways a soldier could avoid combat, but the men still on the line were those prepared to fight, regardless of the consequences. Geller, a kibbutznik, had gone from tank to tank the night before to talk to the men. All the tanks and crews that Israel had at its disposal, he told them, were now committed to battle. The battalion had been engaged in constant combat, but so had all other units and there was no one else to do the job. Whoever was quicker, smarter, and more aggressive would survive. Tank gunner Avi Weiss, who kept a towel at his position to wipe the cold sweat of fear from his hands, was touched by Geller's words. The prickly truth, he felt, was better than the boasting he had been hearing on the radio.

The brigade had finally, two weeks into the war, received machine guns during the night, and the crews were wakened to install them. In Weiss's tank, the men were too tense to go back to sleep. They spent the two hours remaining before dawn chain-smoking and consuming the chocolate and battle rations they had received for the Sabbath. A crewman from an adjoining tank, the company wit, joined them and began telling jokes. Some of the men found themselves laughing too loudly. At dawn, they cleaned and oiled the tank gun. While going through a burned-out tank the day before, crewmen had found that mess kits had survived the blaze intact. Some of the crew now wrote farewell letters to their families and placed them inside their mess kits.

As the morning fog dispersed, the tanks moved up into positions opposite the enemy lines. It was immediately clear to Weiss that the easy victory portended yesterday by the surrender of Egyptian soldiers had been an illusion. Missouri was dark with troops. Armored vehicles in large numbers could be seen deploying. Waves of Skyhawks bombed Missouri and hundreds of Egyptian troops fled the area on foot and in trucks. But thousands of others were digging in and preparing to fight.

Across the canal, Bar-Lev visited Adan late Sunday morning and tried to persuade him, as had Dayan the day before, to turn east in order to reach the Suez Canal before the cease-fire went into effect. Adan, however, reiterated his desire to first continue south and cut the main Suez–Cairo road. Bar-Lev did not press him. Unlike with Sharon, whose suggestions were as often as not rejected, Southern Command and Elazar were inclined to accept Adan's view even when it differed from theirs. When Bar-Lev told Dayan of his conversation with Adan, Dayan said of the division commander: "You can let him decide on the spot. He's thorough and sound."

Two of Adan's brigades were fighting their way briskly south through the Geneifa Hills and the desert to its west, and one was proceeding slowly down the heavily defended strip between the hills and the Suez Canal. Joining this brigade in the afternoon was Maj. Yoram Yair's paratroop battalion, which included the men evacuated from the southern Golan strongpoints on the third day of the war. It was the first unit to reach the southern battlefield from the Golan. The paratroopers were a welcome reinforcement for armor officers who were eager to get crack foot soldiers for the close-in fighting. The "totality of the tank" concept had been buried in Sinai.

Tuvia Raviv's attack on Missouri got under way at 3:15 P.M. One battalion attacked from the south, destroying twenty tanks and overrunning infantry positions before being stopped by minefields and Saggers. Yehuda Geller's battalion attacked from Lexicon Road, southwest of Missouri. His orders were to reach the Artillery Road on the far side of the Egyptian position. When the order was transmitted to the crews, gunner Avi Weiss's palms began to sweat again. The order meant that a score of tanks would have to cross a three mile deep fortified position crowded with antitank weaponry and masses of troops. All that could be done was to reconcile oneself to death. Weiss put a letter from his girlfriend in his pocket and checked his Uzi.

At Geller's command—"Move, move, fire with all weapons, out"—the battalion charged forward.

The widely dispersed tanks moved at high speed, firing as they went. In Weiss's tank, Captain Feibush stood in the turret, firing the newly installed machine gun with one hand and a Kalashnikov with the other. The radio was filled with shouted commands—"Keep abreast, fire, target to left, smash them, keep going." Weiss fired at groups of infantrymen as fast as his loader could insert shells. "They're falling like flies," he shouted. The air seemed to be filled with flying body parts. In the midst of the bedlam, the gunner saw a startled gazelle in his sights. Beyond it, two soldiers were kneeling alongside a suitcase. Weiss fired at them, but before the smoke of the explosion cleared his tank was hit.

Six adjacent tanks had been struck by missiles almost simultaneously. The deputy battalion commander, who was following in their wake, picked up ten survivors, including Weiss and Feibush. Instead of turning back, however, he continued forward, firing as he went, despite the shouts of the res-cued men, most of them wounded, to turn. When he finally did, his tank was hit a glancing blow by a missile, wounding him. A company commander he had taken aboard assumed command but the tank was hit again and set aflame. Most of the men took shelter in an empty Egyptian firing position. Enemy infantrymen closed in but two Israelis with Uzis held them at bay, fir-ing single shots to save ammunition. Captain Feibush was killed in the exchange.

The Egyptians called on the men to raise their hands. A crewman, ignor-ing the cries of his comrades, ran to the tank in an attempt to get to the machine gun on the turret. He was killed before he reached it. The other men in the group, including Weiss, surrendered. Weiss's loader had hidden in an abandoned foxhole with the company commander, the two men covering themselves with sand. Emerging after midnight, they made their way towards the Israeli lines, crawling close enough to enemy positions to hear snatches of conversation. After passing through a minefield, they succeeded in reaching the Chinese Farm and safety at dawn.

Assaulting a fortified infantry position with two dozen tanks was a repu-diation of everything that had been learned in two weeks of battle. As the tank crews realized from the start, the attack was doomed. Only commanders far from the battlefield could have ordered such an attack which may have made sense on a map but not in the field.

Half of Raviv's depleted brigade, twenty-two tanks, had been destroyed. Watching from across the canal, Sharon was beside himself as he watched tank after tank burst into flame. "If your mission is necessary," he would write of the battle, "you accept even the worst casualties. But this was meaningless, suicidal." During the night, however, the Egyptians pulled back almost a mile. As Shazly would acknowledge, the withdrawal was necessitated by Sharon's northward advance on the African side of the canal and the fire that Reshef's tanks were directing from there into Sinai. After three days of grinding combat, the corridor to the crossing point had been widened from two and a half miles to five miles.

The senior command, however, was not yet done with Missouri. Gonen ordered Sharon to send Reshef's brigade back to Sinai to resume the attack in the morning together with Raviv's remaining tanks. Sharon bluntly refused.

"This will constitute failure to carry out an order," warned Gonen.

"Now, really," said Sharon. "Don't bother me with things like that." But Bar-Lev, whose authority Sharon did not presume to challenge, took the microphone and repeated the order.

General Elazar was in a helicopter heading for Northern Command at 10:15 P.M. to monitor the attack on Mount Hermon when he was asked to return immediately to Tel Aviv. Kissinger's notification of the imminent cease-fire had just been received. Meeting with Dayan, Elazar agreed that in the time left, Adan would continue his attempt to encircle the Third Army and another push would be made on Missouri. But the most important thing, said Dayan, was to complete the recapture of the Hermon tonight.

Since the aborted attempt by the Golani Brigade to recapture the mountain spur on October 8, Northern Command had put the operation on hold as it focused on the main battle below. But it was clear to all that before the war was over another attempt would have to be made and at all costs. Strategically, the mountain was a vital platform from which to monitor Syrian deployment and communications all the way to Damascus. It was just as important to deny the Syrians the ability to monitor from there the Golan

Heights and northern Israel. Politically, Israel was determined to prevent the Syrians from winning any territorial gain. Psychologically, it was incumbent upon the IDF to undo the ignominy of the Hermon's fall.

For two weeks, the Golani infantrymen had been heavily engaged in the battle for the Syrian enclave. All the while, they kept looking over their shoulders at the Israeli Hermon. It struck battalion commander Yudke Peled, who had led his men up the western face of the mountain on October 8, that it would be preferable to stage the next attack from the east, starting up from the Syrian enclave rather than from the Golan. From this direction, the 4,000-foot climb was exceedingly steep. But it would bring them directly to the Israeli outpost, perched on the edge of the incline, without the need to fight their way up the ridge again from the west. Brigade commander Drori agreed.

Peled's battalion was pulled off the line and posted in an abandoned Syrian village at the foot of the eastern face. On three successive nights, the battalion commander led his men up a steep spur with full pack to see how they would bear up. He concluded that it could be done. Elazar had given orders to go for the entire crest, including the Syrian Hermon. While Golani would attempt to recapture the Israeli spur, Lt. Col. Haim Nadel's paratroop brigade would attack the prewar Syrian positions.

Paratroop officers proposed that Nadel's force capture the entire mountain, moving down to the Israeli Hermon after taking the crest. This was rejected by Hofi's deputy, Yekutiel Adam, himself a former commander of Golani who insisted that the brigade be permitted to recapture what it had lost. The paratroop officers then suggested that Golani attack from the eastern slope to avoid a recurrence of the October 8 battle—the same view as Peled's and Drori's. This was rejected on the grounds that the eastern slope was too vulnerable to Syrian artillery and too steep to ensure safe evacuation of wounded. Saturday night, October 20, Drori was helicoptered to Northern Command headquarters. A paratroop officer who had preceded him urged Drori to challenge the order. Two weeks of combat showed on Drori's face. "They're going to slaughter your brigade," the paratroop officer said. Drori said he had his orders and would carry them out.

Four hundred Golani soldiers assembled in a grove near the foot of the western slope late Sunday for a final briefing. Drori stressed to them the supreme importance of recapturing the ridge, the only Syrian success not yet erased. The Hermon, he said, was "the eyes and ears" of the country. For the past two weeks, artillery and aircraft had been dropping tons of explosives on the ridge, but the effect was not clear. A reconnaissance team led by Yoni

Netanyahu had climbed an adjacent spur in the morning to observe the Israeli Hermon. It reported seeing only two Syrians on the ridge all day. Air photos likewise offered no indication of a Syrian presence. Either the Syrian paratroopers had been driven off or they were so well disciplined as to keep well hidden on the boulder-strewn slopes by day. It was hard to imagine that they had pulled back without a fight, yet there was hardly a sign of them. "This is either going to be very easy," Peled said to Drori, "or very hard."

An officer told the Golani soldiers that the attack they were about to carry out could be more dangerous than anything they had done until now. Anyone who wanted to stay behind could do so; it would be enough to leave a note in the officers' tent. Sgt. Meir Elbaz, a recently discharged Golani veteran who had rejoined Peled's battalion at the start of the war, did not feel fear. He had read Plato not long before. What is death? it said there. Either dreamless sleep, which we all desire, or afterlife in which we meet Achilles.

Peled's battalion moved off with darkness to the Druze village of Majdal Shams, from where they started their climb. The brigade's reconnaissance company moved up the slopes far to the left. Between the two units, a motorized force led by tanks and a bulldozer prepared to move up the road to the top, waiting until the foot soldiers on both flanks had progressed. A rolling artillery barrage two hundred yards to their front kept pace with the advancing troops, but when shells began to hit too close the artillery was called off.

Peled moved at the head of his column, keeping the pace slow so as not to exhaust the men. They would have to climb 4,000 feet with seventy-five-pound backpacks before reaching the Hermon outpost and they had to be ready to enter into battle at any point along the way. They had climbed nine hours and were two-thirds of the way to the top when a heavy burst of fire cut into the column. A parallel ambush of the motorized column knocked out the lead tanks and half-tracks, blocking the road. The reconnaissance men on the left flank were caught up in a firefight as well and their company commander was one of the first killed.

The Syrians had kept hidden by day for the past two weeks, waiting for the Israelis to return. Only two Syrians had been wounded by the shelling and bombing during that time, the close-packed boulders offering protection.

The two sides fired at each other from a few yards' distance. A dozen Golani troopers would be found dead after the battle with bullet holes through their helmets, a penetration made possible because of the high velocity of the bullets fired from upslope at close proximity.

The Syrians had sniper rifles and night sights but they were also using Israeli machine guns they had taken from the outpost. More than once,

Golani soldiers, seeing the familiar reddish tracers—readily distinguishable from the greenish tracers of Soviet ammunition—and recognizing the rhythm of the machine gun, shouted "Cease fire," believing it was friendly fire from a unit that had gotten ahead of them. When they rose, they were hit.

As he neared the point of contact, Sergeant Elbaz could hear commanders to his front calling on their men to charge. A rush forward would be followed by the sound of sniper fire and the sight of falling figures. The sergeant had picked up a Kalashnikov rifle from a dead Syrian. It had a bayonet attached to it, which he tried unsuccessfully to detach. He was with two other soldiers when they came abreast of someone kneeling in the darkness. It was Colonel Peled. "Move on," said the battalion commander. The three men rose and charged up the slope. A man on one side of Elbaz fell dead. A moment later, the other soldier was hit. Elbaz kept running. He had only tracer bullets, which made him uncomfortably conspicuous whenever he fired. To his front, he saw several figures and fired in their direction. There were shouts, apparently from men he had hit. Rounding a boulder, he came on a Syrian soldier also holding a rifle with a bayonet. Both men sank their bayonets into each other. Elbaz also fired, killing his adversary.

His own wound was not crippling and he was able to continue forward. But as firing around him grew heavy, he went flat. Something exploded overhead and he felt shrapnel ripping into his back. Now, he knew, it was over—the war and life itself. The October cold of the mountaintop embraced him as he lay. To keep warm, he began crawling towards the rear. He came abreast once more of Colonel Peled, still kneeling. The battalion commander was talking into a radio with a calmness Elbaz found hard to comprehend. The officer had a map on his knee, which he was examining with the aid of a tiny light. Elbaz reached an aid station and was carried down the mountain. Plato had not included the possibility of being wounded among his options.

Peled was maneuvering his three companies by radio through steep, barely passable topography in an attempt to outflank the Syrians to his front. Movement was agonizingly slow.

The commander of a company whom Peled directed to the northeast to outflank the Syrians erred and turned northwest instead. Climbing the wrong ridge, he reported himself in place but with no enemy in sight. Peled moved forward to the line of contact in order to better grasp what was happening. His radioman received an urgent request that Peled go back to confer with Drori, who was climbing a short distance behind. Peled ignored the message, not wishing to have the men see him pulling back. Unknown to him, Drori was calling because he had been shot in the chest and wanted to pass on command. Before being carried down on a stretcher, Drori told the officers with him, "You've got to finish this business. Don't dare go down without taking the mountain."

As Peled peered into the darkness for a sign of the lost company, the artillery liaison officer kneeling to his left was fatally shot in the head. Peled's radioman, just behind the battalion commander, was also killed by a shot to the head, and a communications officer to Peled's right toppled over, wounded. Peled put the radio on his own back but a few minutes later he was shot in the side and was carried down the slope.

It was now beginning to dawn. The surviving Golani fighters could for the first time glimpse the enemy. Artillery fire was called down and resistance slowly weakened. An Israeli raised a helmet above a boulder but it drew no fire. Here and there, snipers rose from behind rocks with raised hands as the Golani soldiers pressed forward. The troops moved towards the monitoring station, eliminating final pockets of resistance. At 11 A.M., an officer announced on the radio: "To all stations, to all stations in the world, the Hermon is in our hands."

The price had been steep—55 dead and 79 wounded. Counting the casualties in the failed attack two weeks before, the brigade had paid with 80 dead and 136 wounded to regain the mountain spur.

The paratroop attack on the Syrian Hermon was over too. It had been a very different battle. Instead of scaling the mountain on foot, Nadel's force was airlifted to the crest by helicopter. Two battalions, each of 300 men, were transported in twenty-seven sorties. The helicopters followed a carefully plotted route through wadis that would get them around the Syrian antiaircraft defenses. Artillery batteries laid down a rolling barrage just to the front of the helicopters to suppress any attempt to down the craft with small-arms fire or shoulder-held missiles.

Syrians on the crest saw the helicopters suddenly broach the skyline to their rear. Seven MiGs were downed by Israeli aircraft when they tried to intercede. The Israeli planes also downed two helicopters carrying reinforcements. The airlift was completed by 5 P.M., leaving the paratroopers the entire night to operate. Although the distances to be covered were not great, the thin air demanded slow walking. A helicopter placed seven men, including artillery observers, on the peak of the Hermon from where at night they could see the lights of Damascus.

By 3 A.M., after a series of brief skirmishes, the paratroopers were overlooking the main Syrian observation post, four miles from where they had landed. It had been from this post, 7,800 feet high, that the Syrian paratroopers set out on Yom Kippur to capture the Israeli outpost below. Nadel called down artillery on it for half an hour. When his men attacked, they found that the defenders had fled. Total casualties for the paratroop brigade in the entire operation were one dead and four wounded.

With dawn Monday, October 22, the paratroopers could see smoke from the Golani battle below. At 10 A.M., one of Nadel's battalions began moving along the path leading to the Israeli Hermon to assist. It encountered Syrians fleeing the Golani battle. Several were killed and others taken prisoner. Halfway down, the paratroop force was ordered by Northern Command to return upslope. The retaking of the Israeli Hermon was to remain the Golanis' prerogative.

A cabinet meeting to discuss endgame strategy had gotten under way at midnight Sunday. Mrs. Meir told the ministers she would ask Kissinger to stop off in Tel Aviv on his way back from Moscow. After briefing the cabinet, Elazar begged leave at 2:15 A.M. to return to the Pit to follow the battle for the Hermon. He had not gone far when unspoken thoughts welled up. Executing an about-face, he returned to the meeting and asked for the floor.

The cease-fire worried him greatly, he said. It would halt the IDF just as it was gaining stride. More worrisome, it would permit the Arabs to build up strength for a new round. A resumption of fighting within a few days or weeks was not only possible, he said, but likely. The Egyptians would deploy new SAM batteries, closing off the skies so arduously opened. The Syrians would train crews for the hundreds of new Soviet tanks they had already received, and the Iraqis would send another division. A cease-fire that lasted only a few days or weeks was Israel's worst option. The government must therefore seek guarantees, he said, that this would not happen. He himself would like to have three or four more days to eliminate the Third Army, capture Missouri, and deploy the army along viable new lines.

After the meeting, Dayan received a call from Sharon pleading to have the order to attack Missouri rescinded. Dayan had hitherto refrained from interfering in the disputes between Sharon and his superiors. This time, however, he called General Tal. An appeal from a division commander who believed that a plan was unworkable, said Dayan, could not be ignored. Tal said he would look into it. He called Elazar, waking him from a deep sleep. The chief of staff decided not to fight it anymore. With his assent, Tal called Gonen and told him to give Sharon the option of attacking at Missouri or not. Neither had any doubt what Sharon's choice would be.

Admiral Telem had ordered Captain Almog at Sharm el-Sheikh to attack Ardaka Sunday night. The remaining Egyptian missile boat there constituted a threat to an amphibious operation across the Gulf of Suez that was still an option. Telem suggested that the raiding party this time stand off from the target, which was bound to be protected up close after the previous attack, and use LAW missiles. Almog, a former commander of the naval commandos, decided to lead the operation himself.

Two boats reached the Ardaka channel an hour before dawn and found it unguarded. At 150 yards from their target, fire was opened on them. "Close to firing range," shouted Almog. The designated gunners in the two boats rose at 80 yards and placed the missile launchers on their shoulders. Bracing themselves against the roll, they tried to ignore the enemy fire. Each had five missiles. Each missed with the first four. Almog ordered the boats to close to 40 yards. The last two rounds hit, setting the missile boat aflame. As Almog's boat turned, it ran onto a reef, damaging its propeller. The second boat took it under tow. As they reached the open waters of the gulf, Monday morning was dawning.

In New York an hour later, the Security Council adopted a cease-fire resolution to go into effect at 6:52 P.M., Israel time.

Israel had twelve hours to try to break the back of the Egyptian army.

Thirty-five

CEASE-FIRE

A DAN BEGAN THE NEW DAY AS HE HAD every day for the past two weeks, by addressing his brigade commanders on the radio in a parody of Israel Radio's start to its broadcast day—with the date and a reading from the Psalms.

"This is Monday, 22 October, the seventeenth day of the war. On this day the Levites would chant in the Temple, 'And you shall strike the Egyptians and pursue them to the end.' Should it come to pass that you do not hurry, you will not finish the task. Prepare for orders. Over." Each commander reported readiness and Adan gave them their assignments in down-to-earth military jargon.

The emphasis this day would indeed be on hurrying. But the race would have to be delayed. With the cease-fire imminent, the Egyptians had seized the initiative by staging counterattacks in nearly every sector, often before dawn. In addition, neither artillery nor air support would be available to Adan until 8:30 A.M. because they were being directed at the last SAM bases in the area of Suez City. Adan's plan was to grind up the enemy forces to his front, sever the main Suez–Cairo road, and then, before the cease-fire went into effect, sprint for the canal, fifteen miles east across flat terrain.

The Egyptian Fourth Armored Division had been playing an active role in resisting the Israeli incursion. But now the division commander, Brig. Mustafa Kabil, refused an order from the commander of the Third Army,

General Wasel, to force open the Suez–Cairo road from the west to permit the passage of supply convoys. "The Suez road is cut off, Kabil," said General Wasel, in a message intercepted by Israeli monitors. "Open it for me. You are under my command. Why do you refuse? I'm giving you a clear order." Complaining to war minister Ismail, Wasel said that Kabil's excuse was that Israeli planes would pounce on him if he left the SAM umbrella still deployed in the direction of Cairo.

Adan had positioned himself on a peak offering a broad view of the battlefield. To the north, Gabi Amir's brigade was pushing slowly down the narrow plain between the canal and the Geneifa Hills. To the south, Adan's other two brigades were fighting towards the Third Army's last supply routes. With no more SAMs in the canal zone, the air force was furnishing intensive close support.

Moshe Dayan arrived by helicopter in midmorning. He again stressed to Adan the importance of reaching the canal before the cease-fire. Adan reluctantly called off the southern drive at 2 P.M. and ordered his forces to reach the canal before the cease-fire went into effect half an hour after darkness.

Kissinger landed at Lod International Airport from Moscow early in the afternoon and was driven to the same Mossad facility where less than a month before King Hussein had warned Prime Minister Meir of war. At the start of a fifty-minute tête-à-tête, Mrs. Meir went directly to the heart of her concerns: Had the United States struck an agreement with the Soviets to force Israel back to the 1967 lines? Kissinger assured her there was no such agreement. When he asked if she thought Sadat would survive the military setbacks of the last days, Mrs. Meir said he would. "He is the hero. He dared."

Kissinger told his hosts that he would not make a fuss if military operations continued through the night. He was thus compensating Israel for the four hours lost in forwarding the message from Moscow about the cease-fire agreement. He told Dayan that Israel had been wise not to stage a preemptive strike on Yom Kippur. If it had, Dayan would recall him saying, it would not have received so much as a nail from the United States.

Before departing, Kissinger met briefly with Elazar, Benny Peled, and Zeira and was shown a situation map of the battlefield. It showed the Third Army cut off from Cairo except for a secondary road to the south near Mount Ataka. The map was in error since Adan had halted his drive just short of the main Suez–Cairo road in order to turn to the canal. The generals told Kissinger that the Egyptian and Syrian armies had fought well. Zeira said that the Egyptian Sixteenth Infantry and Twenty-first Armored Divisions had been destroyed and two other divisions, the Fourth Armored and Sixth Mechanized, had been badly hurt. These losses, he said, removed from the Egyptian army its offensive capability. The Syrians, he said, had lost 1,000 of their 1,600 tanks, but Soviet resupply had brought the number back up to 1,400. When Kissinger asked to what they attributed the IDF's successes, Elazar said a wide gap remained between the Israeli army and the Arab armies in leadership and in the quality of the fighting men. Kissinger was impressed by Elazar. "[He] struck me as a man of rare quality, noble in bearing, fatalistic in conduct. He briefed us matter-of-factly, but with the attitude of a man to whom the frenzies of the day were already part of history."

Kissinger would describe his brief stopover in Israel as one of the most moving episodes of his government service. He sensed the nation's exhaustion and the trauma that came with the loss of the sense of invincibility. The way was opening now for diplomacy. But the war and the dying were not over yet.

In Sharon's sector, a tank officer looking north along the Suez Canal saw Egyptian soldiers on the African bank shooting deserters trying to swim across from the Sinai bank. However, Egyptian special forces were putting up stiff resistance in the greenbelt itself as Israeli paratroopers pushed towards Ismailiya. In a dusty village where chickens scattered in front of the armored vehicles the soldiers came upon a farmer, one of the few inhabitants who had not fled. Sharon paused to chat with him. "How many kilos of peanuts do you get to the quarter acre?" he asked. When the Egyptian said 150, Sharon looked surprised. "You should be getting better yields than that," he said. "We get 600 kilos, at least, in Israel." His own father, a farmer, had grown peanuts.

At one point, a small Egyptian training plane which had been fitted out for combat appeared above the tree line and made a run at Sharon and others grouped on a road. The plane did not fire and a burst from an APC's machine gun brought it down. The pilot managed to bail out and was picked up by Israeli troops. Described later by one of the Israelis as a "dandy" with lacquered fingernails, the pilot was brought to Sharon, who asked why he hadn't fired when he plainly had the group on the ground lined up in his sights. The pilot said he hadn't been sure if they were Israelis or Egyptians. When Sharon indicated that he didn't think much of him for not shooting, the Egyptian pilot looked hurt almost to the point of tears.

As his brigades were moving into position for their race to the Suez Canal, Adan received a message from Southern Command which he passed on to his commanders: Radio Cairo reported that Egypt accepted the cease-fire. "We have to hurry," Adan said. They could not begin moving immediately because local resistance was not yet overcome. It was not until 4 P.M., three hours before the cease-fire was to go into effect, that Nir's and Keren's brigades finally began their advance.

It was, Adan would write, a feast for the eyes. "The division was speeding across the plain in a broad, deep structure. The sun was at our back, but vision was obscured by the clouds of dust raised by the charging tanks. The reports were coming in fast and furious, mentioning a thousand and one code names [of locations], so that it was hard to follow. Thousands of Egyptians, I was told, were fleeing every which way."

However, the hands the Egyptians were raising in surrender were still gripping weapons. Adan's officers asked how they should react. There was neither time to teach the Egyptians how to surrender nor time to take them prisoner. Adan said not to fire at them but to keep moving forward and to stay alert in case the Egyptians had second thoughts and started shooting. Colonel Amir's brigade seized a major army base, the Geneifa camp, where thousands of Egyptians wanted to surrender. But there was no time to assemble them.

The air force was no longer available for close support, since it was dealing with masses of planes that Egyptian air force commander Mubarak had thrown into the fray, including training aircraft, in a desperate effort to block the Israelis' final dash. Tank crews watched parachutes, almost all of them Egyptian, floating down from amidst the swirl of aircraft in the sky.

Dusk was descending as the first tanks neared the agricultural belt from the west. Adan ordered each brigade to send a battalion to the canal to stake out an Israeli presence. At 6:50, Bar-Lev asked for a situation report. One unit had reached the canal, said Adan, and two more would soon reach it at other points.

"OK," said Bar-Lev. "In another two minutes the cease-fire is supposed to take effect."

"Repeat, please," said Adan, feigning communications problems. "I can't hear you."

General Magen was replying in the same spirit to a similar message from Ben-Ari. "Are you sure it's today?"

As part of the final lunge, Sharon had received permission in the afternoon to move towards Ismailiya. He ordered Reshef to break through to the
city together with paratroopers in the few hours remaining. Reshef gave
preparatory orders but expressed doubts to Sharon about the wisdom of the
attack in view of the pending cease-fire, the paucity of forces, and the likely
casualties. A senior member of Sharon's staff urged Reshef in a whisper not
to execute the order.

A company of paratroop reservists under Capt. Gideon Shamir led the
way in late afternoon across a still intact bridge spanning the Sweetwater
Canal a mile south of Ismailiya. The paratroopers were taken under fire by
Egyptian commandos lying in ambush and by artillery. Within minutes,
Shamir's company had seventeen dead and wounded. Looking behind him,
the officer saw four tanks from Reshef's brigade get hit by missiles almost
simultaneously and burst into flames. Darkness had already descended when
Shamir was ordered to pull back.

Addressing the entourage of reporters acompanying him, Sharon said:
"The battle to capture Ismailiya could have been effected last night. The
very same forces that conducted it now have been ready for the past forty-
eight hours. Had they begun then, we would have brought about a radical
change in the situation." The reporters were left to decide how much of this
analysis had come from a frustrated soldier and how much from an ambitious politician.

President Sadat had prepared his own endgame gambit—the launch of
Scud ground-to-ground missiles as a strategic marker. As with the firing of
the Kelt missiles in the opening moments of the war, his intention was to
demonstrate that he had a retaliatory option in case Israel contemplated
future attacks on his cities or economic infrastructure. He would not fire the
Scuds at Israel itself, but into the battle zone. He wanted the missiles fired
just moments before the cease-fire went into effect, too late for the Israelis to
retaliate.

The Scuds, however, were in the hands of Soviet units and could not be
fired without Moscow's permission. The Soviet military advisers in Cairo
were inclined to accept Sadat's request, but the Politburo had heretofore
refused the use of the Scuds as long as they were under Soviet control.
According to the only published account of events in the Kremlin during the
war, Ambassador Vinogradov in Cairo called Gromyko to ask what to do but
the foreign minister was not available. The ambassador then asked to speak
to defense minister Grechko. "Go the hell and fire it," said the marshal.

According to Sadat's memoirs, two missiles were fired. According to

Shazly, three missiles were fired at Deversoir. Israeli sources speak of only one missile. It exploded amidst supply vehicles of Yehuda Geller's battered battalion near Missouri, touching off an explosion in an ammunition truck that killed seven persons. When Gromyko learned that Vinogradov had been told by Grechko to have the Scuds fired, he was furious and tried to get permission rescinded. But it was too late. Minutes before the cease-fire went into effect, Egyptian artillery, mortars, and Katyushas unleashed a massive bombardment on both banks of the crossing point, inflicting sixty casualties. According to captured Egyptian documents showing artillery fire plans, 100,000 artillery shells were fired into the bridgeheads on both sides of the canal over the course of six days, besides mortar and Katyusha fire. Hundreds of men were wounded at the crossing point and one hundred killed.

The silence that settled over the battlefield would not last long.

The cease-fire had gone into effect after dark so that not even satellite photos could determine the precise location of the combatants, particularly since the Israelis had been in the midst of a headlong charge. Adan was frustrated at being stopped just as his forces were in position to deliver a knock-out blow. "One way or the other," he would write, "I did not believe the cease-fire would be observed." The impulse among Israeli military leaders after the shock and humiliation of the war's opening days was to go for the kill. Sharon called Begin and asked him to press the government to delay the cease-fire, which, he said, was intended only to save the Egyptian army from destruction. Elazar, in a statement to the fighting forces announcing the cease-fire, added: "From the viewpoint of readiness, you must act as if the war is still going on."

Gen. Dov Tamari, however, believed the troops had had enough. Climbing onto tanks to talk to crewmen, Adan's deputy saw their exhaustion. They had been going virtually round the clock for many days and it was difficult just staying awake. "Their eyes said, 'We've gotten this far and we're still in one piece. Let's end it already,'" he would later say. "With some it wasn't just in the eyes. They actually said it." For a tank company commander who had been fighting since the first day, the most onerous aspect was not physical exhaustion or even the constantly shortening odds of survival but the accumulated sense of loss from comrades killed and wounded. He was flooded with relief at the cease-fire but would have been ready to go on to Cairo without a qualm if the order had been given.

The unit Adan referred to as having reached the canal before the cease-fire was Eliashiv Shimshi's battalion of Centurion tanks, which had participated in the destruction of the Twenty-fifth Brigade. It had this morning overcome an Egyptian ambush, destroying more than twenty tanks without suffering any loss. The battle was a tactical jewel of fire and maneuver, a fitting end to two weeks of war in which the unit had been shaped into a seamless fighting machine. At 4 P.M., Shimshi was informed by brigade commander Arye Keren that he had one more mission. In the three hours remaining before the cease-fire, he was to proceed eastward ten miles and reach the point where the canal touched the southern end of the Bitter Lake. The final stretch of their route would take them through the agricultural strip. Shimshi wanted to get across the strip, filled with potential ambush points, before darkness set in at 6:30. However, the battalion had to fight its way through an Egyptian position on the way and it was not until 6:45 that the battalion entered the strip.

Finding a suitable place for a night laager proved a difficult task. All about them were bogs and mines, not to mention an unseen enemy whose attitude towards the cease-fire was not yet clear. As they drove north along the canal road, Shimshi saw an open field to the left, the size of a soccer pitch. The tanks entered and formed a rectangle, guns pointing outward. Shimshi positioned himself in the hollow center, with APCs carrying an infantry company lined up behind him. Engines were cut and absolute silence descended. The darkness of the night gave way to the deeper darkness of shrubbery and trees beginning twenty to forty yards west of the field. To the east, the waters of the Bitter Lake glittered. Shimshi had wanted to move outside the agricultural belt for the night but Colonel Keren refused. If international observers arrived in the morning, it was important that they find Israeli forces on the canal.

Shimshi assembled his company commanders. They had been through a trying day of battle, he said, but there could be no sleep this night. There was no telling, he said, what forces were out there in the shrubbery and what their intentions were. Shimshi ordered the commander of the infantry company to take two APCs and check escape routes in case they had to hastily pull out. A few minutes after the personnel carriers departed, fire was heard from their direction and a flaring could be seen through the trees. The infantry commander reported that they had been ambushed and one APC set aflame. Shimshi told him to evacuate the men in the burning vehicle and return. The surviving APC had just made it back with one man dead when fire opened on the laager itself—RPGs, small arms, and mortars. The crashing response of the tanks silenced the Egyptians. Shimshi contacted Keren and asked permission to pull out. The brigade commander checked with division and again refused. Once more the Egyptians opened fire and once more the tanks' response silenced them.

In the coming hours, the cycle would be repeated periodically. Shimshi feared that they would run out of ammunition and again requested a pull-out. Again denied. Many of the tanks reported being hit but all continued to function. At about 11 P.M. the first tank reported penetration of an RPG and two wounded. There was a nightmarish helplessness to their predicament—immobilized and surrounded by Egyptian forces they could not see. Shimshi made a point of keeping his voice calm, as if this were just another tactical difficulty of the kind they had overcome so often in the past two and a half weeks. At 1:30 A.M. Shimshi again asked Keren for permission to pull out. There was no point in remaining, he said; the cease-fire was clearly being violated, and if they stayed the results could be disastrous. At 2 A.M., permission was finally granted.

"Start engines," said Shimshi. "Prepare to move out." It was an order the men had been eagerly awaiting for hours. "We'll mount the road and move north," Shimshi said. "At the first junction, we turn left." The map showed a side road there leading across the Sweetwater Canal and on out of the agricultural strip. Several crews reported being unable to move their tanks because of damage from RPGs. Shimshi ordered them to abandon the tanks and find places on others. Delivering a parting volley at the Egyptian infantry, whose fire had intensified with the igniting of the engines, the tanks began filing out onto the road. They had not gotten far when Shimshi's tank was struck by RPGs. The driver swerved and the tank mired in a bog. Shimshi and his crew evacuated the tank and boarded another. Egyptian soldiers were firing at them now from trenches alongside the road. The Egyptians were too close to be hit by the tank's weapons, which could not be depressed sufficiently. An officer standing in the turret next to Shimshi was wounded as he threw grenades. Shimshi himself fired his Uzi.

A personnel carrier ahead of him was set aflame and its occupants scampered aboard others. As the line of vehicles swung around the burning APC, two tanks and an APC ran onto mines at the side of the road. Another tank was caught in a bog and could not extricate itself. Shimshi said to abandon all vehicles that could not be moved rather than try to tow them out.

The company commander with the lead tanks, Maj. Zimran Koren, reported that he had reached the turning but that the side road was blocked by an earthen barrier. Shimshi looked at the map and saw another turning a few hundred yards further north. It too led across the Sweetwater Canal to the desert. He told Koren to head there. The company commander soon called back: "The first tank has reached the canal but there's no bridge."

Shimshi could sense the tension along the column. They had started out only a few minutes before but already half the tanks and APCs were gone and the fire coming at them from the darkness was increasing. The battalion commander looked once more at the map. Koren was clearly at the point marked "crossing." Telling him to remain where he was, Shimshi reported his predicament to brigade. The reply from intelligence, after a pause to check maps, was that there should be a crossing just under the surface of the water. Shimshi told Koren to order the lead tank to descend into the water. The crew was to open hatches and be prepared to jump if the tank went under. A few moments later came the exultant cry—"We're across." The remaining vehicles, firing to either side of the dirt road as they went, hurried across the bridge and out of the greenbelt.

Two miles into the open desert, Shimshi called a halt. The claustrophobic nightmare was over. Around them now were endless expanses. At his request, the men gathered around his tank. They had lost nine tanks and several APCs and every one of the surviving tanks had suffered at least five hits from antitank weapons. But there were only two fatalities and seven wounded. Shimshi commended the crews on their professionalism. The crewmen briefly abandoned professionalism to vent their relief by embracing him.

Other Israeli units were also busy this night. Bar-Lev had ordered his division commanders to start mopping-up operations to achieve territorial continuity between Ismailiya and Suez. "If they don't shoot at us," said Bar-Lev, "we won't shoot at them. If they open fire, of course, we'll respond."

Major Brik was ordered to take the five tanks remaining to him and "steal ground." The cease-fire prohibited shooting but said nothing about movement, according to Brik's battalion commander. (The cease-fire, in fact, called upon the parties to halt all military activity "in the positions they now occupy.") Brik was told to get as far as he could, without firing, before UN observers arrived in the morning.

Brik's company had been fighting from dawn to sunset for the past five days. The nights had been given up largely to preparations for the next day's battle, and the tanks had moved off well before dawn to reach good firing positions. There had been no more than an hour or an hour and a half for sleep each night inside the tanks. Sleep deprivation caught up with them now as they rolled through the night. At about 2 A.M., Brik could fight it no longer and ordered the tanks to halt. "Let's rest for fifteen minutes," he said. They were too weary even to post guards outside, although they were deep inside Egyptian territory. Within a minute, all were sound asleep in their seats.

When Brik opened his eyes, he saw pale blue sky through the hatch. His watch told him it was 5:30 A.M. Rising up in the turret, he saw that they were in the center of a large Egyptian logistics depot. The encampment had shown no lights at night, which is why the Israelis had driven into it without noticing. The Egyptian sentries had assumed the arriving tanks were their own. There were at least one hundred vehicles, including fuel trucks, but no tanks. The Egyptian soldiers in the Israelis' vicinity paid no particular attention to them. After wakening his crews, Brik beckoned to an Egyptian captain nearby. The officer approached and was taken aback when Brik announced to him, through one of his crewmen who spoke Arabic, that they were Israelis. Tell your superior, said Brik, that he must evacuate all this equipment towards Cairo. Sorry, said the Egyptian officer, we were here before you. Brik asked him to call the commander of the encampment. The officer returned with a colonel to whom Brik repeated his demand. The colonel said Brik could not give him orders. "There's a cease-fire," he said.

"Don't get me angry," said Brik. "I have tanks and I can shoot. You with these vehicles can't. I will fire if you don't pull out."

The colonel assembled his officers and within an hour the Egyptian vehicles started to move off. An Egyptian truck driver whose path Brik was blocking honked his horn and the Israeli tank obligingly moved aside. This relatively civil encounter would soon prove an anomaly as the Egyptians began to challenge Israel's interpretation of the cease-fire.

Word of the near destruction of Shimshi's battalion made its way up the Israeli chain of command, feeding the unhappiness with which the cease-fire was being viewed by almost the entire military hierarchy. It was Adan, as the general in command of the most active front, who felt it most keenly. An order was an order but the destruction of the Third Army was a war-winning opportunity. Adan was aware that Dayan, in the Six Day War, had ordered the IDF to halt six miles short of the Suez Canal but that officers in the field had nevertheless brought the army to the water's edge. Elazar himself, as commander of the northern front in that war, had stretched the cease-fire time limits in order to complete the capture of the Golan Heights. Adan concluded that he too must "finish the job" if he was afforded an opening. At about midnight, he informed Gonen of the plight of Shimshi's battalion and noted that there were also other incidents of Egyptian fire. In these circumstances, said Adan, he intended to continue fighting the next day. Gonen replied that Adan was to maintain the cease-fire unless the enemy violated it. Adan took it as a pro forma response from a commander who in fact wanted to continue the fight as much as he did. He spent the remainder of the night preparing his brigades for continuation of the battle the next day on the assumption that the high command would in the end authorize an all-out advance. Shortly after dawn, Colonel Nir reported to Adan Egyptian tank fire in his sector. When Nir suggested checking to see if this was merely a local incident or something broader before reacting, the division commander replied angrily: "Don't make me any armistice here. If they've opened fire at you, take up positions and fire back."

At 8 A.M., Elazar informed Dayan of the Shimshi episode and other shooting incidents. "Last night they destroyed nine of our tanks and now they're attacking in a number of places, trying to grab territory back from us. I want to tell Southern Command that it's free to act in the Third Army's sector." Dayan gave his approval. Just make sure, he said, that the army spokesman points out that Israel is reacting to Egyptian violations of the cease-fire. Unlike Elazar, who believed the cease-fire would prove only a temporary lull, Dayan was convinced that Soviet interest in a cease-fire meant that it would last once it took hold. However, if Israel had its way, it would not take hold just yet.

Dayan's approval opened the way for resumption of an all-out offensive in the Third Army sector. Magen was ordered to cut remaining road links between Cairo and Suez. Implementation was delayed because his division was engaged with Egyptian forces trying to break through from the direction of Cairo to the beleaguered army. Intelligence reported that beyond the attack force, only two armored brigades remained to defend the road to Cairo—Libyan and Algerian units. Magen's division included Dan Shomron's brigade as well as Ran Sarig's, which had come down from the Golan after thirty-three hours on tank transporters. Numbering thirty tanks—less than one-third its normal size—the brigade was the only armored force to be transferred from one front to another. Other units transferred from the Golan to Sinai were Yoram Yair's paratroop battalion and a Katyusha rocket battery.

Adan's division, located closer to the Suez Canal, began its own drive south shortly after noon, routing scattered Egyptian forces in its path. An hour after dark, the lead elements reached the outskirts of Suez City.

Magen's division was by this time on the move. As it approached Adan's sector in the darkness, Adan suggested that its vehicles switch on lights in order to be able to move faster. Hundreds of headlights suddenly lit up the desert. Passing between Adan's tanks lining the road like an honor guard, Magen's force continued the rest of the way in darkness. At midnight, it swung around Mount Ataka and reached the port of Adabiya, headquarters of the Egyptian naval force in the Gulf of Suez. The last road link to the 30,000 men of the Third Army in Sinai was now severed. A major new strategic reality had been imposed on the Egyptian front, with far-reaching implications.

Meanwhile, on the northern front, the Syrian high command was preparing an attack this day—Tuesday, October 23—that was to be the most massive since the initial incursion into the Golan Heights. The Iraqi expeditionary force now numbered two divisions. The Jordanians had likewise doubled their forces and were almost up to division strength. These forces would be thrown into the battle together with all five Syrian divisions, which had been resuscitated with the arrival of hundreds of tanks from the Soviet Union. A brigade of Iraqi mountain troops normally stationed in Kurdistan had reached the front, as well as smaller infantry detachments from Saudi Arabia and Kuwait. Palestinian units had also arrived. In addition, there was the Moroccan brigade which had been fighting alongside the Syrians since the beginning of the war. Dayan's dark vision of Israel fighting the entire Arab world was not far from reality.

The attack was to begin with the landing of special forces, including Palestinian commandos, by helicopter behind the Israeli lines. Tank forces would then attack the Israeli enclave from two directions. The Arabs, by their own estimate, had a 5-to-1 advantage in tanks and artillery and a 4-to-1 advantage in infantry. Assad believed the counterattack would drive the Israelis from the enclave within two days. The plan envisaged a second stage in which the Golan would be recaptured as well. Israel was aware of the pending attack and braced for it. Its units had rested and refitted and were deployed along most of the line on dominant hills.

The acceptance by Egypt of the cease-fire on Monday created a major dilemma for Assad. The cease-fire did not bind Assad, but its implications could not be ignored. Some on the Syrian General Staff favored going ahead with the attack, arguing that if it did so Egypt would feel obliged to continue fighting as well. Even if Egypt stopped fighting, it would take the Israelis several days to shift forces from the Sinai. Others, however, argued that continuation of the war on the northern front would legitimize Israel's efforts to destroy the Egyptian Third Army. In that case, Egypt would not come to Syria's assistance when Israel turned its full might northward, destroying Syria's infrastructure and perhaps attacking Damascus.

In the end, Assad and his advisers decided that the risks outweighed the opportunities. Instead of the twenty-third beginning with a massive artillery barrage heralding the Arab counterattack, as planned, the day passed quietly and ended with Syria's announcement of its acceptance of the cease-fire. The Iraqi government, which objected to a cease-fire, ordered its forces to return home immediately.

With the satisfaction due a man who had been instrumental in wrapping up the Middle East war, Henry Kissinger dropped off to sleep for four hours upon his return home from Moscow and Tel Aviv in the early hours of October 23. When he arrived at his office in late morning, it was to find that the cease-fire agreement had already started to unravel. A message from Hafez Ismail in Cairo informed him that Israel was occupying new positions in disregard of the cease-fire. Another message, from Ambassador Keating in Tel Aviv, reported a troubling conversation with Mrs. Meir. The prime minister said that she had initially rejected a request from her military leaders for two or three days to finish off the Third Army. However, she added, the Egyptians had broken the cease-fire during the night in several places and she had therefore ordered the IDF to resume fighting until the Egyptians stopped shooting.

An alarmed message followed from Brezhnev. Soviet reconnaissance flights had confirmed that Israeli forces were moving south along the canal towards Suez City in what the Soviet leader called "flagrant deceit." Brezhnev wanted the Security Council swiftly convened in order to call on all forces to withdraw to the cease-fire lines. When Golda Meir came on the line a few minutes later, Kissinger suggested that the IDF simply pull its troops back a few hundred yards and announce that it had returned to the cease-fire line. "How can anyone ever know where a line is or was in the desert?" he asked.

"They'll know all right," replied Mrs. Meir.

Kissinger found out what she meant soon enough; the last road links between Suez and Cairo had been severed and the Third Army was trapped. The urgency of the situation was reinforced by still another message from Brezhnev, this one addressed to Nixon. Accusing Israel of "treachery," he asked for joint action to stop the fighting. Kissinger now realized that the

Egyptians' plight must be more serious than the CIA, or the Israelis, had indicated. He informed the Soviets that the United States would support a Security Council resolution reconfirming the cease-fire. "We had no interest in seeing Sadat destroyed," he would write. "Even less so via the collapse of a cease-fire we had cosponsored." Nor did Kissinger wish to lose a heaven-sent opportunity for the United States to elbow aside the Soviets in the Arab world.

In midafternoon, a message addressed to Nixon was received from Sadat himself, the first time since the Six Day War that an Egyptian leader had directly addressed the American administration. He asked for American intervention—even, if necessary, the use of force—to implement the cease-fire. After obtaining from Dinitz an Israeli pledge to observe a new cease-fire if Egypt did, Kissinger informed Brezhnev and Sadat of that in Nixon's name. With the president trapped in the mire of Watergate, Kissinger was signing Nixon's name to diplomatic notes almost as frequently as his own.

At 4 P.M. Tuesday in New York, the Security Council met to reconfirm the cease-fire and direct that UN observers be dispatched to the front. Two hours later, Dayan received a call from the head of the UN Emergency Force in Cairo, Gen. Ensio Siilasvuo. He had received instructions from New York, said the Finnish officer, to send observers to the front to delineate the cease-fire line. Siilasvuo accepted Dayan's suggestion that the new cease-fire take effect at 7 A.M., local time—that is, thirty-six hours after the initial cease-fire was to have gone into effect. Israel's interpretation of cease-fire, however, would continue to prove different from everybody else's.

In the Pit that evening, Elazar mused aloud on the dilemma posed by the cease-fire. Militarily, Israel needed only a few more days in order to bring about the Third Army's surrender and cut off the Second Army as well, bringing about a total Egyptian military collapse. Politically, however, the debt to the United States was too great to ignore. Israel had already received in the past few days forty Phantoms and thirty-two Skyhawks, two-thirds the number of planes that had been lost since the beginning of the war. "That's why we accepted the cease-fire that the United States decided on," he said.

An hour after midnight Adan received from Southern Command his operational orders for the following day, October 24. He was to complete mopping up the greenbelt, cut water pipes laid across the canal to the Third Army, and capture Suez City—"provided it doesn't become a Stalingrad," in Ben-Ari's words. Suez City was a major logistical base for the Third Army and its capture was expected to hasten the army's surrender. Israel took the view that this would be no violation of the new cease-fire if it was launched before 7 A.M. even if the fighting continued after that hour. The Arabs had determined when the war would start and when to call for a cease-fire and the Israelis felt no qualms about adjusting the rules a bit now in their own favor. They also maintained that the cease-fire did not apply to "mopping up" since these operations were not altering the front line, only rear areas.

Adan requested information on the Egyptian military presence in Suez. Intelligence was aware of a commando battalion, two infantry battalions, and an antitank missile company in the city. These were enough forces to put up formidable resistance, particularly in a densely built-up area, but Adan thought it unlikely to happen. During the past two days, Egyptian soldiers had been surrendering in masses, including many officers. Adan was convinced that the fight had gone out of the Egyptian army and that resistance in the city would collapse with the first strong shove. It was an assumption he would have cause to deeply regret.

Thirty-six

SUEZ CITY

L IKE A CAVALRY OFFICER IMPATIENTLY slapping his leg with a riding crop, Col. Arye Keren urged paratroop commander Yossi Yoffe to move at "armor pace."

The two men were conferring at the western outskirts of Suez City where Keren had set up his command post. The tank brigade commander was in charge of the attack on the city. He informed Yoffe that his paratroop reservists would lead the way. He was to start immediately since they were already past the new cease-fire deadline of 7 A.M., October 23.

Yoffe protested. He had only one small map of the city that showed little detail. Nor had he seen air photos. He was being asked to drive straight up the main street of Suez in the nine captured Soviet APCs at his disposal as if there would be no resistance. It was not clear to him on what that confidence was based. The battalion was being sent in blind, the way Mordecai's paratroopers had been at the Chinese Farm.

Suez had almost been emptied of its 260,000 residents during the War of Attrition. But enough residents remained to form a local militia which was part of the force now defending the city.

Pressed by Adan to finish the job before the international observers arrived, Keren had little patience with Yoffe's request to study the situation and draw up a plan. "In the armored corps," said the brigade commander, "we take our orders while we're on the move." Nevertheless, he gave Yoffe

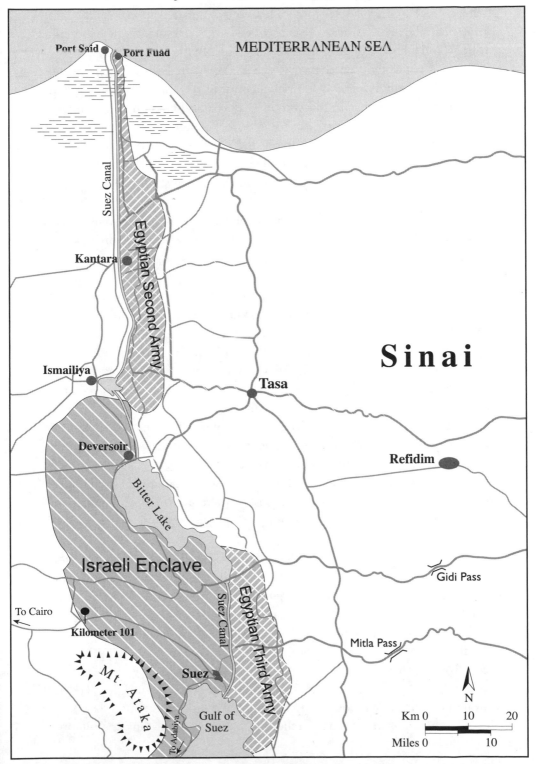

Cease–fire Lines on the Egyptian Front

MEDITERRANEAN SEA

Port Said • • Port Fuad

Suez Canal

Egyptian Second Army

Kantara •

Ismailiya •

Tasa •

S i n a i

Deversoir •

Refidim ●

Bitter Lake

Israeli Enclave

Suez Canal

Egyptian Third Army

Gidi Pass

To Cairo ←

Kilometer 101 ●

Mt. Ataka

To Adabiya

Suez •

Mitla Pass

Gulf of Suez

N

Km 0   10   20

Miles 0   10

half an hour to organize his force. Lt. Col. Nahum Zaken's tank battalion would lead the attack instead, accompanied by its own infantry detachment. Yoffe would follow, dropping off platoons to secure the intersections.

In the battle for Jerusalem in the Six Day War, Yoffe's battalion had captured Ammunition Hill in a night action that was a major turning point in the battle for the city. In this war, it had broken the commando ambush on the road to Fort Budapest. Since being helicoptered across the canal a few days before, it had been fighting in the greenbelt, where it found resistance weak. Learning of their assignment this morning, the men joked that they might save time by driving straight to the mayor's office to accept his surrender.

The capture of the city had neither the strategic nor the psychological importance that made the recapture of the Hermon two days before mandatory. All links to Cairo were already severed. Suez presumably contained supplies for the Third Army across the canal, but the city's capture would make no substantial difference to the fate of that army, now completely surrounded. It was worth making the effort to take Suez only if, as Ben-Ari had stipulated, there would be no serious resistance. The problem was that Adan's division was about to commit itself before finding out.

Zaken's column stretched for more than a mile as it started towards Suez's main avenue, an extension of the Cairo–Suez highway. It was a dual-lane carriageway with railroad tracks running down the center. Lining the street at the city entrance were apartment buildings of three and four stories which gave way to buildings of five and six stories closer to the city center. Zaken was to proceed three miles down the length of the avenue, which ended in a large square bordering the Gulf of Suez. Looking through binoculars, he could see Egyptian soldiers, most of them unarmed, ambling about the edge of the city. Some even raised their hands in surrender at the sight of the approaching tanks.

All twenty-one tank commanders stood in their turrets as the battalion turned down the avenue. The commanders of the fifteen APCs and half-tracks bearing the infantry detachment likewise stood erect to witness this final, almost ceremonial, act of the war. It looked more like a parade than an attack as the armored vehicles proceeded down the avenue. Only the crowds and flags were missing, except for a white flag waved by a few Egyptian soldiers from an alley.

At the second intersection, the victory procession abruptly ended. Grenades rained down from the apartment buildings, gunfire rattled off tank turrets, and RPGs were fired from the alleys. Almost all the tank and infantry commanders were hit within seconds. Zaken, at the head of the column, was unhurt. But when he looked back down the avenue, it seemed that his entire battalion had been wiped out at one blow. Not a single head protruded from the turrets and there was no reply when he tried to reach his company commanders on the radio. Zaken called to crewmen. "Whoever is still alive, enter the commander's compartment and answer." Voices of gunners and loaders began to be heard. They named commanders who had been killed or wounded. Zaken could hear panic in their voices. "Keep moving," he shouted over the din. "Fire all weapons. Get out of the ambush. Keep moving forward."

Maneuvering around two tanks which had been set afire, the rest of the battalion made it to the square at the end of the street. They deployed with their backs to the gulf and their guns facing the buildings and alleys around the square, from which fire came, although less than on the main street. The lead company commander, Capt. Menashe Goldblatt, had lost consciousness after being hit in the shoulder. He recovered now and at Zaken's request made his way from tank to tank to talk to the crews. He found many in shock, with their commanders, and sometimes other crewmen, lying inside the tank wounded or dead. Goldblatt appointed gunners or loaders as tank commanders, assigned them sectors of fire, and directed them to switch their radios from their company frequencies to the battalion frequency so that Zaken could talk directly to them. With fire sweeping the square and no one else afoot in it, Goldblatt tried to keep the tanks between him and the sources of fire.

He found one tank commander who had not been wounded but was afraid to lift his head out of the turret. When persuasion failed, the officer warned him that if he did not begin to function, he, Goldblatt, would fire a shell at his tank. As he moved off, he turned and saw the sergeant's head rising slightly above the turret. The captain, who made several trips through the square on foot during the day, well understood the men's fear. For months after the war he himself would be unable to sleep except in his tank because of the vulnerability he felt outside it.

Zaken organized the transfer of casualties to an APC which sped back up the main street. The Egyptians were taken by surprise and the vehicle made it out of the city unscathed. After depositing the casualties at an aid station, the crew members decided to run the gauntlet again and rejoin the battalion. They made it halfway back before the vehicle was hit by an RPG. One soldier was killed and almost everyone else wounded but the driver managed to turn the vehicle and make it back to the city's outskirts. When a second APC with dead and wounded tried to leave the square, it was turned back by heavy fire. Its commander, however, picked up a report on the radio net that offered a measure of encouragement: "Red boots entering the area." The paratroopers were moving in.

Fire hit the paratroopers' column as soon as it started down the avenue. Yoffe ordered his APC to halt alongside the burning tanks but found that the crews had already been evacuated. The Egyptian fire was too intense for the APCs to continue. An RPG hit Yoffe's vehicle, killing four men and wounding the others, including the battalion commander himself. The vehicles pulled to the side of the street and the paratroopers took cover in adjacent buildings. Most converged on a two-story structure which turned out to be a police station. Two police were killed as the paratroopers burst in, but the rest were permitted to leave.

Fifty of the paratroopers congregated in the building. Lt. David Amit, the ranking unwounded officer, organized the defenses. Men posted at windows and behind a low stone wall in front of the building blocked attempts to storm the police station. Egyptians penetrated a side entrance and approached a room being used as an aid station. The battalion doctor, Maj. Gabi Canaan, rose up from tending the wounded and opened fire on them with his Uzi. Medics joined in overcoming the intruders.

Yoffe, whose leg had been badly ripped, refused morphine so that he could remain alert. At one point, enemy fire suddenly ceased. He listened to the silence for a minute and said, "They're preparing to attack." A hail of RPGs and grenades struck the building, setting a fire on the second floor. Yoffe told Dr. Canaan, "It's time to burn the documents." He was referring to maps and papers that might be useful to Egyptian intelligence. The men, however, repulsed the attack and doused the fire. Yoffe had lost much blood and frequently lost consciousness. During his intervals of wakefulness, Amit consulted with him.

The paratroopers believed that armored forces would break through to rescue them before long. Several attempts were indeed made. As one force of tanks and APCs approached, the men threw furniture out the window to signal their location. But the vehicles were traveling with closed hatches and sped by. The rescue force did, however, spot a second paratroop contingent commanded by Lt. Col. Ya'acov Hisdai, which had entered behind Yoffe's battalion. Hisdai's force consisted of eighty men, most of them wounded. The rescuers succeeded in taking aboard all the wounded but six. Enemy fire curtailed further rescue efforts.

As night approached, Adan ordered armored forces out of the city. They were too vulnerable in the darkness to RPG teams. The evacuation was along the Gulf of Suez shore, which had been cleared of enemy troops. Zaken's battalion had suffered eighteen dead and thirty-five wounded and left three disabled tanks behind.

The two paratroop units—Yoffe's and Hisdai's—were now the only Israeli forces remaining in the city. Adan wanted them to make their way out on foot rather than risk armor in a rescue attempt. Hisdai agreed. Communicating with Keren in the Hebrew equivalent of pig latin to confuse Egyptian eavesdroppers, he asked to have tank projectors beam their lights skyward to indicate the location of the nearest Israeli unit. He himself scouted the route before returning to lead his men out. As they approached the Israeli lines, Hisdai led a full-throated rendition of the Hebrew song "Hevainu Shalom Aleichem [We've brought peace unto you]" to identify themselves.

For Yoffe's men, evacuation was more complex since they were twice as deep inside the city—more than two miles. After dark, the group in the police station was joined by other men from Yoffe's battalion who had found shelter in nearby buildings. There were now ninety men, of whom twenty-three were wounded. With darkness, soldiers dashed out several times to the stranded vehicles to bring in ammunition, medical supplies, and a jerrican of water.

The men were reluctant to leave the security of the building even though shooting had ceased. Colonel Keren tried to persuade Amit to lead them out, but the lieutenant said he preferred to wait for armor to reach them in the morning rather than proceed on foot past buildings filled with enemy troops. He finally succumbed to Keren's increasingly insistent demand, saying he would send the men out in small groups. Keren ruled that out. They must leave in one large group, the brigade commander said, capable both of supporting the wounded and of defending itself if attacked. Keren passed the microphone to Hisdai, who encouraged Amit to do it.

At this point, General Gonen, who was closely following the imbroglio on the radio net, spoke to Amit directly. When the lieutenant explained his reluctance to move out on foot, Gonen told Colonel Keren to attempt an armored rescue in the morning. Exasperated, Keren called Adan to complain that Gonen had spoiled it all after Amit had been persuaded to leave. The division commander called Gonen and explained that a rescue attempt would be too costly. Gonen called Amit back and said it would be best after all to leave on foot.

"Do you have a paper and pencil?" asked the general. Looking at an enlarged air photo of Suez, he proceeded to dictate to Amit the route he should follow out of the city. "Two hundred meters south to the third block of buildings from the corner, then 200 meters west along the alley, then, before the end of the street there's an alley and you go on it 200 meters north, afterwards 250 meters west through a bunch of huts, turn north towards the railroad track, northwest 700 meters you reach a bridge on the [Sweetwater] canal, then you pass a cemetery, then 1,400 meters northwest you reach a crossroad held by our forces. What you have to decide is whether you want artillery or not."

Amit, sitting on the floor of the darkened police building with a flashlight, stopped writing halfway through. What Gonen was proposing would have been difficult enough to follow with a good map by day, but he had no such map and it was night. Furthermore, the proposed route would take them through an area south of their location that Amit knew to be dense with Egyptian troops. He accommodated Gonen by muttering "Yes sir" periodically, but he had no intention of accepting his advice. He would later be told by a sergeant at Umm Hashiba who was with Gonen at the time that the general seemed to see his direct involvement in the rescue as some sort of personal vindication. Amit asked Gonen for an artillery bombardment around the police station itself to clear the area for their departure but said he preferred to move through the city quietly, without artillery accompaniment. He organized the men into squads, each responsible for three wounded men. The squads were to keep distance between each other, so as not to constitute a suspiciously large grouping, but not to lose eye contact. The men moved outside the building and awaited the order to start. However, lookouts reported activity in the buildings around them and said that Egyptian soldiers had set up positions down the street. The report intensified the reluctance among the men to leave the security of the building. Amit, who shared that reluctance, ordered everyone back inside.

The situation looked hopeless. It was becoming apparent that no rescue attempt would be made, even by day. After the casualties they had inflicted on the Egyptians, the paratroopers did not think prisoners would be taken. Some of the men determined to finish themselves off with a grenade or bullet at the last minute if the Egyptians broke in. When Dr. Canaan responded "I'll tell you tomorrow" to a question put to him by a soldier, the soldier said, "Gabi, there won't be a tomorrow." The doctor mustered a smile and said: "You've fought well until now and you'll have the privilege of fighting in many more wars. This story isn't over."

At 2 A.M. Keren cut through all the deliberations. Raising Amit on the radio, he said, "Move out. Report implementation in ten minutes. Out." This was what the lieutenant needed—not a suggestion but an unambiguous order. At this point, Yoffe woke and Amit consulted with him. The battalion commander agreed it was best to leave on foot rather than await the dubious prospect of rescue. As his men watched, the colonel struggled to his feet for the first time since being carried into the building in the morning and took a few tentative steps. "I can walk," he announced. In a scene resembling a mass resurrection, other wounded men, including some in even worse condition than Yoffe, began to rise and hobble about to test their limbs.

Once again, Amit ordered the men to move out. Just two of the wounded had to be carried on stretchers. The remainder walked, some of them supported by comrades. With an artillery barrage keeping down the heads of Egyptians in the vicinity, the column set out behind a point squad unencumbered by wounded to deal with any ambush. Instead of heading south, as Gonen had suggested, the men moved north across the broad avenue and then turned left to follow narrow side streets paralleling it. Broken glass and other debris made it impossible to walk quietly. Cigarettes glowing in the dark revealed the presence of men in surrounding buildings. Several times, Egyptian soldiers passed close, sometimes even emerging from side streets and cutting through gaps in the column. The Egyptians did not challenge the Israelis, either believing they were Egyptian or preferring not to know.

After an excruciating passage lasting almost two hours, the men reached the Sweetwater Canal, the outer point of Egyptian control. They walked along its inner face towards a vehicular bridge marked on the map, ready to fight their way across. A few score yards before the bridge, they came upon a railroad bridge not indicated on the map. They could hear the voices of Egyptian troops guarding the vehicular bridge beyond. But the railroad bridge was unguarded. The paratroopers made their way across it without incident. The Egyptians at the vehicular bridge may well have seen the column, which included wounded men shuffling along. But if so, they chose not to become entangled in a firefight with the war as good as over. The paratroopers reached Keren's tank force on the outskirts of the city just before dawn.

The price paid by the IDF for the Suez misadventure was 80 dead and 120 wounded. The last major action of the Yom Kippur War was over. But the final shots had not yet been fired.

Although all roads to Suez had been cut, Israeli forces had still not established a presence in a six-mile stretch along the Suez Canal north of the city.
At first light on October 25, just after Yoffe's men had reached safety, Captain Brik and his five remaining tanks were dispatched south through the
agricultural strip to close this gap. The company commander was told not to
fire unless fired upon. The cease-fire was officially in effect but the Israeli
command was not interpreting it to mean cease-movement. At the rear of
Brik's tanks was an APC with a squad of paratroopers. Halfway, the commander of the lead tank sighted Egyptian tanks amidst trees to the front. A
moment later, a shell hit Brik's tank, the second in line, destroying the
machine gun and antenna alongside his head but causing him only a facial
cut. "Move left," he shouted to his driver, but there was no response. "He's
dead," called the loader. Brik and the other two surviving crewmen leaped
from the tank before it could be hit again. Meanwhile, the paratroopers
raced through the shrubbery towards the Egyptian tanks. They found them
with hatches opened, abandoned by their crews, and tossed grenades inside.
Brik shifted to another tank, his seventh since the war started, and led the
column on to the outskirts of Suez.

On the first morning of the war, Brik had barely escaped when an RPG
brushed his shirt and set it afire during the commando ambush near
Baluza—the first Sinai fight involving reservists. He had survived the charge
of Assaf Yaguri's battalion on October 8 and many other clashes. He had
now barely escaped again in the very last skirmish of the war. Of the 120
men of the battalion who had started out on Yom Kippur under Yaguri, only
7 were still in action, including Brik and his gunner. Of the original battalion
members and their replacements, 80 had been killed and close to 100
wounded—a casualty rate of 150 percent.

The resumption of fighting in the Third Army sector raised the possibility
that it might be resumed as well in Sharon's sector, where the October 22
cease-fire had meanwhile been holding. As the battle was raging in Suez,
paratroop forces under Sharon, now including Mordecai's battalion, were
ordered to prepare to renew the drive on Ismailiya by capturing vehicular
and railway bridges across the Sweetwater Canal. Strong resistance could be
expected. The units were moving to their start positions when the attack was
called off.

Mordecai ordered his men to make an immediate U-turn in order to
avoid accidental clashes. As the survivors of the Chinese Farm turned back

towards their encampment, soldiers slapped each other on the shoulder. Some grinned. Others had tears in their eyes. "We made it," said one. The war was over.

Despite the disastrous opening of the war for Israel, it held more territory at the end than at the beginning—more territory, indeed, than it had ever held. The Egyptians were holding 1,200 square kilometers in Sinai, 200 less than they had held before the Israeli breakthrough to Matsmed, but the IDF held 1,600 square kilometers west of the canal. The IDF was now within fifty miles of Cairo, twelve miles closer than before. On the Syrian front, it had captured 500 square kilometers and was likewise twelve miles closer to Damascus, now less than thirty miles away.

But even before the Arabs and Israelis could begin debating who won the war and who would pay its price, the superpowers, who had tried to separate them for the past two weeks, began mustering their own armed forces in menacing confrontation with each other.

Thirty-seven

NUCLEAR ALERT

BELIEVING THE WAR ALREADY BEHIND HIM, Chairman Brezhnev was looking forward on the afternoon of October 24 to the festive opening in the Kremlin the following day of the World Congress of Peace Forces, a prestigious conclave in which he would have the kind of starring role he relished. A team of speechwriters submitted drafts of his keynote speech for review and he conferred with colleagues about resolutions to be adopted. An annoyingly dissonant note was sounded by a message that arrived late in the day from Ambassador Vinogradov in Cairo. The Israelis were ignoring the cease-fire, Vinogradov reported, and the Egyptian Third Army was completely cut off. The Egyptians feared that the Israelis were about to descend on Cairo. Militiamen had been mobilized and the population called upon to resist any incursion.

Brezhnev wondered aloud whether Kissinger had made some kind of deal during his stopover in Tel Aviv, a concern that mirrored Mrs. Meir's fear that Kissinger had made a deal at Israel's expense in Moscow. An urgent message arrived from Sadat asking for Soviet observers or troops to be sent this very night. Sadat said he was asking the same of the Americans.

The Politburo decided to send fifty observers, but the suggestion of troops stirred little enthusiasm. A military adventure in which the United States stood with the opposite camp was not an inviting proposition. Chief of staff Kulikov said that by the time Soviet forces had been organized and flown to Egypt, Cairo would have fallen. Nevertheless, there was a consensus that something meaningful had to be done to help Sadat. According to Kremlin chronicler Victor Israelyan, it was decided to hint to the Americans that the Soviets might intervene unilaterally, in the hope that this would make the Americans worried enough to pressure their Israeli clients. In other words, to bluff, since Moscow had no intention of sending troops.

A message from Brezhnev to Nixon was composed in the chairman's study after midnight calling for American and Soviet contingents to be dispatched to the Middle East to ensure implementation of the cease-fire. Then came the trumpet blast. "I will say it straight that if you find it impossible to act jointly with us in this matter, we should be faced with the necessity urgently to consider taking appropriate steps unilaterally. We cannot allow arbitrariness on the part of Israel." If Brezhnev intended to catch Kissinger's attention, he succeeded.

Kissinger had spent the day trying to placate Sadat and the Soviets by assuring them that he was exerting maximum pressure on the Israelis. He was indeed in constant contact with Dinitz, who relayed unconvincing messages from Tel Aviv claiming that it was the Egyptians who were attacking. Kissinger expressed indignation at Israel's violation of the cease-fire.

In Tel Aviv, Elazar was summoned urgently to Mrs. Meir's office. He found her and her senior advisers agitated. Calls were coming in to Dinitz from the White House "every five minutes" to complain of the Israeli actions, he was told. Dinitz had been warned in Nixon's name by Haig that if the fighting did not stop immediately, the president might "disassociate himself" from Israel. Furthermore, Sadat had asked for superpower intervention and there were indications that the Soviets were planning to comply. The chief of staff, still unaware of the extent of the snafu in Suez, called Gonen to pass on the order. "They're shouting in Washington and howling in New York," he said. However, when Gonen requested air support in battles taking place at two points near the Cairo–Suez road where Egyptian tank forces were trying to break through to the Third Army, Elazar gave his approval.

In Washington, Kissinger rejected Cairo's bid for the dispatch of U.S. and Soviet forces to the region. "We had not worked for years to reduce the Soviet military presence in Egypt," he would write, "only to cooperate in reintroducing it. . . . We were determined to resist by force if necessary the introduction of Soviet troops into the Middle East." At 9:35 P.M. he took a call from Ambassador Dobrynin, who said he had received a letter for Nixon from Brezhnev so urgent that he would read it on the phone before sending it over. When Kissinger heard that the Soviets were considering "taking appropriate steps unilaterally," he understood that a major crisis was at hand.

A superpower confrontation was for presidents to manage, not cabinet secretaries, talented though they might be. And Nixon was superb at handling international crises. But it was all the president could do now to hold himself together as the final humiliation of Watergate closed in. In a conversation with Nixon earlier in the evening, Kissinger had found him agitated and talking about the desire of his political enemies not just for his ouster but for his physical death. By the time Brezhnev's letter arrived, the president had gone to bed. When Kissinger asked Haig whether he should be wakened, the White House chief of staff replied firmly, "No." Haig clearly shared Kissinger's feeling that Nixon was in no condition to make weighty decisions.

But decisions had to be made. Kissinger called for an immediate meeting of the senior officials who had been monitoring the Middle East crisis with him since its outbreak. They included defense secretary James Schlesinger, CIA director William Colby, chairman of the Joint Chiefs of Staff Adm. Thomas Moorer, presidential assistant Gen. Brent Scowcroft, and Haig. At Haig's suggestion, the meeting was held in the White House with Kissinger presiding. It got under way at 10:40 P.M. in the situation room in the basement of the West Wing. What followed would be described by Kissinger as "one of the more thoughtful discussions that I attended in my government service."

The forum took the Soviet threat seriously. The CIA reported that the Soviet arms airlift had unexpectedly stopped early that morning. This could mean that the planes were being reconfigured to carry troops. Airborne divisions were known to have been put on heightened alert status, and the Soviet Mediterranean fleet had been reinforced to unprecedented size.

The forum decided to formulate a conciliatory-sounding reply to Brezhnev's letter aimed at drawing the Soviets into talks. At the same time, America's determination not to be stampeded would be signaled by increasing the state of alert in the armed forces from Defcon (Defense Condition) 4 to Defcon 3, the highest state of readiness in peacetime. At 11:41 P.M., Admiral Moorer issued orders to that effect. Kissinger left the meeting several times during the night to confer with Dinitz in the empty lobby of the West Wing. The Israeli ambassador was asked to keep the Israeli government abreast of developments and to report back its reactions. Informing Dinitz of the heightened alert status, Kissinger said it would have a greater impact if Soviet intelligence detected it before the U.S. announcement.

At 11:55 the forum approved a message to Sadat in Nixon's name intended to cut the legs out from under the Soviet threat by persuading Egypt to drop its request for Soviet intervention. The United States, warned the message, would challenge any Soviet force that appeared in the area. "I ask you to consider the consequences for your country if the two great nuclear countries were thus to confront each other on your soil."

During the meeting, it was learned that eight giant Soviet transports were due to fly from Budapest to Cairo within the next few hours. In addition, elements of the East German armed forces were being put on alert. At 12:20 A.M. the forum decided to alert the Eighty-second Airborne Division for possible movement. Five minutes later, orders went out for a carrier task force in the Atlantic to join two others already positioned in the Mediterranean. At 1:45 A.M., the commander of American forces in Europe was told to delay the scheduled return to the United States of troops participating in a NATO exercise. At 3:30 A.M., the Joint Chiefs ordered the Strategic Air Command to have its Guam-based B-52s, capable of carrying nuclear bombs, repositioned to the United States. It was decided not to deliver the reply to Brezhnev until 5:30 A.M. so as to give Soviet intelligence time to pick up the readiness measures and time for the American military to begin implementing them.

Conferring with Dinitz during a break, Kissinger asked how long it would take Israel to destroy the Third Army if there was a showdown. The suggestion that the United States might tolerate, even encourage, such a move astonished Mrs. Meir and her cabinet, which had assembled to receive Dinitz's reports. According to Dinitz, the Americans estimated that if the Soviets intervened, they could fly 4,500 soldiers a day to Cairo. The force was expected to begin moving towards the front in four or five days, when sufficient troops would have been assembled. Kissinger wanted to know if Israel could destroy the Third Army before then. The Israelis were certain they could, since the besieged army no longer had air defenses. Kissinger suggested, according to Dinitz, that the attack not be launched the day the Soviets began to arrive in Cairo but the day after so that it was clear to all which action came first.

Kissinger said he expected Soviet troops to begin landing in Cairo in two days. The Israeli envoy expressed doubt that the Soviets would intervene, noting that since the Second World War Soviet troops had never fought in countries which did not border their own. There's always a first time, said Kissinger. Nevertheless, he asked for Israel's intelligence assessment regarding Soviet intervention. When General Scowcroft, who was party to the conversation, said that Israel had placed Egypt in an impossible position by trapping the Third Army, Dinitz replied that one side or the other had to be in that situation. Now that it was Egypt, Israel had negotiating clout. Kissinger nodded. In Tel Aviv, Mossad chief Zamir reported to Mrs. Meir that there was no sign from his sources that the Soviets were intending to send troops to the Middle East.

Close to midnight, October 24, Dayan called Bar-Lev at Southern Command and was told that all was quiet except in one corner of Suez. Bar-Lev was referring to Yossi Yoffe's trapped battalion. Earlier in the day, Col. Natke Nir had been conferring with his staff officers in the greenbelt when fire was opened on them. Every man in the group was wounded except for the brigade commander himself. By dark, Egyptian pressure on the Cairo–Suez road had ceased and there was no shooting elsewhere at this hour.

It was the first quiet night since cantors had chanted Kol Nidre on Yom Kippur eve nineteen days before. Bar-Lev asked if Dayan could come south in the morning to talk to the division commanders about the political implications of the cease-fire. Dayan agreed but said he might be delayed. "I can't leave Tel Aviv before Golda goes to sleep and she doesn't go to sleep before Kissinger does."

Kissinger was already in bed by the time a messenger arrived at the Soviet embassy at 5:40 A.M. (Washington time) to deliver the reply to Brezhnev's note. Composed in Nixon's name, it said the United States would not tolerate unilateral Soviet action. It expressed hope, however, for cooperation and accepted the idea of a UN truce supervisory force. The message was soft-voiced. The big stick was left dangling behind Washington's back for the Soviets to discover.

Aboard his flagship, the USS *Little Rock,* Adm. Daniel Murphy, commander of the U.S. Sixth Fleet, was showering when an aide rapped on his cabin door shortly before 6 A.M. (local time) to inform him of the Defcon 3 alert. The message added that the carrier *John F. Kennedy* had been ordered through the Gibraltar Strait to join the two carrier task forces already under Murphy's command in the Mediterranean. The *Franklin D. Roosevelt,* which had been maintaining a discreet holding position with its escorts in the western Mediterranean, would now move closer to the Middle East and join up with the *Independence* task force south of Crete. Transport ships bearing 2,000 marines, anchored in Suda Bay on the northern side of Crete, were to join the carrier fleet south of the island, closer to the war zone.

For more than two weeks, the Sixth Fleet had been playing tag with the Soviet Mediterranean squadron as each positioned itself for possible intervention in the Israel-Arab conflict while keeping an eye on the other. Murphy's fleet had increased from 50 vessels to 60. Lookouts monitoring ship movements through the Dardanelles reported surface ships and submarines streaming south; the Soviet squadron's strength increased from 57 ships to 97 following Yom Kippur. This included 16 submarines as well as landing craft for several thousand marines with the Soviet fleet. As the *Kennedy* sailed in from the Atlantic, it was picked up by a Soviet submarine shadow.

The American rules of engagement in this naval face-off, the most massive ever between the superpowers, left it to Murphy's discretion to strike if he determined a Soviet attack was imminent. Murphy calculated that if the Soviet fleet attacked first, it could get off 40 sea-to-sea missiles and 250 torpedoes. If it came to it, however, he was confident that information provided by naval intelligence would enable him to fire the first shots. Murphy reckoned that there was a 40 percent chance of the Soviets attacking. If hostilities commenced, it was his intention to hunt down and destroy every Soviet warship in the Mediterranean, above and below the surface.

Electronic monitors detected Soviet missile systems constantly tracking the American carriers. Murphy kept the *Roosevelt* and *Independence* seventy-five to one hundred miles apart, close enough for their planes to provide mutual support but far enough to determine which one was being painted by Soviet radar. The Americans kept constant air patrol over the Soviet ships. The Soviet fleet, lacking an air arm, shadowed the American vessels with submarines and with destroyers, dubbed "tattletales." Soviet admirals, who had not in the past participated in these close encounters, could now be seen on the bridges of the tattletales, indicating the seriousness with which the Soviets were taking the game. Murphy and his commanders reviewed standing orders for the evacuation of American citizens in the region in an emergency. Of the 60,000 Americans estimated to be in the belligerent countries, 45,000 were in Israel. The marines would play a role in any evacuation.

The closest approach by the Sixth Fleet to the war zone was the positioning of a destroyer off Cyprus, one of a string of picket vessels down the length of the Mediterranean aiding navigation for planes participating in the airlift to Israel.

Within hours of the Defcon 3 alert, Murphy was informed of a change in the deployment of the Soviet fleet. The destroyer "tattletales" had been joined by first-line missile-carrying warships. Washington's alert had been picked up.

At the regularly scheduled meeting of the Politburo this morning, the American alert displaced all items on the agenda. Brezhnev expressed astonishment at the move and rejected a suggestion that it might be connected to his message to Nixon. "What has this to do with the letter I sent to Nixon?" he asked. Podgorny believed it did. "Who could have imagined the Americans would be so easily frightened?" he asked. Marshal Grechko said the Americans had no right under the 1972 Treaty for the Prevention of Nuclear War to alert its nuclear forces. However, none of the Soviet leaders saw a casus belli. "It is not reasonable to become engaged in a war with the United States because of Egypt and Syria," said Kosygin. KGB chief Yuri Andropov echoed that thought. "We shall not unleash the Third World War."

The Kremlin decided to increase military readiness but, except for Marshal Grechko, there was no support for sending troops to the Middle East. Instead, the Soviet leaders reconciled themselves to an Arab defeat. Brezhnev predicted the imminent fall of Ismailiya. "We must tell Sadat that we were right [about the inadvisability of Egypt going to war], that we sympathize with Egypt but we can't reverse the course of military operations." This sentiment was echoed by Andropov. "We tried to hold the Arabs back from starting military operations, but they didn't listen. Sadat expelled our military advisers, but when the Arabs started the fighting we supported them." Brezhnev expressed concern about the possibility of anti-Soviet demonstrations in Cairo.

The meeting was still in session when the reply to Brezhnev's letter formulated in Nixon's name arrived. Its conciliatory tone struck a responsive chord. Brezhnev seized on the message's call for the two powers to act jointly for peace in the Middle East. "That's exactly what we are trying to do," he cried. The Soviet leaders took heart from the statement that the American government was pressing the Israelis to ensure full compliance with the UN resolutions. This, Brezhnev said, was all he had been after.

Then came the key paragraph. "We must view your suggestion of unilateral action as a matter of the gravest concern involving incalculable consequences. It is clear that the forces necessary to impose the cease-fire terms on the two sides would be massive and would require closest coordination to avoid bloodshed. This is not only clearly unfeasible but it is not appropriate to the situation."

Defense minister Grechko responded first. "Why is it unfeasible? A gesture of Soviet-American joint action would have led to an immediate halt to the fighting. Is it not clear? The Americans want to impose their own scenario."

Brezhnev also expressed indignation. "We only said that if the Americans don't agree to act jointly we would have to *consider* taking steps unilaterally. And now, after having unilaterally declared a nuclear alert, they dare to criticize us. Something is wrong with the American logic." There was bewilderment at the absence of any explanation for the nuclear alert, which was not alluded to in the American message.

It was Brezhnev who came up with the most constructive response to the American alert—no response at all. "Nixon is too nervous," he said. "Let him cool down." A conciliatory message was drafted, reaffirming Moscow's objective of bringing an end to the war through joint Soviet-American action and noting that Nixon's agreement for the dispatch of observers obviated the need for unilateral Soviet action.

In Washington, the issue had been defused even before receipt of the new Brezhnev message. Returning to his office at 8 A.M., Kissinger found a message from Hafez Ismail saying that Egypt was dropping its request for Soviet troops in view of the American opposition and would ask the UN instead for an international force. Since UN rules excluded the superpowers from such peacekeeping missions, there would be no Soviet troops.

Nixon woke to discover that while he had been sleeping a global nuclear alert had gone out over his name. When briefed by Kissinger and Haig, he expressed elation at the way events had played themselves out. The crisis, it seemed, was over. Almost forgotten in the sense of relief wafting over both Washington and Moscow was that an army of 30,000 men was trapped in the desert and that Israel had cut off its water supply.

For Israel, the encirclement of the Third Army was psychological nourishment of the kind it had been desperately seeking since Yom Kippur, a reaffirmation of strength after the severest testing in its history. The Israeli cabinet decided Wednesday night to offer passage for the men of the Third Army through the Israeli lines without their weapons, except for officers. The latter were to be held until exchanged, together with the 8,300 Egyptian POWs already held by Israel, for 230 Israeli POWs in Egyptian hands. An alternative proposal put to Kissinger was for both sides to pull back across the canal to their prewar lines. Kissinger said the withdrawal of the Third Army from Sinai would not be acceptable to Sadat. He proposed instead that the Israelis permit food, water, and medicines to reach the beleaguered force while maintaining its encirclement. That way the Third Army would remain Israel's hostage for future bargaining but would not be forced into a humiliating surrender.

There was little sympathy in Israel for that idea. Attempts on Friday by the Egyptians to break out of the pocket and to put a bridge across the canal at Suez City were exploited by Israel to shell and bomb priority targets like command posts and water reserves. American officials reacted angrily. "I hope it's clear to you that you're playing with a superpower confrontation," a Defense Department official said to the Israeli military attaché, General Gur. Kissinger told Dinitz "as a friend" that Israel was playing a dangerous game.

Although Kissinger pressed Israel not to destroy the Third Army, its entrapment was in fact a gift to American diplomacy. It made Sadat totally dependent on the United States if he wished to prevent the army's annihilation. Kissinger told Dinitz that Washington would not countenance the Third Army's destruction. Nixon saw the survival of the Third Army as both an American obligation and the key to luring Egypt from the embrace of the Soviet Union.

Beyond that, the Third Army had become the delicate fulcrum of the endgame Kissinger was attempting to contrive, one in which Egyptian honor would be restored and Israeli deterrence reasserted. He had pushed Israel during the war to strike hard—harder, in fact, than it had initially been able to—in order to demonstrate its military superiority. But once the Israelis had begun smiting the Egyptians, he worked towards a speedy cease-fire that would leave the Egyptians with their dignity intact. Israel, in short, was to emerge quasi-victorious, not triumphant.

The Defense Department proposed that American planes parachute supplies to the beleaguered force. Kissinger preferred to win Israel's acquiescence to supplies passing through its lines and thus possibly open a door to a dialogue between Israel and Egypt. However, Israel was fixated on evening the score with Egypt. Not even the normally farsighted Dayan was ready to see the linkage between the Third Army's fate and the possibilities of peace.

Mrs. Meir took her time—half a day—before responding to Kissinger's urgent call for immediate lifting of the siege. Instead of acquiescing, she suggested that Egyptian and Israeli representatives meet face-to-face to discuss the fate of the Third Army and of the POWs. The Egyptians, she said, could fix the place, the time, and the rank of the representatives. Kissinger saw this as a further stall—no one could expect the Egyptians to agree to direct talks with Israel at this early a stage—but he passed the offer on to Hafez Ismail.

Meanwhile, two developments threatened to undo the delicate web being woven by Kissinger. Nixon, in a desperate bid to shore up his image, called a press conference to describe how he had sure-handedly managed the crisis which touched off the American nuclear alert—the crisis he had in fact slept through. Referring to Brezhnev's threat of unilateral Soviet intervention, he said, "Rather than saying that his note to me was rough and brutal, I would say it was very firm and it left very little to the imagination as to what he intended. My response was also very firm and left little to the imagination of how we would react." Brezhnev, said Nixon, understood American power and understood Nixon. He, Nixon, had after all been the president—continued Nixon—who bombed North Vietnam against all expectations. Kissinger winced as he listened, fearful that Brezhnev would feel called upon to reply in kind by proving his manhood. Haig warned Kissinger not to express his reservations to the president. "He's right on the verge," he said.

The second development was another message from Brezhnev. It did not echo Nixon's swaggering tone and was much milder than Brezhnev's "unilateral action" note two days before. But it expressed deep concern about the Third Army and asked for an American response within a few hours. Brezhnev, having learned his lesson, did not threaten consequences, a restraint that did not imply impotence.

It was time, Kissinger decided, to come down on the Israelis. Calling Dinitz at 11 P.M., he said he was passing on a message from the president. Firstly, the destruction of the Third Army "is an option that does not exist." Secondly, the president wanted an answer by 8 A.M. the next morning, Saturday, October 27, as to whether Israel would permit nonmilitary supplies to reach the trapped force. If the reply was negative, the United States would regretfully support the UN demand for an Israeli pullback to the October 22 lines. This would open the supply routes to the Third Army and in the process significantly worsen Israel's tactical deployment.

In Tel Aviv, Dayan had been telling Elazar and Mrs. Meir that permitting supplies through was the worst of all possible options since it would keep the Third Army intact as a viable fighting force. This would leave Adan's and Magen's divisions hung up between the Third Army in Sinai to their east—which still had bridges capable of carrying it back across the canal—and a new army forming on their western flank, towards Cairo. The preferable option would be to hammer the Third Army into submission. The next-best option was to let it pull back, leaving behind its weapons. If it came to it, however, Dayan was even prepared to let the army take its weapons, as long as it abandoned Sinai. All these thoughts were rendered irrelevant when word was received from Dinitz of Kissinger's ultimatum delivered in Nixon's name.

Reflecting on the war to date, Dayan told the cabinet that the Arabs had surprised him by their steadfastness. "They didn't run, not even when they were defeated in a battle." The minister said the Israeli troops had been superb. They had fought wisely and with determination but too boldly. "It's a wonderful thing and a terrible thing. We have to slow down and think what we're fighting about. When I'm on the other side of the canal I am constantly thinking, What are we doing here? This isn't the Western Wall." Recalling the Australian cavalrymen lost in the battle for Gaza in the First World War, he said, "We generally understand these things a generation later. We should not be shedding blood unless it's necessary."

Five hours before Kissinger's ultimatum to Israel expired, a message arrived in Washington from Hafez Ismail saying that Egypt accepted Israel's offer of direct talks. Kissinger was flabbergasted. "You're from a land of miracles," he told Dinitz. The meeting point set by Cairo was Kilometer 101 on the desert road between Cairo and Suez. The Egyptians designated Major General Gamasy as their representative and stipulated two preconditions for the meeting—a complete cease-fire and the passage of a convoy bearing nonmilitary supplies to the Third Army.

Mrs. Meir accepted both conditions and designated Major General Yariv as Israel's representative. The meeting was scheduled for 3 P.M. Saturday. However, General Gamasy and his party were held up ten miles further west on the Cairo–Suez road by Israeli troops who had not received word of the meeting. It was 1:30 A.M., Sunday, October 28, when the generals finally shook hands in a large tent that had been set up, the first time that representatives of the two countries had ever met for direct negotiations.

More substantive talks would be going on in Washington in the coming days. Acting Egyptian foreign minister Ismail Fahmy showed up in Kissinger's office on October 29 without an invitation and was followed two days later by Mrs. Meir.

On the eve of her departure for Washington, the prime minister had helicoptered south with Dayan and Elazar for her first visit to the front. At Southern Command and at each of the divisional headquarters, she met with the commanders, who described the war from their vantage points. At each stop, the prime minister also met with the troops. Sitting on a chair, she answered questions from soldiers sitting on the ground around her. When she visited Sharon's division and made her entrance alongside Dayan, Elazar, and Sharon, the troops began chanting, "Arik, king of Israel." It was a spontaneous display of affection for a commander at the successful end of a war, but it had political implications not lost on Mrs. Meir and Dayan.

When asked by a soldier why supplies were being permitted to reach the Third Army before Israel's POWs had been freed, the prime minister explained that American pressure left no choice. "It's easier to fight enemies than friends." From time to time, the grandmotherly nature of the visit gave way to disturbing questions. When a soldier asked, "How could we have been so unready?" Mrs. Meir said that she could not give an authoritative answer. She was not an expert on military matters, she said, and relied in this area on the two men sitting alongside her, the chief of staff and the defense minister. Her answer infuriated Lt. Col. Yom Tov Tamir, who still bore emotional scars from the destruction of his tank battalion on the first day of the war. "Because you don't understand these things I lost fifty-eight men?" he shouted. General Gonen, standing alongside him, calmed him down. Anger suppressed during the weeks of combat was beginning to vent.

The question raised by the soldier about the nation's unpreparedness was being asked on the home front with increasing stridency. The two men to whom Mrs. Meir had referred, Elazar and Dayan, would offer conflicting answers to the question the following day. In an appearance before the Knesset Foreign Affairs and Defense Committee, Elazar laid the blame for the initial setbacks squarely on the failure to mobilize the reserves in time. "If we had mobilized," he said, "the war would have lasted three, four, six days. From a terrible opening, the IDF went on to victory, and if there had been enough time it would have magnified it in a way that would have startled the world." There had been mistakes, he admitted, but the structure of the IDF and its preparations for the war had proven sound. There were no previously unknown factors that affected the outcome of the war, he said. It was a statement that ignored the stunning surprise of the Egyptian antitank tactics, the unexpected resilience of their infantry, Israel's neglect of combined arms operations, and the fact that the air force had been impaled by the SAMs.

Dayan disagreed with Elazar on every point. His hard-nosed assessment was that the problem went much deeper than the element of surprise and the failure to mobilize. "The army's operational concept proved incorrect," he said in a meeting with the country's newspaper editors in Tel Aviv. "Even if there had been full mobilization, the tanks could not approach [the enemy without being hit] and the planes could not approach. We estimated that if we have 300 tanks in Sinai and 180 on the Golan, it would be enough. But it was not enough."

Having overcome its initial problems, the IDF had become a formidable fighting machine, he said. "We have three divisions in the south, the likes of which the Israeli people have never seen. If we wanted to, we could reach Cairo. The question is whether that's desirable." Asked whether he feared a renewal of the war, he said, "On the contrary. I very much want a renewal of fighting with Egypt." Israel's present deployment west of the canal—sandwiched between two Egyptian armies and with an overextended supply line—was too awkward to maintain. Dayan wanted to pull back across the canal, but only for a price—the reopening of the Suez Canal and the repopulation of the abandoned canal cities as a guarantee that Egypt would not readily go to war again. If the Egyptians refused, he said, Israel would destroy the Third Army and try to do the same to the Second.

After seeing off Mrs. Meir to Washington, Dayan flew south to consult with the senior command there. He told the generals that he expected the war to flare up again in the next few weeks. This time, he said, "We will have to preempt." The army was strong, he noted. Damaged tanks had been repaired and "the fellows have rested." He did not favor a move towards Cairo, which could provoke Soviet intervention. Instead, he was eager to finish off the Third Army and then tackle the Second Army. He proposed attacking the Third Army even at the cost of a crisis with the United States since the present situation was untenable.

Adan said he believed the Third Army could be overcome in a single night. Sharon advocated steering the talks with Egypt into a dead end and then attacking. Instead of hitting the Third Army, however, he favored attacking the Second Army, which, he said, posed the more serious threat to the Israeli bridgehead. He agreed that it was unwise to move on Cairo. Colonel Reshef favored a feint towards Cairo and then hitting the Second Army. A small number of men under his command, he said, had lost their motivation. Some had been wounded five times already. However, most wanted to bring the war to a decisive conclusion and were prepared to press on, refreshed now after several days' rest. General Tamari did not believe they had the strength to subdue the Second Army.

At a meeting of the General Staff, almost all of the speakers favored resumption of fighting. There were two dissenters. Tal did not see any point in risking additional lives. Zeira said he did not think that destruction of the Third Army would make Sadat more amenable to a settlement, an insightful assessment.

Close to midnight November 2, Elazar ordered Adan to take his division back into Sinai and prepare to attack the Third Army. By dawn, the division had disengaged on the west bank and was streaming eastward across the bridges. The command decision, however, was made in Washington. "You will not be permitted to capture that army," Kissinger told Dinitz. As long as the United States called the tune, there would be no decisive victory. What the Americans were determined to achieve, indeed, was a decisive tie.

The American airlift had been more important to Israel symbolically than militarily. It brought 22,000 tons of supplies compared to 15,000 tons airlifted by the Soviet Union to Syria and Egypt. Only a small part of the material reaching Israel was actually used in the war. The knowledge that it was coming, however, permitted Israel to expend its own stockpiles more freely and cushioned it psychologically. The sight of the giant American transports landing at Ben-Gurion Airport, some forty a day, was a reminder to Israelis that they were not alone at a time when Europe—indeed, the world—was intimidated by the oil boycott.

The Americans had initially hoped to carry out the airlift discreetly so as not to offend the Arabs. The planes were to land at night and depart before dawn. Against the background of the Soviet airlift, however, the operation came increasingly to be seen in post-Vietnam Washington as a reassertion of America's ability to project power—nothing to be bashful about. The delivery of four tanks in giant Galaxies before media cameras was only a symbolic addition to Israel's arsenal, but the muscular preening successfully burnished America's can-do image.

An indirect benefit of the airlift was that it made it easier for President Sadat to ask for a cease-fire by saying he was no longer fighting Israel but the United States—a statement that conveniently ignored the Soviet airlift which had begun before the American airlift. American planes had in fact begun landing only late on October 14, after the tank battle that marked the turning point in the south and after Israel had already shelled Damascus's outskirts.

The strain of the past three weeks was clearly visible on Mrs. Meir's face when Kissinger greeted her upon her arrival in Washington. "The war had devastated her," he would write. On her official agenda were a POW exchange, the siting of the cease-fire line, and the fate of the Third Army. However, the real, unspoken purpose of her visit was to discern whether America's ties to Israel were threatened by Washington's efforts to bring Egypt into its orbit. There had been a worrying development when Kissinger in Moscow worked out the cease-fire resolution with the Soviets without consulting Israel. Was that an omen? In Israel's current state, the prospect of being jilted by its one friend and benefactor was not easy to contemplate.

Kissinger explained that once an Arab country signaled willingness to negotiate peace, America's position shifted to a mediating role that no longer necessarily overlapped all of Israel's positions. If there were no Israeli concessions—such as permitting supplies to get through to the Third Army— there would be no incentive for Egypt to move forward. "Arab intransigence and Soviet pressure had created the illusion that Israel did not have to conduct a foreign policy, only a defense policy," Kissinger would write. "Egypt's turn toward moderation had ended that simple state of affairs. Golda was railing not against America's strategy but against a new, more complicated reality."

The key to future developments lay in Cairo with the man who had just turned the region on its head. Kissinger set out for his first meeting with Sadat two weeks after the fighting stopped. Rapport between the two men was immediate, both appreciating the other's shrewdness and vision and both finding the other worthy of trust.

"I sensed that Sadat represented the best chance to transcend frozen attitudes that the Middle East had known since the creation of the State of Israel," Kissinger would write. The American diplomat tried to convince Sadat that his insistence that Israel pull back to the October 22 line would just lead to protracted debate. Instead, he said, the focus should be on a disengagement of forces in which Israel would pull back from the west bank altogether. The Third Army would meanwhile remain encircled but Israel would be persuaded to permit supply convoys to get through.

"Sadat sat brooding, saying nothing for many minutes," Kissinger would recall. "I was saying in effect that the key to peace was his acquiescence in keeping an Egyptian army cut off in the desert for weeks on end, relying on the assessment of an American he had just met. And then he astonished me. He did not haggle or argue. Violating the normal method of diplomacy— which is to see what one can extract for a concession—he said simply that he agreed with my analysis and my proposed procedure." Kissinger's proposal, which profited from his earlier talks with Fahmy and Mrs. Meir, included the following points:

A formal cease-fire agreement.
The supply of the Third Army via UN checkpoints which would
    replace Israeli checkpoints on the Cairo–Suez highway. Israeli

officers could examine the supplies together with UN officers to ensure their nonmilitary nature.

A POW exchange.

For Israel, the agreement meant that it would be getting its prisoners back without being required to loosen its grip on the Third Army. Egypt, for its part, was ensured that the Third Army would remain intact and that an Israeli pullback across the canal was in the offing. For the United States it meant displacement of the Soviet Union as the dominant foreign influence in Egypt. The agreement was signed on November 11 at Kilometer 101 by Generals Gamasy and Yariv, who were left to work out implementation.

The dialogue begun by the two generals in a desert tent was transformed a month later into a formal international conference in Geneva attended by Kissinger and the foreign ministers of Israel, Egypt, Jordan, and the Soviet Union. For the first time, Arab foreign ministers sat at the same table with their Israeli counterpart. Syria declined to attend, but an empty chair hinted at possible attendance in the future. The conference on December 21 provided the formal framework for a peace process which would unfold in the coming months—not in the stately halls of Geneva but in a sparkling tour de force by Kissinger that came to be known as shuttle diplomacy.

Flying between the capitals of the Middle East—sometimes several capitals in one day—he achieved his first major breakthrough when Egypt and Israel signed a disengagement agreement on January 18 calling for Israeli withdrawal across the canal to a line that would leave the Gidi and Mitla Passes in its hands. Egyptian forces on the Sinai bank would not be required to pull back, as Israel had initially demanded, but the two sides would be separated by a UN buffer zone.

The agreement put an abrupt end to the uneasy cease-fire that had prevailed for ten weeks. Israeli casualties totaled fourteen dead and sixty-five wounded during this "postwar" period. Egypt's casualties were higher, particularly in the sector commanded by Sharon, who ordered his forces to respond with massive artillery barrages to any perceived transgression. (A different view of Sharon was his reaction to the sight of an Israeli reservist major striking a prisoner in a POW camp. According to a senior officer who said he witnessed the incident, Sharon summoned the major to a tent, out of sight of the prisoners, and delivered a stinging rebuke that left the officer's face red.)

The new deployment and Sadat's agreement to reopen the Suez Canal and repopulate the canal cities was what Dayan had proposed in 1970 as the most stable solution in Sinai. In a talk before the Labor Party Central Committee a month after the war, Golda Meir seemed to express contrition for having rejected Dayan's proposal of three years before. "I didn't understand what he was talking about," she confessed. "We should just propose pulling back from the canal?" She did not elaborate but the implications were enormous. Had she accepted Dayan's suggestion, the war could well have taken a very different course—if, indeed, it broke out at all.

A month after the disengagement agreement, the last Israeli troops pulled back across the bridges. It was not without nostalgia that the reservists pulled up their tent stakes. "We'll miss being together," a paratroop sergeant from Colonel Matt's brigade told a reporter at an outpost being evacuated near Ismailiya. "I think some of us wouldn't mind going on living together like in a small kibbutz." In a ceremony of parting from Africa, Lt. Eli Cohen, the first Israeli to step ashore on the west bank four months before, lowered the Israeli flag from a pole set up near the edge of the roller bridge as his comrades set off colored smoke grenades and released balloons.

Israel prepared now to begin the arduous task of rebuilding its army for the next round, whenever it would come. Sadat, however, was still one step ahead. In a gesture that startled Mrs. Meir, the Egyptian leader sent her a personal note through Kissinger. "You must take my word seriously. When I threatened war, I meant it. When I talk of peace now, I mean it. We never had had contact before. We now have the services of Dr. Kissinger. Let us use him and talk to each other through him." Sadat recognized that the recovery of the rest of Sinai was likelier through the allure of peace than the threat of war.

Mrs. Meir's first reaction was suspicion—"Why is he doing this?" she asked Kissinger—but she recovered quickly. In a reply Kissinger took back with him to Cairo, Mrs. Meir wrote, "I am deeply conscious of the significance of a message received by the prime minister of Israel from the president of Egypt. I sincerely hope that these contacts . . . will continue and prove to be an important turning point in our relations."

For Syria's Assad, there would be no such flirtations. Committed to the idea of Israel's nonlegitimacy, he did not contemplate a peace agreement with it. Before returning home, Kissinger stopped off in Damascus to test the waters. Assad said he was prepared to enter into a cease-fire agreement on condition that Israel pull back not only from the enclave it had captured in this war but from half the territory it had captured on the Golan Heights in the 1967 war. Israel had just surrendered to Egypt territory in Sinai that it had captured in 1967—the Egyptian bridgeheads—and Assad demanded no less, even though he held no Israeli territory. He had to show his people, he said, that the thousands of Syrian soldiers killed in the war had not died in vain. Making the best of it, Kissinger told the Israelis that Assad had at least shown a willingness to negotiate.

A month later, the secretary of state returned to the Middle East briefly after Assad agreed to transmit through him the list of Israeli POWs in return for an Israeli counteroffer on the cease-fire. Until now, Syria had refused to say how many prisoners it was holding, let alone give their names. In Jerusalem the next day, when Kissinger handed over the list to Mrs. Meir, she wept and Kissinger put a comforting arm around her. Israel had not known how many of the 140 men missing on the Syrian front had survived. The list contained 65 names, mostly men captured on the Hermon on the first day and downed airmen. Israel held 380 Syrians. The Israeli counteroffer envisioned only a minor withdrawal in the newly captured enclave and none at all on the Golan. Rather than risk negotiations being broken off by transmitting that offer, Kissinger told Assad that the Israelis still needed time to think about it and flew back home. Meanwhile, a war of attrition was going on between Syrian and Israeli forces like the one that had occurred on the Egyptian front before disengagement.

When Kissinger returned to Damascus at the beginning of May, it was for a make-or-break effort that would set new standards for the diplomatic art. Over the course of thirty-four days, he shuttled between Damascus and Jerusalem, with frequent side trips to other Arab countries. He was able to narrow differences down to a strip of territory about a mile wide around Kuneitra. But finally both sides refused to budge any further. Accepting defeat, Kissinger flew to Damascus to take leave of Assad. He had made his farewells and was heading for the door when Assad indicated that he was prepared to make a final concession, a negotiating technique familiar to any bazaar patron in the Middle East. Kissinger flew back to Jerusalem to wrest a final concession there as well.

The agreement arrived at called for Israel to withdraw from the entire enclave captured after Yom Kippur and also from the abandoned town of Kuneitra, which had been on the Israeli side of the Purple Line. Israel gave up smaller patches of land as well along the southern part of the line, including the site of Strongpoint 116, and those parts of the Hermon crest—the Syrian Hermon—it had not held before the war. The Syrians, in turn, agreed to a prisoner exchange, a limitation on the forces both sides could maintain in their forward areas, and a UN observer force between the two lines.

The Syrian army would no longer deploy major forces up against the Israeli line, capable of springing without notice. Assad also pledged that Syria would prevent guerrilla incursions. Syria would honor this unwritten agreement in the ensuing decades, turning the Golan into the quietest of Israel's borders. On June 5, military representatives of the two sides signed the disengagement agreement in Geneva. The Yom Kippur War was officially over on both fronts.

With disengagement in the south, Israel had withdrawn twenty miles from the canal but it still held the bulk of Sinai, to be used as a buffer against war or a trade-off for peace.

There was time now to begin thinking through the lessons of the war. In an unsparing analysis, an armored corps general, Moshe Bar-Kochba, concluded in an article he wrote for an Israeli military journal that the IDF's senior command, wielding formations far larger than any in Israel's history, had had insufficient training in the complex art of war. This, he said, was why it had decided on static defense lines held with minimal forces instead of on a flexible defense. "Future wars will oblige a university-level [military education] and our senior officers are still in grade school," wrote Bar-Kochba, who had served as deputy commander of Laner's division.

Major IDF assumptions had collapsed within forty-eight hours of the war's opening, he wrote, like belief in the reliability of AMAN, in the air force's mastery of the skies over the battlefield, in the low fighting qualities of the Arab armies. Investing more than half the defense budget on the air force, he said, was a miscalculation. If the air force had been allocated twenty planes less, Bar-Kochba wrote, this would have left money for the creation of two more armored divisions, which could have made a critical difference on both fronts.

Given the strategic, tactical, and psychological dimensions of the Arab surprise, Israel's recovery from the edge of the abyss was epic. The IDF destroyed or captured 2,250 enemy tanks. Hundreds of these were captured intact after being abandoned by their crews, mostly on the Syrian front. The IDF would incorporate 400 of them into its own ranks, enough for more than one division. Four hundred Israeli tanks were destroyed. Another 600 were disabled but returned to battle after repairs. Almost every tank had been hit at least once.

Although largely neutralized over the battlefield by the SAMs, the air force had performed spectacularly in air combat. The IAF claimed 277 Arab aircraft shot down in dogfights with the loss of 6 Israeli planes, a 46-to-1 ratio that outdid the 9-to-1 ratio of the Six Day War. In all, the Arab air forces lost 432 planes, including losses to Hawk missiles and antiaircraft fire—not infrequently, their own. Israel lost 102 warplanes, almost as many to conventional antiaircraft fire as to missiles.

Had the superpowers not imposed a cease-fire, Israel's success would doubtless have been even more striking. But the price had been heavy. Israel lost 2,656 dead and 7,250 wounded. Arab casualties as given by a western analyst were 8,528 dead and 19,540 wounded. Israel estimated Arab casualties to be almost twice those figures—15,000 dead (11,000 of them Egyptian) and 35,000 wounded (25,000 Egyptian).

Who won?

Egypt did. So did Israel.

Like a jeweler cutting a precious stone, Sadat had struck with his military mallet perfectly, producing a political process that would lead to the recovery by Egypt of all of Sinai. More important even than territorial gain was the performance of the Egyptian army, which wiped clean the Arab humiliation of 1967.

Politically, Egypt's victory was stunning. But it brought with it an Israeli political victory even more stunning—namely, peace with Egypt itself and the long-awaited breakthrough, however tenuous, to the Arab world beyond.

In terms of morale, Egypt was the clear winner. It had seized the initiative, risking the shattering prospect of another defeat, and emerged honorably.

As for Syria, it had been saved from crushing defeat by the intervention of Iraq. Key elements of Syria's physical infrastructure were smashed and the country would suffer blackouts from the lack of electricity for months after the war. But it won at the negotiating table what it had failed to achieve on the battlefield—Kuneitra. And it did so without having to pay a political price in the form of recognizing Israel. Syria would subside once again after the war into sullen insularity. Unlike Egypt, which rebuilt its heavily damaged canal cities, Syria left Kuneitra in ruins—a monument to ongoing hostility.

In Israel, the abrupt fall from supreme confidence, not to say arrogance, shook the nation to its core. The brutal surprises of the war had confronted it with the prospect not just of defeat but of mortality. The psychological shock found insufficient remedy in military success. Despite the entrapment of the Third Army and the momentum Israel was building up on the road to Cairo, it was Egypt, not Israel, that was gripped by a sense of triumph when the shooting stopped.

Time would bring a different perspective. In military terms, Israel would recognize its achievement in the war as having few historical parallels. Reeling from a surprise attack on two fronts with the bulk of its army still unmobilized, and confronted by staggering new battlefield realities, Israel's situation was one that could readily bring strong nations to their knees. Yet within days it had regained its footing and within less than two weeks it was threatening both enemy capitals. Israel faced not just the Egyptian and Syrian armies but much of the Arab world, and it did so with the arm it had most relied on, the air force, tied behind its back. As a military feat, the IDF's performance in the Yom Kippur War dwarfed that in the Six Day War. Victory emerged from motivation that came from the deepest layers of the nation's being and from basic military skills that compensated for the grave errors of the leadership.

In retrospect, the performance of the Arab armies came to be seen in Israel as less impressive than as first perceived. Still viewing the Arabs through the spectrum of the Six Day War, the Israelis in 1973 were startled by the daring the Arabs displayed and by the way they held their ground. With the passage of time, however, Israel would come to see the Arabs as having "fought bravely, not well," as one armor colonel put it. Disdain for the Arab fighter had given way to respect, but not to a sense that the balance of power was shifting.

Despite Israel's spectacular recovery on the battlefield, its mood at war's end was anguished. It had lost almost three times as many men per capita in nineteen days as did the United States in Vietnam in close to a decade. For the first time in one of Israel's wars, a significant number of its nonfatal casualties—between 10 and 23 percent, according to different studies—suffered from battle shock, in good measure deriving from the initial surprise.

As the reservists returned home, public squares began to fill with crowds—not celebrating Israel's tremendous military achievement but giving vent to the deepest trauma in the nation's history.

Thirty-eight

AFTERMATH

It was a rainy morning in Jerusalem when Motti Ashkenazi took up position across the road from the prime minister's office. Drivers passing through the government center slowed down to look at the bespectacled figure in a windbreaker holding aloft a placard.

"Grandma," it read, "your defense minister is a failure and 3,000 of your grandchildren are dead."

Four months had passed since the Egyptian attack on Budapest, the Bar-Lev fort under Ashkenazi's command. The notion of demonstrating against the government had been with him since he had flung himself down in the sand under the opening Egyptian barrage. Anger at the failure to anticipate the war had been reinforced by anger at the operational unreadiness to deal with it. Now, just two days after his discharge, Ashkenazi had embarked on a campaign of his own.

On the second day of his solitary demonstration, a news photographer happening by took his photograph. The picture was published the next day. The day after that another discharged reservist, who had seen the photograph, wordlessly took up position some distance away with his own placard. With every passing day, more demonstrators arrived.

Two ministers looking out a window before the start of a cabinet meeting studied the growing forest of placards. "They want Dayan's head," said one.

"They want all our heads," said the other.

Most of the returning soldiers bore memories of comrades who did not come back. The friend with whom Ashkenazi had discussed the inevitability of war in a Jerusalem café a few months before, Gideon Giladi, had been killed in his tank trying to open Tirtur Road on the first night of battle in the Chinese Farm at the head of Natan Shunari's paratroopers. The kibbutz mate with whom Yitzhak Brik had ridden off to war Yom Kippur afternoon had been killed alongside him in Yaguri's charge at Hizayon on October 8. Yisrael Itkin, the sergeant in charge of Sharon's APC, had been picked up at Kibbutz Givat Haim by the mobilization bus on Yom Kippur afternoon together with Yehuda Geller, who would lead the final attack on Missouri, and tank commander Yisrael Dagan. Itkin and Geller returned to the kibbutz without Dagan, killed moments before the cease-fire in the final attempt to reach Ismailiya. At Bait Hashita, a kibbutz in the Jezreel Valley, 120 men had gone off to the war, including Shunari and brigade commander Ran Sarig. Eleven did not return, among them the brothers of Shunari and Sarig, the highest per capita loss for an Israeli community.

At a rally in the government center a month after Ashkenazi's solitary appearance, the number of demonstrators reached 5,000. The painful process of working through the nation's trauma was under way.

For Amnon Reshef, the process had begun as soon as the shooting stopped. His brigade had suffered more fatalities than any other Israeli brigade in the war, more than 300. It had borne the brunt of the Egyptian crossing on Yom Kippur and of the battle for the Chinese Farm. With the cease-fire, the brigade was posted to a captured Egyptian air base on the west bank of the canal, where it remained for two months. On Friday nights, after the Sabbath meal, Reshef would retire to a bunker with his officers and choose two to share a bottle of whiskey with him. He would insist that the pair drink until drunk, until they danced or laughed or cried. Sometimes they shouted at him for having let their friends die. In every unit, officers and men vented their feelings in endless discussions. How could they have been so surprised? Why were they so unprepared?

For the nation as a whole, the major instrument of therapy was an inquiry commission set up by the government to answer those questions. It had been clear to Dayan and Mrs. Meir even before the war was over that heads would have to roll—perhaps their own—and that only an inquiry conducted by a body enjoying the highest repute could hope to restore public confidence in the government and the army. Within three weeks of the cease-fire, the president of the Israeli Supreme Court, American-born judge

Shimon Agranat, was asked to head a five-man commission to investigate the events leading up to the war and the setbacks of the first days.

The appointment of the prestigious commission provided a breathing space for the nation to begin pulling itself together. Knesset elections, postponed from October because of the war, were held on December 31. It was too soon for deep-seated voting patterns to have significantly changed. The Labor Party, headed by Golda Meir, won again, although with 5 fewer seats, 51, in the 120-seat Knesset. Mrs. Meir asked Dayan to stay on as defense minister in the new government. He told her that if the Agranat Commission found him in any way responsible for the failings of the war, he would resign. The public, not waiting for the commission's report, had already focused its anger on Dayan, the dashing figure on whom it had rested its sense of security. The public's anger was brought home to him at military funerals when grieving relatives shouted at him, "Murderer."

Attempting to understand the public mood, Dayan accepted an invitation from Motti Ashkenazi's philosophy professor at Hebrew University to meet with the man who had come to symbolize the protest movement. To the meeting at the professor's home in Jerusalem Dayan brought the heads of the Mossad and Shin Bet, the internal security service. The meeting of the country's top security officials and the philosophy student lasted for more than an hour. Only Ashkenazi and Dayan engaged in the dialogue. Neither left a favorable impression on the other.

The IDF, preparing itself for a renewal of fighting, absorbed the massive American arms shipments, most of them arriving now by sea. Accelerated courses for tank crews to fill the depleted ranks of the armored corps were held just behind the front lines. Half the war dead had been tank crewmen. Within a few months, the army would be back to its prewar strength.

Bar-Lev took off his uniform and returned to the cabinet two weeks after the cease-fire, but the southern front was not entrusted again to Gonen. At Dayan's insistence, he was transferred to the command of remote South Sinai until completion of the final Agranat Report—General Gavish leaving that post to return to civilian life. Southern Command was turned over temporarily to General Tal.

Sharon was elected to the Knesset on the Likud ticket but he told Dayan that he would return to the army if appointed chief of staff. Dayan dismissed that possibility although he supported Sharon's bid to retain his reserve commission as a division commander despite Elazar's opposition. In Sharon's farewell address to his troops, he said that victory had been won "despite the blunders and the mistakes, despite the loss of control and authority"—a clear slap at the high command. When Dayan learned of it, he revoked Sharon's commission.

On April 2, 1974, the Agranat Commission published its eagerly awaited preliminary findings. The commission demanded six heads, foremost that of Elazar. "We have reached the conclusion that the chief of staff, Gen. David Elazar, bears direct responsibility for what happened on the eve of the war, both as to the assessment of the situation and the IDF's preparedness." The commission recommended dismissal of Zeira as chief of intelligence for "grave failures," and the removal of his deputy, Brigadier General Shalev, from his post as well. Transfer from intelligence duties was recommended for two other officers, Lieutenant Colonel Bandman, the head of the Egyptian desk at AMAN, and Lieutenant Colonel Gedalia, the chief intelligence officer of Southern Command. General Gonen, said the commission, should be relieved of active duty until the conclusion of its investigation.

As for Mrs. Meir and Dayan, the commission cleared them of all responsibility. Dayan, it noted, had no independent method of assessing the likelihood of war. "The defense minister was never intended to be a 'super–chief of staff' who must guide the chief of staff in the latter's operative area of responsibility." Mrs. Meir, the commission found, had "used her authority properly and wisely when she ordered mobilization of the reserves on Yom Kippur morning despite the weighty political factors involved." The commission stressed that it was judging the ministers' responsibility for security failings, not their parliamentary responsibility, which was outside its mandate.

The absolution of Dayan and Mrs. Meir aroused widespread anger and made public calls for their resignation, particularly Dayan's, even louder. Mrs. Meir had twice during the war refused his offer to step down and she had subsequently defended him against cabinet colleagues calling for his resignation. After the commission's report, Dayan asked her again whether she wanted him to resign. This time she said that the Labor Party leadership must decide. In her memoirs, she would suggest that the commission's harsh findings regarding Elazar and Zeira should have led Dayan to "stick by" his comrades-in-arms and step down. "But he was following a logic of his own," she would write, "and I didn't feel that on such a weighty matter I should give him advice."

She followed her own logic. A week after the report, she announced her resignation, saying she could not ignore the public ferment. Her move obliged the resignation of the entire cabinet, which became effective in June after disengagement on the Syrian front. The new government was headed by Yitzhak Rabin, with Shimon Peres as defense minister.

The Yom Kippur War continued to claim its victims long after the shooting stopped. General Elazar left the army deeply grieved that the Agranat Commission had put the onus of failure upon him while sparing Dayan. He felt that the commission had failed to give proper weight to the critical stabilizing role he had played during the war. It was an assessment that was widely shared. A general who had worked alongside him in the Pit would compare his performance to that of a cruise missile which maintains a fixed altitude relative to the ground no matter how uneven the terrain below. This was no mean feat given the gusts of gloom emanating from Dayan and others, the need to prop up the front commanders in the opening days, and the amount of time he had to spend briefing and keeping up the morale of the political leaders. All this besides fighting a two-front war and dealing with the complex and initially calamitous situation on the battlefields. But as chief of staff he bore the responsibility for failing to recognize the distortions in Israel's military posture before the war. There was a price to be paid for what happened on Yom Kippur and he was inevitably part of that price even though he had been the firm linchpin that held the high command together at a time of awesome stress.

Elazar left with the admiration of his peers and of Mrs. Meir and was appointed head of Israel's national shipping line, Zim. Foreign minister Eban planned to offer him a top ambassadorial post before he himself was dropped from the cabinet. But the war and his dismissal bore heavily upon Elazar. His biographer, Hanoch Bartov, records that shortly after the cease-fire, while still chief of staff, Elazar entered the room in army headquarters where his secretaries worked in order to look for a document. A transistor radio was playing a poignant song sweeping the country, "Would That It Were," which alluded to the pain of the war. It was the first time Elazar had heard it and he stood transfixed. When it was over he strode swiftly back to his office without taking the document. His chief secretary hurried after him. Opening the door, she saw the man whom Mrs. Meir and others had termed "a rock" sitting at his desk, holding his head and sobbing. She closed the door without his having seen her. Two years after the war, he died of a heart attack at age fifty-one.

Although Dayan symbolized for the demonstrators the arrogance that had brought the nation to near disaster he was the most far-seeing of the nation's leaders. His ability to fuse political and military considerations and to think creatively was of the same order as Sadat's. His proposal in 1970 for a pullback from the canal and a buffer zone between the two armies, rejected by Mrs. Meir, would have averted the kind of attack Egypt launched on Yom Kippur, although perhaps not war itself. He was the first to insist on reinforcing the Golan in the days before Yom Kippur. Without reinforcement, the heights would have fallen, something that would have rendered Israel's military position truly catastrophic. His boldness was hemmed by caution, but in the end he had not been cautious enough, failing to press the military to rethink basic assumptions.

If the Six Day War had imbued Dayan with a sense of Israel's power and Arab weakness, the Yom Kippur War made him determined to explore the road to peace. Changing his parliamentary colors by joining the right-wing government of Menahem Begin, which came to power in 1977, as foreign minister, Dayan played a major role in the breakthrough to peace with Egypt.

General Zeira, whose misreading of enemy intentions was the most palpable failure of the war, had a highly rewarding career as an intelligence consultant to foreign governments after his forced retirement from the army. In a book he wrote two decades after the war he argued that the Source, who had passed on to Israel the Egyptian "concept," was probably a double agent—a suggestion dismissed by critics, including ranking Israeli intelligence analysts, as improbable. If the Source was a double agent, why would he have told Zamir on Yom Kippur eve of the coming attack? He had, in fact, given the code word for war by telephone to his handler in Europe some thirty-six hours before war broke out, enough time for Israel to have mobilized much of its reserves if it so chose.

The identity of the Source, one of the most intriguing mysteries of the war, may have been revealed in 2002 by an Israeli writer living in London who alleged that it was none other than Ashraf Marwan, Nasser's son-in-law. Marwan served as a roving troubleshooter for Nasser and then for Sadat, dealing in sensitive intelligence and diplomatic matters. He would become involved in ramified financial dealings in his own right, particularly in England, which made him a very wealthy man. Despite his dismissal of the allegation as "an absurd detective story" it would be given wide credibility. The allegation contended that Marwan was a double agent who faithfully served Egyptian interests by misleading Israel about Sadat's strategy, an echo of Zeira's charge. Following the war, Israeli intelligence agencies investigated the possibility and concluded that the Source was not a double agent, although his motivation remained obscure. In what might be a unique instance in the annals of espionage, the Source could be acclaimed as a hero by the Egyptians and as a savior, whatever his motives, by the Israelis.

Deputy chief of staff Tal had repeatedly differed with Elazar during the war, and after his brief tenure at Southern Command Elazar refused to take his old friend back as his deputy. Instead, Tal devoted himself to development of the innovative Merkava tank, which would be hailed as one of the best in the world. Despite criticism in the Pit of General Hofi's performance, his senior staff officers would maintain that he performed coolly and competently in extremely trying circumstances. He would in time be named head of the Mossad.

The general who won the most fame in the war was Ariel Sharon, although for the wrong reasons. He led the crossing of the canal but he was not, as widely believed, the man who initiated it. A canal crossing had been a central feature of Israeli planning since the Six Day War. The decision to cross was made by Elazar and Bar-Lev, and it was they who chose the most propitious timing—after the Egyptian armored divisions crossed to Sinai and not before, as Sharon advocated. Apart from the crossing operation, it was Sharon's personality, his history, his outspoken criticism of his superiors, and his accessibility to the media that made him the primary focus of attention.

Once across into Africa, it was primarily Adan's war. Sharon would be tied down on the road to Ismailiya in a slow-moving secondary thrust while Adan was deftly maneuvering large armored forces across a broad landscape in the war's strategic endgame. And it was Adan who pushed most effectively for abrogation of the first cease-fire in order to complete the encirclement of the Third Army—a move which fundamentally altered the outcome of the war.

Sharon's merits as a military leader lay in less visible spheres. He was one of the few senior commanders not to be stunned by the surprise attack. Within hours of his arrival at the front he was proposing rescue of beleaguered forts and pushing for a swift counterattack. While the high command was concerned about an Egyptian advance across Sinai towards Tel Aviv, Sharon correctly assessed that the Egyptians would not move out from beneath their missile umbrella. He did not for a moment lose his aggressive instincts and was able to uplift the spirits of the troops in a desperate hour by his very presence.

In retrospect, his call for a large-scale crossing of tanks on the Gilowa rafts before a bridge was erected could be justified because the Egyptians failed to shell the crossing point for more than a day. Had 100 to 200 tanks been brought across during this lull they would have prevented Egyptian infiltration of the greenbelt and permitted a breakout a day earlier. But his superiors cannot be faulted for insisting on a bridge, given the risks involved. Sharon's attempts to refrain from costly attacks on Missouri were justified by Shazly himself, who acknowledged that it was Sharon's advance on the western canal bank that obliged the forces on Missouri to shift northwards. Criticism of him for not widening the bridgehead corridor and bringing up the bridges was uncalled for; the task was simply too big for one division.

Sharon's constant challenging of orders understandably drove his superiors to thoughts of dismissal. But while he attempted to bend orders he never refused an order, except for Gonen's order for a second attack on Missouri towards the end of the war, which was eventually rescinded. There is general agreement that if Sharon had not retired from the army three months earlier and remained as O/C Southern Command, the IDF would not have suffered the intial setback it did in Sinai, and the war would have developed very differently. Clausewitz had someone like Sharon in mind when he wrote: "Happy the army in which an untimely boldness frequently manifests itself . . . Even foolhardiness, that is boldness without an object, is not to be despised . . . It is only when it strikes at the root of obedience, when it treats with contempt the orders of a superior authority, that it must be repressed as a dangerous evil."

The most tragic figure in the Israeli military hierarchy to emerge from the war was Shmuel Gonen. The ignominy of being superseded as commander of the southern front at the height of the war was compounded by his being forced to leave the army after the final Agranat Report. Although the Israeli establishment usually finds suitable jobs for retired generals, he was offered none. Gonen believed Dayan to be responsible for his disgrace and would tell reporters that he had considered walking into Dayan's office and shooting him.

Instead, he spent thirteen years in the jungles of the Central African Republic searching for diamonds with the intention, he said, of becoming wealthy enough to hire the best lawyers in Israel to prove the Agranat findings mistaken and clear his name. He reportedly made and lost one or two fortunes but rejected appeals by family and friends to abandon his obsession. A reporter who visited him in the jungle after nine years found him somewhat mellowed, self-aware, not without sardonic humor, and still sprinkling his conversation with apt quotes from the Talmud. The tough soldier appeared to find satisfaction in coping with the brutal challenges of the jungle rather than nursing his grievances in the cafés of Tel Aviv. Some would see it as a form of penance. He died of a heart attack in 1991 during one of his periodic business trips to Europe. Among the few possessions returned to his family were maps of Sinai, on which he had apparently refought the war during his jungle exile, and a copy of a Kabbalistic work in which the former yeshiva student may have sought explanations for the disaster that had overtaken him beyond what the maps could tell.

On the Egyptian and Syrian sides too, the heads of senior officers were not often garlanded with wreaths. General Shazly, who had so ably prepared his army, had irrevocably angered Sadat by opposing a push to the passes and by his demand that forces be withdrawn from Sinai to meet the Israeli incursion. Six weeks after the war, Shazly was informed by war minister Ismail that Sadat had decided "to end your service in the armed forces." Shazly was named ambassador to London, a prestigious appointment intended not to undermine public morale by the seeming disgrace of a hero. He later became ambassador to Portugal but then went into political exile for years. He eventually returned home to a period of house arrest. The commanders of the Second and Third Armies, Generals Wasel and Khalil, were likewise eased out of the army after the war and appointed to civilian governorships. On the Syrian front, the Druze commander of an infantry brigade that had collapsed during the Israeli breakthrough—Col. Rafik Halawi—was executed even before the war ended. The Seventh Division commander, Gen. Omar Abash, who had failed to break through Ben-Gal's brigade, was alternately reported to have been killed in the fighting or to have died of a heart attack.

The clearest victor in the Yom Kippur War was President Sadat. He had dared, as Mrs. Meir said. Risking all, he had parlayed an audacious military move that restored Egypt's dignity into an audacious diplomatic process that restored its lost lands. Addressing the Egyptian parliament on November 9, 1977—four years after the war—he said, "I am prepared to go to the end of the earth, and Israel will be surprised to hear me say to you, I am ready to go to their home, to the Knesset itself, and to argue with them there." Ten days later, he gave wings to the diplomatic process with a flourish no less breathtaking than the crossing of the canal. Sadat's arrival at Israel's Ben-Gurion Airport at the invitation of Prime Minister Menahem Begin was one of the most dramatic moments in modern Middle East history. On the reception line, Sadat asked Begin if "General Sharon," now agriculture minister, was present. The Egyptian leader smiled when he shook Sharon's hand. "I tried to capture you," he said. "If you attempt to cross to the west bank [of the Suez Canal] again, I'll have you arrested." From the Knesset podium, Sadat proclaimed, "No more war."

Until a few months before his visit, Sadat had seen peace with Israel taking the form of a nonbelligerency pact. Normalization and diplomatic relations, he said, were to be left to future generations, given the bloodiness of the recent past. However, in the end he decided to seek a psychological breakthrough with Israel by going all the way diplomatically. It was imperative for Egypt, he believed, to remove itself from the cycle of the war with

Israel. The country's economy and social fabric could not sustain an endless confrontation—even short of war—involving tremendous military outlays. Although he reiterated in the Knesset his commitment to a comprehensive agreement that included the Palestinian issue, he settled in fact for a separate agreement with Israel in the hope that it would set in motion an irreversible process that would embrace the other relevant Arab parties. Four years after his flight to Jerusalem, Islamic fundamentalists gunned him down in Cairo as he reviewed a military parade marking the anniversary of the war.

The other major victor of the Yom Kippur War was a man who had been six thousand miles from the battlefield. Henry Kissinger had with dazzling statesmanship stage-managed a scenario in which both sides could claim victory while acknowledging, to themselves at least, victory's awful price. It was this realization that made compromise possible. In the process, the secretary of state deftly managed to nudge aside the Soviet Union and tie the leading country in the Arab world to the United States.

The Yom Kippur War had a major impact on the world's armies. The success of the Sagger and RPG in the early days of the war evoked widespread eulogies for the tank. Closer study brought revision. With better armor and different tactics, the tank would continue to dominate the battlefield.

Two senior American armor generals arrived in Israel shortly after the war to walk the battlefields and confer with their Israeli colleagues. For a decade, the United States had been mired in Vietnam, mentally as well as physically. The Soviets had advanced their military doctrine and weaponry during this period, but the American military had skipped a cycle of materiel and tactical upgrading. A Vietnam cease-fire was signed in 1973, and the Americans wanted to learn what the Middle East conflict had to teach about the likely shape of future wars.

The generals found the Yom Kippur War tank battles to have been of unprecedented intensity. The fighting in Sinai and the Golan involved more tanks than any Second World War battle with the possible exceptions of the battle of Kursk in the Soviet Union and the Allied breakout from Normandy. The intensity stemmed not just from the number of tanks but from the lethality of the weapons, their extended range, and their improved accuracy. Entire tank battalions were consumed on the battlefield within hours. What the generals learned would play a major role in the reshaping of the American armored corps.

The future battlefield, they warned in a report upon their return, would be far more crowded with tanks and antitank weaponry than any hitherto known. Combined tank losses on the Arab and Israeli sides in the first week of the war, they noted, exceeded the entire U.S. Army tank inventory in Europe. "Because of the numbers and the lethality of modern weapons, the direct-fire battle will be intense; enormous equipment losses can be expected in a relatively short period of time," wrote one of the Americans, Maj. Gen. Donn A. Starry.

Whereas tanks in the Second World War had fought at an average range of 750 yards, in the Yom Kippur War Israeli tanks were engaging at 2,000 and even 3,000 yards or more. This meant a far broader killing ground. The Sagger greatly increased the deadliness of the battlefield, as did the massive use of RPGs. Lessons the American generals derived from the war included the desirability of opening fire first and at long range, both new ideas for traditional U.S. tank gunnery doctrine.

General Starry's conclusions on the human element were strongly influenced by the Israeli performance. "In modern battle, the outcome will be decided by factors other than numbers," he wrote. "The side that somehow in the course of battle seizes the initiative and holds it to the end will be the side that wins. It is strikingly evident that battles are yet won by the courage of soldiers, the character of leaders, and the combat excellence of well-trained units."

For Israel, however, one of the major lessons of the war was that numbers count. Brigade commander Ben-Gal, who had stood against great odds in the Kuneitra Gap, and General Adan, who led the battle west of the Suez Canal, were among Israeli military leaders who would write afterwards about the quality inherent in quantity.

In the Six Day War, the Israeli air force had achieved one of the most stunning victories in modern military history. In the Yom Kippur War, to the surprise of all, its effect on the outcome was marginal. It trounced the Arab air forces in air combat, conducted strategic strikes in Syria, prevented the Egyptians from foraying out from under their missile umbrella, and kept the enemy air forces from Israel's skies. But the IAF had little impact on the battlefield itself. It was the armored corps that turned the war around.

In the years after the war, the air force would devote itself to conceptualizing an answer to Soviet missile technology. By 1978 it had come up with a plan employing innovative tactics as well as new weaponry and electronic devices, some purchased abroad and some produced at home. Instead of overpowering the missile system, as Tagar was designed to do, the IAF would attempt to outsmart it. When the Lebanese war came in June 1982, the solution was put to the test in Lebanon's Bekaa Valley, where the Syrians deployed a missile system more formidable than the one deployed opposite the Golan Heights in the Yom Kippur War.

Even two decades afterwards, Israel would not reveal exactly how it confronted the SAM array in the Bekaa, but a general outline of the Israeli tactics has emerged. Unlike in 1973, when inability to identify the location of the SAM-6s led to the failure of Dougman 5, the IAF was now able to track the deployment of the Syrian batteries at all times. Most importantly, it had the standoff weapon it had lacked in the Yom Kippur War—smart bombs with cameras that could be launched from beyond the range of the missiles and guided onto target.

According to published accounts, the IAF opened the battle by dispatching drones to send back pictures of the nineteen SAM batteries as well as of the antiaircraft guns guarding them. In an elaborate scenario, planes and drones sent electronic signals activating SAM radars which were being deliberately kept dormant to avoid being targeted. When the radars came alive, their electronic parameters were recorded and instantly fed into airborne and ground-launched missiles that homed in on them before they could be closed down.

With the radars blinded, Israeli warplanes swarmed over the valley and destroyed fifteen of the nineteen batteries and severely damaged three others. When Syrian warplanes rose to challenge them, dozens were shot down, as Israeli air controllers in surveillance planes directed waiting fighter squadrons to the attack. At this stage, with not a single Israeli plane downed, air force commander David Ivri recalled his planes to ensure that the day would not be even slightly marred. Air battles would go on for two days, during which a total of eighty-two Syrian planes were downed in dogfights. Israeli losses were one Skyhawk and two helicopters downed by conventional antiaircraft fire.

The Israeli response in the Bekaa Valley had involved an integration of technology and tactics which American military analyst Anthony Cordesman would call "uniquely efficient." With this stunning display nine years after the frustrations of the Yom Kippur War, the Israeli air force took back the technological high ground which had been lost with the introduction of the SAMs into Egypt and Syria a decade before.

The alarmed Soviets dispatched the deputy head of their air defense command to Syria within a day to examine how the Israelis had done it. Senior military officers in Warsaw Pact nations would, years later, tell Israeli colleagues that the destruction of the missile array in the Bekaa Valley had severely shaken the Soviet leadership, which relied on the SAMs as a shield for the Soviet Union itself against Western air attack. A deputy chief of staff of a Warsaw Pact country would tell General Ivri that the SAMs' vulnerability revealed by the Bekaa raid was one of the factors in the changed Soviet mind-set leading to glasnost and the opening to the West.

For soldiers on both sides of the war, the battles left mental scars that would be long in healing, if healed at all. Lt. Shimon Maliach, who had fought at the Chinese Farm, remained haunted for months by the memory of Lieutenant Rabinowitz and his own unfulfilled promise to rescue him. But Rabinowitz had in fact survived. One of the doctors in the hospital where Maliach was being treated for battle stress found Rabinowitz in a Beersheva hospital and brought Maliach a tape recording from him. After Maliach had woken him from his stupor, Rabinowitz related, he had managed to crawl to the rear. The crippling sense of guilt lifted from Maliach, although not other symptoms of his mental distress.

Two years later, returning from a visit to the Golan Heights, he entered a restaurant in Haifa and noticed a mother and young child sitting at the far end of the room. Across the table from them was a man, his back to the door. He had red hair. The child was about two years old. Maliach thought of the red-haired lieutenant who had told him his wife was about to give birth. He could not see the man's face but ran up to him shouting "Rabinowitz!" It was indeed him. The two men embraced and wept and told each other their stories and wept again. Nodding at his son, Rabinowitz said, "That's why I told you I don't want to die."

When Maliach parted, he did not take Rabinowitz's telephone number. He did not even ask his first name or where he lived. He no longer had unfinished business. Except with God. In the years after the war he would no longer pray on Yom Kippur. He would leave his family in order to spend the day alone, sometimes in an empty apartment, sometimes in the Judaean desert, where he would upbraid God for what he had permitted to happen.

Sgt. Mahmud Nadeh had not despaired of God but he had come to despair of life. Even after the cease-fire, the soldiers of the Third Army remained surrounded in the desert for months on strict rations. Nadeh's company at Botser was isolated from the main body of the Third Army and supplies were uncertain. "We're cut off and entirely dependent on God and the UN," he wrote in his diary. On the same day, in a fanciful bit of escapism, he drew up a list of favorite music, plays, films, and books. Almost all were Western. "Tchaikovsky, 1812 Overture, Napoleon's war" headed the music list. Robert Bolt's *A Man for All Seasons* headed the list of plays, with *The Koran and its Modern Interpretation,* third on his literary list, the only Arabic entry.

On November 27, a month after the cease-fire went into effect, Nadeh recorded that his commander had demoted him to private and struck him for refusing to work because he was ill. Ten days later, he and six comrades slipped away from their unit and crossed the canal at night in an effort to infiltrate through the Israeli lines. In an encounter with an Israeli patrol they were all killed. The diary found on Sergeant Nadeh's body was passed on to intelligence officers. Six years later, two Israeli journalists, who obtained the diary from the army, traveled to a slum dwelling in Alexandria to hand it over to Nadeh's parents, who agreed to publication of excerpts. It included a last will and testament in English. "When the moment comes, remember me," it said. "I fought for my country. Millions of my countrymen dream of peace. It may be that the unknown is beautiful. But the present is more beautiful."

The Yom Kippur War marked a major turning in the Israel-Arab confrontation. By restoring pride to Egypt and a sense of proportion to Israel, it opened the way to the Camp David peace agreement in 1979. Fifteen years later, Israel signed a peace agreement with Jordan. In the ensuing years, the Jewish state would weave discreet economic and political ties with other Arab countries, from Morocco to the Gulf states, as demonization began to give way to realpolitik.

The possibility of renewed war in the Middle East would remain ever present, particularly when the unresolved Palestinian issue inflamed passions. But the Yom Kippur War, despite its disastrous opening for Israel, had enhanced its military deterrence, not diminished it. It is hard to imagine a more propitious opening hand than the one Egypt and Syria dealt themselves in October 1973—achieving strategic and tactical surprise in a two-front war, fought according to plans they had rehearsed for years, and supported by a superpower. Yet the war ended with the Israeli army on the roads to Cairo and Damascus. The chances of Israel ever permitting itself to be surprised like that again would appear unlikely. Israel too had been taught a painful lesson about the limitations of power and the danger of arrogance.

Even before the shooting had completely stopped, there were glimmers of recognition in both camps of the human face in the foxhole opposite.

Amir Yoffe's battalion, positioned on the edge of Suez City, exchanged heavy fire with Egyptian troops despite the cease-fire until a UN contingent arrived on Sunday, October 28, to insert itself between the two forces. As the blue-helmeted peacekeepers deployed, soldiers on both sides raised their heads above their firing positions and looked across at the men they had just been shooting at. The Egyptians were the first to react. Passing through the UN force, they reached an Israeli armored infantry company.

The company commander radioed Yoffe to report his position being inundated by Egyptian soldiers. "Take them prisoner," said Yoffe, assuming that was the reason they had come over.

"They don't want to surrender," said the company commander. "They want to shake hands." Some of the Egyptians kissed the Israeli soldiers they had been firing at a few minutes before. Angry shouts from Egyptian officers brought their men back.

When an army entertainment troupe performed for Yoffe's battalion a few days later, the songs included one written after the Six Day War mocking Egyptian soldiers who fled the battlefield, leaving behind their boots in the sand. Soldiers went up to the performers afterwards and suggested that they drop that song from their repertoire. After three weeks of grueling battle, such easy derision of the enemy was jarring.

The most striking fraternization occurred at the opposite end of the line, near Ismailiya. The morning after the first cease-fire went into effect, Capt. Gideon Shamir was deploying his paratroop company along a spur of the Sweetwater Canal when he saw Egyptian commandos encamped in an orchard one hundred yards away. They were apparently part of the unit with which he had clashed the previous night. The cease-fire was already being violated elsewhere along the line, but Shamir, from a religious kibbutz in the Beisan Valley, wanted to ensure that there would be no more killing in his sector.

Telling his men to cover him, and taking a soldier who spoke Arabic, he descended into an empty irrigation ditch leading towards the orchard. Shamir shouted to the Egyptians as he approached—"Cease-fire, peace"— so as not to take them by surprise. The ditch provided ready cover if needed. The Egyptians, about twenty of them, held their fire as the two Israelis presented themselves. The commandos summoned their company commander, who introduced himself as Major Ali. Shamir told the Egyptian officer that he wanted to avoid shooting. The war was over, he said, and it would be foolish for anyone on either side to be hurt. Ali agreed. He surprised Shamir by saying he believed that Sadat wanted not just a cease-fire but peace with Israel.

In the coming days, soldiers from both sides ventured out into the clearing between the two positions and fraternized. When shooting broke out in adjacent sectors, they hurried back to their respective lines. Initially, when there was shooting at night, the Egyptians fired at Shamir's positions, although they did not do so by day. The paratroopers held their fire, and after a few nights the Egyptians opposite no longer fired either. Before long, the commandos and paratroopers were meeting daily to brew up coffee and play backgammon. Soccer games followed. The men came to know each other's first names and showed off pictures of wives and girlfriends. There was an occasional *kumsitz*, with the Egyptians slaughtering a sheep and Shamir's men contributing food parcels from home.

Word of the local armistice quickly spread and similar arrangements were forged in other sectors. Even Sharon visited to see what was going on. At one point, Ali told Shamir he had permission from his superiors to take him on a visit to Cairo. However, Israeli intelligence officers, fearful that their Egyptian counterparts intended to get information from him, ruled it out. The Israeli intelligence officers, for their part, tried to ascertain from Ali, through Shamir, the fate of Israeli pilots shot down in the area, but without success.

In a discussion between Shamir and Ali that the Israeli officer transcribed immediately afterwards, Shamir asked about an editorial in a Cairo newspaper asserting that Egypt would never recognize Israel. The editorial had been reported on the radio.

"That's just propaganda," said the commando major. "The truth is that we want peace and that we're moving towards it."

"Why doesn't Sadat say so?" asked Shamir.

"Sadat can't say so explicitly. He's a new leader, and although some of the intelligentsia support him, his problem is to win the support of the common people, who are still hypnotized by the figure of Nasser."

A year before, said Ali, he had participated in a meeting of officers with Sadat. Ali was then a captain and the lowest-ranking officer present. "Sadat said that we have to concern ourselves with Egypt's internal development and that if Israel would only show serious intentions of withdrawing from Sinai he would talk with it." Matters had to progress in stages, said Ali. "First the war has to stop. After a year or two we will travel to Tel Aviv and you to Cairo." According to what the Egyptian soldiers told their Israeli counterparts, Ali's uncle was a very senior officer. Some said it was Shazly himself.

The day after the disengagement agreement was signed, Ali brought his battalion commander as well as a colonel whose branch was not made clear. They wanted to hear from the Israeli captain what he thought about the agreement, evidently to probe at field level the seriousness of Israel's declarations. They seemed satisfied by Shamir's assurances that Israel really intended to pull back. Before departing, the Egyptian officers said they hoped that relations between the two countries would come to emulate the relations between Shamir's and Ali's men.

The Egyptian commandos and the Israeli paratroopers were at the spearheads of their respective armies. That these motivated fighters, left to themselves, chose at first opportunity to lay aside their weapons and break bread together on the battlefield said something about what the war had wrought.

After the 1967 war, Egypt perceived that its honor could be retrieved only in a renewed war, while Israel, certain of victory, was not overly intimidated by the prospect. In 1973, both sides emerged from the confrontation with honor intact and a desire not to taste of war again.

The Yom Kippur War had begun with a surprise attack but history, that master of paradox, provided an even more surprising ending, one that left behind on the furrowed battlefield the seeds of peace, however fragile. Not even Sadat, dreaming under his tree in Mit Abul-kum, had conjured up a vision as surrealistic as his journey to Jerusalem.

For Egypt, the war was a towering accomplishment. For Israel, it was an existential earthquake, but one whose repercussions were ultimately healthier than those of the Six Day War. The trauma of the war's opening was not a nightmare to be suppressed but a national memory to be perpetuated, a standing reminder of the consequences of shallow thinking and arrogance. Israel's battlefield recovery, in turn, reflected a society with a will to live and a capacity to improvise amidst chaos. Israel would bear its scars but it would be sustained by the memory of how, in its darkest hour, its young men mounted the nation's crumbling ramparts and held.

NOTES

1. *Footprints in the Sand*

Interviews with Motti Ashkenazi, Meir Weisel, and Mossad official.

Dayan on inherent Arab weakness—address at Israel's Staff and Command College, August 1973.

2. *The Man in the Peasant Robe*

Sadat reshaping Dayan's proposal—remarks by Ashraf Gorbal, Sadat's spokesman, at Yom Kippur War symposium in Washington, published in Parker's *The October War: A Retrospective.*

Saying it with flowers—Sisco in Parker.

All information on Kremlin discussions in this and other chapters, other than those involving Henry Kissinger, is from Israelyan's invaluable *Inside the Kremlin During the Yom Kippur War.*

Ismail's report on his conversation with Kissinger—Gamasy's *The October War.*

Interview with Jehan Sadat—*Yedioth Achronot,* November 6, 1987.

3. *Dovecote*

Dovecote plan—mainly from "Shovakh Yonim" ["Dovecote"], an article by Col. Ze'ev Eitan (res.) in *Ma'archot* 276.

Quotes from Elazar throughout the book are from Bartov's *Dado* and, up to the third day of the war, the Agranat Report unless otherwise noted.

Dusky Light—article by Col. Shaul Shai in *Ma'archot* 372.

Officer uneasy about Zeira's self-confidence—Danny Matt at Ramat Efal symposium.

Information on the Source is principally from Bar-Joseph's *The Watchman Fell Asleep.*

Dayan's comment on the Source—interview with Rami Tal, published in *Ma'ariv*, April 27, 1997.

4. *Badr*

Egyptian preparations are based mainly on Shazly's *The Crossing of the Canal;* Gamasy; and Sadat.

On Israeli awareness of Egyptian use of water cannon—article by Roland Aloni, *Ma'archot* 361.

5. *Illusions*

Background on air force—interviews with Peled, Avihu Bin-Nun; Ehud Yonay's *No Margin for Errors.*

Prewar estimate that the Israel Air Force could lose one plane per missile battery attacked—interview with Benny Peled.

Totality of the tank—Wald's *The Curse of the Broken Vessels;* Luttwak and Horowitz's *The Israel Army;* and a series of articles by Binyamin Amidror in *Ha'olam Hazeh* in 1974–1975. Also, Shimon Naveh, "The Cult of the Offensive Preemption and the Future Challenges for Israeli Operational Thought," in Efraim Karsh, ed., *Between War and Peace.*

Bar-Lev's comments on Arab capabilities—Kermit Guy's *Bar-Lev.*

American general on Israeli gunnery—interview with Gen. Donn Starry.

Armored corps had doctrine for dealing with Sagger—interview with General Adan.

General Tal dismissing request for better antitank weapons—interview with Emanuel Shaked.

Material on Israeli navy—from *The Boats of Cherbourg* by the author.

6. *Summer Lull*

Brezhnev-Nixon summit—Kissinger's *Years of Upheaval.*

State Department official sees fifty-fifty chance of war—Parker.

April 18 meeting at Mrs. Meir's home—Bar-Joseph, Bartov.

Paratroop general—interview with Gen. Danny Matt.

Gonen inspections—interview with Dan Meridor.

Gonen throwing a microphone—Argaman.

Adan on Gonen—interview with Adan.

Egyptian secrecy about the coming war—article by Col. Yohai Shaked (res.) in *Ma'archot* 373.

7. *A Royal Visit*

Meeting of Mrs. Meir and King Hussein—interviews with Lou Kedar, Zussia Keniezer, and Mordecai Gazit.

Zeira's prediction of no war for another ten years—interview with Shmuel Askarov.

8. *Sword from the Scabbard*

Figures on Israeli and Arab armies—Carta's historical atlas.

Eleven warnings received by Israeli intelligence in September—Bar-Joseph in *Ma'archot* 361.

General Zeira's avoidance of ambiguity—Agranat.

General Tal's warning—Bar-Joseph, *Ha'aretz*, December 18, 2002.

Pearl Harbor—article by Roberta Wohlstetter in *Foreign Affairs*, July 1965, as cited by
    Agranat Commission.
Sergeant Nadeh's diary, excerpts in Hebrew translation published in *Yedioth Achronot*,
    September 14, 1975; September 30, 1979.
AMAN material—Bar-Joseph, Yoel Ben-Porat's *Locked On*, interviews with Avi Ya'ari
    and Zussia Keniezer.
On Shabtai Brill—article in *Kol Hair* by Yair Sheleg, September 24, 1993.

9. *Countdown*

Shalev at meeting with Mrs. Meir—Agranat Report.
Forty-seventh Syrian Brigade—Amos Gilboa at Ramat Efal symposium.
Lieutenant Siman-Tov—Agranat Report.
American satellites and CIA—interview with Bruce Reidel.
Sadat-Vinogradov meeting—Israelyan.
Meeting in Dayan's office with Mrs. Meir Friday morning—Agranat Report.
Special sources not activated—Bar-Joseph.
Intelligence bulletin, Friday morning—Bar-Joseph.
Why Bandman added forty-third paragraph—Agranat Report.
General Havidi—interview by Oded Granot in *Ma'ariv Sofshavua* magazine, October
    1993.
Elazar would have mobilized if he had received the warning—Bartov.
General Elazar on October 1–6 being "the most normal week"—Agranat Report.
Gamasy fears Israeli trick—interview with Gamasy by Shmuel Segev in *Ma'ariv*,
    September 24, 1985.
Zvi Zamir missing Kol Nidre—from author's conversation with Zamir.
Zamir's meeting with the Source—Bar-Joseph. (Zamir would confirm to the author
    that Bar-Joseph's version of his meeting with the Source was correct, in contrast
    to others that were published.)

10. *Yom Kippur Morning*

Wake-up calls—Bar-Joseph.
Conversation between Elazar and Benny Peled—interview with Peled.
Elazar's "almost ceremonial" look—Bartov.
Elazar's brothel joke—interview with Shlomo Gazit.
Peled and meteorologist—interview with Peled.
Dayan's refusal to preempt—article by Lt. Col. (res.) Shimon Golan in *Ma'archot* 393.
Mrs. Meir and General Lior—Haber's *War Will Break Out Today*.
Meeting of Zeira and senior staff—interview with Keniezer.
Cabinet meeting—interview with Victor Shemtov.

11. *The Crossing*

Account of Egyptian crossing—Shazly and Gamasy.
Account of forts—interviews with Ashkenazi, Shaul Moses, Yaacov Trostler, Avi
    Yaffe, Meir Weisel, Shalom Hala, Arye Segev, and Menahem Ritterband.

12. *The Humbling of the Tank*

Interviews with Eyal Yoffe, Rami Matan, Gabi Amir, and Reshef.
Most of this chapter is based on the war diary compiled by Amnon Reshef's brigade

and the unit history of Dan Shomron's brigade. Also *Albert* by Aviezer Golan—an account of General Mendler during the war—and the unit history of Amir Yoffe's battalion.
Egyptian antitank defenses—Shazly.
Israel's shortage of firepower—Yisrael Tal's *National Security.*
Oded Marom's story—from talk by Marom at Ramat Efal symposium.
Air photos the air force didn't see—interview with Benny Peled.

13. *Mobilization*

Interviews with Yeshayahu Gavish, Uri Ben-Ari, Yitzhak Brik, Gabi Amir, Motti Hod, Yom Tov Tamir, and Rami Matan.
Ariel Sharon's *Warrior;* Carta's historical atlas; Golan; Adan; and unit histories.
Reserve units reaching front in half the planned time—Lt. Col. Roland Aloni (res.), *Ma'archot* 361.
Ben-Ari keeping an eye on Gonen—interview with Ben-Ari.
Appraisal of Abu Agheila—Binyamin Amidror, *Ha'olam Hazeh,* 1975.
Dayan saying there won't be war for another ten years—article by Sharon in *Yedioth Achronot,* September 24, 1993.
Erez's prediction of 2,500 to 3,000 dead—interviews with Haim Erez and Ami Morag.
Sharon moved by conversations with forts—interview with Yisrael Itkin, who served in Sharon's command personnel carrier.
Conversation between Sharon and Weisel—tape recording by Avi Yaffe.
Destruction of the Egyptian ambush near Baluza—article by Menahem Rahat in *Ma'ariv Sofshavua* magazine, October 1980.
General Hod at Nafakh—interview with Hod.

14. *Syrian Breakthrough*

Interviews with Raful Eitan, Avigdor Kahalani, Avigdor Ben-Gal, Yair Nafshi, Uri Simhoni, Motti Hod, Dennie Agmon, Haim Barak, Shmuel Askarov, Oded Beckman, Zvi Rak, David Eiland, Shmuel Yakhin, Avraham Elimelekh, Yossi Gur, Nir Atir, Yoram Krivine, Amir Drori, Yudke Peled, Yoram Yair, Moshe Zurich, Hanan Schwartz, Zvika Greengold. Also Agranat Report, Kahalani's *Oz 77,* and "The Syrian Attack on the Golan Heights" by Lieutenant Colonel Zvi (res.) (no last name given) in *Ma'archot* 314.
Acquisition of latest Syrian plan a week before war—Bar-Joseph's *The Watchman Fell Asleep.*
Outline of Syrian plan—Brig. Gen. Amos Gilboa (res.), former head of AMAN's Syrian desk, at Ramat Efal symposium, October 2001.
Ben-Shoham not warning of war—Agranat Report, interview with Nafshi.
Erez not knowing that Barak's battalion was behind him—Agranat Report.
Interrogation of Lieutenant Al-Joujoy—article by Alex Fishman, *Yedioth Achronot,* September 19, 1999.
Ben-Gal reluctant to detach one of his battalions—interview with Ben-Gal in *Shirion.*

15. *Darkest at Dawn*

Poor reporting from the field—Shimon Golan at Ramat Efal symposium.
"I'm an atheist"—Sabbato's *Adjustment of Sights.*
Yotser's ascent—interview with Yotser.

Laner: "The battle for the southern Golan is lost"—Bartov.

Tagar—Yonai and interviews with Bin-Nun, Giora Furman, David Ivri, Benny Peled, Amos Amir, Eitan Ben-Eliyahu, Giora Rom.

16. The Fall of the Southern Golan

Interviews with Yair, Krivine, Kahalani, Ben-Gal, Gil Peled, and Drori; Kahalani's *Oz 77*.

Kalish—interview on Israel's Channel Two, May 20, 2001.

Ben-Shoshan: "We've done our bit"—Agranat Report.

17. The Beanstalk

Interviews with Sarig, Bierman, Agmon, Yair, Ben-Porat, Orr, Greengold, Elimelekh, Yakhin, Benny Michaelson, and Drori.

18. The Battle for Nafakh

Interviews with Greengold, Yotser, Barak, Orr, Haim Danon, Ron Gottfried, Agmon, Hanan Anderson, and Zurich. Also the unit history and film produced by Orr's brigade.

Agranat Report.

Among those who would contend that Zvika Greengold saved Nafakh, and the Golan, were Zurich, Ben-Shoham's intelligence officer, and Hanan Schwartz, Ben-Shoham's communications officer.

19. Cut Off

Interviews with Moussa Peled, Avraham Rotem, Beckman, Gur, Yair, Atir, Orr, Motti Katz.

Written sources—Sabbato and unit histories.

Dayan on need to replace Hofi—Arie Braun's *Moshe Dayan and the Yom Kippur War.*

Bar-Lev ordering radios at Northern Command to be shut—Guy's *Bar-Lev.*

Tel Faris bunker—interview with Nir Atir; Uri Millstein's *The Collapse and Its Lessons.*

20. Hand on the Tiller

"Let the line be on the Artillery Road or the Lateral Road"—Braun.

Conversation between Mrs. Meir and Lou Kedar—interview with Ms. Kedar.

Phantom pilot describing Syrian army on Golan—article by Sima Kadmon in *Ma'ariv,* September 24, 1993. Years later, Ms. Kadmon met the pilot, who did not recall his words but apologized for them.

"Take a good look at each other"—article by Ravit Naor in *Ma'ariv,* September 1998. The speaker, Maj. Ron Huldai, would be elected mayor of Tel Aviv in 1998.

The absence of "anticipatory fear"—Dr. Reuven Gal's *The Yom Kippur War: Lessons from the Psychologist's Perspective.*

Battle of San Simon—Bartov.

Sharon's conversation with Gonen—Sharon's *Warrior.*

Events at Fort Orkal—Arye Segev's *Unfulfilled Mission;* interviews with Segev, Ritterband.

Elazar's telephone conversation with Gonen—Agranat Report.

21. Failed Counterattack

Interviews with Adan, Nir, Gabi Amir, Yitzhak Brik, Yom Tov Tamir, and Haim Adini.

Adan's book offers a detailed description of the battle, as does the Agranat Report. Other published material includes "October 8" by Colonel Ze'ev (no surname given) in *Ma'archot* 268, Bartov, Eliashiv Shimshi's *Storm in October*, Millstein, unit histories, and article by Assaf Yaguri in *Yedioth Achronot*, October 10, 1978.

Elazar: "The sky's the limit"—Agranat Report.

Radio communications between Gonen and Adan—Agranat Report.

Quote from Adini comparing a tank charge to an orgasm is from Millstein.

22. *Bomb Damascus*

"There isn't a single tank from there to Haifa"—Bartov.

Attack on Hermon—interviews with Drori and Yudke Peled.

"Sharon seeking votes in Cairo"—Braun.

Meeting at Umm Hashiba—Bartov, Adan.

Dayan on need for "brutal effort" to drive Syria out of war—Braun.

Dayan on entering Damascus—interview with Dayan's aide-de-camp, Arie Braun, by Yigal Sarna in *Yedioth Achronot*, September 17, 1991.

Gonen "not commanding from the saddle"—Binyamin Amidror, *Ha'olam Hazeh*.

Kissinger quip to Dinitz—article by Yigal Sarna in *Yedioth Achronot*, Yom Kippur edition, 1996.

Dismay within air force at poor showing of Israeli armor—interview with David Ivri.

Attack on Damascus—interview with Lapidot.

Basement of Syrian headquarters—interview with Barber.

Description of Joel Aronoff—interview by Arieh O'Sullivan in *Jerusalem Post*, February 4, 2000.

23. *Touching Bottom*

General Tal on war of survival—Bartov.

Israel's nuclear arsenal—Hersh's *The Samson Option*.

"Extreme measures"—article in *Yedioth Achronot*, August 15, 2003, by Ronen Bergnan and Gil Meltzer.

Hizayon—Interviews with Ohr and Strolovitz. Ohr became a professor of rehabilitation medicine at Tel Aviv University. He recalled his ordeal as he sat at his swimming pool in the upscale Tel Aviv suburb of Savion.

Egyptian cameraman—interview with Gohar in Cairo.

"If Arik is in charge . . ."—Avi Weiss's *Prisoner of Egypt*

"Silent patrol"—interview with Matt.

Brom's patrol—interview with Brom's deputy, Zvi Avidan.

Sharon requests permission to cross canal—*Yehioth Achronot*, translated extract, August 2003.

24. *Golan Counterattack*

Interviews with Kahalani, Gil Peled, Ben-Gal, Rak, Nafshi, Sarig.

Entry of reservist rescuers into bunker at Tel Saki—The story was related on Israel Radio by Motti Aviram, one of the men in the bunker. As an archaeologist twenty years later, he excavated the site of Yodfat in the Galilee where the Jewish general and historian Josephus hid in a cave with others after the city's fall to the

Romans 1,900 years earlier, an experience paralleling that of Aviram and his comrades.

Kahalani's *Oz 77*, unit histories.

Assad exhorting division commanders—interview with Mohammed Bassiouni, Egyptian liaison at Syrian General Staff headquarters.

General Jihani—Amos Gilad at Ramat Efal symposium.

Askarov's wound—The bullet entered his forehead and emerged from the rear of his skull. Three doctors said it was hopeless but a fourth decided to operate. Askarov recovered. Though partially paralyzed and speech-impaired, he would walk unaided and drive.

25. *Iraqi Intervention*

Bierman would remain unconscious for two months and undergo fourteen operations but recovered. He became a senior official with the Israel Antiquities Authority, headed by Amir Drori, former Golani commander.

Ben-Gal acceding to Ben-Hanan's request to attack Tel Shams—Herzog.

Ben-Hanan would eventually become commander of the armored corps. Netanyahu was killed in the Entebbe rescue operation in 1976.

Mofaz's raid behind Syrian lines—article by Moshe Zonder, *Ma'ariv Sofshavua* magazine, October 1992. Interview with pilot Yuval Efrat. Mofaz would become Israeli chief of staff and then defense minister. Efrat would become an El Al pilot.

26. *Powers That Be*

This chapter is based largely on Kissinger and Israelyan.

27. *Israel Seeks a Cease-fire*

Interviews with Benny Peled, Gavish, Moses.

"Positions of the Chief of Staff and the Political Level on a Canal Crossing and Cease-fire" by Lt. Col. Shimon Golan (res.), *Ma'archot 327.*

Dayan on Sharon: "What will I get out of it?"—Transcript published in *Yediot Achronot*, August 2003.

Bartov's *Dado.*

Egyptian brigade moved out of SAM umbrella—Shazly.

Israeli Arabs in war—author's reporting for the *Jerusalem Post.*

Naval account based on *The Boats of Cherbourg* by the author.

28. *Decision to Cross*

"Positions of the Chief of Staff and the Political Level on a Canal Crossing and Cease-fire" by Lt. Col. Shimon Golan, *Ma'archot 327.*

Bartov, Braun, Dayan's *Milestones.*

Talk by Zvi Zamir at Ramat Efal symposium.

29. *Stouthearted Men*

Material on bridges from interviews with Avi Zohar, Yishai Dotan, Amikam Doron, Menashe Gur, Ya'acov Even.

Books by Adan, Tal.

Mendler and navy—Golan's *Albert.*

Extracts from Nadeh's diary were published in *Yedioth Achronot* on September 30, 1979.

Soviet involvement in planning canal crossing—Soviet journal *Novia Vrema* as cited in *Bamahane,* an IDF magazine, May 3, 1989.

Sharon conversations with Yael Dayan and Ezer Weizman—Uri Dan's *Bridgehead.*

Estimates of Egyptian tank losses in October 14 attack—oddly enough, Shazly and Gamasy cite the higher figure while Israeli analysts tend towards the lower.

Mrs. Meir had recovered her composure—interview with Victor Shemtov.

Hanan Erez threatening to shoot colonel—interview with Erez.

"They believed"—article by Sharon in *Yedioth Achronot* on twenty-fifth anniversary of the war.

Mitzna briefing his men—article by Yael Gevirtz, in *Yedioth Achronot,* June 17, 1995.

Scene at Umm Hashiba on night of the crossing—article in *Ma'ariv* by Aharon Priel, September 9, 1985.

30. *The Chinese Farm*

Most of this chapter is based on the war diary compiled by Reshef's brigade. Also Yuval Neria's *Fire.* Interviews with Reshef, Matan, Doron, Matt, Eli Cohen, Natan Shunari, Even, Giora Lev, Itkin, and Neria. The latter, awarded Israel's highest medal for his performance in the war, would become a psychologist and a prominent member of Israel's peace movement.

Sharon adjusting his beret—Itkin.

Article on Danny Matt by Simha Aharoni in *Yedioth Achronot,* October 6, 1985.

31. *The Bridges*

Morag's ride—interviews with Morag, Yehuda Tal, and company commander Amnon Amikam.

Bridges—interviews with Even, Lohar, Dotan, Doron, Gur.

Sharon's division—interviews with Erez, Reshef, Lev, Geller.

Paratroopers—interviews with Matt, Yitzhak Mordecai, Yehuda Duvdevani.

Adan's division—interviews with Adan, Tamari.

Article by Eitan Haber in *Yedioth Achronot,* October 1985.

"Lail Hapritsa L'Chava Hasinit" ["Night of the Break-in to the Chinese Farm"], article by Shimon Manueli published by Israel Defense Forces in 1977.

"If they don't put up a bridge soon"—*October Days,* edited by Mordecai Naor and Ze'ev Aner.

Dayan angry at Mrs. Meir's Knesset revelation—Braun.

Lieutenant Colonel Razon and his wounded son—article by Col. Shaul Nagar in *Shirion,* September 2000.

32. *Crossing into Africa*

"Three infiltrating tanks"—Mohamed Heikal's *The Road to Ramadan,* Shazly.

Israel learns that Sadat has taken personal command—Braun.

Sharon at crossing point—interviews with Itkin, Yehoshua Sagui, and Reshef.

Sergeant Barnea's account—article by Barnea in *Ma'archot* 361.

Sharon wanting to smack Bar-Lev—Sharon's *Warrior.*

Yitzhak Brik—interview. As an IDF general in the 1990s, Brik visited an armor training school in Russia where he discovered that the ambush of the Twenty-fifth Brigade was part of the curriculum.

Warning not to use poison gas—Braun.

Attack on Banha—interview with Benny Peled.

33. *Breakout*

Adan; Carta's historical atlas; Sharon; Heikal, Shazly, Gamasy, Sadat.

Interviews—Brik, Bin-Nun, Yehuda Geller, Adan, Nir, Reshef, Lev.

Gilowas—interview with deputy Gilowa commander Amikam Doron.

Mirages fly into SAM-free zone—unit history of Amir Yoffe's battalion.

Bomb explosion near Dayan's APC; Sharon firing with Kalashnikov—interview with Itkin.

Israeli skeleton forces in Sinai—Adan in Ofer and Kober's *Quantity and Quality*.

Major Suleiman—article by Yigal Lev in *Ma'ariv*, October 10, 1981.

34. *Kissinger to the Fore*

Avi Weiss's *Prisoner of Egypt* provides an intimate view of Israeli tank crewmen at the battle for Missouri.

Southern Command monitoring Sharon's units—Braun.

Final assault on Israeli Hermon—interviews with Yudke Peled, Drori.

Paratroop officer's conversation with Drori—Uri Millstein, *Hadashot*, September 24, 1985.

Elbaz's account—interview on Israel Radio.

Paratroop assault on Syrian Hermon—interview with brigade commander Haim Nadel.

Naval commando assault on Ardaka—interviews with Almog and Gadi Kroll.

35. *Cease-fire*

General Wasel complaining about General Kabil—"Aircraft in Ground Support" by Major Y. and Colonel Y. (full names not given) in *Ma'archot* 266.

Their eyes said "Enough"—interview with Dov Tamari.

Prepared to go to Cairo—interview with Rami Matan.

Shimshi's battalion—*Storm in October*.

"Israel wouldn't have received a nail if it had preempted"—Braun.

Egyptian soldiers shooting deserters—interview with Matan.

Sharon and Egyptian pilot—interview with Yisrael Itkin.

Arab odds against Israel on northern front—Iraqi war diary.

36. *Suez City*

Interviews with David Amit, Amiram Gonen, Brik, Mordecai.

Article by Aviezer Golan, *Yedioth Achronot*, September 14, 1975.

Adan, unit histories.

37. *Nuclear Alert*

Interview with Admiral Murphy from *The Boats of Cherbourg*.

"The Arabs didn't run"—Braun.

Yom Tov Tamir shouting at Mrs. Meir—interview with Tamir.

Mrs. Meir regrets not pulling back in 1970—Dayan's autobiography.

Kissinger's comforting arm—interview in *Yedioth Achronot*, September 9, 1991, with Eli Mizrachi, former director of Mrs. Meir's office.

IDF incorporates 400 Syrian tanks into its ranks—Roland Aloni in *Ma'archot* 361.

400 Israeli tanks destroyed in war, 600 damaged and repaired—Tal.

Israelis in battle shock—Gal's *The Yom Kippur War*.

Arab casualty figures—Trevor Dupuy, *Elusive Victory*.

38. *Aftermath*

The Source—The allegation about Ashraf Marwan was made by Ahron Bregman in an interview with the Egyptian newspaper *Al-Ahram* on December 22, 2002, following publication of Bregman's book on Israel, in which he hinted at the Source's closeness to Nasser.

IAF attack on Bekaa in 1982—Yonay, Amos Amir's *Flames in the Sky*, interview with Ivri.

Shimon Maliach episode—article by Avihai Becker in *Ma'ariv*, September 24, 1993.

Fraternization in Suez City—unit history of Amir Yoffe's battalion.

Israeli paratroopers and Egyptian commandos fraternizing near Ismailiya—interview with Gideon Shamir.

A SELECTED BIBLIOGRAPHY

The 2,000-page report of the Agranat Commission, made available to researchers in 1993, is basic to any study of the war, as is Hanoch Bartov's wartime account of chief of staff Gen. David Elazar. Bartov was granted access to extensive records by Elazar. Excerpts from cabinet and General Staff protocols are contained in Moshe Dayan's autobiography and the account written by his aide-de-camp, Arie Braun. The failings of Israeli military intelligence prior to the war are detailed in a highly illuminating book by Uri Bar-Joseph, himself a former intelligence officer. A good account of the battles on the Egyptian front is given in the book by Gen. Avraham Adan.

Official accounts of the war written by IDF historians have not been publicly released as of this writing. However, historians involved in the project have offered important insights into their work in published articles and in lectures.

Dozens of highly useful accounts and analyses of the war were published over the past three decades in *Ma'archot*, Israel's leading military journal. Israeli newspapers also offered a bounty of information. Unit histories were invaluable in reconstructing battles. An often poignant personal dimension is provided in memoirs by combatants, from Israeli tank sergeants to pilots, as well as the diary of an Egyptian soldier found on the battlefield. Eight daylong symposia conducted by the Israeli Military History Association in 1999–2001 produced new insights by senior commanders and researchers.

The Arab side of the war is poorly documented. A notable exception is the war diary by the Egyptian chief of staff, Gen. Saad el Shazly. Unfortunately, books by other Egyptian generals published in English are heavily laden with fantasy, but interviews granted by General Gamasy and Egyptian intelligence officers to the Israeli press offer valuable information. A lively and valuable political account is provided by journalist and Sadat confidant Mohammed Hassenein Heikal. There is nothing authoritative at all from the Syrian side but light is shed on military aspects by outside sources. These include an official Iraqi report on the Syrian front—one of the most straightforward Arab accounts of the war—and articles by former Israeli intelligence officers as well as books by Egyptian and Soviet officials.

Victor Israelyan's inside view from the Kremlin nicely balances Kissinger's book in depicting the superpowers' role in the war.

The written record has been amplified with more than one hundred and thirty interviews.

Books

Adan, Avraham. *On the Banks of the Suez*. San Francisco: Presidio Press, 1980.

Amir, Amos. *Aish ba'shamayaim* [Flames in the Sky]. Tel Aviv: Defense Ministry, 2000.

Argaman, Josef. *Hiver Haya Ha-laila* [Pale was the Night]. Tel Aviv: Yediot Achronot, 2000.

Atlas l'Toldot Medinat Yisrael [Atlas of the History of the State of Israel, 1971–1981]. Jerusalem: Carta, 1983.

Badri, Hassan el, Taha el Magdoub and Mohammed Dia el din Zohdy. *The Ramadan War*. Dunn Loring, Va.: T.N. Dupuy Associates, 1979.

Bar-Joseph, Uri. *Hatsofe Shenirdam* [The Watchman Fell Asleep]. Lod: Zmora-Bitan, 2001.

Bartov, Hanoch. *Dado*. Tel Aviv: Ma'ariv Book Guild, 1978.

Ben-Porat, Yoel. *Neila* [Locked On]. Tel Aviv: Edanim, 1991.

Benziman, Uzi. *Sharon: An Israeli Caesar*. Tel Aviv: Adama, 1985.

Braun, Arie. *Moshe Dayan v'Milkhemet Yom Kippur* [Moshe Dayan and the Yom Kippur War]. Tel Aviv: Edanim, 1992.

Bregman, Ahron. *A History of Israel*. Houndmills: Palgrave Macmillan, 2003.

Cohen, Eliot, and John Gooch. *Military Misfortunes*. New York: Vintage Books, 1991.

Cordesman, Anthony H., and Abraham R. Wagner. *The Lessons of Modern War*, vol. 1, *The Arab-Israeli Conflicts, 1973–1989*. Boulder, Colo.: Westview Press, 1990.

Dan, Uri. *Rosh Gesher* [The Bridgehead]. Tel Aviv: E.L. Special Edition, 1975.

Davis Institute for International Relations. *Milkhemet Yom Hakippurim* [The Yom Kippur War: A New View]. Symposium on the war's twenty-fifth anniversary. Jerusalem: Hebrew University, 1998.

Dayan, Moshe. *Avnei Derekh* [Milestones]. Jerusalem: Edanim, 1982.

Dupuy, Trevor. *Elusive Victory*. New York: HarperCollins, 1978.

Gal, Reuven. *The Yom Kippur War: Lessons from the Psychologist's Perspective*. Zikhron Ya'acov: Israeli Institute for Military Studies, 1987.

Gamasy, Mohamed Abdel Ghani el-. *The October War*. Cairo: American University in Cairo Press, 1993.

Gelber, Yoav, and Hani Ziv. *Bnai Keshet* [The Bow Bearers]. Tel Aviv: Defense Ministry, 1998.

Golan, Aviezer. *Albert*. Tel Aviv: Yedioth, 1977. In Hebrew.

Guy, Kermit. *Bar-Lev*. Tel Aviv: Am Oved, 1998. In Hebrew.

Haber, Eitan. *Hayom Tifrots Milkhama* [War Will Break Out Today]. Tel Aviv: Edanim, 1987.

Heikal, Mohammed Hassenein. *The Road to Ramadan*. New York: Ballantine, 1975.

Hersh, Seymour. *The Samson Option*. New York: Random House, 1991.

Herzog, Chaim. *The War of Atonement*. Tel Aviv: Steimatzky, 1975.

Hirst, David, and Irene Beeson. *Sadat*. London: Faber & Faber, 1981.

Insight Team of the Sunday *Times*. *Insight on the Middle East*. London: Andre Deutsch, 1974.

Iraqi Defense Ministry. *Zva Iraq b'Milkhemet Yom Kippur* [The Iraqi Army in the Yom Kippur War]. Translation from Arabic to Hebrew. Tel Aviv: Ma'archot, 1986.

Israelyan, Victor. *Inside the Kremlin During the Yom Kippur War*. University Park: Pennsylvania State University Press, 1995.

Kahalani, Avigdor. *Oz 77* [Seventy-seventh Battalion]. Tel Aviv: Shocken, 1975.

Karsh, Efraim, ed. *Between War and Peace: Dilemmas of Israeli Security*. London: Frank Cass, 1996.

Kedar, B. Z. *Sipuro Shel Gdud Makhatz* [Story of a Strike Battalion]. Tel Aviv: Tamuz Press, 1975.

Kissinger, Henry. *Years of Upheaval*. Boston: Little, Brown, 1982.

Kober, Avi. *Hakhara Tsvait* [Military Decision in the Arab-Israeli Wars]. Tel Aviv: Ma'archot, 1996.

Kumaraswamy, P. R., ed. *Revisiting the Yom Kippur War*. London: Frank Cass, 2000.

Lanir, Zvi. *Hahafta'a Habasist* [The Basic Surprise]. Tel Aviv: Kav Adom, 1983.

Luttwak, Edward, and Dan Horowitz. *The Israeli Army*. New York: Harper & Row, 1975.

Medzini, Meron. *Hayehudit Hageah* [The Proud Jewess]. Tel Aviv: Edanim, 1990.

Meir, Golda. *My Life*. Tel Aviv: Ma'ariv, 1977.

Meital, Yoram. *Egypt's Struggle for Peace*. Gainesville: University of Florida Press, 1997.

Millstein, Uri. *Krisa V'lekacha* [The Collapse and Its Lessons]. Kiron: Sridot, 1993.

Morris, Benny. *Righteous Victims*. New York: Vintage Books, 1999.

Naor, Mordecai, and Ze'ev Aner, eds. *Yemai October* [October Days]. Tel Aviv: Defense Ministry, 1974.

Neria, Yuval. *Aish* [Fire]. Tel Aviv: Zmora Bitan, 1989.

Ofer, Zvi, and Avi Kober, eds. *Aichut v'Kamut* [Quality and Quantity]. Tel Aviv: Ma'archot, 1985.

Parker, Richard B., ed. *The October War: A Retrospective*. Gainesville: University of Florida Press, 2001.

Peled, Yossi. *Ish Tsava* [Soldier]. Tel Aviv: Ma'ariv, 1993.

Pretty, R. T. *Weapon Systems*. London: Jane's, 1979.

Rabinovich, Abraham. *The Boats of Cherbourg*. Annapolis, Md.: Naval Institute Press, 1988.

Rafael, Gideon. *Destination Peace*. Jerusalem: Edanim, 1981.

Sabbato, Chaim. *Tium Kavanot* [Adjustment of Sights]. Tel Aviv: Yedioth Achronot, 1999.

Sadat, Anwar. *In Search of Identity*. New York: Harper & Row, 1978.

Safran, Nadav. *Israel, the Embattled Ally*. Cambridge, Mass.: Belknap Press of Harvard University Press, 1978.

Seale, Patrick. *Assad: The Struggle for the Middle East*. Berkeley: University of California Press, 1988.

Segev, Arye. *Lo Bitsati et Hamesima* [Unfulfilled Mission]. Tel Aviv: Seder Tselem, 2001.

Sharon, Ariel, with David Chanoff. *Warrior: The Autobiography of Ariel Sharon*. London: MacDonald, 1989.

Shashar, Michael. *Sikhot im Rehavam Ze'evi* [Talks with Rehavam Ze'evi]. Tel Aviv: Yedioth Achronot, 1982.

Shay, Shaul, ed. *The Iraqi-Israeli Conflict, 1948–2000*. Tel Aviv: Defense Ministry, 2002.

Shazly, Saad el. *The Crossing of the Suez*. San Francisco: American Mideast Research, 1980.

Shimshi, Eliashiv. *B'Koach Hatachbula* [By Virtue of Stratagem]. Tel Aviv: Defense Ministry, 1999.

———. *Seara b'October* [Storm in October]. Tel Aviv: Defense Ministry, 1986.

———. *Aifo Ani Nimitsa* [Where Am I?]. Tel Aviv: Defense Ministry, 2002.

Spector, Yiftakh. *Khalom b'Tchelet-Shakhor* [A Dream in Blue and Black]. Jerusalem: Keter, 1991.

Tal, Yisrael. *Bitachon Leumi* [National Security]. Tel Aviv: Dvir, 1996.

Wald, Emanuel. *Klalat Hakailim Hashverum* [The Curse of the Broken Vessels]. Tel Aviv: Shocken, 1987.

Weiss, Avi. *B'Shevi Hamitsri* [Prisoner of Egypt]. Tel Aviv: Defense Ministry, 1998.

Wohlstetter, Roberta. *Pearl Harbor: Warning and Decision*. Stanford, Calif.: Stanford University Press, 1962.

Yonay, Ehud. *No Margin for Errors: The Story of the Israeli Air Force*. New York: Pantheon, 1983.

Zaloga, Steven J. *Armour of the Middle East War*. London: Osprey Publishing, 1981.

Zeira, Eli. *Milkhemet Yom Kippur: Mytos mul Metsiut* [The Yom Kippur War: Myth vs. Reality]. Tel Aviv: Yedioth Achronot, 1993.

Other Sources

War diary of Col. Amnon Reshef's brigade

Tape recordings from Fort Purkan, including conversation with Gen. Ariel Sharon, made by radioman Avi Yaffe

A summation of Israeli air force's role during the war compiled by Lt. Col. Yossi Aboudi, made available by Gen. Benny Peled

Films produced by Yitzhak Mordecai's battalion, Ori Orr's brigade, and the engineering corps

Israel Radio

Israel Television

Unit Histories (listed by names of unit commanders)

Division histories: Raful Eitan; Dan Laner

Brigade histories: Ori Orr, Yossi Peled, Haim Erez, Tuvia Raviv, Dan Shomron, Danny Matt, Natke Nir, Mordecai Ben-Porat

Battalion histories: Amir Yoffe, Emanuel Sakel, Yitzhak Mordecai, Shimon Ben-Shoshan, Ami Morag

Israeli military magazines

Ma'archot

Shirion

Bamahane

Israeli newspapers and magazines

Yedioth Achronot
Ma'ariv
Ha'aretz
Jerusalem Post
Hadashot
Ha'olam Hazeh (an incisive series of articles by military analyst Binyamin Amidror in 1974–75)

Persons interviewed (ranks given were those held at the time)

Northern Command

Maj. Gen. Rafael (Raful) Eitan—division commander
Maj. Gen. Moussa Peled—division commander
Col. Avigdor Ben-Gal—armored brigade commander
Col. Mordecai Ben-Porat—armored brigade commander
Col. Ori Orr—armored brigade commander
Col. Ran Sarig—armored brigade commander
Col. Haim Nadel—paratroop brigade commander
Col. Amir Drori—Golani Infantry Brigade commander
Brig. Gen. Avraham Rotem—deputy division commander
Lt. Col. Uri Simhoni—operations officer, Northern Command
Lt. Col. Avigdor Kahalani—tank battalion commander
Lt. Col. Yudke Peled—Golani battalion commander
Lt. Col. Yair Nafshi—tank battalion commander
Lt. Col. Ron Gottfried—tank battalion commander
Lt. Col. Motti Katz—intelligence officer, Moussa Peled's division
Lt. Col. Chagai Mann—Northern Command intelligence officer
Lt. Col. Pinhas Kuperman—deputy commander, Golan District Brigade
Lt. Col. Aldo Zohar—artillery battery commander
Maj. Giora Berman—tank battalion commander
Maj. Haim Barak—tank battalion commander
Maj. Haim Danon—tank battalion commander
Maj. Hanan Schwartz—communications officer, 188th Brigade
Maj. David Caspi—deputy tank battalion commander
Maj. Zvi Rak—tank company commander
Maj. Yoram Yair—commander of paratroops manning front line
Capt. David Harman—intelligence officer
Lt. Avraham Elimelekh—commander of Outpost 107
Lt. David Eiland—tank platoon commander
Lt. Nitzan Yotser—tank platoon commander
Lt. Zvika Greengold—tank officer
Lt. Gidi Peled—tank battalion operations officer
Lt. Oded Beckman—tank platoon commander
Lt. Hanan Anderson—tank platoon commander

Lt. Yehuda Wagman—deputy tank company commander
Lt. Yossi Gur—commander of Outpost 116
Lt. Shmuel Yakhin—tank platoon commander
Sgt. Nir Atir—tank commander
Sgt. Yoram Krivine—paratrooper

Southern Command
Maj. Gen. Avraham Adan—division commander
Maj. Gen. Yeshayahu Gavish—commander of southern Sinai
Brig. Gen. Barukh Harel—deputy to Gen. Mendler
Brig. Gen. Dov Tamari—deputy to General Adan
Brig. Gen. Avraham Tamir—assistant to General Sharon
Brig. Gen. Uri Ben-Ari—deputy southern front commander
Brig. Gen. Ya'acov Even—deputy to General Sharon
Brig. Gen. Asher Levy—southern front staff
Col. Haim Erez—armored brigade commander
Col. Amnon Reshef—armored brigade commander
Col. Natke Nir—armored brigade commander
Col. Gabi Amir—armored brigade commander
Col. Danny Matt—paratroop brigade commander
Lt. Col. Yitzhak Mordecai—paratroop battalion commander
Lt. Col. Ami Morag—tank battalion commander
Lt. Col. Giora Lev—tank battalion commander
Lt. Col. Yom Tov Tamir—tank battalion commander
Lt. Col. Haim Adini—tank battalion commander
Maj. Meir Weisel—commander of Fort Purkan
Maj. Yehuda Tal—deputy tank battalion commander
Maj. Yehuda Duvdevani—deputy paratroop battalion commander
Maj. Natan Shunari—paratroop battalion commander
Maj. Ilan Oko—deputy to Colonel Even
Maj. Yitzhak Brik—tank company commander
Maj. Zvi Avidan—deputy commander, armored reconnaissance battalion
Maj. Yehuda Geller—tank battalion commander
Maj. Gabi Komissar—Gen. Sharon's communications officer
Capt. Gideon Shamir—paratroop company commander
Capt. Hanan Erez—paratroop officer
Capt. Amnon Amikam—tank company commander
Capt. Yaacov Trostler—commander of Fort Milano
Capt. Motti Ashkenazi—commander of Fort Budapest
Capt. Rami Matan—tank company commander
Capt. Menashe Goldblatt—tank company commander
Capt. Ya'acov Zeira—tank battalion commander
Lt. Yuval Neria—tank company commander
Dr. Avi Ohri—Fort Hizayon
Lt. Shaul Moses—tank platoon commander
Lt. David Amit—paratroop platoon commander
Lt. Eli Cohen—paratroop platoon commander

Sgt. Avi Yaffe—radioman, Fort Purkan
Sgt. Pinhas Strolovitz—Fort Hizayon
Sgt. Shalom Hala—Fort Milano
Sgt. Israel Itkin—commander of Sharon's APC
Sgt. Eyal Yoffe—tank commander
Sgt. Arye Segev—Fort Orkal
Pvt. Menahem Ritterband   Fort Orkal

Air Force
Maj. Gen. Benny Peled—air force commander
Maj. Gen. Motti Hod—liaison to front commanders
Col. David Ivri—deputy air force commander
Col. Giora Furman—chief operations officer
Col. Avihu Bin-Nun—air strike planning
Col. Eitan Ben-Eliyahu—planning staff
Col. Amos Amir—planning staff
Lt. Col. Giora Rom—Skyhawk squadron commander
Lt. Col. Yuval Efrat—helicopter squadron commander
Maj. Arnon Lapidot—deputy Phantom squadron commander
Capt. Avraham Barber—Phantom pilot

Navy
Adm. Binyamin Telem—navy commander
Capt. Ze'ev Almog—commander of Gulf of Suez theater
Lt. Comdr. Gadi Kroll—naval commando

Engineering Corps
Lt. Col. Avi Zohar—pontoon bridge battalion commander
Maj. Yishai Dotan—deputy commander, pontoons
Capt. Amikam Doron—deputy commander, Gilowa raft company
Lt. Col. Menashe Gur—commander of roller bridge
Lt. Eilon Naveh—deputy company commander, rubber boats

Military Intelligence
Lt. Col. Zussia Keniezer—head of Jordanian desk
Lt. Col. Avi Ya'ari—head of Syrian desk
Lt. Col. Dennie Agmon—chief intelligence officer, Eitan's division
Lt. Col. Yehoshua Sagui—chief intelligence officer, Sharon's division
Lt. Col. Chagai Mann—chief intelligence officer, Northern Command
Maj. Amos Gilboa—Syrian desk, AMAN
Maj. Moshe Zurich—188th Brigade intelligence officer
Maj. Ilan Shahar—Seventh Brigade intelligence officer
Capt. David Harman—intelligence officer, Eitan's division
Sgt. Amiram Gonen—Southern Command

Others
Brig. Gen. Emanuel Shaked—chief paratroop and infantry officer
Lou Kedar—assistant to Golda Meir
Mordecai Gazit—director of prime minister's office

Prof. Yuval Ne'eman—physicist, member of defense establishment
Mohammed Bassiouni—Egyptian liaison to Syrian General Staff
Maj. Gen. Shlomo Gazit (ret.)—Israeli military intelligence
Victor Shemtov—health minister
Gen. Donn Starry (ret.)—U.S. Army
Bruce Reidel—U.S. intelligence expert
Mohammed Gohar—Egyptian photographer
Sgt. Dan Meridor—served under Gen. Gonen in 1967
Reuven Merhav—Israeli intelligence community
Benny Michaelson—former chief IDF historian
Prof. Edward Luttwak
Prof. Martin van Creveld, Hebrew University
Prof. Shimon Shamir, Tel Aviv University

INDEX

Note: Page numbers in *italics* refer to maps

ABOUT THE AUTHOR

Abraham Rabinovich worked as a reporter for *Newsday* before joining the *Jerusalem Post*. His work has also appeared in the *New York Times*, the *Wall Street Journal*, the *Christian Science Monitor*, the *International Herald Tribune*, and *The New Republic*, among other publications. He is the author of five previous books, including *Jerusalem on Earth*. Born in New York City, he lives in Jerusalem.